To my parents, wife and daughter for their great support and understanding
Chetan Bajaj

In loving memory of my paternal grandmother and with love to my dear maternal grandmother and parents
Rajnish Tuli

In loving memory of my maternal grandfather and with love to my dear maternal grandmother and parents
Nidhi V Srivastava

10.99

N658.87

Retail
Management

WITHDRAWN

OXFORD
UNIVERSITY PRESS

OXFORD
UNIVERSITY PRESS

YMCA Library Building, Jai Singh Road, New Delhi 110001

Oxford University Press is a department of the University of Oxford.
It furthers the University's objective of excellence in research, scholarship,
and education by publishing worldwide in

Oxford   New York
Auckland   Cape Town   Dar es Salaam   Hong Kong   Karachi
Kuala Lumpur   Madrid   Melbourne   Mexico City   Nairobi
New Delhi   Shanghai   Taipei   Toronto

With offices in
Argentina   Austria   Brazil   Chile   Czech Republic   France   Greece
Guatemala   Hungary   Italy   Japan   Poland   Portugal   Singapore
South Korea   Switzerland   Thailand   Turkey   Ukraine   Vietnam

Oxford is a registered trade mark of Oxford University Press
in the UK and in certain other countries.

Published in India
by Oxford University Press

ISBN-13: 978-0-19-566986-2
ISBN-10: 0-19-566986-X

Typeset in Baskerville MT
by Archetype Typesetting Services, New Delhi
Printed in India by Ram Book Binding House, New Delhi 110020
and published by Manzar Khan, Oxford University Press
YMCA Library Building, Jai Singh Road, New Delhi 110001

PREFACE

Retailing consists of all activities involved in selling goods and services to consumers for their personal, family, or household use. It covers sales of goods ranging from automobiles to apparel and food products, and services ranging from hair cutting to air travel and computer education. Sales of goods to intermediaries who resell to retailers or sales to manufacturers are not considered a retail activity.

Retailing can be examined from many perspectives. A manufacturer of white goods like washing machines and refrigerators has many options to reach out to consumers. It can sell through dealers, company showrooms (Sony World, Videocon Plaza), home improvement stores (Arcus), or hypermarkets (Big Bazaar). The manufacturer will have to decide which retail formats to adopt and whether to go for intensive distribution (sell through many outlets), selective distribution (sell through limited outlets), or exclusive distribution (sell through very few outlets). Next, the manufacturer will have to decide which models to offer through different types of outlets. Having decided on retail distribution, the promotion strategy to attract retailers will have to be finalized.

The retail sector in India is highly fragmented with organized retail contributing to only 2% of total retail sales. The retail sector in developed countries was also highly fragmented at the beginning of the last century but the emergence of large chains like Wal Mart, Sears, and McDonald's led to rapid growth of organized retail and growing consolidation of the retail industry in the developed countries. The rapidly rising income levels and accompanying changes in lifestyle greatly contributed to the growth of organized retail in the West. Today, in India we see a rise in the purchasing power, and growth of a middle class which follows the western lifestyle. Hence, conditions are conducive for the rapid growth of organized retail in India.

However, the Indian environment is different from that of western countries in many ways. Indian cities are congested and a large part of the population is still concentrated in rural areas. The Indian houses are smaller and the Indian consumer is still not used to buying in bulk on weekends. The Indian retail scene is hence very different from that prevailing in the developed countries. As organized retail grows, retail formats, which evolved in the West, need to be modified and new formats suitable to Indian conditions have to evolve. Even as organized retail grows, a large part of Indian retail is still likely to be unorganized. Hence, it is necessary for students and practitioners to understand the difference in the retailing environment and retailing institutions in India.

Organized retail is growing rapidly and we see the emergence of large organized retail chains like Shoppers' Stop, LifeStyle, and Westside. We also find retail malls mushrooming all over the country. The opportunities in retail industry in India will increase since Indian retailing is on the threshold of a major change. Retailing is fast emerging as an important area of study in B-schools all over the world. In India also we see a growing interest in retailing among MBA students in the last few years since the retailing sector is creating many employment opportunities. Till a few years back, retailing was covered as a component of the course on sales and distribution in most Indian B-schools.

However, with the rapid growth in organized retail and increased emphasis of manufacturers on understanding sales at the retail level, the study of retailing has become increasingly relevant. This has led many B-schools to introduce a separate elective on retailing. Today, retailing has become one of the most popular elective courses in many B-schools. Some B-schools are now even offering a diploma and specialization in retail management.

The study of retailing is very important to MBA students interested in employment opportunities with large retail chains. An understanding of retail operations, store location, consumer behaviour, information systems, supply chain, marketing strategies, etc. is very useful in managing store operations. A study of retailing is also useful to students who wish to take up careers in sales, distribution, and related functions in consumer goods and service industries. Sales managers of consumer products firms need to understand the perspective of retailers and design appropriate marketing programmes to attract retailers, particularly when large organized chains become more dominant. Product and brand managers need to understand the factors behind the growth of retail brands to plan effective product and branding strategies.

About the Book

While teaching a retailing course in India, I found that there was no suitable textbook which explored the retailing scene in India. There were a number of foreign textbooks but those were not applicable to the Indian context. There was a real need to have a text which explored the Indian retail scene. This text seeks to fill that void. This book is based on an extensive research on the Indian retailing environment and would be very useful to students pursuing courses on retailing and sales and distribution, as well as executives in retail stores.

The book covers cases, illustrations, and examples from the Indian retail scene and helps the student to understand the Indian consumer and how retail institutions have developed in India. We visited a large number of retail outlets and interviewed retailers and retail executives during our research. We have also drawn material from secondary sources, including articles in magazines and newspapers.

A large number of exercises and project assignments have been included at the end of each chapter to help students assimilate and internalize their learning.

Content and Structure

Chapters 1–3 focus on retailing concepts and retail formats.

Chapter 1 provides an introduction to retailing. This chapter focuses on the functions of retailers and provides an overview of the functioning of the entire distribution chain as also the role of retailers and wholesalers within it.

Chapter 2 covers the various retail formats which have emerged in developed countries and in India. This chapter also discusses how the retail franchising system operates, and presents manufacturer–retailer relationships and non-store retailing operations, such as selling through Internet and selling through catalogues.

Chapter 3 explores the Indian retailing scenario in depth, examines the structure of the Indian retail industry, and studies the retailing and wholeselling organizations. It examines the rural markets and how manufacturers and retailers are reaching out to these markets. This chapter also discusses legal issues related to retailing.

Chapters 4 and 5 of the book focus on retail customers in India and their buying behaviour. Chapter 4 discusses the buying behaviour of retail customers in different buying situations, studies the different stages of the buying process, and how the customer goes about decision-making.

Chapter 5 examines the different ways in which a retailer can segment his market and position the retail store. It discusses demographical and psychographical factors which affect customer behaviour and which can serve as the basis for segmenting markets.

Chapters 6, 7, 8, 9, and 10 of the book focus on the retail mix strategies. Location decision is possibly the most critical decision for a retailer and a key to retail success.

Chapter 6 covers the factors which have to be considered while taking a decision on store location. The various types of shopping centres available in India and location options for retailers are presented. A retailer's analysis of the viability of a site and estimates of the likely traffic are explored. Different theories on selection of retail locations are covered.

Merchandising is at the heart of retailing. Chapter 7 discusses how merchandising decisions are made. This chapter covers the issues of vendor management and development, management of retail inventory, and the development of a buying plan.

Chapter 8 discusses how Indian retailers plan their layout and displays—store interiors, displays, and merchandise presentation. Store layout depends on the product mix and merchandising strategy.

Chapter 9 explores the various pricing strategies adopted by retailers and the conditions in which each of them is appropriate.

Chapter 10 examines and compares the promotion and communications process of retailers and manufacturers. It examines how retailers decide on the promotion objectives and budgets. The promotional mediums being used by Indian retailers to communicate effectively with their customers and their suitability are also examined.

Chapter 11, the last chapter of the book, discusses how Indian retailers are developing relations with their customers. The importance of service quality is examined and various methods to improve services are discussed. This chapter also covers how customer loyalty programmes are developed and managed.

Pedagogical Features

A unique aspect of the book is the large number of illustrations and examples from Indian situations. The book contains cases of major Indian retailers including Subhiksha, Big Bazaar, Margin Free Market, Shoppers' Stop and Westside. There is also a case on franchising, which will help students understand franchising operations and plans of major franchising chains in India. These cases will help students understand the Indian retailing environment and how large organized retailers are evolving their formats and business models. These cases will also help students know about the plans of some major retail chains in India and the constraints and opportunities before them. At the end of each chapter there are concept review questions on major issues covered in the chapter to help students test their understanding of main concepts covered in the chapter. Each chapter also has project assignments on which the students are expected to do a small field study to help them to understand the practical aspects or issues. An instructor's manual accompanies the book.

Acknowledgements

Many people have contributed to the development of this book. However, the authors especially thank the editors of Oxford University Press for the great pains they took to keep them motivated throughout the project and for their suggestions on structuring the book.

Chetan Bajaj is very thankful to Mrs Hema Patil and Mrs Deepa Kuttan, both faculty members at the management programme of Bapuji Institute of Engineering and Technology (BIET), Davangere, for going through the entire manuscript and giving many valuable suggestions. Mrs Hema Patil gave useful suggestions on relationship marketing techniques used by Indian retailers while Mrs. Deepa Kuttan gave some useful suggestions on product and merchandising mix. Both Mrs Hema Patil and Mrs Deepa Kuttan also helped in the preparation of the instructor's manual. Chetan Bajaj thanks the students of MDI, Gurgaon, and BIET, Davangere—especially Nitin, Jayashree, and Amit. He also thanks his family members, including his wife Mrs Nandini Bajaj and daughter Aditi Bajaj, for their great patience. However, he, along with the co-authors, owns the sole responsiblility for any shortcoming in this book.

Rajnish Tuli and Nidhi V Srivastava together thank Professor Amit Mookerjee and Professor A.P. Arora for inculcating a distinctive approach towards learning. They also thank their dear friend and colleague C. Vijayalakshmi and a leading local retailer Dinesh for their inputs and ideas. They would also like to thank their families and dear friends Rakesh and Jyotsna for their encouragement and moral support. They also express their special gratitude to the large number of authors whose work they have cited in the text.

Chetan Bajaj
Rajnish Tuli
Nidhi V Srivastava

CONTENTS

1 RETAILING: ROLE, RELEVANCE, AND TRENDS

Learning Objectives

- To understand the concept of retailing

- To understand the role and relevance of retailing for business and economy

- To identify the activities associated with retailing

- To analyse the key trends that impact the retail sector

- To evaluate the retail sector in the context of the value chain

- To analyse the impact of Internet on the retail sector

Introduction

Which business considers every individual as a customer? Which business accounts for less than 10% of the worldwide labour force and is still the single largest industry in most nations? What is common between Wal-Mart, Amazon, and the small *kirana* stores that dot your neighbourhood?

The answer is retailing, the last link in the chain of production, which begins at the extractive stages, moves through manufacturing, and ends in the distribution of goods and services to the final consumer.

What is Retailing?

The distribution of consumer products begins with the producer and ends at the ultimate consumer. Between the producer and the consumer there is a middleman—the retailer, *who links the producers and the ultimate consumers.* Retailing is defined as a conclusive set of activities or steps used to sell a product or a service to consumers for their personal or family use. It is responsible for matching individual demands of the consumer with supplies of all the manufacturers. The word 'retail' is derived from the French word *retaillier,* meaning 'to cut a piece off' or 'to break bulk'.

A retailer is a person, agent, agency, company, or organization which is instrumental in reaching the goods, merchandise, or services to the ultimate consumer. Retailers perform specific activities such as anticipating customers wants, developing assortments of products, acquiring market information, and financing. A common assumption is that retailing involves only the sale of products in stores. However, it also includes the sale of services like those offered at a restaurant, parlour, or by car rental agencies. The selling need not necessarily take place through a store. Retailing encompasses selling through the mail, the Internet, door-to-door visits—any channel that could be used to approach the consumer. When manufacturers like Dell Computers sell directly to the consumer, they also perform the retailing function.

Retail Industry: North America

Retail is the second largest industry in the United States in terms of both the number of establishments and the number of employees. It is also one of the largest industries worldwide. The retail industry employs over 23 million Americans and generates more than $3 trillion in retail sales annually. In January 2003, the unemployment rate in the retail industry was 6.7%, compared to 6.3% in January 2002.

Wal-Mart is the world's largest retailer and the largest company with approximately US $245 billion in sales annually. Wal-Mart employs more than 1 million associates in the United States and more than 3,00,000 internationally. The second largest retailer in the world is France's Carrefour. Single-store businesses account for over 95% of all US retailers, but generate less than 50% of all retail store sales.

Retailing has become such an intrinsic part of our everyday lives that it is often taken for granted. The nations that have enjoyed the greatest economic and social progress have been those with a strong retail sector. Why has retailing become such a popular method of conducting business? The answer lies in the benefits a vibrant retailing sector has to offer—an easier access to a variety of products, freedom of choice, and higher levels of customer service.

As we all know, the ease of entry into retail business results in fierce competition and better value for customers. To enter retailing is easy and to fail is even easier. Therefore, in order to survive in retailing, a firm must do a satisfactory job in its primary role, i.e., catering to customers. Retailers' cost and profit vary depending on their type of operation and major product line. Their profit is usually a small fraction of sales and is generally about 9–10%. Retail stores of different sizes face distinct challenges and their sales volume influences business opportunities, merchandise purchase policies, nature of promotion, and expense control measures.

Over the last decade there have been sweeping changes in the general retailing business. For instance, what was once a strictly made-to-order market for clothing has now changed into a ready-to-wear market. Flipping through a catalogue, picking the right colour, size, and type of clothing a person wanted to purchase, and then waiting to have it sewn and shipped was the standard practice in the earlier days. By the turn of the century some retailers set up a storefront where people could browse, while new pieces were being sewn or customized in the back rooms. Almost all retail businesses have undergone a similar transition over the years.

Drivers of Change in Retailing

- Changing demographics and industry structure
- Expanding computer technology
- Emphasis on lower costs and prices
- Emphasis on convenience and service
- Focus on productivity
- Added experimentation
- Continuing growth of non-store retailing

The world over retail business is dominated by smaller family run chain stores and regionally targeted stores, but gradually more and more markets in the western world are being taken over by billion-dollar multinational conglomerates, such as Wal-Mart, Sears, McDonald's, Marks and Spencer. The larger retailers have managed to set up huge supply/distribution chains, inventory management systems, financing pacts, and wide-scale marketing plans. In the backdrop of globalization, liberalization, and highly aware customers, a retailer is required to make a conscious effort to position himself distinctively to face the competition. This is determined to a great extent by the retail mix strategy followed by a company to sell its products.

A major development in recent times has been the emergence of varied retail formats that have started operating in most product categories. For instance, there are large department stores that offer a huge assortment of goods and services. There are discounters who offer a wide array of products and compete mainly on price. There are also the high-end retailers who target extremely niche segments.

Each of these types of retailers have their distinct advantages, but it is important to know how these advantages play out. For example, during tough economic times the discount retailers tend to outperform the others; the opposite is true when the economy is doing well. The more successful retailers attempt to combine the characteristics of more than one type of retailing to differentiate themselves from the existing competition.

Significance of Retail Industry

Consumer money drives the economy, and retail is where consumers spend that money. Boutiques, restaurants, discount superstores, mail-order companies, and e-tailers—these establishments are where consumers spend their hard-earned money. When goods are put in the hands, or shopping bags, of consumers, retailers realize revenue—and so do the wholesalers, distributors, and manufacturers that make up the rest of the consumer-goods distribution chain. In addition, retail transactions serve as a means for collecting sales taxes, which support public services of all kinds.

Retail goods are traditionally divided into durable goods, such as furniture, cars, and large appliances, which are expected to last at least five years, and non-durable goods, which include food, clothing, and other categories far too numerous to mention but which eventually form the bulk of the stuff you see on makeshift tables at garage sales.

Retail industry provides immense opportunities to entrepreneurs and workforce as salespeople and clerks, the industry also has opportunities for people interested in determining what goods will be sold, getting these goods to the right place at the right time, and managing the operations, finances, and administration of retail companies.

In today's competitive environment retailers have redefined their role in general, and in the value chain in particular. Retailers act as gatekeepers who decide on which new products should find their way to the shelves of their stores. As a result, they have a strong say in the success of the product or service launched by a business firm. A product manager of household appliances claimed, 'Marketers have to sell a new product several times, first within the company, then to the retailer and finally to the user of the product.'

It is a well-established fact that manufacturers need to sell their products through retail formats that are compatible with their business strategy, brand image, and market profile in order to ensure a competitive edge. The role of retailers in the present competitive environment has gained attention from manufacturers because external parties such as market intermediaries and supplying partners are becoming increasingly powerful. It is necessary for marketers of consumer products to identify the needs and motivations of their partners in the marketing channel. This is especially true in the case of new products.

Consumer companies might improve their new product success rate if they put more effort in creating retailer value as well as consumer differential advantage. If the objectives of a manufacturer are incompatible with those of a market intermediary, such as the retailer, the success of a product is jeopardized.

The increasing number of product categories followed by multiple brands in each category complicate decision-making for both manufacturers and market intermediaries. Retailers want to optimize sales within the limited shelf space, governed by their individual sales philosophy. Retailers undertake risk in selecting a portfolio of products or brands to offer to their customers. Retailers have to make optimum selection of goods to be sold given the following major concerns:

- Selling space available is relatively fixed, and must return maximum profits. If such space is occupied by merchandise that is not moving, it will not result in profit. The retailer may have to resort to substantial price reductions in order to get rid of the unsold stock.

- There is always the risk of non-performance in terms of quality, supplies, etc., which in turn harms the image of the retail outlet.

Retailing is a dynamic industry—constantly changing due to shifts in the needs of the consumers and the growth of technology. Retail formats and companies that were unknown three decades ago are now major forces in the economy. Therefore, the challenges for retail managers the world over are increasing—they must take decisions ranging from setting the price of a bag of rice to setting up multimillion-dollar stores in malls. Selecting target markets, determining what merchandise and services to offer, negotiating with suppliers, training salespeople—these are just a few of the many functions that a retail manager has to perform on a perpetual basis.

Retail Evolution in Hawaii

Retailing was established in Hawaii in the early 19th century but grew somewhat slowly as much of the economy centred around plantations rather than diversified businesses and occupations. By 1900 agricultural employment accounted for roughly 60% of all jobs, while trade activities (retailing and wholesaling) represented only 3% of the total. In the early 20th century, retailing began to diversify along with the economy. Locally operated stores such as Arakawa's and Star Market emerged in this period. In the 1930s, Hawaii retailers experienced their first taste of serious mainland competition with the entrance of Kress and Sears department stores.

The post-World War II recovery period was marked by the emergence of the first major shopping centres in Hawaii, culminating in the opening of the giant (for its time) Ala Moana Shopping Centre in 1959. By the late 1950s, retailing had overtaken agriculture's (declining) share of total jobs. More local chains, such as Foodland, also emerged in this period, and there were new entrants from the US mainland including Longs Drugs and F.W. Woolworth.

Post-statehood retail growth centred on expansion of the shopping centre trend, additional mainland entrants, and a proliferation of businesses tied to the rapidly expanding tourism sector. Between 1970 and 1972, three major new shopping centres opened, namely Kahala Mall, Pearlridge Center, and the Kaahumanu Center in Kahului, Maui. The convenience store trend hit Hawaii in the late 1970s with the opening of the first 7-Eleven Store in 1978. The 1980s saw the opening of neighbourhood 'strip malls' including several in Mililani and Hawaii Kai. Then, as the post-statehood boom peaked in the late 1980s, the first of the membership stores, Costco, opened.

Despite the slowing of the economy in the 1990s, this decade has been most active in retail development and restructuring. Ala Moana Center completed a major renovation in 1990 and entered the upscale fashion market with its Palm Boulevard segment featuring such upscale retailers as Christian Dior, Gucci, and Emporio Armani. For the average resident looking for low prices and variety, the entry of the first *big box* retailer to Hawaii, K-Mart in 1992, was a milestone. The first Wal-Mart followed in 1994. New concepts in shopping centres included the Pearl Highlands Power centre and the Waikele Center above Waipahu, which featured a combination of locally oriented big box retailers and visitor-oriented, factory outlet stores.

The 1990s has also been a period of shake-out in the industry for many retailers who could not weather the slow economy, coupled with the new competition. Local stores such as Arakawa's, Kuni Dry Goods, Gem Department stores, and many small retailers could not reposition themselves in the market in order to survive the more competitive 1990s. Even some mainland chains such as Payless, Pay N Save, Woolworth, and Home Improvement Warehouse disappeared from the local retailing scene. Competition and business conditions in Hawaii were not the primary causes of their demise, but their inability to keep up with consumer and industry trends nationally was a factor.

Source: www.hawaii.gov

Global Retail-industry-related Facts

- Worldwide retail sales are estimated at US $7 trillion.
- The top 200 largest retailers account for 30% of the worldwide demand.
- The money spent on household consumption worldwide increased by 68% between 1980 and 1998.
- Retail sales are generally driven by people's ability (disposable income) and willingness (consumer confidence) to buy.
- The 1998 UNDP Human Development Report points to the fact that global expenditures on advertising are (including in developing countries) increasing faster than the world economy, suggesting that the sector is becoming one of the major players in the development process.

Regional Facts

- Some two-thirds or US $6.6 trillion out of the US $10 trillion American economy is consumer spending. About 40% of that ($3 trillion) is spent on discretionary products and services.
- Retail turnover in the EU was almost 2,000 billion in 2001 and the sector's better than average growth looks set to continue in the future.

- Retail trade in Europe employs 15% of the European workforce (3 million firms and 13 million workers).
- The Asian economies (excluding Japan) are expected to have 6% growth rates in 2005-06.

Consumer Expectations

- Time and quality of life are becoming relatively more important than money; 60% of Americans want to lead a simple life.

- Product performance was found to be the top purchasing criterion, while environmental features were a close second in a survey conducted by the Alliance for Environmental Innovation in conjunction with SC Johnson Wax. *Source:* www.uneptie.org 'Global Retail Industry Facts and Figures', UNEP Meeting of the Retail Industry on Sustainable Development

Retail Industry and Economy

Retail business is the largest private industry, ahead even of finance and engineering, contributing over 8% to the GDP in the West. Over 50 of the Fortune 500 and about 25 of the Asian Top 200 companies are retailers. Thailand and Indonesia, which were affected by the currency turmoil, pepped up the deregulatory measures to attract more FDI in retail business. Japan, under a prolonged recession and protracted downfall in domestic investment, abolished its *Large Scale Retail Store Law* to attract FDI.

Today, in some developed countries, retail business houses have shares as large as 40% of the market. For instance, in Thailand and Brazil the organized retail business has been growing rapidly. In contrast, the organized retail business in India is very small. This is despite the fact that India is one of the biggest markets in the world. Retail business contributes around 10–11% to the country's GDP. It amounts to about $180 billion market and is six times bigger than that of Thailand and four to five times bigger than that of South Korea and Taiwan. India also has the largest number of retailers, about 12 million, though they are mostly small.

The significance of the retail business has increased with the fast growth in the service sector. There has been a dramatic change in the economy's structure post-liberalization. While agriculture continues to be the main springboard for the economy, the manufacturing sector has slumped due to demand recession and liberalized imports. Much of the rapid growth in organized retail business in the developing countries is due to the entry of global retailers. In Thailand, seven of the world's top 10 retailers have made significant investments—Carrefour, Casino, Makro, Royal Ahold, Jusco have set up shop in Thailand. In China, three of the top 10 global retailers, such as Carrefour, Wal Mart, 7-Eleven, have made investments, and in Brazil, the top three global retailers share about 30% of the retail market.

Retail Industry in India

In India, the retail sector is the second largest employer after agriculture. The retailing sector in India is highly fragmented and consists predominantly of small, independent, and owner-managed shops. There are some 12 million retail outlets in India. Besides, the country is also dotted with low-cost kiosks and pushcarts. In 2001, retail trade in India was worth Rs 11228.7 billion.

There has been a boom in the retail trade in India owing to a gradual increase in the disposable income of the middle-class households. More and more players are venturing into the retail business in India to introduce new attractive retail formats like malls, supermarkets, discount stores, department stores, and even changing the traditional look of the bookstores, chemist shops, and furnishing stores. Food sales constitute a high proportion of the total retail sales. The share was 62.7% in 2001, worth approximately Rs 7039.2 billion, while non-food sales were worth Rs 4189.5 billion. However, the non-food retailing sector registered faster year-on-year growth than food sales.

Retail Forecasts in India

The retail business in India is expected to reach Rs 19069.3 billion by 2006, with further growth of organized retailing in both food and non-food segments. The proportion of sales through organized retailing is estimated to increase to around 6% by 2010.

A strong trend in favour of organized retail format is being witnessed in both food and non-food sectors as people are showing preference for one-stop shops. Customers are also looking for ambience and convenience in shopping. This would continue more strongly in the next couple of years. In future, with more dual income families, the consumer's ability to spend will increase, but at the same time, it is predicted that the time available for shopping will go down. In such a scenario, the retailers will have to take steps to develop shopping as an experience, though the more successful retailers will be those that will provide faster services.

Organized Retailing in South Asian Countries		
	Organized retailing	Traditional retailing
Malaysia	50%	50%
Thailand	40%	60%
Philippines	35%	65%
Indonesia	25%	75%
South Korea	15%	85%
China	20%	80%
India	2%	98%

The Emergence of Organized Retail Format in India

India is likely to have over 220 shopping malls by 2006, up from 25 operational malls in 2003, as developers are rushing to encash the booming retail business that is transforming the way Indians have been shopping so far. The shopping mall phenomenon, however, is not likely to be restricted only to metros as malls are also coming up in non-metro cities and larger towns across the country. Nearly a decade after the first signs of organized retail format evolution, India is expecting to develop over 40 million square feet of quality retail real estate space by 2006. The total mall space in six A-Grade cities— Delhi (including Gurgaon and Noida), Mumbai, Bangalore, Hyderabad, Chennai, and Kolkata—is expected to increase to over 21.1 million square feet by 2005. It is also expected to increase in seven non-metro cities—Pune, Ahmedabad, Lucknow, Ludhiana, Jaipur, Chandigarh, and Indore—in the same duration, and the grand total comes to about 26.2 million square feet by 2005.

According to a leading retail magazine, *Images*, the national capital region will account for over 40% of the 26.2 million square feet of the total mall space expected to come up in six metros and seven non-metros by 2005. While Gurgaon currently dominates the organized retail real estate segment in the city, the next two years will see localization of the mall segment with all prominent locations of Delhi slated to have at least one major mall. The financial capital of the country, Mumbai, is also expected to offer the second highest quantum of mall space with close to 4.8 million square feet, scheduled to be operational by 2005-06. Ahmedabad and Lucknow are expected to have over one million square feet of mall space by 2005. Cities like Jaipur, Chandigarh, and Ludhiana are also attracting attention from developers and retailers.

Characteristics of Retailing

Retailing can be distinguished in various ways from other businesses such as manufacturing. Retailing differs from manufacturing in the following ways:

- There is direct end-user interaction in retailing.
- It is the only point in the value chain to provide a platform for promotions.
- Sales at the retail level are generally in smaller unit sizes.
- Location is a critical factor in retail business.
- In most retail businesses services are as important as core products.
- There are a larger number of retail units compared to other members of the value chain. This occurs primarily to meet the requirements of geographical coverage and population density.

Direct Interaction with Customers

Retail businesses have a direct interaction with end-users of goods or services in the value chain. They act as intermediaries between end-users and suppliers such as wholesalers or manufacturers. Therefore, they are in a position to effectively communicate the response and changing preferences of the consumers to the suppliers or sales persons of the company. This helps the manufacturers and marketers to redefine their product and change the components of its marketing strategy accordingly. Manufacturers require a strong retail network both for reach of the product and to obtain a powerful platform for promotions and point-of-purchase advertising. Realizing the importance of retailing in the entire value chain, many manufacturers have entered into retail business by setting up exclusive stores for their brands. This has not only provided direct contact with customers, but has also acted as advertisement for the companies and has provided the manufacturers with bargaining power with respect to other retailers who stocked their product. Retailing provides extensive sales people support for products which are information-intensive, such as in the case of consumer durables.

Lower Average Amount of Sales Transaction

The average amount of sales transaction at retail point is much less in comparison to the other partners in the value chain. Many consumers buy products in small quantities for household consumption. Due to lower disposable incomes, some consumer segments in India even buy grocery items on a daily basis rather than a weekly or a monthly basis. Inventory management becomes a challenge for retailers as a result of the many minor transactions with a large number of customers. Hence, retailers must take care of the average levels of stock, order levels, and the popularity of different brands. The small amount also means that the retailer has to keep a tight control on costs associated with each transaction in the selling process. Credit verification, employment of personnel, value-added activities like bagging, gift-wrapping, and promotional incentives all add up to the costs. One way to resolve this is for the retail outlets to be able to attract the maximum possible number of shoppers.

Theories and Models of Retailing

Dialectic Process

An evolutionary theory based on the premise that retail institutions evolve. The theory suggests that new retail formats emerge by adopting characteristics from other forms of retailers in much the same way that a child is the product of the pooled genes of two different individuals.

Gravity Model

A theory about the structure of market areas. The model states that the volume of purchases by consumers and the fre-quency of trips to the outlets are a function of the size of the store and the distance between the store and the origin of the shopping trip.

Retail Accordion Theory

A theory of retail institutional changes that suggests that retail institutions go from outlets with wide assortments to specialized, narrow, line store merchants and then back again to the more general, wide-assortment institution. It is also referred to as the general–specific–general theory.

Retail Lifecycle Theory

A theory of retail competition that states that retailing institutions, like the products they distribute, pass through an identifiable cycle. This cycle can be partitioned into four distinct stages: (1) innovation, (2) accelerated development, (3) maturity, and (4) decline.

Wheel of Retailing Theory

A theory of retail institutional changes that explains retail evolution with an institutional life cycle concept.

Natural Selection Theory

A theory of retail institutional changes that states that retailing institutions that can most effectively adapt to environmental changes are the ones that are most likely to prosper or survive.

Central Place Theory

A model that ranks communities according to the assortment of goods available in each. At the bottom of the hierarchy are communities that represent the smallest central places (centres of commerce). They provide the basic necessities of life. Further up the hierarchy are the larger central places, which carry all goods and services found in lower-order central places plus more specialized ones that are not necessary.

Point-of-purchase Display and Promotions

A significant relevant chunk of retail sales comes from unplanned or impulse purchases. Studies have shown that shoppers often do not carry a fixed shopping list and pick up merchandise based on impulsive or situational appeal. Many do not look at ads before shopping. Since a lot of retail products are low involvement in nature, impulse purchases of the shopper is a vital area that every retailer must tap into. Therefore, display, point-of-purchase merchandise, store layout, and catalogues become important. Impulse goods like chocolates, snack foods, and magazines can sell much more quickly if they are placed in a high visibility and high traffic location.

Larger Number of Retail Business Units

Location of retail store plays an important role compared to other business units. Manufacturers decide the location on the basis of availability of factors of productions and market. Similarly, retailers consider factors like potential demand, supply of merchandise, and store image-related factors in locating the retail outlet. The number of operating units in retail is the highest compared to other constituents of the value chain, primarily to meet the needs for geographic reach and customer accessibility.

Role of Services in Retailing

Though shopping over the phone and through the Internet have increased rapidly in the past few years, the majority of Indian consumers still visit stores to shop. Stores remain popular because of the need of consumers to be able to see and test products, it is a means of social interaction, the opportunity to compare different brands, and impulse buying. The location of a store is also of great importance in the retail process. Since people are attracted to a particular store, retailers need to keep track of amenities like parking, extended hours of operation, special play areas for children, wash rooms, trial rooms, etc. Besides, efficient customer service is required to make the customer feel comfortable and important.

The characteristics of retailing evolve from the generic functions of a retailer.

Functions of Retailing

Retailers play a significant role as a conduit between manufacturers, wholesalers, suppliers, and consumers. In this context, they perform various functions like sorting, breaking bulk, holding stock, as a channel of communication, storage, advertising, and certain additional services.

Sorting

Manufacturers usually make one or a variety of products and would like to sell their entire inventory to a few buyers to reduce costs. Final consumers, in contrast, prefer a large variety of goods and services to choose from and usually buy them in small quantities. Retailers are able to balance the demands of both sides, by collecting an assortment of goods from different sources, buying them in sufficiently large quantities, and selling them to consumers in small units.

The above process is referred to as the sorting process. Through this process, retailers undertake activities and perform functions that add to the value of the products and services sold to the consumer. Supermarkets in the US offer, on an average, 15,000 different items from 500 companies. Customers are able to choose from a wide range of designs, sizes, and brands from just one location. If each manufacturer had a separate store for its own products, customers would have to visit several stores to complete their shopping. While all retailers offer an assortment, they specialize in types of assortment offered and the market to which the offering is made. Westside provides clothing and accessories, while a chain like Nilgiris specializes in food and bakery items. Shoppers' Stop targets the elite urban class, while Pantaloons is targeted at the middle class.

Breaking Bulk

Breaking bulk is another function performed by retailing. The word retailing is derived from the French word *retailler*, meaning 'to cut a piece off'. To reduce transportation costs, manufacturers and wholesalers typically ship large cartons of the product, which are then tailored by the retailers into smaller quantities to meet individual consumption needs.

Holding Stock

Retailers also offer the service of holding stock for the manufacturers. Retailers maintain an inventory that allows for instant availability of the product to the consumers. It helps to keep prices stable and enables the manufacturer to regulate production. Consumers can keep a small stock of products at home as they know that this can be replenished by the retailer and can save on inventory carrying costs.

Additional Services

Retailers ease the change in ownership of merchandise by providing services that make it convenient to buy and use products. Providing product guarantees, after-sales service, and dealing with consumer complaints are some of the services that add value to the actual product at the retailers' end. Retailers also offer credit and hire-purchase facilities to the customers to enable them to buy a product now and pay for it later. Retailers fill orders, promptly process, deliver and install products. Salespeople are also employed by retailers to answer queries and provide additional information about the displayed products. The display itself allows the consumer to see and test products before actual purchase. Retail essentially completes transactions with customers.

Channel of Communication

Retailers also act as the channel of communication and information between the wholesalers or suppliers and the consumers. From advertisements, salespeople, and display, shoppers learn about the characteristics and features of a product or services offered. Manufacturers, in their turn, learn of sales forecasts, delivery delays, and customer complaints. The manufacturer can then modify defective or unsatisfactory merchandise and services.

Transport and Advertising Functions

Small manufacturers can use retailers to provide assistance with transport, storage, advertising, and pre-payment of merchandise. This also works the other way round in case the number of retailers is small. The number of functions performed by a particular retailer has a direct relation to the percentage and volume of sales needed to cover both their costs and profits.

As a result of these functions, retailers are required to perform the following activities.

Activities Performed by Retailers

Retailers undertake various business activities and perform functions that add value to the offerings they make to their target segments. Retailers provide convenient location, stock, and appropriate mix of merchandise in suitable packages in accordance with the needs of customers. The four major activities, as shown in Figure 1.1, carried out by retailers are:

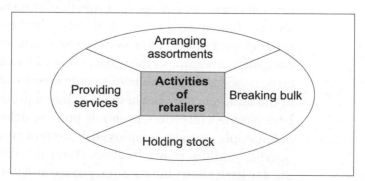

Fig. 1.1   Activities of retailers

1. Arranging an assortment of offerings
2. Breaking quantity
3. Holding stock
4. Extending services

Arranging Assortment

An assortment is a retailer's selection of merchandise. It includes both the depth and breadth of products carried. Retailers have to select the combination of assortments from various categories. The assortments must include substitutable items of multiple brands, SKUs, and price points. They should be distinguished on account of physical dimensions and attributes, e.g., colour or flavour. The small retailer takes assortment decision on the basis of his experience; on the other hand retailers from organized retailing depend on a detailed study of past trends and future projections.

Retailers need to consider certain factors while devising assortment plans for their stores: profitability associated with particular merchandise mix, store image, layout, and the level of compatibility between the existing merchandise. For example, FoodWorld, a leading food supermarket positioned as a one-stop shopping centre, deals in multiple product categories along with all possible variants of brands, stock keeping units, and physical attributes in order to meet the expectations of their consumers and survive in the business. Whereas, Subhiksha, a grocery chain in south India has impressive assortments of only the fast moving brands and SKUs rather than all available variants in the market. Their assortment plan is governed by location, size, and store image (value for money) of their stores.

Breaking Bulk

Breaking bulk means physical repackaging of the products by retailers in small unit sizes according to customers' convenience and stocking requirements. Normally, retailers receive large quantities of sacks and cases of merchandise from suppliers to reduce their transportation costs. In order to meet their customers' requirements retailers have to break or arrange the bulk into convenient units. This entire function of the retailers adds value to the offerings not only for the end customers but also for the suppliers in the value chain. Even in the earlier days of generic and commodity-based trading most of the retailers used to perform this important function in the value chain. This function receives negligible attention from the retailers now due to the introduction of new product categories, such as FMCG and ready-to-wear apparel.

Holding Stock

To ensure the regular availability of their offerings, retailers maintain appropriate levels of inventory. Consumers normally depend on the retailers directly to replenish their stocks at home. Therefore, retailers, on periodic basis, maintain the required levels of stock to meet the regular or seasonal fluctuations in the demand. Retailers need to maintain equilibrium between the range or variety carried and the sales which it gives rise to. Retailers have to face the negative consequences of holding unwanted levels of stock—for instance, too little stock will hamper the sales volume, whereas, too much stock will increase the retailer's cost of operation. Generally, in small towns of India most retailers have arrangements with the nearby warehouses to stock the goods. Some are so small that they have to stock only on the shop floor. Retailers in the organized sector, to a certain extent, are using effective software packages for maintaining adequate levels of inventory. At the same time, retailers avail of just-in-time deliveries with the help of efficient consumer response systems, which reduces the burden of maintaining high levels of stocks.

Extending Services

Retailing provides multiple services to immediate customers and other members of the value chain. The set of services extended by particular retailers may be part of their core product offerings or it may be 'add on' to their product or service. Retailers offer credit, home delivery, after-sales services, and information regarding new products to their customers, thereby making the shopping experience convenient and enjoyable. At the same time, they provide stocking place, reach to the ultimate customers, and information about the concerned target segment to the suppliers. For example, Time Zone, the first organized retail chain of wristwatches in India, started by leading watch manufacturers Titan, set up in all its stores, service centres with proper equipment and trained manpower. This has not only diluted the relevance of service providers in the unorganized sector but has also enhanced the confidence of the customers in the retail services provided by the particular retail chain, as after-sales service is considered to be an integral ingredient of the watch purchase.

Categorizing Retailers

Categorizing retailers helps in understanding the competition and the frequent changes that occur in retailing. There is no universally accepted method of classifying a retail outlet, although many categorization schemes have been proposed. Some of these include classifying on the basis of (a) number of outlets (b) margin vs turnover (c) location (d) size.

The number of outlets operated by a retailer can have a significant impact on the competitiveness of a retail firm. Generally, a greater number of outlets add strength to the firm because it is able to spread fixed costs, such as advertising and managers' salaries, over a greater number of stores in addition to acquiring economies of purchase. While any retailer operating more than one store can be technically classified as a chain owner, for practical purposes a chain store refers to a retail firm which has more than 11 units. In the United States, for example, chain stores account for nearly 95% of general merchandise stores.

Challenges for Retail Banking

Retail banks and markets are at different stages in their evolution. For some, the challenge is to achieve basic operating efficiencies in financial product designing and basic selling skills in the front-line. For some others, the challenge is to find new ways to create income growth, through innovative propositions, differential pricing, or superior delivery. Others are beginning to see the unbundling of retail value-chains, with specialist retail banks, services and financial products businesses coming into existence, and raising fundamental questions about where and how to compete.

Regardless of their market context, all retail banks face a distinct set of management challenges. First, retail banks are typically larger and more complex to manage than most other financial businesses. A typical retail bank comprises massive production, servicing, and retailing operations which need to come together to provide consistent delivery at the point-of-sale or point-of-service. Equally, a retail bank may employ several thousands of people, each of them needing to be motivated and managed to share in the values of the whole. Secondly, the economics of retail banking are complex. The value of products and customers can take a lifetime to be realized, and can easily lead to poor resource allocation decisions and cross-subsidies. In the same way, the economics of delivery are obscure, with no clear division between where money is made along the manufacturing and the retailing value-chain. Thirdly, retail income is under attack. There are few banks left that can feel comfortable that they have a secure, stable home base to rely on. The attack has come not from the Internet retailers, or other entrants, but from other incumbents—whether banks fight to take customers or insurers fight to take their share of the customer's market.

Small chains can use economies of scale while tailoring merchandise to local needs. Big chains operating on a national scale can save costs by a centralized system of buying and accounting. A chain store could have either a standard stock list ensuring that the same merchandise is stocked in every retail outlet or an optional stock list giving the outlets the advantage of changing the merchandise according to customer needs in the area. Because of their size, chain stores are often channel captains of the marketing channel—captains can influence other channel partners, such as wholesalers, to carry out activities they might not otherwise engage in, such as extended payment terms and special package sizes.

Big stores focus on large markets where their customers live and work. They use technology to learn more about their customers and target them with point-of-sale machines, interactive kiosks, and sophisticated forecasting and inventory systems. They tend to stock a narrow range of inventory that sells well and maintain an extensive inventory of the fast selling products. Branding is important to them. Pricing is often a key area of focus for these retailers. Big stores have many strengths, including regional or national reputation, huge buying power, vast inventory, and hassle-free return and exchange policies. Their prime locations, the consistency in their products and services, the fact that they are open when people can and want to shop, and the clear consistent image and identity they develop and maintain challenge the abilities and resources of many small retailers. Perhaps their biggest advantage is their knowledge of their customers. They not only know their customers, but also use that knowledge in every aspect of their business, from inventory selection to store layout.

However, large retailers are not perfect. They have competitive weaknesses that small retailers can exploit. Most offer the same standardized assortments of products nationally. Local managers have little say in inventory selection. Often, sales staff has minimal product knowledge. Staff turnover is extremely high. Most large retailers have little connection with the community they serve. They usually do not offer special services. Larger companies are often slow to recognize and react to changes in their local markets.

Independent retailers can co-exist and flourish in the shadow of the big chains by developing a niche within the diverse market. The niche should be developed on the basis of new or unusual product offerings, superior service, and overall quality. While value is important, price may be less important. Efficient operations, including precise buying practices, is a must. Customer contact within the niche market must be characterized by 'high-touch' service. The key factor is innovation; stores that do not change will perish. The road to success for the independent retailer lies in doing all the things that big chain stores can not or will not do. The successful independent retailers embrace the following principles:

- Be prepared for change.
- Move to a narrower niche market and stop competing directly with the big retailers.
- Learn more about customers and include best customers in a database.
- Invest appropriately in advertising and promotion.
- Charge regular prices and avoid discounting (ensure requisite mark-up).
- Buy with precision and search out speciality suppliers.
- Maintain essential inventory.
- Focus on profit instead of volume (be ready to lose an occasional sale).
- Provide extraordinary service.
- Employ the best possible staff.
- Understand the significance of the Internet.

Gross margin and inventory turnover is another means of classifying retailers. Gross margin is net sales minus the cost of goods sold and gross margin percentage is the return on sales. A 30% margin implies that a retailer generates Rs 30 for every Rs 100 sales that can be used to pay operating expenses. Inventory turnover refers to the number of times per year, on average, a retailer sells his inventory.

On the basis of this, retailers are classified as low margin low turnover—those that cannot survive the competition—and low margin high turnover, exemplified by Amazon.com. Jewellery stores and appliance stores are examples of high margin low turnover stores and only a few retailers achieve high margin high turnover. These retailers are in the best position to combat competition because their high turnover allows them to withstand price wars. The drawback of the classification by this method is that service retailers who have no inventory turnover cannot be encompassed.

One of the old means of classification of retailers is by location, generally within a metropolitan area. Location will be dealt with more extensively in the coming chapters but suffice it to say at this stage that retailers are no longer satisfied with traditional locations within a city's business district but are on the constant lookout for alternate locations to reach customers. Besides renovating old stores, retailers are testing unorthodox locations to expand their clientele. With the advent of the Internet, this area of retailing is likely to undergo tremendous changes in the coming years.

Size is often used as a yardstick to classify retailers because costs often differ on the basis of size, with big retailers having lower operational costs per dollar than smaller players. However, in this sphere too, the Internet may make size an obsolete method of comparison.

Structure and Nature of Retailing Channels

Retailing is the last stage in the distribution process, which comprises all the business operations and the people involved in the physical movement and transfer of ownership of goods and services from the producer to the consumer. A typical distribution channel consists of a manufacturer, a wholesaler, a retailer, and the final consumer. Wholesaling is the intermediate stage—during which goods are sold not to the final consumers but to the business customers for resale.

In some distribution channels, the different activities are performed by independent firms. But most distribution channels have a degree of vertical integration—performing more than one activity. For example, FoodWorld carries out both wholesaling and retailing activities. It buys directly from the manufacturers, has merchandise shipped to its warehouses, and then distributes it to their stores. Some retailers, especially in the clothing business, even design the merchandise they sell and contract its production to manufacturers.

The nature of retailing channels differs in various parts of the world. The US has a retail density that is greater than that of all other countries. A feature of the US system is the concentration of large retail firms—10% of its food and general merchandise retail firms account for over 40% of all retail sales. Some firms are even able to eliminate wholesalers, as they are large enough to operate their own warehouses. Large stores—of over 20,000 square feet—are popular mediums of sale. This combination of large retailers and large stores makes the US one of the most efficient users of the distribution channel.

In Japan, on the other hand, small firms and stores govern the retail sector. The wholesale channel is relatively much larger and independent. To reach all the stores, almost daily, often requires the merchandise to pass through as many as three channels of distribution. Therefore, this reduced efficiency means that in contrast to the 10% of the total labour force employed in this sector in the US, the Japanese use 20% of their workforce.

The European system falls in between that of the US and Japan. Northern Europe is the closest to the US in terms of concentration levels—in some national markets, 80% of the retail sales in food are accounted for by fewer than five firms. In southern Europe, the market is more fragmented with the traditional farmers' market retailing still dominant in some sectors along with 'big-box' formats. Central Europe has seen an increase in retail floor space after the privatization of the retail trade. Privatization has also resulted in a transition from an extremely structured system to one that is highly fragmented, with kiosks rapidly gaining popularity.

In the Indian context, traditionally the small retailers have played a major role in the various sectors with the unorganized players outnumbering the organized ones. However, the past decade has witnessed the rise of chains of supermarkets at both regional and national levels. Some of these stores also have their own line of merchandise, be it clothes, food items, or household articles. The price consciousness among the large middle class also means that large stores that are able to offer discounts on bulk purchases have become more important. The growing pace of lifestyle of the urban consumer and the proliferation of technology has helped popularize online shopping.

Why do these countries differ? The variance is primarily due to three factors: (a) social and political objectives (b) geography (c) market size. The primary objective of Japanese or Indian economy is to reduce unemployment—the large labour force that is available is employed by small labour intensive businesses. Secondly, the population density in Japan and Europe is much higher than in the United States. Thus, these countries have less low-cost real estate available for development of large stores. Thirdly, the US market is the largest in the world and is able to leverage on economies of scale. India is still a growing market and has yet to develop a system as efficient as that of the US.

Trends in Retail Formats

Retail industry is continuously going through changes on account of liberalization, globalization, and consumer preferences. While multi-national retail chains are looking for new markets, manufacturers are identifying, redefining, or evolving new retail formats. The existing retail houses are also gearing up to face the emerging competition from the organized sector and the changing outlook of the consumers. For example, consumer spending is shifting from goods to services. Accordingly the retailers too are fast adjusting to the changing consumer preferences.

Consumers are not only looking for the core products or functional benefits from the retailers but also the non-functional benefits, which need to be compatible with their lifestyles. For example, most of the traditional eating joints in India such as Haldiram, Bikaner, and Sagar Ratna have revised their product offerings and atmospherics on the lines of the multinational chains to compete with them and to serve changed expectations of the consumers.

Mom-and-pop Stores and Traditional Kirana Stores

The retail sector is changing as new store categories have started dominating the marketplace. Mass merchandisers (Wal-Mart, Big Bazaar), discount clubs (Subhiksha), so-called category killers (Home Depot, Vishal chain), and speciality retailers (Time Zone, Tanishq) have all developed successful retail models. At the same time, the small mom-and-pop stores and the traditional department stores, are finding the competition intense. In 2002, while Wal-Mart and Target saw revenues grow (by 12% and 10%, respectively), department stores such as Saks and Federated experienced declining revenues (down 3% and 1%, respectively). But even in the mass-merchandising segment, the competition is fierce, as is evidenced by Kmart's bankruptcy announcement in 2002. Small independent stores, across product categories, is a very common retail format in India, particularly in small townships, but with the emergence of new retail formats they are also undertaking large scale renovations to attract their target consumer segments.

E-commerce

The amount of retail business being conducted on the Internet is growing every year. Indeed, Forrester Research Agency projects e-commerce revenue to rise to $123 billion in 2004, an increase of some 28% over the previous year and for e-tailing to comprise a bigger slice of the overall retail pie (5.6%, up from 4.5% in 2003). Many major retail organizations and manufacturers have online retail stores. Companies like Amazon.com and First and second.com, which helped pioneer the retail e-commerce concept, are now being followed by bricks-and-mortar and catalogue retailers like J. Crew, which are expanding retail e-commerce into new markets.

Wal-Mart: Challenges

Wal-Mart is an extremely successful business model. Indeed, in 2003 the company had a revenue of US $245 billion, more than four times the revenue of Home Depot, the retailer with the next-largest revenue that year. But more and more individuals and organizations are starting to say that the company's growth comes with major costs—to workers, to communities, and to governments. The company is facing serious accusations about its employment of illegal aliens. It has been taken to task for paying extraordinarily low wages—only 38% of full-time employees can afford to purchase a Wal-Mart health insurance plan. The US Equal Employment Opportunity Commission has filed more disability discrimination lawsuits against Wal-Mart than any other corporation. It is the target of the largest class-action suit for sexual discrimination ever filed against a private employer. It has been accused by many of radically changing the communities it enters, by pushing smaller retailers that have deep ties with the community out of business and by putting downward pressure on wages in the community. Already loud, the outcry against Wal-Mart is getting louder.

Department Stores

A few years ago, names like Sears, J.C. Penney, Macy's, and Montgomery Ward dominated malls and downtowns all over America. Over the last decade or so, however, these department stores have suffered badly. In part, this is a result of changing shopping patterns and increased competition from discount stores. It has also come from financial burdens incurred by companies that acquired competing companies and grew too fast. It is unlikely that these players will disappear from the market. However, they should be ready to expect more bumps as the strong get stronger and the weak get absorbed.

Discount Stores

These are giants such as Wal-Mart (the largest retailer in the world, with more than a million employees), Target, and Kmart, as well as membership warehouses, such as Costco. These, along with the category killers, have changed the landscape of both the retail industry and America. Where once mom-and-pop and department stores dominated retail, now the discount retailers and category killers are at the top of the heap. And where once shopping malls, anchored by at least one major department store, used to be the dominant retail presence lining the nation's roads, now it is the behemoth Wal-Marts and Home Depots.

Category Killers

These are the giant retailers that dominate one area of merchandise (e.g., Office Depot, Tower Records, and The Sports Authority). They are able to buy bathroom tiles, file cabinets, electronic goods, or pet food in such huge volumes that they can then sell them at prices even fairly large competitors cannot match. The future of this category is better than that of many of the more general discounters, but the same employment caveats apply. For most job seekers, these companies offer earn-and-learn experiences with vendors and distributors before they move onward and upward.

The Evolution of Marks and Spencer

Financial data drawn from Marks and Spencer's archives and annual reports can be used to identify five phases in the company's sales growth. Early, rather erratic, growth, often through acquisition, gave way to a second phase of store development funded by the Company's floatation in the 1920s. Sales growth in the third phase came substantively through an increase in store size. A fourth phase involved improvements in labour and space productivity. The final and current phase of evolution emphazises diversification.

Speciality Stores

These include Crate & Barrel, the Body Shop, and Victoria's Secret. These stores concentrate on one type of merchandise and offer it in a manner that makes it special. Some are very high-end (Louis Vuitton) while others cater to the price-conscious masses (Old Navy). Many are so successful that department stores have started to emulate their buying, marketing, and merchandise display strategies. Industry experts predict growth in this segment, particularly in home furnishings and home improvement, and it seems to attract many of the best and the brightest in retail. Promotion and responsibility come quickly to those willing to work hard, and in many of these stores the hand of bureaucracy is not heavy.

E-tailers

While most retailers have online storefronts, strictly online purveyors with no bricks-and-mortar counterparts are hoping to snare a percentage of the retail profit. Major players, such as Amazon.com, have generated enough business to cause top brick-and-mortar competitors to come up with their own Internet sites. Traditional retailers like Wal-Mart and Starbucks, hugely successful in their own right, have also set up online stores so as not to miss out on the revenue opportunities that the Internet offers

Relationships Between the Retailers and their Suppliers

Retail sector is critically dependent on its suppliers for the effective operation and profitability of its business.

Like every other marketing decision, the decision about which distribution channels to be used by the manufacturer should be based on all relevant factors. These factors include the firm's production capability, marketing resources, target market, buying patterns of potential customers, and the product itself. After evaluating these factors, the producer can choose a particular strategy for market coverage. The producer then selects the middlemen and channels, the retailer being one of them, to implement the strategy.

Intensive distribution is the use of all the available outlets for a product. Stocking the product in as many outlets as possible is mostly used in the case of convenience goods. *Selective distribution* uses only a portion or percentage of the available outlets in each geographical area. *Exclusive distribution* is the use of only a single retail outlet for a product in a large geographical area. Luxury goods are a good example of this category.

Various socio-economic and demographic factors are considered by the manufacturers for identifying the ideal retail format mix for its products. To exemplify this we use the context of soap category in India and the resultant retail format preferences.

Selection of Retail Format Mix by Manufacturers in the Soap Category

Soap is primarily targeted towards women as they are the chief decision-makers in soap purchase. Medicated positioning like germ killing and anti-bacterial are marketed to families. Manufacturers use various kinds of retail formats for distributing their products rather than using a particular kind of retail format. About 75% of the soaps are bought through these different types of outlets.

Kirana store: This is the most common source for buying soap, which usually forms a part of the month's grocery list. Consumers exhibit loyalty to these stores. These stores are largely dependent on proximity to consumers' homes. Here consumers buy over the counter and do not have an option of browsing through display shelves.

Pan-Beedi shops: These are small shops, almost like handcarts, and are primarily set up to dispense cigarettes and chewing tobacco. One can find such shops at every corner and they are the main source of soap purchase for the lower socio-economic classes. These kinds of shops exist by the dozen in rural areas.

Department stores in India: There are very few department stores and the 'Indianised' version of department stores are called 'Sahakari Bhandars.' It is still a fairly new concept. Department stores have good display counters and this is the only place where consumers get a first-hand experience of shopping and choosing from the available options. Here soap prices are also discounted below the retail prices.

Electronic Commerce: Impact on Pharma Value Chain

In recent years, the role of electronic business and electronic commerce in the supply chain and logistics systems for the retail trade sector has been considerable, especially in general merchandising and pharmaceutical retailing.

Electronic data interchange (EDI) systems, based on either proprietary or Internet technologies provide the glue or information infrastructure to hold the value chain together. The exchange of information is as important as, or more important than, the exchange of physical goods, in the general merchandise value chain. The value chain in the general merchandise business consists of manufacturers, importers, distribution channels including couriers, truckers, logisticians, trading houses, wholesalers, department stores, other general merchandise stores, and, of course, the consumer.

The pharmaceutical value chain consists of manufacturers of prescription drugs (brand name and generic drugs), manufacturers of non-prescription drugs (brand name and generic drugs), wholesalers, hospitals, distribution channels (couriers, etc.), physicians, drug stores and other outlets, and the consumer. Manufacturers sometimes deal directly with pharmacists and sometimes sell their products through wholesalers. Internet-based technologies helped retailers and third-party logistics firms to access their respective information systems through the Internet.

The general merchandising and the pharmaceutical retailing industries are heavy users of electronic commerce. Paper systems have largely been replaced by electronic systems including Electronic Data Interchange (EDI) and Internet-based systems.

Electronic systems have been instrumental in streamlining the supply chain and logistics operations of the retail sector. As soon as orders are received from customers, instructions are sent electronically to suppliers and distribution centres to ship the order either from the warehouse or the plant. Orders for 'big-ticket' items such as fridges and stoves are communicated directly to the manufacturer and shipped to a central distribution centre and subsequently sent to a retail location or to the customer's home address.

Inventory costs are being passed down the supply chain, as manufacturers are able to make better decisions on product flow based on collaborative Internet-based networks between suppliers and retailers. Suppliers are better informed whether or not to stock key items in their warehouses. The end result is reduced inventory costs and better product flow.

Logistics managers are placing greater emphasis on external functions and demand-pull systems that are customer oriented. In the past, they concentrated exclusively on internal logistics functions including warehousing, transportation, etc.

Retailers are benefiting from improved logistics systems, which utilize central distribution centres in key locations and electronic systems to keep track of the movement of goods and the repair needs of the equipment (tractors, trailers, etc.).

Some retailers perform all their transportation logistics internally as they believe that they have a competitive advantage in this area. Other retailers contract out this function, which allows the retailer to concentrate on its core business.

While EDI systems are still important, retailers are generally moving to Internet-based systems or plan to do so in the near future. Internet-based systems are more cost effective and efficient. Suppliers do not have high up front costs for equipment and software. Internet-based systems are better able to work with a myriad of suppliers, retailers, distributors, agents, intermediaries, and customers.

Internet-based systems support mass customization of products and a management structure that operates collaboratively with all players in the value chain.

Source: Industry Canada 2000, Logistics and Supply Chain Management: Sector Competitiveness Framework.

Retail Strategy

Retail strategy indicates how the firm plans to focus its resources to accomplish its objectives. It influences the firm's business activities and its response to market forces, such as competition and the economy. There are six steps involved in the development of a retail strategy. They include:

(1) Defining the business of the firm in terms of orientation towards a particular sector

(2) Setting short-term and long-term objectives with regard to image and profitability

(3) Identifying the target market towards which to direct efforts on the basis of the customers' characteristics and needs
(4) Deciding the broad direction the company must take in the future
(5) Implementing an integrated plan that encompasses all the aspects of retailing like pricing, location, and channel decisions
(6) Evaluating and revising the plan depending on the nature of the internal and external environment

Retail Concept

It is essentially the marketing concept of a customer-centred, company-wide approach to developing and implementing a strategy. It provides the guidelines, which must be followed by all retailers irrespective of their size, channel design, and medium of selling. The retailing concept covers four broad areas and is an essential part of the retailing strategy.

(a) *Customer orientation:* The retailer makes a careful study of the needs of the customer and attempts to satisfy those needs.
(b) *Goal orientation:* The retailer has clear cut goals and devises strategies to achieve those goals.
(c) *Value driven approach:* The retailer offers good value to the consumer with merchandise having the price and quality appropriate for the target market.
(d) *Coordinated effort:* Every activity of the firm is aligned to the goal and is designed to maximize its efficiency and deliver value to the consumer.

The retailing concept, though simple to adopt, is not followed by many retailers who neglect one or more of the points enumerated above. There must be a proper balance of all the aspects of this concept for the retailer to achieve success. The retailing concept, while important, is limited by its nature as it does not cover the firm's internal capabilities or the competitiveness of the external environment. It however remains an important strategic guide.

The retailing concept can be used to measure the retailers' performance through three parameters: the total retail experience, customer service, and relationship retailing. The total retail experience refers to all the ingredients of a customer's interaction with the retailer. This includes all activities from parking to billing. If some parts of the retail experience are unsatisfactory, the shopper may decide not to patronize that particular outlet. Therefore, it is necessary for a retailer to ensure that every element in the experience must aim at fulfilling customer expectations. This experience means different aspects for different types of retailers—for an upper-end clothing retailer this might imply the presence of plush interiors and air conditioning while a discount store needs to have adequate stock.

One of the biggest challenges for the retailer today is to devise new ways of attracting customer attention to be able to position themselves differently from competitors. Many novelties in retailing, for example, the theme restaurants, have emerged and there is a battle to snare the customer's attention. Sometimes though, elements of the retail experience can be beyond the control of the retailer, like the levying of sales tax or the speed of online shopping.

Customer service refers to the tangible and intangible activities undertaken by a retailer in combination with the basic goods and services it provides. It is part of the value-driven approach adopted by retailers in a bid to differentiate themselves and occupy a strategic position. Among the factors that drive a firm's customer-centric approach are store hours, parking access, sales personnel, amenities like a recreation area for children, and coffee shops. Different people evaluate the same service in various ways. Even an individual may do so at different times due to intangibility. People's assessment of a particular service is based not necessarily on reality but on perception.

Keywords such as customer orientation, innovation, and flexibility have become 'must-haves'.

International Retailing—Steps for Expansion

1. *Quantification:* of the opportunity
2. *Market assessment:* to go or not to go
3. *Cultural differences:* how to deal with them
4. *Competition:* level, quality, and positioning
5. *Price analysis:* defining the right pricing for the new market
6. *Gross margin:* quantifying cost of goods and identifying sourcing alternatives
7. *Regulatory issues:* identification and cost-effective solutions
8. *Logistics planning:* how to flow goods efficiently to the new market
9. *Systems integration:* between the head office and a new international division

10. *Head office and company structure:* options for managing the international operation
11. *Proforma development:* defining the RoI based on cross-border operating benchmarks
12. *Entry strategy and location analysis:* from overall strategy to predictive modeling
13. *Implementation services:* including such services as staff and executive recruiting, media and public relations management, import/export logistics, and warehousing and distribution coordination

These words have been repeated like mantras for decades now but rarely have they been put into practice. The service mentality frequently encountered in the Indian retail sector can still be unpleasant, even to those customers willing to make purchases. The realization that the services provided do not suit the prices demanded impels rationally acting customers to switch to the discounters. Stand-alone businesses and the owner-managed specialist stores are suffering the most and, at least in urban India, appear to have passed their zenith. Many retail companies have now realized that the competition for the purchasing power of the customers has long crossed the boundaries of their own narrow sectors. New competitors have been courting the attention of customers and trespassing on the traditional territory of the retail companies.

Some of the major criteria for the right customer approach are as follows:

- Creating the right environment
- Listening to customers
- Providing rewards to the best customers
- Realizing the lifetime value of consumers

The concept of lifetime value of consumers is employed in relationship marketing. Retailers need to establish relationships with existing customers to motivate them to return regularly. The ongoing process of identifying and creating new value with individual customers over the lifetime of a relationship is relationship marketing. It is mutually beneficial in nature creating a win-win solution for both the retailer and the consumer by allowing the retailer to be profitable and giving the consumer value. This is especially important because it is much harder to attract new customers than it is to retain old ones. It is a blend of product, quality, and services.

Relationship marketing uses the event-driven tactics of customer retention marketing, but treats marketing as a process over time rather than a series of single unconnected events. By moulding the marketing message and tactics according to the lifecycle of the customer, the relationship marketing approach achieves very high customer satisfaction and high profits. Using the relationship marketing approach, the retailer must customize programmes for individual consumer groups and the stage of the process they are going through as opposed to some forms of database marketing where everybody would get virtually the same promotions, with perhaps a change in offer. The stage in the customer lifecycle determines the marketing approach used with the customer. A simple example of this would be sending new customers a 'welcome kit,' as an incentive to make a second purchase.

The Changing Face of Retailing

This section deals with some of the current trends in the world of retailing and delineates some of the major predictions for retailers and customers alike. It consists of two parts: (a) role of the Internet in retailing and (b) branding through retailers.

Role of the Internet

The Internet has opened a new world of opportunities for retailers. It offers a way to grow an existing retail business and increase exposure in the marketplace. Retailers of any size can get even more successful through the Internet with an effective service and sale site. The Web also offers a way for retailers to fill the gaps of their brick and mortar stores by offering more service online for their existing customers.

Considerable attention has been focused on the Internet and its commercial potential for retailers. However, two key areas of confusion emerge for retailers. First, what role can the Internet play in retail marketing? Some academics assert that the Internet will provide a new retail format, usurping the traditional dominance of fixed location stores.

Alternatively, some see the Internet performing a supporting role for existing marketing activity. Whichever role is adopted, it may ultimately determine consumer demand for online shopping and thus the development of 'cyber retailing'. This raises the second area of confusion; speculation concerning the actual size, growth, or future potential of the 'cyber retail market'. Which retailers are online and are they using the Internet strategically or tactically as a marketing tool?

This information is critical for retailers developing Internet marketing strategies, and may help to identify the sectors or variables that hold most potential for online retailing. It could also expose any retailer weaknesses or threats to existing retail formats.

The Internet has been used in three main ways to facilitate retail marketing. Basically, it is a means of communicating information about the retail organization, its products, and services. At the next level, it is used as a more proactive marketing tool, inviting consumers interactively to access the website to gain more product information to facilitate their buying decision-making process.

At the same time it provides valuable consumer data to retailers to enable greater targeting. US retailers view the Internet as a communication tool for attracting new customers, penetrating new markets, promoting the company's brand, and improving customer retention. The third level involves retailers actually selling products online through transactions with the consumers, providing an additional channel to an existing store or mail order operation.

Internet retailing offers a retail experience that is totally different from fixed location retailing. Comparison and price shopping across a greater number of sites will be easier and could be achieved within minutes. More and more consumers are beginning to use the Internet for research in the early part of the buying decision-making process. But in India there is still hesitation in buying directly on the Web.

Most carry out research on the Internet and subsequently purchase the product by store or order on the telephone. In India, growth of retail formats is tardy because of the time taken for establishing the physical infrastructure, providing the consumer time to adapt to the new methods of delivery. The retailers with a strong and established brand presence, effective physical distribution relationships, and capital investment in traditional formats may be less inclined towards expansion into a non-store, electronic format.

Does the Size of a Retail Organization Play a Big Part in its Easy Adaptability to the Internet?

It has been suggested that small retail organizations are most likely to adopt the Internet due to its greater flexibility, limited resources and, lack of economies of scale, encouraging collective marketing via small business networks. While it appears that the size of the organization may be a critical factor in influencing a retailer's adoption of the Internet, the US experience indicates otherwise—a survey of the top US retailers suggested that smaller companies were less likely to be online.

Some scholars suggest that the larger retail organizations feel most threatened by the Internet and are now attempting to exploit the new medium to reinforce their market presence. Alternatively, it could be that the larger retailers, because of their comparative advantage in terms of skilled manpower and financial resources, perceive that they are best placed to exploit the commercial potential of the Internet.

Is the Product/Service Offered also a Prime Determinant of Cyber Retailing?

The type of shopping activity may further indicate the product groups most likely to succeed on the Internet. Convenience shopping and speciality goods may offer varying attractions to the online consumer. Evidence from the US experience of Internet retailing indicated a preference for electronics and other related products. In addition to PC peripherals, banking services and books and magazines accounted for nearly half of Internet sales in the US, whereas grocery shopping was considered to be less compatible with Internet shopping. In contrast, the Internet retail structure in the UK tends to be dominated by the food sector.

Retailers are increasingly turning to Web-based tools for better communication with suppliers and clients, and to keep a closer eye on inventory. Led by big US discounters like Wal-Mart and Target, the industry has developed intricate supply-chain systems. Software to help avoid excess stock and data mining technologies to gather information about customers' purchasing habits is now in common use in the West. Internet-based tools can make a huge difference, resulting in cost savings of several million dollars across the entire supply chain.

The Web allows even small suppliers to plug in, whereas earlier systems would have required expensive hardware to allow them to communicate electronically with big retailers.

Tools such as the Syncra Systems' Web-based software cautions the suppliers in real-time when a discrepancy shows up between their production forecasts and the retailers' buying forecasts, allowing both players to plan more efficiently. Software like IBM WebSphere can help lower clients' out-of-stock and improve inventory turnover—the rate at which goods move off store shelves. Retailers can make more money when they are able to lessen the frequency of running out of popular products and increase the speed at which a product sells.

Increasingly, retailers employ just-in-time processes that minimize their stockholding by feeding their EPOS (electronic point of sale) data into EDI (electronic data interchange) systems. The way this works is that when stock on the shelf falls to the pre-defined re-order quantity, it places an order electronically to the supplier. The EDI systems may also complete other elements of the transaction electronically, such as order acknowledgement, invoicing, and payment. As retailers make considerable administrative cost savings by trading with suppliers electronically, many require that suppliers are EDI-enabled.

Most retailers in India are now familiar with IT features like e-mail and websites. But this is only the tip of the IT iceberg, and the ubiquitous microchip has thrown up a plethora of less well-known business applications as well as multiple software packages for computerization of systems, which can have a spectacular impact on the bottom line.

What could Limit the Success of Cyber Retailing in India?

Some of the main factors will be concerns about lack of secure payment methods, access restrictions, and various technological restrictions. The success of e-tailing or retail on the World Wide Web will largely depend upon the competitive pricing and penetration of Internet connectivity and availability of broadband services in India's widespread households. Consumer predisposition toward the Internet as a new retail format may also constrain future growth. Consumer demand for the Internet is a key component that may ultimately drive widespread adoption of the Internet by retailers. The ultimate success of the Internet will depend on whether the Indian consumer has access and how they use or perceive Internet shopping.

Branding Through Retailers

In many countries today, the biggest retailers dominate the consumer environment. Although the Internet and the catalogues allow manufacturers to sell directly to the public, these media currently only deliver a niche market opportunity. In its turn, retailing is a highly competitive market, usually with a small number of very large retailers vying with each other for the top position. Also, in comparison to manufacturing, retailing is not that profitable.

Retailers do make a considerable mark-up on manufacturers' prices, but often their net profits are significantly below those made by the larger manufacturers. In a cluttered, fragmented media environment, the store now plays a prominent role as both a medium and a mediator between the brand and the consumer.

Over the last few years, the largest fast moving consumer goods (FMCG) manufacturers have been increasingly threatened by the large retailers because, without them, they would not be able to reach their customers, in terms of both logistics and consumer communications. The role of retailers as communicators for a particular brand is important—advertising is effective not only because it directly persuades consumers to buy a brand, but because it persuades retailers to allocate that brand with extra shelf space or 'facings'.

This conveys to the consumers that the brand is much in demand, and therefore probably worth buying. Large retailers have started developing their own product brands that are displacing many manufacturer-branded goods. Therefore, manufacturers must be able to build strong brands and maintain relationships with retailers.

How do Retailers Choose which Brands to Display?

Most retailers seek to maximize the profit they make from each square yard/metre of shelf space. The increasing number of similar products on the shelves endangers manufacturers and market intermediaries alike. Therefore, the selection of the right products for the shelves becomes essential to retailers for their market success. Major retailers use store-planning software to optimize the mix of products on the shelf in order to generate maximum returns.

The latest trend is for retailers to consider appointing category managers, whereby suppliers bid for the right to manage an entire category of products, both their own and competitors', by offering the highest guaranteed rate of return to the retailer. Some of the categories of products that are stocked by a retailer are: profit earner—where the brand earns more profit than its competition; traffic builder—where the brand attracts more traffic; and image builder—where the brand has greater image impact than the competition.

Why do New Products Fail in the Market?

The role of retailers in obtaining new product success is crucial because they assume the role of a gatekeeper who decides which new products find their way to the shelves. It is therefore necessary for manufacturers of consumer products to explore the needs of their partners in the marketing channel. Product quality, product novelty, compatibility, and launch strategy related factors have previously also been found to impact new product adoption by retailers. Competitive pressure measures and market variability also appear to be important factors for retailers when deciding about whether or not to adopt a new product.

How can Manufacturers Maximize Brand Exposure in a Given Retail Outlet?

Some of the factors include:
- Number and size of physical 'facings' on the shelves
- Prominent positions in the store (check-outs)
- Multiple positions within the store and promotional opportunities outside the store (shop windows)
- Identified brand areas (branded racking, dispensers, cabinets)
- In-store shop floor promotions (e.g., tastings, demonstrations, leaflets)
- In-store advertising (shelves, floors, walls, ceilings, counters, dispensers)
- Promotions and packaging (tell your customers a story)
- Inclusion in the retailer's communication process

Lifestyle Clustering

The proliferation of choices available and the growth of personal style possibilities are creating a new kind of store that acts as a 'choice editor' for shoppers. A large part of what the store stands for is communicated through limiting the brands and types of products they carry. The trend is now towards grouping products by lifestyle as opposed to the type of product is proving to be an effective tactic for retailers. Rather than working through traditional category management, like putting all the shampoos together and all the skin creams together, retailers are creating lifestyle clusters inside their stores, for example all low fat-food, beverages, snacks, and other food products in one section.

Vertical Retail Concepts are on the Rise

The boundaries between simple store concepts along traditional lines and verticalist or shop-in-shop concepts are fluid and are reflected in modern store construction concepts, which make the customer the focus of attention to a greater extent than in the past and help the retailers stage-manage the product. The challenge for them involves finding a future-oriented mixture of system and individuality, without alienating their important target group of walk-in customers with too sharp a profile.

Alliances with specialists raises the levels of competence and customer frequency. An example can be taken of the grocery retailing business, which is fast merging with the convenience-shopping concept. The basic idea behind this concept involves bringing the sale of non-food articles like newspapers, magazines, paperbacks, etc., with food, snacks, and beverages.

Retailers and marketers are not just focusing on temporary price reductions, feature ads, and displays, but are often going beyond these tactics to adopt strategies that are changing the face of retailing to accommodate and alter the way consumers think and behave. Changes in the retail environment are making today's stores one of the richest, most complex vehicles for communicating with consumers. The new face of retail is changing the way shoppers think about the retail brand, as well as the products featured within the store. The new strategy of gaining access to the consumer is LIM, 'Less Is More'.

In the clothing retail business, for example, this involves a deliberate reduction in the number of models presented per square meter of sales surface area and is considerably more successful in this respect than surfaces with a higher number of models per square meter of sales surface area.

This has brought about the concept of 'retail ecology' in which retail environments are studied along with how shoppers interact with specific environments. Once the ecology of the retail space is known and understood, it can be used to make the shopping trip more efficient, more intuitive, and more effective for shoppers

Consumption-related Mega-trends

There are certain trends in consumption behaviour that have a direct and significant impact on the business strategy and profitability of retail business. These trends relate to the changing demography, increasing individualization, increasing computerization, increased mobility, increased demand in terms of sustainability, and dematerialization.

Demographically, there is an increase in the number of consumers with greater purchasing power and more migrant consumers. In the West there is a fall in the number of young and increase in the number of senior consumers. In India there are more young consumers than senior consumers. The composition of households is also changing with the increase in smaller and newer forms.

There is also an *increase in consumer power* both on an individual and on a collective basis. It is reflected in demand-led production and focus on narrow niches. There have been consumption changes from acquiring to experiencing. The retail industry has tried to respond to these trends by greater focus on customer service and retail atmospherics.

Technology has facilitated the move towards online consumption and making consumption *independent of time (24/7) and space*. Product and price comparison is easier. With process globalization setting in, consumers want a broad selection of products, and consumption of imported products has increased. Faster and easier mobility has contributed to the *rise of leisure commuter*. The frequency of holidays has increased. There is also increased consumption en route (stations, gas stations, and airports). Internationalization of business has caused a rise in international business trips.

There has been an increase in the *demand for high quality and sustainable products*. While expenditure on bio-dynamic and healthy food products has increased, people now long for 'honest', 'original', and 'green' products and services. Preference for eco-tourism, recycling and alternative environment-friendly modes of transport are on the rise. This will doubtless have implications on retail merchandise and brand stocking decisions, store positioning, and packaging.

Many retail outlets like Body Shop, Fab India, and Khadi and Village Industries Commission (KVIC) outlets are such examples. The latest trend of *dematerialization,* where experiencing services has become more important than acquiring them, is increasingly becoming popular. This has been accompanied by the rise of digital goods (like MP3 music).

Drivers of Success in the Retail Sector

This section essentially puts together different ideas introduced in the chapter and attempts to elucidate some of the fundamental factors that are necessary for success in the retailing industry today.

With the growing competition both on and off the Web today, it is becoming increasingly difficult for retailers to survive in the new economy. A new revolution is taking place. And for retailers to thrive today, they must possess revolutionary thinking. This type of thinking involves a desire to embrace change within their organization. Changes include a more focussed approach to strategic planning, advanced marketing skills, a stronger customer focus, and enhanced exposure on the World Wide Web. Faced with an environment where it is hard to raise prices or sales volume, retailers are seeking subtler ways to increase profits.

Customers are the Driving Force In Change

With two-income families, busier schedules, and less time to shop, retailers must also offer more convenience than ever before. Today's busy consumers have less free time. It is becoming harder for people to find time to shop in a leisurely manner. Excellent customer service of the 21st century is all about offering more convenience and education to customers. They want to shop when it is convenient to them.

Customers are becoming more demanding and less forgiving as their shopping options increase in number, size, and variety. They are less interested in the lowest price or the biggest selection and more interested in finding solutions to their problems. They seek and demand unexpected services and the store goes the extra mile to meet their demands. Consumers get bored quickly and expect retailers to blend shopping, eating, and playing into the retail equation.

Retailers may want to offer added convenience by extending their hours of operation, improving their website purchasing, or by speeding up check-out lines. Retailers must learn how to sell diversely to multiple generations and genders. This investment in customers will yield more sales and greater loyalty.

The key to success in retail is two pronged—knowing what the customer wants, and providing what the customer wants just as it is required in the most cost-efficient manner. The first requires customer intimacy, that is, the combination of soft market research (focus groups, laddering, psychographics), with hard data analysis—trends, patterns, statistical clustering, and demographics.

The second requires a supply chain that is efficient and just-in-time. It requires the information to flow quickly and purposefuly from the point of sale to the supplier, while integrating the logistics provider. Today, the scope for improvement is tremendous. Currently, most of in-store personnel time is spent on non-sales activities and margins have been squeezed down to 1% for many items.

Retailers must encourage their sales staff and allow them to personalize relations with the customers by spending more time listening to each customer and understanding their needs. Smaller retailers can get to know their customers by name and learn more about their families and personal interests to make stronger one-on-one connections. Larger or corporate retailers may offer shopper-friendly terminals that will help consumers locate what they are looking for without searching for the sales help. User-friendly kiosks will offer self-service to customers.

Re-evaluating the Marketing Plan

Along with the growth in competition, both on and off the Web, advertising prices too will continue to rise. Retailers will stand out as leaders and authorities in their respective markets by focusing their advertising efforts on the benefits of a changing customer base. Mass advertising has become less effective as many retailers advertise from just one sale to the next. The word *sale* has been overused and is becoming a less effective vehicle to drive traffic into retail stores today. Even corporate discount merchants have discovered the need for a more upscale image to reach a larger customer base. For example, Target, a worldwide mass discount retailer, has learned how to effectively use a more upscale image to build a strong branded image with their customers.

Generic advertising is becoming less and less effective to stand out from the crowd, and a strong public relations campaign has become a more effective way to get customer attention for many retailers. Public relations is often perceived as a stronger approach and in some cases an even less expensive one. Retailers may become known as experts in their niche industries by writing articles for local or international publications or getting interviewed on radio and TV.

Advanced Education for Retailers is Critical for Growth

Innovative retailers have discovered that to improve and adjust to changes quickly within their environment, they must continue to learn and become cutting-edge to move ahead of their competitors. They must begin to work on their businesses by getting out and seeking opportunities for growth. Attending seminars, meeting other retailers, and learning from both will add to the competitive edge that retailers must have today. Business is changing so rapidly that smart retailers are now learning as much within one year as they had in the past five years altogether. As this trend continues, innovative retailers on the move towards future growth are attending more focused retail seminars and workshops to be aware of the latest marketing trends, sales skills, and new business strategies within the changing industry.

Strong Visual Recognition

Retailers today must take on a new approach to be successful since visual marketing has become increasingly important to drive more sales. About 70–80% of the buying decisions in mass retailing today are made at the point of purchase. Therefore, it is extremely important for retailers to learn how to focus on their customers' needs and to view their business through their customers' eyes. To build an effective business image, retailers must be aware of all the details that make up an overall consistent and effective image. In a matter of seconds, prospective customers begin to scrutinize every detail of a business from a retailer's business card, displays, employees, or directly through their website. A business image is always perceptible.

The Workplace Challenge

Employees will be even more difficult to come by as information technology and other high-paying professions lure applicants who would have taken retail positions. Retailers will counter this threat by hiring more part-timers and being more flexible with hours, or by choosing to pay a lot more. Retailers may foresee this challenge by offering more continued education, greater appreciation, and motivation for their employees. Regular manager and sales staff meetings are necessary to build a strong relationship. Retailers should accept inputs from their employees and encourage them to have independent thinking.

Planning for Success

The retailing world of tomorrow will be very different from today. To survive in retailing one must begin to plan for the evolution and shifts in the industry. Strategic planning, which is a combination of strategic thinking and long-range planning, is the key to planning for success. It can be a retailer's blueprint to achieve the goals and plans for future growth. In addition, strategic planning can increase the focus on marketing approach and also help to build a supportive team of employees.

The Last Word

In contrast to the situation a few years ago, competitive advantages in the retailing sector today, once achieved, are only of short duration unless they are accompanied by superb management quality or based on a unique position. The efforts required to maintain such advantages are incomparably greater. Against this backdrop, cooperation will have a decisive effect on the future of the retail sector. The necessity of achieving market power, as well as the drive for size, profitability, and efficiency, will continue to produce profound changes in the retail sector in the future. This means, for the majority of companies acting in the market, the companies which do not master a particular market or category/niche will have no chance of survival. It also means that non-organized retail businesses in particular will have to struggle more than ever in future to justify their ongoing existence. Overall, the opportunities are shrinking for traditionally structured retailers to maintain themselves against vertical players and companies external to the sector.

The manner in which India's retail industry is shaping up, the foreseeable future indicates that large retailers would most certainly cut into a sizable share of the branded market, which was hitherto largely controlled by small players. The trend of large national chain stores replacing small independent retailers is continuing unabated. Rapidly growing catalogue and Internet usage confront small retailers with new challenges and dramatic changes that force them to adapt rapidly or perish. As a result, small retailers will feel the pinch of high markups and may shift to lower price point merchandise. Thus, they would be required to sell larger volumes in order to compensate the high price point drop. The independent stores that survive and prosper will be those who: (1) recognize and act on their competitive strengths and weaknesses; (2) understand who their customers are and what they want; and (3) identify and fill a viable niche in the marketplace.

Small retailers will also have to match the ambience provided by their larger competitors. They may opt for different business models like speciality stores, fixed price shops, or discount stores. A few may consider switching to large format stores and enhance their capabilities in terms of range, merchandise and price points. Some retailers might even be forced to move to different categories or even change their line of business. In a similar manner, large stores might turn to operating out of small format outlets with speciality offerings, catalogue showrooms, transit stores, and satellite warehouses for parent showrooms.

The tendency towards integration into a common value chain will increase significantly in future and will become an essential component of strategies between companies. Tough negotiation of conditions will give way to considerations as to how, for example, a prompt and predominantly regional sourcing strategy can guarantee product range and sales policies adequate to customer requirements and how synergies may be realized in sales and marketing. Retail concepts with the potential for future success are based exclusively on a close network of all parties involved in the process chain. Lone fighters do not stand much of a chance, unless they have a dominant position in the market on account of their innovative leadership or strong brand image.

In the Indian market in particular, concepts focused on emphasizing value-for-money considerations will accelerate the polarization of the market across all sectors and will outperform their respective market segments.

Summary

Retailing is defined as the conclusive set of activities or steps used to sell a product or service to consumers for their personal or family use. It is responsible for matching individual demands of the consumer with supplies of all the manufacturers. The word 'retail' is derived from the French word *retaillier*, meaning 'to cut a piece off' or 'to break bulk'. Some of the key aspects of retailing are direct customer interaction, small unit size of sales, point-of-sale promotions, criticality of location, and emphasis on customer service.

The retailer performs various functions like sorting, breaking bulk, holding stock, channel of communication, storage, advertising, and certain additional services. Retailers can be classified on the basis of number of outlets, margin vs. turnover, location, and size. The key drivers of change in the retail sector are the changing demographics and industry structure, expanding computer technology, emphasis on lower costs and lower prices, accent on convenience and service, focus on productivity, added experimentation, and continuing growth of non-store retailing.

It is important for retailers to carefully plan their strategy. In this context the following steps to plan the retail strategy need to be followed: (a) defining the business of the firm in terms of orientation towards a particular sector; (b) setting short-term and long-term objectives with regard to image and profitability; (c) identifying the target market towards which to direct efforts on the basis of the customer's characteristics and needs; (d) deciding the broad direction the company must take in the future; (e) implementing an integrated plan that encompasses all the aspects of retailing like pricing, location, and channel decisions, and (f) evaluation and revision of the plan depending on the nature of the internal and external environment.

Concept Review Questions

1. What is retailing? Enlist the retail activities carried out by retailers.
2. Discuss briefly various types of retail formats.
3. What are the drivers of changing face of retail structures in the developing world, particularly in the context of India?
4. What is the role of Internet technology in redefining the retail industry in the entire value chain?

Project Work Assignment

1. Identify the retail functions of the following types of retailers:
   (a) Mom-and-pop store (*kirana*)
   (b) Department grocery store
   (c) Independent apparel store
   (d) Franchised food outlet

2. Identify the nature of Internet usage by two retailers in different product categories in your city. Also analyse the reasons for using this new interface.

3. Compare the nature of retail formats employed and their impact on retail penetration of any two FMCG companies.

Case Study

Retailing in Perishables: Compulsions and Impact of Consolidation

In recent years the fresh fruits and vegetable value chain has gone through a process of re-structuring, having considerable impact on food retailing format. Stable food prices, slowing growth in at-home food spending, the increasing share of expenditure on food service channels, and the growth of food sales by non-traditional retailers, including online shopping options, have heightened competition among grocery retailers. Many food retailers have opted to merge, citing cost savings and efficiency gains in order to compete better.

Fresh fruit and vegetable market in the US was estimated in 1990 at around $ 83.5 billion. Over the last decade the US food system has experienced the entrance of new competitors playing by new rules, placing greater competitive pressure on conventional food retailers. Chief among these new competitors are mass merchandisers introducing supply chain management, a procurement model designed to streamline the distribution system by eliminating non-value-adding transaction costs. Increasing investment of European supermarket chains in the US market has likely reinforced this trend, as many European chains have advanced further in the implementation of supply chain management compared to conventional US retailers. As they have invested in the US system, they have gradually begun to modify the US procurement model, including a greater reliance on private labels.

More recently, retailers have been faced with the challenge of positioning themselves in a market place that offers nascent business to consumer food marketing choices (online food shopping) and emerging e-commerce procurement options, both of whose impacts and roles are as yet uncertain. The future role of business-to-business e-commerce in fresh produce is particularly unclear given the perishable nature of the products and differences in quality and volumes both intra- and inter-seasonally. While the dry grocery industry long ago adopted EDI, this system never functioned in the volatile produce sector, which operates more through personal relationships rather than automated procurement systems.

Still, as buyers grow, there are compelling reasons to streamline fresh produce procurement and firms are beginning to attempt to treat fresh produce like other food commodities with more stable pricing and volumes. The recent emergence of retailer-shipper procurement contracts is a part of this process and demonstrates the introduction of supply chain management methods in the US fresh produce system. E-commerce platforms tailored to the fresh produce sector have the potential to become successful alternatives to EDI.

The new competitive pressures have contributed to retail and wholesale consolidation as firms seek efficiency gains through mergers and acquisitions to strengthen their competitive positions. As the leading retailers and wholesalers have grown, they have begun to exercise greater buying power, including in the procurement of fresh produce. Greater buying power has caused an increase in the level and types of fees and services being required from fresh produce suppliers and is leading to more closely coordinated relationships between buyers and sellers. Suppliers are changing by adopting information technology and developing the systems and services capable of serving the needs of the few larger buyers. Given the costs associated with a higher level of services and the need to more-or-less match the scale of larger buyers, supplier's consolidation is beginning to occur, whether through ownership or strategic alliances.

Finally, consumers are in the driver's seat, increasingly demanding more services, including convenience in food-purchasing and preparation, taste, quality, safety, and variety. This presents both challenges and opportunities for firms at all levels of the fresh produce marketing system.

Consolidation in Food Retailing

From 1992 to 1999, the four largest food retailers' share of grocery store sales rose from 15.9% to 29% while the share of the eight largest retailers increased from 24.9% to 42%. Most of these gains occurred after 1996, when a number of firms consolidated.

Today there are ten integrated wholesale-retailers (defined in the box on grocery retailing channels) each with over 1000 stores and selling over US $1 billion in fresh produce annually. For each of the two largest supermarket chains, fresh produce sales are estimated to exceed US $4 billion. Clearly, the buying power of these groups is impressive with half of US food sales now accounted for by these 10 integrated wholesale-retailers. Suppliers who are not equipped to sell to these very large buyers must focus their efforts on the remaining, more fragmented portions of the food system, both retail and other.

Consolidation in Food Wholesaling

Consolidation is also occurring rapidly among merchant food wholesalers, many of whom have acquired specialized fresh produce wholesalers, as well as merging with general-line grocery wholesalers. Acquisitions and mergers continue to reshuffle the ranks of the leading companies. Supervalue/Rich Foods, a voluntary chain—a type of integrated wholesaler-retailer—has aggressively acquired firms to become the largest grocery wholesaler, with sales of US $22 billion in 1999 and serving some 4,400 stores. Fleming Cos, the largest wholesaler until 1996, is now at number two with sales of US $15.1 billion in 1999, serving over 5,500 grocery stores and 279 of its own corporate food stores.

While the food-service distribution industry continues to experience a high level of merger activity, it remains relatively fragmented, with the top 10 specialized food-service wholesalers accounting for 25% of the US $147 billion in total food-service wholesale sales in 1998, while the top four firms had 21% share. Fragmentation in the food-service wholesaling industry is because of the huge number of final users served.

While there are about 30,600 supermarkets in the US there are over 627,000 commercial food-service outlets, and around 112,000 non-commercial outlets. In addition, while large retailers predominantly buy fresh produce directly from shipping point, avoiding wholesalers, food-service buyers still rely greatly on wholesalers and terminal markets. Sysco Corporation is by far the largest food-service wholesaler, with sales of US $17.4 billion in 1999, up from US $14.8 billion in 1997. While Sysco distributes a full line of food and non-food products, fresh produce now accounts for 6% of its sales, equivalent to about US $1 billion. In August 2000 Royal A's US food-service acquired PYA/Monarch, creating a group with combined annual sales of US $10.7 billion and making it the number two player in this segment.

As consolidation occurs in food-service channels, buyers will procure greater volumes of fresh produce directly from shipping point, just as retailers have increasingly done in recent decades. Since much of the product moving through wholesale markets is destined for food-service users, as large foodservice buyers grow in importance, wholesalers will need to become more service-oriented if they are to retain these customers.

Impact on Produce Suppliers

Retailers expect efficiency in the procurement of many products, including produce, as a result of mergers. By purchasing more volume, retailers hope to lower the per-unit cost of goods by negotiating lower prices. In return, retailers may develop partnerships with preferred suppliers, concentrating volumes with these firms, potentially benefiting suppliers with more predictable firm level demand. When demand and supply are more closely coordinated, buyers and sellers can work together to stimulate sales, and achieve more consistent volumes and quality. On the other hand, as price takers in a low margin business, many shippers feel that they have little ability to absorb lower FOB prices, reporting that volume discounts are not cost-justified for commodity-based fresh produce shippers (as opposed to shippers of value-added produce like packaged salads).

Retailers also expect reduced marketing and selling costs as a result of relationships with preferred suppliers. Suppliers and distributors are being asked to help retailers with the design and provision of category management, effective design of promotions, promotional allowances, and special packaging. To make this type of marketing support function, effective retailers should share sales data with suppliers in order to better evaluate promotions, seasonal effects, price responses, and other characteristics of consumer demand. However, till now it is mainly the mass merchandisers that aggressively share information with shippers, reducing the effectiveness of supply chain management in conventional retail channels. Clearly, firms on both sides of the retail–shipper interface are still in the initial phases of capturing the potential benefits of partnering.

Although the economic effects of the recent mergers on fresh produce have not yet been determined, many suppliers fear that competition will erode. To date, many recently merged chains are still in the process of integrating their buying systems and some still buy produce on a division basis (with divisions defined along the lines of the incorporated chains), lessening the effect of consolidation. However, this is changing with corporate purchases growing in importance at most chains. Grower-shippers will increasingly face fewer but larger buyers as consolidated food retailers reduce the number of buying offices and combine orders into larger volumes. Produce suppliers have also cited new marketing and trade promotion practices, such as slotting allowances and fees, as evidence that produce buyers may enjoy an unfair advantage in bargaining with suppliers. However, recent research by USDA and UC Davis has shown that most fresh produce shippers of commodities, as opposed to value-added fresh-cut produce, are not paying slotting allowances, at least to date.

Still, produce suppliers will be challenged to meet the needs of food wholesalers and retailers that adopt supply chain management practices. Many smaller grower-shippers may form joint ventures, cooperatives, or other alliances to better serve large retailers. Other produce suppliers may seek niche markets, either product or buyer-derived in order to meet the procurement needs of different sizes and types of buyers. For example, niche markets exist for speciality fruits and vegetables or organically grown products, and independent retailers and upscale restaurants can be profitable niche markets for high quality produce of all varieties.

The fresh produce industry has clearly embarked upon a path leading to greater vertical coordination of the distribution system via more supply chain-oriented procurement models, despite the fact that conventional retailers are lagging behind mass merchandisers in this regard. The explosive growth of the Supercenter format is a compelling force that will continue to move conventional retailers in this direction.

1. Identify the nature of structural changes experienced by the entire value chain for perishable products.

2. Analyse the factors that have contributed to structural changes in the value chain for perishable products.

3. Analyse the response of the traditional retailers to meet the consolidation effort at various levels of value chain.

4. What kind of benefits retailers foresee through the vertical consolidation in the perishable food chain?

References

1. Pricewaterhouse Coopers 1999, 'Food for Thought', Special Insert 30(1), July.

2. www.merceroliverwyman.com, 'Retail Banking Industry: Challenges'.

3. Industry Canada 2000, 'Logistics and Supply Chain Management: Sector Competitiveness Framework'.

4. Lindstrom, Martin 1999, 'The Role of Retail in the Internet Age', www.clickz.com, July 1.

5. Majumdar, S. 2002, 'FDI in retailing: India as a supermarket', *Business Line*, Tuesday, Sep 17.

6. *The Times of India* 2004, 'India to have 220 malls by 2006', Wednesday, April 14.

7. Berman and Evans 1989, *Retail Management: A Strategic Approach*, Macmillan Publishing Company, New York, NY.

8. Lusch and Dunne 1990, *Retail Management*, South-Western Publishing Co., Cincinnati, HO.

9. Levy and Weitz 2002, *Retailing Management*, Tata McGraw-Hill Publishing Company Ltd., New Delhi

10. www.kpmg.de 2003, 'Trends in Retailing 2005—An Outlook for the Food, Fashion and Footwear Sectors'.

11. www.nacsonline.com 2004, 'Retailers of the Future Could Become "Choice Editors"', Feb. 23.

12. www.mudvalley.co.uk 2002, 'Branding through retailers'.

13. Cathy, Hart, Neil, Doherty, Fiona, Ellis-Chadwick 2000, 'Retailer adoption of the Internet Implications for retail marketing', *European Journal of Marketing*, vol. 34, No. 8, p. 954.

14. Morganosky, M.A. 1997, 'Retailing and the Internet: a perspective on the top 100 US retailers', *International Journal of Retail & Distribution Management*, vol. 25, No. 11, pp. 372–77.

15. Bill, P. and Bill, R. 2000, 'How Independent Stores Can Survive in Your Community', *Let's Talk Business*, UWEX Center for Community Economic Development, Issue 51, November.

2 RETAIL ORGANIZATION

Learning Objectives

- To understand the various methods of classifying retail formats

- To analyse the recent changes in the structure of retailing

- To explain the ownership patterns of retail organizations

- To understand the operational structures associated with retail organizations

- To evaluate retail classifications based on the length and depth of merchandise

- To discuss retail classifications based on the nature of service

- To discuss retail classifications based on the type of pricing policy

- To evaluate retail classification based on the type of retail location

- To analyse retail classification based on the method of customer interaction

Introduction

The term retail organization refers to the basic format or structure of a retail business designed to cater to the needs of the end customer. Recently, some scholars have started referring to India as a nation of shopkeepers. This epithet has its roots in the huge number of retail enterprises in India, which were over 12 million in 2003. About 78% of these are small family businesses utilizing only household labour.

Even among retail enterprises that employ hired workers, the majority of them use less than three workers. There are only 14 companies that run department stores and two with hypermarkets. While the number of businesses operating supermarkets is high (385 in 2003), most of these have only one outlet. The number of companies with supermarket chains is less than ten.

A large portion of consumer expenditure in India is incurred on basic necessities, especially food related items. Hence, it is not surprising that food, beverages, and tobacco accounted for as much as 71% of retail sales in 2002. The remaining 29% of retail sales were in non-food items. Sales through supermarkets and department stores are small compared to overall retail sales.

However, their sales grew much more rapidly (about 30% per year) during the review period. As a result, their sales almost tripled during this time. This high acceleration in sales through modern retail formats is expected to continue during the next few years with the rapid growth in numbers of such outlets in response to consumer demand and business potential.

As we see, various components of retail marketing mix indicate diverse strategic motives of the retailers. This gets reflected in the preference for different types of retail formats. Specific retail format analysis is important in these phases of strategic planning: selecting an organizational mission, choosing an ownership alternative, defining the goods/services category, and setting objectives.

Retail firms may be independently owned, parts of a retail chain, operated as a franchisee, leased departments, owned by manufacturers or wholesalers, consumer-owned, or co-operative societies.

A retail unit could be owned by:

- Manufacturer (e.g., company owned retail outlets)

- Wholesaler (e.g., Vastra outlet in Rajouri in New Delhi)
- Independent retailer (Chanakya Sweet Shop near Hazratganj in Lucknow)
- Consumer (consumer owned grocery stores in many residential societies)
- Co-operative society (e.g., Mother Dairy milk booths in Delhi)
- Government (e.g., Cottage Emporia)
- Ownership shared among franchiser and franchisee (e.g., Archies Gallery)

Although most Indian retailers fall in the category of small-scale units, there are also some very big retailers. According to a study by Economic Times Intelligence, the Confederation of Indian Industry, and Tata Strategic Management Group, organized retail sales in India were Rs 135 billion in 2000 and are estimated to grow to Rs 460 billion by the year 2005. Organized retail stores are generally characterized by large, professionally managed store formats providing goods and services that appeal to customers, in an ambience that is conducive for shopping and provides a memorable experience to customers.

From positioning and operating perspectives, each ownership format serves a marketplace niche and presents certain advantages and disadvantages. Retail executives must not lose sight of this in playing up their strengths and working around their weaknesses.

The Changing Structure of Retailing

All dynamic developments in retailing, from the birth of departmental stores in the last century to the recent emergence of warehouse clubs and hypermarkets, have been responses to a changing environment. Changing customer demand, new technologies, intense competition, and social changes create new opportunities even as they shake up existing business. In the remainder of this century and into the next, the turbulent environment in which retailers operate will most likely accelerate the pace of change. Technological advances, changing demographics, and shifts in consumer preferences and shopping expectations will bring undreamt of changes in the structure of the industry.

Discount Stores—the Next Retail Revolution in India

Retailing is going through a transitional phase in India. The corner place grocery store, which was the only choice available to the consumer, is now giving way to international formats of retailing. The traditional food and grocery segment has seen the emergence of supermarkets/grocery chains (FoodWorld, Nilgiris, Apna Bazaar, Subhiksha), convenience stores (ConveniO, HP Speedmart), and fast-food chains (McDonald's, Domino's).

The emergence of new retail sectors has been accompanied by changes in existing formats, as well as the introduction of new formats for setting up these stores:

- Hypermarts are large supermarkets, with an area of 3500–5000 sq. ft.
- Mini supermarkets have an area of 1,000–2000 sq. ft.
- Convenience stores have an area of 750–1000 sq. ft.

In fact, the retail business formats have been changing very fast, mainly due to technological influences. The Internet and the Web technologies have created a myriad of opportunities for the Web-based business model of retailing. This has created a competition for the retailer with its own self. Besides, the challenge for the retailer now is to keep abreast of these latest formats in order to maintain and grow its share of market and compete within its band of retailers.

A key impact of technology has been provision of greater information to the customer. Hence, a big challenge for the retailer in the information savvy world of today is that the opportunities for price differentiation have nearly vanished. With the wealth of information which the customer has, it becomes imperative for the retailer to differentiate itself qualitatively by superior customer services or better value for money to the customer.

For this purpose, the retailer has to constantly innovate in its customer services and re-design its value pack to the customer to keep ahead of its competition. Simultaneously, technology is also prompting efforts towards product and service differentiation. As highlighted in the point above on customer awareness, this throws up a major challenge to the retailer—service or store experience re-design and realignment with the support of latest available technologies and, thus, make the overall customer experience more satisfying and fruitful.

To this end, it is seen in the West that there is focus on customer convenience and services in the retail stores.

Bharat Petroleum: Making a Difference through Innovative Retailing

Bharat Petroleum's efforts have all along been to build a profound understanding of customer needs and relentlessly work towards fulfilling these needs. Bharat Petroleum is consciously working towards providing added value to customers, both in fuel and non-fuel areas.

Bharat Petroleum's efforts began with remodelling and upgrading retail outlets to world-class standards back in 1996. Retail outlets have been equipped with state-of-the-art modern infrastructure, including the multi-product dispensers to pre-set price and quantity of fuel and Electronic Air Gauges facilitating precise inflation of tyres. Attractive canopies are suitably designed to provide shelter and adequate lighting of the forecourt at most retail outlets.

On the non-fuel front, Bharat Petroleum has introduced the Errand Mall concept successfully at select markets. Called the 'In & Out', these malls offer the customer a broad range of facilities and brands to choose from. ATMs, cybercafe, courier services, laundry, photo studio, music, fast food, greeting cards, courier services, bill payments, movies/entertainment tickets, etc. have made Bharat Petroleum's retail outlets a happening place and indeed a rewarding experience for motorists.

Bharat Petroleum has also pioneered the concept of convenience stores at select petrol pumps that operate under the name 'Bazaar'. These Bazaars provide a wide range of convenience items and fast food to customers in a clean, air-conditioned, and friendly environment.

Source: www.bharatpetroleum.com

Already, banks, airlines, and hotels are enabling customers to pay bills and plan their vacations at home through cable TV and videotext systems. It is now possible to buy a variety of products and services without even entering a store. Electronic inventory systems have spawned discount stores that offer the same merchandise as traditional department stores do but at much lower prices.

Speciality stores have carved out a niche by offering greater selection and better services than department stores with limited merchandise lines offer. Off-price retailers have made a year round business out of leftover merchandise and factory overruns. Retailing firms that once occupied a unique position, such as traditional department and discount stores, are now being squeezed by more innovative firms.

To understand the changes in retailing business in a better way, we will now examine the theories of change in retailing.

Theories of Structural Change in Retailing

Retailing has always been a dynamic industry, and new retail firms have brought innovative approaches into retailing, changing the industry as they entered, developed, and grew. Home shopping clubs like those offered on cable TV channels are an example of how new retailers can introduce new business formats to the industry. These retailers, presently, are in an entry stage called *development and introduction.*

Time will tell whether consumers will accept this new way of doing business. Those retailers that are successful enough to survive the development and introduction stage enter the *growth stage.* The rapidly growing off-price retailer T.J. Maxx is an example of a retailer in the second stage of development.

As the business grows, it moves gradually into the maturity stage, in which competition intensifies and strategies must be developed to maintain the existing market share. Most department stores today are in this stage of development. Stores that cannot compete effectively move into the *decline stage* and eventually go out of business.

The traditional variety stores such as Ben Franklin are now in decline. The entire process can take just a few years or decades, depending on competitive conditions. Understanding how and why this process occurs is essential for success in the industry. We will examine three theories of how firms change and, in doing so, change the industry. Although the theories differ, they speak about the same problem. In retailing, change is not a matter of chance; it is a virtual certainty.

The Wheel of Retailing

The *wheel of retailing* is one of the better known theories of structural change in retailing. It was proposed by Malcomb McNair at Harvard University. It is basically a theory of cyclical or circular development. The wheel of retailing concept describes how retail institutions change during their evolutionary life cycles. New retailing institutions enter the market as low-status, low-margin, and low-price operations.

As these retailers achieve success, attempts are made to increase their customer base and sales. Products are upgraded, facilities are improved, and new services are added. Prices and margins are increased to support these higher costs. New retailers enter the market to fill the low-status, low-margin, and low-price niche. The cycle begins again. Hence, the retail store types pass through stages of growth and decline.

A retail store type emerges, enjoys a period of accelerated growth, reaches maturity, and declines. The wheel of retailing theory has been criticized because it does not explain all changes in retailing. In fact, many stores do not begin as low-price, low-service outlets.

The Dialectic Process

A second theory holds that retailing evolves through a dialectic process—the blending of two opposing store types into a superior form. For example, speciality stores offer specialized merchandise, a wide array of services, and attractive surroundings to a large and diverse market.

The blending of these two formats produces the speciality discount store. Silo, Home Depot, and Highland Superstores offer both a wide array of customer services and a broad assortment of specialized merchandise in attractive surroundings.

Natural Selection

According to the theory of *natural selection*, retail stores evolve to meet changes in the micro-environment. The retailers that successfully adapt to technological, social, demographic, economic, and political/legal changes are most likely to grow and prosper. The variety store is often cited as an example of a retail format that failed to adapt to changing times.

Today, these once successful retailers have almost died out. In contrast, television home shopping networks are likely to expand and grow because they are responding to changes in the lifestyles of the consumers.

Because it takes into account macro-environmental forces, the theory of natural selection is more inclusive than those of the wheel of retailing and the dialectic process, which are based solely on a profit–cost analysis. Yet all three theories suffer from a lack of emphasis on customer taste, wants, desires, and expectations. By gravitating to those stores that best meet their desires and needs, and shunning those that do not, consumers exert a powerful force on the evolution of retailing as does any other part of the macro-environment.

The retailers will succeed only by knowing their customers well. Consumers expect retailers to provide timely and fashionable merchandise at a convenient location and at a reasonable price. They expect value not only in the goods they buy but also in the total shopping experience, which includes pleasant atmospherics, well-trained and courteous salespeople, and special touches like live entertainment.

Classification of Retail Units

Conceptual classification of a business unit provides the marketers with strategic guidelines, useful in the design of retailing strategy. Besides, retail businesses are extremely diverse, and there are quite a few types of retail units. Therefore, retail units are classified on multiple dimensions such as margin, turnover, size, type of product sold, nature of ownership, geographical locations, kind of customer interaction, level of services provided, etc.

Bases for Classification of Retail Units

Retail firms can be classified into various format types based on the following criteria:

- *Nature of ownership:* The three basic legal forms of ownership are sole proprietorship, partnership, and limited liability company (private and public).
- *Operational structure:* The retail operational structures can be classified into the following three types: the independent trader (usually operating only one retail outlet); the multiple or chain store; franchising and the consumer co-operative.
- *Length and depth of merchandise:* Retail units differentiate themselves on the basis of the range and variety of merchandise they maintain in their stores. Some retail businesses offer a wide range of goods. On other hand, some deal only in a specific product category with a minimum range of merchandise within that product category.
- *Nature of service:* Lately, with the growing emphasis of retailers on service mix in their entire retail mix, retailers are classified on the basis of level and kind of services extended by them to their customers. Recently, in India many retail outlets have been converted to or built as self-service units, and are providing services

such as delivery, credit, gift-wrapping, repairs, etc. Hence, many former self-service retailers are now looking at ways of gaining competitive advantage by adding new customer services.

- *Type of pricing policy:* Some retailers choose to emphasize the low price rather than the service element of their retailing mix. Others choose to price their offerings above the competition, knowing that they will generate business on the basis of some other attribute such as convenient location, premium merchandise mix, or distinctive image.
- *Type of retail location:* Under this, retailers are classified according to their store's geographical location. With the increasing cost of central business district centre sites, limited parking facility, and traffic congestion, many retailers have out-of-town locations, whilst others have preferred to locate in 'cluster' locations in downtown centres.
- *Method of customer interaction:* Traditionally, most of the retail interactions or transactions have been conducted by face-to-face contact in retail stores. However, a significant number of retailers are generating retail sales by non-store retailing operations such as mail order catalogues, telephone selling, vending machines, door-to-door selling, or mobile vendors.

Some of the formats that emerge out of these classification schemes overlap but they are all relevant, given the specific marketing situations. The conventional and most common classification of retail organizations is based primarily on the nature of products, operational structure, and range of merchandise.

Retailers Classified on the Basis of Ownership

One of the first decisions that the retailer has to make as a business owner is how the company should be structured. This decision is likely to have long-term implications, so it is important to consult with an accountant and attorney to help one select preferred ownership structure.

In making the choice, the following aspects need to be considered:
- Retailer's vision regarding the size and nature of his business
- The level of control he wishes to have
- The level of 'structure' they are willing to deal with

- The business's vulnerability to lawsuits
- Tax implications of the different ownership structures
- Expected profit (or loss) of the business
- Whether or not one is required to re-invest earnings in the business
- Retailer's need for access to cash from the business for personal use

We now take an overview of the four basic legal forms of ownership for retailers:

1. Sole proprietorship
2. Partnership
3. Joint venture
4. Limited liability company (public and private)

Sole Proprietorships

The vast majority of small businesses start out as sole proprietorships. These firms are owned by one person, usually the individual who has the day-to-day responsibility for running the business. In this case, the retailer owns all the assets of the business and the profits generated by it. He also assumes complete responsibility for any of its liabilities or debts. In the eyes of the law and the public, the retailer is one and the same with the business.

Advantages of Sole Proprietorship

- Sole proprietorship is the easiest and least expensive form of ownership to organize.
- Sole proprietors are in complete control and, within the parameters of the law, may make decisions as they see fit.
- Sole proprietors receive all income generated by the business to keep or reinvest.
- Profits from the business flow directly to the owner's personal tax return.
- The business is easy to dissolve, if desired.

Disadvantages of Sole Proprietorship

- Sole proprietors have unlimited liability and are legally responsible for all debts against the business. Their business and personal assets are at risk.

- Sole proprietorship may be at a disadvantage in raising funds and are often limited to using funds from personal savings or consumer loans.
- Sole proprietorship may have a hard time attracting high-calibre employees or those that are motivated by the opportunity to own a part of the business.
- Some employee benefits such as the owner's medical insurance premiums are not directly deductible from business income (only partially deductible as an adjustment to income).

Partnerships

A partnership is a common format in India for carrying out business activities (particularly trading) on a small or medium scale. A business unit is generally carried out through a partnership. There is no restriction on a company's participation in a partnership, but this is rare in practice. In a partnership, two or more people share ownership of a single business. As in case of proprietorships, the law does not distinguish between the business and its owners in partnership. The partners should have a legal agreement that sets forth how decisions will be made, profits will be shared, disputes will be resolved, how future partners will be admitted to the partnership, how partners can be bought out, or what steps will be taken to dissolve the partnership when needed. It is hard to think about a 'break-up' when the business is just getting started, but many partnerships split up at crisis times and unless there is a defined process, there will be even greater problems. They must also decide up-front how much time and capital each partner will contribute, etc.

Advantages of a partnership:

- Partnerships are relatively easy to establish; however, time should be invested in developing the partnership agreement.
- With more than one owner, the ability to raise funds may be increased.
- The profits from the business flow directly to the partners' personal tax returns.
- Prospective employees may be attracted to the business if there is some incentive to become a partner.
- The business usually will benefit from partners who have complementary skills.

Disadvantages of a partnership:

- Partners are both jointly and individually liable for the actions of the other partners.
- Profits must be shared with others.
- Since decisions are shared, disagreements can occur.
- Some employee benefits are not deductible from business income on tax returns.
- The partnership may have a limited life; it may end upon the withdrawal or death of a partner.

For tax considerations:

- A partnership is an entity for tax purposes.
- Double taxation can be avoided where the partnership is evidenced by a deed specifying the individual shares of partners.

Entity or Conduit   Under the general law, a partnership is not a separate entity distinct from the partners, but for tax purposes a partnership is an entity. Double taxation is avoided in the manner described below.

Taxable Income   In the case of a partnership evidenced by a deed in which the individual shares of the partners are specified, the taxable income of the partnership is computed in the same manner as that of a company. Salary, bonus, commission, and other remuneration payable to working partners and interest payable to partners according to the partnership deed are deductible to the specified limits in computing the partnership's taxable income and included in the taxable income of the applicable partner.

The partnership pays tax on the balance profits at 40% (30% on long-term capital gains). (It is proposed to reduce the capital gains tax to 20%.) The balance profits are not taxed when in the hands of the partners. A partnership not evidenced by a deed in which the shares of the individual partners are specified is taxed like a joint venture.

Taxation of Foreign Partners   A foreign partner is taxed in the same manner as an Indian partner. Membership of a non-resident company in an Indian partnership, if permitted by the Reserve Bank of India, would create a permanent establishment. The tax treaties generally do not specifically address partnerships. However, the permanent establishment and business profits articles are relevant to non-resident corporate partners. The article on elimination of double taxation enables non-resident partners to claim relief for double taxation in their country of residence.

Types of Partnership

Partnerships can be of various kinds as discussed below.

General Partnership   Partners divide responsibility for management and liability, as well as the shares of profit or loss according to their internal agreement. Equal shares are assumed unless there is a written agreement that states differently.

Limited Partnership and Partnership with Limited Liability 'Limited' means that most of the partners have limited liability (to the extent of their investment) as well as limited input regarding management decisions, which generally encourages investors for short-term projects, or for investing in capital assets. This form of ownership is not often used for operating retail or service businesses. Forming a limited partnership is more complex and formal than forming a general partnership.

Joint Venture

A joint venture is not well defined in the law. Unless incorporated or established as a firm as evidenced by a deed, joint ventures may be taxed like association of persons, sometimes at maximum marginal rates. It acts like a general partnership, but is clearly for a limited period of time or a single project. If the partners in a joint venture repeat the activity, they will be recognized as an ongoing partnership, and will have to file as such and distribute accumulated partnership assets upon dissolution of the entity.

VLCC: Joint Venture Partnership

VLCC is India's leading chain of health, beauty, and fitness centres. It is managed and operated by its parent company, Curls and Curves (India) Ltd (CCIL), a Rs 600 million group. For opening its centres it enters into a joint-venture partnership with the interested party. The joint venture partners are assigned a dedicated team of professionals for ensuring smooth functioning of their business. The team is designed to take care of most of the business needs of the partner—right from customer relations to the financial integrity. VLCC operates and manages the business for the partner and the partnership is on a profit sharing basis.

VLCC invites joint venture collaborations for the following businesses:

- VLCC Slimming & Beauty Centre
- VLCC Workout Factory (Fitness Centre)
- VLCC Institute
- Beauty Shops (Retail Outlets for VLCC Products)
- VLCC Just for Men (Men's Saloon)
- VLCC Beauty Centers
- VLCC Health Kitchens

VLCC has many successful joint venture partnerships across India. An increasing number of partners joining hands with the company have achieved a reasonably high rate of interest on their investment, the average rate of return on investment ranging from 25% to 36%.

Source: www.vlcc.co.in

Taxable Income   The taxable income of a venture is determined in the same manner as in a company. Interest and remuneration payable to the ventures are treated as profit participation and added back in arriving at the venture's taxable income.

Taxation of a Foreign Venturer   A foreign venturer is taxed in the same manner as an Indian venturer, subject to the higher tax rate in the case of a non-resident corporate venturer.

Limited Liability Company (LLC)

The LLC is a relatively new type of hybrid business structure that is now permissible in most states. It is designed to provide the limited liability features of a corporation and the tax efficiencies and operational flexibility of a partnership. Formation is more complex and formal than that of a general partnership.

The owners are members, and the duration of the LLC is usually determined when the organization papers are filed. The time limit can be continued if desired by a vote of the members at the time of expiration. LLC's must not have more than two of the four characteristics that define corporations: limited liability to the extent of assets; continuity of life; centralization of management; and free transferability of ownership interests.

Classification of Retailers on the basis of Operational Structure

Retail businesses are classified on the basis of their operational and organizational structure. Operational structure defines the key strategic decision of retail entity, whether to hire employees and manage the distributed sales function internally or to reach customers through franchised outlets owned and operated by local entrepreneurs.

Retail businesses need to examine the economic and organizational trade-offs between independent ownership and franchise chain affiliation. In Indian retail set-up, independent retail organization structures are well established and often a single family designs, builds, manages, and operates the entire retail unit. After liberalization, only retail chain and franchising have evolved as strong options with retailers as modes of retail operational and organizational format.

Retailers need to evaluate various options in terms of investments, cost savings related to economies of scale, and potential demand-enhancing and reputation benefits. At times, it is possible for chain-affiliated outlets to obtain higher returns compared to a franchise, since in the latter case the agent is required to share some returns with the upstream firm. In taking such decisions, retailers need to consider outlet characteristics, market conditions, and incentive effects. Retail firms can be classified into five heads on the basis of their respective operational structures:

1. Independent retail unit
2. Retail chain
3. Franchise
4. Leased departments
5. Co-operatives

Independent Retail Unit

The total number of retailers in India is estimated to be over 5 million in 2003. About 78% of these are small family businesses utilizing only household labour. An independent retailer owns one retail unit. In the US, there are almost 2.20 million independent retailers, accounting for nearly 40% of total retail store sales. The presence of higher number of independent retailers can be attributed to multiple macro and micro reasons. A key macro-level factor is the long history of non-industry-based economic growth, whereas, an important micro-factor is the need to have low capital and licensing requirements.

Competitive Advantages and Disadvantages of the Independent Retail Format   Independent retailers have a variety of advantages and disadvantages. The competitive advantages of an independent retailer are as follows.

- There is a great deal of flexibility in choosing retail formats and locations, and in devising a strategy. Because only one store location is involved, detailed specifications can be set for the best location and a thorough search undertaken. Uniform location standards are not needed, as they are for chain stores, and independents do not have to worry about being too close to other companies' stores. In setting a strategy, an independent retailer has great latitude in selecting a target market. Because most of the independent retailers have modest goals, small customer segments may be selected rather than the mass market. Product assortments, prices, store hours, and other factors are then set consistent with the market.
- As independents run only one store, investment costs for leases, fixtures, workers, and merchandise can be brought down. In addition, there is no duplication of stock or individual functions. Responsibilities are clearly delineated within a store.
- Independents often act as specialists and acquire skills in a niche goods/service category. They are then more efficient and can lure shoppers that are interested in specialized retailers.
- Independents exert strong control over their strategies and the owner-operator is usually present on the premises. Decision-making is usually centralized and the levels of management are minimized.
- There is a certain image attached to independents, particularly smaller ones, which the chains find difficult to capture. This is the image of a personable retailer with a comfortable atmosphere to shop in.
- Independents are able to sustain consistency in their efforts since only one geographic market is served and just one strategy is followed. For example, there cannot be problems due to two branch stores selling identical items at different prices.
- Independents have 'independence'. Owner-operators are usually in full charge of their business and do not have to fret about

stockholders, board of director meetings, and labour unrest. They are often free from union work and seniority rules. This can enhance labour productivity.

- Owner-operators usually have a strong entrepreneurial drive. They have personal investments in their businesses, success or failure has huge implications for them, and even their ego is involved.

Some of the disadvantages of independent retailing are as follows.

- In bargaining with suppliers, independents may have less power because they often buy in small quantities. They may even be bypassed by suppliers or the products made available to them may be limited. Reordering may also be tough if minimum order requirements are too high for them to qualify. To overcome this problem, a number of independents, such as hardware stores, have formed buying groups to increase their power in dealing with suppliers.

- Independents typically cannot gain economies of scale (low per-unit costs due to handling of many units at a time) in buying and maintaining inventory. Due to financial constraints, small assortments are bought several times per year rather than large orders once or twice per year. Thus, transportation, ordering, and handling costs per unit are high.

- Operations are often very labour intensive, sometimes with little computerization. Ordering, taking inventory, marking items, ringing up sales, and bookkeeping may be done manually. This is less efficient than computerization (expensive for some small firms in terms of the initial investment in hardware and software although costs have fallen significantly). In many cases, owner-operators are unwilling or unable to spend time on learning how to set up and apply computerized procedures.

- By virtue of the relatively high costs of TV ads and the large geographical coverage of magazines and newspapers (too large for firms with one outlet), independents are limited in their access to advertising media and may pay higher fees per ad compared to regular users. Yet, there are various promotion tools available for creative independents.

- A crucial problem for family-run independents is an overdependence on the owner. Often, all decisions are made by this person, and there is no continuity of management when the owner-boss is ill, on vacation, or retires. The leading worries at family-run firms involve identifying successors, the role of non-family workers, and management training for family members. Long-run success and employee morale can be affected by overdependence on the owner.

- There is a limited amount of time and resources allotted to long-run planning. Since the owner in intimately involved in daily operations of the firm, responsiveness to new legislation, new products, and new competitors frequently suffers.

Retail Chain

A chain retailer operates multiple outlets (store units) under common ownership; it usually engages in some level of centralized (or coordinated) purchasing and decision making. In the United States, there are roughly 90,000 retail chains that operate about 6,50,000 establishments.

The relative strength of chains is great, and their popularity is rising, even though the number of retail chains is small (4% of all US retail firms).

The dominance of chains varies greatly by the type of retailer. The retailers that own and operate multiple outlets generate 75% or more of total categories sales from department stores, discount department stores, and gross restored. On the other hand, stationery, beauty salon, furniture, and liquor store retailers with multiple outlets produce far less than 50% of total retail sales in their categories.

Competitive Advantages of Retail Chains   There are a number of competitive advantages for a chain retailer:

- Many chains have bargaining power with suppliers due to their volume of purchases. These chains receive new items as soon as they are introduced, have reorder promptly filled, get proper service and selling support from suppliers, and obtain the best prices. Large chains may also gain exclusive rights for selling certain items and may have suppliers that make goods under their own brands. Sears has suppliers that produce appliances with its Kenmore name and tools with its Craftsman name.
- Chains can achieve cost efficiency by doing wholesaling functions themselves. Buying directly from manufacturers and in large

volume, shipping and storing goods, and attending trade shows sponsored by suppliers to learn about new offerings are just some of the wholesaling activities that can be fulfilled by chains. Thus, they can sometimes bypass wholesalers, with the result being lower supplier prices.

- Efficiency in multiple store operations can be gained through shared warehousing facilities; large purchases of standardized stole fixtures, employee uniforms, and so on; centralized purchasing and decision-making; and other factors. Chains generally give the headquarter executives broad authority for overall personnel policies as well as for buying, pricing, and advertising decision.

- Chains, because of their resources, can use computers in ordering merchandise, taking inventory, forecasting, ringing up sales, and bookkeeping. This increases efficiency and reduces his overall costs.

- Chains, particularly national or regional ones, can take advantage of a variety of media, including TV, magazines, and traditional newspapers. Large revenues and geographical coverage of the market allow chains to utilize all forms of media.

- Most chains have defined management philosophies. Strategies are detailed and employee responsibilities are clearly defined. Continuity is usually ensured when managerial personnel are absent or retire because there are qualified people to fill in and succession plans in place.

- Many chains spend considerable time and resources in long-run planning. Frequently, specific staff is assigned the planning on a permanent basis. Opportunities and threats are carefully monitored.

Disadvantages of Retail Chains

- Once chains are established, their flexibility may be limited. Additional non-overlapping store locations may be hard to find. Consistent strategies must be maintained throughout all branches— prices, promotions, and product assortments must be similar for each store. For chains that use centralized decision- making, there may be difficulty in adapting to local needs, such as taking into account differences in the lifestyles of urban, suburban, and rural customers.

- Investments may be high. There are multiple leases, fixtures, product assortments, and employees. The purchase of merchandise may be costly because a number of store branches must be stocked.

- Managerial control can be hard, especially for chains with geographically dispersed branches. Top management cannot maintain the kind of control over each branch that independents have over their single outlets. Lack of communication and time delays in making and enacting decisions are some other problems.
- Personnel in large chains may have limited independence in their jobs. In many cases, there are several management levels, unionized employees, stockholders, and boards of directors. Some chains empower their personnel to give them more independence to be able to better address special customer needs when they arise. As the director of the SBDC at the University of Memphis said: 'The key similarity between children and chains is this. The more you have—children or stores—the less attention you have for each one, so you have to empower those more and trust them more. They won't turn out to have the same personality, but if you raise them right, they'll each do you proud in their own way.'

Franchising

Franchising involves a contractual arrangement between a *franchiser* (which may be a manufacturer, a wholesaler, or a service sponsor) and a retail *franchisee*, which allows the franchisee to conduct a given form of business under an establishment's name and according to a given pattern of business. In a typical arrangement, the franchisee pays an initial fee and a monthly percentage of gross sales in exchange for the exclusive rights to sell goods and services in a specified area. Franchising is a retail organizational form in which small businesses can benefit by being part of a large, multi-unit, chain-type retail institution.

There are two types of franchise systems—product/trademark based and business format based. In product/trademark franchising, the franchisee acquires the identities of the franchisers by agreeing to sell the latter's products and/or operate under the latter's names. Franchisees operate rather autonomously from their franchiser. Although, they must adhere to certain operating rules, set store hours, choose locations, determine store facilities and displays, and otherwise run the business. Product/trademark franchising represents two-thirds of retail franchising sales. Examples are auto dealers and many gasoline service stations.

In the business format of franchising, there is a more interactive relationship between franchisers and franchisees. The franchisees receive assistance on site location, quality control, accounting systems, startup practices, management training, and responding to problems, besides the right to sell goods and services. The use of prototype stores, standardized product lines, and cooperative advertising let these franchisees achieve a level of coordination previously found only in chains. In recent times, most of the growth in franchising has involved business format arrangements which are common for restaurants and other food outlets, real estate, and service retailing. Due to the small size of many franchisees, they account for more than 75% of outlets, though just one-third of total sales. McDonald's is a good example of a business format that works on franchise arrangement.

Size and Structural Arrangements in Franchising   Retail franchising began in the United States in 1851, when Singer Sewing Machine first franchised dealers. It did not become popular until the early 1900s, when the underfinanced auto makers started using franchising to expand their distribution network.

Although auto and truck dealers still provide more than one-half of all US retail franchise sales, few retail sectors have remained unaffected by franchising growth. In the United States, there are now 2,500 retail franchisers doing business with 250,000 franchisees. They operate 600,000 franchisee and franchiser-owned US outlets, employ several million people, and generate over one-third of total store sales.

In addition, hundreds of US-based franchisers currently have foreign operations, with tens of thousands of outlets. Today, a large number of franchisees operate as chains. The main forms of franchisee-operated chains are:

- *Manufacturer-retailer*   A manufacturer gives independent franchisees the right to sell goods and related services through a licensing agreement. For example, both Raymonds and Liberty Shoes have entered into franchise agreements with retailers. Conditions imposed on retailers as part of the franchise agreement relate to exclusively stocking the manufacturer's brands, standardization of store décor, content of and reimbursement of advertising, and promotion expenses.

- *Wholesaler-retailer* It can take the form of voluntary offer of a franchise to the retailer or a cooperative association of retailers themselves.

  In case of the *voluntary system*, a wholesaler sets up a franchise system and grants franchise to individual retailers. In case of the *cooperative system*, a group of retailers set up a franchise system and share the ownership and operations of a wholesaling organization.
- *Service-sponsor retailer* It operates when a service firm licenses individual retailers to let them offer specific service packages to consumers. An example of this is VLCC, India's leading chain of health, beauty, and fitness centres. It is managed and operated by its parent company, Curls and Curves (India) Ltd, a Rs 600 million group.

Competitive Advantages and Disadvantages of Franchising

Franchisees receive several benefits by investing in successful franchise operations:

- Individual franchisees can own retail enterprises with relatively small capital investments.
- Franchisees acquire well-known names and goods/service lines.
- Standard operating procedures and management skills may be taught to the franchisees.
- Cooperative marketing (e.g., national advertising) is often used that could not otherwise be afforded.
- Franchisees obtain exclusive selling rights for specified geographical territories.
- Franchisee purchases may be less costly per unit due to the volume bought by the overall franchise.

  Some potential problems do exist for franchisees:

- Over saturation could occur if too many franchisees are in one geographical area; the sales and profits of each unit would then be adversely affected.
- Due to overzealous selling by some franchisers, the income potential and required managerial ability, initiative, and investment of franchiseed units may be incorrectly stated.

- Franchisees may be locked into contract provisions whereby purchases must be made through franchisers or certain approved vendors.
- Cancellation clauses may give franchisers the right to void individual franchisees if provisions in the franchise agreements are not met.
- In some industries, franchise agreements are of short duration.
- Under most contracts, royalties are a percentage of gross sales, regardless of the franchisee's profits.

The preceding factors contribute to constrained decision-making, whereby franchisers can exclude franchisees from or limit their involvement in the strategic planning process.

Key Aspects of Franchising

- A national or global presence can be developed quickly and with less franchiser investment.
- Franchisee qualifications for ownership can be set and enforced.
- Money is obtained when goods are delivered rather than when they are sold.
- Agreements can be drawn up requiring franchisees to abide by stringent rules set by franchisers.
- Because franchisees are owners and not employees, they have a greater incentive to work hard.
- After franchisees have paid for their franchised outlets, franchisers still receive royalties and may sell products to the individual proprietors.

Potential Problems in Franchising

- Franchisees could harm a firm's overall reputation if they do not adhere to company standards.
- A lack of uniformity among outlets could adversely affect customer loyalty.
- Infrastructure competition is not desirable.
- The resale value of individual units is affected if franchisees perform poorly.
- Ineffective franchised units directly injure their franchisers' profitability from selling services, materials, or products to the franchisees and from royalty fees.

- Franchisees, in increasing numbers, are seeking independence from franchiser rules and regulations.

Leased Department or Shop-in-shop

It refers to department/s in a retail store that are rented to an outside party. Usually this is done in case of department and speciality stores and also, at times, in discount stores. The proprietor of a leased department is usually responsible for all aspects of its business (including fixtures) and normally pays the store a percentage of sales as rent. The store has operating restrictions for the leased department to ensure overall consistency and coordination. In China, most department stores are 100% leased departments or 'shops-in-shops'.

In most situations, these departments or shop-in-shop (S-in-S) formats are used by the existing stores-based retailers to broaden their merchandise or service offerings into product categories requiring highly specialized skills or knowledge, which is not possessed by the retailer himself. Thus, leased departments or S-in-Ss often operate in categories that are on the fringe of the store's major product lines. They are most common for in-store beauty salons, banks, photographic studios, jewellery, cosmetics, watch repair, and shoe repair departments. They are also gaining popularity in the shopping centre food courts.

Competitive Advantages and Disadvantages of Leased Departments From the stores perspective, having leased departments has a number of benefits:

- Store personnel might lack the merchandising ability to handle and sell certain goods and services.
- The market can be enlarged by providing one-stop customer shopping.
- Leased department operators pay for inventory and personnel expenses, thus reducing store costs.
- Personnel management, merchandise displays, reordering of items, and so on are undertaken by the lessees.
- A percentage of revenues is received regularly by the lessor.

Potential Pitfalls from the Stores' Perspective

- Leased departments may use operating procedures that conflict with those of the stores.

Timex Watches Experiment with Shop-in-Shop

Timex Watches Ltd, the Indian subsidiary of the US-based watch giant, is focusing on the 'shop-in-shop' retail format in department stores for greater penetration into the Indian markets. The company has decided to set up 140 such stores, christened Club Timex Stores, by the end of 2004. At present, Timex has 62 shop-in-shop retail outlets in India. The strategy is to cash in on the mall revolution that is reaching its pinnacle in India. Though initially they plan to target the metros, equal focus is likely to be on the B and C class towns as well. They plan to hit 23 cities with this format.

- Lessees may adversely affect the store's image.
- Customers may blame the stores rather than the lessees for their problems.

Advantages for Leased Department Operators

- Existing stores are usually well known, have a large number of steady customers, and generate immediate sales for leased departments.
- Some costs are reduced through shared facilities, such as security equipment and display windows.
- There are economies of scale (volume savings) through pooled ads. The lessees' images are aided by their relationships with popular stores.

Problems for the Lessees

- There may be inflexibility as to the hours they must be open and the operating style they must utilize.
- The goods/service lines they are allowed to offer will usually be restricted.
- If lessees are successful, the stores may raise the rent or may not renew leases when they expire.
- The in-store locations may not generate the sales expected.

A leased department may be viewed from two perspectives: as an element in a shopping centre and as a part of a franchise system. In the context of shopping centres, a leased department operates in a rented area, with a given traffic flow, to conduct its business.

The lessee must examine the character of the traffic flow and its relationship to the chosen target market; the lessor must examine the extent to which the leased department will either create added traffic or be a parasite and live off the traffic generated by other parts of the store. The franchise analogy relates to a leased department's ability to blend with the merchandise philosophy of another retailer and the need to set a broad policy for all departments, so that the store's image is not injured by one operator.

Co-operative Outlets

Co-operative outlets are generally owned and managed by co-operative societies. In this context the detailed example of Kendriya Bhandar in India is being discussed.

Kendriya Bhandar   The Central Government Employees Consumer Cooperative Society Ltd, operating by the name and form of Kendriya Bhandar (a welfare project of Govt of India, under the Ministry of Personnel, Public Grievances and Pensions), is a network of 112 stores (out of which 102 are self-service stores) and 42 Fair Price Shops located in Delhi, Mumbai, Chennai, Hyderabad, Bangalore, Trichy, Cochin, Tirupati, Daman, Gwalior, Jaipur, Mussoorie, Lucknow, Faridabad, Kapurthala, Noida, Manesar and Chandigarh and a fleet of four Mobile Shops in Delhi, which provide service to the customers in such colonies where stores of Kendriya Bhandar do not exist. It also supplies a wide range of office requirements, including stationery, furniture, and computers, etc. to the government departments and other offices.

Largest Consumer Cooperative Society   Kendriya Bhandar has the distinction of being the largest consumer cooperative society in the country in terms of membership. It has more than 77,000 members inclusive of Associate Members. The co-operative, which retails consumer goods, groceries, stationery, office equipment, and furniture, reported a turnover of Rs 261.60 crores during 2001-02.

Objectives   Kendriya Bhandar was set up in 1963 as a welfare project of the government for the benefit of central government employees, their families, and other customers. Its objectives are as follows.

- To provide essential commodities of daily needs to the customers at reasonable price—representing assured standards of quality and value for money
- To play an effective role in the public distribution system and to become a pacesetter in retail market
- To assist the government in holding the price line and ensure distribution of scarce commodities at controlled prices
- To create an attractive and congenial shopping environment for customers

Sales Performance Kendriya Bhandar has registered phenomenal growth in the recent past as shown in Table 2.1. Starting with an annual sales turnover of mere Rs 52 lakhs in 1963–64, the Bhandar registered a record sales turnover of Rs 228.71 crores in 1998–99 with a net profit of more than 3 crores.

The management has pursued the policy of serving the consumers by providing essential commodities at reasonable prices. This has become possible on account of the efforts directed towards higher efficiency, better productivity, and more cost-effective operations.

Major initiatives taken recently Computerization has been further extended. Now heads of all the departments, viz. accounts, stationery, consumer, grocery, public relations, and vigilance have their own personal computers. Local area networking (LAN) has been provided in the accounts department and the stationery department VSNL Internet service has been introduced at the head office and P-block.

Keeping in view the professionalism of the Society and with a view to further developing its human resources, Kendriya Bhandar has taken the lead in setting up a training lounge in Kendriya Bhandar itself. Training courses are being conducted with the cooperation of Delhi Cooperative Training Centre, the Institute of Marketing and Management, and the National Institute of Sale (NIS) for the staff regularly to improve their skills and equip them to discharge higher responsibilities.

A sales promotion scheme for the shareholders has been introduced. Every year, an attractive gift is given to all shareholders and employees as an incentive.

Table 2.1: Total sales of Kendriya Bhandar during the last five years

Year	Sales
1994–95	Rs 117.58 crores
1995–96	Rs 138.88 crores
1996-97	Rs 186.60 crores
1997-98	Rs 205.89 crores
1998-99	Rs 228.71 crores

Benefits to Consumers   Kendriya Bhandar has been able to maintain competitive prices for the various products sold by it as compared to those prevailing in the market and also in the sister organizations. Selling prices prevailing in Kendriya Bhandar are treated as a benchmark. The Society closely controls its selling prices. Margins are being constantly reduced so as to pass on greater benefits to the customers. The ratio of gross profit to sale on the grocery items is less than 3%.

For better quality control, pre-testing of all grocery items before distribution to stores has been introduced, and testing of random samples picked up from the shelves of stores is frequently undertaken. Kendriya Bhandar has set up a food-testing laboratory at its headquarters in collaboration with FICCI. Samples are also tested at Government's Regional Testing Centre at Okhla and other laboratories. These steps ensure that the quality of goods sold is maintained for better consumer satisfaction. Another step in this direction is the introduction of alphanumeric cash machines at all the stores in Delhi. The machine prints the name of the item, price, and other relevant information about the product.

As a symbol of the Bhandar's responsiveness to the requirements of customers, complaint/suggestion books with numbered pages have been provided in all stores to enable the customers to convey their complaints/suggestions. These are promptly attended to so as to provide better services to the customers. Efforts are being made to provide postage-paid postcards to customers for communicating their suggestions or complaints to them.

Target Market   A recent survey conducted by Kendriya Bhandar reported that about 48% of the customers of the store were state and central government employees, who in effect constitute just around 1% of the total population of the country. The ministry then realized that there is the vast untapped corporate sector, which presents a great potential for the Kendriya Bhandars to leverage its national network and improve its share of non-governmental business.

Revised Positioning   Kendriya Bhandar has drawn up a blueprint for growth and expansion by opening more stores.

As the face of retailing in the metros and mini-metros is changing and more and more shopping malls with their swanky air-conditioned ambience are taking the place of shabby and small mom-and-pop stores. Needless to say, this has changed consumer perceptions about what shopping should be all about. This may well be among the main reasons the ministry feels that the Kendriya Bhandars could do with an overhaul.

The plan also envisages the Bhandar offering its customers a better shopping experience through improved ambience in the stores and expanding the range of products it has to offer. The cooperative is improving the internal layout of its stores, to give customers a more enjoyable shopping experience.

Hence, the entire chain is being classified into 'gold', 'silver', and 'copper' standard stores, the classification being dependent on the amenities, goods, and ambience each store offers. The Kendriya Bhandar consumer cooperative stores have grown from just one store in 1963 to the present 119.

Government officials say that around Rs 8 million will be spent on doing up eight stores in Delhi alone. There is a strong consideration of positioning Kendriya Bhandar as the Indian version of the American $1 stores, where any of the goods stocked cost $1 or less. The first version of such a store, the Kendriya Bhandar at Netaji Nagar in Delhi, opened on 19 September, 2002.

Classification of Retailers on the basis of Retail Location

Retailers have also been classified according to their store location. Retailers can locate their stores in an isolated place and attract the customers to the store on their own strength—such as a small grocery store or paan shop in a colony, which attracts the customers staying close by. Or it may locate its store in a central business district or a downtown centre where there are a large number of retail establishments and retailers are in a position to avail retail synergies. Retailers have multiple choices within a business district, they may either locate their stores in the large shopping centres in the heart of the city or smaller shopping complexes in a suburb.

Classification of retailers on the basis of location is discussed below:
- Retailers in a free-standing location

- Retailers in a business-associated location
- Retailers in specialized markets
- Retailers at airports

Free-standing Retailers

Retailers located at a site which is not connected to other retailers depend entirely on their store's drawing power and on the various promotional tools to attract customers. This type of location has several advantages including no competition, low rent, better visibility from the road, easy parking, and lower property costs. But there are disadvantages also such as difficulty in attracting customers, no shared costs as in a shopping centre, and lack of variety for shoppers. We find free-standing grocery stores in colonies and dhabas or food chains on highways. Free-standing stores can be classified as neighbourhood stores or highway stores.

Neighbourhood stores are located in residential neighbourhoods and serve a small locality. They sell convenience products like groceries. On the other hand, highway stores are located along highways and intersections of two highways, and attract the traffic passing through these highways. The dhabas found on most Indian highways is a fine example of highway stores. We now have attractive motels coming up on highways, where there are good parking facilities, fast-food restaurants, and dhabas. For example, the Haldiram's outlet on the Delhi–Jaipur highway and the McDonald's outlet on Delhi–Ludhiana highway.

Retailers in a Business-associated Location

In this case, a retailer locates his store in a place where a group of retail outlets, offering a variety of merchandise, work together to attract customers to their retail area, and also compete against each other for the same customers.

Business associated location can be further classified as unplanned business districts and planned shopping centres.

Unplanned Business Districts   An unplanned business district is a type of retail location where two or more retailers locate their stores together, as shown in Fig. 2.1, on individual considerations rather than

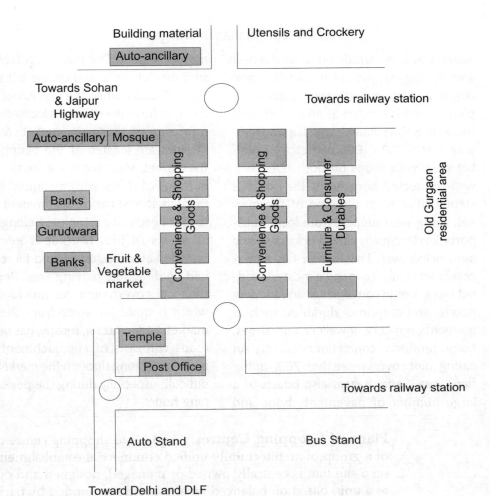

Fig. 2.1:   Sadar Bazaar: an unplanned shopping centre

on the basis of any long-term collective planning. An unplanned district generally provides certain advantages like availability of a variety of goods, services, and prices; access to public transport; nearness to commercial and social facilities; and pedestrian traffic. However, an unplanned business district has certain limitations which have led to the growth of planned shopping centres like congestion, out-dated facilities, lack of space for large outlets, parking problems, and high rentals.

Sadar Bazaar in Gurgaon

Sadar Bazaar is considered to be the best and the biggest market in Old Gurgaon city. It is a huge destination market for people, and is located at around 50 kms towards Sohna-Palval and Jaipur Highway. It is a 700 –1000m stretch of market area, with shops on both sides. It is well-connected because of the city bus station situated at one end of the market, along with support from local transportation (manually driven rickshaws and auto rickshaws). This market has an excellent retail mix, covering almost all product categories in convenience and shoping goods, and consumer durables, such as garments, grocery, jewellery and shoes, home products, confectioneries, etc. An eating joint covers more than 70% of the floor area. Sadar Bazaar also boasts of a large number of pavement shops and mobile traders. The main vegetable and fruit market is situated on the left side of Sadar Bazaar, while the consumer durables and furniture market is located on the right side of the main market. Medical facilities are located at the periphery of the market. Most shops are old fashioned in terms of decor with minimum investment in atmospherics. This market caters to the needs of customers belonging to all walks of life. Market is generally crowded and congested, and till recently had no designate parking area. Recently, the local government has provided one, which is quite far away from the main market. Sadar Bazaar, mostly, has unclean roads with lots of encroachments that make navigating through the market quite difficult, especially during the peak shopping hours.

Planned Shopping Centres A planned shopping centre consists of a group of architecturally unified commercial establishments built on a site that is centrally owned or managed, designed and operated as a unit, based on balanced tenancy, and surrounded by parking facilities. In India, Connaught Place was developed initially as a planned business district to serve the city of New Delhi; similarly the various sector markets in Chandigarh were developed in a planned way. Recently, we see the emergence of planned shopping centres and malls on Western lines. In India, we can classify planned shopping centres into two categories: regional shopping centres and neighbourhood/community shopping centres. These classifications are discussed in detail in Chapter 6.

Retailers in Specialized Markets

Besides the above location-based classification, we also have in India retailers who prefer specialized markets, particularly traditional independent retailers or chain stores. In India, most of the cities have specialized markets famous for a particular product category. A wide variety of merchandise is available within those product categories in such markets.

For example, in Chennai, Godown Street is famous for clothes, Bunder street for stationery products, Usman street for jewellery, T Nagar for ready-made garments, Govindappan Naicleen street for grocery, Poo Kadia for food and vegetables. This is true for most of the urban centres in India such as Chowk area in Lucknow is famous for food and cotton embroidery work. These places provide an established retail area to the prospective retailers to start a particular business, where they have to make little effort to attract consumers to the retail site.

Another peculiar type of retailers found in India are the ones who operate from periodic market, which is established at particular places on a particular day of the week. The retailers operating in these markets have a mobile set-up, which they keep moving from one marketplace to another depending on the day of the week. Most of these markets operate in evening hours. Such markets serve the lower and middle-income classes.

These are very popular with the large population of labourers, who have migrated from the rural areas to work in the cities since it provides them merchandise in accordance with their requirements at low prices and at convenient hours. Now, even the large urban population including the double-income group families have started patronizing these retailers since they provide convenience and low prices. This is a rural retail format, which is now very popular in the Indian cities.

Bombay Selection

Bombay Selection, a leading retail store in Indian women's ethnic-wear in Delhi, preferred to locate all its stores in the specialized retail centres in the National Capital Region. For example, their first store was located in Karol bagh—the leading central business district centre known for apparel trade, especially for women. They chose to locate their second outlet in Delhi at Rajouri Garden, another unplanned centre known for ethnic wear. Their latest store has come up in Metropolitan Mall, a planned shopping centre positioned as a women-centric shopping destination.

These periodic markets are even availed by retailers with well-established set-ups in regular markets, along with mobile traders, as these markets attract consumers from large trade areas, have limited credit transactions, involve very limited infrastructure-related costs, and carry low overheads. Only a nominal fee has to be paid to the local government bodies.

Airport Retailing

For quite some time, duty-free shops and news-stands dominated the small amount of commercial space provided at airports. Lately, serious efforts are being made to design new airport facilities in order to incorporate substantial amounts of retail space. And efforts, just as intense, are being undertaken by retailers to tenant that space. Developers and retailers are realizing that retail sales at airports bring in, on an average, US $1,137 per sq. ft.

This is due to the unique market that airport shoppers provide, ranging from guilty parents who forgot to buy something for their kids to vacationers who want to bring home souvenirs of their trips. It is also being realized that for many time-strapped travellers, the only glimpse of a host city they get is the airport that they visit, giving the airports undivided control of the perception of those cities.

An impressive display of high-end local and national retailers makes a great impression, and more often than not, results in substantial contributions to the local economy. Generally, airport retailing focuses on duty-free/travel value products, souvenirs and gifts, restaurants and bars, services (banks, currency exchange, telecommunications), car rental, etc.

The key features of airport retailing are:
- Large groups of prospective shoppers
- Captive audience
- Strong sales per square foot of retail space
- Strong sales of gift and travel items
- Difficulty in replenishment
- Longer operating hours
- Duty-free shopping possible

Variety of Merchandise Mix

Retail merchandising has come a long way in India since the days when general stores (kirana) that stocked everything from groceries to stationery and small shops that sold limited varieties of products (such as clothes, furniture, medicines, etc.) reigned supreme.

There are many different retail stores in India—convenience stores, supermarkets, hypermarkets, department stores, brand stores, and discount stores characterized by the variety of merchandise mix offered by a respective retail format. The consumer can choose between different stores for different needs. Retail units, on account of variety of merchandise mix, can be classified as follows:

(a) Department stores
(b) Discount stores
(c) Speciality stores
(d) Hypermarkets

Department Stores

It is a large retail store organized into a number of departments, offering a broad variety and depth of merchandise, commonly part of a retail chain. Usually, department stores are located within the planned shopping centres or traditional upmarket downtown centres. The leading fashion department stores in India are Ebony, Globus, LifeStyle, Pantaloon, Shoppers' Stop, and Westside. All of them are multi-product stores. Ebony has seven stores, Globus has four stores, LifeStyle has three stores, and there are 12 Pantaloon Family Stores.

Ebony: Department Store

Ebony opened its first store in 1994 at South Extension, New Delhi. Today, it is successfully running eight stores, across seven Indian cities. Ebony is today among the largest retail players in India. Ebony is characterized by an ambience that is comfortable, unobtrusive, and spacious. The first organized retail player to make its entry into Chandigarh and Noida, Uttar Pradesh, with two large format stores each spread across 35,000 sq. ft, Ebony also has one store at Rajouri Garden in New Delhi and one each in Ludhiana and Jalandhar in Punjab. The Amritsar store, which opened in October 2002, and the Faridabad store in January 2003, are the most recent additions to a venture that originated at South Extension in New Delhi.

Ebony provides a wide range of high quality products to choose from among well-known apparel brands, household items, cosmetics and personal care products, jewellery, fashion accessories, books and music, stationery, household items, furnishing, crystal ware, and even prams. The home floor at each store is truly a homemaker's delight, with products ranging from crockery and kitchen appliances to the finest linen, bathroom accessories, furniture, carpets, and gardening equipment. A number of these products are imported and exclusive to Ebony. Sourced from across the world, these products are a reflection of Ebony's endeavour to offer superior merchandising mix at the most affordable prices. Apart from a wide range of products Ebony has innovative marketing tie-ups with Lifespring, Planet M, etc. These companies dispense their products inside the various Ebony outlets.

Source: www.ebonyclick.com

Pantaloon Stores

Pantaloon Retail India Ltd (PRIL) is the flagship company of the Pantaloon Group. In 1997, it launched its first department store in Calcutta.

The company now owns and operates 14 mega stores/family stores on the department store format. They operate in Ahmedabad, Chennai, Hyderabad, Kolkata, Nagpur, Pune, Secunderabad, Kanpur, and Thane. Stores are characterized by a broad variety, deep assortment, and considerable customer service. The stores are organized into separate departments selling men's, ladies', and children's clothing and accessories. These stores also have a household section housing textiles, furnishings, and gift items.

Its leading brands are John Miller, Annabelle, T- 2000, Ajile, Scotsville, Bare, Honey & Pantaloons.

Shoppers' Stop: Launch at Malad at InOrbit Mall

Shoppers' Stop, India's premier fashion and lifestyle destination, has launched 'BUZZ', the designer stores, at its new store at Malad at InOrbit Mall. The 6th in Mumbai and the 14th Shoppers' Stop in the country the store offers the customers a truly unique, enjoyable, and international shopping experience. Color Studio is a completely new concept in the genre of cosmetics and makeup which is being implemented for the first time in India. The store, a combination of international design standards, services, and products, will cater to the over one-million customer base in and around Malad. The store boasts of a series of 'FIRST TIME' and 'UNIQUE' services marking, a revolutionary change in the Indian retail arena.

- *Colour Studio:* An International array of colour cosmetics (Shiseido, Nina Ricci, Elizabeth Arden, Clarins, Bourjois, Pupa, Chambor) offering make-up consultation, tips, make-over sessions, etc.

- *Nail Studio:* Mavala, a Swiss brand offering nail care and grooming services
- *Hair Studio:* L'Oreal's expertise in hair styling and colouring .
- *Buzz:* Designer Gallery housing Prêt lines from nine leading designers—Priyadarshini Rao, Anshu Arora Sen, Rocky S, Raghuvendra Rathore, Ravi Bajaj, Rohit Bal, Shantanu and Nikhil, Ashish Soni, and Suneet Varma. The designer wear is available at an affordable price starting from Rs 745 onwards for women's wear and Rs 1200 onwards for menswear.
- Javed Habib's hair salon
- *First Citizen Members' Lounge:* For the first time, the most privileged customers of Shoppers' Stop (First Citizen members) will have an exclusive lounge for themselves. Spread across 600 sq. ft of comfort, the lounge is armed with comfortable seating space, magazine section, and a cafeteria close by.
- A 1000 sq. ft footwear section with some of the leading international and Indian brands for men, women, and kids. The brands available are: STOP, Catwalk, Class Apart, Kittens, Red Tape, Florsheim, Marco Ricci, Lee Cooper, Portland, and Caterpillar.
- *DIY–Do it Yourself:* Private label from Shoppers' Stop offering ready-to-stitch women's ethnic wear. Graduates from NIFT would offer fashion consultation to customers from 1st March for two weeks.

Customers can choose from over 350 brands and avail of superior services and a great ambience, all under one roof. To fulfil distinct needs, the store will offer a complete range in men'swear, women's wear, kids' wear, home furnishing, footwear, leather accessories, soft luggage, cosmetics, jewellery (Fine & Fashion), and accessories. It also has an offering for mothers to be from 'The Mom Co'. The shopping experience will get more interactive and fun with the constant promotional activities that will be held with the aim of maintaining high customer excitement at the store.

Recently in India, many leading independent retailers of the cities and even new entrants are indicating preference for autonomous department stores. For example, Appeal, a leading fashion store in west Delhi and the Baniya store in Jammu offer a wide range of products such as gifts, dry fruits, sports material, apparel, home fashion, curtains, bed sheets, etc. Customers are free to move around the store unlike the traditional counter set-ups in India.

Various departments within the store have a designated selling space allocated to them, including a point-of-sales terminal to transact and record sales, and salespeople to assist customers. A majority of the department stores in India possess women's, men's, kids', fashion accessories, and kitchenware and home fashion departments. Some departments, to provide convenience to their customers in the browsing and selection of merchandise, have further sections within the specific department on the account of attributes of the product category, for example, women's departments have sections on ethnic/Western, formal/casual, and accessories.

Department stores provide a distinctive shopping experience to customers on account of services (home delivery, credit card, restaurants, cloakroom, and changing room, etc.) extended along with core offerings and atmospherics of the retail store. Pricing of the offerings is relatively high due to trained sales staff, range of merchandise offered and services, and high capital investments. Department stores, generally, opt for centralized buying taking into consideration the preferences and tastes of the consumers. In case of multiplicity of departments within stores, each department carries out its own buying in accordance with the demand patterns of their customers.

Some department stores deal only in specific product category on account of variety and brands available in particular product category, examples being Arcus in Gurgaon and the Food Bazaar chain of grocery stores.

Department Store Format in General Merchandise Industry in China: Phases in Evolution and Development

Slow Development Period: 1900–89

China's first department store was set up in 1900 in north-east China's Harbin. Many more were set up since then, yet they were less than 100 by 1989. However, they were making profits due to short supply in the market, the nation's planned economy, and their monopoly in the market.

Rapid Growth Period: 1990–95

Due to China's economic reforms, profit margins at department stores attained record growth of 10.11% and 9.71% in 1994 and 1995 respectively. A large group of general merchandise enterprises emerged during the 1990–95 period, with the number of department stores in 1995 becoming six times higher than in 1990. Large GDP growth, ever-increasing market supply, and people's living standard improvements prompted the establishment of a series of modern and renovated department stores.

Maturing Period: 1996–2000

The blind expansion of the general merchandise sector resulted in slender profit margins for operators, and price wars became the key tool for operators to win the market share. The serious competition caused a group of department stores to go bankrupt. Only the highly competitive stores survived. In 1996, six large department stores were closed. Having learnt lessons from these failures, the surviving general merchandise players devised strategies to manage competition.

Adjustment Period: 2000–Present

Department store operators carried out strategic adjustments and restructuring. Many large department stores were changed into shopping centres, while most of the small and medium-size ones turned into speciality stores in fields such as household electric appliances, jewellery, and furniture. Some retail enterprises also entered the retail chain sector. However, the general condition of the industry was still not positive, as department store sales volumes and profits witnessed a sharp decline from 2000 to 2002.

According to statistics from the China Commerce Association, in 2001, 104 of China's top 500 department stores were in the red. And the sales volume of general merchandise enterprises only made up 50% of the total consumer retailing volume in 2002, down 30% from 2001.
Source: China Daily 2004, April 16.

Discount Stores

Retailers offering a broad variety of merchandise mix, limited or no service, and low prices are characterised by low margins, heavy advertising, low investments on fixtures, limited support from sales people, etc. Discount stores prefer shopping centres that provide space at lower rents as they attract customers from other adjoining stores in the shopping centre.

S Kumar's: S-MART Discount Chain

S Kumar's group is scheduled to come up with its discount retail chain, S-Mart, in 12 cities in the next 18 months. The USP of S-Mart is brands for less. Every item in this store will be sold at a discount. As of now, the discount levels will range from 10–15%. For certain category items, such levels may also go up to 50–70%. The store will stock more than one lakh items across 15–20 product categories. Garments, electronic items, leather goods, furniture, furnishing, cosmetics, accessories, and, fast moving consumer goods are some of the focused areas.

All these will be picked up from a host of national and international brands. S-Mart will provide the right environment for value shopping by offering surplus and off-seasonal items at a much lower price.

Source: The Economic Times 2001, October 2.

In India, the 'discount store' concept works with a difference. Indian consumers are price conscious, interested in the best of the offerings, that is, the brands at least price. One needs to classify stores on the basis of perpetual discount stores (Subhiksha and Margin Free, etc.), extent of discount, category-wise discount, item/brand wise discount, GP-based discount, general discount, loyalty discount, special discount, festival discount, stock clearance discount, and fixed amount discount. Vendor partnership is an essential element in the success of the operations. A store's operations and inventory management need to be very efficient and effective to keep the running expenditure under control. Display should be self-explanatory to guide the customer in his buying decision. Price tags should be pasted depending on the commodity so that they are visible irrespective of the category of merchandise.

Margin Free Markets

Margin Free Markets is the largest retail chain in the state of Kerala and one of the leading retail chains in India. The first outlet of this chain started functioning on 26 January 1994 at Thiruvananthapuram. There are currently more than 275 franchisees of Margin Free Markets spread all over south India. The outlets are franchises and are not actually owned by the chain. The Consumer Protection and Guidance Society currently control Margin Free Markets, which is a registered charitable institution that started functioning in 1993. The consumers are assured of quality, quantity, and fair price of the goods sold through the Margin Free Markets. Any retailer can upgrade his shop to a Margin Free outlet by sending in an application to the society. If his application is accepted, he has to make the neces-

sary investment as required. These shops deal in the entire gamut of goods required by a home for its monthly consumption, viz., grocery, food and non-food FMCG items, fruits and vegetables, consumer goods and household articles. Margin Free outlets are typical discount stores, offering one-stop-shop convenience and self-service facility at significant discount to its customers. Most of these customers, in time, turn out to be its permanent customers by taking discount cards, which permit them to obtain larger discounts than the non-card holders. The necessity to offer protection against the rising prices gave birth to the idea of Margin Free Markets. An enthusiastic entrepreneur, named Mr N. Ravikumar, conceived the idea. The idea turned out to be an instant success in Kerala especially because Kerala is more of, a 'consumer' state than a 'producing' state. Kerala depends on her neighbouring states for her consumer needs. Due to the large number of inter-mediaries involved and the transportation costs, the prices are high and there is a wide fluctuation in the prices of grocer-ies, fruits, and vegetables. Groceries and FMCG goods are brought directly from the production units of the neighboring states. In the process of direct purchase from farmers and manufactures, the in-termediaries are removed and a part of the margin or 'profits' earned is disbursed among the consumers. The distribution to the different outlets under the chain is taken as a collective responsibility and is done with the objective to reduce the to-tal transportation costs.

Subhiksha

Chennai-based Subhiksha started its serv-ice in 1997. Beginning its journey from a single store, at present this retail chain has 143 stores spread across the length and breadth of Tamil Nadu and Pondicherry, and had earned a total turnover of Rs 235 crore in 2002–03. Subhiksha expects to close the current fis-cal with a total turnover of Rs 290 crore.

The chain expects to earn a total turno-ver of about Rs 1200 crore in 2008–09 as it plans to expand to other larger metros like Bangalore, Delhi, Bombay, and Ahmedabad. The retail food and pharmacy chain plans to have 550 stores in the next five years with an anticipated investment of about Rs 145 crore for the expansion plan. Under the first phase of expansion, they plan to open 50 stores in Bangalore during the period from April to Decem-ber, 2004. The second phase of expansion will see setting up of 140 stores in Delhi, which would take place in 18 months from April 2004. They also plan to expand to Mumbai by setting up 140 stores, and about 80 stores in Ahmedabad. The aim of Subhiksha, is to set-up an outlet every 2 km in residential areas, where the average monthly income is more than Rs 4,000. The retail outlets under this chain are mainly organized on the concept of a discount store that meets all the monthly household needs of a family. Subhiksha not only serves its customers through its outlets alone but also meets their demands through the home delivery concept, and, currently, the company makes around 16,000 deliveries every month. It is also planning to expand the number of outlets in Tamil Nadu to 135 by the end of this year from the current 104 across 23 cities and towns in the state. In Chennai itself Subhiksha has 60 outlets. The retail company would also expand the number of its warehouses to 15 across the five states from the present two in one state and will employ around 8,000 people over the next three years. Its current staff strength is around 1,500.

Speciality Stores

Speciality stores stress on one or a limited number of complementary product categories and extend a high level of service to their customers. In India, the traditionally independent retailers in the specialized market centre operate in a particular product category, as these centres attract large crowds. Such specialized retail operations provide expertise, economies of scale, bargain, and image to the particular stores.

Recently, with the advent of organized retailing, many companies and retail chains have opted for this retail format such as furniture (Gautier), durables (Vivek's), watches (Titan), etc. In particular, this kind of retail format appeals to lifestyle product categories such as apparel, watches, home fashions, and jewellery, etc. The largest penetration of organized retail would possibly happen in this format in categories such as health and beauty, home improvement, and IT products, etc.

Khadder: Khadi Speciality

Kolkata-based Tropical Clothing Company Private Limited owns khadi garments retail outlets under the brand name Khadder. These stores specialize in the khadi-based merchandise with limited depth. They have five outlets in the country, in Kolkata, Patna, Chandigarh, and the recently-opened two outlets in Bangalore. They are looking forward to expanding their outlets in other cities such as Ludhiana, Dehradun, Gurgaon, Mumbai, and New Delhi. Being one of the pioneers in the area, Khadder currently has around 70% of its garments in the women's wear segment with prices ranging from Rs 299 to Rs 569. The entire branding exercise of Khadder has been undertaken largely by word-of-mouth along with participating in a few promotional events.

Footwear: Speciality Store

Lakewood Malls Private Limited (LMPL), the retail division of the Hiranandani group, is now planning to get into the speciality stores category through footwear retailing. According to the IMAGES Retail Report 2001, the footwear industry in the country is valued at about Rs 8,500 crore out of which the organised footwear retailing forms about 20% of the business. The proposed store would be placed in Powai in the Haiko Mall, which already houses the Haiko Supermarket and Planet M. This store would be spread over 15,000 sq. ft, will cater to the masses and will have over 50 brands of footwear under one roof, from Bata to Bally. Prices will start at a phenomenal low of Rs 40! This store would be equipped with all footwear and allied products. The outlet will stock over 35,000 pairs of footwear, 15,000 pairs of socks, shoe polishes, shoe laces, brushes, shoe cleaners, in-soles, etc. The store will also have in-house cobblers who would (if required) alter shoes as per customers' requirements, besides an in-house pedicure corner wherein one could get one's feet cleaned and massaged with natural oils. The range would consist of shoes, sandals, chappals, sneakers, including Kohlapuris, Mojris, Jootis from Punjab to Hawai chappals. The merchandise would also consist of some exclusive brands from Europe and other parts of the world. The store would also have an artificial track of approximately 100 feet, where the customers can trial run before deciding to buy any sports shoe. There would also be a repair section, where footwear would be repaired at nominal charges, irrespective of its place of purchase.

Supermarkets and Hypermarkets

A hypermarket is a very large retail unit offering merchandise at low prices. Superstores have a sales area of about 25,000–50,000 sq. ft, while hypermarkets have a selling area of over 50,000 sq.ft. Hypermarkets are characterized by large store size, low operating costs and margins, low prices, and a comprehensive range of merchandise.

Hypermarkets own spacious parking facility exclusively for their customers and employees. AC Nielsen pointed out the major challenges hypermarkets will confront for survival from traditional downtown centres and wholesalers in the market. Hypermarkets are still at an experimental stage in India. The challenge ahead with marketers is to build themselves as service brands by integrating distinct consumer offerings and aggressive mass media campaigns as a core holistic strategy. In this regard, the hypermarkets need to demonstrate the concept of prolonged shopping as a functional mode of entertainment to the Indian consumers, to ensure the success of emerging retail format. Therefore, the success of hypermarkets depends on the transition the Indian consumer makes from activity-based shopping to planned-out leisure shopping.

RPG, a leading corporate house in organised retailing, decided to experiment with just one hypermarket, called 'Giant', which was set up in Hyderabad in June 2001. A separate company, Great Wholesale Club, was created for the ownership and management of the Giant chain.

The first Giant was a 50,000 sq. ft store located on a 120,000 sq. ft site. It stocked over 20,000 products. While groceries accounted for about 60% of sales, the store also sold a large number of other products like consumer durables, garments, and luggage. At Giant one could get groceries, fresh fruit, vegetables, home appliances, white goods, luggage, and anything one wanted at discounted prices.

Giant would offer three levels of discounts across every product sold in the store, 365 days in a year. The discounts would range from 4% to 40% on the maximum retail price. Price, comfort, convenience, quality, correct quantity, and service are just few of the benefits of what you can experience at Giant. Apart from the wide product range, the Giant store would also have a bakery, music world and a gifts and novelties counter. The central theme of this retail format is the widest range being offered at discounted prices, i.e. 'Badaa Choice Chota Price'.

Pantaloon's Big Bazaar: Hypermarket

The Rs 275 crore Pantaloon Retail (India) Ltd launched hypermarkets under the brand name 'Big Bazaar' at Phoenix Mills premises in Mumbai with an area of 50,000 sq. ft in April 2002. The company also planned to set up two additional hypermarkets with a capacity of 53,000 sq. ft each in Mulund and the western suburbs by the end of 2002. Pantaloon Retail (India) set up three hypermarkets in Bangalore, Hyderabad, and Kolkata in October, 2002. The company is investing Rs 12–14 crore in setting up each hypermarket by sourcing funds from preferential equity and the balance through debts.

The hypermarket in Mumbai will enable the company to generate Rs 75 crore to Rs 100 crore by 2003 end. The company targets the footfalls to increase to 50,000 per day by 2003 end. The management described hypermarket as a market which is big in size, offers a large variety of merchandise at competitive prices, and accommodates a multitude of customers. Big Bazaar is competing with retailing from a street seller to a premium outlet. Big bazaar offers over 1,70,000 items in over 20 product categories. In short, there is something for everyone. As regards promotional and marketing strategies, the management has positioned (USP) Big Bazaars in Mumbai on the lines of global discount chains like Wal-Mart and Carrefour and the unique selling proposition for Big Bazaar would be selling apparel and accessories to the whole family besides dress material, suitings and shirtings, sarees, home textile and furnishing, home needs, plasticware and thermoware, kitchen needs, food and grocery, utensils and steel, luggage, gifts and stationery, and medicines and opticals among others at minimal pricing targeted at the middle-end of the market. Big Bazaar will also offer distinct services such as car parking, a trolley system, and a convenience store to the customers.

Source: The Financial Express 2002, January 30.

The store had a turnover of Rs 850 m (US$ 18 m) in the financial year 2002–03. Besides selling directly to customers, Giant also sells to other businesses such as hotels, restaurants, contractors, and small retailers. Such business-to-business sales form about 25% of the revenues.

RPG stated that it has taken seven years for the FoodWorld chain to generate revenues of about Rs 3.5 bn; the expectation is that Giant revenues will reach Rs 20 bn within the same period.

Over the next three years, RPG plans to set up at least 15 Giant stores. This time it plans to go national, with stores in cities such as Mumbai, Kolkata, Chennai, Bangalore, Delhi, and Visakhapatnam. However, given the large size of the properties required—about 50,000 to 60,000 sq.ft for each store—these are necessarily long-gestation projects.

FoodWorld: Supermarket

The FoodWorld chain has grown rapidly over the past seven years and there are now 90 stores. Most FoodWorld stores are located in Chennai and Bangalore, and the chain is focused on the south. FoodWorld had to shut down the first three supermarkets it opened in Pune. The average size of the stores varies from 4,000 to 5,000 sq. ft. The initial focus on Chennai and Bangalore was partly because Spencer already had prime properties in these two cities. FoodWorld's turnover was Rs 3 bn (US$ 62m) in 2002–03. Its business has been delivering operating profits for the last two years. A major aspect of FoodWorld's strategy was to develop its supply chain and source as much as possible directly from producers. It deals directly with a number of top fast-moving consumer goods (FMCG) companies such as Hindustan Lever (a subsidiary of Anglo-Dutch consumer goods giant Unilever), Henkel, Coca-Cola, Godrej, Sara Lee, Tropicana, and Colgate and also procures many commodities (such as rice, pulses, fruits, and vegetables) from as close to the source as possible. A large number of contract farmers supply fruits and vegetables directly to FoodWorld. Another important strategy is the emphasis on private labels. Here, the focus has been primarily on the non-lifestyle area, including generic products like ketchups, jams, garbage bags, and so on. Private label sales account for about 30% of total sales. The company plans to increase the number of FoodWorld supermarkets to 125 by March 2006 but will remain focused on the south. Today, a typical FoodWorld supermarket is around 4,000 sq.ft. During the next few years, the company is planning to experiment with two different store formats near the same hubs. FoodWorld is looking at large

superstores measuring 12,000–15,000 sq. ft. These would offer a larger variety of fruits and vegetables, fresh produce, and general merchandise. The company is looking for suitable properties but FoodWorld says that the number of such 'super FoodWorld flagship stores' will be small—five or six at the most.
Source: Economic Intelligence Unit Limited 2004.

The retail entities primarily selling services to their customers rather than products are in retailing of services. Services also play a crucial role in the retail mix of the retail firms selling merchandise as a core product. The main differences between retailing of products and retailing of services are on account of the intangibility, simultaneous production and consumption, perishability, and inconsistency.

As disposable income rises, consumers' spending shifts from purchasing of essential products to services, which enhances consumers' quality of life. Service retailers are an inevitable part of the markets, such as cineplex, cobbler, barber, tailoring (clothes), financial services, etc.

With time, the old set of service retailers re-positioned their outlets and a new lot of service providers, such as health centres, old-age home, consultancy services, courier services, education centres, theme parks, dance bars, coaching centres, etc., emerged and thrived. The emergence of such strong service retailing can be attributed to the changed lifestyle of the customers in the last few years; for example, the ageing population depends on health centres or old-age homes, the young population with an impressive pay package is looking for avenues for leisure, and families with double income are looking for services for their day-to-day living.

Today, the leading national services companies such as banks, insurance, airlines, hotels, health care, etc. are in retailing. Most of these services have national coverage. Whereas lawyers, doctors, dry cleaners, plumbers/electricians have local markets to serve, with the advent of organized markets these retail set-ups are all set to cater to the large markets.

Recently, in India many business organizations such as hospitals, education centres, banks, insurance companies have started incorporating retail marketing mix at branch level to attract customers and meet competition from new players. Most of these organizations

VLCC

VLCC is the world's first slimming, fitness, and beauty corporate to get the ISO 9001:2000 certification. It has established a new benchmark for the company, ensuring the delivery of top-notch international quality services and products to consumers. VLCC is also the first company of its kind, globally, to have been awarded the SA: 8000 (Social Accountability) certification and ISO 14001 for being an environment-friendly company.

That VLCC is one of India's most recognized brands in its own right is an acknowledged fact and this is reinforced by its recent induction into the world-wide hall of fame for brands by being awarded the international Superbrand status. This recognition is not easy to obtain since the tag is given only to brands which offer the consumers significant emotional and physical advantages over its competitors for which consumers are willing to pay a significant premium.

Shaping the confidence of hundreds and thousands of people with its 'Look Good, Feel Great' credo, VLCC today is a 60-centre strong company in the slimming, beauty, and fitness industry with a presence in 35 cities across the country.

have started taking into consideration the customer's experience at the servicescape in terms of delivery, location convenience, atmospherics, etc. Some companies even devise their retail marketing mix in accordance with the local needs of the markets, for example, McDonald's in India has sufficient arrangements for the customers to visit their outlets and enjoy food within the outlet, whereas in the West they do not have such arrangements.

Retailers usually provide merchandise and services to their customers. The mix of services and goods varies across the retail formats in retail industry according to the level of competition, store image, target segment, etc. Some retail formats have self-service provisions, with no assistance from salesforce, in order to provide merchandise at low price. On the other hand, particular retail formats such as speciality stores and franchised outlets provide a set of multiple services, such as free home delivery, salesforce, alterations, returns, and adjustments along with the core merchandise to the customers.

Method of Customer Interaction

Retail units can be classified into two groups on the basis of the nature of interaction between retailers and customers, namely store retailers and non-store retailers. Retail transactions are carried out through face-to-face interaction between retailers and customers in the case of retail stores. Whereas non-store retailers sell to the customers in the absence of a retail store (direct selling), sometimes interactions between two entities take place without face-to-face interaction (Internet, TV, mail catalogue). Most of the non-store retailing mediums are well-known on account of the medium used by them to interact with their customers.

Store Retailers

Store retailers operate from fixed point-of-sale locations to attract a high volume of walk-in customers. Retail stores have extensive displays of merchandise and use mass-media advertising to attract customers. They sell products and services to the customers for personal or household consumption, but some retailers also serve business and institutional clients such as office supplies stores, computer and software stores, gasoline stations, banks' branches, building material dealers, and electrical supplies stores. In addition to selling products, some store retailers also provide after-sales services, such as repair, alterations, and installation.

Non-Store Retailers

Non-store retailers approach their customers and market merchandise with methods such as the broadcasting of infomercials on TV channels, the broadcasting and publishing of direct-response advertising (Internet), the publishing of traditional and electronic catalogues, door-to-door solicitation (direct selling), in-home demonstration, temporary displaying of merchandise (stalls in melas, tradefairs, periodic markets, etc.), and vending machines. The methods of transaction and delivery of merchandise vary across types of non-store retailers. For example, non-store retailers that reach their customers using information technologies can receive payment at the time of purchase or at the time of delivery, and the delivery of the merchandise may be done by the retailer or by a third party, such as the post office or a courier. In contrast, non-store retailers that reach their customers by door-to-door solicitation, in-home demonstration, temporary displaying of their offerings (stalls), and vending machines receive payment and deliver the merchandise to the customer at the time of the purchase.

Electronic Retailing

Electronic retailing has been acknowledged as one of the formidable non-store retail formats in the retailing industry since the arrival of mail order retailing in the nineteenth century. E-tailing is considered to be the fastest-growing sector of the retail industry. Internet retailing has grown from a mere US $350 million to US $3 billion in volumes in less than a decade. E-tailing is estimated at about Rs 12 crore. In percentage terms, e-tailing is a mere 0.3% of the total retail business in India in 2000.

The study by McKinsey and Confederation of Indian Industry (CII) points out that the growing consumer base and the development of e-commerce infrastructure are indicating a trend in favour of e-tailing. The number of Internet users in India is estimated at four million. These users are young, well-educated males with a monthly income of over Rs 15,000 and are concentrated in the top 10–20 class A cities. Women, who constitute over 50% of the US market, are still a small but growing percentage of users in India. It is predicted that for grocery a significant share of the existing phone-based ordering and home delivery system—which accounts for 10–15% of the total grocery purchases in major metros—is likely to shift to e-tailing.

Internet retailing had a positive impact on the economy of the nation in particular and the world at large. In India, it will be a mixture of e-tailing and retailing that will work. With time, companies are working hard on reaching out to their consumers with the help of Internet.

It helps prospective customers to acquire information about the offers or retailers at minimal cost in terms of travelling time and cost involved. The capital and labour devoted to stores, salespersons, inventories, etc. are freed up for other productive applications in the economy.

Internet retailing appeals to marketers and retailers on account of the following factors:

- Internet retailers can avoid expensive capital investment on stores and in store fittings, sales persons, and inventory holding costs.
- Internet retailers depend on IT integration from their store-front to order processing all the way back to their suppliers. This will help to reduce the costs of acquiring and delivering throughout the value chain, which in turn help the marketers to share benefits with customers.

- Internet retailing widens the market to be served and provides national or international presence.

According to the KSA Technopak's annual consumer outlook 2000, the consumers feel more comfortable in buying certain items on the Internet. An illustrative list of consumer items with a percentage of the consumers are: books and music 47%, home furnishing 29%, sports apparel 25%, casual clothes 21%, shoes 14%, groceries 9% and tailored clothes 9%. It has been identified that for successful e-tail strategy one needs to have five elements: a distinctive brand, an integrated channel strategy (supply chain), optimal merchandise mix, an efficient distribution system, and a provision for understanding and using consumer insights.

In order to meet the demand of their customers efficiently and effectively electronic retailers need to have perfect infrastructure. It includes the following:

- Proper systems to handle individual and rapid responses, whether it is in taking orders or in handling queries, complaints, and returns and adjustments.
- Logistics—an e-retailer has to take the offerings to the individual customer. In e-retailing, a shipment is possibly of a single item, to an individual customer. Hundred per cent accuracy is a must in

---

E-Retailing Challenges

Penetration of credit cards is much higher and people use them more frequently in the USA. In goods such as apparels, retail gross margin is as high as 65%, whereas in India it could be somewhere between 35% and 40%. This margin is enough to take care of credit card costs among other things. In FMCG, the margins are even lower at 10% or still lower in India. Hence, e-tailing might not catch on so fast in India.

It is important for a consumer to be comfortable before using a credit card at the website. They are a convenient way of paying online. In fact, they are one of the best ways of paying online. However, there are certain security aspects which are a cause for concern. Hence e-tailers would have to look at an alternative form of e-cash. Currently, lack of technology is preventing this from happening.

Source: The Financial Exepress 2004, Excerpts from 'Internet is a Superior Alternative', April 11.

this case. At the same time to keep per unit distribution costs down is also an important issue.

- Conversion—if the customer does not find exactly what he is looking for, the system must have sufficient provisions to suggest alternatives so that the customer is not lost.
- To ensure a site accessible at all times, page download time must be minimized, the site must be easy to navigate, and the clicks per purchase must be minimized.

Fabmall: E-Retailer

Fabmall was incorporated as a company in December 2002. However, it has a history of operations much older than that. In September 1999, six professionals came together to set up Fabmart (www.fabmart.com) as a focused online retailing company and since then it has built itself as a strong online brand. With a mixture of good merchandise and focus on customer service, fabmart.com has been able to build a loyal customer base, both within and outside India.

In January 2002, keeping in mind the emerging retailing trends worldwide, where many successful global retailers (Walmart, JC Penney, Nordstrom, Tesco, etc.) were vigorously employing a multi-channel (physical stores, telephone orders, Internet etc.) approach to retail customers, Fabmart also decided to expand into a physical chain of grocery stores, apart from electronic retailing. As this initiative took off, more business opportunities started emerging, each of them opening up fresh revenue streams.

To ensure that all such initiatives receive adequate focus and resources, and also to make sure the company reflected the new ethos and business priorities, Fabmall is planning to focus aggressively on several business areas:

- Electronic retailing—with a mixture of category based stores and a growing assortment of merchants using the advanced online technology platform to create their own online web-store fronts.
- Web services—using the skill sets built up over the last three years to offer corporates a combination of services like payment gateways and Web-based BPO (business process outsourcing) solutions.
- Physical grocery chain—a chain of grocery supermarkets in Bangalore with plans to expand into multiple cities and with a mixture of different physical retailing formats.

During this period, Fabmall has also built up a reasonable customer base outside India, primarily amongst NRIs (non-resident indians), who use Fabmall regularly to send gifts back home in India to their friends and relatives. Many have also used Fabmall to order gifts and jewellery for shipping outside India as well. Fabmall is now launching a fully revamped International store with great merchandise for shipment all over the world.

Products

They currently ship out Indian jewellery and ethnic gifts and handicrafts outside India. They also have select books like the Amar Chitra Katha comics. Since a lot of items are sold online and are restricted to sale within India, Fabmall is unable to offer a more comprehensive catalogue at the moment.

Mode of Payment

They accept all international Diners, Master, Visa, and American Express cards. In certain cases, customers paying through credit cards may also be asked for some additional information. This is part of their standard due diligence process. They use 128-bit SSL encrypted secure links for the Citibank online payment gateway.

Shipping Information

All international orders are shipped through FedEx. There is a shipment charge of US$ 14 per shipment. However, jewellery and non-jewellery products cannot be shipped in the same shipment.

Source: www.fabmart.com

Catalogue and Direct Mail Retailing

It is a form of non-store retailing in which retail units communicate about their merchandise or service through a catalogue. This retail format is new to Indian retail industry and is at a very nascent stage of its development. In the West, catalogue retailing became popular among marketers and retailers to tap rural markets, which lacked access to the retail centre/stores. Later, with the emergence of the double-income families with limited time at their disposal, catalogue retailing proved quite successful.

Direct mail retailing is a non-store retail format in which retailers communicate with their customers using mails/letters or brochures. Retailers directly mail advertising material to their existing or potential customers with the objective of selling goods or services.

Catalogue retailing is classified into two, namely general merchandise-catalogue and speciality-catalogue retailing. General merchandise catalogue offers a wide variety of merchandise (for example grocery) that is periodically mailed to the customers. On the other hand, speciality-catalogue retailers or marketers focus on particular product categories, for example, cosmetics or designer wear.

Catalogue sales have experienced dramatic growth in United States and Canada and similar expansion is expected to occur in India.

The factors that contribute in the success of catalogue retailing are:

- Convenience—customers can shop when it is convenient for them.
- Time-saving—one saves resources on account of time and travelling cost and parking problems.
- Information—relevant product information is available in detail.
- No time limits—there is no undue pressure to buy unlike the retail store shopping.

There are two main types of catalogues differentiated by their target audience—consumer and business-to-business. Catalogues can be used to present a range of products in an organized manner to motivate the recipient to buy, to present a company's entire line of merchandise, or to create an identity, image, or niche for the company.

Advantages of selling via catalogues are:

- A catalogue can project the company's identity niche.
- There is space for unlimited product display.
- Catalogue allows for low overheads and reduced cost of sales.
- The marketer has total control of the selling process.
- Accurate inventory control as well as timely and accurate analysis can take place.
- Toll-free telephone lines and call centres enable the business to operate 24 hours a day, seven days a week.
- Customer reach is unlimited by geographical location.
- Modern direct marketing techniques allow prospective clients to be targeted, based on their known interests.

Direct Selling

It is a retail format which involves personal contact between salesperson/retailer and customers at any convenient place, be it his home, office, or club. It also includes the phone interactions between retailers and customers. The salesperson needs to demonstrate the product, to take orders, and to deliver the product selected by the consumer.

This retail format is considered highly interactive in nature, which is compatible with retailing of the products high on information and search attributes such as jewellery, cosmetics, vacuum cleaner, etc. Worldwide, the direct selling industry does an estimated sale of US $

83 billion annually. Direct selling is practised in 165 countries of the world. Total direct sales people worldwide rose from 37 million in 1999 to over 40 million in 2000. The USA has the highest number of direct salespeople at 11 million. Indonesia is second with 4.2 million salespeople.

India was the fastest growing market in 2000 in terms of revenues from direct selling, registering a 54% growth. Total sales through direct selling in India is estimated to be at Rs 13.74 billion. Amway is the largest player in India with annual sales exceeding Rs 5 billion. Trends that have increased the use of direct marketing include:

- Increasing number of women in the workforce
- High costs of driving, including traffic congestion and parking problems
- Shortage of retail help (salesforce) at retail stores–limited or no help at self-service stores
- Long checkout lines
- Toll-free telephone numbers to place order or register complaints
- Availability of credit through proliferation of credit cards
- Growth of computer power and communication technology
- Increasing time pressure on consumer.

Direct-selling companies do away with wholesalers, retailers and other middlemen in the supply chain, thereby reducing their distribution and advertising costs. Direct selling has minimal support of advertising and large dependence on word-of-mouth publicity.

Methods of Direct Selling   The three common methods of direct selling are:

1. *Person-to-person selling:* Representatives of companies and manu-facturers (independent contractors) sell services and products di-rectly to people at home, office, or workplace, on a one-to-one basis.

2. *Party-plan or group presentations:*   A system by which sales are made to individuals who are part of a group. The sales person invites a 'hostess' to hold a 'party' for eight to ten prospective customers, usually at home, but it can also be at an office or workplace. The emphasis of the party is to have an enjoyable time products are

attractively displayed whilst the independent contractor talks about the various products and allows the audience to 'feel' products (touch, smell, taste, etc. depending on the product being demonstrated).

3. *Multilevel network:* It is a system for selling goods or services through a network of distributors. Under this format salespeople serve as distributors and also recruit other people to become distributors in their network. The multilevel network programme works through recruitment. Prospective salespeople are invited to become distributors, sometimes through another distributor of the multilevel network company's products and sometimes through a generally advertised meeting.

A distributor with a multilevel company receives commission through the sales of the products and through recruiting other distributors and receiving a portion of the income these distributors generate. The distributors that join under an existing distributor are called his/her downline. The distributor that is originally recruited fresh is called his/her upline.

There are certain strategic business advantages of direct selling. Some of them are as follows:
- Reduced cost for the seller
- Lower prices for the buyer
- Large geographical coverage
- Convenience for customers
- Ability to pin-point customer segments
- Ability to eliminate sales tax for some
- Ability to supplement regular business without additional outlets

Television Shopping

It is a retail format in which existing and prospective customers watch a TV programme demonstrating products and then placing order for the same by telephone, e-mail, and Internet. There are three types of television shopping, namely cable channels meant for shopping, infomercials, and direct-response advertising shown on TV.

Infomercials are TV programmes that mix entertainment with product demonstrations and then interested customers place orders by telephone or e-mail. However, direct-response advertising includes advertisements on TV that provide details about merchandise and an opportunity to order.

The Indian TV retailing is estimated at Rs 50 crore, with an annual growth rate of 20%. The key players in the Indian market are Asian Sky Shop (ASK), TSN, TVC, TSNM, Telebrands (India), and Star Warnaco, the last one being an international player. ASK and TSN are Rs 20 crore companies each, with the balance Rs 10 crore being shared by other players in the market.

In India, the infomercial and the 30–60 minute capsule is fairly common. However, the Indian TV shopping retailers have neither set up a channel dedicated to television, nor do they intend to do so, due to the limited size of the market.

Vending Machine Retailing

It is a form of non-store retailing in which products or services are placed in a machine and dispensed to customers when they deposit cash or use plastic money (credit or debit card). Vending machines are found everywhere; compared to store retailing, vending machines offer consumers greater convenience 24 hours a day, and have replaced many services formally requiring a human interface.

The first commercial coin-operated vending machines were introduced in London, England, in the early 1880s. They dispensed post cards. In 1888, the Thomas Adams Gum Company introduced vending machines in the United States. The machines were installed on the elevated subway platforms in New York City and sold Tutti-Fruiti gum.

Vending machines soon offered everything, including cigars, postcards, stamps, etc. In Philadelphia, a completely coin-operated restaurant called Horn & Hardart was opened in 1902, which operated until 1962. A company called Vendorlator Manufacturing Company of Fresno California made a series of classic vending machines during the 1940s and 1950s that mostly sold Coca-Cola and Pepsi. The expensive equipment and labour required to stock and service vending machines makes this a costly channel of distribution, and prices of vended goods are often 15–20% higher than those in retail stores.

Summary

The term retail organization refers to the basic format or structure of a retail business designed to cater to the end customer. Retailing has been a dynamic industry, and new retail firms have brought innovative approaches to retailing, changing the industry as they entered, developed, and grew. Various theories of structural change like the wheel of retailing, the dialectic process, and the natural selection are used to understand the changes in the retail industry.

Retail organizations can be classified on the basis of ownership, operational structure, length and depth of merchandise, nature of service, type of pricing policy, type of retail location, and method of customer interaction. On the basis of ownership they can be classified into sole proprietorship, partnership, joint venture, and limited liability company. In terms of operational structure retail organizations can take the form of independent retail unit, retail chain, franchise, leased departments, and co-operatives.

On the basis of location, there could be retailers in free-standing locations, business-associated locations, specialized markets, and airports. In terms of merchandise mix, retail outlets could be classified as department stores, discount stores, speciality stores, and hypermarkets. Various types of non-store retail practices have also become common. Mainly, they take the form of direct selling and marketing, temporary display of merchandise, vending machines, and online retailing.

Key Terms

1. **Catalogue retailer:** A type of non-store retail format in which retailers communicate with customers using catalogues sent through the mail.

2. **Convenience store:** These are small retail units that are well-located, food-centric, and operate for long hours.

3. **Department:** It is refered to a section of a retail unit with a particular type of merchandise.

4. **Department store:** It is a retail unit dealing in a wide variety and assortment of goods, extends multiple services, and is organized into various departments for different product categories.

5. **Direct-mail retailer:** A type of non-store retail format in which retailers communicate directly with customers using letters and brochures sent through the mail.

6. **Direct marketing:** Non-store retail format in which customers are approached through print or electronic media (non-personal medium) and then order the products by telephone, mail, and the Internet.

7. **Direct selling:** A retail format in which a salesperson approaches a prospective or existing customer directly at a suitable location (home or office) and demonstrates a product—if needed, takes an order and delivers the same to the customer.

8. **Discount retail store:** A retail unit selling general merchandise with wide variety, limited services, and low prices.

9. **Electronic retailing:** A retail format in which the retailer and the customer communicate with each other through an interactive electronic network such as Internet.

10. **Franchisee:** The owner of a retail store in a franchise agreement.

11. **Franchising:** A contractual agreement between a franchisor and a franchisee that allows the franchisee to operate a retail outlet using a name and format developed and supported by the franchisor.

12. **Franchisor:** The owner of a franchise in a franchisee agreement.

13. **Hypermarket:** A very large retail store that offers low prices and combines discounts and superstore food retailer in one building.

14. **Infomercials:** A TV programme that mixes entertainment with product demonstrations and solicits orders placed by telephone from consumers.

15. **Joint venture:** A business entity formed when a retailer pools resources with a local retailer to form a new company in which the ownership, control, and profits are shared.

16. **Leased department (shop in shop):** An area in a retail unit leased or rented by a retailer or management. The leaseholder is responsible for the entire retail mix of the concerned department (speciality or discount) and pays rent to the store as per agreement.

17. **Lessee:** The entity signing the lease.

18. **Lessor:** The entity owning the property that is for rent.

19. **Manufacturer–owned store:** A retail store owned and operated by the manufacturer.

20. **Multilevel direct marketing:** Retail format in which people sell directly to customers and recruit other people to become distributors in their network.

21. **Non-store retailing:** It is a form of retailing not conducted from the store. It is carried through computer interfaces, vending machines, direct selling, and direct marketing.

22. **Retail chain:** A firm that consists of multiple retail units under common ownership and usually has some centralization of decision making in defining and executing strategy.

23. **Speciality store:** A retail store offering limited number of complementary merchandise categories and providing a high level of services.

24. **TV shopping:** A retail format in which customers watch a TV programme demonstrating a product and then place orders for the merchandise over phone.

25. **Vending machine retailing:** A non-store retail format in which merchandise is stored in machine and dispensed to customers when they deposit cash or use a credit card.

26. **Vertical marketing system:** All the levels of independently owned businesses along a channel of distribution. Products and services are distributed through one of the three

types of systems: independent, partially integrated, and fully integrated.

27. **Wheel of retailing:** A cyclical theory of retail evolution whose premise is that retailing units evolve from low-price/service/margins to higher price/service/margins operations. This then provides scope for new discount stores.

Concept Review Questions

1. What do you understand by classification of retail units? Outline the importance of classifying retail units.

2. List all possible bases of classifying the retail business.

3. Discuss the types of retail units and their respective characteristics on the basis of ownership.

4. What are the differences among retail units operated under the following types of ownership structure: retail chain, franchising, and joint venture?

5. What do you understand by co-operative retail format? Enlist its state of operation in the Indian retail industry.

6. What are the types of retail formats on the basis of their location and the merchandise variety they are offering? Discuss each classification with the help of an example (retail store) from your city.

7. What are the different types of retail units on the basis of method of customer interaction?

Project Work Assignments

1. Identify the types of retail formats on the basis of ownership existing in the central business district of your city. Select at least one store under each type of ownership, and identify and enumerate the differences between them on account of their respective retail marketing mix.

2. What are the best possible retail formats you propose for the following product categories on account of type of location and merchandise variety for a semi-urban township and a metro city?
   - Books
   - Cosmetics
   - Personal computers

3. Design the retail marketing strategy for launching an e-retail store for traditional gold jewellery to tap the NRI customers.

4. Which will prove to be the most appropriate retail format for a expansion strategy for your successful designer furniture store?

Case Study

Big Bazaar : The Indian Wal-Mart

Retail Industry

The last decade has experienced a fundamental change in the Indian retailing industry structure, with a very perceptible shift from unorganized kirana and small independent shops to organized retailing such as retail chains and franchised outlets.

This gradual shift is attributed to increased purchasing power along with aspirational demands of a segment driven by exposure to the Western world because of media. An NCAER study shows that only 0.25% of total population falls in the category of earnings above Rs 5,00,000. Most of the organized retailers are targeting this supra-niche segment for higher margins.

Retail sector witnessed the entry of concepts like Shopper's Stop, Crossroads, Globus, FoodWorld, and discount chains like Subhiksha. Pantaloon Retail (India) Ltd (Pantaloon) is one of such listed companies to enter this business, with a presence in both discount shops (Big Bazaar) and retail stores (Pantaloon outlets).

Background

Pantaloon Retail (India) Limited is today recognized as one of the pioneers in the business of organized retailing in the country with a turnover of over Rs 400 crores in the financial year ending June 2003. The company is headquartered in Mumbai with zonal offices at Kolkata, Bangalore, and Gurgaon (Delhi). It has 4 kinds of stores; 14 Pantaloon Family Stores, 7 Big Bazaar discount hypermarkets, 6 Food Bazaar large sized supermarket stores, and Gold Bazaar Stores with over 6.5 lakh sq.ft retail space across Kolkata, Mumbai, Thane, Pune, Hyderabad, Bangalore, Nagpur, Ahmedabad, Kanpur, Chennai, and Gurgaon (Delhi).

Pantaloon Retail India Limited is the flagship company of the Pantaloon group promoted by Mr Kishore Biyani. It has been one of the pioneers in organized retailing in India. It began its retailing operations in India way back in 1987. Currently, it manufactures and sells ready-made garments through its own retail outlets and two discounting stores.

The company plans to diversify into the business of discounting in a big way, which is targeted at the growing middle class segment. It has India's second largest retail chain with 17 retail outlets and two discounting stores branded as Big Bazaars across the country at an estimated retail space of 4,01,300 sq.ft. The company plans to double its retail space in the next couple of years.

Pantaloon has come up with an excellent revenue model, focussing on 'value for money' segment. Pantaloon plans to target the upper middle and the middle class segment, which forms the large chunk of Indian population. This segment is very price conscious and always looks out for value for money. Pantaloon has already opened two discount stores at Hyderabad and Calcutta. It also plans to sell household items through its discount stores along with apparels. Since the company has got strong brands like John Miller and Pantaloon, coupling it with the discount store model would boost the sales to the larger population.

Pantaloon successfully launched its discount store chain (branded as Big Bazaar), which targets the large and growing upper-middle and middle class of Indian society. This is totally in contrast to the other organized retail players, which focus on high net-worth of individuals. Pantaloon has the second largest selling space amongst the retailers. Big Bazaar offers products and services such as a chemist, a photography shop, a bakery, financial products, automobile accessories, bicycles, and electrical hardware among other items—the range is vast and fulfils practically every need of the consumer under one roof. This is backed by complete automation of the retail outlets. After completion of the central hub at Mumbai the company's operations would be fully integrated which would give its operating efficiency a boost.

Big Bazaar has strong own brand names in its portfolio across product categories. The brands include Pantaloon, John Miller, and Bare. Higher percentage of 'own brand' sales improves margins, thus reducing the break-even level of sales. Big Bazaar has diversified from apparels to household items in its discount stores. This has enabled them to enlarge their basket of offerings.

Expansion Plans

This concept of discount stores resemble the Wal-Mart strategy. In India and especially in metro cities like Mumbai, Bangalore, Calcutta, and Hyderabad, where the population is dense and consists of a high middle-class population, the concept of discount stores is gaining a lot of acceptance. The company plans to expand rapidly. The next year it plans to open its stores in Mumbai and Delhi at critical locations.

It has plans to open three Big Bazaars (discount stores) in 'A-class cities' like Bangalore. Pantaloon has already bagged substantial retail space in Hyderabad (60,000 sq.ft), Kolkata (35,000 sq.ft), and Bangalore (40,000 sq.ft). In Mumbai it acquired 50,000 sq. ft area at each of its locations at Lower Parel, Mulund, and the western suburbs.

Challenges

The key challenges facing the company are as follows:

- **Fund raising**—The company acknowledges that expansion plans of the company cannot be met from internal resources. This means that the company has to tap external sources to fund expansion. The company has recently allotted shares to promoters at SEBI formula price. It plans to borrow heavily to fund its expansion plans. As a consequence of increased interest payment and depreciation expense, the net profit margins would remain flat.

- **Competition**—Although there are a few stores operating in this segment such as Giant in Hyderabad, it is mostly international chains such as Wal-Mart and Carrefour that are the better known names as discount stores worldwide. Meanwhile, the general retailers in Mumbai are not too pleased about the concept of discount stores. Claims a retailer at a south Mumbai outlet, 'We can't figure out from where such stores get their margins. It must have a feasible revenue model to sustain the venture.'

The company is facing limited competition from the organized retailers but strong competition exists from the downtown center's unorganized

---

'Grocery Shops to Fight Malls'

The local traders—grains, provisions and dry fruits sellers—have chalked out an interesting strategy to counter the 'mall effect'. They are buying goods in bulk from manufacturers and passing on the discount they get on bulk purchases to customers. The shopkeepers had to do a rethink on selling strategies after they lost business to malls like Big Bazaar and Food Bazaar, which sell goods below maximum retail price (MRP).

To increase their bargaining power vis-a-vis suppliers, the traders have decided to form an association that will be called Ghatkopar Retail, Provision, Kirana, and Dryfruits Merchants Association. The traders' organization, which will be formally launched in April, promises to protect the interests of the traders as well as the customers. 'The membership drive is on in full swing and the response is encouraging.'

So far, we have enlisted the support of 100 traders from the suburb,' says Amubhai Ghelani, proprietor of Ghelani Stores in Hingwala Lane. Ghelani says once the association is in place, the traders will not be at the mercy of suppliers. He further says that malls like Big Bazaar are able to sell products at lower prices because the MNCs and corporates sell them the products at discounted rates. ' We don't get the products at lower rates

and so we cannot pass on the benefit to our customers,' he explains. With more than 100 members already enlisted, the traders are now working on the finer points of the scheme for retaining customers. 'The association will place orders with suppliers on behalf of all the traders. Since the orders will be placed in bulk, the cost price will decrease and we will pass this benefit to our consumers,' says Vinod Chedda of Food Spot on Tilak Road. Once the plan is in place, Ghelani expects to sell branded products at rates that are 2–8 % lower than the present rates. Citing one example, Ghelani says, 'If small traders buy a product worth Rs 100 from suppliers, the same will cost only Rs 80 if purchased in bulk.' Commenting on the benefits a trader can derive from this association, Ghelani says, 'Apart from benefitting loyal customers, the association will be in a better position to take up disputes with suppliers and major companies. A lone trader does not have the will or the resources to fight his case.' 'The association will be a blessing in disguise for the traders,' says Chedda. He explains that often manufacturers decline to take responsibility for damaged or faulty products that have been sold to customers. 'This tarnishes the image of the trader, though he is not directly responsible for the fault. The association will take up the issue with the manufacturers on behalf of the customers. This will strengthen the goodwill between traders, manufacturers, and the customers.' Adds Kantibhai Shah of Vijay Dal Mill in Ghatkopar (W), 'The

association will also take up the problems customer faces with the trader.'
Source: Manthan Mehta 2004, 'Grocery shops to fight malls', March 9, www.midday.com

retailers. With respect to Mumbai, with the presence of Giant Hypermarket, which is also competing on the price platform, Big Bazaar is experiencing competition from the similar kind of retail format. Discount stores in Mumbai are wooing the value-for-money-oriented consumer.

Whilst Big Bazaar's positioning has been 'Isse sasta aur kahin nahin'(Nowhere else you get it cheaper). Giant's positioning is 'Bada choice chota price'(Big choice small price.), However, both appear to claim to be the cheapest but neither is planning to cut prices on any of its lines to attract customers from the other. That's probably because of the different locations that they are in—Lower Parel and Malad, respectively.

Giant offers maximum reduction on food items, sanitation products, and apparels. The reduction ranges between 10–15%. Big Bazaar on the other hand gives more discounts on buckets, luggage, and non-stick cookwares, all of which, it claims, are around 15–20% cheaper. In the apparels section, it claims prices are lower by 50%.

'Our proposition, "Isse sasta aur accha kahin nahin" encapsulates our business model of a discount store concept which our customers have accepted,' said the marketing manager, Big Bazaar. 'Our model is a high-volume, low-margin business, more of a mass-market model', said the marketing manager, Giant Hypermarket. Giant offers discounts, which range from 3–20% whereas Big Bazaar has discounts in the range of 2–60%. The larger discounts are usually on their in-store brands rather than the established mega brands.

1. Evaluate the retail format of Big Bazaar and discuss its business strategy.
2. Identify and analyse the recent challenges faced by Big Bazaar. Suggest strategies to overcome them.
3. Devise a strategic plan for small retailers to be able to face challenges posed by retail formats like that of Big Bazaar.
4. In the context of Big Bazaar retail mix strategy, evaluate the scope for organized retailing in India.

References

1. *Milestones*, an ORG-MARG publication.

2. www.anderson.ucla.edu.

3. Dutt, D. 2004, 'An Outlook for Retailing in India, Vision 2005' (From a presentation by KSA Technopak at MDI Gurgaon in January and February).

4. Kotler, Philip 2000, *Marketing Management*, 10th Ed., Prentice Hall of India Pvt Ltd, New Delhi.

5. Knight Frank India Research (Mumbai) 2002, 'Searching for space', *Praxis Business Line*, January.

6. Chandrasekhar, Priya 2001, 'Retailing in India: Trends and opportunities', *Business Line: Catalyst*, February 15.

7. Devasahayam, Madona 1998, 'Big Deal', *Praxis Quarterly Journal on Management*, August, Vol. 2, No. 2.

8. Majumdar, S. 2002, 'FDI in retailing: India as a supermarket', *Business Line*, Tuesday, Sep 17.

9. Kannan, S. 2001, 'Huge potential awaits retailing', *Business Line*, Thursday, September 13.

10. Jagannathan, V. 2001, 'Vivek's—a store more reputed than the brands it sells', *Business Line*, February 5.

11. Bhushan, R. 2002, 'The show begins here', *Business Line*, Thursday, December 26.

12. www.ipan.com

13. www.indiainfoline.com

14. Aroor, S. and Singh, S. 2004, 'Market Dynamics: Cigarette Retailer As The New King', *The Financial Express*, Net Edition, May 4.

15. *Delhi Economic Indicators*, 2000–2001.

16. *SPICE* 2003, Vol. 1 No. 7.

17. Gupta, R., 'Pharma retailing gains momentum in India', www.galtglobalreview.com

18. www.retailyatra.com

19. www.bata.com

20. www.prweb.com

21. www.retailbiz.com

22. Chandran, R. 2003, 'Kodak India rejigs retail strategy', *Business Line*, Friday, October 3.

23. www.titan.com

24. www.emediaplan.com

25. www.indiareacts.com

26. Salil Panchal and Morpheus Inc. 2003, 'What is VAT? And why VAT', www.rediff.com, April 12.

27. www.morepen.com

28. www.theindiatravelguide.com

29. www.smallindustryindia.com
30. www.thaneweb.com
31. www.economictimes.indiatimes.com 2004, Citibank to increase presence in India, April 19.
32. www.bharatpetroleum.com
33. Jagannathan, V. 2003, 'Retail reality tales', www.domain-b.com , March 11.

Retail Organization   117

28. www.retailindustry.com.

30. www.theworldbank.org.

31. www.cci.nml.com, 'India.shopper.com, 2004, Giorgio to increase presence in India', 19...

32. worldbank.jsp-release.com.

33. Japanmakret News 2004, 'Retail realty rates', www.domain-b.com, March 11...

3   RETAIL IN INDIA

Learning Objectives

- To understand the present retailing scenario in India

- To analyse various retailing formats in the Indian context

- To examine the growth and development of organized and traditional retail formats in India

- To analyse the nature of retailing in rural India

- To become aware of the developments in the retail sector with respect to various product categories

- To discuss the key challenges faced by the retail industry in India

Introduction

The retail industry in India is largely unorganized and predominantly consists of small, independent, owner-managed shops. Retailing is India's largest industry in terms of contribution to GDP and constitutes 13% of the GDP (gross domestic product). There are around 5 million retail outlets in India. There are also an unaccounted number of low-cost kiosks (tea stalls, snack centres, barber shops, etc.) and pushcarts/mobile vendors. Total retail sales area in India was estimated at 328 million sq. mt. in 2001, with an average selling space of 29.4 sq. mt. per outlet. In India, the per capita retailing space is about 2 sq. ft., which is quite low compared to that of the developed economies.

In 2000, the global management consultancy AT Kearney put retail trade at Rs 400,000 crore (1 crore = 10 million), which is expected to increase to Rs 800,000 crore by the year 2005—an annual increase of 20%. According to a survey by AT Kearney, an overwhelming proportion of the Rs 400,000 crore retail market is unorganized. In fact, only a Rs 20,000 crore segment of the market is organized. There is no integrated supply chain management outlook in the Indian traditional retail industry.

Food sales constitute a high proportion of the total retail sales. The share was 62.7% in 2001, worth approximately Rs 7,039.2 billion, while non-food sales were worth Rs 4189.5 billion. However, the non-food retailing sector registered faster year-on-year growth than the food sales sector. The trend to market private labels by a specific retail store is catching on in India as it helps to improve margins. The turnover from private labels by major retail chains was estimated at around Rs 1200 million in 2001.

Table 3.1:   Growth in retail outlets (millions)

Year	Urban	Rural	Total
1978	0.58	1.76	2.35
1984	0.75	2.02	2.77
1990	0.94	2.42	3.36
1996	1.80	3.33	5.13

Source: www.indiainfoline.com

Table 3.2: Composition of urban outlets

Retail Outlet	Composition
Grocers	34.7%
Cosmetic stores	4.0%
Chemist	6.3%
Food stores	6.6%
General stores	14.4%

contd

contd

Retail Outlet	Composition
Tobacco, pan stores	17.0%
Others	17.0%

Source: www.indiainfoline.com

Table 3.3: Composition of rural outlets

Retail Outlet	Composition
Grocers	55.6%
General stores	13.5%
Chemists	3.3%
Others	27.6%

Source: www.indiainfoline.com

Organized Retailing in India: Challenges

Legal procedures such as time-consuming process in title clearance, requirement of numerous lease deeds in the case of multiple ownership, and difficulties in conversion of normal land into commercial use are some of the basic difficulties impairing the development of organized retailing in India. To open a large store, an organization has to acquire as many as 10–15 clearances from several government agencies, which involves a lot of time and resources.

Even local laws do not permit opening of stores beyond 7:30 p.m. (for example in Delhi) and on Sundays and holidays. It stands contrary to the strategy of modern retail centres, as they attract shoppers on weekends and late hours on weekdays, and offer a whole new shopping experience, which includes entertainment, and food courts under one roof. Shoppers' Stop, which pioneered modern retailing in India, has recently obtained permission to extend shopping hours up to 9.30 p.m. on all days including national holidays for its outlet at New Delhi's Ansal Plaza.

The retail industry is also facing problems on account of labour laws, which do not facilitate part-time employment in the organized sector.

Emergence of Organized Retailing

Organized retailing in India represents a small fraction of the total retail market. In 2001, organized retail trade in India was worth

Chennai: The Centre of Organized Retail Boom

Chennai has experienced the organized retail boom. This is despite its perception of being a traditional, conservative, and cost conscious market. FoodWorld, Music World, Health and Glow, Subhiksha, and the likes, are a few of the successful names in the retail business that started their chain of stores from Chennai. Factors such as reasonable real estate prices, strong presence of MNCs, healthy industrial growth, increase in the number of double-income households, growth of the middle class, increase in the purchasing power of the consumer as well as the need for a better shopping experience have all led to the growth and sustenance of this industry in Chennai.

Rs 11,228.7 billion. Modern retail formats are showing robust growth as several retail chains have established a base in metropolitan cities, especially in south India, and are spreading all over India at a rapid pace. However, space and rentals are proving to be the biggest constraints to the development of large formats in metropolitan cities since retailers are aiming at prime locations.

In urban India, families are experiencing growth in income but dearth of time. More and more women are taking up corporate jobs, which is adding to the family's income and leading to better lifestyles. Rising incomes has led to an increased demand for better quality products while lack of time has led to a demand for convenience and services.

The demand for frozen, instant, ready-to-cook, ready-to-eat food has been on the rise, especially in the metropolitan and large cities in India. There is also a strong trend in favour of one-stop shops like supermarkets and department stores.

Rural India continues to be serviced by small retail outlets. Only 3.6 million outlets cater to more than 700 million inhabitants of rural India. Here, provision stores, paan shops, and ration shops are the most popular vehicles of retailing. Apart from this, there are periodic or temporary markets, such as haats, peeth, and melas, that come up at the same location at regular time intervals.

The McKinsey report predicts that FDI will help the retail businesses to grow to US $ 460–470 billion by 2010. There has been a strong resistance to foreign direct investment (FDI) in retailing from small traders who fear that foreign companies would take away their business, lead to the closure of many small trading businesses, and result in large-scale unemployment. Therefore, government has discouraged FDI in the retail sector. At present, foreign retailers can enter the retailing sector only through restricted modes. Global players in the retail segment have been entering the market for a while now. Players that entered before the easing of restrictions on FDI in retail had to come through different modes, such as joint ventures where the Indian partner is an export house (e.g., Total Health Care); franchising/local manufacturing/sourcing from small-scale sector (e.g., McDonald's, Pizza Hut); cash and carry operations (e.g., Giant), and licensing (Marks & Spencer's).

India Ranked No. 5 in Emerging Retail Markets

The global retailing sector is increasingly regarding India as an attractive investment destination, at least in terms of potential, since FDI in retailing is banned. The country has emerged fifth in a global ranking of emerging destinations in the retail sector, rising one notch over its previous year's rank. The Global Retail Development Index (GRDI), developed by AT Kearney, has ranked Russia and Eastern Europe as the most attractive destinations for food and general merchandise retailers who have international expansion plans. The GRDI is an annual ranking of retail investment attractiveness among 30 emerging markets including countries like Hong Kong, Indonesia, Thailand, Malaysia, and Hungary. As modern retail has reached a saturation point in many developed countries, global retailers like Carrefour and Wal-Mart have expanded in other regions, with Asia being a key market.

India was ranked sixth in last year's ranking while China had been ranked first. China has dropped down two places to third rank, primarily because of the methodology adopted for the ranking. The index ranks a country on economic and political risk, modern retail area per 1,000 inhabitants, the number of international retailers in the country, and time pressure, that is, the difference between the country's GDP growth and modern retail area's growth.

From these factors, a rank between 0 and 100 is given, with 100 indicating that there is a huge opportunity to be exploited. Russia has got 72 marks while India has got 65, losing out mainly due to country risk. Since FDI is not allowed, global retailers do not have direct access to the Indian markets. Yet, organized retail in its existing form is growing at a fast rate.

The ET Knowledge Series, 'Changing Gears: Retailing in India', has projected India's organized retail trade in 2002 at Rs 160 billion, which is estimated to have grown by about 15–18% during 2003. China has attracted several global retailers, with a nearly 13% increase in retail space annually but the 'window of opportunity is closing fast', according to AT Kearney. This is why China has slipped in rank. Russia has gained because its economy has become stronger, inflation levels have dropped, retail density is very low with only six international retailers present there and the retail sector is booming.

Though India's fifth rank represents a huge opportunity for global retailers, restrictions on FDI inflows mean that this market will be out of bounds for direct entry. The GRDI report says that FDI is heavily regulated, retail ownership by foreign companies is limited, and taxes are relatively high.

Source: Ravi Ananthanarayanan 2003, Times News Network, August 28.

In the sections below we provide an overview of the trends and formats in the traditional and modern retail sector in India.

Traditional Retail Formats

Traditional retail formats refer to those formats that have long been part of the retail landscape of India. They include formats like kirana and independent stores that are typical of the unorganized retail sector across product categories and also the most administratively organized form of Indian retailing—co-operatives and government—controlled retail institutions (like the public distribution system and cottage emporiums). In terms of professional management and efficiency of integration with the value chain, the traditional retail formats are better classified under the unorganized retail sector.

There are predominantly two types of traditional retail formats, namely:
- Kirana and independent stores
- Co-operative and government-owned stores

Independent and kirana stores have emerged with the spread and density of population. Historically, they are traced to the generation of surplus in agriculture that needed to be sold to obtain other essential commodities by the producer. This was accompanied by the emergence of a trading class in India.

Co-operative stores in India are the result of the co-operative movement that can be traced to the pre-independence period. They emerged as a reaction to the feudal system and attempted to place the fruits of labour in the hands of the producer himself to make him self-reliant. The co-operative movement was strengthened after independence; yet it was largely successful in western India. Government-owned and/or–operated stores emerged after independence because of their increased role in business and their responsibility towards the socio-economically weaker sections of the society, and for preservation of handicrafts, promotion of tourism, ensuring fair prices, and distribution of essential items. In the sections that follow, the above formats are discussed in detail.

Kirana and Independent Stores

Generally, the *kirana*, mom-and-pop, and family-owned retail stores represent the retail business in India. These are usually shops with a very small area, stocking a limited range of products, varying from region to region according to the needs of the clientele or the whims of the owners.

About 78% of these retail stores are small family-owned businesses utilizing only household labour. Even among the retail enterprises that employ hired workers, the bulk of them use less than three workers. According to ORG-MARG, a small retailer is defined as one with an average turnover between Rs 17,500 and Rs 52,500 per annum.

These are low-cost structures, mostly owner-operated, have negligible real estate and labour costs, and little or no taxes to pay. Consumer familiarity that runs from generation to generation is one big advantage enjoyed by the traditional retailing sector. The retailer to consumer ratio is very low with many such shops often located close to people's residence thus making location and convenience a major factor for their popularity. However, the retailer offers credit facilities depending on the size of his business and seeming credibility of his customer.

Branding is not the key decision criteria for a majority of customers at the traditional retail outlets, particularly in the small townships and rural India. Traditional retailers play a significant role in the purchase decision, influencing both the product and the brand perception.

Conventionally, retailers source the merchandise from wholesalers and sell it to end-users. Manufacturers distribute goods through carrying and forwarding agents to distributors and wholesalers. The merchandise price gets inflated to a great extent by the time it reaches from the manufacturer to the end-user. The new wave of competition has had a healthy effect on traditional retailers. Many are trying to introduce self-service formats, attractive atmospherics, services such as home delivery, and even telephone-based order delivery. Many experts have referred to this as the 'boom in retailing'. However, there are three aspects of boom in retailing in India:

(a) The emergence of newer, specialized, and bigger retail formats in urban India with greater focus on 'experiential' aspects of shopping. This has been prompted by a more demanding consumer, higher disposable incomes, entry of foreign brands in the Indian market, and entry of Indian business houses in the retail sector.

(b) Deeper and wider penetration of retail network in rural India prompted by greater recognition of the potential of rural markets especially in the FMCG and consumer durables sector.

(c) Redesigning the retail mix by the traditional retailers as a sign of greater maturity of the sector and also the rub-off effect of the developments in the organized sector.

The Indian retail sector has traditionally been structured around three small retail entities—the grocer, the general store, and the chemist. The grocer stocks non-packaged, unbranded/generic commodities such as rice, flour, pulses, salt, etc. The grocery stores located in neighbourhood centres or central business districts also sell branded and packaged fast moving consumer goods (FMCGs).

The general store stocks only branded and packaged FMCGs. These are generally located prominently in the neighbourhood centres and residential areas. The chemist, apart from dispensing pharmaceutical products, sells branded FMCGs such as personal care products and health foods. Alongside the three retail outfits, exist a large segment of smaller, unorganized players—paan-beedi stores which stock products in sachets, batteries, confectionery, and soaps; bakeries and confectioners; fruit juice/tea stalls; ice-cream parlours; electrical, furniture, and hardware stores; and non-food boutiques. There are a large number of hawkers, carts, and stalls within the main markets or localities and street corners, and many door-to-door sellers such as vegetable vendors.

The small independent retailers in India play a crucial role in the entire value chain. Their importance has been well acknowledged among the marketers and the customers. This is primarily because of the increase in stock-keeping units (SKUs) over the past years. According to ORG-MARG's retail audit, in 1996, the number of packs more than doubled in the 57 core FMCG categories such as white toothpaste, detergent powder, and cold cream.

That apart, there have been 19 new FMCG categories (between 1990 and 1996) like branded atta, anti-ageing creams, and dishwashing pastes that have introduced 1378 brands and 2579 SKUs at the retail counter. This SKU proliferation has caused intense pressure on shelf space. Marketers, therefore, have been forced to seek width in distribution rather than depth. So, the small retailer is playing a significant role as a distribution channel for FMCGs in the existing and the new settlement areas in urban areas.

Importance of Unorganized Retail Sector in the Value Chain

The war for cigarette marketing has been reduced to a three-by-two-feet-space retail outlet. That is the size of the board on which cigarette makers can advertise at retail outlets. With the advertising ban now in effect, cigarette retailers have lunged up the value chain and are now elevated to be the premium publicity battleground between cigarette makers.

Cigarette makers like Godfrey Phillips India (GPI) are rushing to forge exclusivity contracts with cigarette shops for better display of their products and fliers. Market leader ITC says it already has exclusivity arrangements and will work within this before it can come up with something new and innovative later. More goodwill strategies include both GPI and ITC shipping display boards to retailers, which say that cigarettes will not be sold to people under 18.

For starters, 'Cigarettes will not be sold to persons below 18 years of age, and the panwadis who violate this will be prosecuted' (in Hindi). Now that would seem like just a clause from the Tobacco Bill. It is actually part of the point-of-sale (PoS) material that cigarette companies like GPI are shipping out to retail outlets as a goodwill gesture. Though the Bill says that retailers are required to carry these statutory signs, it does not say that cigarette companies are required to supply these to retailers. GPI is supplying over four lakh retail outlets with the warning sign—the beginning of the retailer's new exalted status.

GPI senior vice-president (corporate affairs) says the signs are 'to help retailers comply with the new government directives which require them to display such a sign.' ITC senior executive vice-president says, 'We will supply such boards to our retailers. We will also advise them on these signs and help in translating exactly as per the government directive, so that they are not harassed.' According to the government directive, cigarette companies are allowed to have two boards advertising their products at retail outlets and merchandising racks.

Considering that cigarette shops are the only place now left where cigarette companies can advertise their products, the fight for space has narrowed down considerably. ITC and Godfrey Phillips were the major point-of-sale advertisers even before the advertising ban came into effect.

GPI will also forge exclusivity contracts with retailers across the country for better display of its products and publicity boards than others. 'The retailer is now absolute king,' KSA Technopak chairman says. 'Cigarette retailers tend to gain from other means of brand promotion—glow signs, cigarette shelves and even empty cartons supplied by cigarette companies.' *Source:* Shiv Aroor & Sangeeta Singh, 2004, 'Market Dynamics: Cigarette Retailer As The New King', *The Financial Express*, Net Edition, May 04.

Independent Neighbourhood Stores for FMCG Products

The concept of independent neighbourhood stores for FMCG products has survived and thrived due to plenty of factors such as:

- **Locational convenience**

  These stores are normally located in geographical proximity to consumer's home or workplace making shopping convenient. Locational convenience of retail formats becomes very important in the Indian context because of the following reasons.
  - Indians lack storage space at home and therefore make frequent trips to nearby retailers.
  - Indian consumers prefer fresh grocery rather than keeping bulk and use stale ones.
  - India has low motorised vehicle penetration levels (48.5% in 1995–96) in comparison to bicycle. Therefore, people prefer to buy from a nearby store rather than spending on public transport to buy from the main market.

- **Value added services**

  Small independent stores provide a lot of complementary services along with core offerings such as credit facility, home delivery, returns and adjustments, etc. Some retailers are well aware of the preferences of consumers and even advise them on the selection of product or brand.

- **Cost involved**

  These conventional retail units require very low investments initially, as most are owned by retailers or are protected tenants. These units have limited running expenses as family members provide their services to manage day-to-day operations.

- **Importance in value chain**

These stores have been acknowledged as the most important retail format in the value chain of FMCG companies. These outlets are used extensively not only to dispense products but also to stimulate demand. Therefore, companies generally provide POP material, banners, and refrigerators, and manage the display of their offerings effectively.

Source: The Indian FMCG Sector 2002, ICRA.

Supply chain integration does not quite matter in the case of a small retailer because of the small scale of his operations. Retailers normally prefer to deal directly with wholesalers with whom they are able to negotiate rates and payment terms.

Retail consolidation (consolidation of buying power) among supermarket/hypermarket/chain stores operators is unlikely to hurt the interest of small retailers simply because it is likely to affect manufacturers/suppliers directly, who do not want to compromise on the retail penetration against few large volumes to a few big retailers. Small retailers are patronized by customers on account of low prices and services they offer.

Small retailers provide a wide variety of facilities to their customers, such as telephone order, credit facilities, home delivery, customization on account of offerings and packaging, and specific products procured on order (in case of stock-outs). More importantly, they are available next door to offer personalized service. In this way, they are able to develop a strong relationship with his customers, who, over a period of time, become extremely loyal.

Cooperatives and Government Bodies

India has a large number of retail stores run by cooperative societies and government bodies across product categories. Such initiatives were taken for various socio-economic factors, primarily, to promote industries and generate employment opportunities in rural areas.

The examples of organized retailing format in India are the Super Bazaars and the Kendriya Bhandars along with the administered price public distribution system. These stores were among India's earliest endeavours into organized retailing with a user-friendly store format, large variety, and reasonable prices.

However, these were characterized by average customer service, bureaucratic timings, and poor upkeep. In a similar manner, cooperative movement in various industries such as dairy products also led to the emergence of organized retail chain in leading cities of India, such as Mother Diary outlets in Delhi and Parag in Lucknow. At the same time, government-established retail chains too provide effective marketing infrastructure to small-scale industries engaged in handicrafts and local goods such as KVIC stores in entire India, and state emporiums in the leading cities.

However, since the 1990s, there has been a reduction in government support for cooperatives. In 2002, there were about 35,000 outlets run by cooperatives.

Some of the popular retail institutions that are controlled and managed by the co-operative or government institutions are discussed below.

Mother Dairy, Delhi, and Fruit and Vegetable Project, Delhi

Mother Dairy, Delhi, and the Fruit and Vegetable Project, Delhi, set up by the National Dairy Development Board (NDDB) in 1974 and 1986, respectively, were merged to form Mother Dairy Fruit and Vegetable Limited (MD F&V) in April 2000.

The new company, a wholly owned subsidiary of NDDB, is involved in marketing and distribution of milk, milk products, and horticulture produce. The company's dairy plant handles more than 1.3 million litres of milk daily and undertakes its marketing operations through 636 own milk shops and more than 6,500 retails outlets in and around Delhi. Ice-cream market under the brand name 'Mother Dairy' has a 41% market share in Delhi.

The company markets horticulture produce in fresh, frozen, and processed form under the brand named 'SAFAL' through a chain of 263 own fruit and vegetable shops and more than 20,000 retail outlets in various parts of the country. Fresh produce from the producers is handled at the company's modern processing facility in Delhi with an annual capacity of 120,000 MT.

A state-of-the-art fruit processing plant, a 100% EOU, set up in 1996 at Mumbai, supplies quality products in the international market. The company's unique distribution network of bulk vending booths, retail outlets, and mobile units gives it a significant competitive advantage.

Safal: Fresh Fruit and Vegetable Outlets

The fruit and vegetables unit of the National Dairy Development Board (NDDB) was set up in 1988 with the objective of ensuring a direct link between the farmers and the consumers. The aim is to ensure that the customer gets the highest quality produce. The processed products of the unit are marketed with the brand name 'Safal'. The Safal group acts as a link between the farmer and the consumer in the procurement process that benefits both.

The farmers get the most remunerative price and the consumers get the best produce at a reasonable price. A large and ultra-modern central distribution facility has been set up to handle fresh and frozen fruits and vegetables. Initial cleaning, grading, and sorting are done, followed by cooling, to ensure its freshness till the product reaches the consumers. Specially designed modern retail outlets, the first of their kind in India, have been set up at various localities in Delhi and Mumbai, to market good quality fruit and vegetables at reasonable prices directly to the consumers.

As many as 279 specially designed modern retail outlets have been set up in and around Delhi to market fresh and frozen fruits and vegetables directly to the consumers. Each shop caters to a large number of customers and has a capacity to sell 1,600 kilos of fruit and vegetables a day. The shops are equipped with electronic machines that automatically weigh the produce and print item-wise bills.

Public Distribution System in New Delhi

The public distribution system (PDS) ensures the distribution of essential items such as selected cereals, sugar, and kerosene at subsidized prices to holders of ration cards. The PDS also helps to modulate open-market prices for commodities that are distributed through the system.

The Department of Food and Civil Supplies, Govt. of Delhi, manages the PDS in Delhi for regulating supply and distribution of, and trade and commerce in, essential commodities with a view to maintaining or increasing supplies thereof, and securing their equitable distribution and availability at fair prices by enforcing the Essential Commodities Act, 1955, and various Control Orders made thereunder.

The main items distributed through the PDS are cereals, such as rice and wheat, and essential items, such as sugar (only for people

Table 3.4: Important indicators of PDS—Delhi

S.No.	Item	1998-99	1999-2000	2000-2001
1	No. of Cards (in'000')	3353	3599	3689
2	No. of Cereal Units (in'000')	30721	33090	33948
3	No. of Sugar Units (in'000')	17793	19345	1589
4	Fair Price Shop (in number) (i+ii)	3214	3228	3165
	(i) Urban	2811	2853	2818
	(ii) Rural	403	375	347
5	No. of Licensed Shops of Kerosene Oil	2342	2372	2501

below poverty line) and kerosene. According to the Department of Food and Civil Supplies, there were 3,165 PDS outlets in Delhi in March 2001. Of these, 2,818 outlets were in urban areas and 347 in rural areas. On an average, each Fair Price Shop handles 1,000 ration cards. The number of households in Delhi that have ration cards increased from 23.62 lakhs in 1990–91 to 36.89 lakhs in 2000–2001 (Table 3.4).

Central Cottage Industries Emporium

The Central Cottage Industries Emporium (CCIE) is a Government of India undertaking to promote sales of artisanal goods to tourists as well as local customers. There are six stores across the country, by the same name, all keeping up the tradition of displaying and selling crafts from various regions of India.

The government runs the Central Cottage Industries Emporium, which has branches in each major city. These are well-appointed, multi-storeyed complexes containing a selection of handicrafts from every corner of the country. In order to provide attractive markets in urban centres and right prices to the artisans and craftsmen, the government launched the CCIE to provide them with an alternative retail channel.

India has, over the centuries, kept its arts and crafts alive—ivory, brass, silver, copper, gold, jewellery, silks and brocades, leather goods, carpets, excellent woodwork items, precious and semiprecious stones, blue pottery, and an unending list of other goods.

The central and state governments run various cottage and handicraft emporiums across the country. In Delhi, the Central Cottage Industries Emporium and the various state emporiums are located in Connaught Place. Cottage Emporium, as also many other such stores in the country, accept all major international credit cards. Each branch has an air freighting section where bulky purchases are delivered right at the customer's doorstep.

These emporiums retail a wide variety of product categories, which they procure from every part of India. They offer a rich variety of silk with special colours and weaves.

The heavy Kanjeevaram silks of the south, the soft and the richly brocaded ones of Beneras, the light silks from the east, the golden-hued 'muga' of Assam, 'tanchoi' from Surat, the magical tie-and-dye of Rajasthan and Gujarat, the 'ikat' or 'patola' of Orissa, and artifacts in bronze, brass, ivory, marble, or wood—statues, lamp shades, chairs, delicate filigree work on ivory and silver, marble inlaid with precious coloured stones, enamel work; 'kundan' or 'mina' jewellery of Rajasthan, silver from Orissa and pearls of Hyderabad—the entire range of rich handicraft products of India can be obtained from them. This is especially useful for the shopper in a hurry.

In New Delhi, an entire street—full of state government emporia—on the Baba Kharag Singh Marg provides the shoppers with virtually everything that is available in the country. They bring to the customers a wide selection of textiles, leather goods, art and artifacts, and the best of everything that a particular state offers. There are other emporia too like the Handloom House which sell equally good and genuine things.

Modern Retail Formats in India

Formats that have emerged or become popular in the 1990s are classified as modern retail formats. In terms of professional management and efficiency of integration with the value chain, these formats are classified as part of the organized retail sector in India.

Franchised Outlets and Company-owned Stores

Economic liberalization, competition, and foreign investment since the 1990s led to the proliferation of brands, with both foreign and

Indian companies acquiring strong brand equity for their products. Hence, franchising emerged as a popular mode of retailing. Sales of franchises grew at a rapid pace of 14% per annum over the review period. In 2002, there were over 5,000 franchised outlets.

The other major retailing organization format in India is 'chain stores'. In 2002, there were about 1,800 chain stores. Among the various organizational formats, sales of chain stores grew at the fastest pace, with sales growth during the review period averaging 24% per year.

There has been a boom in organized retailing in India owing to a gradual increase in the disposable incomes of the middle-class households.

More and more new or established companies in other trades are coming into the retail business in India, contributing to the introduction of new formats like malls, supermarkets, hypermarkets, discount stores, department stores, and even changing the traditional looks of bookstores, company-owned stores, chemist shops, and furnishing stores.

For example, Bata India Ltd is one of the largest and oldest retailers in organized retail sector, with 1,600 footwear stores spread across the country, and a retail turnover of Rs 6 billion in 2001. Bata enjoyed almost a monopolistic presence in the organized footwear market until the 1980s.

However, of late, retailing has become one of the most active sectors in India for almost a decade now. It has been undergoing a metamorphosis of sorts with the entry of big organized players in a largely traditional unorganized market. However, organized retail in India does not cover more than 2% of the retail trade. Moreover, most organized retail formats have emerged in the metros and on their outskirts. Hence, they have not thrown up a major challenge to the unorganized retail formats, except for inducing a positive shift in their strategy in terms of greater focus on experiential aspects and ambience.

The emergence of organized retailing in India has been influenced by factors such as the increasing purchasing power of consumers, increased variety of options, more brand awareness, consumer interest in quality, and the increasing economies of scale, along with the aid of modern supply and distribution management solutions.

The most interesting facet of this revolution is the non-food segment, which has given the urban consumer the power of choice while catering

to their changing needs and lifestyles. These new sectors include lifestyle
and fashion retailers, such as Shoppers' Stop, Globus, LifeStyle, Westside,
etc.; apparel retail, such as Wills Lifestyle and Landmark; books, music,
and gift retailers, such as Archies, Music World, Crosswords, etc.; and
drugs and pharmacy retailers, such as Health and Glow, Apollo. These
segments have taken retail into diverse areas, offering the consumer a
wide range of goods and pleasant shopping experiences.

The success of large malls such as Crossroads in Mumbai, Spencer
Plaza in Chennai, and Ansal Plaza in Delhi has encouraged a number
of developers to join the retail bandwagon. Malls, supermarkets, and
various internationally successful formats are bringing about the retail
boom in cities like Gurgaon, Mumbai, Bangalore, and Chennai.
Affordability, variety, and attractiveness seem to be the key offerings
of the retailing chains.

Organized retail in India is looking to change the face of the market
with local, national, and international chains trying to create a space
for themselves.

The traditional food and grocery segment has seen the emergence
of supermarkets and grocery chains such as FoodWorld, Nilgiris, and
Apna Bazaar; convenience stores like Convenio and HP Speedmart
are increasingly found at petrol pumps; and fast-food chains like
McDonald's, Dominos, Nirulas, etc. and coffee shops such as Barista,
Cafe Coffee Day etc. are expanding fast and wide.

Pubs such as Geoffrey's, and speciality eateries such as Copper
Chimney and Mainland China are creating a niche for themselves
and are expanding their franchise. Besides, the food and grocery sector
now accounts for 14% of total organized retail, after clothing and textiles
(at 36%), and watches and jewellery (at 17%). Food and grocery retail
offers the biggest opportunity for growth, and even the provided levels
of investment are high, says the KSA study.

Geographical Markets

There is considerable variance in economic prosperity levels among
various Indian states, which is linked to the overall wealth creation
from agriculture, trade, and industrial development. Accordingly, there
are affluent and poor districts in most states, classified according to
their market potential.

At the national level, India has 500 active districts (excluding Jammu and Kashmir), of which the top 150 districts (Class A) account for 78%, while the next 150 (Class B) account for 15% of the national market potential for a wide category of goods. The remaining 200 districts (Class C), which have 40% of the geographical share, are backward and account for only 7% of India's market potential. The spread of affluent and non-affluent districts is uniform in all the four regions. However, the eastern, north-eastern and central regions of India have the largest share of backward districts.

Retailing in Rural India

An important phenomenon in India's consumer culture is the emergence of the rural market for several basic consumer goods. Three-fourths of India's population lives in rural areas, and brings one-third of the national income. This rural population is spread all over India in about 0.6 million villages. This simply shows the great purchasing potential of rural India. It has also brought the much-needed volume-driven growth for companies, particularly in the FMCG sector.

Also, the rural market has been growing steadily over the years and is now bigger than the urban market for FMCGs (53% share of the total market), with an annual size, in value terms, currently estimated at around Rs 50,000 crores (Table 3.6). It is a definite boon for the companies who have already reached the plateau in their business curve in urban India and are seeking new ways to increase sales.

As per the National Council for Applied Economic Research (NCAER) study, there are as many 'middle income and above' households in the rural areas as there are in the urban areas. There are almost twice as many 'lower middle income' households in rural areas as in the urban areas. At the highest income level there are 2.3 million urban households as against 1.6 million households in rural areas (Table 3.7).

According to the NCAER projections, the number of middle- and high-income households in rural India is expected to grow from 80 million to 111 million by 2007. Nearly 45% of rural Indians are literate (men 59%, women 31%), and 33% of all villages (0.21 million) are connected by pucca roads. In all, there are more than 3.8 million retail outlets in rural India, averaging 5.8 shops per village (the term 'shop' refers to any type of premises–huts, stalls, shacks, etc., that sell goods). But despite the high rural share in these categories, the rural penetration rates are low, thus offering tremendous growth potential to the companies, (Table 3.5).

Table 3.5: Rural market penetration levels selected goods

Durable	Rural share %	Product	Penetration %
Refrigerator	24.30	Coffee	7
Black and white television	62.65	Biscuits	60.1
Washing machine	14.64	Toilet soap	91.6
Pressure cooker	51.51	Toothpaste	35.6
Instant water heater	2.04	Talcum powder	16.4
Mixer/grinder	27.43	Hair oil	16.0
Colour television	28.77	Shampoo	39.8
Scooter	28.56	Razor blade	47.1
Motorcycle	47.87	Skin cream	15.5

Source: NCAER, 2001

Table 3.6: Rural FMCG market: a snapshot

Category	Total size #	% Growth*	Rural size (Rs. crore)
Toilet soap	7500	13.4	6021
Body talcum power	940	23.65	793
Toothpaste	2080	23.5	1441
Tea	6500	10.97	4955
Health beverages	908	28.54	601
Electric bulbs	750	9.4	354
Cigarrettes	7662	13.09	6442
Packaged biscuits	2500	6.79	1323

Figures in Rs crore for 1998–99

* Annual growth rates compounded for last five years (1998-2003)

Source: Business Intelligence Unit and NCAER, 1998–99

Table 3.7: Percentage of Rural Households

Income group	1994–95	2000–2001*	2001–2006*
>Rs1, 06,000	1.6	3.8	5.6
Rs 77,000-1,06,000	2.7	4.7	5.8
Rs50, 001-77,000	8.3	13.0	22.4
Rs 25,001-50,000	26.0	41.1	44.6
<25000	61.4	37.4	20.2

* 2000–2001 and 2001–2007 projections are based on 7.2% GDP growth

Source: NCAER

Most manufacturers and marketing companies have a distribution arrangement for villages through village shopkeepers.

While it is necessary for marketers to select a particular distribution channel in rural areas in accordance with the characteristics of the product—consumable or durable—the shelf-life of the product and other factors have to be kept in mind. The challenges for the marketers and retailers are immense in rural India on account of poor logistics, limited storage and transport facilities, inaccessible markets, and high level of demand concentration.

In such circumstances, the significance of retail network increases in the entire rural marketing system. Therefore, one needs to have good understanding of the role of rural retailers in rural India. As we know, retailers undertake a wide range of activities such as determining consumer needs, finding a supplier, buying, transporting, pricing, and promotion exercise.

No doubt the retailer is a key source of information for the entire range of entities from manufacturers, wholesalers, buyers, etc. As per a study conducted in the eastern UP belt, almost 30% of retail outlets were managed by females. More than 70% of retailers from rural areas depended on the nearest feeder centre for their purchases, 20% preferred the haat or mela, and the rest preferred the city.

Product lines displayed and sold by retailers indicated that differences persisted from village to village. Each village represented its preferences, which were quite different from these of the adjoining villages. While big-retailers were dealing in 60 to over 100 items, small retailers were dealing in only 30 items.

Fifty per cent of the products sold by retailers are packaged ones, which clearly shows that penetration and receptiveness towards packaging has increased in the rural market. Even local manufacturers started providing packaged commodities. Margins are the major determinants of the brands to be sold.

Regarding the selection of products, brand, quantity, etc., retailers prefer to collect information from and give due importance to the advice of co-retailers. The supplier leads the show, as nearly 60% of the retailers depend on them for selection of brand or merchandise to be sold. Retailers enjoy a compatible relation with suppliers as suppliers inform them about new product arrivals, discounts, gifts, etc., and, above all, the assurance of replacing the product if not sold by the retailer. Consumers and advertisements also provide information to the retailers.

Therefore, the selection of supplier becomes crucial in the overall strategy of rural retailers. Retailers favour big suppliers in the trade centre (feeder market). Reasonable pricing is preferred by most of the retailers, followed by variety in the products offered and credit facility. It is strange to find that credit facility is desired only by a few retailers, as they believe they end up paying more when making purchase on credit. At the same time, credit facility is not offered very frequently.

In order to maintain regular sales, retailers follow a strict schedule. Thirty per cent visit market (feeder centre) daily, 40% visit market weekly for replenishing the stock, 20% visit bi-weekly, and rest as per need. It is not compulsory that the retailer himself will go for making purchases, he may ask favour of fellow retailers, relatives, or even neighbours. This not only saves his time but also is economical. In order to attract customers, retailers also provide credit facilities.

As most of the regular customers are neighbours and relatives, credit facility becomes an integral part of retail transactions. Seventy per cent prefer cash credit transaction, whereas the rest 30% go for cash transaction.

Retail network is an important link between a consumer and a producer. They provide information regarding quantity of pack, promotional schemes, influence of advertisement, consumer feedback, etc. Doubts in respect of credit facility still persist. Retailers are going for diversification in product line. Female-owned shops are coming up. The study of retailer's behaviour, requirements, and network is crucial for strategy in respect of the rural market.

Existing retail formats available in rural India are retail outlets within village, feeder centre or market, melas, haats and shandies, and hawkers (mobile retailers). Covering 5.57 lakh villages for distribution appears to be a formidable task. Most of the corporates have concentrated their efforts on rural areas which have a population of 2,000 persons or above. The percentage of such villages is merely 10% of the total number of villages in India. Therefore, for villages with less than 2,500 population, the distribution has been left to the initiative of the shopkeepers and dealers in larger villages and to the shopkeepers of smaller villages (within the village retail set-up).

At the same time, the age-old mobile department stores, namely haats/shandies, etc., (periodic markets), play an exceptional role in reaching to the rural consumers. Rural consumers have sufficient opportunities to make a choice not only in respect of products and brands but also regarding retail formats (haats, retail outlet within villages, hawkers, and feeder centres)

Retail Outlets Within Villages

These are basically run at low scale, mostly as a secondary business activity. They deal in limited product and limited brand variety within each product category. The number of retail outlets is subject to the population of villages in India. Villages with less than 500 may not even have one shop. Rural areas having a population of more than 1500 enjoy a strong parallel retail format set-up.

Periodic Markets (Shandies/Haats/Jathras)

Periodic markets are traditional places where the rural consumers congregate as a rule. While shandies/haats are held on a particular day every week, periodic markets are normally timed with religious festivals. These places attract a large number of itinerant merchants, and temporary shops are set up to sell all kinds of goods.

The importance of haats in the lives of the rural people is evident from the fact that 81% of the buyers are regular visitors to periodic markets. Fifty eight per cent visit haats to buy specific products although more than half of them have similar products available in their villages.

Most of the companies, across product categories, are already busy formulating their rural marketing strategy to tap the potential before competition catches up. The companies with years of experience in the urban markets are facing serious problems in rural areas in respect of distribution strategy. These limitation are attributed to various factors such as:

- Inadequate infrastructure (road, railway connectivity) with highly dispersed and thinly populated villages that need huge expenditure to establish distribution channels
- Inability of the small rural retailers to invest in stocks for multiple products or brands
- Limited or traditional medium of communication and other sales promotion difficulties
- Low per capita income and social, economic, and cultural differences of the rural masses as compared to the urban segment
- Low level of exposure to different product categories and product brands

One of the major challenges for companies is to ensure availability of the product or service through the present distribution channel. India's 6,27,000 villages are spread over 3.2 million sq. km; about 700 million Indians live in rural areas, and approaching them is not an easy task with the existing retail infrastucture. However, given the poor state of roads, it is an even greater challenge to regularly transport products to the far-flung villages.

Any serious marketer must strive to reach at least 13,113 villages with a population of more than 5,000. Marketers must trade-off the distribution cost with incremental market penetration. Over the years, India's largest MNC, Hindustan Lever, a subsidiary of Unilever, has built a strong distribution system, which helps its brands to reach the interiors of the rural market.

To service remote villages, stockists use autorickshaws, bullock-carts, and even boats in the backwaters of Kerala. Coca-Cola, which considers rural India as a future growth driver, has evolved a hub and spoke model to reach the villages. To ensure full loads, the company depot supplies twice a week to the large distributors who act as hubs.

These distributors appoint and supply once a week smaller distributors in adjoining areas. LG Electronics defines all cities and towns, other than the seven metro cities, as a rural and semi-urban market. To tap these unexplored country markets, LG has set up 45 area offices and 59 rural/remote area offices to cater directly the needs of the rural consumers.

The problems of physical distribution and channel management adversely affect the service as well as the cost aspect. The existent market structure consists of the primary rural market and retail sales outlet. The structure involves stock points in feeder towns to service these retail outlets at the village level. But it becomes difficult to maintain the required service level in the delivery of the product at the retail level.

One of the ways could be using company delivery vans, which can serve two purposes—it can take the products to the customers in every nook and corner of the market and it also enables the firm to establish direct contact with them and thereby facilitate sales promotion. However, only the bigwigs can adopt this channel.

Retail Strategy with Respect to Specific Product Categories

Till now we have discussed the trends and development in the retail sector in India in general. However, the retail sector represents a variation in the level of development and preference for the formats based on product categories. This is the result of the product category characteristics or the companies operating in the specific categories, or both.

Product categories differ in terms of percentage share of markets, level of risk and relevance for the consumer, and the expectations and requirements of customer service. They also vary in terms of cost of operations and investments required by the retailer, the margins available to him, the nature of competitive environment, and the complexity of supply chain.

For example, in product categories where the risk and relevance aspect is emphasized by the consumer, retail formats are driven by the need for better customer service and provision of adequate information to the customer. This is also true for financial services retailing. Similarly, in case of product categories characterized by a competitive market situation, discounters are likely to emerge, and low versus high focus on service may emerge as the differentiator.

Consumer requirements in terms of convenience and accessibility has led to the popularity of kirana and neighbourhood stores for grocery products. For the same reason many petro-retailers have discovered the utility of 'convenience stores' as part of the petro-retail outlet.

Hence, in the following sections we discuss the Indian retail sector with respect to some important product categories. The product categories have been selected to provide a representative profile of retailing in India in terms of nature of predominant formats, requirements for customer service, and utilization of other retail mix elements. In the sections that follow retail strategy has been discussed with respect to the following product categories:

- Food
- Restaurants
- Health and beauty product
- Home furniture and household goods
- Clothing and footwear
- Durable goods
- Petro-retailing in India
- Retail banking
- Leisure industry

Retailing in the Food Category

Food sales account for 63% of the total sales, growing to 10 lakh crores from 3.81 lakh crores in 1996. Urbanization, double-income families, increased household incomes, and the convenience of one-stop shop with good ambience drive growth for organized and upmarket retail format/stores in food retailing. The number of food retail outlets has increased at the rate of 33% from 1996 to 2001, as shown in Table 3.8.

There are a large variety of retailers operating in the food retailing sector. This is not surprising considering the enormous size of the market for food. However, traditional types of retailers, who operate small, single outlet businesses mainly using family labour, dominate

Table 3.8: Number of retail outlets in India

Year	1997	1998	1999	2000	2001
Food Retailers ('000 outlets)	2943	3123.4	3300.2	3480	3682.9

this sector. In comparison, supermarkets account for a minuscule proportion of food sales.

This is because of the competitive strengths of the traditional retailers. These include low operating costs and overheads, low margins, proximity to customers, long opening hours, and additional services to customers (such as home delivery). Nevertheless, supermarket sales expanded at a much higher rate than other retailers. This is because a greater number of higher income Indians prefer to shop at supermarkets because of convenience, higher standards of hygiene, and attractive ambience.

The first visible sign of change in food retailing was seen in the mid-eighties. Around that time, a few new food stores were set up in all the metro cities in India. Calcutta was the only exception where it started a little later. We had, at that time, a feal leading food stores such as 'Morning Stores' and 'Modern Stores' in Delhi, 'Nilgiri' in Bangalore, 'Food Land' in Mumbai, and 'Spencers Food Stores' in Chennai.

In Mumbai, the Garware group, during the late eighties, had set up a large food store, which is now reported to have been closed down. But Food Land is still operating. Co-operative stores like 'Apna Bazzar' in Mumbai and 'Kendriya Bhandar' in Delhi were very successful and are now operating many outlets in all the strategic localities in the city.

Most food retail players in the organized sector have been region-specific as far as geographical presence is concerned. Take the case of RPG Group's FoodWorld, Nilgiri's Margin Free Market, Giant, Varkey's and Subhiksha, all of which are more-or-less spread in the southern region. Sabka Bazaar has a presence only in and around Delhi; names such as Haiko and Radhakrishna Foodland are Mumbai-centric; and Adani is Ahmedabad-centric.

The organized food and grocery retail chains that are planning to go national require significant investments. Retailing within this sector is not just about the front-end but also involves complex supply chain and logistics issues. The sector has not seen too many big entrants. The industry requires a lot more players.

Fast-food Retail Chain with Foreign Collaboration

Nanz Group of West Germany, a two-and-half-billion-dollar food retail store chain, was roped in a joint venture with Goetze (an Escort group company) and all due clearances were obtained, which paved the way for setting up of the first foreign food retail store in India. Later on, the 'Marsh' food chain of USA also joined it by taking 30% equity in the joint venture. There are now about 20 food stores under 'Nanz' operating in northern India alone—some directly owned and some franchised. The first 'Nanz' store opened at South Extension in 1990. Even after eight years of the store's existence the company is still in the red.

FoodWorld: Challenges in Expansion

FoodWorld was the first mover in the organized retailing sector. The chain has no plans to venture beyond the southern region just yet. FoodWorld wants to focus on the southern markets and achieve saturation. It has a current sales figure of Rs 350 crore. The major hurdles in the expansion plan are high set-up costs in terms of setting up of buying/distribution infrastructure, which are gradually amortized over a larger number of stores. At macro level, the obstacles in looking at a pan-India model for grocery are the federal nature of the country, the weak infrastructure, and the major variances in eating habits in different parts of the country. One will have to replicate the retail administration costs for at least each region, and therefore the gestation period of the project becomes huge.

The major formats being followed for organized food retailing in India are supermarkets, discount stores, fresh product outlets, speciality stores, convenience stores, and off-price retailers.

Supermarkets

There is a lack of universally acceptable definition of supermarkets. In terms of its key features, supermarkets have the tendency to limit themselves largely to food, to be located in congested areas (rather than on the outskirts as many of the early supermarkets did), and to appeal to consumers through lowered costs of distribution on staple products and well-known brands, rather than acting as dumping grounds for the surplus stocks of manufacturers who could not find a profitable market elsewhere.

In this context, the retail mix of supermarkets in India is quite similar to those in the West. However, Indian supermarkets are smaller in size. Many traditional Indian grocery retailers are adopting this format.

The example of FoodWorld, the popular supermarket chain, is discussed below.

FoodWorld   FoodWorld is one of the biggest retail chains in India. The RPG group opened the first FoodWorld outlet on May 9, 1996, at Chennai, which was a 2400 square feet store. It is the only national chain having foreign direct investment to the extent of 49% that is permitted in India. Now FoodWorld operates as a 51:49 joint venture with Dairy Farm International of the Jardine Matheson Group, a US$ 4.5-billion retail giant operating in the Asia-Pacific markets with the requisite experience.

FoodWorld has decided to concentrate more on local areas rather than going for a nationwide presence in its expansion plans at the beginning. South India was chosen, with focus on Bangalore and Chennai, and later on Hyderabad.

They identified areas within the city with more than 4,000 households in a 2-km radius with an average monthly income of more than Rs 4,000. The important variables considered while setting up an outlet are choosing the right location, sourcing the merchandise, and recruiting a trained workforce.

A typical store is about 3000–3500 sq. ft in size and carries about 5,500 items. FoodWorld handles on an average 600 customers per day per store, which translates to 1.5 million transactions per month. It is estimated that the chain serves more than three lakh families.

As on 1st November 2003, FoodWorld had 89 outlets spread across Tamil Nadu, Karnataka, Andhra Pradesh, Kerala, and Maharashtra (Pune). Its product portfolio includes grocery of all kinds, fresh foods, viz., fruits and vegetables in fresh/chilled/frozen form, food that can be directly consumed, food and non-food FMCG products, and general household merchandise like buckets, cups, shelves, etc. Indian-made foreign liquor is also sold at certain outlets.

FoodWorld follows the strategy selling around 100–120 items at any point of time below the maximum retail price (MRP). This strategy is generally applied for essential items or the items to which the customer attaches more value. In addition, there are also lots of schemes and offers to attract and retain customers. For procurement it follows the model of 'hub and spoke'.

The purchase for each state is done collectively to reduce costs. The distribution to each outlet is done by FoodWorld in such a way as to reduce the total handling costs. To source its daily requirement of fruits and vegetables, FoodWorld participates in the early morning auctions at the major wholesale markets and has a set of suppliers who then grade, clean, pack, and label the products in time for early morning dispatch to the stores.

At peak season, the fruit and vegetable shelf in a FoodWorld store stocks around 125 items, making it the widest range available under one roof in this category. FoodWorld's share of the organized retail market in the cities in which it operates is 62%, clearly a dominant share. The firm expects the number of FoodWorld stores to increase to 125 by 2005. A smaller version, FoodWorld Express is also planned to be launched in future.

Discount Stores

Retail stores that sell products at prices lower than those asked by traditional retail outlets are defined as discount stores. Some, such as department stores, offer a wide assortment of goods; others specialize in such merchandise as jewellery, electronic equipment, or electrical appliances. Food stores are also operated on the discount principle.

Subhiksha offers an interesting example of a discount store.

Subhiksha Chennai-based Subhiksha started its service in 1997. Beginning its journey from a single department store, at present this retail chain has 143 stores spread across the length and breadth of Tamil Nadu and Pondicherry. It earned a total turnover of Rs 235 crore in 2002–03.

Subhiksha expects to close the current fiscal with a total turnover of Rs 290 crore. According to Mr R. Subramanian, the Managing Director of Subhiksha Supermarket and Pharmacy, the chain expects to earn a total turnover of about Rs 1200 crore in 2008–09 as it plans to expand to other larger metros like Bangalore, Delhi, Bombay, and Ahmedabad.

The retail food and pharmacy chain plans to have 550 stores in the next five years with an anticipated investment of about Rs 145 crore for the expansion plan. Under the first phase of expansion, they plan to open 50 stores in Bangalore during the period from April to December 2004.

The second phase of expansion will see setting up of 140 stores in Delhi, which would take place in 18 months from April 2004. They also plan to expand it by setting up 140 stores in Mumbai and about 80 stores in Ahmedabad. The aim of Subhiksha is to set up an outlet every 2 km in residential areas where the average monthly income is more than Rs 4,000.

The retail outlets under this chain are mainly organized on the concept of a discount store that meets all the monthly household needs of a family. Subhiksha not only serves its customers through its outlets but also meets their demands through the home delivery concept, and currently the company makes around 16,000 deliveries every month. It is also planning to expand the number of outlets in Tamil Nadu to 135 by the end of this year from the current 104 across 23 cities and towns in the state. In Chennai itself Subhiksha has 60 outlets.

The retail company would also expand the number of its warehouses to 15 across the five states from the present two in one state and will employ around 8,000 people over the next three years. Its current staff-strength is around 1,500.

Speciality Stores

Speciality stores are concept shops which offer single-themed merchandise, such as fashion apparel and accessories, skin care products, books, etc. An example of Speciality food store in India is MTR.

MTR   It was way back in 1976 that MTR (Mavalli Tiffin Room) ventured into the business of retailing of groceries and other household general items by opening a department store. Because of the popularity gained by the company in this period, the MTR Group did not face much problem in making the consumers readily accept the products sold by its department store. Taking this lead it has grown by leaps and bounds.

The firm now has three stores in Bangalore, which solely deal in its products. Officials at MTR say, 'with a view to make the products available, products are designed in all sizes—small, medium, and big according to the needs of the end users'. Target customers of the group are mainly the working women. MTR opened its exclusive retail outlet in Bangalore in 2001 and currently has three similar outlets.

The company plans to open one unit in Chennai. With the basic strategy of making the product available to the target customers, MTR also distributes its products through various department stores and convenience stores.

With a wide range of product categories and with a consistency in good quality products, MTR has made its successful presence in south India and also in places like the USA, the UK, the Gulf, the Far East (Singapore, Malaysia), and Australia MTR brands in some categories hold market leadership in south India.

After being highly successful in south India, MTR decided to tap the western and northern markets of India. The number of working women are more in these regions and it has launched a number of new products aimed at the western and northern markets. Though the entry of multinationals is feared by many domestic industries, MTR with its deep penetration of outlets feels otherwise.

Mr Sadananda Maiya, Managing Director of MTR, says, 'The management of MTR feels that the entry of MNCs will hardly have an impact on Indian food business for the simple fact that it is highly difficult to change the food habits'. However, in line with the trend, they have been offering various 'ready-to-eat' products.

Restaurants

The food service sector in India consists of approximately 22,000 registered restaurants with sales of over US $15,000 per month. In addition, there are more than 1,00,000 roadside restaurants (dhabas) in small stalls in cities and on highways and 1,700 registered restaurants in hotels. The institutional sector consists of hospitals, prisons, defense establishments, schools, company canteens, railways, and airlines.

Generally, restaurants cater to the numerous ethnic groups in India, each of which has distinct food habits. However, the foreign mass media have had an impact on the food habits of the Indian consumers. They are shifting away from traditional Indian food served in restaurants and are increasingly turning to hotels and restaurants that serve foreign foods. Restaurant chains are creating awareness about their services and brands.

As a result, speciality and theme restaurants are opening more frequently than typical traditional Indian food restaurants. Speciality restaurants in India serve a focused menu of Chinese, Italian, Thai, or Mexican food. The fast-food industry, after a slow start, has registered prolific growth in recent years. Most US fast-food chains—McDonald's, KFC, Domino's Pizza, Pizza Hut—along with local chains such as Nirulas and Pizza Inn are doing good business in major urban areas and are now spreading to smaller cities.

Pubs and independent bars are also becoming popular among higher income Indian consumers in India's major metropolitan cities. Increasing demand from middle-class consumers is expected to spur robust growth in value-for-money restaurants. Although most restaurants source their raw materials locally, products such as frozen potato fries, speciality cheeses, some meat and fishery products, and condiments and flavorings are often imported.

In the following sections, some traditional food joints in India are discussed.

Apna Ghar

Apna Ghar, with a just-about-4-feet entrance, is located right opposite the International Book House in Deccan Gymkhana, Pune. Started by Nana Thorat to provide quality snacks to college students and office-goers at affordable rates (all items are priced between 4 and 6 rupees), this little desi fast-food joint has made quite a mark.

Every morning, the outlet serves people standing at the entrance. People queue up to eat the delicacies. Favourites are *pohe*, *sabudana khichdi*, *misal*, *upeet*, and of course the superb *shira*. Apart from the delicious food, the nice thing about this place is its cleanliness and efficient service. The retailer has given due importance to customer service and consistency in quality of offerings.

The store's spiritual atmosphere is also reflected by the boards on the walls with *Bhojan mantra* and *Gayatri mantra*. An ideal place to sit before you sip the delicious *Taak*—chilled buttermilk with ginger, jira, salt, and assorted spices.

Traditional retail outlets are quite popular in the eating joints category in India. To an extent, it is due to their ethnic cuisine, customer service, and low prices. The traditional eating joints are quite well known for their specialized preparations and customization as per local tastes. These outlets generally operate at low costs in central business districts (CBD) and neighbourhood centres. In the section below we discuss the famous traditional eating joints at Chandni Chowk—a leading CBD in Delhi.

Chandni Chowk, Delhi : Old Formats Coexist

The eating joints in Chandni Chowk are famous not only in Delhi, but all over India. Most of these date from the last century, some even earlier than that. Handed down from father to son, many of these businesses are now being managed by the 4th or 5th generations. They include halwais (confectioners), namkeen (spicy savouries) shops, chaatwalahs, and many others.

Quality is a top priority, with some even preparing their own spices and using only butter and pure ghee. More often than not, each shop has its own recipes (which are treated like family heirlooms) so that even though two shops may provide the same product, the flavour will differ. Strapped for space, one has to sit or stand in rather cramped arrangements. Some of the more famous shops in Chandni Chowk have been discussed below.

The Ghantewala Halwai

It is one of the oldest sweet shops in Chandni Chowk. More than two hundred years old, the Ghantewala is a landmark in itself. The shop is known for its quality of sweets available, the one most in demand being *sohan halwa* (Indian traditional sweet), made from dry fruits, sprouts, and sugar. This sweet shop has a long history stretching back to the year 1790. Sumer Chand Jain, the present patriarch of this family business, says the name of the shop came from the Mughal era.

'Ghantee' in Hindi means a huge bell. Legend goes that when the royal procession used to move down the road, the emperor would stop and be offered the delicacies from the sweet shop. The emperor's elephant would also be offered sweets. In a short time, the animal came to know the shop so well that, procession or no procession, it would refuse to pass through the road and shake its head until the compulsory offering of sweets was made! The bells hanging from the elephant's neck would tinkle melodiously in the process, and from there the shop acquired its name.

There is another Ghantewala Shahi Halwai near the famous fountain. Originally from the same family, the business has now been divided. This shop is also famous for its dry fruits, *sohan halwa*, *barfis*, and *namkeens*. Presently, the shop is owned by the 11th generation.

Natraj's Dahi Bhalle—Natraj Cafe

A typical Punjabi delicacy prepared from *dahi* (curd) and *bhalle* (a doughnut shaped item made of ground pulses). It is an all-time favourite with the crowds that throng the outlet in Chandni Chowk. Dating back to 1940, the shop also provides seating space and is patronized by many famous politicians and film stars.

With time they have expanded their list of offerings. It now includes south Indian and north Indian traditional dishes like *masala dosa, idli, wada* with *sambhar* and *coconut chutney*. North Indian food includes *thali* with a variety of vegetables, curd, *papad, tawa chapaties*, and pickles, which has been its hallmark for the last 50 years. Today, it is known as Natraj Café.

Kanwarji Bhagirathmal Dalbhujiawallah

More than 150 years old, this shop is well known for its *namkeens* like *dalbhujia* (fried pulses), *aalu ka lachha* (spicy fried potato sticks), and sweets like *barfi* and *imarti*. The shop is famous among the locals simply as 'Kanwarji'. It was established 175 years ago by the great grandfather of the present owner Laxmi Narayan Gupta. The shop is especially busy during Diwali and makes 12–14 types of sweets and savouries. They are more popular for namkeens, such as *shahi mixture* and *samosas*, but their sweets (mithai) has loyal followers too. Favourites include *pista loj, misri mawa (kalakand), and sohan halwa*.

Gianiji ka Falooda

Famous for its *rabri falooda* (milk starch and rice noodles served with crushed ice), the shop dates back to the time of India's independence. Extremely particular about their product's quality, the owners manufacture their own ice from filtered water. Lately, ice creams have also been included in the menu.

Near the Fatehpuri Mosque are the two famous confectioners— 'Meghraj and Sons' and 'Chainaram'. The former dates back to more than a 100 years ago whereas the latter was established in 1948. Both shops offer exotic Indian sweets and other fried food stuff.

Health and Beauty Product Retailers

With growth in incomes, Indians have been spending more on health and beauty products. Currently, India has over 5 million retailers, of whom 15% are chemists. As in the case of other retailing sectors, small single-outlet retailers also dominate sales of health and beauty products. Most of the independent retailers in this segment have introduced value-added services for the consumer, such as home delivery, prescription records, and reminder services.

In addition, pharma stores consist of self-diagnostic equipment, natural foods, baby care products, skin care, and toiletries among other things. However, in recent years, a couple of retail chains specializing in health and beauty products have sprung up. For instance, the customer-friendly environment makes the Lifespring chain of health and beauty stores a perfect example of captive retailing—organized retailing with much emphasis on the environment the goods are sold in.

Besides the regular pharmacy, Lifespring also offers a large variety of lifestyle-related health products like health foods, health drinks including power drinks, and self-help diagnostic items. GlaxoSmithKline (GSK), the leading pharma company, launched its pharma retail stores by the name 98.4°. Such developments are unprecedented in Indian pharma industry, pointing to the fact that the Indian healthcare business is progressing towards a new era.

The Apollo Hospitals group has over 70 round-the-clock retail outlets in India striving to maintain a stock of prescription drugs, OTC medicines, and other health and body-care related products. The pharmacy business has, as part of its expansion plans, tied up with Indian Oil Corporation (a Fortune 500 company) to set up convenience stores across its retail gas stations in India. Additionally, the retail business is moving towards offering e-prescription based services to the end user and the doctor. The Apollo group has initiated most ambitious initiatives in Apollo clinics across India and its neighbouring countries. These centres were incorporated to deliver family-focused primary healthcare services.

Competition Among Retail Chains

The total domestic pharmaceutical industry is estimated to be worth US$3.19 billion and is projected to grow at 10% annually. Advent of new retail formats in pharma retail industry has become highly competitive with the entry of more and more, players. Recent developments, such as pharmaceutical major, Morepen Laboratories' acquisition of the retail chain Lifespring, and new launches—98.4° from Global Healthline and Consumer Retail Services (CRS) Health Division from SAK

Industries—exemplify this new trend. SAK CRS has rolled out branded outlets under the name 'CRS Health—The Wellbeing Place'. SAK CRS is aiming to operate 150 outlets in the country in the next five years, while Global Healthline is planning to open 40–50 stores under the 98.4° brand over the next three years.

According to India's leading market research company ORG-MARG, 'The future trade channel will evolve in such a way that there will be value migration from suppliers to retailers, the reason being the proximity retailers will have with the end customer. As the role of the intermediary diminishes, retailers will become stronger in their negotiating powers than manufacturers and the only way for companies to keep this bargaining power is to enter into retailing themselves.'

Source: Gupta, R., 'Pharma retailing gains momentum in India', www.galtglobalreview.com

Apollo Health and LifeStyle Limited (AHLL) plans to establish initially a nationwide chain of more than 250 primary healthcare centres through franchisees. These clinics would be equipped to provide a one-stop solution to the primary healthcare needs of the family as a whole, and would provide tele-consultation, diagnostic, and pharmacy services.

The independent players also, cover retail industry for beauty services, with only few organized retail formats, such as Shahnaz, Lakme-Lever, VLCC, and Health and Glow. Significant focus of these centres is on sales counters, beauty advisors, and dealer aids.

Lakme's expert service is the core component of their services, across 44 Lakme Beauty Salons, due to its vision of offering a complete beauty solution to consumers. Multinational cosmetic players, such as Avon, Oriflame, and Amway use multi-level-marketing successfully to tap the cosmetic products market. Avon Beauty Products (Avon Beauty), the wholly owned Indian subsidiary of New York-based Avon Products Inc., plans to further explore the Indian mass market in the Rs 1,724-crore direct selling segment.

The company, which has products that cater to Sections B and C households, plans to introduce products for Section D households as well. Avon Beauty's lipsticks are priced at Rs 40 and above, while its least expensive nail enamel costs Rs 25, which is comparable to the prices of competitive brands. Avon Beauty recorded total sales, which includes sales of make-up, skin care, and fragrance products, of Rs 100 crore in 2002.

Oriflame Operations

Oriflame operates through distributors who buy products from the company and sell to the customers. A distributor registers with the company for a fees of Rs 250. After registration he/she is given a start-up kit with sample products in sachets and vials and some literature. The distributor places an order (minimum order size) with the company. The distributor then sells the products to its customers. The distributor marks up the price by 25% to sell at the Maximum Retail Price. This is one level of the distribution channel.

The distributor can introduce more people into the network and become a sponsor for another person. A sponsor can have his/her own network of distributors. This is a multi-level distribution system. At the end of each month the company calculates what is called a group volume, and for different slabs of volume it gives back to the entire network a discount, which can be up to a maximum of 21% of the business volumes. Further, the company also gives bonus over and above a certain volume level.

Hence, any distributor with Oriflame earns through both his direct sales as well as his network. Many a time this network money can be really big, so the distributors have to invest a lot of time in keeping their network motivated.

Make-up products are the company's fastest selling items, followed by skin care and fragrance products. Avon Products has set a growth rate target of 25–30% for 2003, lower than the 34.5% growth rate achieved in 2002. This is attributed to the slowdown in the FMCG segment. Analysts opine that Avon Beauty has a 5% share of the Indian market for cosmetic, fragrances, and skin care products.

In an era propelled by the changing lifestyles and increasing health consciousness of the Indian consumer, expenditure on healthcare is bound to increase, particularly due to changing lifestyles. Habits such as the consumption of packaged food products mean getting various nutritional deficiencies.

Considering these lifestyle changes, pharma companies are foraying into 'health outlets', particularly in major cities, where a combination of health services such as a health bar, fitness centre, beauty parlour, and spa are adjunct to a pharmacy where various health and beauty-related products are offered.

Consumers are also driven to organized and branded retail chains in order to avoid spurious and fake offerings prevalent in this industry.

Consumers can be assured of buying genuine products at these stores without worrying about issues such as expiry of drugs and billing, and so on. At present, they account for only a tiny share of sales of these products. However, as Indians spend more on such products in future, their business will undoubtedly expand substantially. There is also scope for entry of more such chains.

The example of Lifespring, a leading pharma chain, is discussed below.

Lifespring: Health and Beauty Place

Dr Morepen acquired Lifespring, the renowned chain of health and beauty stores, from Total Care Pvt. Ltd. Lifespring is an internationally styled, health and beauty chain of retail stores offering a range of nearly 15,000 domestic and international brand under one roof.

Lifespring is operating under the umbrella brand of Dr Morepen, which now plans to expand its franchise into a retail format, in order to come closer to the end consumer. Under Dr Morepen's banner, the Lifespring stores have become 'peppier', 'happening', and certainly more health-oriented.

Lifespring currently has six stores spread across Delhi at high retail density areas like South Extension, Rajouri Garden, Basant Lok, Greater Kailash, Karol Bagh, and I.P Extension.

Each store consists of three sections: Personal Care and Beauty, OTC and Prescription Medicines, and Optical Center. The pharmacy at the store offers a little more than a traditional chemist store. These are manned by trained and knowledgeable pharmacists, who are at customers' service at all times to advise them on products and prescriptions. A large range of herbal medicines, vitamins, dietary supplements, as well as health foods are also available.

Other Healthcare Products

Home healthcare products comprise pregnancy pillows, anti-snore pills, adjustable walking sticks and frames, and other specialized products. Lifespring provides a range of self-help health products, including diagnostic equipment such as BP Monitor kits, glucose monitors, and weight monitors among others.

It retails oral care products such as tooth polishes, smokers' toothpaste, and cavity guards. Its key foot-care products include foot creams and sprays, corn caps, anti-fungal powders, and massage sandals. Lifespring's first-aid products include wound care products, support, and braces.

The pharmacy also keeps informative literature on common illnesses and cures in order to educate and inform the customers.

Health Bar at Lifespring

One of the latest additions to the store is its health mocktails like Earthquake, Guilt Free, Tango Spice, and Silver Spring at an ergonomically designed health bar. Customers are offered these exotic drinks in a relaxed atmosphere, while one can go around shopping.

Health Foods at Lifespring

A wide range of health foods comprising products like natural teas, health snacks, health chocolates, juices, low cholesterol, and low caloried diet items now form an important part of Lifespring offerings, giving a chance to the customer to enjoy the complete health package under one roof—food, drinks, and medical equipment.

Beauty Products at Lifespring

Lifespring retails a range of cosmetics both Indian and international brands. Before buying the customer can even try them. All make-up can be tested before purchase. The beauty section also consists of products related to skin care, hair care, manicure products, cosmetic aids, perfumes, etc. Here too, trained staff is present to guide and educate customers on purchase and usage of products.

Eye Care at Lifespring

Bausch and Lomb has opened eye care centres at Lifespring. These centres offer free eye check ups for entire families. Customers can also choose from a wide range of colour contact lenses, spectacles, and sunglasses.

Infant Care at Lifespring

Lifespring has a whole section for infants. Products like baby food, diapers and clothing, nursery equipment, and educative safety toys. Pur, a leading manufacturer of baby care products, launched its range in India through Lifespring. It includes specialized products like anti-colic bottles, toothbrush training sets, bottle sterilizers, medicine feeders, and orthodontic teats in silicon and latex. A new international range of first year's product for newborns, infants, and toddlers has also been recently added.

Hence, Lifespring has emerged as a leading pharma chain in Delhi.

Clothing and Footwear Retailers

Numerous clothing and footwear shops are to be found in Indian cities and towns, especially in shopping centres and markets. Industry experts estimate the total apparel market in India to be to the tune of Rs 48,000–50,000 crore. Of this, branded apparel is only to the extent of Rs 9,000–10,000 crore.

Overall, analysts expect the market to grow at 10–15% per annum and the footwear retail market is around Rs 15,000 crore but both are overcrowded with small and major players. These are a mix of traditional and modern stores. Traditional outlets are family-owned business units, generally small in size and cramped, with little emphasis on alluring displays, and advertising depends on word-of-mouth or only on their strong customer relationship.

They basically stock a limited range of unbranded or local and popular items. This set of retailers depend on local wholesalers or traders from manufacturing centres such as Ludhiana, Surat, and Lucknow for specific kind of clothing, and Agra, Jaipur, and Kanpur for shoes. Retailers usually position their stores on the basis of pricing, quality, and variety of the merchandise and extend various services to their consumers such as credit, home delivery, selection of products at home, tailoring facility, alteration, returns, and adjustments.

Retailers prefer to attend to their regular and loyal customers themselves rather than letting the salespeople to attend them. A large number of such retailers are located in the central business districts or main markets of the cities, and only a limited number of independent retailers own massive retail units with designer décor and impressive layout, known as 'showroom'.

Independent Speciality Store: Seasons

'Seasons', Mumbai's biggest (5,000 sq. feet) and only retail outlet dedicated to Indian ethnic wear. Seasons offers semi-Indian wear for cocktail parties to straight cut lehangas for mehandi (traditional marriage ceremony) and short kurtis (ladies shirts) with lots of sequins and crystal work to add a little extra shimmer and glow on bride's face. One can shop for all the ceremonies from 'Haldi (engagement ceremony) to Honeymoon' under one roof. Established in 1995, it is one of the biggest outlets in the western suburb of Santacruz. The store has its own research unit designing staff, craftsmen from various parts of the country who give that additional ethnic touch to dresses. Lots of shimmer and hand embroidery is the speciality of Seasons.

Seasons accepts that western wear is 'in' but Indians cannot give up ethnic wear as far as weddings are concerned and there is no substitute for bridal saree or lehanga. Seasons has its own manufacturing unit so one can look for international stitching standards. Seasons annual calendar is one thing everyone looks forward to. Bipasha Basu, Gauri Pradhan, Aditi Govtrikar have all been the faces of Seasons. And one cannot ignore the larger-than-life billboards of Seasons in all over Mumbai.

Source: www.retailyatra.com

These outlets deal in un-stitched or ready-to-wear or both kinds of offerings. With time, few of the leading independent retail stores from the unorganized sector have established themselves as successful retail chains such as Nalli, Kumarans from Chennai, and Bombay Selection, Meena Bazaar from Delhi, Sant Footwear from Ludhiana, and Delco, and Metro from Delhi.

Small townships and rural areas of India have a large number of retail stores selling clothes, basically unstitched stuff for the entire family. These outlets are very small in size, have provisions for customers to sit inside the shop with retailers and select the merchandise.

The traditional retail set up has been distinctively classified on account of occasion-specific dressing (formal, casual, and party/wedding), sex (menswear and women's wear), etc. Just as in the case of food retailing, there are also a large number of retailers selling clothing and footwear in temporary markets (periodic markets in urban and rural areas). Because of their rock-bottom prices, which are much lower than prices of branded products, they attract a large number of customers.

In contrast, modern clothing and footwear stores are spacious with attractive window displays and use of mannequins. Most of the manufacturing companies, in order to achieve maximum level of retail penetration and to drive bargain, are using all possible retail formats

Shilpi: Example of a Boutique

Shilpi is considered as a haven for the connoisseur of handloom sarees. It was started by Arundhati Menon and Bamini Narayanan, 20 years back, when the concept of boutique was new to Chennai. From a kid's shop with 165 square feet area, Shilpi is now a name to reckon with in boutiques. Block printed sarees, hand painted sarees, and embroidery sarees are available at the store. Handloom sarees from all the states of India such as Andhra, Tamil Nadu, Orissa, and West Bengal with their unique patterns are on display. They have their supplies from the weavers directly. Shilpi has regular clients from all over the world, who are besotted to the beauty of Indian sarees. It also has designer salwars, churidhars, kurtas, and caftans to please the young generation. Apart from these, household linen like cushion covers, bedspreads, printed and handwoven, and bed covers are others specialities here. Customers can walk in and select their entire range of household linen. They export high quality tablemats to Dubai, Singapore, and Kuala Lumpur.

in the organized sector such as franchise, retail chain, company-owned outlet, etc.

Apparel and footwear retailing has identified various types of retail formats within the organized retail sector such as retail chain, franchise, company-owned stores and department stores, etc. In the branded clothing segment, leading companies are going for exclusive showrooms with trendy and attractive ambience to enhance the shopping experience of their shoppers; for example, Raymonds has 263 outlets, Madura Coats has 100 stores, while Grasim has 106 stores.

Benetton is also available in over 100 outlets. Even state-owned KVIC that runs the Khadi chain of stores has 7,000 stores. Footwear company Liberty, with a turnover of about 350 crores, sells through 350 exclusive Liberty showrooms and more than 4000 multi-brand stores spread all over India.

But the retail stores are neither owned nor managed by a company. On the other hand, Bata, a leading footwear company, sells through over 4,700 company-owned retail stores spanning almost every continent, and over 1,00,000 independent retailers and franchisees distributing Bata footwear, the Bata banner is one of the world's most familiar sights. Bata operates four core formats of stores: City Stores, Superstores, Family Stores, and Value Stores.

Bata: Store Formats

Bata operates four core formats: City Stores, Superstores, Family Stores and Value Stores.

Bata City Stores

Bata operates stores in many of the world's fashion capitals. Bata City Stores offer urban customers the best in today's fashion footwear and accessories. These stores are in prime locations, and provide a high level of customer service, exclusive fashion shoelines with complementary accessories, and contemporary shopping environment to discerning shoppers.

Bata Superstores

Bata Superstores offer a wide assortment of fashion, casual, and athletic footwear for the entire family. Located primarily in urban and suburban shopping malls, these stores offer high value by providing good quality shoes at reasonable prices in an assisted-service shopping environment.

Bata Family Stores

Bata is the world's leading family footwear chain. Whether in Prague or Singapore, customers have learned to depend on Bata for a wide assortment of comfortable, durable, and fashionable footwear for the entire family at reasonable prices. The products are primarily of the Bata brand, with a carefully selected assortment of articles from other local and international brands. For footwear, handbags, hosiery, shoe care products, Bata Family Stores are a trusted source around the world.

Bata Value Stores

Bata Value Stores—outlet centres, Bata Bazaar stores and depots—offer an incredibly wide assortment of very affordable footwear for the entire family. The shopping environment is a self-service format for ease of shopping. Footwear is attractive and durable, specifically selected, and sourced to meet the needs of the value conscious consumer.

Source: www.bata.com

For instance DCM Benetton is the licensed franchisee of United Colours of Benetton in India. The chain operates through company-owned, franchised, and multi-brand outlets.

In apparel retailing, a retailer has two choices: either create his own brand or sell other brands. Own brands definitely offer higher margins over non-store brands. Margins in apparel retailing could be anywhere between 40 and 50%. Independent retailers usually prefer to sell multiple brands rather than some specific brand.

In the section that follows the example of Kala Niketan, a leading clothing store at Mumbai, and The Loft, the biggest footwear store, are discussed.

Kala Niketan, the Clothing Store at Mumbai

The story of Kala Niketan began way back in the pre-independence days, when it was a 200-sq. ft shop. It has come a long way today in terms of both size and merchandise. 'Had it not been my father who threw me out of the house, this dream would not have been realized', recalls Shri Jayantibhai. He is the owner of Kala Niketan, the very shop which had employed him as a sales boy. It was this dream and sheer hard work which spelled the success of Jayantibhai. 'The customer is like God,' he says.

Kala Niketan, as it stands today, is a world of elegance and extravagance housing some of the most exquisite silks sarees and fabrics. Selecting the best available silks from all over the country, Kala Niketan has a wide range of embroidery, beadwork, and brocades. The weavers are master craftsmen, weaving exquisite patterns into the fabrics in a myraid of colours and designs. Kala Niketan claims, it is the pioneer of tailor-made sarees and over the years has had a royal clientele to boast of for many kings and heads of states have been its major buyers.

Today, fashion designers such as Karl Lagerfied, Issey Miyake, Gianni Versace, and Yves St Laurent are catered to by Kala Niketan in the traditional fabrics. From wedding ensembles to anything one can think of in terms of silk, Kala Niketan has the answer to it.

With the dream of making forays into the foreign markets, Kala Niketan group has set up K.N. Dyers and Printers Pvt. Ltd with its own design studio. It creates its own signature silks called K.N. Prints which are sold both in the domestic and the international market. Its silk scarfs come in an array of innovative designs. Of late, the group has diversified into ready-made menswear as well as designer wear. Apart from the various kinds of sarees from different parts of India, the store has launched a unique collection of sarees inspired by the Hindustani classical music, called Hansdhwani sarees. Kala Niketan has an export division known as Kala Darshan. Kala Kendra wholesales cotton sarees as well as shawls.

The store sells not only fabrics and garments but also chic accessories such as jewellery and bags to match one's outfit.

The Loft: Biggest Footwear Store in India

The Loft, the biggest footwear store in India, is currently running two stores in the country. The chain plans to open another five such stores in every metropolitan city of India by next 2–3 years. The store has been positioned as a complete foot-care retailer.

Their focus is to deal with merchandise only for the part of the body below the calves. Its second store at Banjara Hills, Hyderabad, is a grand 22,500-sq.ft shoe store, which the company prefers to call a category killer. With this size, the store will be the second such store in India, after the one in Mumbai owned by the same group. To give an international feel, a Canadian architect was appointed to design a modern shoe store. The store is built in three levels, with each level having two circumferences. The outer circumference is a walled storage area and the inner circumference is the display area.

The lower level of the store houses the formal and party wear for men and women, while the middle level houses the sports wear, leisure wear, and accessories like socks, shoe polishes, and laces. The upper level has an exclusive children's footwear, along with a big section of home wear and Indian ethnic wear, and a special infants section. The lower level has a special section for exclusive shoes, with price points ranging from Rs 5,000 to 15,000.

The middle level is expected to be embellished by a 160-feet jogging track made of Astroturf, so that the buyers of the sports shoes can actually jog around the track to see how well the shoes fit them. Moreover, a 49-feet wall on the upper level would be reserved for socks, which would house almost 15,000 pairs of socks. This will be in addition to over 1,00,000 pairs of footwear of more than 120 brands. The store plans to house all the quality brands—Bata, Gaitonde, Woodland, Lotus Bawa, Liberty, Reebok, Nike, Adidas, Red Tape, Rockport, Lee Cooper, Tuffs, Madam Phoenix, Clarks, Barker, Florshiem—you name it and the brand would be there.

This has positioned the store as a footwear and foot care supermarket. With all this, the store would be positioned as a value for money and MRP store with price points starting from Rs 40 to 15,000 per pair. However, this store will draw people from all the sections of the society.

And this is not all—on the anvil is a complete foot care solutions section for the customers. The foot care services would include a pedicure centre, Doctor Scholl's corner, dealing with acupressure shoes and shoes for handicapped people, help kiosks for educating the customer on foot care and selecting the right kind of shoes, and finally a cobbler's corner for shoe repair. The store would also stock some well-known brands of foot care products including foot talcum powder, foot massage gel, anti-odour creams, etc.

Since footwear industry is not an organized business in India, from day one 'THE LOFT' planned to work on a quick response (QR) model, where goods would be directly delivered by the vendors to the stores and there would be no stocking except on shop floors. While the industry works on an average stock turn of twice a year, the store is pitching for a stock turn of at least 5.5 times a year. Once successful, the company plans to replicate this model across five other metros in India by 2005–06.

Department Stores in the Apparel Category

For many foreign and private brands, department stores offer the ideal retail format for the apparel product category. Given the relatively high prices of leading brands, traditional retailers are reluctant to stock premium goods. Until now department stores have been few and far between in India. There are fewer than 100 department stores. But department store chains are now growing, reflecting the fast pace of modernization in the Indian retailing industry as a whole.

Prior to economic reforms that began in 1991, department stores did not seem a viable business in India because of the relative lack of branded consumer goods available in the market. While a few outlets that called themselves department stores did exist, these were nowhere close to international standards.

It was only during 1992–93 that the first department store that could be compared to counterparts abroad was set up in Mumbai by Shoppers' Stop. Today, there are about eight major department store chains selling across product categories such as apparel, cosmetics, fashion accessories, home fashion, and furniture.

Customers patronizing department stores in India are predominantly from the upper-middle and high-income classes, since such stores mainly stock premium brands. To cater to their customers' growing appetite for foreign brands most department stores stock a range of these.

Indeed, because of their late development in India, department stores are still considered by most Indians as exclusive shopping outlets that stock premium, high quality, and fashionable products.

Most department stores have spent a lot of money on state-of-the-art IT systems. These have covered all areas of operation, such as merchandise management, interaction with vendors, and stock planning. This has helped stores manage the complexities of interacting with a large number of suppliers, running many stores and warehouses, and selling a huge number of products to many customers.

In the clothing segment, many department stores have been selling their own brands in addition to other well-known Indian and foreign brands. Private labels are much more profitable and also enable stores to offer substantial price discounts and promotional offers to attract customers.

Department Store Chains

Shoppers' Stop   In 2002–03 the company's revenues amounted to Rs 3 billion (US$ 62 million). There are currently 13 Shoppers' Stop stores. Five of these are located in Mumbai while the others are in Bangalore, Chennai, Hyderabad, Delhi, Gurgaon, Kolkata, Jaipur, and Pune. The plans of the company are to nearly triple the number of stores to around 35 by 2007.

Pantaloon   Pantaloon Retail operates 14 Pantaloon department stores in Kolkata, Mumbai, Pune, Chennai, Hyderabad, Nagpur, Ahmedabad, and Kanpur. These stores generated sales of Rs 1.7 billion in 2002–03. The size of each outlet is significantly smaller than those of most other department stores chains. Before venturing into the department store business in 1997, the company was involved in manufacturing and retailing apparel.

LifeStyle International   LifeStyle operates the 'LifeStyle' chain of department stores. There are seven stores in Chennai, Bangalore, Hyderabad, Gurgaon, and Mumbai. Sales during 2002–03 amounted to Rs 1.4 billion. The company, which started operations in 1999, is owned by non-resident Indians and is a part of the Landmark group, based in Dubai. By 2007, the company plans to increase its network to 14 stores with sales of Rs 6.5 billion.

Trent   Trent (short for Tata Retail Enterprises), part of the Tata group, started its retailing operations in 1998 by acquiring the department

Nalli: The Saree Retail Chain

The Nalli, was established in the year 1928 and has done business for more than 70 years in textile and retail markets. It was started as a small retail store for silk sarees in Chennai by a young man called Nalli Chinnaswami Chettiar in the year 1928. The family-run shop did steady business until his grandson Nalli Kuppuswamy Chettiar took over. In a radical departure from convention, Kuppuswamy decided that the shop would not do any discount selling. Nalli, the shop soon built up an image of unrivalled quality at reasonable prices, its roster of loyal clients also grew multifold. Nalli's focus of business has also become broader.

In the last 10 years, the Nalli Silk Sarees has made geographical expansions by opening retail outlets in Delhi, Bangalore, and Mumbai. It has also started an exquisite shopping paradise of about 50,000 sq.feet in the heart of Chennai. The quality products of Nalli silk sarees and its reputation have spread worldwide. Nalli has retail outlets in various parts of India and also has offices in USA, Canada, and Singapore.

store that Littlewoods of Britain was running in Bangalore. It operates the Westside chain of stores. Trent's revenues amounted to Rs 1.1 billion in 2002–03. The company has 14 stores, known as 'Westside', in 10 cities. A unique feature of Trent is its strategy of relying almost entirely on private labels, which account for as much as 90% of sales.

Retail chain is another type of organized retail format in the retailing of apparel and footwear. It involves a number of similar establishments under one ownership. This format is common among family-owned business and enables them to expand their business and avail of economies of scale on account of bargaining with suppliers and harness the emerging potential of the market.

The spread of retail chain stores is taking placing more within the cities they belong to or at the most in the nearby areas as in the case of Bombay Selection and Meena Bazaar. The national level spread of retail chain stores in apparel and footwear has been very limited such as Nalli (international spread–USA, UK, Singapore), Kumarans, etc.

Home Furniture and Household Goods Retailers

The size of the Indian furniture retail market is estimated at around Rs 30,000 crore. The home furniture and household goods retailing sector in India is dominated by small retailers. Despite the large size of this market, very few modern and large retailers have established specialized stores for these products.

Most of the retail players are independent retailers with small infrastructure. These traditional retailers provide customized services to their customers in regard to designing of the furniture, material to be used, and mode of payments (cash, credit, or instalments).

With time, in the big urban centres, retailers have introduced impressive changes in terms of having huge stores, displaying some prepared furniture to attract customers, using interior experts, and providing distinctive ambience. Most of the Indian cities have specified market areas for furniture retailers; they usually have proper sections within the central district markets. On similar lines, household goods retail stores are prominently run by independent retailers.

These stores are normally located in the main market of the city. A good number of retailers sell household goods, particularly plastic goods, from periodic markets in urban and rural centres. However, there is a considerable potential for the entry or expansion of specialized retail chains and it is likely that this will happen during the next few years.

Organized furniture retailing is gaining more space in India, helped by the entry of international brands and changing consumer preferences. The neighbourhood carpenter or the upgraded craftsman

---

Arcus Home Store Chain

The Arcus home development store chain has one store each at Lower Parel, Mumbai, and Gurgaon near New Delhi. Arcus is planning to open two stores in Mumbai and one each in Bangalore and Hyderabad. While Arcus' Gurgaon store has been functioning for quite some time, the one in Mumbai started operations only recently. The company has a turnover of Rs 25-30 crore. The retail store sells a variety of products including sanitary ware, electrical items, furniture, ready-made kitchens, paints, and white goods. Arcus has tied up with many residential developers to showcase its products. For instance, it has an exclusive arrangement with the Gurgaon-based developer Unitech. The US-based retail chain Home Depot is the largest home development retail chain in the world. Arcus has followed the Home Depot model.

Source: www.retailbiz.com

who designs with an eye on foreign trends no longer satisfies the consumer with international exposure. These branded stores are characterized by huge expanses of exclusive designs, a multitude of colours, and sky-high prices.

They offer everything including furniture, linen, mirrors, lights, and other décor offerings. These up-market stores are no longer just focusing on furnishing, but also on 'home dressing'. According to the latest KSA Technopak Consumer Outlook Survey, durables purchases peak in the 20–34 years age group—double-income couples setting up households are possibly the driving force.

For instance, in 1998, the Gautier brand (owned by Groupe Seribo of France) was launched across India through a network of exclusive outlets and became the first national player of organized retailing of home furniture. It was the time when India was opening up to the concept of home dressing. Today, Gautier is the market leader in organized furniture retailing.

The brand was nurtured carefully for five years and it has become synonymous with exquisite French style, elegance, comfort, and practicality. The Gautier range in India comprises bedroom, living room, and dinning room furniture, which are made available through a countrywide network of 55 outlets including far-flung areas like Guwahati and Siliguri.

Durable Goods Retailers

Traditionally, independent retailers cater to the needs of customers and manufacturing companies to reach the end consumers in India. These retail outlets basically deal in multiple brands and limited variants in them, with no loyalties to a specific brand. The only determinants to select merchandise mix are margins, advertising, and demand for the particular brand. These retailers also provide a good number of services to their customers including after-sales services, home delivery, and credit facility.

Kodak India: Retail Strategy

The US$ 12-billion Eastman Kodak is focusing its energies on India, with an objective to ensure availability of offerings 'within an arm's reach,' of their potential segment. The company has redefined its distribution strategy, which not only covers physical network, but also the presentation—as stores in India, typically had bad flooring, bad lighting, and poor customer service. So Kodak wants to improve the quality of the store, the service and the product, and greatly enhance retailer-customer interface. It began with Kodak Express, the one-stop shop and photo-finishing site which was launched world-wide in 1990; in India, the 1,300 outlets in more than 300 metros and mini-metros are aimed at amateur photographers. The Kodak PhotoShop—a branded neighbourhood studio-store also for the amateur customer—which was conceptualized in India, and replicated in China, Pakistan, and Bangladesh. Launched in 2002, there are over 7,500 Kodak PhotoShops across the country today. India has one of the largest networks of Kodak Express and PhotoShop outlets on the Eastman Kodak map, and the network contributes to more than 54% of Kodak India's photography business. Broadly, Kodak adopted an FMCG-style distribution operation for photographic film, with 600 distributors to cover all towns with a population of over 1 lakh. So film was taken into grocery, novelty, medical, and lifestyle stores—ranging from an Express shop-in-shop outlet in Big Bazaar, to products sold at cash tills at FoodWorld stores.

Source: Rina Chandran 2003, 'Kodak India rejigs retail strategy', *Business Line*, Friday, Oct 03.

Even today in the purchase of the durable products, Indian consumers in smaller towns give weightage to the advice of retailers regarding models and brands. Therefore, companies along with multi-branded independent retailers are exploring other retail formats such as franchise outlets, company-owned outlets, and department stores to cater to the new segment in leading cities looking for distinctive shopping environment and extensive variety in durable shopping.

For instance, Titan, India's leading watch brand which uses design, technology, and people for unchallenged market leadership, distributes its products through various types of retail formats such as independent retail outlets, franchised stores (Time Zone), company-owned stores (World of Titan), exclusive (Sonata Store), and discount stores (Titan Value Mart). These retail formats vary on account of merchandise mix, pricing, brand portfolio, atmospherics, and service assistance.

World of Titan

World of Titan is a stylish showrooms chain in India, characterized by international ambience and a staggering choice of over a 1000 watches and trendy accessories. The store extends special treatment by delivering gifts to the customers and offering gift vouchers to their loved ones. The store also has its successful loyalty programme, Signet Club, with lots of privileges.

Time Zone

These stores bring together the country's leading watch brands under one roof, providing shoppers with a variety of brands, looks, and price ranges backed by efficient after-sales service. Time Zone stores are a chain of trusted franchised watch shops. Conveniently located, these 142 Time Zone stores across 89 towns offer shoppers the complete watch shopping experience.

Titan Value Mart

These outlets sell surplus stocks of Titan watches at reduced prices, offering fabulous value for money with the same warranty as a regular, full-priced watch.

Sonata Stores

Titan is running exclusive stores for the Sonata watch range. Sonata outlets have an authorized service centre for Sonata and Titan brands.

Source: www.titan.com

The entry of a large number of foreign consumer durable companies into the Indian market during the 1990s, after the government liberalized the foreign investment and import policies, transformed this sector dramatically. A larger variety of consumer electronic items and household appliances became available to the Indian customer.

Competition among companies to sell their brands provided a strong impetus to the growth of retailers operating in this sector. Retailing of white goods experienced the emergence of organized retail houses in south India, such as Vivek and Jainsons. These outlets were established in order to provide a one-stop shop to customers to buy goods from a wide variety at low prices.

In the following sections we discuss two examples of a leading retail chain—Vivek's and Sony India (in terms of its emerging retail strategy).

Vivek's

Vivek's is a durable goods retail chain with Rs 140-crores turnover (consisting of Vivek's Rs 108 crore and its subsidiary, Jainsons, with a turnover of Rs 32 crore). The store has a workforce of nearly 700 people in Chennai alone and nearly 1,046 suppliers in the city. Its main products are television, refrigerators, and washing machines. Of late, music systems are catching up.

Mobile phones and IT-related items are also picking up. The average customer turnout at Vivek's in Chennai is 1,000 customers per day.

On the New Year Day it touches nearly 40,000. The peak seasons at Vivek's is New Year and Diwali. Mostly the middle-and the upper-middle-income groups prefer to shop here. Between 1965 and 1995, the company owned just three showrooms in Chennai. The number went up to 16 by 2000. The Vivek's chain commands better faith and brand equity than that of the brands it sells. It is common to hear, 'I bought a new television at Vivek's,' omitting the brand name.

In order to expand its operation, Vivek took over Jainsons, a competing chain with 14 showrooms, in 1999 for an undisclosed sum. The Jainsons acquisition gave Vivek an immediate presence in the small towns of Tamil Nadu, apart from eight showrooms in Chennai. The reasons for keeping two chains, instead of merging them into one, are to cater the different sets of customers and establish distinctive store images.

There are around 200 consumer durable outlets in Chennai alone, competing against Vivek's. The proliferation of consumer durable brands is squeezing the small dealers as they lack the financial muscle to stock all brands. This, in turn, augurs well for retail chains like Vivek's, Jainsons, Vasanth and Co, Chennai, and Vijay Sales, Mumbai. The acquisition of Jainsons gave Vivek's a good bargaining power with its 75 suppliers. It centralized the sourcing and availed of cash discount.

Further, the increased competition amongst suppliers resulted in better margins for Vivek's. This hastened the breakeven point of each new showroom. In Chennai, Vivek's has a market share of 17%; 6% in the rest of Tamil Nadu; and 8% in Bangalore.

Product-wise in the Chennai market, Vivek's commands 10% of the television market, and 15% and 18% of the refrigerator and washing machine markets, respectively. With its presence in all the major cities/towns of Tamil Nadu through its two chains, and five showrooms under Vivek's name in Bangalore, Vivek's is now setting its foot in Andhra Pradesh by opening one showroom each in Hyderabad, Vizag, and Vijayawada.

The management is planning to achieve a target of 200 showrooms through the franchisee route by rewarding high performers with a licence. But before embarking on that, the company needs to streamline its supply chain management and make investments in IT systems.

Sony India's Emerging Retail Strategy

Sony India, the wholly owned subsidiary of Sony Corporation, Japan, is now changing its retail formats after seven years of presence in India. At the same time, the company wants to strengthen its distribution network and also invest in logistics management. Sony India has a distribution network of nearly 2,000 dealers and distributors in major locations in the country. Apart from this, it has 54 Sony Exclusive outlets and 39 Sony World outlets.

The retail change includes the introduction of a new retail format called Pro Shop and also upgrading, renaming, and expanding the existing formats. While Sony India sells directly to retailers located in the four metro cities and Bangalore, 20 distributors supply to multi-brand outlets located outside these five cities.

The company acknowledges that today shoppers look out for some unique shopping experience. Further, as the products attain more technical sophistication, it is more of technology selling that happens at the retail end than selling brands. Pro Shop will retail exclusive lifestyle products like home theatre and car audios, throughout the country.

Pro Shop will join Sony India's retail structure that consists of multi-brand outlets, Sony Exclusive outlets (exclusive dealers selling only colour television [CTV] and audio models) and Sony World, the mega store showcasing the company's entire product range. Pro Shop is just one part of Sony's market expansion strategy. The other part consists of upgrading the existing Sony Exclusive outlets and renaming them as Sony Zone, expanding the Sony World outlets, and the Web initiative.

Sony Zone, modelled along the lines of Sony World, will be small in size and located in upcountry markets. The company plans to increase such outlets to 500 from the existing 29. While it is a big leap with regards to the Sony Zone format, the company is also on its way to increase its franchisee-owned mega concept format, Sony World.

Given the wide range of products manufactured by Sony Corporation, small dealers found it difficult to stock and sell everything. However, the company was at a loss as it was not able to push its entire basket of products. This resulted in the Sony World concept, the one-stop shop for all Sony products. Showcasing the entire range of Sony India's products, the centrally air-conditioned franchisee-owned Sony World is normally 3,000–4,000 sq. ft in size, sporting a uniform interior layout, and a lighting scheme to offer shoppers a unique shopping experience.

Sony World showcases the company's entire product range: colour televisions (CTV), audio systems, digital camera range, handycams, DVD players, floppy diskettes, telephone instruments, dry cell batteries, and so on. The Sony World, which opened in 1998, contributes about 30% to the Calcutta turnover and is ranked amongst the top five performers for Sony India in that region.

The other beneficial offshoot of Sony World is in holding the price level of Sony products in a city. The idea is to have one Sony World store in all the towns with a population of 10 lakh and above. By 2005, Sony will have 50 Sony World outlets, which in turn would contribute around Rs 300 crore to its turnover.

Today, 82% of the company's Rs 670-crore turnover comes from multi-brand outlets, 7% from Sony Zones and Sony Exclusives, and 11% from Sony Worlds. Though the Sony World stores were expected to stock Sony India's entire product range, in practice it did not happen.

Even today, at some shops, products of normal usage like floppy discs and microtapes are not available. Correcting this anomaly, all Sony World outlets will have an Internet-enabled computer to help shoppers to buy their requirements and also the latest Sony products from Sony Singapore. Sony website has been redesigned to facilitate Internet shopping.

Many non-resident Indians (NRIs) use the company's website to gift Sony products to their relatives and friends. 'To ease the supply chain management we will be networking all our outlets with the Singapore office.' In order to popularize Sony World, the company has doubled its promotion spend to Rs 4 crore with commercials to be aired on television channels and ads inserted in newspapers. For the company as a whole, the ad-spend is around 5% of the turnover.

Petro-Retailing in India

Globally, petro-retailing has transformed from only petro-products to multi-products and services. India is also showing signs of aligning with global trends in petro-retailing with increasing revenue from non-fuel related products. This is largely the result of increasing competitive forces that are reducing margins and profitability.

The pressure on margins has mainly come from changing consumer needs and expectations and entry of new players in the marketplace. In the Indian market, company owned and company operated (COCO) outlets occupy the highest percentage; for example, it is 60% for BPCL, 50% for HPCL, and 28% for IOCL.

The key market segments in this sector are defined as metros, semi-urban, highways, and rural. COCO is predominant in metros. dealer owned and dealer operated (DODO) outlets are fast gaining share in all the above segments. The retail models in this sector change based on the balance of supplier–customer power. Petro-companies prefer the shift from COCO to DODO in order to reduce costs.

Recently, many petro-retailers are providing for supermarkets and convenience stores along with many other value-added services at the petro-stations. In future, franchising is likely to emerge as an important format in petro-retailing since it would help companies in eliminating the capital investment in land and also ensure quality standards. The example of Bharat petroleum is discussed below.

Bharat Petroleum: Making a Difference Through Innovative Retailing

Bharat Petroleum's efforts have all along been to build a superior understanding of customer needs and relentlessly work towards fulfilling these needs. Bharat Petroleum is consciously working towards providing added value to customers, both in fuel and non-fuel areas.

Recognizing that the basic need of the customer is pure quality and correct quantity of fuels, as one of the major initiatives in this direction, Bharat Petroleum has triggered a virtual movement at select retail outlets (petrol pumps) to guarantee pure quality and correct quantity to its customers. This 'Enhanced Fuel Proposition' movement, which is the sign of a new revolution, has been gaining nation-wide momentum after its initial launch at a few centres. Retail outlets enrolled in the movement display the 'Pure for Sure' signage very prominently at the outlet.

Bharat Petroleum's efforts began with remodelling and upgrading retail outlets to world-class standards back in 1996. Retail outlets have been equipped with state-of-the-art modern infrastructure, including the multi-product dispensers to pre-set price and quantity of fuel and electronic air gauges to facilitate precise inflation of tyres. Attractive canopies are suitably designed to provide shelter and adequate lighting of the forecourt at most retail outlets.

On the non-fuel front, Bharat Petroleum has introduced the errand mall concept successfully at select markets. Called the 'In & Out' , these malls offer the customer a broad range of facilities and brands to choose from. ATMs, cybercafes, courier services, laundry, photo studio, music, fast food, greeting cards, bill payments, movies/entertainment tickets, etc. have made Bharat Petroleum's retail outlets a happening place and indeed a rewarding experience for motorists.

To make life more convenient and rewarding for customers, Bharat Petroleum has introduced the 'Petro Card' for individual customers and the 'SmartFleet Card' for fleet owners. Using the Petro Card entitles the customer to 'PetroMiles' under the 'PetroBonus' rewards programme.

Bharat Petroleum has also pioneered the concept of convenience stores at select petrol pumps that operate under the name 'Bazaar'. These Bazaars provide a wide range of convenience items and fast foods to customers in a clean, air-conditioned, and friendly environment.

Retail Banking

After the reforms, banking services have changed from a seller's to a buyer's market. The face of the Indian consumer is changing. This is reflected in a change in the urban household income pattern. The direct fallout of such a change has been a change in the consumption patterns and hence the banking habits of Indians. Besides, bank's financial compulsions have forced them to focus more clearly on retail banking.

Big corporates are bypassing banks and raising money through the debt market and commercial papers, which are cheaper than bank credit. Therefore, banks are being forced to look at the mid-corporates. But, this is a risky strategy as the risk is concentrated and delinquency is higher. To compensate, most banks have devised strategies to go in for retail banking as a major thrust area.

The risk here is distributed and there is a huge market to be tapped. Some of the banks which have been aggressive in this area are HDFC Bank, ICICI Bank, State Bank of India (SBI), and Corporation Bank. With the retail banking sector expected to grow at a rate of 30%, players are focussing more and more on retail and are waking up to the potential of this sector of banking.

Citibank Expansion Plans

Citibank, the foreign banking major, has established its franchisees for all the customer segments and locations in India, with a target to grow its retail customer base to over 10 million. The bank has registered a growth in profits from country operations by 45–50% in the last few years and now plans to increase its presence through 300 centres and in 35 cities in two years. Citibank expects to get 6–7 branch licences annually and increase its presence in the top 35 cities over the next 24 months. Citibank is also tripling its network of CitiCard Banking centres, which combine ATMs and self-service phone and internet banking. The bank had been able to extend home loans to seven new cities, while personal loans would be available in 30 cities. Citibank maintains a leadership position in credit cards business along with lowest loss rates across the industry. Citigroup operates in India through 31 Citibank branches in 22 cities and another 170 branches and sales points of its NBFC arm CitiFinancial.

Source: 'Citibank to increase presence in India', APRIL 19, 2004 www.economictimes.indiatimes.com

However, Indian banks have shown little or no interest in innovative tailor-made products. They have often tried to copy process designs that have been tested, albeit successfully, in the West. In case of foreign banks, regulatory restrictions prevent them from expanding their branch network. So these banks often take the direct selling agent (DSA) route whereby low-end jobs like sourcing or transaction processing are outsourced to small regional players.

To be successful in retail banking, banks need to revamp their business model to (a) build a large-volume, highly scalable operation, (b) package and deliver products rapidly in a dynamic market, (c) leverage effectively on multiple delivery channels (branch, internet, ATMs, etc.) with a view to containing the cost of operations, and (d) build collaborative relationships with providers of related financial products and services and move towards converting the network of bank branches into 'financial supermarkets'.

In this context some of the recent trends in retail banking are discussed below.

Multi-Channel Distribution

Multi-channel distribution refers to delivery of services using a multiplicity of channels like Internet, ATMs, telephone, etc. Till now, delivery channels were viewed in terms of cost and technology. Delivery channels were devised focussing mainly on time and place advantage to the customers. The promise of lower transaction costs, increased sales productivity, and more convenient service has lured banks into setting up new delivery channels. The goal for the banks' senior management is to turn today's 'all things to all people' branch network into a highly differentiated system for delivery of multiple products.

Most of them are aggressively adopting information technology in branch operations and services to offer multiple delivery channels, which include 'anytime banking' through ATMs, 'anywhere banking' through networking of branches, and tele-banking. Further, many banks have begun offering Internet banking facilities. ATMs still remain the most successful delivery channel followed by telephone banking and Internet banking. With about 9000 off-site and on-site ATMs installed, banks are effectively reaching out to a large customer base at a substantially lower cost. A transaction costs Rs 35–45 if done with physical presence of the customer at a branch, Rs 7 through a cheque, and Rs 2 on the Internet.

These new creations have resulted in different channels of distribution of banking products and services. The transaction simplicity through these channels is drawing people to these banks, not just for banking products but for other ancillary products such as payment of utility bills and insurance premium.

In India there are around 4,500 ATMs and if they continue to grow at the current pace, there will be around 35,000 by the end of the year 2005. The cash movement through ATMs is between Rs 35,000 and Rs 45,000 crore each year. It is important for banks to manage interactions among channels as rigourously as they manage each channel in isolation.

Call Centres (Support Services)

Banks have picked up the nuances of getting closer to the ultimate customer and separated the sales and service functions. With call centres, services are being offered by stimulating customer interaction. The initiation of such call centre services was much appreciated but very few changes have been effected since then and they are losing their efficacy. The model being the same since its inception, data are increasingly built around it. With such a huge database, calls are being queued up, causing irritation to customers due to high waiting time.

Technology

Technology underlies the above two features. This is taken to be the cutting edge among banks and for real product differentiation the public and private players are becoming tech-savvy. With increasing emphasis on technology, banks try to take its advantage and venture into new areas of cross-selling their products through various channels.

The cost savings and the ease of effecting a transaction through technology are increasingly recognized and are compelling banks to carry the same to almost all the dimensions of banking. Incidentally, the more advanced the technology, the higher the cost savings generated with a much wider coverage, which results in quicker, cheaper, and reliable service. However, one should not get lost in the maze of new technologies as statistics do not support the proposition of technology aggression. (The number of people accessing Internet is 7 per 1000 people, using personal computers are 6 per 1000. Cellular subscribers are 6 per every 1000. Urban population is 27.9% of the total population and this is expected to grow to 32.2% by 2015).

This reminds one of better channel synchronization and integration but not proliferation. Banks should allow the earlier facilities to sink into the culture of the customers before any new facilities are launched. Also, the earlier facilities should be embedded with services so that customers not only appreciate new technology, but are also in a position to operate.

Rural Exposure

What is happening on the rural front? Why is there a reduction in the number of new bank branches? Is it because the rural areas suddenly lacked in potential or they lacked in infrastructure for banking in such areas. Looking at the statistics, the scenario seems to have changed drastically after the Narisimham Committee proposal in 1991. It has forced the philosophy of free markets and could successfully circumvent the intentions of the Government about building a stable financial system unique to the Indian economy.

The following matrix depicts the rural banking scenario on different parameters. Between March 1994 and March 2000, the number of bank offices in rural areas (population below 10,000) came down from 35,329 to 32,734, while the number of branches in semi-urban areas (population between 10,000 to 1,00,000) rose from 11,890 to 14,723. The figures have been going up in urban areas (population between 1 lakh and 10 lakh) and metros (population above 10 lakhs) from 8,745 to 10,447 and 5,839 to 8,557, respectively. However, around 98.5% of the rural borrowers still look to informal financing with credit limits below Rs 2 lakh. Today, agricultural lending by commercial banks has almost equalled the outstanding personal loans of rural consumers.

In the section that follows, the retailing thrust of the banking giant State Bank of India (SBI) is discussed.

SBI—Retailing Thrust

Consider some of the other developments at SBI. A few months back it appointed McKinsey & Co to take a close look at its century-old business processes and make necessary changes for faster decision-making; in early June it networked its 1,600 automated teller machines across the country. The bank has launched a facility for its customers to pay utility bills. It has also made an agreement with its strong trade unions on full-fledged computerization.

Clearly, the proverbial sleeping giant of the Indian financial sector is waking up. SBI has 9,000-odd branches. Its associate banks have another 5,000. SBI is omnipresent in India. A branch of the SBI family can be reached in 20 minutes by car from any human habitation in India. Even after the successful implementation of the voluntary retirement scheme in 2001, SBI has 2,08,000 employees on its payroll. The family staff strength is around 300,000. SBI's net interest margin (the difference between interest paid on liabilities and interest earned on assets) is 2.95% against nearly 3.5% that the world's best banks enjoy.

There are only two ways of reducing transaction costs: by increasing the volume of business and putting the right technology platform in place. The bank seems to be aggressively attacking both fronts. On the volume game, the bank is targeting retail lending in a big way. Its domestic loan portfolio grew by 15.2% last year. But under this umbrella, retail loans grew by 37.5%. Again, within the retail segment, housing loans jumped by 48%. At Rs 24,350 crore (Rs 243.50 billion), the bank's personal loan segment is the largest single asset portfolio (if one excludes the statutory priority sector advances).

SBI enjoys enormous advantages over the competition by virtue of its relatively lower cost of funds and wider reach. But it never encashed this advantage. The aggressive new private and foreign banks have already taken away corporate employees' accounts in the metros. Still, there are virgin territories like small and medium enterprises, traders, and the untapped service sector to set up ATMs to help students deposit their fees.

This is one of the ways in which the bank hopes to woo back younger customers who have steadily deserted the bank for lack of innovation and apathy to technology. The volume war can be won only if SBI is able to put the right technology platform in place. But this is easier said than done for a bank of its size. By March next year, it plans to have 3,000 ATMs.

Close to 4,000 of its branches are now fully computerized and this number will go up to 6,800 by September next year. But the real work on the technology front will start only when the bank interconnects these islands, across the country. The interconnectivity project is set to take off in August next year.

The plan is to connect at least 3,000 branches by 2005 and 6,800 in due course of time. The blueprint for connectivity—which will be done through satellite and underground cable networks by linking about 2,500 of the branches to a central server and hooking the rest to the branches—is the most ambitious project in the world. No global bank has seen such a large connectivity project. Sakura Bank in Japan had made a similar attempt, though the number of branches to be connected was much lower.

After the technology platform is ready, the SBI will have to address the most critical area—the quality of manpower. Out of 208,000 employees of the bank, roughly 50,000 are officers and another 55,000 sub-staff, while the rest are clerks and cashiers and so on. A substantial chunk of the officers are actually clerks-turned-officers and even messengers-turned-clerk-turned-officers. The transition from manual banking to technology banking will never be easy for them. Simultaneously, SBI needs to infuse fresh talent into its organization. This is only possible if it raises salary packages and allows lateral entry at various levels.

One of its subsidiaries, SBI Caps, has recently recruited 50 young finance professionals who in turn have been posted at SBI on deputation. SBI needs to recruit at least 5,000 such professionals right now while the existing unskilled employees can be redeployed selling insurance products, credit card, mutual funds schemes, home loans, and car loans over the counter at 14,000 branches. This way, the financial powerhouse can also leverage its group strength, which it has never done seriously.

Leisure Industry

Rising household incomes due to economic growth spurred consumer expenditure on leisure and personal goods in India. There are specialized retailers for each category of products in this sector. A few retail chains also emerged particularly in the retailing of movies, amusement parks, and music products. Another key feature of this sector is the popularity of franchising and retail chain arrangements.

Traditionally, consumers used to consider shopping activity to downtown centre or other city, to a great extent, as an outing for them and their family. Most of the shopping centres are well characterized with the presence of centres of entertainment such as cinema hall, zoo, circus, many other small units for entertaining kids such as swings, 'bi-scope', etc. For example, Hazratganj, a leading shopping centre of Lucknow, is marked with three cinema halls, a zoo, many eating joints, and mobile vendors with swings for kids.

All these set-ups are fast getting eroded or getting confined to traditional or backward areas of the cities, especially in the metros. Leading townships are experiencing a complete revolution on account of leisure industry with the emergence of cyber cafés, music outlets, theme parks, cineplexes, resorts, clubs, etc.

Leading Leisure Groups

Inox Leisure Ltd, plans to invest Rs 200 crore in setting up a series of multiplexes across the country. While two Inox multiplexes are already operational in Pune and Vadodara, Mumbai, Kolkata, Bangalore, Hyderabad, Chennai, and Gurgaon will follow. In all, 12 establish-ments of Inox multiplexes are in various stages of completion and are expected to be operational by 2004-end. The Inox multiplex in Pune already claims an average occupancy of 65%.

The Delhi-based Satyam Cineplexes is investing Rs 80–85 crore in its cineplex venter in Delhi alone. It has launched its first four-screen, 40,000 sq. ft multiplex in the Capital—the largest multiplex in north India. Satyam proposes to venture into Mumbai and Chandigarh, and add another two multiplexes in Delhi within 18 months.

The 3Cs (Competent Cine Court), floated by the Rs 550-crores Competent Group of Companies, includes a 325-seat auditorium, and a food court comprising six speciality restaurants under one roof in Delhi. The Competent group is planning to replicate its 3Cs model with a similar cineplex-cum-food court in Delhi, followed by Lucknow and Amritsar.

Leisure industry has been witnessing the advent of multiplexes as consolidated entertainment centres in urban India—in the form of movie theatres, restaurants, and shopping arcades—all under one roof. Industry estimates project that, on average, 1,000 new screens are expected in the next few years and that the cost of developing entertainment complexes of about 50,000 sq. ft works out to Rs 15–20 crore.

PVR was a pioneer in the field of cineplex. The company launched India's first multiplex—PVR Anupam 4. It was the first cinema company to introduce computerized ticketing through use of international box office software in its cinemas; the first cinema to accept credit cards in India against tickets; and the first to offer cinema tickets on Internet with online-payment-gateway for payment.

The company had a turnover of Rs 41 crores in 2001–02, which is expected to rise to about Rs 60 crores in 2002-03, and with the growth envisaged, the turnover in the next 3 years is expected to be over Rs 250 crores. The latest addition is the 7-screen multiplex in the city of Gurgaon in the NCR (national capital region), which is touted to be the fastest-growing suburb in India. PVR Priya, which was a 25-year-old cinema and is considered one of the best cineplexes in Delhi, was completely renovated and brought into the fold of PVR in January 2000. PVR Priya boasts of highest box office collections in the city of Delhi after PVR Saket. Priya has once again become an attractive destination with the presence of other outlets like Reebok, TGIF, Pizza Hut, McDonald's, Nirulas, Barista, Benetton, Modern Bazaar, Wills Lifestyle, etc.

PVR Limited (operating as PVR Cinemas) has successfully raised private equity from ICICI Venture as part of funding to support its Rs 100-crore expansion plan in March 2003. ICICI Venture has invested

Rs 38 crore in PVR Limited, the balance coming by way of Rs 40 crore debt funding, and the rest in accruals.

This represents the most significant investment in the Indian cinema industry in recent times and bears testimony to the immense faith ICICI has reposed in the business model, promoters, and management team of PVR. Further, PVR Cinemas will be unveiling India's largest multiplex in the city of Bangalore. The cinema is situated at Koramangala and is a part of the 3,50,000 sq. ft family entertainment complex being developed by the Prestige Group.

The company will also be setting up a five- and eight-screens multiplex in Juhu and Mulund in Mumbai, and a five-screens multiplex in Hyderabad. In the Capital and NCR, it plans to open a boutique cinema at Plaza and a two-screen cinema in Faridabad. The company has ambitious plans of setting up many more multiplexes across the country and has already signed sites in cities like Indore, two more sites of 8-screen multiplexes each in Goregoan and Phoenix Mills Mumbai, and two sites in Delhi, one being a three-screen in East Delhi Mall and another for a five-screen in Saket.

The case of PVR really demonstrated the changing face of retailing of movies in India, which is graduating from earlier conservative, non-AC, immovable chairs, with limited parking space to modern, well-equipped, and state-of-the-art facilities for consumers.

In a world of changing needs, accelerating pace, advanced technology, and shrinking distances the Internet is becoming integral for communication, entertainment, and information. With the proliferation of the Indian Internet user base there is a significant growth in the numbers of cyber cafes across India. Retailers are positioning their centres not only as centres of communication but also as recreational points by adding some other services such as tea, coffee, snacks, etc. Cyber Cafes are an important access route in India (See Table 3.9). The Web is indeed becoming a household name, specially amongst the upwardly mobile Indian—a fact that holds tremendous promise for e-commerce activities.

It is estimated that at the peak time there were more than 5,000 cafes in Mumbai. On an average, they have four to six computer terminals. More than 1.5 million people are dependent on cyber cafes in Mumbai. On an average there are 15,000 computers in the public

Table 3.9:   Point of access

Net accessed from	% on a Working Day	% on a Holiday
Home	25	47
Cyber Café	30	27
Work	29	07
Others	16	19

Source: www.emediaplan.com

domain. The industry is very fragmented, so it is difficult to make sound estimates.

Satyam Infoway, a subsidiary of Satyam Computer Services Limited, launched 'Sify i-way', the country's largest network of Internet browsing centres (cyber cafes). Today, the chain has over 1,780 cafes in more than 60 cities and these numbers are growing rapidly. The broadband connectivity at the i-ways has ensured that the browsing speeds are superior to those at the local cyber cafes. These centres are providing quality service at nominal price.

Vertical Marketing System in Indian Retailing

A vertical marketing system consists of all the levels of independently owned business entities along a channel of distribution/value chain. Products and services are normally distributed through one of these types of vertical marketing systems: independent, moderately integrated, and fully integrated.

In an independent vertical marketing system, there are three levels of independently owned forms: manufacturers or suppliers, wholesalers or distributors, and retailers. It is the most common vertical marketing system in India, across product categories, because of large-scale unorganized operations at the retail level. It is a form of vertical marketing system in which independent entities at different levels of the value chain operate contractually to obtain the economies of scale and market impacts that could not be obtained by unilateral action.

Such a system is often used if manufacturers or retailers are small, intensive distribution is within a group, customers are widely dispersed, unit sales are high, firm resources are low, channel members want to share costs and risks, and task specialization is desirable. Under this system, the identity of the individual business entity and its autonomy to operate remain intact. The three principal types of contractual systems are franchise system, retailer sponsored cooperative, and wholesaler sponsored cooperative. Independent vertical marketing systems are prominently in use by many stationery stores, gift shops, hardware stores, grocery stores, and chemist shops.

The partial integrated vertical marketing system is a form of vertical marketing system designed to control a line or classification of merchandise as opposed to an entire store's operation. The most common form of the system is when a supplier or producer and a retailer manage complete transactions and shopping, storing, and other channel functions in the absence of any independently owned intermediary (wholesaler/distributor). The vertically aligned companies, even though in a non-ownership position, may work together to reduce the total systems cost of such activities as advertising, transportation, and data processing.

This system is most compatible if the producers and retailers are large, selective, or exclusive distribution is sought, unit sales are moderate, company resources are high, the greater channel control is desired, and existing wholesalers are too expensive or unavailable. Such integrated systems are often used by furniture stores, restaurants, computer retailers, mail-order, and direct-selling firms. This system is also adopted by the retail chains and department stores widely.

A fully integrated vertical marketing system is a form of vertical marketing system in which all or most of the functions from production to distribution are at least partially owned and controlled by a single entity. Corporate systems generally operate in manufacturing units, warehouse facilities, and retail outlets.

In simple words, a single company performs all production and distribution functions without the aid of any other firms. In the past, this system was usually employed only by manufacturers, such as in Avon, Goodyear, and ModiCare. At Sherwin Williams, the paint manufacturer, its 2250 company-owned stores account for 57% of the firm's sales. Today, a good number of retailers are having fully integrated systems as many independent apparel stores have their own manufacturing units and retail outlets.

For example, Wills Lifestyle apparel stores are owned and managed by ITC group. A fully integrated vertical marketing system can be termed as a corporate vertical system where a firm has total control over its strategy, has direct contact with final consumers, has higher retail mark-ups without raising prices (by eliminating channel members), is self-sufficient and does not rely on others, has exclusivity over products and services offered, and keeps all profits within the company.

Raymond's exclusive chain of showrooms (Formal) maximize product visibility, enhance brand image, have exclusivity over brands, and control retail prices. However, there may be some difficulties with a fully integrated system, including heavy investment costs and a lack of expertise in both manufacturing and retailing and even distributing to other retail formats if the company is banking on a mix of retail formats.

In India, most of the firms use a dual vertical marketing system, whereby they use more than one type of channel arrangement. Thus, Titan has a fully integrated system for its World of Titan exclusive company-owned stores, Value Mart discount stores, Time Zone (partially integrated vertical system, franchise arrangement), and independent stores approached through well-established dealer networks as a part of independent vertical marketing system.

Challenges in Retail Business in India

The retail industry in India is in a phase of transition and hence is likely to face a whole new set of challenges. For one, generating large, free cash in flows for expansion is not easy. Retail margins are already wafer-thin, compared to those in other markets like the Middle East. The management of LifeStyle, which runs over 200 stores there, says its net profit margins after tax in India are 4–5% compared to about 10% in the Middle East.

There are enough recent examples of chains that tried ramping up too fast too soon. Barista, Domino's and Shoppers' Stop all fell into a cash trap. So deciding the right pace of expansion is quite critical.

Most retailers are trying to increase margins. For instance, RPG group has started sourcing its fresh produce directly from the farmers. About 350 farmers in Karnataka are doing contract farming for RPG.

Everybody going from this. The farmers get a guaranteed offtake and 46–48% of the price which the consumer pays (up from the earlier 40%). As for FoodWorld, now sourcing half of its total fresh produce directly from these farmers, it can sell it 15–20% cheaper than the market.

Also, in apparel, it is not easy to find suppliers who can match the capacities that a fast-expanding chain like Shoppers' Stop needs. The management feels that every time customers ask why they do not have a product or a size, they end up with egg on their face. That is why store labels come in and so do international labels, which offer gross margins of 40%.

Then, there's the other bugbear: too many department stores, too many exclusive outlets, all too close to each other. There is also a lack of sufficient differentiation. This could make it hard to build store loyalty. Besides, customers do not prefer to travel for more than 20 minutes to visit a store. So, building higher levels of traffic when catchments are shrinking is a tough challenge.

Retailers in India also face certain challenges in terms of the real estate, legal, workforce-related and certain other issues. They have an impact on the costs and efficiency of operations of the retail business.

Real Estate

Location is considered to be a key component of the retail strategy of any store. It also guides the direction and success of retailing industry in general. Indian retail units have to struggle on account of the shortage of real estate for new projects and even retail space in central business districts is out of reach for retailers due to price and high demand. Some of the new retail projects initiated by private houses are suffering on account of lack of cooperation from the local bodies in respect of security, hard infrastructure (power, roads), and public transportation facilities. In such conditions, retailers are ending up with incompatible retail property at high price. Poor state of retail estate in India can be attributed to the following factors.

- Stamp duties on transfer of property is very high and inconsistent throughout India. Stamp duties are taxes payable on every conceivable documented transaction. It is a form of revenue for a state, that is why it varies from state to state.

- The Urban Land Ceiling Act and Rent Control Acts were repealed just a few years back, but it has distorted property markets in urban centres, leading to exceptionally high property prices, particularly of retail property in central business districts.
- The presence of pro-tenancy laws make it difficult to remove a tenant or tenants. The problem is multiplied by tedious and long-drawn procedures to clear titles of ownership.
- Land use conversion is time consuming and complex, particularly in case of new shopping centers, which are coming up on out-of-town agricultural land.
- Huge costs are involved in terms of time and money in legal processes for property disputes.
- City urban planning projects smaller commercial plots and this, together with rigid building and uncertain zoning laws, hinders the procurement of retail property.
- Non-residents are not allowed to own property except if they are of Indian origin. Foreign-owned Indian companies can own property for business purposes.
- Foreign investment in real estate business is prohibited except for integrated township development, wherein 100% FDI is allowed with prior government approval.

Work Force

The traditional independent retailers that practice child labour have come under stringent provisions of the law forbidding child labour. Therefore, dependence on adult and experienced workforce will definitely increase their cost of operations. On the other hand, the organized retailers are facing multiple challenges on this front, such as limited supply of trained workforce and labour laws hindering operations in accordance with their business requirements. The labour laws that protect store workers are not flexible enough to support the organized formats of retailing.

Some local government bodies, after a series of requests, recently extended permission to shopping centres to operate up to 9.30 p.m. on all days including national holidays. For example, the New Delhi government provided such a permission to Ansal Plaza. But extended

Legal Hurdles Impair Organized Retail

H.S.Narula, chairman of Ebony Retail Holdings Ltd, says, 'The time-consuming process in title clearance, requirement of numerous lease deeds in the case of multiple ownership, and difficulties in conversion of normal land into commercial use are some of the basic difficulties encountered by the retail community.' To open a large store, an organization has to acquire as many as 10 to 15 clearances from several government agencies that are plagued, as always, with red tape, inefficiency, and corruption.

Source: www.indiareacts.com

working hours stand contrary to existing labour laws. One of them is that workforce can only be employed for a specified number of hours and, therefore, to operate stores for a longer interval of time the retailers have to depend on multiple-shift duties. Being subject to seasonal demand cycle (festive and end of year), these stores prefer to have part-time arrangement, which is not permissible under the existing laws. This increases the store's cost of operation.

It is a fact that the retailing industry is in its starting phase in our country. The benefits of organized retailing will only be felt once an equitable scale is achieved. This, to a large extent, depends on the store size, the walkthroughs, bills per customer per year, average bill size, and the revenue earned per sq. ft. But, besides resources and bottomline, a variety of other aspects need to be in place for tasting success. The need for qualified and trained manpower is of utmost importance.

What is VAT?

VAT is a multi-stage tax levied at each stage of the value addition chain, with a provision to allow input tax credit (ITC) on tax paid at an earlier stage, which can be appropriated against the VAT liability on subsequent sale. VAT is intended to tax every stage of sale where some value is added to raw materials, but taxpayers will receive credit for tax already paid on procurement stages. Thus, VAT will be without the problem of double taxation as prevalent in the present tax laws. Presently VAT is followed in over 160 countries. The proposed Indian model of VAT will be different from VAT as it exists in most parts of the world. In India, VAT will replace the existing state sales tax system. One of the many reasons underlying the shift to VAT is to do away with the distortions in our existing tax structure that carve up the country into a large number of small markets rather than one big common market. In the present sales tax structure, tax is not levied on all the stages of value addition or sales and distribution channel, which means the margins of distributors/dealers/retailers are not subject to sales tax at present. Thus, the present pricing structure needs to factor only the single-point levy component of sales tax and the margins of manufacturers and dealers/retailers, etc. are worked out accordingly. Under the VAT regime, due to multi-point levy on the price including value additions at each and every resale, the margins of either the re-seller or the manufacturer would be reduced unless the ultimate price is increased.

The VAT system ensures lesser paperwork for the retail community. There will be no local statutory forms under VAT. The existing sales tax system requires dealers to maintain an account of sales and purchases, and the VAT system also requires maintenance of only such accounts. Further, the Central Sales Tax Act would be amended and there would be a single-page return form common for local and central Acts. The return would be required to be filed quarterly, as is being done currently.

Importance of VAT

In India, particularly the trading community has accepted and adopted loopholes in the present tax system administered by the state or the centre. If VAT comes in, it will close avenues for traders and businessmen to evade paying taxes. They will also be compelled to keep proper records of their sales and purchases. Many sections hold the view that the trading community has been amongst the biggest offenders when it comes to evading taxes. Under the VAT system, no exemptions will be given and a tax will be levied at each stage of manufacture of a product. At each stage of value-addition, the tax levied on the inputs can be claimed back from the tax authorities.

At a macro level, VAT system, if enforced properly, forms part of the fiscal consolidation strategy for the country. It could, in fact, help address the fiscal deficit problem and the revenues estimated to be collected could actually mean lowering of the fiscal deficit burden for the government. The International Monetary Fund, in its semi-annual World Economic Outlook 2003 release, expressed its concern over India's large fiscal deficit— 10% of the GDP. Further, any globally accepted tax administrative system will only help India integrate better in the World Trade Organization regime.

Source: Salil Panchal and Morpheus Inc. 2003, 'What is VAT'? And why VAT' www.rediff.com, April 12.

In order to survive in today's tough retail climate, companies must continually innovate ways to create stronger, more direct links with their customers. At the same time, retailers must focus on the most demanding customers who want customization, value, and service.

New store designs must assault the consumer's sense of sight, sound, taste, touch, and smell—preferably all at the same time. In this environment merchandising and especially displays are more important than ever as being on top-of-the-mind will keep the brand growing.

According to a McKinsey report, if appropriate reforms are carried out, this sector is capable of creating eight million jobs in the next 10 years, and it can also provide job opportunities for people transitioning from agriculture. On the FDI (foreign direct investment) front, although a number of retail players have been advocating FDI in the retail sector, one needs to understand that just by allowing FDI in retail one should not expect the investments to pour into this sector in India. The FDI policy needs to be framed in such a way that it attracts foreign players to invest in India. FDI will bring in not only the much-needed capital to fuel growth but also sophisticated systems and know-how and will shorten the learning curve.

In fact, the challenges of urban and rural retailing will keep marketers busy for much of this millennium.

Summary

The retail industry in India is highly unorganized and predominantly consists of small, independent, owner-managed shops. Retailing is India's largest industry, accounting for 13% of the GDP (gross domestic product). There are around 5 million retail outlets in India. Food sales constitute a high proportion of total retail sales.

There are three aspects of 'boom in retail' in India. (a) The emergence of newer, specialized, and bigger retail formats in urban India with greater focus on 'experiential' aspects of shopping. This has been prompted by a more demanding consumer, higher disposable incomes, entry of foreign brands in the Indian market, and entry of Indian business houses in the retail sector. (b) Deeper and wider penetration of retail network in rural India prompted by greater recognition of the potential of rural markets especially in the FMCG and consumer durables sector. (c) Redesigning the retail mix by the traditional retailers as a sign of greater maturity of the sector and also the rub-off effect of the developments in the organized sector.

The traditional retail formats refer to retail formats that have long been part of the retail landscape of India. They include formats like kirana and independent stores that are typical of the unorganized retail sector and also the most administratively organized form of Indian retailing—co-operatives and government controlled retail institutions.

Formats that emerged or became popular in the 1990s are classified as modern retail formats. In terms of professional management and efficiency of integration with the value chain, these formats are classified as part of the organized retail sector in India. They generally include franchised outlets and company-owned stores. In rural India, the outlets within villages are generally part of the secondary business activity. Periodic markets in the form of shandis and haats are highly popular.

There are product-category-specific variations in the development of the retail sector in India.

Concept Review Questions

1. Give a brief sketch of evolution of retailing industry in India.
2. What are the different types of traditional retail formats in the Indian retail sector?
3. What is the relevance of traditional retail format such as kirana and small independent stores in the entire value chain in the backdrop of Indian industry?
4. Discuss broadly the drivers for the emergence of the organized retailing and new retail formats in Indian retail industry.
5. What are the challenges faced by the retailers from the organized and unorganized retail sectors?
6. Enlist the types of retail formats that exist in the following product categories.

Project Work Assignments

1. Visit two villages near your city and identify all the possible types of retail formats existing there and give the details regarding their retail mix.
2. Identify the drivers for the two small independent retailers in different product categories who have recently redesigned retail marketing mixes in their stores.
3. Interview the mobile vendors in different product categories in urban centres to understand their retail model and its importance to the marketers.
4. Evaluate the changes experienced by particular product industries (FMCG, vegetables, pharma, etc.) in the types of retail formats employed in India over the period.

Case Study

New Retailing—The Thane Experience

Introduction

Thane is a city in the western Maharashtra state. It lies on the Thana river in the north Konkan coastal lowland, on the mainland of the Deccan Plateau. Located about 30 km from the central business district of Mumbai (formerly known as Bombay), Thane has developed as one of Mumbai's suburbs. Industries in Thane manufacture a wide variety of products, including woolen fabrics, dye stuffs, drugs, pencils, glassware, cotton textiles, and handloomed fabrics. Major rail lines and a national highway link Thane with Mumbai and other cities and towns. The nearest airport is in Mumbai.

According to the 1991 Census, the population of the district was 52.49 lakhs. During 1981 to 1991, this population increased by 56.59%. This increase in population was the highest in the State for this period. The rural population of the district was 35.36% and the urban population of the district was 64.64%. Out of the total urban population, 73.13% lived in Thane, Kalyan, Ulhasnagar, Bhivandi, and Vasai Cities. The literacy rate in the district was 69.54%, which was higher than the State's rate of literacy at 64.9%. The male literacy rate of the district was 77.56% and the female literacy rate of the district was 60.28%, both higher than that of the State rate, 76.6% and 52.3% respectively. The district is ranked sixth in the state in literacy. The density of population in the district was 549 persons per sq. km, which was much higher than the state density rate of 257 persons per sq. km.

Occupational Structure

According to the 1991 Population Census, the total working population in the district was 1,961,704 persons, which was 37.37% of the total population of the district. Out of the total workforce, 30.75% were engaged in agriculture and allied activities, 1.19% in manufacturing, service, and cottage industries, and the remaining 30.69% in other activities. Women constituted 22.89% of the workforce in the district.

Infrastructural Facilities

Infrastructural facilities are the main source of industrial development in the district. Thane district is ranked third in the list of industrially developed districts in the state. More than 50% of the economic and social development of the district is on account of its progress in industrialization. The MIDC has developed 10 industrial estates in the district.

The high rate of development in the district is due to its proximity to Mumbai and its port, the transportation and subsidy facilities provided by the state government, and also the uninterrupted power supply by the atomic energy plant at Tarapur in the Palghar taluka of the district.

As per the 1991 Census, the total population of Thane district was 52.49 lakh. The male and female population were 27.93 lakh and 24.56 lakh respectively. Rural and urban population comprise of 18.56 lakh and 33.93 lakh respectively. Density of population was 549 persons per sq. km. The literacy rate for the district was 69.54%, which was higher than the state literacy rate of 64.9%. As per the 1990 Economic Census, the total working force of the district was 8.06 lakhs. Out of which 7.87 lakh were engaged in non-agricultural activities. Only 19,258 persons were working in agriculture. This shows that in Thane district industries provide the main activity and agriculture is the secondary activity.

Thane District at a Glance

S. No.	Particulars	Unit	Thane
1.	**Area**		
	(a) Geographical Area	Thousand Hect.	934
	(b) Forest Area	Thousand Hect.	346
	(c) Cultivable Area	Thousand Hect.	380
2.	**Population (1991)**		
	(a) Rural	In '000's	1856
	(b) Urban	In '000's	3393
	(c) Total	In '000's	5249
	(d) Schedule Caste	In '000's	272
	(e) Schedule Tribe	In '000's	951
	(f) Density	Sq. Km	549
3.	**Talukas (1998–99)**	Nos	13
4.	**Cities**	Nos	23
5.	**Villages**	Nos	1697
6.	**Rate of Literacy (1991)**		
	(a) Male	Percentage	77.56
	(b) Female	Percentage	60.28
	(c) Total	Percentage	69.54
7.	**Roads**		
	(a) National Highway	Km	226
	(b) State Highway	Km	1194
	(c) District Roads	Km	1850
	(d) Village Roads	Km	2566
8.	**Railway**	Km	346
9.	**No. of Post Offices**	Nos	405

contd

contd

S. No.	Particulars	Unit	Thane
10.	No. of Telegraph Offices	Nos	64
11.	No. of Telephone Exchanges	Nos	564221
12.	Bank Branches (Scheduled)	Nos	360
13.	Bank Branches (Co-op.)	Nos	155
14.	Existing Indl. Estates	Nos	10
15.	Large Scale Units	Nos	1548
16.	Small Scale Units (PMT) (Upto March 2000)	Nos	10813
17.	Growth Centres	Nos	02

Note:- N.A. = Not Available

Source:-

1. District Statistical Abstract (1998–99)

2. Lead Bank (Thane District) Annual Credit Plan (1999–2000)

New Thane

After India's independence, Thane grew slowly and became an industrial town only in the 1960s and 70s. There was also a corresponding growth in trade, transport, and construction activities, which picked up tremendously in the 80s. The city was always in the news for the development activities

What happened over the next few years was a radical transformation of the city, long perceived by many to be the untidy, backward suburb of Mumbai, to a clean and green entity. Clogged gutters were cleared and covered with footpaths. Roads were broadened and concretized. Trees were planted and encroachments removed. Today, Thane is fast growing as a residential city as many builders have chosen it for their upcoming projects.

Fed up with the dirt, traffic, pollution, and general chaos of Mumbai, they were looking for a place to stay with decent amenities, and Thane fitted the bill perfectly. The all round development of the city attracted builders like Hiranandani, Kalpataru, the Tatas, Godrej, Soham, and Seth. Most builders started offering amenities that attracted the working middle class and upper middle class to Thane.

As a result, the city started sprouting pockets that were visibly upmarket. It is estimated that in the past five years, there has been an addition of approximately 20,000 middle to upper middle class housing units in Thane.

Also, there are 20–25 housing projects currently at various stages of completion at different areas in Thane.

Another inherent advantage that Thane had was that it was well linked to almost any part of Mumbai because of the excellent Eastern Express highway. Thane has emerged as one of the major shopping destinations. It is experiencing a large-scale development of shopping malls and multiplex theatres.

The city is experiencing a growth in population and also the inhabitants' spending power has increased manifold. Thane lacked the places where people could spend their money. Local population still had to drive down to Mumbai to shop at good retail centres.

Recently, leading brands across product categories established their outlets in Thane, such as McDonald's, Pantaloons, Planet Fashion, Crocodile, Lee, Dominoes, Lee Cooper, Arrow, and Reebok. The advent of national retail chains, across product categories, are driving the changing face of the retail formats of Thane city.

We will now discuss the establishment of a few new stores and restructuring of the existing retail formats by leading independent retail stores on lines of organized retailing.

Maria Supermarket

'Maria supermarket' has registered itself as the most attractive shopping destination among the local population. Mr Thomas started it on 13 April 2002. The store is located at a central location it a prime area, with parking facility. The idea to start such a unique concept came up when he visited a supermarket in Germany. The store is positioned to extend services in accordance with the shoppers' needs and also provide them with a luxurious atmosphere.

The market has all the consumer goods like grains, stationery, ready-made snacks, bottled food items, and many more items including vegetables. Maria supermarket is the first ultramodern supermarket of Thane, with a wide range of products. It has all the Indian and imported products like chocolates and biscuits.

A variety of garden foods like wafers, cheese balls, maggie, chocolates, butter, cheese, soft drinks, fresh fruits, etc. are kept. The pricing is below maximum retail price with a lot of discount schemes. Free home delivery is offered to people who place an order above Rs 1,000.

The management is further planning to introduce fast food corners, just like a mini restaurant where people can come and enjoy themselves. In future, they are also planning to open a banquet hall above the super-market. The banquet hall will be centrally air-conditioned with a capacity of about 200 people.

Milan Saree Centre

Milan sarees and dress shop was started by Mr Nagjibhai Shah 25 years ago at the Ambedkar Chowk. It was a low-profile retail venture. Today, Milan is a prominent landmark in the station area. Pravin, son of Mr Nagjibhai, changed the layout of the small shop about 10 years ago. Milan was turned into an exclusive sarees shop and fast-emerged as a speciality retail.

Milan's working hours are from 9 a.m. to 9 p.m. and it has an off day on Monday. They accept credit cards and also have the home delivery scheme. Accessibility is still a problem, but as one enters, one is amazed by the length and depth of the variety of goods at display. Being positioned as an exclusive saree shop, Milan carries the comprehensive range of sarees from highly premium to regular every-day wears.

The store holds a wide range of sarees such as silks, Kanjivaram, Paithani, wash and wear, cottons, etc. They have also been trendsetters for certain exclusive sarees like Vamini, Patola, Ghadwal, etc. Exhaustive ranges, plush interiors, and warm service with personal attention have made Milan a favourite amongst Thaneites for a long time. They also provide dry-cleaning of silk sarees to prevent any damage of the material and thus ensure a long life for the exquisite garment. Milan's is success initiated the opening of several other shops of its kind in this city.

Celebration

Celebration, an exclusive showroom of gifts and other related accessories, was started on 22 September 1998; since then it has become a meeting point for most of the young Thaneites. Mr Sanjay Shah, a 26-year-old entrepreneur, started this wonderful gift showroom. The shop has every item in the gifts section. It has greeting cards of all the reputed companies like Archies, Hallmark, Expression, etc. for all occasions.

They have gifts like showpieces, soft toys, lamps, crystals, sceneries, crockery, games, perfumes, watches, brass items, key chains, chocolates, cosmetics, antique novelties, audio cassettes and CDs, and special items of Feng Shui. Other than these it also has many decorative items for home such as flower vases, wall hangings, etc. It also sells leather items like handbags, wallets, and purses. Sales people of the store are very experienced and help customers in their purchase decisions.

Mr Shah has no worries about any competition in this field since they have quality and unique products. This showroom has all the products according to the trend and they always try to keep something new with them, which helps the store to satisfy the customer's needs and make him feel unique and different from others. Mr Shah says that he wants his customers to be praised for the gifts they give to the others, which will definitely make them happy.

Mriganaini

Mr Sharma started the Mriganaini boutique, a one-stop ladies wear shop, in 2001. Mriganaini houses an extensive range of ladies wear including ready-to-wear, dress materials, nighties, etc. All these are available in the latest forms, patterns, styles, and colours. Mriganaini provides stitching facilities to its customers interested in made-to-order apparel as per their specific preferences. This work is done from the latest fashion and embroidery books.

They also offer machine and hand embroidered clothes. Dress materials bought from here can be stitched at their in-house tailoring and embroidery facility. Costume, jewellery, and hair accessories are also on hand to complement the attire. The store also carries cosmetics (Indian and imported), nail enamels, lipsticks and perfumes of all quality companies. Shoppers are provided with personal attention and proper product guidance. Prompt service and the informal atmosphere make shopping at Mriganaini an experience in itself. One can get ones dress stitched on the same day, at a very little extra cost, which is of excellent quality.

Millenium Mall

Mr Manish R. Mehta started the Millenium Mall on 21 April 2002, in Hari Niwas, keeping in mind the needs of the people around. Millenium Mall is distinctive for its exquisite and ethnic interiors, extensive range of products, and is totally unique from the other competitors. The showroom is very spacious and has two floors.

The ground floor mainly consists of products like eatables, soaps, cool drinks, etc., while the first floor consists of cosmetic and leather products. The Mall has neatly defined sections so that people find it easy to locate desired products or brands. Mr and Mrs Manish Mehta manage the working of the mall with the assistance of nearly 10 staff members.

They also have well stocked sections devoted to eatables, grains and pulses, cosmetics, perfumes and deodorants, stationeries, leather purses and wallets, chocolates, shampoo, tissue papers, home made products like biscuits, cool drinks, pickles, etc. Other than these there are also products such as imported biscuits and chocolates.

They also offer free home delivery service. Mr Manish always makes it a point to introduce all the new products in the market. Prices of merchandise are comparatively less in comparison to other shops in Thane. In future, management is planning to introduce some more products like gift items and toys. They also have schemes like a glass free on goods purchased worth Rs 100.

Wood Plaza

The people behind Wood Plaza are the brothers Jayant and Dhanji. Right from the start, Wood Plaza created a niche in the market with exquisitely designed contemporary furniture for home and office. One of the largest furniture showrooms in the city, Wood Plaza is covering an expanse of 6500 sq. ft. The store offers bedroom set, study table, dining set, office furniture in wood and metal, etc. Wood Plaza has a provision for incorporating the suggestions of the customers' in designing the furniture.

---

1. Evaluate the external environment of the city Thane in respect of retail industry.

2. Identify the factors which have re-defined the retail development in Thane City.

3. What are the common marketing mix features of recently opened stores across product categories and how are they in compatibility with the served market segments?

4. On what dimensions you perceive that local retailers have re-designed their retail mix to meet competition from organized retail chains?

References

1. *Milestones*, an ORG-MARG publication.
2. www.anderson.ucla.edu

3. Dutt, D. 2004, 'An Outlook for Retailing in India, Vision 2005' (Form a presentation by KSA Technopak at MDI Gurgaon in January and February).

4. Kotler, Philip 2000, *Marketing Management*, 10th Ed., Prentice Hall of India Pvt Ltd, New Delhi.

5. Knight Frank India Research (Mumbai) 2002, 'Searching for space', *Praxis Business Line*, January.

6. Chandrasekhar, Priya 2001, 'Retailing in India: Trends and opportunities', *Business Line: Catalyst*, February 15.

7. Devasahayam, Madona 1998, 'Big Deal', *Praxis Quarterly Journal on Management*, August, Vol. 2, No. 2.

8. Majumdar, S. 2002, 'FDI in retailing: India as a supermarket', *Business Line*, Tuesday, Sep 17.

9. Kannan, S. 2001, 'Huge potential awaits retailing', *Business Line*, Thursday, September 13.

10. Jagannathan, V. 2001, 'Vivek's–a store more reputed than the brands it sells', *Business Line*, February 5.

11. Bhushan, R. 2002, 'The show begins here', *Business Line*, Thursday, December 26.

12. www.ipan.com

13. www.indiainfoline.com

14. Aroor, S. and Singh, S. 2004, 'Market Dynamics: Cigarette Retailer As The New King', *The Financial Express*, Net Edition, May 4.

15. *Delhi Economic Indicators*, 2000–2001.

16. *SPICE* 2003, Vol. 1 No. 7.

17. Gupta, R., 'Pharma retailing gains momentum in India', www.galtglobalreview.com www.morepen.com

18. www.retailyatra.com

19. www.bata.com

20. www.prweb.com

21. www.retailbiz.com

22. Chandran, R. 2003, 'Kodak India rejigs retail strategy', *Business Line*, Friday, October 3.

23. www.titan.com

24. www.emediaplan.com

25. www.indiareacts.com

26. Salil Panchal and Morpheus Inc. 2003, 'What is VAT? And why VAT', www.rediff.com, April 12.

27. www.morepen.com

28. www.theindiatravelguide.com

29. www.smallindustryindia.com

30. www.thaneweb.com

31. www.economictimes.indiatimes.com 2004, Citibank to increase presence in India, April 19.

32. www.bharatpetroleum.com

33. Jagannathan, V. 2003, 'Retail reality tales', www.domain-b.com , March 11.

34. Jagannathan, V. 2000, 'Sony India to restructure, expand distribution" www.domain-b.com, March 25.

35. *Business Line*, 'Sony set to expand retail presence', Friday, March 7.

36. *Business Line* 2004, 'Sony India aims to achieve Rs 1,100-cr turnover', Sunday, May 2.

30. www.thaneweb.com

31. www.economictimes.indiatimes.com 2004, 'Citibank to increase presence in India', April 19.

32. www.bharatpetroleum.com

33. Jagannathan, V. 2003, 'Retail reality tales', www.domain-b.com, 11 March.

34. Jagannathan, V. 2000, 'Sony India to restructure, expand distribution', www.domain-b.com, 25 March.

35. *Business Line* 2003, 'Sony set to expand retail presence', Friday, Mar 07.

36. *Business Line* 2004, 'Sony India aims to achieve Rs 1,100-cr turnover', Sunday, May 02.

4 RETAIL CUSTOMER

Learning Objectives

- To demonstrate the importance of knowledge of consumer behaviour for the success of retailing strategies

- To discuss the factors that influence consumer behaviour

- To outline the stages of consumer decision-making and its impact on retail strategies

- To discuss the various levels of consumer decision-making

- To outline the type of consumer decision-making process

- To discuss the factors which affect the nature of consumer decision-making

- To discuss the influence of situational variables on shopping behaviour

Introduction

Consumer buying behaviour refers to the buying behaviour of the ultimate consumer. Consumer behaviour is the study of how consumers make decisions to use their respective resources such as time, money, and effort for buying, using, and disposing goods and services. The behaviour of humans as consumers is complex. Marketers' understanding of the drivers of consumers' buying behaviour will help them to serve their customers effectively and efficiently and attract new customers. In the retailing context marketers are required to understand customers' shopping behaviour, which includes decision variables regarding, among other things, brand selection, shopping timing, and choice of retail format and store.

Consumers' shopping behaviour can be understood by analysing the factors that affect behaviour. These factors could be demographic, psychological, environmental, or related to the lifestyle of the customer. It is equally important for the retailer to identify the various stages in the consumer decision-making process and the major influences at each stage. This would make possible an effective retail marketing strategy.

Saravana Stores Versus Shoppers' Stop

The retailing success of Saravana stores in comparison with Shoppers' Stop is considered one of the distinctive retail successes in modern times. Shoppers' Stop has outlets in six cities and a total floor space of over 2,25,000 sq. ft. Its outlets are air-conditioned, well maintained, and have inviting store displays. Their advertising campaign is considered to be one of the best in the industry and the staff is well dressed and articulate. They have good loyalty programmes, and their service is reasonably quick and efficient. They have spacious, pleasant cafes with a variety of different snacks and beverages from leading brands.

On the other hand, Saravana stores have only one outlet in Chennai, consisting of three divisions. It has a lower middle-class clientele and a total space of around 25,000 sq. ft. The exterior of the outlet has not even been white washed for many years. There is a huge crowd round the clock. Goods are piled on top of one another (sofas, plastic chairs), or displayed all along the wall (garments, textiles). Signboards within the stores have a slightly peremptory note: for example, 'Trials not allowed' or 'Pay money at the counter only'. The staff is dressed in untidy uniforms, and courtesy towards customers is not expected from them. Billing and delivery can take almost 20 to 25 minutes. The eatery at the top of the garment section has no tables and chairs. It sells a total of about eight items—coffee, tea, and cold drinks included.

Shoppers' Stop has a total turnover of Rs 160 crore. Saravana Stores has a total turnover in excess of Rs 600 crore—earned from 20,000 customers per day.

Saravana in Chennai basically targets daily wage earners or govt employees. Many of them have roots in villages or small towns from where they have migrated to Chennai. For them the environment in and around Shoppers' Stop does not seem very inviting. It does not map with their existing perception of the market they usually shop in. The tremendous depth and range of merchandise at Saravana Stores suit all pockets and all tastes. Saravana Stores is a very close prototype of melas and shanties where lower middle-class or migrants from rural area used to shop. The indifferent service atmosphere suits the customer very well. It also means that no one will interfere with him while he inspects the displayed goods at his leisure. The eating joint has no infrastructure; customers at Saravana sit with the rest of the family on *duries* on the floor—just like at home. The anchor no doubt is price, which even attracts people from the middle class. A 20 to 30% saving is attractive by any standards.

The retail marketing mix of Saravana Stores and Shoppers' Stop is focused on different sections of the market. However, both indicate the primary goal required for successful retailing—the satisfaction of target consumers. In order to achieve this task retailers are required to have a better understanding of consumer benefits, their perception and attitudes, and how they influence the development of successful retail marketing strategies.

Consumer Behaviour

Consumer behaviour is the understanding of how consumers make decisions to use their resources such as time, money, and effort for buying, using and disposing goods and services.

In the retail context, marketers would specifically be more interested to know about consumers' shopping behaviour, which involves an understanding of decision variables regarding when, where, and what to shop (shopping timing, choice of retail format and store, etc.). Such decision variables are the factors to be considered by the retailer while taking decisions regarding the above criteria.

For instance, in case of pickle, marketers will be interested in finding out the type of pickle consumers intend to buy (single vegetable/fruit or mixed, spicy or not, oily or dry, veg or non-veg); the brand preference (national, private, generic); the reason for using (to add taste, for food preparation, to eat along with snacks); the place of purchase (super bazaar, convenience store, vendors, home made); and frequency of purchase (weekly, biweekly, monthly). On the basis of various alternatives to consumer needs, marketers evolve the best possible marketing mix to attract the target market.

Therefore, shoppers' response to retail marketing mix has a great impact on the firms' success in the long run. As described by Cohen (1991), in consumer buying behaviour analysis the marketing mix inputs (or the four Ps of price, place, promotion, and product) are adapted and focused upon the consumer. Individual consumers consider each element of retail marketing mix in relation to their culture, attitude, previous learning, and personal perception.

Many a time consumers' patronize more than one retail outlet for the same product. The consumer is influenced by both the intrinsic and extrinsic factors. Intrinsically, his needs, motives, perceptions, and attitudes tend to influence what he purchases and where he purchases. However, extrinsic influences such as family, social class, the culture, and economic factors will also affect his behaviour. With the understanding of these elements retailers or marketers would be well placed to devise their retail marketing mix in accordance with their respective target segments.

To understand what and from where do the shoppers shop, it is important to analyse the reasons that prompt shopping behaviour.

Why do People Shop?

It has been suggested that consumer shopping activities are influenced by personal and social motives. Consumers' motives are important and positively related to their pleasure and satisfaction while shopping in terms of retail choices.

Personal Motives

- Role playing—shopping activities are learned behaviours and are expected or accepted as part of one's position or role, such as mother or housewife.
- Diversion—shopping can offer a diversion from the routine of daily life and is a form of recreation.
- Self-gratification—shopping may be motivated not by the expected utility of consuming, but the utility of their buying process itself. Thus, emotional states or moods may explain why or when someone goes shopping.

- Learning about new trends—shopping provides consumers with information about trends and movements and product symbols reflecting attitudes and lifestyle.
- Physical activity—it involves considerable amount of exercise.
- Sensory stimulation—shopping can provide sensory benefits such as looking at and handling merchandise, listening to the sounds (e.g., noise, music) and smelling scents.

Social Motives

- Social experience outside home—shopping can provide opportunities for seeking new acquaintances, encounters with friends, or just 'people watching'.

Shopping as a social experience

- Communication with other similar interests—it provides opportunity for interactions with other customers or sales people.

- Peer group attraction—certain stores provide a meeting place where members of peer group may gather.
- Status and authority—shopping may provide an opportunity to attain status and power by being waited.
- Pleasure Bargaining—shopping may offer the enjoyment of gaining a lower price through bargaining comparison shopping or visiting special sales.

Having understood why do people shop it is important to analyse the factors that affect the consumers' decision making process regarding what, when, and from where to shop.

Factors Affecting Consumer Decision-making

A consumer's purchase decision tends to be affected by the following four factors:

1. Demographic
2. Psychological
3. Environmental
4. LifeStyle

DEMOGRAPHIC FACTORS	PSYCHOLOGICAL FACTORS
Gender	Motives
Age	Perception
Occupation	Learning
Education	Attitude
Family size	Personality
Income	
ENVIRONMENTAL FACTORS	**LIFESTYLE**
Physical Environment	Activities and interests
Social Environment—culture,	Nature of occupation
sub-culture, social class	Availability of leisure

Fig. 4.1   Factors affecting the consumer decision-making process

Demographic Factors

Demographic factors are unique to a particular person. They are objective, quantifiable, and easily identifiable population data such as sex, income, age, marital status, etc. It also involves identification of who is responsible for the decision-making or buying and who is the ultimate consumer. Even Saravana Stores and Shoppers' Stop, as discussed earlier, have focussed themselves on respective segments based on demographic factors such as income, age, family size, gender, occupation, education, nature and number of vehicles owned, etc. This aspect is covered in detail in the next chapter (Chapter 5).

Psychological Factors

Psychological factors refer to the intrinsic or inner aspects of the individual. An understanding of consumers' psychology guides the marketers' segmentation strategy. For example, consumers respond differently towards the same retail marketing mix due to their respective motives, personality, perception, learning, level of involvement, and attitude.

Indian Working Women and Dressing

Study findings indicate maximum usage of ethnic salwar-kameez (34.3%) by Indian working women at the workplace. This dress is generally tailor-stitched. But the branded offerings are not far behind. formal shirts with trousers (28%) are the second most widely used workwear; then comes Indo-Western kurta (10%) followed by formal shirt with jeans (6.9%), t-shirt with jeans (6.2%), and finally the traditional sari (5%).

Income-group-wise analyses of findings show salwar-kameez being most widely used across all major sections of working women. Usage of rest of the dress combinations also conform to the overall scores except for the Sari that takes dominance over Indo-Western Kurta among the Rs 10,001–15,000 monthly income category of respondents. The overall income-level impact on usage of different dress combinations is however quite insignificant. The study then assesses the age factor impact.

Amongst the youngest group of working women, aged 21–25 years, formal shirt with trousers emerges as the most widely used dress combination with 208 weighted points. The jinx is finally broken. The age factor clearly appears to have a distinct impact on fashion lifestyles of working women.

Source: G.D. Singh & Tulika Sen 2003, 'What Women Want', www.imagesfashion.com, May.

Motives

A motive is an internal energizing force that orients a person's activities towards satisfying a need or achieving a goal. Actions are affected by a set of motives, not just one. If marketers can identify the relevant motives then they can develop a better retail marketing mix.

Maslow's hierarchy of needs is one of the best frameworks used in this respect. It consists of the following five needs:

1. Physiological
2. Safety
3. Social
4. Esteem
5. Self-actualization

Retailers are required to determine the need level of the consumers to have a sound understanding of what motivates consumer preference towards a particular retail format or store.

An instance of satisfaction of social needs is presented when, in rural India, consumers regularly visit periodic markets not only to purchase goods or services but also to enjoy an outing with family and friends and to participate in local festivals and other activities.

In Chennai, it is considered a status symbol if women shop for silk sarees from Kanchipuram (a town famous for *Silk work*) avoiding a long list of leading silk saree stores in Chennai even though they offer better selection and at times lower prices. This occurs due to customers' desire to satisfy their esteem needs.

In Indian metros, consumers are replacing milk vendor or milk store (traditional-independent) with Mother Dairy products, which they have to collect from their retail outlets at comparatively higher price, because of the emerging concerns about the quality of milk. This is largely an outcome of the consumers' safety needs.

Perception

Perception is the process of selecting, organizing, and interpreting information inputs to produce meaning. Recognition, selection, organization, and interpretation of particular stimuli is a highly individual process subject to individual needs, values, and expectations. A stimulus is any unit of input to any of the senses. The same stimulus may be perceived differently by different set of customers based on their unique personal and situational context. Hence, the indifferent service offered at the Saravana stores may be perceived positively by a certain set of customers due to the opportunity it provides them to look up the products at leisure. However, another set of customers may perceive it negatively, assuming it to be a reflection of the lack of interest of the store management in the needs of the customers.

Shoppers tend to seek out favourable information on products which are compatible with their needs, values, and expectation. They prefer to avoid unpleasant information. For instance, they prefer to pay more attention to advertising message that is in consonance with their value system and prefer to ignore a message that is in contradiction with their cultural values. This is done primarily to avoid the creation of cognitive dissonance. During Diwali most of the retail stores announce discounts and various other promotional schemes. Customers become highly uncomfortable if they do not get a good bargain at a particular market known for offering deals. Examples of some such markets are Palika Bazaar and Sarojni Nagar in Delhi, Linking Road in Mumbai, and Palton Bazaar in Dehradun.

Indian consumers initially perceived McDonald's outlets as costly and were not well aware of its product offerings. To overcome this perception among prospective consumers, McDonald's management introduced a seven-rupee softy ice cream to attract the shoppers. Retailers or marketers design the retail marketing mix to ensure patronization of the retail store or format by the target segment and/or to attract new customers.

Learning

Learning is the process through which a relatively permanent change in behaviour results from the consequences of past behaviour. There are various theories regarding the processes involved in causing such a permanent change in behaviour. Some of these theories are classical conditioning, operant conditioning, vicarious learning, and mere exposure.

Classical conditioning results from the association of two stimuli in the environment that work together to create an unconditioned response. The two stimuli in the environment are referred to as conditioned and unconditioned stimuli. The repeated association of conditioned and unconditioned stimuli may, in due course, lead the conditioned stimulus to produce the unconditioned response. Initially, self-service (conditioned stimulus) was resisted by Indian consumers particularly in smaller townships, but with repeated occurrence of benefits such as low price and fast service (unconditioned stimulus) people became more frequent visitors at eating joints (unconditioned response) with the policy of self-service.

Operant conditioning occurs when a person learns to associate its behaviour with the consequences or results of the behaviour. There are positive and negative types of operant conditioning. When a dog shakes its master's hand it gets a biscuit. If you work hard and study, you will get good grades. These are both positive parts of classical conditioning. Similarly, when a customer shops from an up-market store and receives appreciation from his peer group, the behaviour is likely to be reinforced, provided he values the opinion of his peer group. Operant conditioning is different from classical conditioning because the former is a learned behaviour and not a conditioned response.

Vicarious learning is defined as change in behaviour due to experience of others which could be a model, celebrity, or a member of the family or peer group. This is popularly used in case of advertising and publicity by ensuring the association and endorsement of specific retail outlets by celebrities, examples being Priety Zinta with PVR cinema in Delhi, Jackie Shroff with IBP of Indian oil, and Shilpa Shetty with P.P. Jewellers.

Mere exposure effect, in case of retailing, may occur in case of development of an emotional preference for previously unfamiliar retail outlets because of frequent exposure to that store from personal or impersonal sources. For example, Shoppers' Stop is briefly mentioned as a radio show's sponsor each week on various FM channels.

According to all these theories, a permanent change in behaviour is caused by information and experience. Therefore, to change consumers' shopping behaviour retailers need to provide them with new or modified information about aspects such as the nature of the store, product profile, shopping environment, etc. For example, most of the middle- and upper middle-class women prefer to shop for jewellery from their trusted local shop patronized by their family for generations. Tanishq, by its positioning strategy and increased awareness among women about the quality, authenticity, returns and adjustments (crucial in gold purchase), and variety in their store, attracted a good crowd in metros.

Time Zone, the first organized retail network for watches, was introduced by Titan. Before the advent of Time Zone, watches were sold through the unorganized retail set up. Time Zone has made sustainable efforts to educate people about the availability of wide variety, multiple brands, and authentic products at their franchised outlets.

Attitude

Attitude is consumers' predisposition to respond favourably or unfavourably to an element of retail mix or the retail mix in its entirety. It comprises knowledge and positive and negative feelings about an object or activity. The object could be tangible or intangible, living or non-living. An individual learns attitudes through experience and interaction with others.

Consumers' attitude towards a store and its products greatly influences the success or failure of a retail outlet's marketing strategy. Consumers' personality and lifestyle influences attitude and attitude change. Consumers screen information that conflicts with their attitudes. There is a difference between attitude and intention, and ability to buy. For example, in India consumers have a positive attitude towards pizza. But its limited availability and high price restrict people from enjoying it frequently. Amul, the leading milk cooperative in India, found it an economically viable gap and introduced pizza at Rs 20. The offering was supplemented with extensive retail penetration.

Fishbein's *multi-attribute model* proposes that attitude towards an object is based on the summed set of beliefs about the object's attributes weighed by the evaluation of these attributes.

$$A_b = \sum_{i=1}^{(n)} b_i e_i$$

Where A_b equals the brand, b_i equals the belief that performing behaviour B leads to consequence $_i$, e_i equals evaluation for consequence $_i$, and n equals the number of salient consequences.

As a rule, marketers want their consumers to perceive their brand as: (1) possessing positively evaluated attributes (i.e., when e_i is positive, b_i is positive), and (2) not possessing negatively evaluated attributes. Both approaches are commonly employed in advertising for favourable attitudes. For example, Big Bazaar is most strongly advertised as a department store with low prices, and consumers are also told that the variety and quality of offerings were given due consideration.

Fishbein's model is extremely helpful to retailers in, besides other things, devising their advertising strategy because it provides the reasons for consumer preferences, identifies unfulfilled needs, and provides suggestions for new products.

Theory of reasoned action says that a person's behaviour is determined by his attitude towards the outcome of that behaviour and by the opinions of the person's social environment. Ajzen and Fishbein proposed that a person's behaviour is determined by his intention to perform the behaviour and that this intention is, in turn, a function of his attitude toward the behaviour and his subjective norm. This is more clearly explained through the following example:

Attitude: 'I think I must shop for furniture from the outlets selling branded imported furniture.'

Subjective Norm: 'I bet my friends would be impressed by the branded furniture labels.'

Intention: 'I want to shop for furniture at the outlets selling branded imported furniture.'

Behaviour: 'I am going to the outlets selling branded imported furniture to make the purchase.'

Indian Consumers

J. Walter Thompson's (JWT) study identifies eight core, underlying truths about Indian consumers that significantly influence their attitudes and behaviour. The eight most significant norms moulding attitudes and behaviour, according to the study, are:

1. Entrepreneurial
2. Speed and lightness in all aspects of life
3. Enjoyment
4. Religion and spirituality for physical and mental health
5. The family as a brand
6. The 'nowness' of life
7. Manipulation and powerplay for family harmony and
8. Getting more out of less

There is also an increasing penchant for 'lightness' among families, be it in terms of being more casual than traditional, seeking lightness in the kitchen through convenience foods and ready-to-use masalas, or looking for lightness in terms of convenience— purchase through supermarkets and home delivery systems. More than the need for a product or service, it was found that Indian consumers today lay greater emphasis on the experience and enjoyment that come with it. Enjoying the simple pleasures of life, working to earn that enjoyment, and enjoying the small dreams that come true with the help of brands, new products and services are the top priorities among Indians.

The study also revealed that although people are willing to spend money, their expectations of return from every rupee spent are much more than what they were earlier. Consumers today are seeking better deals and better bargains, and are looking to get more than they bargained for, not just from a product but also from the entire experience.

Source: www.aandm.com 2003, 26 September.

Personality

Personality refers to all the internal traits and behaviours that make a person unique. Uniqueness is derived from heredity and personal experience. In the retail context, consumers' consistent and enduring patterns of shopping behaviour represents a set of consumer characteristics which is used to target segments. Examples of such consumer characteristics are:

- Workaholism
- Compulsiveness
- Self-confidence
- Friendliness
- Adaptability
- Ambitiousness
- Dogmatism
- Authoritarianism
- Introversion
- Extroversion
- Aggressiveness
- Competitiveness.

Traits affect the way people behave. Marketers try to match the store image to the perceived image of their customers. For example, Indian consumers give due importance to retailers' image to a great extent while selecting the store. This holds true even for branded goods.

This is because Indians value relationship and try to attribute importance to relationship even in formal interactions. For example, most households in semi-urban areas depend on a particular set of retailers for their needs, right from grocery items to durable purchases.

Environmental Factors

Environmental factors cover all the physical and social characteristics of a consumer's external world, including physical objects (goods and outlets), spatial relationships (location of the shopping centre and merchandise in stores), and the social factors (opinion leaders, the person's family, co-customers, reference groups, social class, and culture). The environmental factors influence consumers' wants, learning, motives, etc., which in turn influence affective and cognitive responses and, among other things, the shopping behaviour of the individual.

The environment can be analysed at two levels—macro and micro. The macro environment includes large-scale, general environmental factors such as economic conditions with easy credit facility for durable goods and vehicles. Today, consumers in India are buying goods on easy installments. There has been an increase in the population owning vehicles. This has made it viable to locate shopping centres out of city, such as Metropolitan, DLF City centre, Sahara Mall on Mehrauli-Gurgaon Highway, and Fun Republic in Mumbai and Ahmedabad. The repeal of Land Ceiling Act and liberalization and poor performance by stock markets has led to shift of funds towards trading and organized retail business. This has helped the Indian consumers to experience new kinds of formats with excellent and varied facilities.

These environmental drivers have a general influence on behaviour, for instance, when the state of the economy influences collective purchases of household items, automobiles and investment options.

The microenvironment refers to the more tangible physical and social aspects of an individual's immediate surroundings. Examples of physical environment include aspects such as nature of the market structure (planned or unplanned), temperature controlled environment, visual merchandise and display, roads and other infrastructural components. For instance, the congested lanes in the shopping centre and the transportation facility available are important aspects of the physical environment. Such factors have an immediate influence on consumers' buying and shopping behaviour. For example, consumers with cars normally avoid congested lanes (Chandni Chowk and Karol Bagh in Delhi). In north India people prefer shopping at noon time in winters and in the evening in summers.

The social environment includes all social interactions among people. Consumers interact with friends, relatives, and salespersons regarding prospective or past purchases and sometimes observe others (family members or friends) buying and using the products. Consumers learn from both types of social interactions—participation and observation.

Leisure

Qwiky's, Barista, and Café Coffee Day are providing a comfortable place to teenagers, young professionals, families, and working couples in cities to relax and unwind while sipping coffee. A similar function is performed by existing institutions like *adda* in Calcutta, *chaupal* in rural area, and roadside coffee or tea shops. The popularity of such coffee bars is also due to the fact that it provides an alternative to people uncomfortable with roadside *chaiwallas* (tea shops) or the formal setting of five-star coffee shops and restaurants. It is also popular among youth from middle-class families as they find it easier to get pocket money for visiting a coffee bar than for a beer bar.

Café Coffee Day store in Chennai

It is acknowledged that culture, subculture, and social class along with face-to-face social interaction among small groups of people such as families and reference groups are components of social environment, which influence values, beliefs, attitudes, emotions, and behaviour of individual consumers. Social interactions with fellow workers, family, and friends have significant influence on consumers' perception and therefore on behaviour.

For example, people learn acceptable and appropriate behaviour and acquire many of their values, beliefs, and attitudes through direct social interaction with family and reference groups. The influence of family is specially relevant in case of brand and store preference and loyalty.

In the Indian context, many studies claim that women play a major role in the need identification phase. Children have a major say in brand selection while the head of the family largely decides on financial matter and selection of the store.

In urban areas, Indian women are the key decision-makers for garments and food items for the entire family. In rural India, the male members of the family perform most of the city-based shopping. The female members participate in decision-making related to product and brand selection.

Hence, retailers need to provide the appropriate product profile and service environment as per the preference of shoppers and key decision-makers.

Men—The Major Decision-makers

In India consumption-related family decision-making in all areas—ranging from which cars to buy to what cloth manufacturers to patronize—is dictated by men when it comes to the most upscale market segment in India.

Who decides?

	Self	Spouse	Joint	Family	Elders	Children
Buying a house	25%	5.8%	20.8%	30.1%	14%	0.4%
Child's marriage	7.7%	5.9%	21.8%	18.7%	11.5%	4%
Own marriage	20.4%	2.5%	6.2%	22.4%	29.7%	0.9%
Child's education	15.1%	6.6%	34%	12.5%	5.6%	4.6%

Taking a loan	31.4%	5%	24.3%	18.1%	9.2%	0.6%
Fixing monthly budget	24.2%	10.3%	33.3%	18.5%	11.2%	0.6%
Buying entertainment durables, such as TVs	21.4%	8.2%	33.4%	26.7%	7.4%	1.6%
Buying durables such as washing machines	19.3%	10.7%	33.3%	26.2%	8.2%	1%
Deciding on holiday destinations	20.6%	6.1%	28.4%	31.8%	4.5%	5.6%

The male member of the family seems to play a major role in deciding the monthly budget or whether to take a loan, but when it comes to deciding whom he should marry, it is still the older people in the family who play a key role.

Interestingly, people in the six metros surveyed seemed to show entirely different tastes in watching television. The average number of channels watched were five and an average of 100 minutes of television is watched a day, with 30 minutes devoted to news.

News and sports are the most preferred programme genres, followed by general entertainment. However, 29% of the respondents in Delhi preferred news channels, while only 14% of those surveyed in Bangalore preferred news. Bangaloreans prefer watching sports with a high rate of 34%.

Source: 'Horizon 2003', a study by BBC World, conducted by market research agency NFO-MBL across six top Indian metros (www.rediff.com, May 02, 2003)

For example, McDonald's in Delhi attempted to attract entire family at their outlets by targeting kids. This they did by arranging concessional trip to their outlets directly from nearby schools. Since kids play a major role in the decision of the family regarding entertainment and food-related outings, this strategy proved to be a great success.

Retailer as Referral

In urban townships' consumers tend to have a closer association with most retailers of all the possible products they consume. Therefore, brands have limited influence on their decision-making irrespective of the product category. This is because of the characteristic of the Indian society, where most of the retailers are considered strong reference groups. This ensures trust in the transactions between two entities. Some of the retailers tend to be associated for generations with a particular family. Therefore, personal relations is an important characteristic of retail marketing in India.

Social Class

Social class is referred to as the classification of members of a society into a hierarchy of distinct status classes, so that members of each class have relatively similar status and members of all other classes either have more or less status. Social class of an individual is then determined by variables such as education attained, occupation, wealth, and ownership of assets. Market research has established a link between social class and consumer attitudes concerning shopping behaviour. For example, most of the upmarket clubs or resorts, such as Sutlej Club in Ludhiana or Mahindra and Mahindra resorts, before granting membership to their facility, expect prospective members to fulfil certain conditions. Most of these conditions are meant to determine if their social status matches that of their existing members.

Street vendors preparing local snacks

Middle class and higher sections of society prefer to shop for grocery items once a month from a particular shop. They, therefore, look for packaged products to maintain their quality during the storage period.

They usually prefer stores with wide variety and those which possess most of their requirements. On the other hand, lower sections of the society usually shop for such items on a daily basis. They are also not very particular about the shop from which the purchase is to be made.

In urban centres, the re-emergence of the periodic markets is attributed to the immigration of rural sections of society and the labour class. They perceive urban retail set-ups as costly and find themselves in an alien environment while shopping in retail outlets selling the same product range which they buy from periodic markets.

Social status of an individual plays an important role even in determining the frequency of purchase. Most of the middle-class people prefer to buy fresh vegetables and fruits from the vegetable market in morning time on a daily basis even though it may be available at a higher price. On the other hand, lower classes prefer to buy vegetables and fruits in the evening at lower prices. Similarly, the lower class prefers to buy snacks prepared by street vendors rather than going to a snack bar.

Customer Classification and Preferences

Upper Elite Class

Those who have inherited wealth. This class is less than 0.1% and have preference for antiques, jewellery, homes, vacations, higher education, fitness, beauty treatment, traveling, etc.

Lower Upper Class

These are the people who have earned wealth due to their exceptional ability and who are neo-rich. They prefer to spend on cars, big home, good school education for their children, etc.

Upper Middle Class

These are career-oriented professionals and corporate managers who prefer to spend on education, books, cloths, furniture, home appliances, etc.

Middle Class

These are average-pay white-collar class of society who prefer to spend on popular and trendy products, personal vehicles, branded goods, good homes, college education for children, entertainment, etc.

Working Class

These are again average-pay blue-collar class of society who prefer to spend on unbranded goods, cheap food and liquor, etc.

Lower Class

This class of people would prefer to spend on necessities from local market and local unbranded goods.
Source: www.retailyatra.com

Culture and Sub-culture

Culture refers to the set of values, ideas, and attitudes that are accepted by a homogeneous group of people and transmitted to the next generation. Culture also influences the nature of retail advertising. Culture determines what people wear or eat, and where and how do they reside and travel. India is known for its cultural diversification specifically based on language, symbols, religion, rituals, and customs.

In India, religion is not the only basis for segmentation as is the case of the Arab world. Hindus and Muslims do not form a homogeneous group to enable consistent marketing mix. There are three significant influences on the local culture, Westernization, emergent national cultural styles, and popular culture. The pre-independence Western way of living was patronized by the feudal class and high-ranking civil servants. Later it seeped into the upper and middle classes. During the freedom struggle and revival of political nationalism a new nationalistic style emerged. Some aspects of it persist even today—swadeshi, cultural nationalism, boycotting of foreign goods, spartan living, etc. Lastly, popular culture, largely an output of the mass media, is a unifying factor. The impact of films (Hindi, English, and regional), TV, radio, and newspaper has reshaped images and attitude of the masses.

Consumers in semi-urban India are not very attracted towards credit offered by banks or companies for acquiring the consumer durable. For the purchase of consumer durable like CTV, microwave, CD system, two wheelers, etc., many consumers prefer to obtain credit facility from a known person in their social circle, such as a relative, friend, or well-known retailer. Hence, some retailers in the semi-urban areas started the system of a pool party where a person is required to pay a monthly instalment for the product acquired at a monthly party organized by the retailer. This party comprises most people from the social group of the concerned members. Here retailers obtain the assured payment of their instalment because the social group creates sufficient pressure on the individual concerned and his family for such payments. A defaulter is not given due respect in Indian society. This system involves no paper work for retailers and consumers in comparison with bank loans.

Modernization has taken roots in India. However there is still a lot of conformity to the traditional value system. This is more true in case of preferences related to food. McDonald's and Pizza Hut revised their offerings as per the preferences of the Indian consumers. While pork is against the religious tenants of Muslims, many Hindus avoid non-vegetarian food. Hence, appropriate changes were made by multinational food chains in their cooking medium, processes, and cuisine.

Inox multiplex in Baroda attracting elite crowds

Similarly, in western India, most of the restaurants advertise the availability of *Jain Thalli* (a unit of offering) to attract the Jain community, which constitutes a major chunk of the population and is also a profitable consumer segment. Fast-food eating joints such as Pizza World are offering 'Jain Pizza', which includes baby corn, capsicum, and paneer.

Eating joints in India while offering non-vegetarian dishes have to provide information on the manner particular animal was chopped, because individuals following certain religions are prohibited to consume meat chopped in certain ways.

Indian Food Habits

American fast food giants are fast finding out that if they want to tap into the huge Indian market, the key is to 'Indianize' the American food. Just a little twist to the recipe here and a little touch to a side dish there and they are on their way to acceptance. KFC added rice pulao and a little bit of spicy tomato gravy along with its chicken 'Hot and Crispy'.

Vegetarian offerings are derived from the Indian market. The impressive vegetarian selection offers 'Spicy Paneer' pizza with chunks of seasoned paneer, capsicum, and hot red paprika. Incidentally, the vegetarian selection is as wide as the non-vegetarian menu. And on the non-vegetarian menu, chicken takes the predominant position, with a splattering of pork and lamb.

Indianization of McDonald's

Values represent the core level of culture. Values are defined as mental images that affect attitudes of individuals, which in turn influences their respective behaviour in a specific situation or

Khadder

Khadder is a popular store in Bangalore that specialises in dresses for women. It is owned by a Kolkata-based company. It gives a fine example of trying to incorporate the cultural values of Indian women in their garments. They noticed a very unique taste characteristic of Indian women in the extra-large (XL) garment size-group. Unlike their Western counterparts, Indian women in this size-category do not want the contours of their body to get highlighted and are consciously looking for dresses that would conceal them. The solution? Khaddar decided that all of their offerings in this range would have straight-cuts. It worked.

environment. Values are considered as guidelines for behaviour. In contrast, customs and rituals are considered the usual and acceptable ways of behaving. This has an impact on the effectiveness of many retail strategies. For instance, many middle-aged women irrespective of age and religion feel uncomfortable when asked for their names while placing the order or when intervened by a male salesperson while surfing in the retail store.

Similarly, while practising direct selling, Eureka Forbes salespersons take ample initiative to meet a male member of the family when they try to approach their prospective consumers as some Indian women are uncomfortable interacting with unknown individuals.

Lifestyle

Lifestyle refers to an individual's mode of living as identified by his or her activities, interests, and opinions. Lifestyle variables have been measured by identifying a consumer's day-to-day activities and interests. Lifestyle is considered to be highly correlated with consumer's values and personality.

An individual's lifestyle is influenced by, among other things, the social group he belongs to and his occupation. For example, double-income-no-kids (DINKS) families in metros shop very regularly at the super malls because of the limited time at their disposal, and they also look for entertainment while shopping on weekends. At the same time, they are higher spenders than, for e.g., single-income families.

A study by imagesfashion.com highlights that Indian working women have to balance their wardrobe collection based on requirements of

Table 4.1   Dress working women prefer for different occasions

Occasions	Western wear	Ethnic wear	Total
In Office	66.7	31.3	100
At Home	77.8	20.2	100
To Party	69.7	30.3	100
While Shopping	85.9	11.1	100
During Festivals	3.1	93.9	100
Family Occassions	17.2	80.8	100
While Travelling	89.9	10.1	100

Source: G.D. Singh & Tulika Sen 2003, 'What Women Want', www.imagesfashion.com, May.

different occasions related to professional workplace or family gathering.

To cater to their specific requirements, different brands have emerged. In ethnic wear, there are just a handful of quality brands like Nalli, Kumarans, Bombay Selection, and Meena Bazaar. They have positioned themselves to meet the need for ethnic wear at family or festive occasions. On the other hand, W (women store) and Khadder are trying to infuse global styling and design functionality with salwar kameez. It has created a women's career wear brand that is retailed in a smart, modern format that appeals to the lifestyle of their target segment.

Stages of the Consumer Decision Process

When people buy things, they engage in a decision-making process. Decision is defined as the selection of an option from two or more alternatives. By understanding their needs and concerns as they progress through the decision-making cycle, marketers can build better and more successful retail marketing mix. The consumer decision-making process is the process consumers go through when they decide to make a purchase. In the retail context, a marketer is concerned about shopping decisions like what, when and where, how, and from whom to purchase, and the frequency of purchase.

Let us take the example of a consumer interested in buying a new audio system. The first step in this process is of course to recognize the need for a new system. Though one may have an idea of which system one would like to possess, one probably would also want to look for some information in order to narrow down to a few alternatives.

One may go online to investigate manufacturers, resellers, and independent consumer organizations, ask friends and colleagues for advice, and may even visit a few stores.

Consumers compare options and finally decide to purchase what seems to be the best alternative based on a set of criteria like design, features, price, after-sales service, etc. The consumer is also concerned with the decision as to the place of purchase; the various options could be an independent retailer with multiple brands, a specialist retailer in audio products (Bose), a company-owned retail outlet (Digital Samsung, LG Home), or a net shop (Indiatimes.com and Rediff.com etc.). Prospective consumers have to decide about the market they would prefer to visit, with whom should they go for the purchase, and the mode of payment for the purchase. Retailers have to address these issues while communicating their retail mix to the target segment. The five common stages (as shown in Fig. 4.2) of the buying or shopping process have been identified as need identification, information search, evaluation of alternatives, purchase decision, and post-purchase behaviour. Post-purchase behaviour may take the form of cognitive dissonance.

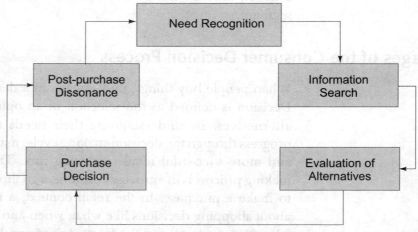

Fig. 4.2   Stages of the decision-making process

Need Recognition

Need recognition occurs when a consumer realizes a significant gap between his or her present state and some desired level of state. Social and physiological stimuli arouse the consumer about his specific need. The consumer also has to acknowledge that a certain set of goods can satisfy felt desire or shortage. This leads to the need for a particular good or set of goods, which in turn translates into desire for a particular product or service. To satisfy this desire the consumer looks for possible sources to shop for the specific offering. Therefore, decision regarding particular retail formats, private or national brands, and retail stores follows the awareness of the need for a good or service.

Needs are classified as simple or complex. Simple need recognition is referred to as a problem that occurs frequently or periodically and can be solved through known ways. For instance, housewives depend on nearby retail shops (Kirana) for their immediate grocery requirements. Complex need recognition is referred to as a problem, which is faced infrequently by the consumer and evolves over time. For example, purchase of colour television and other consumer durables.

Marketing communication is devised to make the consumer aware of the problem and then highlight the solution provided by them. For example, these days both national food chains and eating joints in the unorganized sector are providing home delivery facility to their customers.

Marketers attempt to create two kinds of demand, primary and secondary. In case of primary demand, marketers encourage consumers to use a particular good, service, or retail set-up regardless of the brand they choose. Such needs are often encouraged in the early stages of a product's life cycle. An example is the advent of shopping mall as a new place of shopping in India. Secondary demand, which refers to the situation where consumers are stimulated to prefer a specific retail outlet to others, can occur only if primary demand already exists. For example, Pizza Hut, Pizza Corner, Dominos, and Pizza Express are marketing themselves as the best places to have pizza. In this case, retailers or marketers make a sustainable effort to convince their target segment that their specific need can be satisfied best by their offerings.

Information Search

Once the individual has acknowledged a need or problem, he or she looks for information to resolve the need in consideration. Information search is the process where the prospective buyers examine their environment for appropriate information to make a sound decision.

Shoppers, at times, enjoy looking for information and keeping a record of new developments. This they may do just for pleasure or to collect information for future use. For instance, opening of a new garment store, or a promotional scheme by a leading store. This is termed as ongoing search. On the other hand, a section of consumers looks for specific information for satisfaction of very specific needs. This stage is termed as prepurchase search.

An individual looking for information tries to evolve various possible alternatives that are likely to solve his or her problem. The individual enlists various alternatives that may address the problem encountered in the previous step of decision process. For example, a college going student listed all possible eating joints along with offerings available, price, timings, etc. in order to take his friends out for a treat next week on his birthday.

An individual usually derives or acquires information from two sources, namely internal and external. A person's past experience accompanied with shopping exposure might provide him with substantial guidelines to make the current decision with the help of his or her internal memory. At the same time, a consumer with no or limited prior experience has to indulge in extensive information search from the external environment in order to evolve the list of all possible alternatives and list of criteria to solve the present problem. An

Information Search

Mahindra Krishi Vihar was set up not only to sell inputs such as seeds, pesticides, and fertilizers but also to rent out agricultural equipment assisting in commercial farming in rural areas. The runaway success of MKV centres is due to the guidance it gives to the farmers at all possible stages of farming regarding what to purchase, in what quantity, and how to use it effectively. Before the emergence of such facilities, farmers used to avoid the usage of new technology or end up using the wrong ones. Therefore, agricultural firms tapped their target segment at the information stage of decision-making.

individual depends on various external sources to collect information regarding a new purchase. This information could relate to the kind of model, technology, or retailer that will be most able to solve the problem. External sources are grouped as sponsored sources such as mass media, retail sales people, and consultants. Non-sponsored sources are primarily family, friends, and public relations.

Consumers invest time in information search in proportion to the perceived risk associated with the particular purchase, and importance of purchase. For example, if grocery items are purchased from a well-known retailer, the risk associated with the transaction is minimized. In case of purchase of unbranded garments from a tourist place, proper information search is required from friends or family members who are acquainted with the place.

Evaluation of Alternatives

After information search for the required product, the consumer is expected to take a final decision on one of the choices. The search also helps the consumer to acquire knowledge about the criterion to be used to evaluate the various alternatives evolved at the information stage. For example, in Gurgaon some management students enlist the following restaurants for entertaining friends: Haldi Ram, Nirula's, McDonald's, Punjabi Hut, Pizza Hut, Pizza Corner, etc.

Purchase Importance

In India, most of the durable goods and expensive goods such as jewellery and garments (for marriages) are purchased from the well-known retail outlets, as there are very limited number of brands in these product categories. Therefore, people are well assured on account of performance of the product they are buying from a particular retailer.

Even for the durable products, people in small towns give due importance to the say of the retailers as they buy most of their durables from one shop.

Things are now changing in metros, where people who migrated from other towns have to depend on friends, mass media, etc. to ward off the associated risk with every prospective purchase.

Strand Bookstall

Strand bookstall in Mumbai, instead of opening a new store, added a cafeteria to attract readers. It later added toys, stationery, and magazines and extended a

40% discount scheme on all books. This helped the store to meet the emerging competition from Crossword book chain. Today, Strand enjoys a mailing list of 78,000 loyal customers and remains committed to providing them with a 'reader-friendly environment'.

The alternatives, which are actively considered during the consumer decision-making process, constitute the individual's evoked set. The evoked set comprised retail outlets already in the memory and distinctly added from the retail environment (mass media, friend, etc.) with respect to a particular product purchase. The evoked or consideration set consists of a subset of retail outlets which the consumer is exposed to, remembers, and is compatible with.

It is essential for all retailers or marketers to ensure that their brand finds place in the consideration set of the target segment. The various factors responsible for a brand's failure to find a place in the consideration set are lack of familiarity (selective exposure to advertising media), not appropriate in terms of quality, attribute, positioning, etc., impassive offering (may lack special benefit), prove to be overlooked (may be due to lack of clear positioning), and incompetence (with respect to the particular need).

Retailers require an effective marketing programme, especially in terms of their communication strategy in order to inform and position the store as per the needs of the target segment. At the same time, retailers need to revise its offerings and attributes as per the changing preferences of their target segment.

Evoked Set

With the advent of Sagar Ratna (popular south Indian food joint) and McDonald's, and renovation and repositioning by Bikaner (Indian fast food joint) in Rajouri (New Delhi), Wimpy's the oldest eating joint in the region lost its position from the consideration set of the consumers. This is attributed to the following factors: Sagar Ratna offered competent south Indian food, McDonald's was unbeatable on fast foods such as burgers, and Bikaner provided a varied cuisine from south Indian to north Indian snacks (tikki, pao bhaji, sweets, etc.) along with fast foods in a new upmarket ambience.

On the other hand, Wimpy's has not positioned itself strongly against the competition. It had no unique offering or attractive physical environment to attract the customer.

Consideration Set

McDonald's has introduced not only varied vegetarian offerings in India but also introduced some potato-based preparations for their burgers to find place in the consideration set of their customers, many of whom prefer to eat out frequently but largely order vegetarian food and opt for potatoes with their breads.

It is possible that after revising the list in the evoked set an individual is left with two or more convincing and attractive alternatives, say, in case of selection of an eating joint. He or she then requires a criterion to evaluate the existing options and their relative salience.

W Store

W store, which deals in professional women's dressing range, highlighted their offering ethnic salwar kameez with a Western flavour. This ensured that their store found a place among women who were interested in Western dresses but were also looking for the Indian touch. Prior to this they used to depend on tailors to stitch such dresses for them.

The criterion to evaluate the particular retail mix element is very subjective. It usually evolves during the information search stage. For instance, a set of management students in Gurgaon mentioned the following decision variables to evaluate a particular set of eating joint.

Variables used for retail format or store:
- Adjustments
- Advertising
- Air-conditioning
- Carryout to car
- Check cashing
- Cleanliness
- Coupon redemption
- Credit
- Customer complaints
- Delivery
- Display
- Door man or automatic door
- Drinking fountain

- Gift certificates/guarantees
- Operation hours
- Interior decorative service
- Layaways
- Layout and appearance
- Lighting
- Location convenience
- Merchandise
- Message service
- Music
- Play room or areas
- Rest rooms and lounges
- Special orders
- Unit pricing
- Bill payment

After criterion formulation, a person rates all the alternatives on the important attributes from the most favourable to the least favourable.

After evaluating or rating various alternatives on important attributes, an individual can shortlist the best possible retail outlet (an eating joint for taking his friends out for a treat).

Purchase Decision

After evaluating various alternatives, an individual is in a position to focus on the preferred product category, good, retail outlet, or brand. This is followed by a purchase decision by the consumer. Final choice from multiple alternatives leads to the purchase stage or decision. This

Rural Consumer

In rural India, consumers prefer village shops for making purchases for their urgent needs. They prefer to purchase in small quantities, preferably on credit. This helps them avoid the transportation cost associated with periodic markets. It is also difficult to avail credit facility in such markets.

They consider periodic markets as fit for quantity purchases on cash, which in turn provides an opportunity to bargain and obtain a greater variety to make better choices.

involves an exchange of cash or credit note for the ownership or usage of offering. It is the purchase stage which generates revenue for the retailers and marketers in the value chain.

In the retailing context, the purchase stage plays the most important role in consumer decision-making with regard to place of shopping. In the Indian context, one can obtain many products from multiple retail outlets or formats. For example, Paras Pharmaceutical's OTC brands—Krack, Moov, Borosoft, Itchguard, and D'Cold etc.—are available not only from the chemist shops but also at grocery stores and outlets selling cosmetics etc. In the same way, Harvest Gold is offering its confectionery products not only from confectionery shops but also through its own mobile vendor network.

In case of garments and durables purchase, customers have to decide not only about the nature of store (independent, multiple branded, exclusive, company owned, etc.) but also the place of shopping—the traditional market or out of town shopping mall or neighbourhood market.

With all these retail options available with consumers, retailers have to make a serious effort to understand the decision variables, which influence consumer choices and the role played by situational variables among various consumer segments.

The extensive research on store image provides an insight into some of the aspects considered by shoppers while selecting or evaluating the viability of patronizing any particular store. These factors are as follows.

- *Physical characteristics* such as store size, location, appearance, and convenience of store layout.
- *Social interaction* such as between sales people and customers, co-customer behaviour.
- *Assurance* such as warranty, adjustment or returns, complaint handling, and alteration if required.
- *Policy* such as operating hours, payment options, loyalty programmes, parking, and so forth.
- *Merchandise* such as product category, brand spread, length and breadth, quality, style, price level, and SKU's.

Big Bazaar

Big Bazaar was the second hypermarket that opened in Hyderabad. It provides not only a comprehensive product range but also merchandise at low margins, along with a wide range of facilities considered better than that of high street markets or equivalent to department stores.

Big Bazaar even highlighted in their communication their key USP 'Isse sasta aur achha kahin nahi' (nowhere else it is cheaper or better).

The particular good or service is likely to be purchased by the prospective customer in case he is satisfied by the respective retail set-up on parameters discussed above.

Post-purchase Dissonance

After purchasing a particular good or service or visiting an outlet, consumers evaluate its performance against their expected level of satisfaction on account of important attributes. For example, in case of a multiplex theatre a consumer is expected to examine the experience on account of sound effect, air conditioning efficiency, other consumer behaviour, etc.

This kind of evaluation is likely to lead to three possible outcomes.

(a) Actual performance meets expectations, leading to a neutral response. Hence, the individual may like to evaluate it further.

(b) Performance exceeds expected levels, resulting in satisfaction. This may lead to repeated purchase and positive word-of-mouth publicity.

(c) Performance may fall short of the expectations, resulting in dissatisfaction. This may lead to discontinuation of purchase of the particular good or from the retail outlet.

In case of post purchase evaluation, the basic concern of the consumer is to reassure himself that he or she has opted for the best available option from amongst various alternatives. This helps to minimize the post-purchase cognitive dissonance.

In order to ensure long-term customer relationship, most retailers or marketers operate programmes to minimize the post-purchase dissonance through various innovative schemes. For example, customers are requested to fill up feedback forms after their purchases. This serves many purposes. This helps to make the customer feel important, take his suggestions to make improvements, extend invitations to special events, and offer special packages for celebration of birthdays and anniversaries.

Types of Consumer Decision-making

Consumers cannot devote extensive time to accessing and inferring information for purchasing all the products they want to use. As they become used to solving some of their problems, purchases for the purpose become routinized. Similarly, for many of their needs they depend on others to conduct the purchase.

For some goods they are required to go through an extensive search for information. Essentially natural, consumers' decision-making varies with the level of involvement and familiarity with product usage and its purchase.

On the basis of the nature of decision-making one can classify the purchases into three categories:

- *Routine buy* refers to those transactions where the buyer reorders from a regular store without any modifications and on a routine basis. For example, normally Indian households buy their grocery stock from a particular retailer. For instance, newspapers, bread, milk, and high frequency items are purchased from regular shops in their vicinity.
- *Modified rebuy* refers to those transactions where buyers want to modify product specifications, prices terms, or suppliers. It usually involves more time and information. For example, if a particular product is not available at the regular shop, the customer may seek advice from the retailer concerned. In case he does not give credence to the retailer's advice, he may start gathering information from other sources to shortlist retailers for the subsequent purchase.
- *New product purchase* refers to those transactions where a buyer purchases a product or considers visiting a particular retail outlet for the first time and therefore requires an extensive amount of information to be obtained and evaluated. This is largely true for infrequent purchases. For instance, if one desires to purchase a home theatre system, one may look for the extensive information

to compare various offers. One would also be required to evaluate various dealers and retail outlets on issues related to after-sales service and delivery of the product.

On the basis of effort required for purchase or the level of involvement, one can categorize the nature of consumer decision-making into four levels, namely extensive problem solving, limited problem solving, routinized response behaviour, and impulse buying. It is strongly correlated to the kind of product that is purchased.

The four levels of consumer decision making are:

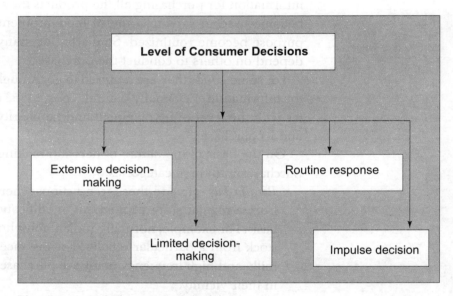

Fig. 4.3   Level of consumer decisions

- *Extensive decision-making/complex high-involvement* —this kind of decision-making usually happens for unfamiliar, expensive and/or infrequently bought products. These transactions involve a high degree of economic/performance/psychological risk. Examples include purchase decision for cars, homes, computers, and education. For such transactions, an individual has to spend a lot of time seeking information and making the decision.

    The information sources one uses for such purchases are mass media, friends and relatives, store personnel, etc. For such decisions consumers go through all the stages of the buying process.

- *Limited decision making* happens when an individual purchases a product occasionally and is required to look for a different brand or retailer for a product one is used to because of non-performance or non-availability. This requires a moderate amount of time for information gathering. Examples are clothes, utensils, crockery— essentially those products where the consumer is aware of the product class and not the brand.
- *Routine response/programmed behaviour* is observed in case of low-involvement, frequently purchased, and generally low cost products. They require very little search and decision efforts and are purchased almost automatically. Examples include grocery items from a particular retailer.
- *Impulse buying* relates to those purchases that do not involve any conscious planning. Example could be a soft drink purchase that occurs due to the sighting of the advertisement or the product at the outlet.

A particular product does not always remain confined to one category of the decision-making behaviour. A product can shift from one category to the next. For example, selecting a restaurant may involve extensive decision-making for someone not used to dining out, but limited decision-making for someone used to frequent dining out. The occasion for the diner, whether it is anniversary celebration, or a regular meal with a couple of friends will also determine the category of decision making involved. Therefore, most of the eating joints locate their outlets at all the possible destination shopping centres.

Consumer Decision Rules

Heuristics, decision strategies, and information-processing strategies constitute some of the decision rules used by the consumer to facilitate store and brand choices. These rules reduce the burden on the limited resources (economic and non-economic) of a prospective consumer in making complex decisions by providing guidelines that make the process of decision making less wearing.

Consumer decision rules are classified into two categories, namely compensatory and non-compensatory.

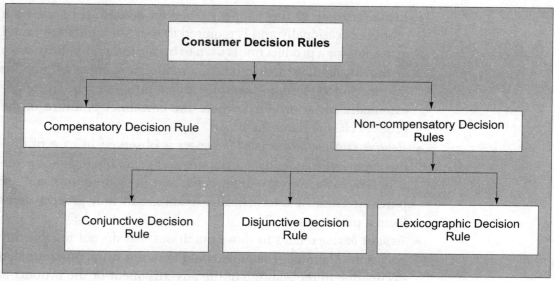

Fig. 4.4 Classification of consumer decision-making

Compensatory Decision Rule

On the basis of compensatory decision rule, a shopper evaluates store or brand alternatives in respect of each salient attribute and assigns weight or summated score for each store or brand in a consideration set. The computed value reflects the store's relative edge as a potential purchase choice. The proposition is that the shopper will select the store or brand that scores the highest among the options evaluated. Table 4.2 clearly shows that while selecting a particular restaurant a prospective shopper will select Haldiram in comparison with McDonald's and Bikaner.

Table 4.2 Compensatory evaluation of restaurants

Features	McDonald's	Haldiram	Bikaner
Cuisines Available	5	8	8
Service	8	6	7
Price	7	9	8
Distance	7	8	4
Atmospherics	5	5	6
Total	32	35	33

Compensatory decision rule is characterized by allowing a positive evaluation of a store or brand on one attribute to compensate or make for a negative evaluation on some other attribute. For example, a positive perception of the cuisines available (merchandise mix) at the Haldiram outlet has offset a negative perception of atmospherics.

Non-compensatory Decision Rules

In comparison with compensatory decision rule, non-compensatory decision rules do not allow consumers to balance positive assessment of store on one dimension against a negative evaluation on other dimensions. For instance, in case of restaurant selection, negative rating on atmospherics (Haldiram) would not be offset by a positive assessment of its merchandise mix (cuisines variety). For example, if a student's choice of a restaurant was based on variety of cuisines, a non-compensatory decision rule would have dropped McDonald's before evaluating on other dimensions.

Three non-compensatory rules are considered briefly here:

Conjunctive Decision Rule

Here the shopper establishes a specific, minimal acceptable level as a cut off point for each dimension. If a particular prospective store falls below the cut off point on any dimension (evaluative criteria), it is dropped from the consideration set.

This helps the shopper to evolve or acknowledge acceptable options from multiple alternatives, which can be further evaluated with the help of other decision rules to select the restaurant to be visited.

Disjunctive Decision Rule

While applying this decision rule, a prospective shopper sets up a specific, minimal acceptable level as a cut off point for each dimension. Under this rule the shopper accepts the store or brand if it meets or exceeds the limit established for any one dimension.

In this case also the shopper may have to resort to other decision rules to decide on the final selection of store from a refined set of alternatives.

Lexicographic Decision Rule

In this rule a shopper first ranks the dimensions in terms of their perceived salience or importance. The shopper then compares the various brand alternatives in terms of a single attribute that is considered most important. If one brand scores sufficiently high on this top-ranked dimension (regardless of the scores on any of the other attributes), it is selected and the process ends. When there are two or more surviving brand alternatives, the process is repeated with the second highest ranked dimension (and so on), until reaching the point that one of the brands is selected because it exceeds the others on a particular dimension.

The understanding of this decision rule helps the retailers and marketers to devise their marketing strategy in general and communication strategy in particular. One has to have an in-depth understanding of the decision rules employed by its target segment while selecting a particular store. This will provide indication about not only the level of involvement and concern of the shopper for a particular purchase but also the mechanism used to decide the final store.

According to a consumer survey, nine out of ten shoppers who go to a store for frequently purchased items pose a specific shopping strategy for saving money. The following consumer segments have been identified on the basis of the specific shopping rules followed by them.

- *Practical loyalists:* comprise shoppers who look for ways to save on the brands and products they would buy anyway.
- *Bottom-line price shoppers:* comprise shoppers who buy the lowest-priced items without regard for brand.
- *Opportunistic switchers:* comprise those who use coupons or sales to decide among brands and products that fall in their evoked set.
- *Deal hunters:* comprise those shoppers who look for the best 'bargain' and are not brand loyal.

Influence of Situational Variables on Shopping Behaviour

A shopping situation is a particular act of buying behaviour occurring at a specific point in space and time. An interesting example would be a customer seeking service at the Lakme beauty parlours—these beauty parlours are open to customers on all the seven days of a week, from 10 a.m. to around 7 p.m., in the midst of soft lights while the strains of sarangi and sarod soothe the customers' frayed nerves, which is simply a behaviour setting. The situation serves as an interface between the person (e.g., salon consumer) and the stimulus-object (beauty treatment such as facial, pedicure, etc.) and all those factors defining that interface constituting situational variables.

Situational variables refer to all those factors particular to a time and place of observation which do not follow from a knowledge of personal (intra-individual) and stimulus (choice alternative) attributes. Such attributes range from store location and layout to time of day and the presence (or absence) of others. These can be classified into four distinct dimensions of situational influence:

1. Physical setting
2. Social setting
3. Temporal perspective
4. Task definition

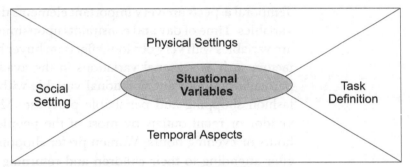

Fig. 4.5   Dimensions of situational variables

Physical Setting

The physical setting covers geographical location of the retail but might equally be seen in terms of the environment in which the consumer reads a catalogue, or accesses a shopping centre and a particular store. Shoppers who travel for half an hour or more are considered 'far shoppers'; those who travel for less than half an hour are considered 'near shoppers'. At the same time, shoppers who usually shop before 3 p.m. are designated 'early shoppers', and those who usually shop after 3 p.m. are designated 'late shoppers'.

It also subsumes influences on behaviour resulting from environmental conditions, such as weather or climate, placement of merchandise, access to information in a store, and background music or colour scheme.

Social Setting

The social setting describes the presence or absence of others, together with their social roles, role attributes, and opportunities for interaction. Therefore, it encapsulates everything – security staff in the shopping centre or store, opportunities for interaction with sales staff, friends or relatives accompanying the consumer on the shopping trip and even to proximity of other customers present in the store or servicescape.

The shoppers who are accompanied by other people are considered to be 'social shoppers'; those who are unaccompanied are designated 'solitary shoppers'.

Temporal Aspects

Temporal aspects are very important elements that affect the situational variables. Time of day and constraints upon time available for shopping are variables with very obvious effects on buyer behaviour, for instance, factors such as seasonal variations in the available product range—a particularly important situational variable within the context of both fashion shopping and perishable purchase. Milk is purchased from vendor or retail outlets by most of the people in India in morning hours or evening hours. Women prefer shopping in post-lunch hours after attending to their children and returning before the rest of the family reaches home. Therefore, retailers open their shops in accordance to shopping hours of their target segments. Shoppers who spent less than an hour were considered to be 'quick shoppers'; those who spent more than one hour or more were designated 'slow shoppers'.

Barista

Barista positioned its outlets as a place where people meet each other in an environment, which fulfills both their social and intellectual needs. The music is not too loud and encourages conversation, and the person behind the counter is non-intrusive and friendly. Any consumer knows that even when it is crowded at Barista, you will have your share of privacy. This is because the other consumer is not listening in; he is too involved in himself.

Task Definition

Task definition is more individual-specific and encompasses cognitive and motivational indications of the shopping situation, effectively capturing situational influences on the task definition, information search, and evaluation stages depicted in traditional consumer decision-making models. The difference in the degree of information processing behaviour varies for practical or hedonistic products, products for self-consumption versus gift purchases for others, etc.

For example, a young executive going alone for dinner will choose an eating joint that offers hygienic food at low prices with quick service. The same person may choose an upmarket restaurant with inviting décor, ambience, and compatible social surroundings when he is on a date with his girl friend. Low prices and quick service may actually be dysfunctional, in such a situation.

Many sections of the Indian middle class usually prefer to purchase garments for day-to-day use from retailers dealing in unbranded merchandise at lower prices. However, they prefer to visit an outlet offering branded products which are normally higher priced when they need to shop for a special or festive occasion such as Diwali, Id, marriage, etc.

The sound understanding and importance given to the influence of situational variables in devising the retail marketing mix will ensure the effective and profitable output to the retailers.

Consumers' image of a retail outlet plays an important role in determining the nature of shopping behaviour. In this context, it is important to understand the factors that affect the image formation of a retail store along with the process of its formation.

Consumers' Image of Retail Stores

A consumer's image of a store is the summation of his attitudes towards various aspects of that store. Retail marketers have provided considerable importance to consumers' attitude and images in store selection and rejection. Every retail store possesses an individuality that differentiates it from its competitors. A retailer must devise a strategy to communicate its individuality or personality across to its target segments to build their confidence in its merchandise and services.

Consumer decision-making is a process of matching self-images with the image of relevant retail store to meet their specific needs. It is argued that where there is some degree of congruity of individual's self-image and his image of a store or brand, there is a strong possibility of positive behaviour towards that particular store or shopping centre. The measurement of consumers' images of the store and measurement of consumers' self-images aid retailers in segmenting the consumer population into groups by demographic characteristics or patronage practices based on differences in the image of the retail store or shopping centre.

It is important to discuss the factors influencing the development of these attitudes. Figure 4.6 depicts the process of attitude formation and the resultant image (defined as constellation of attitude). Attitude and image formation takes places within and is affected by the physiological, sociological, and psychological environments. Within these environments the individuals' perceptions, motivations, interpersonal responses, traits, and concept of self interact to form attitudes towards various dimensions of the retail store. These attitudes in turn affect the person's perception, motivation, interpersonal response traits, and self-concept. The summation of all relevant attitudes is termed as the image of the retail store.

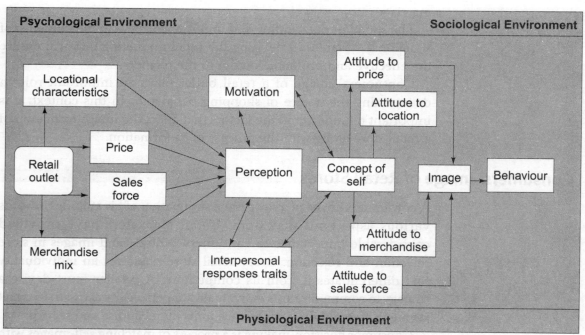

Fig. 4.6   Image development (Adapted from Wyckham (1967), p. 334.)

Retail Image Dimensions

To measure the image of a retail store or shopping centre, it is essential to identify and aggregate the relevant consumer attitudes. Lot of work on factors influencing consumers' attitudes towards stores in terms of shopping practices and in terms of store characteristics has been done in the West but it is an emerging field in the developing countries. The most comprehensive presentation is Fisk's 'conceptual model' in which he summarises store qualities as cognitive dimension (see Fig. 4.7 of store image). These dimensions can be used to identify relevant attitudes and assist in the development of measurement instruments for a particular retail store.

Dimension	Determinants
1. Locational convenience	1. Access route 2. Traffic barrier 3. Travelling time 4. Parking availability
2. Merchandise suitability	1. Number of brands stocked 2. Quality of line 3. Breadth of assortment 4. Depth of assortment 5. Number of outstanding departments in the store.
3. Value for price	1. Price of a particular item in a particular store 2. Price of same item in another store 3. Price of another item in the same store 4. Price of same item in a substitute store 5. Trading stamps and discounts
4. Sales effort and store services	1. Courtesy of sales clerks 2. Helpfulness of sales clerks 3. Reliability and usefulness of advertising 4. Billing procedures 5. Adequacy of credit arrangements 6. Delivery promptness and care 7. Eating facilities

5. Congeniality	1. Store layout
	2. Store décor
	3. Merchandise displays
	4. Class of customers
	5. Store traffic and congestion
6. Post-transaction satisfaction	1. Satisfaction with good in use
	2. Satisfaction with returns and adjustments
	3. Satisfaction with price paid
	4. Satisfaction with accessibility to store

Fig. 4.7   Department store image

These dimensions do not constitute an exhaustive list of retail store characteristics for every store to measure the store image. One has to revise the list in respect of the product category they are in, the retail format they have adopted, and the competition they are facing along with characteristics of their target segment. For example banking retail institutions, restaurants, and fashion stores will have to work out the specific characteristics which will be relevant in their context to measure their respective image.

Image concept is most relevant in respect of the retail sector because of consumer intimacy with the store and awareness of the retail store. Unlike the producers whose primary contact with the immediate consumer is through his offerings and communications, the retailers relate directly to the consumer through physical premises, sales force, offerings, and services. Thus, customers develop personal images of retail stores and centres based on their experience.

Retailers can avail the understanding of the store image by their target segment by devising or revising their corporate objectives and store operations. For example, McDonald's has positioned itself in India as a 'Family Restaurant' as in India most of the individuals prefer outings with family. Whereas the Big Bazaar discount store, to overcome this notion among Indian masses that low priced products are of poor quality, stressed on 'Sabse sasta sabse achaa'. On the other hand, conflicting activities within the store may result in an image which lacks 'sharp definition' and restricts market expansion and retention of the existing customer base.

Indian Shoppers

Time of day is considered a physical dimension rather than a temporal one. Shopping in the Indian market during the daytime is a rather different physical experience than shopping during the evening hours. Consequently, it is hardly surprising that the Indian shoppers tend to visit the market in the later part of the day rather than the earlier and hotter daytime, especially during summers. Whereas, during winters consumers prefer to shop during day time before sunset. There would be no such distinction in the climatically controlled Malls emerging in India, particularly in the metros. Consequently, the time of day situational variable may undergo a metamorphosis as the years pass. In India, retailers, in particular service providers, highlight the fact that their outlets or stalls possess superior cooling fans to beat the heat. For example, in the last two years, most of the Cineplexes in the major cities carried out a drive to introduce effective air conditioning systems in their theatres to attract the crowds during morning or noon hours in north India.

Another constraining factor is poor availability of transportation. The private car is only owned by 11% of the Indian population. This reflects the sheer inconvenience of carrying too many purchases over a longer distance using two-wheelers, bicycle, scooters, or public transportation as the primary mode of transportation.

A higher proportion of shoppers in India prefer to purchase products other than food or beverages in the company of their relatives or friends. There may be marketing implications to this phenomenon. One interpretation is that in the Western countries a mall visit can be a recreational activity—given the comfortable and pleasing environment (*physical surroundings*)—whereas in India a visit to an open traditional market carries a more specific purchase intent (*task definition*). From a retail-marketing point of view, the difference in the layout of the two sites dictates a particular shopping behaviour. Malls are equipped with restaurants, cafes, food courts, and other places to eat. Customers are thus encouraged to interrupt their shopping and eat or drink while sitting down comfortably. On the other hand, even though the traditional market has many stalls providing food and beverages, these items are consumed right next to the outlet selling other products or while the customer is walking around the market. Thus, a marketer might be able to stimulate additional sales by providing enhanced physical surroundings. For example, leading traditional eating joints in India such as Haldiram, Bikaner, and Nirulas regularly carry out a massive drive to renovate their stores layout and provide comfortable infrastructure and inviting ambience to attract consumers to their stores.

Jewellery: Organized Players

Pantaloon Retail (I) Ltd recently launched Gold Bazaar—its fourth retail division at Big Bazaar, Lower Parel, Mumbai, and the second in the city. Pantaloon is driven by its philosophy of 'Rewrite Rules— Retail Values'. Gold Bazaar is a unique concept with six unique benefits in terms of what it offers to its customers. This was set up in acknowledgment of the fact that Indian consumers always preferred independent jewellers which remain associated with the family for generations. Such jewellers offered the benefit of trustworthiness, credibility and special prices for their regular clients. Gold Bazaar seeks to offer similar benefits through various price-off schemes and institutional support designed to generate trust and credibility.

The six benefits designed to overcome inhibitions of customers are:

- A certificate announcing the purity of the gold along with the HALL MARK (BIS)
- Offering a standard rate chart on 'making charges'
- Making charges 20% less as compared to the market rate
- An all risk/perils insurance cover from ICICI-Lombard
- Excellent buy back schemes
- Testing gold for purity on a non-destructive Karat Meter before the customer so as to ensure the quality of the gold they buy

The USP of Gold Bazaar is the purity of the gold offered. Just like Big Bazaar and Food Bazaar, Gold Bazaar too is being offered as a value-for-money destination. Keeping in mind the traditional mindset of Indian customers, Pantaloon endeavours to offer customers a transparent transaction—something which has never been offered before in gold retailing in India. Every piece of Jewellery has the guarantee of purity by way of HALL MARK from BIS (Bureau of Indian Standards).

Moreover, at Gold Bazaar customers can check the purity of the gold by means of a karat meter using the XRF technique. A certificate of purity issued by Roentgenanalytik Messtechnik GmbH would accompany every purchase made at the store. The store is also likely to be the only one to put up a standard rate chart for 'making charges', thereby simplifying the calculation for the cost of the ornament.

Gold Bazaar's six unique benefits also include exchanging old jewellery for new with guaranteed 0% weight loss, giving customers complete satisfaction and true value for their money. A life-long after sales service is also provided which includes cleaning, polishing and repairing services. Should the customer be dissatisfied with the purchase made, there is a 15-day money back guarantee—no questions asked.

The frequency of market/mall visit can be influenced by actions of the managers of the market/mall and the individual establishments. Inducements as prizes, drawings, special sales, or other encouragements may be offered to increase frequency of visit. The more frequently a consumer patronizes a market/mall, the greater the opportunity for purchase. For example, stores such as Ebony and Shoppers' Stop introduce coupons and redemption cards which can be availed of within a particular duration from the date of issuance. Some eating joints introduce happy hours and discounts and gifts to attract the customers during lean periods of the day.

Some retailers and malls also organize special events, exhibits, contests, and special sales. For example, Rajouri market organizes the FM contest in association with Radio FM channel in their market every fortnight on weekends to attract youngsters. Even the retailers along with the mobile traders organize the periodic market, which attracts masses. In some of these ways retailers can encourage people to come at varying periods of the day or week.

Time spent in the market/mall is also deeply related to shopping behaviour. The longer a patron can be persuaded to remain in the market the greater the likelihood of effecting a purchase. Special displays of merchandise, presence of celebrities, or announcements of special promotions are frequently used to encourage longer visits. Similarly shopping malls introduce a special section for kids so that while they remain occupied their parents can spend more time at the shopping centre. Some retail outlets frequently arrange some programmes with well-known personalities to attract potential customers to their store. For example, the Planet M chain of music stores regularly organizes the events by inviting personalities from Hindi film industry.

Sample of a Customer Profile and Analysis

Customer research helps a retailer in defining the customer segment he can and should serve and how he can serve them more effectively and profitably. A useful customer research would like to find answers to the following questions.

- When do customers like to shop?
- How do customers like to pay?
- What quality of merchandise do customers usually prefer?
- What type of store has the maximum appeal for my customers?
- How do customers handle servicing of the mechanical products purchased by them?
- Who does most of the buying in the homes of my customers?
- What is the income level of my average customer?
- What is the age profile of my average customer?
- What is the general attitude of my customer towards his community?
- How does my customer react to new and different merchandise or promotional activities?
- What major changes has my customer made in the last two years?

Based on the above customer profile, retailers will have a good idea of how to serve the needs of the target market. This would also enable the retailer to suitably tailor the advertising to appeal to the target market. Advertising in various local publications could then be a good way to reach this segment.

Depending on the product or service, the customer profile study should include information relevant to the target market. Many companies seek out information on a potential user's lifestyle, loyalty, and spending habits. Businesses that advertise heavily want to know the media habits of potential customers as well. All the information that will help the retailer to promote and sell his product better should be included in the customer profile study.

Summary

An understanding of consumer behaviour is important in order to formulate and im- plement effective retail marketing strategies. Consumer behaviour refers to the understanding of how consumers make decision to use their respective resources such as time, money, and effort for buying, using, and disposing goods and services. Consumer behaviour in turn is affected by various factors specific to the consumer and the external environment. These factors could be classified as intrinsic and extrinsic; the former deals with motives, perceptions, and attitudes of the consumers, and the latter deals with influences such as family, social class, culture, and economic environment.

Another classification of factors that affect consumer behaviour refers to personal, psychological, and environmental influences. Personal factors are unique to a particular person and largely refer to demographics such as age, marital status, sex, and income. Psychological factors refer to intrinsic aspects of the individual, such as motives, perception, learning, attitudes, personality, and lifestyle. Environmental influences refer to the physical and social characteristics of a consumer's external world, including physical objects, spatial relationships, and social factors.

Consumer decision-making process refers to the stages consumers go through when they decide to make a purchase. It consists of five stages—need recognition, information search, evaluation of alternatives, purchase decision, and purchase evaluation. Needs could be simple or complex based on the frequency of their occurrence. Information search could be prepurchase or ongoing search which, in turn, could be derived from internal and external sources. Consumers invest time in information search in proportion to the perceived risk associated with the particular purchase and the importance of purchase. Alternatives from the evoked set are then analysed to take a final decision from various choices. It is essential for all retailers to ensure that their outlet finds a place in the consideration set of the target segment for they need to inform and position the store as per the needs of the target segment.

In the retailing context, the purchase stage involves decision with regard to the place of shopping, which relates to the nature of store as well as the nature of market—traditional market, shopping mall, or neighbourhood market. Shoppers consider aspects like physical characteristics, social interaction, assurance, and nature of merchandise, and policies like operating hours, payment options, loyalty programmes etc., while selecting or evaluating the viability of patronizing any particular store. Purchase is followed by evaluation of performance against expectations.

Nature of consumer decision-making also varies with the level of involvement and familiarity with product usage and its purchase. Based on types of purchase, transactions can be classified into routine buy, modified rebuy, and new product purchase.

On the basis of efforts required or the level of involvement, consumer decision-making can be classified into extensive problem-solving, limited problem-solving, routinized response behaviour, and impulse buying.

Key Terms

1. **AIOs:** Activities, interests, and opinions—the psychographic variables used in market segmentation.

2. **Attitudes:** Positive, neutral, or negative feelings an individual has about the economy, politics, offerings, institutions, etc.

3. **Cognitive dissonance:** Doubt that occurs after a purchase is made.

4. **Consumer behaviour:** Involves the process by which persons determine whether, what, where, how, from whom, and how often to purchase goods and services.

5. **Consumer satisfaction or dissatisfaction:** The overall attitude a person has about a offering that has been purchased.

6. **Consumer decision process:** Stages a consumer goes thorough in buying a good or service; need recognition, information search, evaluation of alternatives, purchase, post-purchase behaviour.

7. **Culture:** Distinctive heritage shared by a group of people. It passes on beliefs, norms, and customs.

8. **Custom:** A norm that is derived from a traditional way of doing things.

9. **Demographics:** Objective, quantifiable, easily identifiable, and measurable population data.

10. **Evaluative criteria:** The dimensions used by consumers to compare competing product alternatives.

11. **Evoked set:** Those products or brands already in the memory plus those prominent in the retail environment.

12. **Impulse buying:** A process that occurs when the consumer experiences a sudden urge to purchase an item that he or she can not resist.

13. **Involvement:** The degree of motivation to process product-related information during buying decision process.

14. **Learning:** A relatively permanent change in the behaviour caused by experience.

15. **LifeStyle:** Ways that individual consumers and families live and spend time and money.

16. **Motivation:** An internal state that activates goal-oriented behaviour.

17. **Motives:** Reasons for consumer behaviour.

18. **Norms:** The informal rules that govern what is right or wrong.

19. **Perceived risk:** The belief that use of a product has potentially negative consequences, physical, social, or economical.

20. **Perception:** The process by which stimuli are selected, organized, and interpreted.

21. **Personality:** A person's unique psychological makeup, which consistently influences the way the person responds to his or her environment.

22. **Psychographics:** It focuses on how physical environment is integrated into the consumer's subjective experience.

23. **Social class:** Informal ranking of people based on income, occupation, education, and other factors.

24. **Reference group:** Influence of people's thoughts and behaviour. They may be friends, family members, personalities etc.

25. **Target market:** Customer group that a retailer seeks to attract and satisfy.

26. **Value:** Represented by the activities and processes a value

27. **Word-of-mouth:** The information transmitted by individual consumers on an informal basis.

Concept Review Questions

1. In what ways the knowledge of consumer behaviour is essential for the success of retail strategies?
2. What are the factors that influence consumer behaviour in retail banking?
3. What are the stages of consumer decision-making and its impact on retail strategies? Specify with an example.
4. What are the types of consumer decision-making process? Explain with an example.
5. Discuss the factors which affect the nature of consumer decision-making?
6. State the influence of situational variables on shopping behaviour in a planned shopping centre?

Project Work Assignments

1. Identify the differences in consumer behaviour while shopping for any two identified grocery items at a local Kirana store (referred to as mom-and-pop stores) and at a department-store. Identify differences among consumers from different socio-economic levels while shopping for identified items. Collect the observational data along with interviews of the retailers into get insights in shopping behaviour?
2. Carry out a field study to understand
   - the factors which influence Indian middle class customers to shop in malls
   - the shopping patterns and consumer purchasing behaviour in malls
3. List the variables which motivate the consumer to patronize the periodic markets in the urban areas. Carry out a consumer survey and also collect inputs from retailers operating in periodic markets for the purpose.
4. Carry out an in-depth interview of two to three women in your locality to describe the purchasing behaviour of Indian middle-class women when buying expensive jewellery?

Case Study

Rajat Gandhi, the dynamic CEO of a large amusement park, is watching the last show in a new multiplex. There is a sizeable crowd in the auditorium. He observes that four other shows are running in parallel halls, all attracting large crowds. On the way back home he wonders if it would be a good idea to diversify by setting up a multiplex chain. He reasons that before he takes a decision he should understand why people prefer to see movies in such multiplexes, driving long distances even though the tickets are high priced.

Next day, Gandhi summons Mehta—a known cinema distributor in the region, over dinner, to understand the dynamics of the business and identify the reasons behind the growth of multiplexes. Mehta mentions that the multiplexes are going to change the way movie exhibition business will operate. Multiplexes like PVR in Delhi and R World and Fun Republic in Ahmedabad are changing the cinema experience. Watching of movies can be clubbed with shopping, eating out, and other entertainment activities. People prefer to view movies in multiplexes for a variety of reasons— these provide a pleasant ambience, have excellent equipment and comfortable seating arrangements, etc. The likelihood of getting a ticket also increases since five or six movies are being simultaneously screened.

The economics also favours the multiplex business mode when compared to a single-hall theatre. A single-hall theatre with a seating capacity of 1200 would need around 50% occupancy to recover its operating costs. Thus, shows drawing less than 600 customers would be loosing money. In the present scenario when many movies are flopping on the box office, this becomes a very risky proposition since movie rights are purchased a week or multiple weeks in advance. In contrast the multiplex offers much greater flexibility. A multiplex has theatres of different sizes. Successful movies can be screened in bigger halls or in multiple halls while those not doing well can be shifted to smaller theatres. A multiplex owner can also shift the movies from larger to smaller theatres as the popularity of the movie declines. Besides the flexibility in size of the auditoriums, the multiplex also has flexibility regarding timing of the shows. The shows in different auditoriums can be timed to commence at different hours. Many multiplexes have shows commencing every hour at one or the other of its auditoriums. This gives greater flexibility to the customers.

The multiplexes, especially those belonging to a chain of multiplexes, have enormous bargaining powers with distributors. They can negotiate on movie rights and sometimes even on launch dates for movies. Multiplexes can negotiate rights to screen blockbusters while single-hall theatres have to often wait for the blockbusters to be taken off the multiplexes. Cinema goers are, however, not too keen to wait for the blockbuster movie to be screened at a single-hall theater. If the single-hall theatre owners do not wish to wait for the movie to be taken off the multiplex, they have the choice of running less popular movies, which again is not a very welcome option.

However, the multiplex can succeed only if it attracts a large crowd. The rates charged are relatively higher because of the ambience. A multiplex has to become a destination for the middle-class customers to be viable. Smaller towns and rural areas would not generate such a large flow of traffic to a destination. Hence, single-hall theaters are likely to remain viable in such towns. The lower income groups in metros may also not be able to afford the multiplexes and may continue to patronize the single-hall theater.

Rajat Gandhi has a sharp business sense.

He reasons that a large chain of multiplexes can negotiate better rates with distributors, plan promotions more efficiently, and gain economies in ticket printing and other operational costs. Gandhi feels that emergence of such large chains will lead to a gradual consolidation of movie exhibition business. Mr Gandhi is however worried about the large number of multiplexes coming up. It is estimated that over 300 multiplexes will come up in the country in the next two to three years. Ajay Bijli's PVR group, which set up India's first multiplex PVR Anupam in Delhi, has set up multiplexes in two more locations in Delhi, and in Bangalore, Mumbai, and Gurgaon. The Mumbai-based Inox group has five multiplexes in Mumbai, Pune, and Baroda. In Ahmedabad alone there are over twenty multiplex screens. The proliferation of multiplexes has resulted in an intense competition. When PVR Anupam opened, it attracted customers from across the city; similarly R World, located 20 kms outside Ahmedabad, attracted customers from the city. When the multiplexes first came up in India in the late 1990s, they were destinations that attracted customers from across the city and suburbs. But now with a large number of multiplexes opening up, their catchment area is becoming much smaller. With the establishment of many other multiplexes in Ahmedabad, traffic to R World has declined. The problem is often compounded by the concentration of multiplexes in a locality, for example, a large number of multiplexes have come up at Gurgaon near Delhi and at Lokhandwala in Mumbai.

Gandhi wondered how he can differentiate his multiplex chain. Stand-alone multiplex screens lack appeal and may not pull crowds in large numbers. Hence, many multiplexes were coming up as part of an entertainment centre. For example, Fun Republic promoted by Zee developed the multiplex as a part of an entertainment centre allocating only about 35% area to auditoriums. The remaining is set aside for synergistic retail outlets such as bookshops, music shops, the eateries, and department stores. Others like the PVR are looking out for entertainment centres spanning food and retailing. They seek malls coming up across the country. Gandhi surveyed the scene abroad and found that in United States the multiplexes were often driven out of business by the giant megaplexes with 20 screens. The large megaplexes enjoyed enormous bargaining power with film distributors and offered a destination location.

Gandhi felt that he has to understand the consumer psychology and behaviour before deciding on the model for his multiplex chain. How does an Indian customer view the movie experience? Would they drive long distances to view a movie? Would they combine a visit to a movie with shopping? What types of retail outlets would have greater synergy with cinema? Will the customer viewing a movie be only interested in entertainment activities like eating out and visiting a music store or a book store or will he or she also like to shop for groceries and garments?

Gandhi wondered if he should target his multiplexes to young upper-class males and females who have high purchasing power and like to visit happening places for fun and relaxation with close friends or in groups. In that case, he has to develop entertainment centres catering to the interest of this segment—they would contain eateries, music shops, and book shops. If he targeted families, he wondered if they would combine shopping of grocery and other items with watching of the movie. Gandhi examined the possibility of setting up megaplexes with 20 screens which enjoyed high popularity in the United States. He reasons that for these to be successful they have to attract customers from large catchment areas. Will the Indian customer drive long distances if provided a unique experience? Gandhi feels that he needs to visit multiplexes in a few large metropolitan cities and observe the cinema watching habits of consumers across the country more closely. He picks up his mobile and asks his travel agent to book him on the next flight to Bangalore.

1. What are the factors which influence customers to view movies in multiplexes vis-a-vis single-screen theatres?

2. Will multiplex chains dominate the movie exhibition business in future or will single-hall theatres be able to hold on?

3. How should Mr Gandhi go about taking a decision on whether to establish a chain of multiplexes?

References

1. Riti, M.D. 2003, 'Consumer behavior: Men still major decision-makers', www.rediff.com, May 2.

2. Rao, S.L. and Natarajan, I., Indian Market Demographics: The Consumer Classes, *National Council for Applied Economic Research (NCAER)*, New Delhi, p. 242.

3. Chandran, R. 2003, 'JWT study casts new light on consumer attitudes', http://www.hinduonnet.com/bline/, Apr 10.

4. Lobo, A. 2001, 'No frills Superstore', *Business India*, March 5-18, pp.110.

5. Sarkar, R. 2002, 'The Roots of Success', *Businessworld*, Febuary 4, pp. 20–26.

6. Parekh, A. 2001, 'Songs In Store', *Business India*, August 6-19.

7. Gangadhar, V. 2003, 'A bookstall stands tall', www.blonnet.com/life, Feb 17.

8. Shenoy, M. 2001, 'The brew catches on', *Business India*, August 16-29, pp. 114–116.

9. Rastogi, P., 'Food for Thought', *Businessworld*, September 11, pp. 44–49

10. Rajshekhar, M. 2001, 'Of Crowds and Sensibilities', *Businessworld*, March 5, pp. 46–48.

11. Kumar, N. 2002, 'A low price for success', *Business Standard:* The Strategist, June 18, p. 1.

12. Fisk, G. 1961-1962, 'A Conceptual Model for Studying Consumer Image', *Journal of Retailing*, vol. 37, Winter.

13. Wyckham, R.G. 1967, 'Aggregate Department Store Images: Social and Experimental Factors,' *Changing Marketing System*, Ed. Reed Moyer, American Marketing Association, Chicago.

14. Kerlinger, F.N. 1965, Foundations of Behavioural Research, Holt, New York.

15. Tauber, E.M. 1972, 'Why do people shop?' *Journal of Marketing*, vol. 36, October, pp. 47-48.

16. Peterson, L. 1992, 'The Strategic Shopper', *Ad week's Marketing Week*, March 30, p. 18?20.

5 RETAIL MARKET SEGMENTATION

INTRODUCTION

MARKET SEGMENTATION

THE BENEFITS OF MARKET SEGMENTATION

STAGES OF THE CONSUMER DECISION PROCESS

SEGMENTING, TARGETING, AND POSITIONING

CRITERIA FOR EFFECTIVE MARKET SEGMENTATION

KINDS OF MARKETS

DIMENSIONS FOR SEGMENTATION

MARKET TARGETING—CHOOSING THE SEGMENTS TO FOCUS

CUSTOMER PROFILE

SURVEY OF BUYERS' INTENTIONS

MARKET SEGMENTATION IN INDIA

Learning Objectives

- To understand the meaning of market segmentation

- To appreciate the benefits of segmenting markets

- To outline the criteria for market segmentation

- To examine the dimensions on which markets can be segmented: demographic, psychographic, and behavioural

- To understand how to identify and select target markets

- To understand how to develop profiles of target segments

- To examine market segmentation practices followed in India

Introduction

A market is a group of potential customers with similar needs who are willing to exchange something of value with sellers offering various goods and services that can satisfy these needs. The marketer has the option of either approaching the entire set of customers with a uniform marketing approach or adopting a differentiated approach for different sets of customers. While the former refers to mass marketing, the latter refers to the strategy of market segmentation.

The argument for mass marketing is that it creates the largest potential market, which can lead to higher sales. Mass marketing approach can also lower costs since the retailer does not have to spend on specific communication and promotional programmes. This can result in higher margins and profitability.

However, with increase in competition, the mass marketing approach may not be feasible. Consumers have many shopping options today. A consumer can buy groceries from a neighbourhood store or a large supermarket; she may buy jewellery from a speciality store or from a large department store. The proliferation of distribution channels and retail formats is increasing competition and forcing retailers to focus their selling efforts on select groups of customers. Each type of retail format offers distinct benefits in terms of product variety, pricing, shopping ambience, etc., which appeals to a particular group of customers. Today, even while buying clothes, customers can choose between traditional stores with unbranded range, upscale speciality stores (Raymond, Lacoste, Nalli), no-frill discount 'Box' stores (Wills, Marks and Spencer), and discounted stores (Big Bazaar, Giant). They can shop in conventional supermarkets, super stores, combination stores (Ansal Plaza, Cross Roads, Globus), and factory outlets (Levis, Adidas, etc.).

Hence, retailers are required to understand the various criteria that can be adopted for segmenting the market and the benefits offered by each segment. Based on this analysis, the retail marketer can select one or more of the segments as the target market and position his outlet as per the profile of the targeted segment. Availability and analysis of customer data, specific to the market concerned, facilitates the process of segmentation.

Market Segmentation

Market segmentation is the process of dividing the heterogeneous total market into small groups of customers who share a similar set of wants. Each of these smaller groups possesses somewhat homogeneous characteristics. As in case of marketers in other businesses, marketers in the business of retailing may also seek the benefits of market segmentation depending on his unique market and business context. A retailer may divide women customers into two segments, working women and housewife, if it finds that these two groups have different sets of needs. Segmenting is thus an aggregating process—clustering people with similar needs into a market segment. A segment is a relatively homogeneous group and hence responds to a marketing mix in a similar way. Different groups or segments require different promotional strategies and marketing mixes because they have different wants and needs. A niche is a more narrowly defined group seeking a distinctive mix of benefits.

Marketers usually identify niches by dividing a segment into sub-segments. For example, the retailer may divide the segment of working women into two sub-segments, those with children and those without children.

Segmentation helps the retailer to customize the product/service and tailor its promotional campaigns. This helps it to reach out to and meet the specific needs of a narrowly defined customer group. Segmentation of markets is imperative and often crucial to the development of effective marketing programmes in today's competitive marketplace. The impetus for market segmentation is heterogeneous customer needs and shopping behaviour/patterns, which no single retailer is in a position to serve as per their desired level of needs.

The Benefits of Market Segmentation

Retailers segment the market to identify specific groups of customers in their trade area on whom their selling efforts can be concentrated. Such focused selling efforts are aimed at making the retailer the preferred destination for such identified segments for the products or services it deals in and to develop a dominant position in the target segments. Following are the benefits of segmenting the market, also shown in Fig. 5.1.

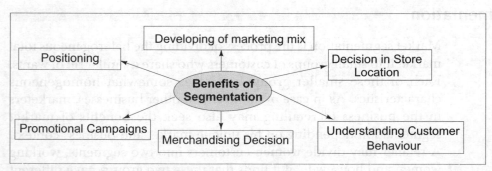

Fig. 5.1   Benefits of segmentation

- *Development of marketing mix:* Segmentation helps a retailer in identifying the target population and developing a customized marketing programme in terms of product/service offering, pricing strategy, and promotional programme.
- *Store location decision:* Segmentation helps a retail chain in deciding locations for its new stores. The retail outlets can be located where there is a concentration of the target population.
- *Understand customer behaviour:* Segmentation helps a retailer to gain insight into why the target group acts the way it does. The buying behaviour of the target segment can be understood once the market is segmented. This can help in the development of an effective marketing strategy.
- *Merchandising decisions:* Segmentation helps a retailer in merchandising decisions. Merchandising is essentially the skill that decides which items will go on the shelves. An understanding of preferences of target segments is essential for a successful merchandising programme.
- *Promotional campaigns:* Segmentation helps the retailer in developing more effective and accurate promotional campaigns.
- *Positioning:* Segmentation helps a retailer in positioning itself in the market. Thus, Shoppers' Stop and Crossroads have targeted the upper income class while Westside has targeted the larger base of middle and upper middle-class consumers.

Segmenting, Targeting, and Positioning

Retail marketers are required to recognize the three stages of market segmentation: segmenting, targeting, and positioning (STP) (Kotler 1984). According to this approach, illustrated in Figure 5.2, the segmentation process begins with the aggregation of customers into groups to maximize homogeneity within, and heterogeneity between, segments.

Once the market segments are identified, detailed profiles of customers in each segment should be developed. Such profiles would include demographic information on age, income level, education, etc., on psychographic variables such as motives, attitudes, perceptions, values, and beliefs, which help to understand customers' lifestyle and behavioural information such as customers' shopping and

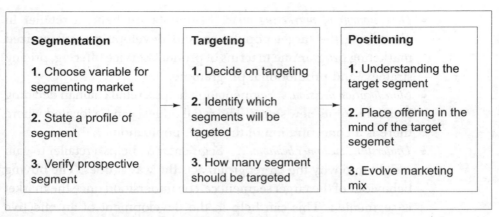

Fig. 5.2   Stages in marketing segmentation

consumption habits including product usage, frequency of purchase, etc. Customer profiles help the retailers in understanding the behaviour of target markets. The retailers should also be constantly looking for the emergence of new segments and search new dimensions on which the markets can be segmented. After the markets are segmented and profiled, the retailers have to decide which segments to target and focus on and how many segments to target. The retailers have to evaluate the attractiveness of each segment by estimating its size, rate of growth, etc.

Before selecting the target segments it should also ensure that needs of the target segments match with retailer's business model— its product range, promotional programme, etc. After the target segments are identified and chosen, the retailer has to develop its positioning strategy. For effective positioning, a detailed understanding of the needs of the target segment is necessary. Market research may be carried out to get such an understanding. Finally, an appropriate marketing strategy has to be developed to create positive perceptions in a customer's mind and achieve the desired market positioning.

Criteria for Effective Market Segmentation

Effective market segmentation can provide a base for developing a sound marketing strategy. But market segmentation is a challenging task. If a retailer identifies and segments its market on variables that influence purchase decision for its products and services, segmenta-

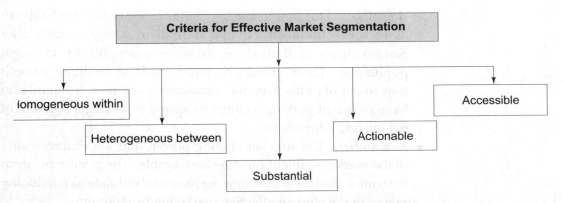

Fig. 5.3 Important characteristics for effective marketing segmentation

tion can become a sound platform for developing an effective marketing strategy. Otherwise, segmentation may prove to be a futile exercise.

For market segmentation to be effective, the identified segments must satisfy the following criteria.

- *Homogeneous within:* The segments into which the market is divided should be homogeneous within. The customers in a segment should have similar needs and wants and follow similar buying behaviour as much as possible so that their needs can be addressed through a uniform marketing programme.
- *Heterogeneous between:* The customers in different segments should be as different as possible with respect to their needs and buying behaviour. This will help a retailer to focus its efforts on its identified target segments.
- *Substantial:* The market segment or segments that a retailer plans to target must be large enough and have enough discretionary income to help the retailer to be profitable. Stores like Bombay Stores and Lifestyle, which target higher income groups, should ensure that there is a significantly large population of such high-income groups in their trade area before locating a store.
- *Actionable:* The segmenting dimensions should be useful for identifying customers and deciding on marketing mix variables. Barista targets youngsters who seek to enjoy a coffee in a fashionable outlet; it should be accessible to its target customers.

- *Accessible:* The target market segment must be reachable so as to serve them effectively. A mall in a city suburb, like Koramangala in Bangalore, must be accessible to its target population. There should be good roads to facilitate smooth movement of traffic from the surrounding colonies. It should also have sufficient parking facilities to appeal to its target segment of car-owning consumers.
- *Measurable:* The size, purchasing power, and the characteristics of the market segment must be measurable. The retailer needs to determine the size of the target segment and estimate its purchasing power to develop an effective marketing programme.

Types of Markets

A market is any group of existing or potential buyers of a product. There are three major types of markets—consumer, industrial, and re-seller:

- The consumer market includes individuals and households who buy goods or services for their own use. Grocery and stationery items are among the most common types of consumer products.
- The industrial market includes individuals, groups, or organizations that purchase products or services for direct use in producing other products.
- The re-seller market includes middlemen or intermediaries, such as wholesalers and retailers, who buy finished goods and re-sell them for a profit.

Retailing is associated with that aspect of the transaction where the final customer in the value chain purchases products or services for self-consumption. Our focus in this chapter is on segmentation of retail markets which deal with consumer products.

Consumer products are those products that are intended for the ultimate consumer. Consumer products can be sub-divided into four sub-groups:

- *Convenience products:* Convenience products are products that are purchased frequently but on which the consumer is not willing to spend much time or effort. These include staples like packaged foods, milk, bread, and emergency products like medicine, umbrellas, etc.

- *Shopping products:* Shopping products are products that a customer feels are worth the time and effort to compare with competing products. These include furniture, clothing, washing machines, television sets, etc.
- *Speciality items:* Speciality products are consumer products that the customer makes a special effort to purchase. The consumer is willing to search for such speciality products. Any branded product that customers insist on by name is a speciality product.
- *Unsought items:* Unsought goods are products that potential customers do not yet want or know about. Customers do not buy such products unless promotion shows their value. Life insurance and encyclopedias are examples of unsought products.

A retailer has to understand the product class it is dealing with in order to understand customers' buying behaviour and to be able to segment markets.

Dimensions for Segmentation

A retailer must decide on product-market dimensions for segmenting the market, which might be useful in planning marketing strategies. Customers can be described by many specific dimensions. Table 5.1 shows a comprehensive list of dimensions useful for segmenting consumer markets. A few dimensions are demographic; others are geographic, psychographic and behavioural. In segmenting the total market, the retailer must first decide which combination of segmenting dimensions to use. For example, a retailer may use a geographical dimension to define its trade area, a demographic dimension to identify its customers, and a behavioural dimension to understand their buying practices.

Table 5.1   Dimensions used to segment markets

1	**Sex**	8.	**Family size**
	Male, female		2, 3, 4, 5, more
2.	**Age**	9.	**Family life cycle**
	0–5, pre-school		Young, single

contd

contd

	16–12, pre-teen 13–19, teenage 20–30, young … …		Young, married, no children Young, married, youngest Pre-school Older, no children at home
3.	**Marital status** Single Married Separated Widowed	10.	**Religion** Hindu Muslim Christian, etc.
4.	**Income** < Rs 5,000 … …. Over Rs 10,00,000	11.	**Social class** Upper-upper Lower-upper Upper-middle Upper-lower, etc.
5.	**Occupation** Professional Manager Labour Student Businessman Homemaker	12.	**Housing** Owned Rent
6	**Education** Primary Secondary Intermediate Graduate Professional degree	13.	**Geographic** Rural Suburban Urban Metro Driving time
7.	**Type of family** Nuclear family Joint family		

Geographic Segmentation

In case of geographic segmentation, the market is divided into geographical units such as nations, states, regions, countries, cities, or neighbourhoods. Retailers in India have often segmented markets by cities and focused on metros and large cities. Globus started its first

Table: 5.2   Top 5 money-spending priorities of SEC A and SEC B by region

West	North	South	East
Grocery	Grocery	Grocery	Grocery
Eating out	Personal care	Eating out	Apparel
Books and music	Eating out	Apparel	Savings
Personal care	Books and music	Books and music	Personal care
Savings	Savings	Savings	Eating out

Source: Consumer Outlook 2002, KSA Technopak

store in the metropolitan city Chennai as well as the mid-sized city of Indore to gauge market potential in cities of different sizes. Subhiksha has stores in Chennai, at short distances, serving the nearby colonies. A study done by KSA Technopak in India among segments SEC A and SEC B revealed that while the four regions—north, south, east, and west—had consensus on top-spending priorities, their preference order(Table 5.2).

Demographic Segmentation

In case of demographic segmentation, the market is divided into groups based on demographic variables such as age, religion, gender, income level, social class, family size, occupation, education level, and marital status. The retailer should segment the market on variables which reflect interest, need, and ability of the customer to patronize a particular kind of shopping centre or retail outlet. Thus, an apparel retailer like Benetton may segment the market by gender, while an up-market department store like LifeStyle may segment market by income class. The major objective of analyzing demographic characteristics is to locate the market, whereas psychological and socio-cultural indicators help in understanding the buying behaviour. In India, most market research agencies prefer to segment on the basis of socio-economic class (SEC A, SEC B, and SEC C) rather than income per se. In this context, it is also important to continuously monitor the preference patterns of each of the segments due to fluidity in the socio-economic situation facilitated by economic development. For instance, the KSA Technopak study (Table 5.3) states that the difference between SEC A and SEC B has narrowed down and, hence, there could be a need for looking at some other segmentation criteria.

Age is very popularly used as a basis of segmentation of product categories that receive a differentiated consumer response on such basis. The KSA Technopak study (2002) states that the youth (15–24 years) in India is emerging as a core target customer for lifestyle products like personal care, music, books and magazines, entertainment parks, movies and theatre, and eating out. It also states that relative spending of youth with respect to older age groups is on the increase since 1999.

In terms of occupational status, a significant segmentation basis has been the spending habits of professionally employed women as compared to housewives. The KSA Technopak study (2002) states that the overall spending of working women is about 10% more than that of a housewife, and that the former spend much more on lifestyle products (Table 5.4).

Table: 5.3   Ratio of SEC A spending to SEC B spending for 14 product categories

Category	Ratio of SEC A Spending to SEC B Spending	Trend
Home appliances	1.74	▼
Personal care	1.68	
Savings and investment	1.65	
Books and music	1.59	
Vacation	1.59	▼
Clothing	1.41	
Eating out	1.37	▼
Accessories	1.30	▼
Footwear	1.28	▼
Home textiles	1.28	▼
Grocery	1.27	
Household durables	1.16	▼
Movies and theatre	1.14	▼
Audio/Video	1.09	▼

Source: Consumer Outlook 2002, KSA Technopak

Table: 5.4   Ratio of spending of working women to that of housewives

Category	Ratio of Spending of Working Women to that of Housewives
Eating out	1.5
Books and music	1.7
Gifts	1.7
Mobile phones	2.5
Movies	2.8

Source: Consumer Outlook 2002, KSA Technopak

Family income can also be used as an effective basis for segmentation. Large shopping malls located on the outskirts of a city like the Metropolitan Mall in Gurgaon with state-of-the-art facilities, and tenants like McDonalds, Shoppers' Stop, Reebok, Marks and Spencer, etc., which sell an extensive range of premium brands, can segment market on demographic basis focusing on family income. They can target professionals, married, aged between 30 to 45 years old with young children, and with incomes more than Rs 4,00,000 per annum. Tupperware targets middle-class, married women in their thirties, keen to make some money through marketing its products.

Family

Retailers can target bachelors or families. They may also target various family set-ups like joint families, nuclear families, DINKS (double income no kids), etc. Nirula's, a restaurant chain in Delhi, has positioned itself as a family joint providing pleasant experience and fun while Mc Donald's has positioned itself as a family joint which provides a reliable and safe dining experience. Many retail outlets and shopping malls that target families have begun to provide play areas for children so that the parents can better enjoy the shopping experience.

Social Classes and Preferences

Upper Elite Class

Those who have inherited wealth. This class is less than 0.1% and have preference in antiques, jewellery, homes, vacations, higher education, fitness, beauty treatment, traveling, etc.

Lower Upper Class

These are people who have earned wealth due to their exceptional ability, are neo-rich, and prefer to spend on cars, big home, good schooling, education for their children, etc.

Upper Middle Class

Career oriented professionals and corporate managers are the people who prefer to spend on: Education, books, cloths, furniture, home appliances, etc.

Middle Class

These are average pay white-collar class of society who prefer to spend on popular and trendy products, cars, branded goods, good homes, college education for children, entertainment, etc.

Working Class

These are average pay blue-collar class of society who prefer unbranded goods, cheap food, liquor, etc.

Lower Class

This class of people would prefer to spend on necessities from local market and local unbranded goods.

Source: www.retailyatra.com

Retail Spenders

Fifteen per cent of the purchases of the upper elite class were of foreign make mostly bought from abroad during foreign travel.

The 3 million Indian upper class families with average household income of about 4–5,00,000 is the next segment, wherein average per person spending was about Rs 5000. This segment accounted for more than 17% of the total spending on clothing and about 28% on branded clothing. Eight per cent of it was spent on gifts. The largest spender on clothing was the middle class with an average per household spend of Rs 3750. Overall it accounted for about 55% of the total clothing consumption in the country. The middle class consists of about 315 million people, which is also the largest consumer of unbranded as well as tailor-made clothing. This is the segment that is likely to switch over to branded wear in quite a few categories within next 2 years. An important observation in this segment is its high spend on kidswear. All children of

this class go to schools and buy a minimum of two sets of uniform a year.

The rest 141 million households put together spent less than what was spent by 0.4 million house-holds of the super-rich segment. The 'Age Group wise Spending' study shows how much spending was done by different age groups in the year 2001–02. Out of 1037 million people (by September 2001) it was expected that 537 million were male and 500 million were female consumers. In above 14 years age group there were 353 million male and 328 million female consumers. The table once again shows the strength of the Indian youth in their numbers as well as in consumption capacities. While in men, age group 25–34 was the strongest segment with 83 million consumers (24% of total men population) accounting for 30% of its spending on clothing, in women, age group 15–24 was the highest spender with 97 million consumers(30% of total women population) accounting for 32% of women's clothing purchases. These two, being the marriageable age groups, make substantial purchases of clothing. Thirty five years and above age groups in both men and women went for almost similar spending.

Psychographic Segmentation

When a retailer segments markets based on psychographic characteristics it divides buyers into different groups based on their lifestyle, personality, or values. Lifestyle is a distinctive mode of living. It gets reflected by activities performed (work, social, and hobbies), interests (family, job, sports and fashion), and opinion (politics, education, and social issues).

In major Indian cities, Indian Coffee House provides good quality coffee at a very modest price. It targets customers above 40 years, interested in discussing politics, intellectual issues, or business matters while sipping coffee. On the other hand, Café Coffee Day and Barista target youngsters from high income families looking for fun, with their up-market décor and attractive layout.

Values

Value refers to belief systems that go beyond behaviour or attitude. Values are stable and occupy a central position in a person's cognitive system. Values are determinants of attitudes and behaviour, and provide a stable and inner oriented understanding of consumers. For example, an individual may value ambition and honesty, which in turn determines his attitude and lifestyle.

Benetton, the apparel retailer, has targeted customers who value protection of environment. It encourages recyclable packaging and re-fill services. Benetton also contributes a fraction of its profits to environment related causes, protection of forests, afforestation programmes, etc.

Cultural Values

Retailers like Planet M encourage their staff to greet the customers and suggest support in product selection. While some customers appreciate such services others consider it an intrusion in their privacy. The latter sentiment is at times echoed by women shoppers from certain conservative families.

Value and Lifestyle Segmentation

Unlike traditional segmentation, value and lifestyle segmentation (VALS) begins with people instead of products and classifies them into different types, each characterized by a unique style of living. It then determines how marketing factors fit into their lives. This perspective provides a three-dimensional view of the target consumer.

VALS is a relatively new concept, pioneered by SRI International, a management consulting firm in California. This model was later modified in 1989 and renamed VALS-II which segmented the American consumers into 8 consumer profiles.

Some of the uses to which value and lifestyle segmentation has been put are:

- To identify whom to target and find niche markets easily
- To locate where concentrations of a retailer's group lives
- To gain insight into why the target group acts the way it does
- To improve and introduce products that are in harmony with customers' values
- To target marketing and advertising campaigns more effectively and accurately
- To position products more accurately in the marketplace

VALS Segmentation Applied to India

The Self-driven Materialists

This group represents people who are ambitious and practical. They are self-driven individuals constantly striving to achieve success in terms of materialistic possessions as well as social recognition. As consumers, they are reluctant to be extravagant and do not indulge themselves. They are not reciprocative to discounts and sales and do not indulge in excessive buying of garments and jewellery during the festive season.

A look at the demographics show that 14.8% of the population of SEC A and B lies in this group. Ninety per cent of the population is more than 25 years old. Fifty seven per cent of the group are graduates. A majority of the people are from the service class.

The Independent Explorer

This group comprises fiercely independent people. They are broadminded, loyalists, not excessively ambitious, and unorthodox in their behaviour. Not materialistic in their approach to life, they equate success with job satisfaction. Family and friends do not influence the choice of brands they purchase and celebrity endorsements too do not make an impact on them. They believe that branded products offer more benefits than unbranded products.

Twenty four per cent of the population lies in this group. A majority of the people lie in the age groups 18–24 and 25–34 and 42% of the total people are post graduates, which goes to explain the independent nature of this group. This is a group represented by young people.

The Passive Traditionalists

People who are the epitome of tradition and conservatism define this group. Indian values, as well as belief in the Indian system, are strongly embedded in these people. They prefer job security to progress in career or job satisfaction and are averse to risk. They are family oriented and most of their leisure activities are centred on the home. As a consumer, they prefer to buy brands that their families bought and are not open to purchasing any foreign brands (nationalists). Not experimentative, they generally plan their purchases and do not indulge in impulse buying.

Demographically 12% of SEC A and B lie in this group. Fifty one per cent are graduates and 41% of the people are in the age group 35–49, which explains the conservative nature of the group.

The Enthusiastic Experimenters

Individuals belonging to this group are enthusiastic in nature. These people are ardent followers of fashion, trends, and fad (in vogue). They are the consumers who are ever ready to try out new brands and products (experimentative). These are the kind of people who would shop in supermarkets or make their purchases via teleshopping/e-commerce. They are more likely to be seen at a McDonald's or a Pizza Hut rather than at a roadside pav-bhaaji stall. Impulsive people, they like to indulge themselves through excessive buying-purchases usually comprising of designer brand names. They tend to purchase heavily during festive seasons and are attracted by sales and discounts.

About 14.1% of the population belong to this category. The enthusiastic nature of the group could be attributed to the fact that 50% of the people are in the age group 18–24.

The Opinionated Realists

These people are self-centred and consider no one else but themselves. They are loners, very uncomfortable in groups. They are broadminded only when it concerns issues which don't have an immediate effect on their lives as individuals. They are not quick to accept new media/product/ideas. They do not experiment much but believe that branded products do offer better quality than unbranded ones.

Demographics reveal that this is a fairly large group of 21%, very evenly spread out in the age groups 18–49. Fifty nine per cent of the people have been educated till the higher secondary level. This group is predominantly made up of the affluent business class.

The Mature Sensibles

This group believes in traditional values and systems like joint families and are religious, though they do not follow rites and rituals regularly. They are polite, well-mannered people who prefer a formal work environment. They have a high degree of respect for institutions of authority and social decorum. Their hobbies and interests revolve around their homes and they are not very experimentative. As consumers, they are not easily influenced and as a result are not reciprocative to discounts and sales. They are very cautious and logical in their approach. They are not biased towards products that are branded, insist on value for money, and yet are quality conscious.

Representing 14.1% of the population this group is evenly spread across all age groups. Graduates make up 50% of this group.

Behavioural Segmentation

In this customers are divided into groups based on the way they respond to, use, or know a product. Products and services are purchased for a variety of reasons. A girl may buy a dress to make a fashion statement, or she may buy it as a casual wear. Retailers must determine reasons for purchase. Marketers can compile information on behavioural variables such as occasions, benefits, user status, usage rate, etc. to understand the customer-purchasing behaviour before finding a suitable basis for segmenting the market.

Reason/occasion for purchase: For example, many Indians paint their houses just before the Deepawali festival leading to higher sales of paints during Deepawali. A retailer may segment market on the basis of purchase occasions and target customers purchasing paints during Deepawali with special offers.

Frequency of purchase: Some customers purchase vegetables on a weekly basis; others purchase it every day. A retailer can segment market on frequency of purchase and target customers who desire fresh vegetables every day.

Quantity of purchase: Some customers purchase in bulk occasionally while others buy in smaller volumes more frequently. In rural India, many consumers purchase goods on daily basis in small quantities; a retailer may target such customers.

Product usage: Markets can be segmented on the basis of usage—heavy drinkers drink beer regularly on a daily basis; some others drink on weekends; and others are occasional drinkers. A retailer may target heavy drinkers.

Loyalty status: Some customers patronize a particular store; others shop for best bargains. A retailer may segment the market by loyalty status and target customers who are loyal with special offers. Most large retailers including Shoppers' Stop and LifeStyle have cards for regular shoppers on which discount and other benefits can be availed.

Buyer readiness stage: A retailer may segment the market by the buyer's readiness to purchase a product. Some customers may be innovators and early adopters of sophisticated telecom products; others may be laggards. The retailer may target the innovators.

Source of purchase: Some customers may prefer purchasing in a neighbourhood business district; others may prefer purchases in a mall during weekends. A retailer may segment the market by customers' choice of shopping locations.

Market Targeting—Choosing the Segments to Focus

Once a retailer has segmented the market, he has to identify the segments for focussing the marketing effort. While choosing target segments, a retailer has to measure the attractiveness of the segment and its capacity to serve the segment. In evaluating segment attractiveness, a retailer has to estimate the size of the segment, its purchasing power, its growth rate, presence of competition, etc. In this context, marketers may opt for an untapped segment or choose to operate in a segment where there are already existing players. Such a decision would depend on the respective profitability of each segment besides factors such as the retailer's capacity to serve the segment and the degree of accord between the requirement of the segment and retailer's product offerings and marketing mix. Crossroads in Mumbai identified its target clientele as the upper middle-class customers, projecting daily walk-ins of about 10,000 people. To serve the target customers visiting the mall a floor was devoted to each of the four shopping categories—women, kids, men, and home furnishings. Anchor stores—McDonald's and Pantaloon—were placed in front inside the mall.

It is important to identify not just the target customers but also the kind of customers who are likely to visit the store, who are likely to make purchases, and those who are likely to continue as repeat customers (Fig. 5.4). Incidently, all the visitors to the store may not be members of the identified target market. Many retailers in India are missing the big picture and concentrating their efforts primarily on customers who make purchases. Retailbiz (Oct. 9, 2003) reports that in India only about 15–20% of the so-called target customers walks into the store and as much as 80–90% do not even enter the store—a clear case of major error in customer identification. Amongst those who go to the store, only one-third end up buying, and two-thirds go to the shop next door—a case of poor merchandise and service. Thus, a target customer base of 100 is reduced to a buyer base of 5. Out of these 5 buyers, only 2–3 are repeat customers.

Many retailers in India, instead of looking at a potential of 100 customers, are looking at maximizing their share among the five customers.

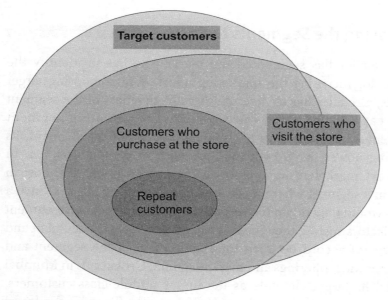

Fig. 5.4 Levels of customer identification

KSA Technopak conducted a research to identify the gain and effort at each stage and found that the gain–effort ratio reduces exponentially from step I (identification of target customers) to step IV (ensuring repeat purchase). Hence, efforts are minimal and usually one-time in step I (identification of target customers) and II (ensuring customers visit the store) and gains are much higher. In step III (ensuring customers make a purchase) and IV (ensuring repeat purchase), it takes a lot of effort, almost on an ongoing basis, and gains are disproportionately low. Therefore, Indian retailers must pay increasing attention to more precise identification of the target customer base (step I). Behavioural segmentation, discussed earlier, is quite useful in this context.

A retailer should ensure that the customers patronizing the store should mix well. Retailers focusing on elite upper class segments should not simultaneously try to attract lower class segments. Similarly, the retailer targeting trendy youngsters should not simultaneously target the traditional shoppers. This can often result in inconvenience to both groups of customers.

The Crossroads Experience

Crossroads opened in Mumbai in 1999. Initially, it attracted 30,000–40,000 people during week days and 100,000 customers during weekends. Most of the visitors were browsers and not serious customers. The high numbers put enormous pressure on mall's infrastructure and disconcerted the posh clientele targeted by Crossroads. The mall management restricted entry by requiring visitors to produce a credit card, visiting card, cell phone, etc., or pay a entry fee of Rs 60 to be refunded against purchases. The traffic fell drastically to only 6000 to 8000 per day. Premium outlets like the jewellery shop and hi-fi equipment vendors were elated with the reduction in traffic. The bookshop and the music store, which depend on large traffic, were however badly hurt. Fountainhead, the bookshop, moved out in 2001. The lesson to be learned is that a mall management should target tenants whose clientele comes from the same target segments.

Profitability of Segments in Branded Apparel Market in India

Market segments such as men's ready-to-wear and sports clothing have begun to evolve in recent years and look potentially profitable. Men's clothing accounts for 70% of all branded apparel sales (which is pegged at Rs 4,000 crores), compared to 22% of children's wear, and 8% of women's wear. This trend is expected to continue, with men's branded apparel slated to grow by 30% a year, against 10% for both women's and children's clothing.

Mr. B. S. Nagesh, Chief Executive Officer, Shoppers' Stop, feels that markets for retail branded women's wear have still a long way to go. Branded apparel forms at best 3% of the women's clothing market and around 13% of their apparel market. Western clothes for women, easier to standardize, are restricted to students in urban markets and a minority of women executives. It is estimated to be less than 10% of women's apparel market, implying a market size of Rs 60 crores at best. The kids' wear market (organized and unorganized) is estimated at Rs 6,000 crores. The branded players are targeting 10-12% of this market, leaving the balance to the unorganized market and small-scale regional/local labels.

Source: Mckinsey 2000,Report on India's Retail Sector, The Hindu, November 9.

Customer Profile

After deciding on target segments, a retailer must develop detailed profiles of customers in the identified target segments. Market research may be necessary to develop customer profiles. The profiles help the retailer in understanding the needs of the target segments and its shopping behaviour. Such an understanding can help a retailer in the development of effective marketing strategies and programme.

The customer profile may contain the following information.

Customer Demographics

Data about the target segment may be collected on demographic characteristics such as age, sex, income levels, educational background, and professional background.

Family Decision Making

When families are the target customers, the retailer needs to understand the decision-making processes in the family. In such situations, different family members can play different roles as initiators, influencers, deciders, buyers, consumers, and evaluators. For example, while purchasing a TV set for use by the entire household, the wife may have acted as the initiator by proposing the idea, while the elder son, who may be an engineer may have evaluated the different options available, the daughter may have influenced the choice of brand, the husband may have acted as the final decision maker, and the selection of retailer and the act of buying may have been completed by the younger son. In many cases, one person may play all the six roles. A retailer should have an understanding of the decision-making processes and buying roles among the target family segments.

Psychographics

The retailer has to profile its consumers' lifestyles and values. The various activities pursued by target segments such as sports, adventure, worship, etc., as well as their interests, hobbies, opinions, and values may be profiled to get a better understanding of the target segment. For example, the customers of Café Coffee Day are youngsters who like to move around in groups, live a fast active life, and entertain friends. The typical customer at Westside may be a sophisticated middle-class lady who values her independence, shops for best products, and is looking for good value for her money, and who may not believe in taking large credits/loans.

It entirely depends on the retailers or marketers to decide which segmentation criteria will be most helpful in segmenting the market. They can consider the following table to explore the options.

Geographic	_____Yes	_____No
Demographic	_____Yes	_____No
Psychographic	_____Yes	_____No
Behaviourist	_____Yes	_____No

Purchasing Behaviour of the Target Population

The retailer should also develop a detailed understanding of the purchasing behaviour of the selected target segment. It should compile information regarding purchase motivation, the cultural influences on purchasing behaviour of the target segment, etc. Information may be compiled about the following.

Purchase Motivation

Research has found that consumers' behaviour is directed towards the satisfaction of various needs and desires. The decision to buy or not to buy often comes from what one anticipates as the consequences of one's decision. Consumers tend to choose the alternative with the highest perceived net rewards. The retailer should understand the purchase motivation of the target segment. For example, a young man may buy a fashionable brand of shirt from Shoppers' Stop to announce

Case Study Example: McDonald's

Positive Consequences	Negative Consequences
• Children indulgence.	• Not an essential food item
• Consistent and effective service.	• Limited offerings

to his colleagues and friends that he has come of age or has been successful at his work. He may also visit a Barista outlet to make a fashion statement.

Purchasing Process

In India, many people buy grocery items from shops located near their house on a rotating credit facility. This is also the case with some non-food purchases. For high involvement purchases such as jewellery and consumer durables, many consumers often depend on retailers with whom their family may be dealing for many generations. Consumers, especially in semi-urban areas, are not very comfortable with plastic money and do not prefer bank credit. However, credit facilities are very important for increasing sales of consumer durables. An innovative approach very common among middle-class families in India is financing of durables purchase through a kitty. Kitty has become quite common in India among middle-class families. A number of ladies form a kitty club where a fixed amount is contributed to the kitty every month by every member. There is a draw of lots every month, when a member gets her entire contribution during the year at one go by turns. The money thus obtained is often used for purchasing household durables. Retailers often facilitate organization of such kitty clubs to facilitate sale of durables and help the buyers get trade discounts for purchases from the concerned companies.

Source of Purchase

With the emergence of multiple retail formats, retailers are not only concerned about the reasons behind customers patronizing the particular store but also looking for the decision variables which influence customers' choice of particular retail formats for meeting specific requirement. Customers' choice of shopping locations depends on time utility and place utility. Time utility refers to availability of products and services at convenient hours or in case of urgent requirements. Place utility refers to the benefits of shopping at particular shopping locations due to availability of a wide range of products, low prices, shopping ambience, or entertainment options. Time utility and place utility are further elaborated below

Time Utility The choice of format is influenced by time utility—consumers buy from outlets which are accessible when they need to purchase. In rural India, consumers prefer to purchase from shops within the village when they need a limited range of frequently used products urgently. They prefer to visit feeder centres or periodic markets in nearby towns for planned purchases on a periodic basis. In cities, people purchase daily consumer items (bread, milk etc.) from nearby stores, whereas they prefer to visit well-known markets for purchase of a major part of clothes and durables. For examples, people from a major part of north India shop for clothes from Karol Bagh and Chandni Chowk in Delhi, especially for special occasions (marriages, festivals, etc.).

Place Utility Customers prefer outlets which sell products they seek at the place they want to buy. Customers evaluate each shopping centre on the functional utility it provides in terms of product variety, price range, parking, transportation and other facilities, bargaining possibilities, quality, entertainment options, services provided, and scope for returns. They select shopping centers which provide a desired set of utilities. An understanding of the utility desired by the target segment can help a retailer choose an appropriate location. Similarly, knowledge about the preferences of the target customers provide inputs to developers of shopping centres on appropriate tenant mix, need for parking facilities, recreational facilities and rest rooms, organizing events, managing common area, cleanliness, etc. To understand the concept of place utility we can consider why periodic markets, often called haats, are popular in rural India. Customers in villages prefer to visit periodic markets in nearby towns or villages for purchasing due to various economic and non-economic benefits, such as product variety and choice, low prices, bargaining options, discounts, etc., which are not common in the shops located within the villages. The attractiveness of these periodic markets, or the place utility of such periodic markets, has also increased since they serve as a place for socialization and entertainment centres where nautanki, dances, and magic shows are performed.

Consumer demands on place and time utility will vary according to the product they wish to purchase. For convenience products used on daily basis like soaps, detergents, food products, and medicines, time utility is important. Place utility is more important when buying shopping products like clothes, furniture, utensils, etc.

Survey of Buyers' Intentions

The retailer can develop an effective merchandising plan and other elements of the marketing mix if it has detailed information on requirements of its target segment regarding choice of products, price they are willing to pay, type of packaging they prefer, the promotional mediums to which they are exposed, type of promotional campaigns that will influence them, their purchasing behaviour, etc. Market research should also provide insights into competitors serving the segment, the strengths and weaknesses of competitor's merchandising mix, their marketing strategies and plans, etc. Retailers can collect information about this segment on

- Frequency of customer visit to store
- Weekday/weekend shopping patterns
- Store selection criteria: how they go about selecting the store
- Spending per visit: how much the customer spends on an average during each visit
- Planned vs unplanned shopping: items purchased in a planned way and impulse purchases
- Store loyalty: do they patronize a few stores or shop around for bargains

Retailers should also identify retail attributes and their importance to the customers, and rank these on a scale of high, medium, low, or not at all as shown in Table 5.5.

Table: 5.5 Retail attributes and their importance to customers

Retail attributes	Very high	High	Medium	Low	Not at all
Price					
Quality					
Brand					
Variety of merchandise					
Salespersons					
Special offers					
Promotional offers					
Packaging					
Location					
Guarantees/adjustments					
Store décor					
Payment terms					
Styles					
Models					
Information					
Infrastructure facilities					
Speed					
Ambiance					

Such a research will help the retail organization understand whether its target segment is price sensitive, it is looking for good quality, or location of store is most important. It will help identify primary segments that offer the most promising opportunities in accordance with the retailer's strengths and situational constraints. It will also help them to develop strategies and execute programmes tailored to the unique needs of the targeted segments and allocate its marketing resources in the most effective and efficient manner.

Retailers adopting market segmentation can enjoy a variety of benefits. The customer and competitor analyses of the segmentation approach that is required allows the retailer to become more attuned to the behaviour of both. The result can be a better understanding of customers' needs and wants, allowing greater responsiveness in terms of the retail marketing mix. The enhanced appreciation of the competitive situation also allows the business unit to better understand the appropriate segments to target and the nature of competitive advantage to seek.

Market Segmentation in India

The Indian consumer market with its plethora of demographic, psychological, and other strategic variables presents an ideal arena for segmentation to be an attractive, viable, and a potentially profitable strategy. Today, most marketers in India use segmentation models based on demographics, geo-demographics, SEC data, and benefits and usage.

McDonald's focuses on middle and upper-class families in the Indian market. To attract consumers from lower middle class, it introduced seven rupee offerings (ice creams) to increase footfalls, with the hope of converting the customer so attracted into regular customers for other standard offerings. McDonald's also introduced the vegetarian products to target the large population of vegetarians in India who avoid non-vegetarian diet on account of religious and health beliefs.

McDonald's Socio-Cultural Segmentation

McDonald's acknowledged the voice of the consumer in India. The Indian consumer is 'Indianizing' McDonald's (as opposed to McDonald's 'Americanizing' India), and if this is indeed happening, the effects are already starting to be seen. The veggie burger (McVeggie) developed for the Indian market has been introduced in New York City. Not only have Indian consumers altered the product offerings to fit in with their own values, beliefs, traditions, and culture, they have also gone beyond this to influence the product offerings of the multinational back in the other parts of the world.

Dhabas on Indian Highways

The dhabas (eating joints) all along the Indian highways segment their market in a different way. Some focus on serving exclusively to the truck, bus, and taxi drivers with minimum facilities for boarding and lodging and have simple décor. They are positioned on low price, healthy and rich traditional food, and minimum comforts. Other dhabas/motels serve the needs of passengers travelling by road transport. These are well-managed outlets high on basic services such as rest rooms, cleanliness, and interior décor, and along with traditional food they serve Chinese and Western food. These outlets are available at various price points.

Consumers travelling by their own four wheelers usually visit the up-market eating joints whereas people traveling on public transportation prefer average-priced eating joints. Thus, the dhabas segment their market on the basis of profession, income level, mode of transportation used, and traffic count.

Haveli Dhaba

Haveli Dhaba on the Ludhiana–Jalandhar highway provides travellers a place to eat and relax in a homely atmosphere. It has a seating arrangement on the floor using mattresses and muddas (Indian traditional variant of chair without back), uses utensils of steel, serves Punjabi food, and is very economically priced. Haveli provides Punjabi food in a Punjabi ambience. It targets customer segments used to or interested in Punjabi cuisine.

Similarly, Chokhi Dani in Jaipur and Vaishala in Ahmedabad provide local ethnic cuisine in an ethnic manner.

Nescafe launched its own retail outlets, offering various variants of coffee in the north Indian market to develop the taste of the consumers who are habitual tea consumers. By providing coffee at a low price in an attractive setting it attempted to convert them into consumers of coffee and thus, increase the size of its market. Nescafe targeted the segment not interested in or capable of paying high prices at Barista or Café Coffee Day outlets.

Malls like City Center and Metropolitan Mall in Gurgaon have introduced cineplexes to attract customer segments, which view shopping as an entertainment these customers seek to combine shopping with entertainment.

In the year 2002, DCM Benetton India repositioned itself from a casual-wear brand to a wardrobe option, and redesigned stores as per its international format. In 2003, it attempted to target a niche audience through its concept stores. Benetton recently launched its pilot 'Baby-on-Board' store, which targets mothers-to-be and kids, as well as the 'Accessories' and 'Adults-Only' store in Gurgaon. The Baby-on-Board store, which is targeted at young urban upwardly mobile parents, has a product line which includes infant and maternity wear, educational toys, strollers, car seats, fashion wear for moms-to-be, newborns, babies and kids up to 12 years of age. The Accessories store, on the other hand, sells luggage, bags, sunglasses, and vanity cases, and the Adults-Only store showcases Benetton's apparel collection for men and women.

The launch of the concept stores did raise questions on feasibility, considering the nascent stage of the retail industry in India. The company felt that such a strategy would enable it to target a consumer segment that is well-travelled and more aware of international fashion trends. It would also enable the company to offer a more complete product line to different target segments. For this purpose, the company intends to create strategic business units for each line—mothers-to-be and kids, adults, and accessories.

This strategy of concept stores makes sense when there is an opportunity to grow certain segments of the assortment. In some cases, a part of the range may be mature enough to be spun off as a separate brand, with its own speciality format. In the current scenario in India, where so many malls are emerging in the metros and other cities, such a retail segmentation strategy may allow United Colors of Benetton the flexibility to manage its store portfolio more effectively with the right-sized formats in these malls, rather than be constrained by a single large footprint format.

Many retailers, internationally, have limited-line stores in addition to full-line stores. Baby Gap and Gap Kids from Gap is one example of an apparel brand operating multiple formats for different segments. Marks and Spencer also operates food-only stores in the UK in addition to its full-line stores which have both food and non-food lines. This allows it to reach consumers with the food offer, where perhaps the opportunity for the full-line stores is limited. However, in India, there is a reverse trend of brands moving out of their concept stores to large formats. Madura Garments' brands Van Heusen, Louis Philippe, and Allen Solly, which have had their concept stores for some time, are now coming together under the Planet Fashion umbrella. Essentially, segmentation strategies are driven by assessment of market potential. Hence, Benetton's Baby-on-Board store which is targeted at mothers-to-be and kids is likely to draw footfalls as Indian parents in metros have experienced an increase in their disposable incomes. Besides, there is a rise in philocentric tendencies in Indian families to facilitate a higher spend on specialized products for their children. However, it would be interesting to see whether an exclusive accessories store would make much business sense for the company.

Retail Segmentation Strategy of Benetton in India

An exclusive mother-and-child store equipped with an array of products, an outlet for accessories, and an adults-only store—retail segmentation is the new thrust of DCM Benetton India. After undergoing a retail makeover just over a year ago, when it redesigned stores as per its international format and also repositioned the brand from a casual-wear brand to a wardrobe option, the company is now looking at targeting a niche audience through its concept stores. It now has 85 exclusive outlets across the country.

Benetton recently launched its pilot 'Baby-on-Board' store, which targets mothers-to-be and kids, as well as the 'Accessories' and 'Adults-Only' store in Gurgaon. The Baby-on-Board store, which is targeted at young urban upwardly mobile parents, has a product line which includes infant and maternity wear, educational toys, strollers, car seats, fashion for moms-to-be, newborns, babies and kids up to 12 years of age. The Accessories store, on the other hand, sells luggage, bags, sunglasses and vanity cases, while the Adults-Only store showcases Benetton's apparel collection for men and women.

The company feels that the Indian consumer is well travelled and more aware of international fashion trends. Therefore, there is a need for more specialized products and that the market is ripe for this venture.

Vivek Bharatram, Chairman and Managing Director, DCM Benetton India Ltd feels, 'The idea is to capitalize on our new category launches by opting for a distribution model that would enable us to make available a complete product line and experience for different target segments. This in turn would help us in driving demand and the brand's growth. This also fits in with our plans to bring the international UCB experience to India.'

Bharatram says, this strategy of having concept stores along with its existing chain, Colors of Benetton stores, falls in line with its international retail format. 'Internationally, Benetton follows formats that emphasize a complete retail experience through its mega stores, offering a complete fashion and lifestyle range along with the concept stores that have a unique product line.'

Arvind Singhal, Chairman, KSA Technopak, says that Benetton's strategy of retail segmentation is fundamentally sound, as there is enough opportunity in the market to segregate.

While the pilot stores in Gurgaon are company-owned stores, Benetton plans to stick to its original franchisee model for other concept stores. Since the concept stores in Gurgaon have received a good response and the company is planning to set up similar stores in other metros and a few mini-metros such as Bangalore, Hyderabad, Pune, and Chandigarh. A lot depends on the company finding the right partners who are comfortable with its retail format. For instance, Benetton has certain retail policies—for example, they do not do consignment sales. They produce to order based on seasonal lines and theme, which the franchisee has to be comfortable with.

The company has invested Rs 3 crore in the accessories store and the mother-and-kid store. The Benetton accessories and specialized baby products would only be restricted to the concept stores. Since the products at the concept stores are targeted at a niche segment, the company does not plan to retail these products at multi-brand outlets (MBO). In fact, Benetton is available in MBOs only in smaller towns where it is impractical to sustain an exclusive store format.

For marketing the concept stores, the company will start with a mood-oriented campaign in print and then look at promoting the stores. The company feels that the stores in mega malls and high streets are advertisements in themselves, largely due to the overall ambience and the depth of the product offering.

The company expects that the new retail strategy would add about 5 to 10% to the company's bottomline in 2003. They grew at 17.5% in 2002–03. The sales for the year were Rs 80 crore.

The company claims that the brand's repositioning last year from a casual-wear brand to an international wardrobe option has worked well for the company. This is reflected in the fact that even during a recessionary period they managed to grow at a rate of 17.5%, which is well above the industry standard of 5–10% in the same period.

Along with expanding its concept store presence in Delhi and other major markets, Benetton India will also look at reorienting its corporate framework to ensure that each segment is fully optimized. They intend to create strategic business units for each line—mothers-to-be and kids, adults, and accessories.

As Bharatram says, 'The retail segmentation is a decision to bring the international shopping experience to India. This strategy will help us in re-emphasizing our worldwide positioning and to envision Benetton as a wardrobe brand that does extensive fashion options and represents a special combination of excellent styling and quality.'

Source: Ajita Shashidhar 2003, 'The Benetton Makeover', *Business Line*, August 07.

The growth and development of multiplex theatres in India represent an interesting experience in segmentation. Though patterned along the 'shopping mall' model of the multiplex as developed and prevalent in the West, and sustained by the retail boom unleashed by the economic liberalization policy of 1991, the Indian multiplex site sports all the features of an up-market turf. Most multiplexes in India offer a curious mix of parallel, regional, and art cinema along with both domestic and foreign mainstream cinema. This distinguishes them from the multiplexes in the West. The latter operate in more developed markets characterized by deeply entrenched segmentation which extends into film exhibition as well. Multiplexes in the West largely focus on the 'blockbuster' films. Similarly, various single-screen cinemas in India identify themselves with particular types of films, say the Hindi '*masala*' and blockbuster, the English, or the porn movie. On the other hand, the multiplexes in India have capitalized on an inclusive tendency to motivate and assemble diverse audiences in terms of their movie preferences. However, they have largely segmented in terms of income and lifestyle categories. Multiplexes in India have remained an urban, largely middle and upper middle-class leisure pursuit, with its highly priced tickets excluding the masses crowded in the lower regions of the income graph. Spatially too, these multiplexes can mostly be spotted in affluent neighbourhoods, within the easy reach and concentration of young audiences. It is quite possible that, in the future, multiplexes may enhance segmentation and result in branded theatres exhibiting particular fare, say the art, mainstream, foreign films, or maybe even documentaries.

Recently, segmentation has also caught the fancy of cyber café owners in India. This is primarily to take advantage of the 150% growth projected for the sector. Many big, branded players such as HCL Comnet, Mantra Online, Satyam Infoway, etc. have set up chains of branded Internet parlours or cyber cafes. A key element of their strategy is to find a niche and clearly define their audiences and services. A study by KSA Technopak states that the players in India have started segmenting the cyber cafes primarily into two categories: one for utility-oriented customers—the middle and junior level business executives—and the other the experiential kind which will offer allied services for the non-business users . While Mantra Online is planning to segment its cafes into business and residential categories, a Delhi-based player Netxss is planning to focus on Net-banking. On the other hand, Delhi State Industrial Development Corporation Ltd (DSIDC) is specializing in facilitating e-governance in Delhi through its 16-cyber cafes in the city. It is intended to be used by the customers to pay their electricity and water bills online.

An extremely effective segmentation and targeting experience in India has occurred in case of the petrol retail sector. The petrol retail experience, until recently, was uninviting, with the station being nothing more than a place to tank up, and cash being the preferred payment mode. In recent times, however, the outlets have seen a complete facelift, with new multi-fuel dispensers, better trained attendants, and service elements. The product offering has widened to include blended fuels, branded fuels, high-octane fuels, lubes, groceries and more. The outlet itself is expanding to include grocery stores, cafes, bank ATMs, internet kiosks, etc., giving the customer more reasons to spend time and money at a location that offers more than just fuel. Credit cards, debit cards, and loyalty cards are also widely accepted. These changes gave the customer reasons to build preference among the three companies (IOCL, BPCL, and HPCL) and their brands. In this context, BPCL launched PetroBonus, its customer loyalty programme, in September 1999. This enabled data capture of the profile and transactions of about 1.2 million card holders across 43 cities by 2003. Using data mining on the database thus generated, BPCL started segmenting members by activity level and created targeted communication and offers to activate members, significantly driving up revenues within the existing member base. Data analysis also revealed a segment of members with abnormally high usage. It turned out that this segment was that of fleet owners who were giving PetroBonus cards to their truck drivers for fuelling up. After understanding the distinct needs of fleet owners, BPCL designed and launched the Smart Fleet programme in early 2001. Similarly, most players in the retail petrol sector are launching co-branded cards to move towards more niche segments that target lifestyle or special interest groups.

This amply demonstrates the realization among a few recently deregulated sectors of the Indian economy that profitable marketing strategy can evolve from effective segmentation achieved through extensive research.

An Images India and KSA Technopak study claims that most retailers of branded apparels in India have concentrated on the male segment, while a huge untapped opportunity exists in the women's and children's segments (Table 5.6).

Table: 5.6   Estimated market size for certain categories of branded apparels for women and children

Product categories for women and children	Estimated market size for branded apparels (Rs Billion)
Salwar Kameez	10
Lingerie	10
Maternity wear	10
Petticoats	16
Infant clothing	10
School uniform	6
Total potential	62

Source: KSA and imagesfashion.com

As seen from the examples above, in most product categories, the retail sector in India has been quite alive towards utilizing the opportunities offered by various market segments. However, with the growth of organized retailing, focus on more micro-segments may be expected.

Summary

The mass marketing approach, where the retailer targets the entire population in his trading area with a uniform marketing mix is becoming infeasible with the increase in competition. Under market segmentation approach the retailer divides the market into homogeneous groups, selects target segments to focus, and develops a customized marketing mix as per the requirements of the targeted segments.

Market segmentation helps the retailer in understanding customer requirements and in developing an appropriate marketing mix. It helps the retailer in merchandising decision—deciding what to stock and in what quantities. Understanding requirements of target segments also helps in developing an effective promotional programme. An understanding of target market segments can also help a retailer in locating its stores where there is concentration of customers belonging to target segments.

Market segmentation is successful if the segments selected are homogeneous within, and heterogeneous between, which means that the customers within a segment should have uniform requirements, but these should differ from requirements of customers in other segments. The size of the segments should be measurable and substantial so that the retailer can target them profitably. The segments should be actionable, which means the retailer should be able to identify customers in each segment so as to reach out to them.

Markets can be segmented on geographic, demographic, psychographic, or behavioural variables. Under geographic basis it can be divided by cities, states, regions, etc. Segmentation on demographic variables would mean dividing the market by age, income, gender, occupation, social levels, etc. Markets can also be divided by psychographic variables based on customer lifestyles. Finally, the markets can be divided on behavioural variables like product usage, occasion of purchase, benefit sought, and retailer loyalty, etc.

After segmenting the market, the retailer has to identify target segments to focus its marketing efforts. This would require measuring the potential of each segment and its accord with retailers' product offerings. Next, the retailer has to develop its positioning with the target segment, which means the way it should be perceived by the target segment. The retailer has to develop detailed profiles of customer requirement for each of the target segments to develop sound marketing strategies. It should collect information on customers' buying behaviour, shopping patterns, loyalty to the retailer, quality and service desired, media choice, etc. Such detailed information about its target segments will help the retailer develop an effective marketing strategy.

The retailers in India have tried to understand the specific requirements of the Indian customers, which can be quite distinct, and develop innovative strategies to satisfy these needs.

Key Terms

1. **AIOs:** Activities, interests, and opinions the psychographic variables used in market segmentation.

2. **Attitudes:** Positive, neutral, or negative feelings an individual has about the economy, politics, offerings, institutions, etc.

3. **Consumer behaviour:** Involves the process by which persons determine whether, what, where, how, from whom, and how often to purchase goods and services.

4. **Consumer satisfaction or dissatisfaction:** The overall attitude a person has about a offering that has been purchased.

5. **Culture:** Distinctive heritage shared by a group of people. It passes on beliefs, norms, and customs.

6. **Custom:** A norm that is derived from a traditional way of doing things.

7. **Demographics:** Objective, quantifiable, easily identifiable, and measurable population data.

8. **LifeStyles:** Ways that individual consumer and families live and spend time and money.

9. **Motives:** Reasons for consumer behaviour.

10. **Personality:** A person's unique psychological makeup, which consistently influences

the way the person responds to his or her environment.

11. **Psychographics:** It focuses on how physical environment is integrated into the consumer's subjective experience.

12. **Reference group:** Influence of people's thoughts and behaviour. They may be friends, family members, personalities, etc.

13. **Target market:** Customer group that a retailer seeks to attract and satisfy.

Concept Review Questions

1. What is market segmentation? Why is segmentation becoming increasingly important?

2. Which criterion must be satisfied for a segmentation approach to be effective?

3. What are the benefits of market segmentation for a retail chain like Barista?

4. Which geographic and demographic variables should a hyper-market like Giant consider while segmenting its markets?

5. Which psychographic and behavioural variables must a large music store like Planet M or Music World consider while segmenting markets?

6. What factors must a retailer consider while identifying and selecting target segments?

7. How does a detailed market profile of target segments help a retailer in developing appropriate marketing strategies?

Project Work Assignments

1. List all possible dimensions along which the market can be segmented by :

   (a) a readymade garment store and

   (b) a tailoring shop.

2. Profile the customers who are likely to visit traditional eating joints and up-market branded eating joints (Pizza Hut, McDonald's, etc.)

3. A multinational company which plans to sell branded consumer durables in the Indian market through company-owned outlets has to develop a segmentation strategy. How should the company segment the market? Identify segments to focus on.

4. Develop a segmentation plan for a large department store planning to sell lifestyle products with outlets in central markets of major metros.

Case Study

The meeting at the five star deluxe hotel in Delhi has stretched into a late Saturday evening. The hostess arrives at the table with drinks. Ganesh reaches out to fill his glass and looks out of the window to see the beautiful skyline of the great metropolis. Seated around a conference table are Ganesh and three other promoters of a new mall, coming up at Gurgaon, discussing intensely about their target customers.

Ganesh Sood: There are three malls already in Gurgaon and five more malls are coming up besides our mall all within a radius of 3 kms.

Sudarshan: Do you think that this area can support 8 to 10 malls. I think there will be very intense competition when all these malls come up.

Ganesh Sood: The three malls are doing excellent business. They have reversed the flow of traffic. Earlier, residents of Gurgaon used to go to Delhi for their weekly shopping. Now people from nearby colonies in south and west Delhi are coming to Gurgaon for shopping and recreation. The air-conditioned facilities, attractive ambience, and easy parking facilities have made these malls very popular. These malls provide a one-stop shopping and entertainment option. But I agree that when the five new malls come up there will be intense competition for the same group of customers.

Ranjan Ghosh: The two malls DLF City Centre and Metropolitan Mall are right opposite on Mehrauli–Gurgaon road. They have up-market stores and attract upper middle-class and upper-class customers. On weekends about 10,000 people visit these malls. About 75 to 80% of them are from colonies in south and west Delhi stretching up to a distance of 20 to 25 kms. The third mall Sahara Mall is about a kilometre. away. The anchor store here is the large discount hypermarket–Big Bazaar. Sahara Mall attracts middle-and even lower middle-class customers. While Metropolitan Mall and City Centre have a large mix of foreign stores and franchisee chains as tenants, Sahara mall has mostly Indian tenants.

Ganesh: I read that City Centre and Metropolitan Malls attract a relatively higher percentage of college crowd and young bachelors while the Sahara mall attracts a greater percentage of families and married female customers.

Prakash Jain: That is because in Metropolitan Mall and City Centre there are many pubs where youngsters can relax; then there are eateries like Barista, Pizza Hut, McDonald, Subway, etc. There are multiplex screens where these youngsters enjoy watching the movies. It is really an ideal setting for youngsters and young couples. Sahara Mall attracts families and female shoppers looking for bargains and pleasant shopping experience while looking for a wide range of goods.

Ranjan Ghosh: Another interesting thing is the relatively greater focus of DLF City Centre on female segment and Metropolitan Mall on men's segment. DLF City Centre has outlets catering to women's fashion like 'W', Madame, and Karar, all focusing on women-dressing, and Kelly shoes also focusing on women segment. Metropolitan Mall has relatively focused more on men segment with Reebok, Shoppers' Stop, etc.

Sudarshan: DLF City Centre has also focused on outlets popular in Delhi and national capital region like Mehrasons, Bombay Selections, Meena Bazaar, etc., while Metropolitan Mall has attracted relatively more national and multinational retail chains like Marks & Spencer, Reebok, Lacoste, etc. The eating joints in Metropolitan Mall like McDonald's, Pizza Hut, and Subway are also multinationals.

Sudarshan: We have to carve out a distinct positioning and become a preferred destination for some segment of population if we are to attract traffic when all the 8 malls are functioning in our vicinity.

Ranjan Ghosh: I agree with Sudarshan; we should create a distinct positioning to be able to attract a particular segment of population. I think we have to identify an innovative dimension on which to segment the market.

Ganesh: But a large mall like ours planned on a 150,000 sq. ft area cannot confine itself to a narrow segment. We need to have a mass market appeal. A mall like ours should get daily walk-ins of about 8 to 10 thousand people.

Sudarshan: I agree that our segment should not be narrowly defined. Yet, we should ensure that a large chunk of our customers should patronize the mall and visit it frequently. With the large choice available in the vicinity, this can only happen if the customer finds something unique about our offer.

Prakash Jain: We should create a distinct positioning also to attract the right mix of retail tenants to our mall. Look at the experience of Crossroads in Mumbai. When the mall opened in 1999 it attracted footfalls of 40,000 on week days and about a lakh on weekends. Most visitors were curious onlookers and conversions (ratio of customers who purchase) were low.

Now the mall attracts only 5,000 to 6,000 customers a week but the conversions are much higher.

Sudarshan: I recollect how huge crowds came to Cross Roads mall when it opened; it had become a major sight seeing venue for local people not having experience of malls earlier. The huge crowds had become unmanageable and the management had to introduce a high entry fee to control the rush. After the introduction of entry fee the footfalls fell sharply.

Ganesh: I hear that with the fall in foot falls in Cross Roads the book store Fountainhead found its operations unviable and shifted out in 2001. The music store Groove also found the going tough. Books are low margin items and are mostly impulse purchases. They need greater traffic flow.

Prakash Jain: But premium outlets like the jewellery shop and hi-fi equipment vendors were elated when the traffic to the mall dropped. Now they had fewer but more serious customers. While the conversion ratio was very low in 1999 when most visitors were only window shoppers, it rose significantly in 2001 when traffic became thin. Such outlets attract serious customers and are profitable only if they offer an ambience where customers can shop at leisure and get excellent services.

Sudarshan: We should hence ensure that customers of a particular interest and lifestyle visit our mall, and that he or she is delighted by the services and experience we offer and becomes a regular visitor to the mall.

Ranjan Ghosh: We should also look at major retail tenants who would like to open their outlets in our mall and the positioning they enjoy before taking a final decision.

Praksh Jain: Yes, but we must decide on some innovative ways of segmenting the market and identifying the target segments. Some of the retailers in the West have segmented their markets on demographic or geographic basis, while others have segmented on the basis of psychographics or individual lifestyle, or on behavioural dimensions.

Ganesh: I think that the segments we finally decide to target must represent a significantly large part of the population. We should also ensure that we are able to communicate our offerings to these segments.

The meeting is over but the four promoters are still worried about the segmentation approach and positioning strategy for their upcoming mall as they drive back to their respective residences. Ganesh drives past the malls in Gurgaon on his way back and thinks about his meeting with the press tomorrow as he passes. Can he use the meeting to promote the new mall and its positioning?

---

1. Should the promoters of the planned new mall go for market segmentation or practice mass marketing? If they decide to segment the market how should they go about segmenting the market and identifying the target segments?

2. How should the promoters of the planned mall identify the right mix of retail outlets? How can they attract such outlets to the mall?

3. How can the promoters communicate the positioning of the mall to its target audience?

References

1. Belk, R.W. 1975, 'Situational Variables and Consumer Behavior', *Journal of Consumer Research*, 2, December, 157–164.

2. Claycampo, H.J. and Massy, W.F. 1968, 'A Theory of Market Segmentation', *Journal of Marketing Research*, 5, November, pp. 388–394.

3. Beane, T.P. and Ennis, D.M. 1987, 'Marketing Segmentation: A Review', *European Journal of Marketing*, 21, No. 5, pp. 20–42.

4. www.tribuneindia.com 2002, ' "Haveli", a concept *dhaba* in Jalandhar, which from its menu to the music, decor and ambience reminds of yesteryear's Punjab, and awakens rich memories', July12.

5. *India Today* 2003, 'Household Survey: Census 2001', July 28, pp. 34–42.

6. Chattopadhay, R. 2001, 'The Mall as the Playing Field', *Business Standard, The Strategist*, Tuesday, Febuary 6, p. 3.

7. Kotler, P. 1997, *Marketing Management: Analysis, Planning, Implementation, and Control*, Prentice-Hall Inc., New Jersey, USA

6 RETAIL LOCATION STRATEGY

Learning Objectives

- To demonstrate the importance of store location for a retailer

- To outline the process of choosing a store location and to discuss the various criteria for evaluating general retail locations and the specific sites within them

- To examine the type of store locations available to a retailer: isolated store, unplanned business district, and planned shopping centre

- To show how the types of goods sold influence location decision of a retailer

- To discuss the concept of trading area and techniques to analyse its potential

- To discuss the different theories which explain the historical patterns of retail location

Introduction

Location is the most important ingredient for any business that relies on customers. It is also one of the most difficult to plan for completely. Location decisions can be complex, costs can be quite high, there is often little flexibility once a location has been chosen, and the attributes of location have a strong impact on a retailer's overall strategy. In

India, most retailers prefer to own the property rather than avail of the desired property through lease or rental. This makes the location decision even more critical. Choosing the wrong site can lead to poor results and, in some cases, insolvency and closure.

In India, with the emergence of large retail chains, some small retailers would also need to have a re-look at their location decision. A small grocery store located on a street and doing a good business may suddenly face problems if a large supermarket opens up across the street. Although the small store features personal service and long hours, it cannot match the supermarket's product selection and prices. A large supermarket or a discount store can offer lower prices since they get economies of scale in purchasing and operations. The reasons for locating a store in a certain place vary with the type of business. For example, in case of a restaurant or retail business, one prefers an area where there is sufficient parking, a good flow of walk-in and drive-by traffic, and little competition. In this chapter we will cover a range of important issues that retailers must consider before committing themselves to a particular location.

Importance of Location Decision

The importance of the location decision is due to the following factors.

Location is a major cost factor because it
- Involves large capital investment
- Affects transportation costs
- Affects human resources cost, e.g., salaries

Location is a major revenue factor because it
- Affects the amount of customer traffic
- Affects the volume of business

The traditional inclination of Indian retailers to own property further increases capital investment and this along with the penchant of Indian retailers to continue their business at the same location makes the location decision even more important.

The terms 'location' and 'site' are often used interchangeably but there is a distinct difference between the two. 'Location' is a broader concept, which denotes the store and its trading area from where a majority of its customers originate, while a site refers to the specific building or part of the building where a store is located. A location decision is influenced by the flow of pedestrian and vehicular traffic, which determine the footfalls in a retail store. Footfalls refer to the number of customers who visit a store in a defined time period. It is possible (in fact, it is all too common) for a store facility to have good location characteristics and poor site characteristics, or vice-versa. For example, a store may satisfy characteristics of a good location, the targeted customer segments may be residing or working in the vicinity of the store or passing by, but it may display poor site characteristics because of lack of good parking facilities. Location and site characteristics should interact in a positive and synergistic way with a store's merchandising, operations, and customer service characteristics. For example, a designer men's store located in an upmarket shopping centre or a mall near posh residential colonies, housed in an attractive building with adequate parking facilities, offering a wide selection, and providing excellent ambience and customer service, can be said to have tied its entire marketing mix in a synergistic manner. This may result in high profits. Hence, it is important that retailers understand the location decision in the context of stores operations and marketing strategy.

Levels of Location Decision and its Determining Factors

A retailer has to take the location decision, as shown in Fig. 6.1, basing on three aspects:

1. Selection of a city
2. Selection of an area or type of location within a city
3. Identification of a specific site

The factors which influence these decisions are discussed in the following sections.

Selection of a City

The following factors play a significant role in the selection of a particular city for starting or relocating an existing retail business:

- *Size of the city's trading area:* A city's trading area is the geographic region from which customers come to the city for shopping. A city's trading area would comprise its suburbs as well as

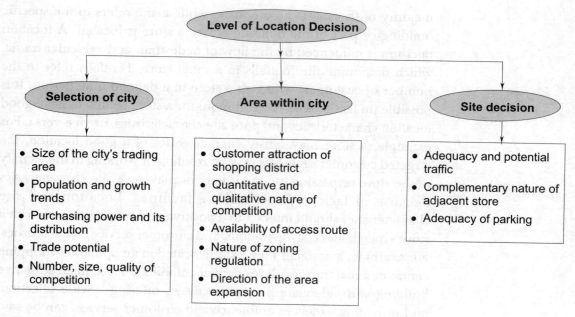

Fig. 6.1 Levels of location decision

neighbouring cities and towns. Cities like Mumbai and Delhi have a large trading area as they draw customers from far off cities and towns.

- *Population or population growth in the trading area:* The larger the population of the trading area, the greater the potential of the city as a shopping location. A high growth in population in the trading area can also increase the retail potential.

- *Total purchasing power and its distribution:* The retail potential of a city also depends on the purchasing power of the customers and its distribution networks in its trading area. Cities with a large population of affluent and upper middle-class customers can be an attractive location for stores selling high-priced products such as designer men's wear. The fast growth in purchasing power and its distribution among a large base of middle class is contributing to a retailing boom around major cities in India.

- *Total retail trade potential for different lines of trade:* A city may become specialized in certain lines of trade and attract customers from other cities. Moradabad has become an important retail location for brassware products while Mysore is famous for silk saris.

- *Number, size, and quality of competition:* The retailer also considers the number, size, and quality of competition before selecting a city. Unlike other large department store chains in India, Globus opened its first store in the mid-sized city of Indore, where it became popular being the only large department store.
- *Development cost:* The cost of land, rental value, and other retail developmental costs also affect attractiveness of a city as a retail location. In India, large organized retail chains like FoodWorld and Subhiksha preferred to start their activities in metros such as Chennai and Bangalore since the land value and other developmental costs were more reasonable in these cities than in Mumbai and Delhi.

Many large retail chains operate on a hub and spoke concept. There is a central warehouse, which acts as a hub and services the stores located around it (Fig. 6.2). This arrangement enables bulk purchases through the central warehouse and makes the supply chain more efficient. The retail chains operating on this concept saturate a city or a region with their stores before moving to another city or region. This also helps them in focussing their resources on building awareness and brand loyalty in select regions or cities. In India, large grocery chains like Food World and Subhiksha have organized their stores around this concept. We find concentration of Food World stores in and around a few cities like Chennai, Bangalore, Hyderabad, and Pune. Similarly, Subhiksha first located its stores around Chennai. Margin Free Market has located its stores in the state of Kerala, where it has built up a strong position.

Margin Free Market and Nilgiris

Margin Free Market, the Kerala based retail chain which specializes in the sale of grocery and toiletry product's has targeted the middle- and lower middle-class consumers and scripted a reasonable success story. It has over 250 stores located in small towns in Kerala. It was the first retailer in India to cross a turnover of Rs 500 crore. It would have liked to come up in North India earlier if it wasn't for steep real-estate costs. The Bangalore-based Nilgiris, which specializes in bakery and dairy products, has begun to look for franchisees in Delhi, Mumbai, and Kolkata, 'but the right location and right partners are absolutely essential' for the success of the venture as per Nilgiri's management.

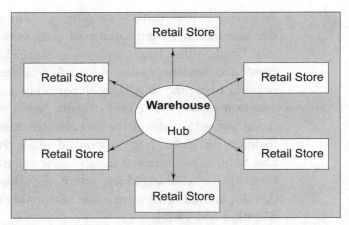

Fig. 6.2   Location of a warehouse (hub) and retail store (spokes)

Selection of an Area or Type of Location within a City

In the selection of a particular area or type of location within a city, evaluation of the following factors is required.

Customer attraction power of a shopping district or a particular store: Major shopping centres like Chandni Chowk in Delhi, Colaba in Mumbai, and Commercial Street in Bangalore attract customers from far off, while small shopping centres located in colonies attract customers from immediate neighbourhood.

Quantitative and qualitative nature of competitive stores: Retailers would like to evaluate the product lines carried by other stores, number of stores in the area, etc. before selecting the area. Thus, Nai Sarak in Delhi would be a suitable location for retailing paper and stationery products since it has become a specialized market for these products.

Availability of access routes: The area or shopping centre should provide easy access routes. There should not be traffic jams and congestion. MG road in Bangalore provides easy access from different parts of the city and hence has become popular.

Nature of zoning regulations: The retailer should also consider the zoning regulations in the city. They should examine the plans of zoning commissions and municipal corporations regarding the development of shopping centres, residential areas, flyovers, etc.

Direction of spread of the city: The retailer should consider the direction in which the city is developing while selecting the location. For example, Mumbai's suburbs and Navi Mumbai are growing at a fast

Zoning and Levy can Make or Mar Prospects of a Particular Location

McDonald's outlet located on the outskirts of Ludhiana on the Delhi–Ludhiana highway was presented as a destination location for consumers in Ludhiana and for highway travellers. With the implementation of a new municipal order, a check post was established just before the Mc Donald's store. Every vehicle passing through the highway from Ludhiana had to now pay tax for using the highway before reaching the McDonald's outlet. This reduced the attraction of the outlet for customers in the city of Ludhiana who had to now pay the highway tax for reaching this outlet. This adversely affected the volume of traffic coming from Ludhiana city and the outlet's profitability.

rate. Gurgaon to the south of Delhi has similarly grown into an attractive retail location.

Selection of a Specific Site

The choice of a specific site is particularly important. In central and secondary shopping centres, non-anchor stores depend on customers coming to the market and the traffic generated by anchor stores. Large stores in turn depend on attracting customers from the existing flow of traffic. Where sales depend on nearby settlements, selecting the trading area is even more important than picking the specific site. The following factors need to be considered while selecting a specific site.

Adequacy and potential of traffic passing the site: The volume of vehicular traffic and pedestrian shoppers who pass by the specific site should be assessed since they represent the potential customers.

Ability of the site to intercept the traffic flowing past the site: The vehicular or pedestrian traffic moving past the site would be attracted only if it represents the segment the store is targeting. Thus, a large number of school children moving past the site may not mean much to a store selling designer menswear. The presence of other shopping centres or stores in the vicinity can also influence the ability of the site to attract the flowing traffic.

Complementary nature of adjacent stores: The site will have greater potential if the adjacent stores sell complementary products. Thus, a store selling school uniforms would have greater potential if adjacent stores sell school books, stationery, etc.

Bombay Store

Bombay Store is a reliable place to shop for handloom cottons, woollens, silks, furnishings, linen, and handicrafts. It is perceived as a showcase of Indian culture and heritage made available under a single roof. Bombay Stores started with 12 stores in India, all located on the famous M.G. Roads in different cities. Recently, a store has been set up at a strategic airport location in Mumbai. Bombay Stores have now become a destination location for Indians, NRIs, and foreign customers seeking traditional and ethnic handicrafts from India in an attractive setting. The popularity of this store and its products is now making the management consider the possibility of opening similar stores at other locations in India and abroad which are frequented by the target population of Indians, NRIs, and foreigners likely to be interested in traditional Indian handicrafts and related products.

Adequacy of parking: Before finalizing a site it should be ensured that there are adequate parking facilities available in the vicinity, especially if the store expects substantial vehicular traffic.

Vulnerability of the site to unfriendly competition: The retailer should consider if unfriendly competition can emerge, for example, in the form of a large discount store which resorts to aggressive pricing strategies which can threaten the nearby retailers. In USA, many retailers had to close or relocate when Wal-Mart set up its stores in the neighbourhood. In India, small retailers will have to reconsider their location decision when large supermarkets like Food World or discount stores like Big Bazaar open up in the neighbourhood.

Types of Retail Location

A retailer has to choose among alternate types of retail locations available. It may locate in an isolated place and pull the customer to the store on its own strength, such as a small grocery store or paan shop in a colony which attracts the customers staying close by. Or, it may locate in a business district where there are a large number of retail establishments. If it decides to locate its store in a business district, it may have a choice ranging from the large shopping centres in the heart of the city or smaller shopping complexes in a suburb.

The various options available to a retailer in India are shown in Fig. 6.3 and discussed below:

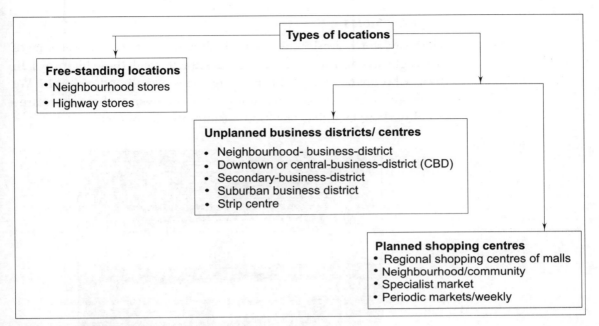

Fig. 6.3 Types of retail locations

Free-standing Location

Where there are no other retail outlets in the vicinity of the store and, therefore, the store depends on its own pulling power and promotion to attract customers. This type of location has several advantages including no competition, low rent, often better visibility from the road, easy parking, and lower property costs. But there are disadvantages also such as difficulty in attracting customers, no shared costs like in a shopping centre, and lack of variety for shoppers. We find free-standing grocery stores in colonies and dhabas on highways. Free-standing stores can be classified as neighbourhood stores or highway stores.

Neighbourhood Stores

Neighbourhood stores are located in residential neighbourhoods and serve a small locality. They sell convenience products like groceries. Now, even the large organized sector stores, which pull customers from across the city, are also coming up in suburbs or away from major markets as free-standing locations. For example, Kemp Fort and LifeStyle stores are free-standing stores in Bangalore away from major markets of the city.

Highway Stores

Highway stores are located along highways or at the intersections of two highways and attract customers passing through these highways. In India, the dhabas found on most highways are a good example. We now have attractive motels coming up on highways where there are good parking facilities, fast-food restaurants, dhabas, etc.

Ebony store in Ludhiana: free-standing location

Business-associated Location

These are locations where a group of retail outlets offering a variety of merchandise work together to attract customers to their retail area, but also compete against each other for the same customers. This type of location can be further classified as:
- Unplanned business districts
- Planned shopping centres

We describe below the various types of unplanned business districts and planned shopping centers prevalent in India.

Unplanned Business Districts/Centres

An unplanned business district is a type of retail location where two or more retail stores locate together on individual considerations rather than on the basis of any long-range collective planning. Thus, we may find four to five shoe stores, three to four medical stores in a cluster, but no grocery store. An unplanned district generally provides certain advantages like availability of a variety of goods, services, and prices; access to public transport; nearness to commercial and social facilities;

and pedestrian traffic. However, an unplanned business district has certain limitations such as congestion, older facilities, lack of space for large outlets, parking problems, and high rentals, which have led to the growth of planned shopping centers. In India, most of the business districts or shopping centres have come up in an unplanned fashion. A few like Connaught Place in New Delhi and the various sector markets in Chandigarh were developed in a planned way initially, but the later growth of these shopping districts has taken place mostly in an unplanned way.

There are four kinds of unplanned business districts in India: the central business district, the secondary business district, the neighbourhood-business-district, and the downtown business district. A brief description of each follows.

Downtown or Central Business District (CBD)   A CBD is the hub of retailing activity in a city. Stores located in CBD usually have a trade area that varies according to the size of the city or town. The CBD draws customers from across the city and suburbs. CBDs in major metros like Delhi and Mumbai even draw customers from far off places. In major metros like Delhi and Mumbai we find two or more CBDs, each serving different sections of population. For example, Cannaught Place in Delhi, Colaba in Mumbai, and Commercial street in Bangalore are upmarket CBDs serving the upper and upper middle-class customers across these cities, while Chandni Chowk in Delhi, Kalbadevi-Bhuleswar in Mumbai, and Chickpet in Bangalore serve

A central business district in Mumbai

middle income class customers across these cities. Other examples of

CBD are Park Street, New Market, Bora Bazaar in Calcutta, and Chawra Bazaar in Ludhiana.

Some of these shopping districts like Connaught Place have shown a combination of planned and unplanned growth. While Connaught Place was initially established in a planned way to serve the residents of New Delhi, its later growth has been mostly in an unplanned manner.

Khan Market : Shopping Centre Image

Khan Market, a genteel market in the heart of Delhi, has turned into India's costliest tract of high-street retail. At Rs 220 per sq. ft, Crossroads in Mumbai comes a poor second. The rate for the anchoring front shops in Khan Market has already touched Rs 400 per sq. ft, and may go up more in future. The average shop space is small—well under 1,000 sq. ft—yet, landlords can easily take home a lakh and a half.

But this is no where in comparison to global main street rentals. Fifth Avenue and East 57th Street in Manhattan share the first place as the world's most expensive retail location as per last year's edition of *Main Streets Across the World*, an annual report by Cushman & Wakefield. With rents $700 per sq. ft, the New York retail destination is 20% more expensive than Paris ' Avenue des Champs Elysées.

The basic cause why rents are increasing is the transformation of this regular provisions and services market into a lifestyle destination.

A cloth store has made way for an upscale watch store, an NGO store specializing in handmade baby clothes has made way for Subway, an odds and ends shop has morphed into a glitzy footwear store, a crockery store has transformed into a bank ATM, a bicycle shop has made way for Big Chill, a trendy cafe, and a scrap station now stocks trendy bags and luggage.

The first refugee market (people who came from Pakistan) in the capital, Khan Market, was built to service bureaucrats and politicians who live around it. So there were fresh produce stores, repair shops, regular groceries, clothing merchants, the odd bookstore, a music store, a crockery shop, a toy shop, etc.—almost one or two of each category. Fifty years ago, a typical annual lease would be a princely Rs 150 for the entire shop with Rs 50 as deposit. The average consumer was either the diplomat, bureaucrat, lawyer, or politician.

Post liberalization, the change was first noticed. The consumer base grew to include long-staying foreigners who chose to live in the upscale Amrita Shergill Marg, Golf Links, and Jorbagh. Indeed, there was a running joke among the shop owners that 'the memsahibs would shop at Khan Market for fresh vegetables while the chefs and bearers would go to INA.' Predictably, everything was at a 30% premium compared to INA. Even imported packaged foodstuff.

Khan market was also successful in attracting the fashion fraternity and up-

wardly mobile, rich young teens and young call centre employees with loads of time to hang about during the day.
Source: Chandralekha Roy 2003, Times News Network, www.economictimes.com, Dec. 20.

Secondary Business District   These are composed of an unplanned cluster of stores often located on a major intersection of a city. They attract customers from a large part of the city. Some of the major

Secondary market in a semi-urban city

secondary business districts include Dadar in Mumbai, Lajpat Nagar, Karol Bagh, and Kamla Nagar in Delhi, and Koramangla in Bangalore.

Neighbourhood Business District   Stores located in a neighbourhood business district form a small cluster and serve the neighbourhood trading area. Most colonies in cities and towns in India have such clusters of shops.

Suburban Business District   Stores located on the town's periphery have lower rents, often rely on traffic generated by the downtown, and may sometimes offer parking facilities. The malls in Gurgaon near Delhi are good examples. In Mumbai, Bandra-Andheri is a major suburban business district.

Planned Shopping Centres

A planned shopping centre consists of a group of architecturally owned or managed stores, designed and operated as a unit, based on balanced

Store location in a planned shopping centre

tenancy, and surrounded by parking facilities. In India, Connaught Place was developed, initially, as a planned business district to serve the city of New Delhi; similarly, the various sector markets in Chandigarh were developed in a planned way. Recently, we have seen the emergence of planned shopping centres and malls on Western lines. In India, we can classify planned shopping centres into two categories: regional shopping centres and neighbourhood/community shopping centers.

Regional Shopping Centres or Malls   Regional shopping centres or malls are the largest planned shopping centres; often they are anchored by two or more major department stores, have enclosed malls, serve a large trading area, and have high rents. They attract customers from across the city and suburbs. Major regional shopping centres or malls in India include Crossroads in Mumbai, Ansal Plaza in Delhi, Spencers Plaza in Chennai, and Metropolitan Mall in Gurgaon.

Crossroads in Mumbai

Community shopping centre in DLF City, Gurgaon

Neighbourhood/community Shopping Centres   Neighbourhood/community shopping centres usually have a balanced mix of stores including a few grocery stores a chemist, a variety store, and a few other stores, selling convenience goods to the residents of the neighbourhood. The markets in various sectors in Chandigarh are planned neighbourhoodshopping centres.

Specialized Markets   Besides the above general markets, we also have specialized markets. In India, most of the cities have specialized markets famous for a particular product category. A wide variety of merchandise is available within those product categories in such markets. For example, in Chennai, Godown Street is famous for clothes, Bunder street for stationery products, Usman street for jewellery, T Nagar for ready-made garments, Govindappan Naicleen street for grocery, Poo Kadia for food and vegetables. This is true for most of the urban centres in India. These places provide an established retail area to the prospective retailers to start a particular business, where they have to make little effort to attract consumers to the retail site.

Periodic Markets   Another peculiar type of market found in India is the periodic market, which is established at particular places on a particular day in a week. The retailers operating in these markets have mobile set-ups which they keep moving from one marketplace to another depending on the day of the week. Most of these markets operate in evening hours. Such markets serve the lower and middle income classes. These are very popular with the large population of labourers who have migrated from the rural areas to work in the cities, since it provides them merchandise in accordance with their requirements at low prices and at convenient hours. Now, even the large urban population including the double income group families have started patronizing these markets since they provide convenience and low prices. This is a rural retail format, which is now very popular in the Indian cities. These markets are mostly associated with the name of the day it is held on. A market organized on Monday for example would be called Som Bazaar (Som means Monday). These periodic markets are even availed of by retailers with well-established set-ups in regular markets, along with mobile traders, as these markets attract consumers from large trade areas, have limited credit transactions, involve very limited infrastructure related costs, and carry low overheads. Only a nominal fee has to be paid to the local government bodies.

Chowk area in Lucknow known for its Indian snacks

Types of Consumer Goods and Location Decision

Another factor that affects site selection is the customers' perception of the goods sold by a store (Bucklin 1963). Consumer goods are generally grouped into three major categories: convenience, shopping, and speciality goods. We discuss below how the type of goods sold by a retailer may influence its location decision.

Convenience Goods

Convenience goods usually imply products that carry a low unit price, are purchased frequently, involve little selling effort, are bought by habit, and are sold in numerous outlets. Products like candy bars, cigarettes, and milk are generally categorized as convenience goods.

Subhiksha Supermarket

Subhiksha Trading Services, promoters of the Subhiksha supermarket (grocery and cosmetics products) and pharmacy chain has chalked out a major expansion strategy of setting up one outlet, within every three–four kms, in major cities in Tamil Nadu. The company, which has opened 53 retail chain stores within Chennai itself since its inception in 1997, is opening 24 more stores in other cities in Tamil Nadu. This includes five in Coimbatore, Madurai, and Tiruchi, three in Salem, and one each in Erode, Kalpakkam, Vellore, Tiruvallur, Arakonam, and Chengalpattu. But Subhiksha has not positioned itself against established players like Nilgiris or Food World in retail marketing, who have set up air-conditioned outlets at destination locations. Rather it aims to kill competition from unorganized small retailers by its aggressive pricing strategy. Subhiksha offers discounts of up to 10% on MRP for most products. Such aggressive pricing policy is possible because a large grocery chain like Subhiksha enjoys economies of scale due to bulk purchases, and often purchases directly from the manufacturer thus eliminating the margins of middleman. Subhiksha plans to open 350 outlets in Gujarat, Maharashtra, Karnataka, and Andhra Pradesh by the end of 2004.

For stores handling convenience goods, like a supermarket, the quantity of traffic is most important. The corner of an intersection which offers two distinct traffic streams and a large window display area is usually considered a better site than the one in the middle of a block. Convenience stores located in central business districts, such as low-priced, ready-to-wear stores or a chemist, have a limited ability to generate their own traffic. Convenience goods are often purchased on impulse in easily accessible stores in the neighbourhood.

Shopping Goods

Shopping goods usually imply products with a high unit price, which are purchased infrequently and involve more intensive selling effort on the part of the store owner. Price, quality, and features of such products are compared across stores by customers. Shopping products are often sold in only selected franchised outlets. Examples of such products are men's suits, automobiles, and furniture.

For stores handling shopping goods, the quality of the traffic is more important. While convenience goods are purchased by nearly everyone, certain kinds of shopping goods are purchased by only certain segments of shoppers. Moreover, it is sometimes the character of the retail establishment rather than the type of goods it sells that governs the selection of a site. For example, Shoppers' Stop, which sells branded products to upmarket customers, may prefer to locate in a suburb or in a mall, which is accessible to car-owning consumers, while Westside, which sells mostly own brands and has a middle-class clientele, prefers to locate in central business districts or major secondary business districts frequented by its target customers.

In many cases, buyers of shopping goods like to compare the items in several stores. The consumers buy these goods infrequently and deliberately plan their purchases. Hence, the consumers are willing to travel some distance to make shopping comparisons. As a result, stores offering complementary items tend to locate close to one another. An excellent site for a shopping goods store is next to a department store or between two large department stores when there is a heavy flow of traffic between them. Another good site is the one between a major parking area and a department store.

A large retailer, dealing in shopping goods, can have a much wider trading area and can generate its own traffic. In such a case, easy accessibility from residential areas is important. A retailer offering

---

Westside Stores

Trent Limited (TL), which runs Westside (Bangalore, Ahmedabad, Chennai, Hyderabad, Kolkata, Mumbai, Pune, and Delhi) stores, has added one more 16,000 sq. ft. location in Delhi at Alankar, Lajpat Nagar. Westside has spacious stores, each ranging between 10,000 and 20,000 sq.ft. Compared to the competition, the Westside business model is different. Most other chains have gone for the multi-label format, but Westside run by the Tatas decided to market its own labels. Unlike Shoppers' Stop or Pyramid, which have targeted the upper 5% of the population with expensive brands, Westside has looked at the larger base of middle- and upper middle-class consumers which account for 25% of the population. Pantaloons and its sister concern Big Bazaar also target the middle class. With most of the other department stores fighting for a piece of the high-price pie, Westside has the field open to itself. Therefore, Westside has located its store in the high streets or central business centres of the city to attract middle-class customers. On the other hand, Shopper's Stop often preferred to locate its store within malls at a distance from the traditional market or in suburbs to attract car-owning customers looking for high-end branded products in all the categories.

shopping goods, however, should not locate too far away from potential customers. A study conducted by Wal-Mart in USA showed that 79.6% of the shoppers to its discount stores lived within a radius of eight kilometres, while 16.1% stayed within a 16 kilometres radius. In India, we can expect majority of customers to be concentrated in an even smaller region since roads in most cities are highly congested. The magnitude of the trading area for a shopping goods store can be determined by a customer survey, automobile license checks, sales slips, charge account records, store deliveries, and the extent of local newspaper circulation.

Speciality Goods

Speciality goods usually imply products with high unit price (although price is not a purchase consideration) which are bought infrequently, which require a special effort on the part of the customer to make the purchase, for which no substitutes are considered, and which are generally sold in exclusively franchised outlets. Examples of such products are precious jewellery, expensive perfume, fine furs, and so on, of specific brands or name labels.

Speciality goods are often sought by customers who are already 'sold' on the product, brand, or both. Stores catering to this type of consumer may use isolated locations because they generate their own consumer traffic. Stores carrying speciality goods that are complementary to certain other kinds of shopping goods may desire to locate close to the shopping goods stores. In general, the speciality goods retailer should locate in the type of neighbourhood where the adjacent stores and other establishments are compatible with the speciality store's operations.

Trading Area

A trade area is a contiguous geographic area from which a retailer draws customers that account for the majority of a store's sales. A trade area may be part of a city, or it can extend beyond the city's boundaries, depending on the type of store and density of settlements surrounding it.

The trade area can be divided into two or three zones. The dimensions of these zones depend on the size of store, its location, and nature of merchandise it deals in.

Westside store in Mumbai central business district

The primary zone is the geographical area from which the retail outlets or the shopping centre derives 60 – 65% of its customers.

The secondary zone is the geographical area of secondary importance in terms of customer sales, generating about 20% of an entire sale of the outlet.

The tertiary zone (the outermost ring) draws the remaining 10–15% customers who occasionally shop at the store or shopping centre. The customers are attracted from the tertiary zone because of lack of adequate retail centres near their place and attraction of a destination location, or because the specific shopping centre is on the way or near to their workplace.

Trade Area Analysis

A thorough analysis of trade area is necessary to estimate market potential, understand customer profile, competition, develop merchandising plan, and focus promotional activities. Increasingly,

---

Crossroads

Initially, when the Crossroads mall opened in Tardeo in central Mumbai, footfalls were as high as 30,000 everyday. But most were merely window-shoppers, with a measly 10% actually buying anything. The reason? The lopsided tenant mix, which ranged from stores targeting middle class like Panta-loon to up market stores like Pallazio. To achieve a distinct positioning and attract consumers of the desired profile a mall should have a uniform mix of tenants. The developers of a mall should take into consideration the profile of population in its catchment area before deciding on the tenant mix.

---

retailers are using geographic information systems (GIS) software in their trade area delineation and analysis. GIS combine digitized mapping with key locational data to graphically depict such trade area characteristics as the demographic attributes of the population, data on customer purchases, and listing of current, proposed, and competitor's locations. Thus, GIS software lets retailers research the attractiveness of alternate locations and see findings on computer-screen maps.

Market Potential

In estimating the market demand potential, retailers consider factors that are specific to their product line. Hence, often there is a variation in the criterion used by retailers for market estimation. Some of the important indicators of market demand are as follows.

Population Characteristics and its Trends   Population characteristics such as geo-demographics, psychographics, and behavioural characteristics are used to segment markets. Considerable information about an area's population characteristics can be acquired from secondary sources. Retailers can access data regarding population size, population density, and number of households, income distribution, sex, education, age, occupation, and mobility. The information on behavioural characteristics can be obtained by carrying out a primary study measuring store loyalty, consumer lifestyles, and store patronage.

Purchasing Power and its Distribution   The average household purchasing power and distribution of household income can significantly influence selection of a particular retail area. Thus, as purchasing power rises, the population is likely to exhibit an increased demand for luxury goods and more sophisticated demand for necessities.

Business Climate   Retailers should take into account the employment trends of the market because a high level of employment drives up the purchasing power. It is in the interest of retailers and developers to determine which geographical areas are growing rapidly and why.

For instance, Noida and Gurgaon have become favourable retail locations among retailers because of the existence of industrial units and software parks. This kind of understanding will help the retailers to devise their merhandise and expansion strategy.

Competition   The level and nature of competition in an area also influence the selection of a particular retail location. On the basis of levels of competition, trade area can be classified into three types—saturated, under-stored, and over-stored.

Locational Strategies of Some Department Stores in India

The Mehrauli–Gurgaon road area has started attracting a large number of department stores. Roughly a kilometre before an intersection called Iffco Chowk, LifeStyle and Shoppers' Stop have opened their stores in malls squarely opposite to each other. About 500 metres away, Sahara Mall has come up. In this mall, Pantaloon Retail has opened both the stores —Big Bazaar and Pantaloon. Nearby, three other shopping malls are nearing completion. This clustering seems full of opportunities for developers and retailers.

None of this is unique to Gurgaon either. In the Mumbai suburb of Malad, Shoppers' Stop and LifeStyle have opened in the same mall. In Mulund, another Mumbai suburb, they are anchor tenants in adjacent malls. In a third suburb, Lower Parel, LifeStyle is opening a store next to Big Bazaar and Pantaloons. Pantaloon is opening eight new stores in Chennai, Kolkata, Ahmedabad, and Nagpur. In Kolkata, a Shoppers' Stop store just opened close to Pantaloon's outlet.

This is an interesting development in terms of department stores trying to cluster together? Till now, most of the upmarket department stores have sought locations far away from competition. However, now the strategy seems altered. It is important to look at the reasons for such a strategy.

As catchments become smaller, retailers are being forced to open stores in each of the emerging catchments. Every retailer looks for a large floor space, ranging between 20,000 and 30,000 sq. ft. That kind of space is either not available in downtown neighbourhoods, or is expensive. Everyone is looking at places where new construction is going on, that is, suburbs like Gurgaon and Mulund. Take the example of Shoppers' Stop. It began in the early 90s with one store in the Mumbai suburb of Andheri. This solitary property pulled in shoppers from Bandra to Borivli. Today, with Mumbai having more cars than it has roads, only people living between Juhu and Jogeshwari are happy travelling to the store. So Shoppers' Stop added stores in Ghatkopar, Bandra, and Kandivli. Shortly, it is planning to open three more in Malad, Mulund, and Juhu.

None of these properties are likely to be stand-alone department stores. For one, there are hardly any buildings where a stand-alone store can be erected. Also, between a mall and a stand-alone store, the former will pull in far more people. And, as the mall developers know each other's plans, they try and place their mall as close as possible to any potential retail hub. That explains the clustering.

The impact of this proximity on the department stores seems to be interesting. For instance, in Gurgaon, about 25,000 of the households that populate this suburb fit the target profile of both Shoppers' Stop and LifeStyle. The LifeStyle store needs about 3,000–4,000 walk-ins every day (averaged over the week) to break even. So what is likely to happen when all the other malls, all targeting much the same SEC A consumer, open? Some fear that this may lead to attrition in the near future.

However, most retailers do not think that attrition is on the cards. They allude to Singapore's Orchard Street, where 10 or so malls co-exist on the same stretch of road. Of these, they say, just three

malls have a distinctive positioning. There is little differentiation between the others. But, such is the collective noise level that enough traffic is pulled in to make the place viable. That is what everyone is banking on in Gurgaon too. A developer feels, 'as competition comes in, some of these 25,000 households will move to the other stores. But the noise levels will increase, and we will start getting consumers from Delhi.' As he says, 20–25% of his consumers already come from Delhi.

Similarly, Pantaloon's management feels that the business might drop initially as people check out the new stores. Ultimately, however, they feel, the holy trinity of eating out, movies, and shopping will pull in people from beyond Gurgaon.

The DT mall, where LifeStyle has come up,has already opened its multiplex. Across the road, at the MGF mall, PVR is opening its multiplex. At the Sahara Mall, an Imax is coming up. Barista has opened in both DT and MGF malls. Similar is the case with eatery chain Ruby Tuesday. 'Organized retail', says a developer, 'is about to strike hard at the traditional high streets'. People, he says, will prefer to come to a Mehrauli–Gurgaon Road than go to a Karol Bagh or a Sarojini Nagar market.

But this may not be all that simple as per the retailers in shopping districts. While retailing and entertainment can be a heady mix, it remains to be seen if people will be willing to travel to other catchments far away once similar propositions come up closer.

One could take the example of the property Shoppers' Stop is developing in

Juhu. It is the anchor tenant in an entertainment complex, replete with restaurants and movie screens. That is the template which Shoppers' Stop plans to follow in Delhi and Bangalore. Once that happens it remains to be seen if people would still want to travel the extra miles to Gurgaon? Most feel that the high street at Gurgaon will work as long as traffic keeps coming from Delhi. But as stores come up in south Delhi, the tap may be turned off.

Some retailers feel it is simply a question of differentiation. For example, Big Bazar is targeting a wider market than Shoppers' Stop and LifeStyle. Globus and Westside, too, are similarly distinct. However, the distinction between Shoppers' Stop and LifeStyle is much more blurred. While the former is stronger in menswear, the latter is strong in women's wear, children's apparel, shoes, and home furnishings.

However, there is not much that the stores can do when they operate in a mall than a stand-alone store. Unlike earlier, when they operated out of stand-alone department stores, the retailers do not have much control over their fate today. A lot depends on the tenant mix of the mall they are in. That becomes a problem since mall developers start by signing on the anchor tenant and then look for other tenants. Hence, the stores are essentially laying a wager. At best, the anchor stores can suggest the tenant mix they would like to have. Concepts like mall management are very nascent in this country today. Most developers see it as a simple real-estate play and aim to sell off the property. Right now, little thought is being given to differentiation, and all malls are targeting the SEC A. Over time, it is expected, this will change.

Source: M. Rajshekhar 2003, Conflict Street: India's department stores are entering each other's markets, and a new era of competition, www.businessworldindia.com, March 24.

A saturated trade area offers customers a wide variety of merchandise, which also ensures impressive profits for retailers in the market. Customers tend to prefer these areas because of the variety of merchandise offered and competitive pricing. Therefore, retailers who find location characteristics compatible with their marketing mix prefer to establish their stores at such locations. Examples in this context are Nirula's, McDonald's, Pizza Corner, and Pizza Hut in India.

Retailers located in a saturated trade area look for head-to-head competition. They develop methods and internal systems that allow them to successfully compete with others. They believe locating in places enjoying competition ensures high footfalls, which can be converted into sales with sustained marketing efforts.

Under-stored trade area is one that has too few stores selling specific merchandise to meet the needs of the segment efficiently. Subhiksha's early success was based on its location strategy of opening stores in small towns and residential neighbourhoods in Chennai that were relatively poorly served by the existing retailers. Today, these stores are registering high market share and drawing traffic from surrounding settlements.

Over-stored trade areas are characterized by the presence of multiple retailers in a specific product category. An example is Nai Sarak in Delhi, which is well known all over India for its educational books

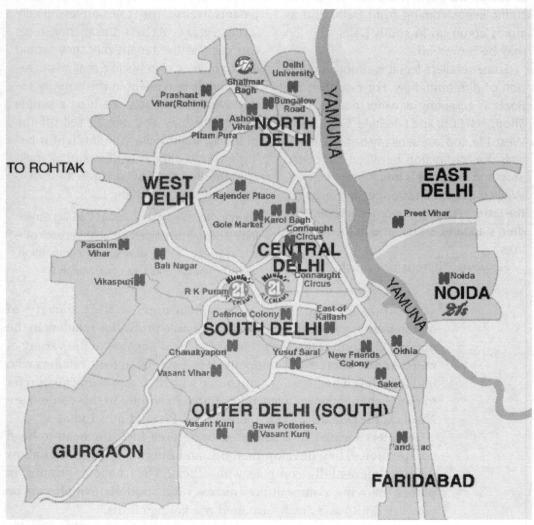

Network of Nirula's outlets in Delhi

and stationery products. These areas pose great challenges for new entrants in terms of investment and efforts in attracting customers. In India, most of the over-stored trade areas are traditional markets with limited space for new retailers and high rentals.

Peer Pressure and Competition   The importance of support of public and the already existing business in adjoining area is evident from the following example. Sonepat–Delhi national highway is one of the busiest highways in the country; therefore, it has immense economic potential for dhabas (eating joints). An entire stretch of one kilometre on this highway near Delhi has no outlet serving non-vegetarian stuff in spite of many customers visiting there being non-vegetarian. Social norms have ensured that non-vegetarian outlets do not set shops on this stretch.

DT cineplex in a planned shopping centre in Gurgaon

Site Selection Analysis

With the advent of new retail formats in India such as planned shopping centres and malls, emergence of free-standing department stores, hypermarkets, etc., and further development of traditional business districts and other unplanned shopping locations as discussed earlier, a retailer is presented with a wider choice of locations. Consideration of all the options keeping in view the product mix, customer profile, and overall business model presents an enormous challenge. A retailer has to consider the following factors while selecting a site:

- Kind of products sold

- Cost factor
- Competitor's location
- Ease of traffic flow and accessibility
- Parking and major thoroughfares
- Market trends
- Visibility

Kind of Products Sold

For stores dealing in convenience goods, the quantity of traffic is most important. The corner of an intersection, which offers two distinct traffic streams and a large window display area is usually a better site than the middle of a block. Convenience goods are often purchased on impulse from easily accessible stores. For stores dealing in shopping goods, the quality of the traffic is more important. The emergence of several apparel factory outlets within a short stretch on the Delhi–Jaipur highway, at Mahipalpur market in Delhi, is driven by this factor. Stores carrying speciality goods that are complementary to certain other kinds of shopping goods may desire to locate close to the shopping goods stores. In general, the speciality goods retailer should locate in the type of neighbourhood where the adjacent stores and other establishments are compatible with his or her operation.

Cost Factor in Location Decision

Location decision on cost considerations alone is risky. Space cost is a combination of rent or mortgage payment, utilities, leasehold improvements, general decoration, security, insurance, and all related costs of having a place to conduct business operations. Traditionally, the retail community placed great importance on owning the place since this was considered prestigious in the business community. However, there are many periodic retail markets in India, which operate on particular days of the week. The retailers operating in these periodic markets keep shifting from place to place and do not own any property; instead they pay a small rental for their set-up in each market. This supports their model of selling goods at very low margins. With the emergence of new forms of retail formats such as franchising, malls, and department store, the dependence on rent or lease is increasing.

Competitor's Location

The type and number of competitors is another important factor. The presence of major retail centres, industrial parks, franchisee chains, and department stores should be noted. Intense competition in the area shows that new businesses will have to divide the market with existing businesses. If one is not able to offer better quality and competitively priced products, one might reconsider that particular location. An excellent location may be next or close to parallel or complementary businesses that will help to attract customers.

Ease of Traffic Flow and Accessibility

These two factors are more important to some businesses than others. Consider the nature of the business you are planning to open and your potential customers. Retailers selling convenience goods must attract business from the existing flow of traffic. Studying the flow of traffic, noting one-way streets, street widths, and parking lots, is hence important. The following factors have to be considered: parking availability, distance from residential areas or other business areas, traffic congestion, side of street, width of street, part of the block, and neighbours. Evaluate how accessible the site is for walk-in or drive-by traffic as well as the amount of pedestrian traffic and automobile traffic that goes by the proposed location.

Parking and Major Thoroughfares

Parking is another site characteristic that is especially a cause for concern in densely populated areas. When evaluating the parking that exists at a retail site, there are two considerations: parking capacity (the number of cars that can be parked), and parking configuration (the way the parking lot is laid out, the direction of the travel lanes and spaces, landscaping, etc.). There are several ratios that are generally used to determine the adequacy of a parking lot. While different ratios exist for different types of retailers or service providers, the ideal ratio for food stores is in the magnitude of 7–8 cars per 1,000 square feet of food store. This means that a 10,000 sq. ft food store would have an ideal parking lot that could accommodate between 70 and 80 cars. Parking lots are generally designed on the basis of 400 sq. ft per car (which includes drive lanes, spaces, etc.). Thus, the ideal parking ratio for a food store is about 3:1 or 3 sq. ft of parking space for every square ft of store. However, it should be noted that an ideal ratio hardly

Parking Problems

On the Gurgaon–Mehrauli road three planned shopping malls have come up. This has caused traffic bottlenecks. These malls measure up to international standards on most parameters but for poor parking facilities. A major problem faced by the management, shoppers, and public living in adjoining areas is that of inadequate parking facilities in particular on weekends, when a large number of shoppers also from Delhi visit these malls.

ever exists in real life—especially in densely populated areas. Obviously, the more suburban the location, the greater the emphasis should be on maximizing parking availability. Urban stores generally get a significant amount of their business from walkers, bikers, and shoppers who use public transportation to and from the store and, thus, can get by with a lower parking ratio.

As to parking configuration, there are several considerations to be followed. First, a parking lot should be laid out so that the driving lanes are perpendicular (and the spaces are parallel) to the storefront in order to facilitate shoppers to walk between their cars and the store door. Secondly, food shoppers usually like to park in reasonably close proximity (within 300–350 feet) to the main entrance/exit of the store, and within the sight of it.

Market Trends

Evaluate the community from a broad, futuristic perspective. Local newspapers are a good source of information. Discussions with business owners and officials in the area can also help. Make use of information available through the Chamber of Commerce. Is the community receptive to change and will a new business be welcome? Does the community depend on a single firm or industry? If so, is it prospering? Is there sufficient demand in the local market to support a new business?

McDonald's

The first McDonald's outlet in India was opened at Jaipur. McDonald's selected Jaipur since it is one of the most important tourist destinations in India attracting a large number of foreign tourists. McDonald's was targeting foreign tourists already accustomed to McDonald's and its offerings. Later McDonald's opened a large number of outlets in metros including Delhi and Mumbai.

High street market with parking facilities in a central business district

Visibility

Visibility has a varied impact on a store's sales potential. It is important when a shopper is trying to find the store for the first or second time. Once the shopper has become a regular customer, visibility no longer matters. But consider this fact: one in five families moves every year,which means that some part of a community's population may be 'shopping' in a new store. It follows that, if a store cannot readily be seen, new residents of an area (or prospective shoppers) probably will not choose it. Another aspect of visibility relates to travellers and passers-by. Generally speaking, a store's trade area accounts for 75–90% of its business. This means that about 10–25% of a store's business comes from beyond its trade area. With respect to this component of a store's business, visibility takes on added importance.

No one type of location is better than the others. Many retailers, such as the Delhi-based retailers Mehrasons and Nirula's have been

McDonald's located in Fun Republic to attain maximum visibility

successful in all types of locations. The following factors can be used to list a particular retail site:

- Is there a need to be in the middle of traffic flow of customers as they pass between the stores with the greatest customer pull?
- Who will be the store's neighbours?
- What will be their effect on stores sales?
- How much space is needed?

Based on experience, the amount of space required can be determined to run the expected level of operations. The amount of space will determine rent. Many retailers need to rethink their space requirements when locating in a shopping centre. Rents are generally much higher and, therefore, space must be used efficiently.

Selection of a Particular Shopping Centre or Market Area

The following considerations influence the selection of a particular shopping centre:

- Merchants' association
- Landlord responsiveness
- Zoning and planning
- Lease terms
- Building layout

Merchants' Association

A merchants' association can be very important in promoting and maintaining the business in a given area. The presence of an effective merchants' association can strengthen business and save money through group advertising programmes, group insurance plans, and collective security measures. Some associations have induced city planners to add highway exits near their shopping centres. Others have lobbied for and received funds from cities to remodel their shopping centres including extension of parking lots. Merchants' associations can be particularly effective in promoting stores using common themes or events and during holiday seasons. The collective draw from these promotions is usually several times higher than what a single retailer could have mustered.

Responsiveness of the Landlord

The responsiveness of the landlord plays an important role in the selection of a particular location. Prospective retailers expect landlord's acknowledgement on the following issues: placement and size of signs, maintenance and repairs, and renting the adjacent retail space. To have an idea about the responsiveness of the landlord, the retailer can gather information from the existing tenants on the following factors:

- Does the landlord return calls in a reasonable period and send service people quickly?
- Is it necessary to nag the landlord just to get routine maintenance done?
- Does the landlord just collect the rent and disappear or is he or she sympathetic to the needs of the tenants?
- Does the landlord have any policies that hamper marketing innovations?

Retailers can also approach the previous tenants of the location to find information about what businesses they were in and why they left? Did they fail or just move? What support or constraints did the landlord create? If the opportunity presented itself, would they be retail tenants of this landlord again?

Zoning and Planning

The zoning commission will provide the latest 'mapping' of the retail location and surrounding areas under consideration. This will help a retailer to take care of the following issues:

- Are there restrictions that will limit or hamper retail operations? For example, the Ludhiana–Delhi McDonald's has faced such restrictions.
- Will construction or changes in city traffic or new highways present barriers to your store?

For example, in New Delhi, the construction of the flyover near AIIMS has reduced the number of footfalls at the central district centre, South Ex. But it led to the increase in footfall at nearby planned shopping centres, as consumers started avoiding a particular lane where construction was going on because of traffic congestion.

Will any competitive advantage currently available at the location being considered be diminished by zoning changes? Development of new markets like Rohini and Punjabi Bagh in Delhi will impact the flow of customers to well-established shopping centres of west Delhi such as Tilak Nagar market and Rajauri Market. Similarly, the establishment of malls in suburbs of Bangalore like Koramangala will reduce traffic to traditional shopping centres like Commercial Street and Brigade Road.

Most zoning boards, along with economic/regional development committees, plan several years in advance. They can probably provide valuable insights to decide among alternative retail locations.

Leases

Directly related to zoning is intended period of stay and lease the agreement. Before entering into any lease agreement, retailers should collect information on future zoning plans and decide how long it will be viable to run business at a particular location. The following should be considered while evaluating a lease agreement.

- If business is successful, is expansion possible at this location?
- Is lease agreement flexible, so the retailer has an option to renew after a specified number of years? (On the other hand, the retailer may seek another location.)
- Is rent subject to sales volume (with an upper ceiling) or is rent merely fixed?
- Does it put unambiguously in writing the promises the property owner has made about repairs, construction and reconstruction, decorating, alteration, and maintenance?
- Does it contain prohibitions against subleasing?

Building Layout

Retailer has to consider, in particular, the following factors before selecting a particular shopping centre or building: the age and condition of the shopping area or centre, the condition and adequacy of all mechanical systems, remodelling needs, storage availability, security needs, restrictions on alterations and improvements to the property, responsibility for the cost of utilities, responsibility for maintenance and repair, conditions related to insurance, payment of maintenance expenses, renewal of the agreement, etc.

Estimate of Store Sales

A retailer with some past experience in the same merchandise line for which a store is planned can make a reasonable estimate of sales volume if the following information is available (in lieu of past personal experience, the trade association may be of help).

- Characteristics of individuals who are most likely to be store customers (from pedestrian interviews)
- Number of such individuals passing the site during store hours (from traffic counts)
- Proportion of passers-by who will enter the store (from pedestrian interviews)
- Proportion of those entering who will become purchasers (from pedestrian interviews)
- Amount of average transaction (from past experience, trade associations, and trade publications)

One retailer divides the people who pass a given site into three categories: those who enter a store; those who, after looking at the windows, may become customers; and those who pass without entering or looking. Owing to prior experience, this retailer is able to estimate from the percentage falling into each classification not only the number who will make purchases but also how much the average purchase will be. If out of 1,000 passers-by each day 5% (fifty) enter the store and each spends an average of Rs 200, a store at that site, which operates 300 days a year will have an annual sales volume of Rs 3,00,000.

How to Make a Traffic Count

Knowledge of the volume and character of passing traffic is a very essential parameter for the selection of a location. Flow of traffic along with factors such as parking facilities, operating costs, location of competitors, etc. are important determinants of success for a retail store. To evaluate the traffic available to competitors, traffic counts at competitor's sites can also be conducted. Data from a traffic count should not only show how many people pass by, but generally indicate what kinds of people they are. Analysis of the characteristics of the passing traffic often reveals patterns and variations not readily apparent from casual observations.

For counting purposes, the passing traffic is divided into different classifications according to the characteristics of the customers who would patronize the store. Whereas a drug store is interested in the total volume of passing traffic, a men's clothing store is obviously more concerned with the amount of male traffic, especially men between the ages of sixteen and sixty-five. It is also important to classify the passing traffic based on purpose. A woman on the way to a beauty salon is probably a poor prospect for a paint store, but she may be a good prospect for a chemist. The hours at which individuals pass by are often an indication of their purpose. In the early morning hours people are generally on their way to work. In the late afternoon these same people are usually going home from work.

To determine what proportion of the passing traffic represents potential shoppers, some of the pedestrians should be interviewed about the origin of their trip, their destination, and the stores in which they plan to shop. This sort of information can provide a better estimate of the number of potential customers. Techniques for making pedestrian and automobile traffic counts are discussed below.

Pedestrian Traffic Count

In making a pedestrian count one must decide who is to be counted, where the count should take place, and when the count should be made. In considering who is to be counted, determine the types of people who should be included. For example, the study might count all men presumed to be between sixteen and sixty-five. The directions should be clear as to the individuals to be counted so the counters will be consistent and the total figure will reflect the traffic flow.

As previously indicated, it is frequently desirable to divide the pedestrian traffic into classes. Quite often separate counts of men and women and certain age categories are required. A trial run will indicate if there are any difficulties in identifying those to be counted or in placing them in various groupings.

The season, month, week, day, and hour influence the traffic flow and should be considered before deciding when the count should be taken. For example, during the summer season there is generally an increased flow of traffic on the shady side of the street. During a holiday period such as Diwali or Dussehera, the traffic density is higher. The patronage of a store varies by the day of the week too. Store traffic usually increases during the latter part of the week. In some communities, there is heavier traffic on factory pay days and days when social security checks are received. The day of the week and the time of day should represent a normal period for traffic flow. Pedestrian flow accelerates around noon as office workers go out for lunch. Generally, more customers enter a downtown store between 10 a.m. and noon and between 4 p.m. and 7 p.m. than at any other time. Local customs or other factors, however, may cause a variation in these expected traffic patterns. The day should be divided into half-hour intervals. Traffic should be counted and recorded for each half-hour period of a store's customary operating hours. If it is not feasible to count the traffic for each half-hour interval, the traffic flow can be sampled. Traffic in the representative half-hour periods in the morning, noon, afternoon, and evening hours can be counted.

Automobile Traffic Count

A growing number of retail firms depend on drive-in traffic for their sales. Both the quantity and quality of automotive traffic can be analysed in the same way as is done in case of pedestrian traffic. For the major streets in urban areas, the city engineer, the planning commission, the state highway department, or an outdoor advertising company may be able to provide data on traffic flows. However, this data needs to be modified to suit specific needs. For example, one should supplement data relating to the total count of vehicles passing the site with actual observation in order to evaluate such influences on traffic such as commercial vehicles, people changing shifts at nearby factories, highway traffic, and increased flow caused by special events or activities.

Retail Location Theories

Several theories have been developed to explain the pattern of urban settlement and development of retailing institutions. These can be broadly classified into three approaches:

1. Central place theory
2. Spatial interaction theory
3. Land value theory

Central Place Theory

The central place theory was established by Christaller (1966) and Lösch (1941) more than sixty years ago. The theory has played an important role in the explanation of urban systems.

This theory attempts to explain the spatial distribution of settlement, i.e., the spatial pattern of urbanization. It states that a central place and its market area best express this pattern of settlement. The central place is specialized in selling various goods and services. The threshold level for a store is the minimum area from which it must draw traffic to be viable. The range is a sphere of the settlement of consumers travelling to the central place. This is shown in Fig. 6.4.

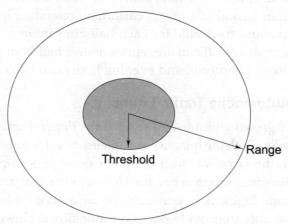

Fig. 6.4   The threshold and market range

Retailers prefer to serve consumers who live within a range where cheaper delivery prices can be possible. The range shows average maximum distance from the store to consumers willing to purchase. Each central place has its own specific market area.

The range of a store should be at least equal to its threshold area. The store will earn profits only if its range is larger than its threshold. If the retail store has a big threshold it needs a much bigger range, covering a larger population. Therefore, the locations of stores are hierarchical based on these thresholds.

Spatial Interaction Theory

Spatial interaction is defined as the flow of goods, people, or information among places, in response to localized supply and demand. This has also been expressed, somewhat more formally, as complementarily—a deficit in one place and a surplus in another. Transferability is the possibility of transport at a cost that the market will bear (the cost of transport is less than the opportunity cost of not transporting). In other words, spatial interaction theory is based on the attractiveness of alternative shopping areas against the deterrent effect of distance.

It discards the assumption made by central place theory that behaviour is explained by consumers using the nearest offering of goods or services.

Retailing-related applications of spatial interaction theory date from the pioneering studies of William J. Reilly (1931). Reilly stated that 'The likelihood that a city (or shopping centre) will attract shoppers from a hinterland increases with the size of the city (or shopping centre) and decreases with distance from the city (or shopping centre)'. The 'law of retail gravitation' can be supplemented with knowledge of the location and size of competing centres to develop a boundary around each centre beyond which it is more likely that a shopper will go to another centre. Reilly's law of retail gravitation, which suggests that R, the retail attractiveness of a central place (or shopping centre) j to a potential customer residing at i increases proportionately with the population P (or size in square feet) of j, and increases inversely with the square of the distance ij:

$$R_j = k P_j / D_{ij}^2$$

Note that whether we are using population or size in square feet, the implication is that the greater possibility of finding more of the goods/services needed, with only one trip, is a powerful attraction to a customer of a particular place.

Huff (1963) was first to propose a spatial interaction model for estimating retail trade areas. He believed that consumers patronize competing shopping areas as the basis of their overall 'utility'. He stated that when consumers have a number of alternative shopping opportunities they may visit several different stores rather than restrict patronage to a particular store. Therefore, each store within a geographic area with which the shopper is familiar has some chance of being patronized. The probability increases with the size of the outlet and decreases with distance.

Land Value Theory

Land value theory, also known as bid rent theory and urban rent theory, achieved recognition from the work of Haig (1927). It is used for analysing and explaining the arrangement of urban land uses and the location of economic activities within cities. Haig emphasised that competition for an inelastic supply of land ensures that, in the long run, all urban sites are occupied by the activity capable of paying the highest rentals, and land is thereby put to its 'highest and best' use. The location of various retail formats depends on the competitive bidding for a particular site.

The price a bidder is likely to pay will depend on the use which will be made of the site. For example, a commercial user will earn more from the land and, therefore, be willing to pay a higher price than an industrial user, who in turn may pay more than a residential user. Generally, the more central the location, the more desirable will be the plot, and higher will be the price, as different users will bid to purchase the land. Retailers require access to consumers more than any other land use function and will be prepared to pay very high rents for city centre locations. The bid rent demand from retailers will fall sharply as the distance from the city centre increases. This is shown in Fig. 6.5. The retail sector will be further segmented into different demand schedules, with some willing to bid higher rents. Department and speciality stores selling designer wear, for example, are likely to attach greater importance to a central location than a convenience store or a grocery retailer.

Alonso (1964) developed models on utilization of land on the basis of Haig's work. He constructed bid rent curves for each land use function, their slope reflecting the sensitivity of that activity (use of land) to changes in accessibility. With the objective of attracting most of the customers from adjoining areas of central sites, retailers are prepared to bid high rentals, but the amount they are willing to spend is inversely related to the distance from the central business district.

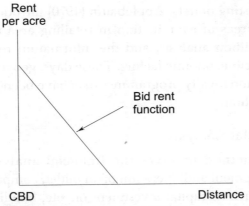

Fig. 6.5 The bid rent function

Location Assessment Procedures

There are four established retail location assessment procedures in practice to determine the best possible retail location for the prospective retail outlet:

1. Checklist analysis
2. Analogue analysis
3. Financial analysis
4. Regression analysis

Checklist Analysis

The checklist consists of a simple framework covering relevant factors regarding geo-demographics, shopping behaviour, competition, cost (capital and variable), and accessibility to the particular site. It is informal in approach and provides a picture about the location viability in the mind of the retailer. The extensive checklist was prepared by Lindquist (1974-75) and Martineau (1958).

Analogue Analysis

It attempts to predict the economic performance (turnover) of a particular site by assessing its potential against the already running stores after incorporating differences between the proposed site and the existing outlets. Applebaum (1970) introduced this method. The main areas of examination in retailing area are customer surveys, competition analysis, and the information regarding demographic and socio-economic factors. These days, geographic analysis systems (GIS) and loyalty programmes data have been used in the assessment of location.

Financial Analysis

This method involves the financial analysis in respect of the development and operation of an outlet, comparing the development costs such as capital investment on site, building, and variable costs against expected returns. Competitive analysis and shopping behaviour are not considered in this method.

Regression Modelling

For retail location decision, multiple regression models have been developed around a number of determinants such as demographics (d), accessibility (a), competitive environment (c), and trade area characteristics (t) to estimate the potential turnover of the prospective outlet.

We can state the relationship among dependent and independent variables as follows:

Turnover = f (d, a, c, t)

The regression coefficients testify the effects of each decision variable on turnover, and the corresponding beta weights show the relative relevance of each determinant.

Retail Area Development

Retail area development is a complicated process. Retailers alone are not responsible for the development of new sites. It involves the participation of many other entities, such as brokers and financial intermediaries; there are four important interest groups that can work individually and in partnership to overcome the challenges and obstacles in the development of new retail markets or increasing the attractiveness of an existing retail site.

The four key players are:

- The public (residents, community-based organizations)
- Developers

Fig. 6.6 Key players in retail area development

- The Government (elected officials and professional staff)
- Retailers

It is retailers in partnership with developers that drive the development of a particular retail site or centre. This requires support from the public bodies and government at the same time, as shown in Fig. 6.6. In general, the key points that influence retail development in new or existing markets are:

- Law and order situation and security provision
- Settlement standings
- Purchasing power
- Build out/rehabilitation costs
- Site attractiveness
- Scope of expansion
- Parking facilities
- Operating or maintenance costs
- Construction and development costs
- Lack of hard infrastructure (water, electricity, and road connectivity)

Summary

A retailer may make a location decision in three steps: first he selects a city, next he identifies an appropriate area/location within a city, and finally he selects a specific site. While selecting a city, a retailer considers factors like population of the city, purchasing power, nature of competition, rental values, and value of property, etc. While selecting an area or shopping centre in a city, a retailer considers attractiveness of different locations with respect to his product line, nature of competition, growth prospects, access routes available, etc. Finally, while selecting a site, a retailer assesses the potential of the site to attract traffic, its visibility, nature of products sold by adjacent stores, parking facilities, etc.

A free-standing store is isolated and not adjacent to other stores. It attracts traffic on its own strength. An unplanned business district is a shopping area with two or more stores located together. The store composition is decided by individual retailers rather than in a planned way by a central agency. There are broadly four types of unplanned business districts, namely central business district, secondary business district, suburban business district, and neighbourhood business district. Most of the traditional markets in India are unplanned business districts. A planned shopping centre is centrally owned or managed and has a balanced mix of shops. The planned shopping centres and malls are coming up in India in a big way in last few years.

A trade area is the geographic area from which a retailer draws customers. The trade area consists of three parts: primary, secondary, and tertiary. The primary trade area is closest to the store and accounts for a majority of its customers; the secondary trading area lying beyond the primary trading area draws the second highest volume of customers; and the tertiary trading area is the furthest from the store and draws the least number of customers. An analysis of a store's trading area is useful to estimate

sales potential, identify the profiles of customers, and develop marketing strategies.

We also discussed various techniques to estimate automobile and pedestrian traffic. An accurate count is a very important determinant of sales potential. Care should be taken to ensure that counting is done at representative hours, and seasonal and hourly patterns should be understood. The count should consider the volume of traffic as well as profile of the consumers passing in terms of age, sex, etc.

Finally, we discuss the three approaches, which explain pattern of urban settlement and location of retailing institutions namely, central place theory, spatial interaction theory and land value theory. The Central place theory suggests that a central place and its market area best express the pattern of urban settlement. A customer prefers purchasing from the nearest central place. The spatial interaction theory suggests that larger cities and shopping centres have a larger trade area. The customer is willing to travel a greater distance, to a larger shopping area, providing greater variety. The land value theory or bid rent theory states that competition for an inelastic supply of land ensures that in the long run all urban sites are occupied by activities capable of paying the highest rent. Location of retail formats depend on their ability to bid, those generating highest margins bidding for the high-priced central locations.

Key Terms

1. **Analogue approach:** A method of trade area analysis also known as the 'similar store' or 'mapping' approach.

2. **Anchor store:** A large, well-known retail

store located in a shopping centre serving as an attraction force for customers to the shopping centre.

3. **Central place theory:** Christaller's theory of retail location suggesting that retailers tend to locate in a central place. As more retailers locate together, more customers are attracted to the central place.

4. **Central business district (CBD):** A shopping area located in the central downtown area or another area in the city with a concentration of business.

5. **Convenience goods:** Goods that consumers put a minimum amount of thought into while purchasing.

6. **Demographic variables:** Population characteristics that are used to describe consumers, such as age, income, education, and occupation.

7. **Drive-in location:** A special case of free-standing sites that are selected for the purpose of satisfying the needs of customers to shop in their car.

8. **Factory outlet stores:** A limited-line store owned and managed by the manufacturer, often offering production overruns, seconds, and returned merchandise at competitive prices.

9. **Retail format:** The total mix of merchandise, services, advertising, and pricing policies and practices, location, store design, layout used to implement a sustainable competitive advantage.

10. **Free-standing location:** A retail store that stands alone, physically separated from other retail stores.

11. **Huff's model:** A gravitational model which helps estimate the trade area. It considers the size of the shopping centre, how long it would take to travel to each centre, and the type of products the consumer is looking for.

12. **Hypermarket:** A very large retail store that offers low prices and combines a discount stores and a superstore food retailer in one warehouse-like building.

13. **Lifestyle:** An individual's manner of living.

14. **Location analysis:** The use of demographic, economic, culture, demand, competition, and facilities data to determine the area where a retail store will be placed.

15. **Reilly's law:** A gravitational model states the distance a customer will travel to shop, based on the population of the shopping area and the distance between those areas.

16. **Shopping goods:** Goods for which customers are willing to search and compare for price, service, or brand.

17. **Site:** The specific location selected for a retail store.

18. **Speciality goods:** Those goods for which customers have a preconceived need and for which they will make a specific effort to come to the store to purchase.

19. **Target market:** The customer profile of a segment of the people within a geographic area that the store decided to serve.

20. **Trade area:** The retail trade area is the geographic area within which the retail customers for a particular kind of store reside.

21. **Zoning:** The regulation of the construction and use of the building areas of a municipality.

Concept Review Questions

1. From the retailer's perspective, compare the advantages of locating in an unplanned business district versus a planned business district?

2. What are the factors a retailer should consider before selecting a final site for locating his store?

3. What are the factors that a large department store like Shoppers' Stop should consider before finalizing its location?

4. What factors should a *supermarket* chain consider while considering whether to locate as a free standing store on an important street or in a large upcoming mall?

5. How does a developer setting up a mall estimate parking requirements?

6. How do characteristics which define an optimum location for a store selling convenience, shopping, and speciality products differ?

7. How does the land value theory explain the location of retailers in central districts and in the far flung colonies?

Project Work Assignments

1. Interview a retailer in your locality to identify the decision factors used by him to analyse the suitability of the site for locating the store.

2. Compare the retail location strategy of two leading retail stores in your city dealing in the same product category.

3. Identify the factors that attract retailers to establish a temporary set-up in the periodic market near your locality.

4. Identify the list of factors which differentiate the location decision of a retailer of readymade apparels and a gift shop.

Case Study

Dinesh looks outside his first store outlet at the Metropolitan Mall in Gurgaon near Delhi. He sees the two MBA students approaching him for an interview. The students Neetu and Smita had mentioned that they were preparing a case on retail location as part of their MBA studies. Dinesh had readily agreed for the interview. He has opened his second watch outlet in the Metropolitan Mall in Gurgaon just 15 days back; while he is confident about his choice of the Metropolitan Mall as an ideal location for his outlet he is not sure if this outlet will do as well as his first outlet, about 7 to 8 km away at Sadar Bazaar market in Gurgaon.

Neetu: Thanks a lot for granting the interview. Can you please tell us about your outlet at

Sadar market in Gurgaon?

Dinesh: I started retailing in watches in 1994 under the name Ram & Avatar Sons in Sadar market. When I started there were 15 shops selling watches in the Sadar market, now there are about 20 to 25. But Ram & Avatar Sons is the largest and best known. In fact we are the largest watch outlet in the whole state of Haryana.

Smita: You get customers from all over Gurgaon?

Dinesh: You would be surprised to know that my customers come from as far as 50 – 60 kms south of Gurgaon from neighboring towns like Rewari, Pataudi, and Bhiwadi. You may know that Sadar Bazaar in Gurgaon is the destination market for people from this large region. I have customers from all sections of the population from small children to old citizens belonging to all income categories. I keep a large variety of branded watches and am a franchisee of Time Zone. I have expanded my outlet in Sadar and now it is spread over two floors. I plan to add two more floors to the Sadar Bazar outlet.

Neetu: Why did you plan to open an outlet in Metropolitan Mall?

Dinesh: In Sadar market there is too much congestion now; car owners find it difficult to find parking space. They now prefer to shop in the malls where there is abundant parking facility. Besides, these newly upcoming malls provide a much more pleasant shopping experience. I expect such customers would now prefer to shop in the World of Watches—the name I have chosen for this new outlet.

Smita: Do you expect your customers to shift their purchases from Ram & Avatar Sons in Sadar market to the World of Watches outlet in the Metropolitan Mall?

Dinesh: I expect a very small percentage of my customers to shift their purchases from Ram & Avatar Sons to World of watches. As I mentioned many of my customers come from far off places to the south of Gurgaon from small towns. The Sadar market is much more accessible to these people since the railway station and bus terminus are nearby. I don't expect more than 15 – 20% of my customers at Ram & Avatar Sons to shift their purchases to these malls and shop at Word of Watches

Neetu: Then why have you set up this new outlet in the Metropolitan Mall?

Dinesh: I expect most of the customers of Word of Watches to come from colonies in south and west Delhi. I expect that 80% of my customers will be from Delhi. I do not get customers from Delhi at my Sadar market outlet. So you can see that I am targeting a totally different segment of customers.

Smita: Why do so many people come to your shop from colonies in Delhi some of which are more than 20 km away. After all there are many watch retail outlets in Delhi.

Dinesh: They do not come to my shop alone. They come to these malls from Delhi for recreation and shopping. You can see that these malls provide a very pleasant air-conditioned shopping environment. The mall also has abundant parking facilities and is convenient for people owning cars. Because of that they attract people from Delhi. Besides that many people from Delhi work in Gurgaon; they also prefer to do their shopping in these malls.

Neetu: What else would be different about your customers in Sadar market and here?

Dinesh: My customers in Sadar market are from a cross-section of the society, most of them use public transportation. I expect my customers at the Metropolitan Mall to be from upper middle class and middle-class income groups. The customers here would generally be car owners. Also I expect a large number of my customers here to be younger in age.

Smita: Why do you expect younger crowd to come to this shop?

Dinesh: This mall attracts youngsters because of the presence of a large number of eating joint, pubs, and cineplexes. There are 4–5 pubs near my shop.

Neetu: Did you do any survey before deciding on this location?

Dinesh: I am in business for long. I understand the needs of my customers and, hence, I could identify the customers who would prefer to shop here. I met a lot of shop owners in the mall and also had discussions with my customers. I estimated the daily walk-ins to be around 6000 to 8000 going up further on week ends. As this Mall becomes popular, I expect to do good business.

Neetu: You have chosen the first floor location rather than locating on the ground floor of the mall where the customer traffic is higher why?

Dinesh: The rentals on the ground floor are almost double; I don't expect to do enough business to recover the high rentals on the ground floor. Besides, as you might have seen, the shops on the first floor are smaller and more in number. Since there are larger numbers of shops on the first floor, a broader range of merchandise would be available. That will attract a lot of customers to the first floor. Besides, there are many pubs on the first floor which would attract youngsters.

Neetu: How many customers do you expect at World of Watches every day?

Dinesh: I expect about 400 to 600 walk-ins every day, if the conversion ratio is about 8–10% I will be happy.

Smita: Are these figures based on market research?

Dinesh: I did not do any formal market research; these figures are based on my discussions with other shop owners and my long experience in the field.

Smita: Is there any difference in your business strategy between here and your Sadar market outlet?

Dinesh: I keep a wide range of branded watches and provide repair facility at both these outlets. However, at Sadar I keep more of lower priced brands like Sonata. Here, I plan to keep more of high-priced branded watches. I sell Titan, Timex, Casio, and Citizen brands of watches in Sadar. Here, I am also planning to introduce premium brands like Pierre Cardin and Espirit. The average value of watch I sell in Sadar is priced around Rs 1000/-. Here I expect the average price of a watch sold to be around Rs 2,000/- to Rs 2,500/-.

Neetu and Smita: Thank you very much sir; this has been a great learning opportunity for both of us.

As Neetu and Smita drive back to their college hostel they discuss about their interview.

Smita: Dinesh is certainly an intelligent businessman but I wonder if he has taken the right decision by opening his second outlet in the Metropolitan Mall. I also wonder if Dinesh has made a right decision by locating on the first floor.

Neetu: The Metropolitan Mall attracts a lot of footfalls but I wonder if the people visiting this mall would purchase watches from here. If watches are purchased as impulse products, I suppose the large walk-in crowd would be attracted. I would like to discuss with our professor if watches are convenience, impulse, or shopping products.

1. Has Dinesh done adequate market research before deciding on the location of his second outlet? What else could he have done?

2. Should the watch outlet have been located on the ground floor instead of first floor— what data/information is needed before taking this decision?

3. What are the advantages and disadvantages of a location in a mall like the Metropolitan Mall compared to a location in a central business district like Sadar Bazar?

References

1. BucKlin, L.P. 1963, 'Retail Strategy and the classification of goods', *Journal of Marketing*, 27, 53–54.

2. Christaller, W. 1966, *Central Places of Southern Germany*, Prentice-Hall, Englewood Cliffs, NJ.

3. Lösch, A. 1941, Die räimliche Ordnumb der Wirtscharft, Gustav Fischer, Jena.

4. Reilly, W.J. 1931, *The Law of Retail Gravitation*, Knicker-bocker Press, New York, NY.

5. Huff, D.L. 1963, 'A Probabilistic Analysis of Consumer Spatial Behaviour', *Emerging Concepts in Marketing*, Ed. William S. Decker, American Marketing Association, Chicago, pp. 443–461.

6. Haig, R. 1927, Regional Survey of New York and Its Environs, New York City Planning Commission, New York.

7. Alonso, W. 1964, Location and Land Use, Harvard University Press, Cambridge, MA.

8. Lindquist, J.D. 1974–75, 'Meaning of Image: A Survey of Empirical and Hypothetical Evidence', *Journal of Retailing*, 50, pp. 29–38.

9. Martineau, Pierre 1958, 'The Personality of Retail Store', *Harvard Business Review*, 47–55.

10. Applebaum, W. 1970, *Shopping Center Strategy*, International Council of Shopping Centers, New York.

11. Rajshekhar, M. 2003, 'Conflict Street: India's department stores are entering each other's markets, and a new era of competition', www.businessworldindia.com, March 24.

12. Roy, C. 2003, Times News Network, www.economictimes.com, Dec. 20.

7 PRODUCT AND MERCHANDISE MANAGEMENT

Learning Objectives

- To understand the role of product and merchandise management in retail business

- To analyse the significance of retail branding, especially in the context of private labels

- To discuss the nature of merchandise budgeting and unit planning

- To identify the constraining factors in merchandise management

- To describe the steps in model stock plan

- To identify the types of suppliers and explain their selection criterion

- To explain the tools used for measuring merchandise performance

Introduction

Product and merchandise management is a key activity in the management of retail business. It drives the business strategy of the retailer and has immense cost and profit implications. A related issue is also the management of retail brands and the decision to offer retailer's private labels along with, or instead of, national and local brands. While product management deals with issues related to the kind of products sold by the retailer, merchandise management concerns itself with the selection of the right quantity of the product and ensuring its availability at the right place and time. This involves a careful planning of merchandise mix and its financial implications are reflected in the merchandise budget. The product and merchandise plan is drawn keeping in mind various factors that influence shopping behaviour and the strategic and cost concerns of the retailer.

Product Management

Products are critical to a retail firm's existence and profitability. They constitute the basis of exchange transactions between retailers and customers. Products, in a retailing context, are defined as anything sold and purchased in a retail transaction. Hence, it could constitute goods, services, places, events, ideas, etc. A product could be tangible or intangible. Examples of outlets selling intangible products are service-focussed stores like beauty parlours, massage parlours, gymnasiums, banks, and other advisory services. Some of them may sell goods as well—beauty parlours and gymnasiums may also sell some personal care products and health formulations. Some of them could be their private labels while some could be outsourced from other manufacturers. It is also possible that in due course the goods component of the retail business may become more profitable than the service component. The opposite may hold true for goods-based retail outlets that offer some services as well. For typical retail outlets, services may take the form of home-delivery service, entertainment and child-care facilities, information and advisory services like interior designing services provided by home-solution product retailers, etc. Lakme Lever has started relying on beauty advisors at sales counters to push the sales of its products.

Product management, in the context of retailing, may be defined as a set of decisions related to the selection and removal of products from the retailers' portfolio, along with the related product and market analysis.

Role of Product Management in Retail Business

Product management is critical to the success of retail business. Identification of the products to be retailed forms the core component of the retailer's business plan. Hence, it determines business profitability to a large extent. There are different cost implications in sourcing various kinds of products. Besides, there are varied demand patterns and competitive factors for different product categories.

Product management by the retail firm is critical to the satisfaction of consumer needs. Satisfaction of consumer needs is important to the success of retail operations. Selection of the product is designed to meet some unmet needs of the customer. For example, every shopping centre, whether planned or unplanned, has at least one eating outlet, a grocery shop, and a chemist shop. This is primarily because they are largely retail convenience products where accessibility is a prime concern. Besides, the retailer must update himself with the changes in product categories and product innovations and should also be flexible enough to alter product profiles accordingly. For example, most fast food joints offering Indian cuisine have also started incorporating Chinese menu as well. The PVR Cinemas in Delhi have begun offering *Nachos*, a popular Mexican snack, from their outlets. It felt this to be important since many of its patrons were globe-trotters or at least people who had had an exposure to various cuisines. Besides, *Nachoes* had already started appearing on the shelves of many department stores and *supermarkets* in India.

Product management is also an implementation of the segmentation strategy of the retailer who attempts to attract the target segment through the product profile and the specific pricing strategies. For example, if a retailer seeks to exploit the potential in the kid's segment, the product profile would consist of categories like toys, kids' garments, baby strollers, car seats, baby cots, etc. Besides, changes in the product profile is an effective strategy followed by many retailers to innovate on their existing offers and in many cases to *re-position* their store.

Levi's Product Strategy in France

Out with unisex, in with jeans for women only. That is part of Levi's new strategy in France. Hoping to lift sales in its vital European market, Levi Strauss last week opened its first jeans boutique for young women. The company then plans a gradual dividing of the sexes in other stores, with many just for women, many for men. The new store in Paris, called 'Levi's for Girls', will be aimed at women between 19 and 25 years of age, though the company readily admits that the average customer is more likely to be 15 to 22. Levi Strauss also plans to transform its Paris flagship into a store for men only. This is all part of a broad plan to have multiple outlets for different corners of the market.

Source: The Herald, Tuesday, September 30, 2003

Display of ladies apparel at Pantaloon store

The Pantaloon Store in Mumbai—The Product and Brand Profile

Pantaloon Retail (India) Limited is recognized as one of the pioneers in the business of organized retailing in India. The company is headquartered in Mumbai, with zonal offices in Kolkata, Bangalore, and Hyderabad. Its mega retail store at High Street, Phoenix Mills (Lower Parel), Mumbai, is spread over 50,000 sq. ft and has an international look with an Indian feel.

The store consists of three floors. The ground floor caters to women, offering fashion and leather accessories, cosmetics, perfumes, jewellery, etc. The women's section also houses international brands like L'Oreal, Maybelline, Gucci, Jane Shilton, etc. There is a designer gallery, Springboard, which houses prêt collections of eminent designers such as Rohit Bal, Anshu Arora Sen, Sonali Mansingka, etc.

The first floor caters to both women and children. It offers ladies' apparels, teens' apparels, children's apparel, ethnic wear, lingerie, infant necessities, ladies/children footwear, toys, eye-wear, watches, etc. It also houses international brands such as BIBA, Annabelle, Oye, Jockey, Catwalk, Popeye, Disney, Espirit, Funskool, and Barbie.

The second floor caters to men, which includes formals, smart casuals, denims, men's accessories, etc. The men's section houses international brands like Nike, Hugo, Reebok, Levis, Scullers, Arrow, Black Berrys, etc. It is a one stop family store for all the well-known brands.

Source: www.retailyatra.com

The Product Selection Process

The product selection process involves a review of the performance of the existing product range. This exercise aids in deleting some products or assists in revising various aspects of product portfolio. A retailer is required to consider various issues related to the selection of products to be retailed. These relate to the type of products to be retailed, life cycle of the products, trends in the product category, and its strategic fit with the retailer's business. Broadly, it helps to identify the opportunities to bring in new products or product-related attributes to meet the changing preferences of the target customers.

Product performance review *utilises* information collected from secondary and primary sources such as sales report, product profitability reports, quality reports, return figures, promotional campaign results and plans, product–market trend information, and consumer research. These tools are used regularly by the retailers in the organized sectors, as they possess most of such information about each product. However, retailers in the unorganized sector take such decisions on the basis of experience and through observation of movement of a particular product from the specified shelf.

Product range review assists retailers to go in for possible decisions such as:

- Deletion of a product
- Increase in variety and range
- Identification of new suppliers
- Additions to product features
- Review and revision of promotional campaign

A corollary of effective product management is brand management. The nature of product assortment is an active ingredient in building a strong retail brand.

Brand Management and Retailing

Of the top ten strongest brands in the world, five are retail brands. Brand management poses several challenges to the retailer. The key issues in retail branding are:

- brand management of the retail outlet; and
- deciding whether or not to opt for the strategy of self own branding.

Retailers may also choose to adopt a multi-pronged strategy.

A strong retail brand and a strong private label strategy can be an effective tool to differentiate the stores and the shopping experience. The ten strongest brands in the world are given below:

The ten strongest brands in the world

Coca Cola	Wal-Mart
McDonald's	Ford
Sony	Levi's
Nike	Gap
Microsoft	Amazon

Strong retail brands have a sharper definition of their brand identity in terms of the following criteria:

- Who am I?
- What do I do?
- How am I different from others?
- Why buy me?

The sharper this focus, the stronger is the retail brand.

A retailer's brand is valuable since it enhances reach and endurance with the consumer, and ensures a more focused strategic plan. The elements of a store brand are shown in Fig. 7.1. In many cases 'store' as a brand is stronger than the 'brands' stored within. In the retail boom that India is going through, many manufacturing brands are losing their identity to retail brands. For example, a customer, when coming out of a Pantaloon showroom after buying a Peter England shirt, is heard saying, 'I bought this shirt from Pantaloons,' instead of saying, 'I have bought a Peter England shirt.' So here Pantaloon may have become a stronger brand than Peter England. Hindustan Lever had also observed a similar phenomenon when their products were being sold through Hallmark outlets.

A store brand evolves from the following seven components: product assortment, location, visual merchandising, experience, price, format, and service. In this context, the strongest retail brand in India is considered the neighbourhood kirana store. It draws its brand strength from location, defined in terms of accessibility, experience, price, and service. Due to their location they are in a better position to provide home delivery services. Besides, due to constant interaction with their customers they are in a better position to maintain close relationship with them. This enables them to offer better services to the customer, often at negotiated lower prices. The department stores and supermarkets, which are entering the Indian market recently, draw their brand strength largely from visual merchandising, format, product assortment, and location. Location contributes to brand perception in terms of the brand image of the shopping centre itself.

Fig. 7.1   Elements of a store brand

Own Branding

Own branding occurs when a retailer sells products under the retail organization's house brand name. A KSA Technopak study confirms what has already been popularly understood—consumers see retail labels as brands. Own branding can be of two types, integrated own branding and independent contracting. Integrated own branding occurs when the retailer also manufactures the branded retail products. This ensures greater control over quality and delivery. Some examples are the Raymonds, Bose, and Sony retail outlets in India. Independent contracting occurs when the retailer procures the products from other suppliers though, they are sold under the label of the retail house. This strategy is quite popular in product categories like grocery, garments, shoes, and even some electronic goods.

Pantaloon and LifeStyle

Pantaloon and LifeStyle are two powerful retail chains in India. Both are increasingly becoming aware of the competitive challenges in the retail business. One way that they are trying to increase margins is by pushing their own in-house labels. In Big Bazaar (from the Pantaloon stable), for instance, gross margins on grocery and food products from in-house labels is around 4% higher than on competing brands. As a result, the company has been pushing these products, which constitute

25% of its sales currently. A similar tactic is being followed at LifeStyle. The company has developed its own brands like Splash, Nexus, and 2Extremz in the apparels department, which currently make up about 11% of the company's business.

Source: Surajeet Das Gupta 2003, Shopping in style, *Business Standard,* www.businessstandard .com July 26.

Significance of Own Branding

Private label sales have showed an increase in terms of both value and volume across countries. A study by A. C. Nielsen reveals that of the 28 countries surveyed, private label share of product categories such as food, drink, personal care, and household ranged between 5% and 20% in value terms in most countries. In most countries reviewed, both household and food categories showed the highest private label penetration levels, as is expected from products whose brand loyalty is lowest. Private labels were found to be less developed in drinks and personal care products, reflecting the strength of branding in these two categories.

Private labels at FoodWorld

A well-run private label brand enhances store profitability by increasing pressure on branded manufacturers. Lower marketing cost also reduces profitability of the private label brand. Purchase prices can be significantly lower and can be used to increase margins or offer products at lower prices. It ensures better control over price, delivery, and quality, and also ensures a strong brand identity for a retailer. In fact, national brands are increasingly feeling a threat from private labels.

However, retailers need to exercise caution in cases where the national brands are too powerful and the product category is considered a high-risk purchase by the consumer. Besides, private labels may not always be considered feasible where the minimum order sizes are too small. An effective private label programme should include all elements of the value proposition—price, quality, and product differentiation.

The strategic intent of retail product and brand management is executed through effective merchandise management.

Merchandise Management

The primary function of retailing is to sell merchandise. One of the most strategic aspects of the retail business is to decide the merchandise mix and quantity to be purchased. Merchandise management is the process by which a retailer attempts to offer the right quantity of the right product at the right place and time while meeting the retail firm's financial goals. Merchandise management is the analysis, planning, procurement, handling, and control of the merchandise investments of a retail operation. The components of merchandise management are shown in Fig. 7.2.

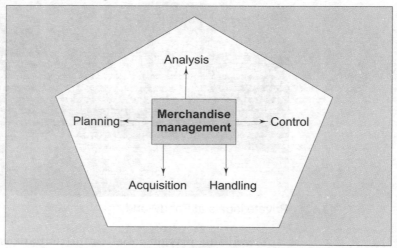

Fig. 7.2   Components of merchandise management

Merchandise analysis expects retailers to identify the target segment prior to determining their needs in order to buy the required merchandise. Merchandise planning consists of establishing objectives and devising plans for obtaining merchandise well in advance of the selling season.

Merchandise control involves designing the policies and procedures in order to determine whether the stated objectives or goals have been achieved. Planning is the process of establishing performance guidelines, whereas control is the process of checking how well a management is following those guidelines. The objectives range from the corporate strategic objectives to the micro-level objectives regarding the merchandise assortment, stocking, and re-order.

The merchandise mix represents the full range of mixture of products a retailer offers to its target consumers. Developing the merchandise mix provides a retailer with one of the means to segment the total market and appeal to a select group of consumer segments.

Merchandise mix management covers decisions on a host of key parameters, also shown in Fig. 7.3, such as merchandise variety, assortment, and support. This would lead to an appropriate combination of product lines, product items, and product units. Merchandise variety is the number of different product lines that a retailer stocks in the store. Merchandise assortment refers to the number of different product items the retailer stocks within a particular product line. Merchandise support deals with the planning and control of the number of units the retailer should have on hand to meet the expected sales for a particular product. Merchandise budget is a financial tool for planning and controlling a retailer's merchandise inventory investment.

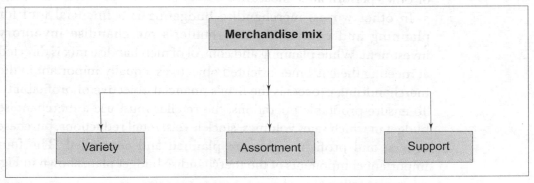

Fig. 7.3   Key dimensions of the merchandise mix

Merchandise Specialization

At times, retailers choose to specialize in a single kind of merchandise and choose to carry a very deep assortment. For example, in the Chandni Chowk market in Delhi a particular lane is referred to as the Paranthe Wali gali. *Paratha* is an Indian bread savoury. All the retail food outlets only sell different variants of *parathas* with a vegetable curry and pickle. Sometimes they may also serve a simple dessert. The customers are attracted to the lane primarily because of its specialization. This is also the reason for its popularity. Similar examples are seen in many parts of India—shops selling *Chikan* embroidered material and garments in the Chowk and Aminabad markets of Lucknow, shops selling bandhni material and garments in Jaipur, etc. Specialization is their best advertisement.

Similarly, many shops may choose to specialize in a particular kind of merchandise without sensing the need to carry a deeper assortment. An example is the *Tunde Kabab* in Lucknow, offering just two variants of this non-vegetarian delicacy along with an Indian bread to go along with it. Its unique preparation has become best advertisement and the outlet has become popular nationally and internationally. This kind of specialization also offers immense benefits in terms of logistics and resultant cost savings. A similar example is offered by many shops in Hyderabad selling only the famous Hyderbadi *biryani*.

Merchandise Budget

Merchandise budget is referred to as a financial plan that indicates how much to invest in product inventories, usually stated in rupees per month. Earmarking of merchandising budgets is considered to be a vital component of the planning phase. Usually, a budget states the amount allocated for each product, based on the pre-set profitability or other performance measures.

In other words, merchandise budgeting is a financial tool for planning and controlling the retailer's merchandise inventory investment. While planning and control of merchandise mix is directed at meeting the customer-oriented objectives, equally important in the merchandising process is the firm's financial objective of profitability. To ensure profitable operations, the retailer must use a merchandise budget in which sales volumes, stock levels, retail reductions, purchase orders, and profit margins are planned and controlled. The four important components of the merchandise budget plan, shown in Fig. 7.4, are as follows.

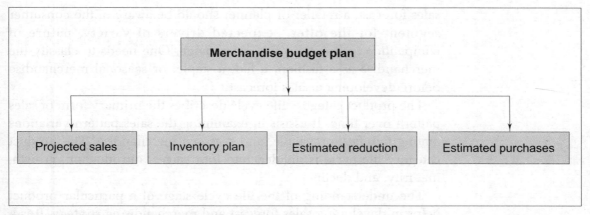

Fig. 7.4   Components of merchandise budget plan

1. Projected sales
2. Inventory plan
3. Estimated reductions
4. Estimated purchases

These aspects of merchandise budget require due consideration from the retailer or the concerned decision-maker.

Projected Sales

Budget planning starts with the development of a sales plan, this shows the expected or projected rupees volume of sales for each merchandise or department. Sales forecasting helps the management in a forecast of expected sales. Without having information on how much is to be sold, the retailer cannot determine how much to buy. Mistakes made at this stage will be reflected in the entire budgeting plan and may incur huge losses to the management in the future.

In India, most of the retail set-ups in the unorganized sector, irrespective of product category they are in, make a sales forecast on the basis of the past experiences, intuition, trends in related goods markets, information from the suppliers or co-retailers, and customers. Sales forecast requires sufficient understanding of the product or service one is dealing with. The upcoming organized retail set-ups are banking on the management tools to determine their projected sales.

Usually, product categories experience an expected sales pattern: sales start at low, then increase gradually, stabilize, and finally decline. It is important to understand that the pattern experienced varies from one product category to another product category. While making the sales forecast, a retailer or planner should be aware of the consumer segment for the offer, expected drivers of variety, nature of competition, promotion, and price range. One needs to classify the merchandise as a fashion, a fad, a staple, or seasonal merchandise before developing a sales forecast.

The product category life cycle describes the primary form of sales pattern over time. It assists in examining the sales pattern variations among fad, fashion, staple, and seasonal merchandise. The product category life cycle is divided into four stages: introduction, growth, maturity, and decline.

The understanding of the life cycle stage of a particular product helps in developing sales forecast and merchandising strategy. It is a well-known fact that the product category life cycle stage affects the retail marketing mix such as target market, variety, place, price, and advertising. The life cycle stages and the corresponding strategy variables are shown in Table 7.1.

The target market for a newly introduced product is usually the high-income innovator. For example, cellular phones, introduced in India in 1996, targeted the high-income professionals or the business class. It was, no doubt, very expensive in comparison to the other modes of communication. With time, as the category reached the early and late stages, they became more appealing to the middle-income, mass-market customers who were the target market for discount stores. This clearly shows how a new entry in the market enlarges its market as it moves along its life cycle.

The variety available in cellular phone was small at its introductory stage. However, today the Indian retail market is experiencing a huge expansion with a wide range of choices based on colour, product features, and price levels.

Distribution intensity refers to the number of retailers carrying a particular category. In the introductory stage, a product is distributed from a limited number of outlets. For example, in India, colour television was initially acquired by people in the metros. Even after 20 years of introduction of CTV in Indian markets, most of the semi-urban areas acquired it from the adjoining cities. In the same manner, cell phone was earlier available in major cities only but today even the smaller cities have a good number of unorganized retailers along with company-owned outlets in this sector. It is often observed that as the new offer gains popularity in the growth and maturity stages, retail penetration increases. At the same time, when certain products like pagers experience decline in sales, fewer or no retailer intends to stock the product.

The pricing strategy for a newly introduced product can be either high-skimming or low penetration, depending on the type of category and the level of distribution penetration. As new offerings in limited supply are available from a limited number of stores, they enjoy high prices. For example, initially pizza offered in the Indian markets enjoyed premium prices as they were available from a limited number of branded retail outlets, but as pizza gained popularity and new retailers joined the market, this resulted in increased supply and reduced the prices of pizza.

Amul Enters Pizza Market

Amul, India's best-known dairy co-operative, is now making international fast food majors like Dominos and Pizza Hut jittery.

If the response they have generated in Ahmedabad and now New Delhi is any indication then Amul's pizzas are set to take Indian cities by storm.

Going by the serpentine queues that form outside the Amul outlet that opened in Ahmedabad last week, there is hardly any room for doubt that its pizzas are already a rage.

The Gujarat Co-operative Milk Marketing Federation, the Rs 20-billion co-operative and proud owners of the Amul brand of milk and milk products, opened its first pizza outlet at Surat, in south Gujarat, about a month ago.

Opening pizza outlets was part of a pilot project and a dairy in Surat was a test case.

'We enjoy 75 per cent of the cheese market. The idea was to further popularise our cheese,' GCMMF managing director B. M. Vyas told IANS from Anand, about 75 km from Ahmedabad.

Priced a mere Rs 20 a piece, Amul pizza was a runaway success, prompting the GCMMF to go for a bigger plan that includes opening 3,000 outlets in 300 cities across the country.

Amul Pizza from its retail outlet

Outlets have opened in New Delhi even as trade inquiries are pouring in at Anand. The GCMMF plans to open outlets in cities where it already has strong presence. Ahmedabad alone may have about 100 outlets this year.

'Of course we want to sell more cheese,' said brand manager Pawan Kumar. The GCMMF sells about 3,500 tons of Amul cheese annually. Kumar expects its sales to go up by about 1000 tons.

The runaway success of the outlet at Royal Sweet Mart, off the upmarket CG Road in Ahmedabad, has only reinforced GCMMF's resolve to take its pizzas across India.

Vyas says that the federation will position its pizza as a mass consumption product and will leverage its countrywide distribution network to promote it.

Mushroom, margarita, tomato-onion and fruit are some of the toppings that Amul offers to begin with.

That the GCMMF is pretty serious about its latest venture is obvious because it has included the 'Jain pizza' among its offerings.

The Jain pizza will not have any root produce like onion, ginger or garlic in the dressing. This keeps in mind the fact that the Jain community does not consume roots.

With projected sales of 100 pizzas a day at each outlet in the very first year, Amul will indeed have a tall order at hand.

Source: Pradeep Mallik 2001, Indo-Asian News Service, www.rediff.com, July 23.

The understanding of category life cycle stage helps in predicting sales. For example, the choice of distribution intensity or pricing strategy in the introduction stage or growth stage will influence whether the product will have high or modest sales. For example, if embroidery work declines, retailers are expected to maintain less stock and carry limited advertising. This will lead to decrease in sales. It indicates clearly that the stage of life cycle a particular product category enjoys will indicate the sales expected in future. The product life cycle curve is shown in Fig 7.5.

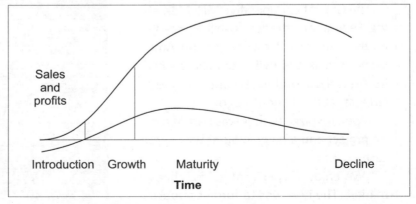

Fig. 7.5 Product life cycle

Table. 7.1 Life cycle stages

Strategy Variable	Introduction	Growth	Maturity	Decline
Target Market	High-income innovators	Middle-income	Mass Market	Low-income
Variety	One basic offering	Limited variety Product features	Greater Variety	Less Variety
Penetration	Limited or extensive	More retailers	More retailers Multiple retail formats	Fewer or no retailers
Price	Penetration or skimming	More price level	Lower prices	Lower prices
Promotion	Informative, induce trial	Persuasive	Competitive	Limited

Retailers are required to incorporate the variations on the category life cycle while developing sales forecast. The special categories of product life cycle are style, fashion, fad, staple, and seasonal. The distinctions to be noticed among them are whether the category passes through four stages or many seasons, whether a specific style sells for many seasons, and whether sales vary from one season to the next.

A style is a basic and distinctive mode of expression, appearing in a field of human endeavour. Styles popularly appear in clothing (formal, western, casual) and art (classical, realistic, abstract). Style can last for generations, going in and out of vogue. For example, Indian working women feel more comfortable in the modified version of Salwar Kameez which looks similar to business suits. A fashion is currently accepted or is a popular style in a given field. Fashions pass through four stages: distinctiveness, emulation, mass fashion, and decline. For example, different movie themes (social, action, family-oriented, romantic, and period movies) have been popular in India during different stages from 1960s to 1990s.

Till a decade ago, it was popular among the upper and middle class to watch movies in cinema halls followed by dinner in a restaurant. Now it has become more fashionable to watch movies on video system at homes.

Fads are fashions that come quickly into public view, are adopted with great zeal, peak early, and decline very fast. The sales generated are short-lived, often lasting less than a season. For example, the craze for imported sports and decorated material from China, hairstyles, and fashion accessories. They tend to attract those who are looking for excitement or want to distinguish themselves from others.

Offerings within the staple product category are in continuous demand over an extended period of time. Sales forecast for the staple items are fairly easy and mechanical compared to those for fashion merchandise. Estimating sales of staple items requires extension of sales trends from the past into the future. However, for fashion merchandise, past trends along with other issues (colour patterns, duration of season) play crucial role.

Exponential smoothing is a forecasting technique in which sales in the corresponding period in the past are weighted to forecast future trends. This technique provides due weightage to unexpected increments or decrements without ignoring the historical average since the variation could be a random occurrence:

The following formula takes into account the two sales forecasting objectives of being responsive and ignoring random occurrence:

New forecast = Old forecast + α (Actual demand − Old forecast)

The Greek letter alpha (α) is constant between 0 and 1 that determines the influence of actual demand on the new forecast. When demand is increasing or decreasing sharply, high values of alpha, such as 0.5, cause the forecast to react quickly. Low values of alpha, such as 0.1, are appropriate when demand is changing very slowly. Therefore, if value of alpha is too high, an unsteady sales forecast results because of overreaction to random changes in trend. On the other hand, if alpha is too low, the forecast will always lag behind or move ahead of the trend.

In India, even staple items like groceries experience the impact of seasonality or festival periods. Demands for various products tend to rise around festive seasons; and the demand for a product concerned varies from region to region. For example, during Diwali the consumption of sugar, milk, and milk products increases among Hindu families. During Id festival, among Muslims, a similar phenomenon is experienced in case of sugar and semolina to make the popular desserts. Therefore, the retailers, based on their specific locational context, need to incorporate these trends while making sales forecast.

Inventory Plan

Inventory management plan provides information regarding sales velocity, inventory availability, ordered quantity, inventory turnover, sales forecast, and quantity to order for specific SKU. Inventory plan assists retailers in scheduling orders to vendors after considering trade-off between carrying cost versus the cost of ordering and handling the inventory. The more they purchase at one time, the higher the carrying costs, but the lower the buying and handling costs.

The inventory plan helps to devise the stock support levels for a specific sales period. Most widely used methods to determine the stock support levels, also shown in Fig 7.6, are: beginning-of-the-month ratios, weeks' supply method, the percentage variation method, and the basic stock method.

The stock/sales ratio (BOM) method relates inventory on the first of the month to the planned sales for that month. This method is quite easy to use but requires retailers to have a BOM stock-to-sales ratio. This ratio informs the retailers about the quantity of inventory needed at the beginning of the month to support the month's estimated sales. The ratio is calculated as follows:

BOM = planned monthly sales * desired stock/sales ratio

A ratio of 1.5, for example, would indicate retailers that they should maintain one and one-half times that month's forecasted sales on hand in inventory at the beginning of the month.

Stock-to-sales can be obtained from internal or external sources. In the Indian context this is not possible in case of retailers belonging to the unorganized sector as they do not maintain a good accounting system. At the same time, there are very limited or no retail trade

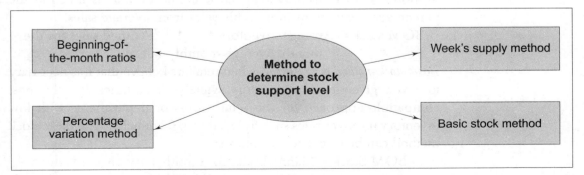

Fig. 7.6   Methods to determine stock support levels

associations which maintain such data. Recently, a few fashion, grocery, and pharmaceutical retail stores have been benking on this methos to determine the amount of stock necessary to support the projected sales. *The week's supply method* is for determining stock levels that states that the inventory level should be set equal to a predetermined number of weeks' supply, which is directly related to the desired rate of stock turnover. The predetermined number of weeks' supply is directly related to the stock turnover rate desired. It is the most widely used by the retailers in the urban and rural areas, where inventories are planned on a weekly basis and in which sales do not fluctuate substantially. This method sets stock levels in direct proportion to sales.

The illustration of week's supply method:

Number of weeks to be stocked = Number of weeks in the period/Stock turnover rate for the period

Average weekly sales = Estimated total sales for the period/ Number of weeks in the period

BOM stock = Average weekly sales * Number of weeks to be stocked

This method allows a retailer to replenish stock frequently, preventing stockouts, and therefore avoids inconvenience to the customers.

Percentage variation method is for planning necessary stock support levels in which stock levels are adjusted based on actual variation in sales. This method is more appropriate for the product categories which experience frequent fluctuations and high yearly turnover rates such as six or more times a year.

Percentage variation method assumes that percentage fluctuations in monthly stock from average stock should be half as much as the percentage fluctuations in monthly sales from average sales.

BOM stock = Average inventory * ½ [1 + (Planned sales for the month/Average monthly sales)]

Basic stock method is preferred when retailers believe that it is necessary to have a given level of inventory available at all times. It is the most compatible approach for the retail stores or departments with low inventory turnover rates such as less than 6.0 annually. The basic stock method can be calculated as follows:

BOM Stock = Planned sales for month + Average inventory – Average monthly sales

Estimated Reductions

Retailers are required to provide for retail reductions along with sales forecast and inventory support levels. Retail reduction is anticipated sales below the list price. Retail reductions are classified into three types of sales below price: markdowns, discounts, and shortages. Markdown is defined as reduction in the original list price to encourage sales of the product. Discounts are reduction in the original retail price given to special customer groups, such as loyal customers. Shortages are reductions in the total value of inventory that results from damages to merchandise, shoplifting, or pilferage. The retailers on the bases of their past experience on retail reductions make adequate arrangements while evolving merchandise budgets.

Estimated Purchase Levels

At this stage a retailer is supposed to devise an actual budget for planned purchase. In other words, planned purchases refer to planned purchases that must be made at the beginning of each month. Here a retailer or planner uses information compiled at the initial stages of merchandise budget planning.

Planned purchases are calculated as follows:

> Planned monthly sales
> + Planned monthly reductions
> + Desired end-of-the-month stock
> ---
> = Total stock needs for the month
> − Planned BOM stock
> ---
> = Planned monthly purchases

The planned monthly purchases figure informs buyers how much they need to spend to support anticipated sales levels considering existing inventories.

Merchandise Planning in Units

The most important component of merchandise planning is stock keeping unit (SKU) plan after merchandise budget plan. Customers categorize retail businesses according to the merchandise mix offered. Permutation and combination of various SKUs take on certain characteristics in the mind of the customers and influence their shopping behaviour in the retail setting. Therefore, it is very crucial for any retail business to channelize its merchandise budget to evolve and

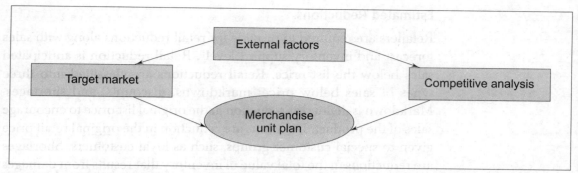

Fig. 7.7 Influence of external factors on merchandise unit plan

acquire the optimal merchandise mix. To a great extent, the merchandise mix defines the strategic question of retail format they are working in or want to work in. Merchandise mix must be in season, the right model, the right style, the right size, the right colour, the right fabric, the right brand, and so on.

Merchandise mix from the perspective of the shopping centre also plays an important role to attract the customers, as it is crucial for the success of the individual retail store. From the point of view of a shopping centre, it is the tenant mix which drives the merchandise mix of a particular retail area.

In this section, we will cover the merchandise mix in the context of the retail store. Retailers or managements have to give due consideration to external factors while formulating the unit plan of merchandise. The impact of external factors on merchandise unit plan is shown in Fig 7.7.

Target Market Analysis

Retailers need to incorporate demographic, shopping behaviour, and psychographic data. This understanding provides a clear explanation of the market situation and its implications for the merchandise mix. For instance, planned centres attempt to control the merchandise mix through the selection of tenants in the shopping centres. Selection of tenants is done based on, among other things, preferences and patronage behaviour of the section of the segment that the shopping centre management intends to serve profitably. For example, DLF City centre shopping mall in Gurgaon has evolved its merchandise mix around female ethnic and formal wear in garments, footwear, etc., by providing retail space to the local brands from the national capital region (Delhi). This indicates that they are targeting middle-aged women looking for popular local brands at competitive prices. However, the Metropolitan Mall in Gurgaon, operating in the same catchment area, prefers tenants who provide merchandise of international brands specifically for menswear. This different approach towards the selection of tenants by shopping centres directly depends on the kind of target segment the particular shopping centre is interested in serving.

On the similar lines in rural India, periodic markets and semi-urban markets are supposed to stock different kinds of merchandise mix in comparison to village retail shops on account of quantity, variety in merchandise lines, and depth and breadth of goods as they cater to not only local customers but also customers from the adjoining villages, who are interested in a variety of goods not available in the villages. Retailers' understanding of their respective target segments will help them to evolve the effective merchandise unit plan. Similarly, in hypermarkets like Giant, as much as much as 65% of the retail space is devoted to food and groceries. But in Big Bazaar, only 30% of the revenues come from this segment. The company contends that this is the percentage that most households spend on food.

Retailers analyze information related to their target segments on the following basic aspects:

- Who is the shopper and consumer of their products, services, and brands—national or private labels
- Segments of shoppers/consumers based on the patterns of shopping and consumption behaviour
- Characteristics of various consumer groups and differences between segments
- Consumers' preference or opinion on products, services, and brands offered by the retailer
- Consumers' complaints and suggestions
- Characteristics of non-patronizing consumer segments
- The number of non-patronizing buyers
- Reasons for not patronizing the store
- To what extent merchandise mix can influence their patronizing behaviour.

The various consumer characteristics that influence the shopping behaviour, shown in Fig. 7.8, are: geographical, demographic,

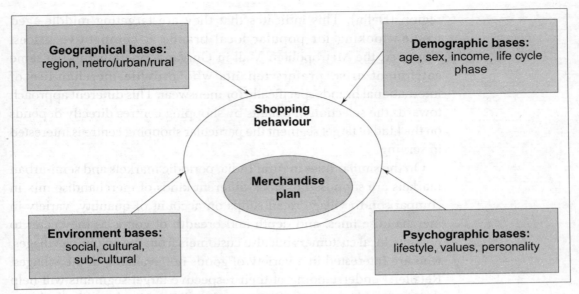

Fig. 7.8 Consumer characteristics that influence the merchandise plan

environmental, and psychographic aspects. These influences on shopping behaviour in turn determine the nature of merchandise plan.

Competition Analysis

Competition analysis covers evaluation of the competitive retail stores in the trade area. The firm is expected to identify the merchandise strengths and weaknesses, voids and opportunities, and bases its merchandise mix planning with required competitive edge. It assists retail stores in devising marketing mix in response to these factors.

The market and competition analyzes are used to articulate a market positioning that identifies the retail store position vis-à-vis its competition, defines its target customers, and describes a viable approach for its merchandising and marketing mix. Therefore, the understanding of market and competitive factors guides the retailers or marketers effectively in the formulation of the optimal merchandise mix. For instance, most of the Indian urban centres have specialized market lanes, which are known for their offerings in a particular product category. Examples are Chowk area in Lucknow, which is known for Chikan work and vegetarian and non-vegetarian Indian snacks; Nai Sarak (new lane) in Delhi is famous for books; Zaveri Bazaar in Mumbai is considered India's biggest jewellery market; Gaffar Market in Delhi is famous for imported merchandise in multiple product categories from electronics to decorative materials. To establish a retail venture in such markets requires huge investment in terms of owning or renting a shop, to be able to maintain a wide variety of inventory as most of the retailers maintain a comprehensive stock covering almost all brands and available SKUs. A retailer may attempt to enter a shopping centre where a wide variety of product categories are already available. In such a case, he needs to identify the major competitors and their respective advantages drawn on the basis of merchandise mix alone. This will help him to plan a competitive merchandise and to meet any unmet demand. For instance, Time Zone retail chain operating throughout India offers all the leading brands of watches with comprehensive ranges available in each brand. They have positioned their retail chain against the big retailers in the unorganized sector on the basis of a comprehensive merchandise mix, including authorized service centres of the respective brands which the consumer expects to be located under one roof.

The optimal merchandise mix consists of three dimensions within a merchandise line; it consists of a group of products that are closely related because they are intended for the same end use, are sold to the same customer group, or fall within a given price range.

The merchandise plan is also determined by competitive factors like number, types, and positioning of the anchor store and non-anchor stores, and size and nature of the market area in which the particular retailer is operating his/her business (see Fig. 7.9).

Today, some retailers manage categories, or lines, as a strategic business unit. When using category management, buyers are no longer concerned with Gross Margin on Inventory Investment (GMROI) for just the single product but would be concerned with the GMROI for the entire line or category.

Merchandise Differentiation

Westside, the fashion department store, does not deal in cosmetics and perfumes as distinct from other fashion department stores such as Shoppers' Store and LifeStyle. This has not only positioned them differently from the competitors but has also provided financial and physical (space) resources for their core ready-to-wear garment merchandise.

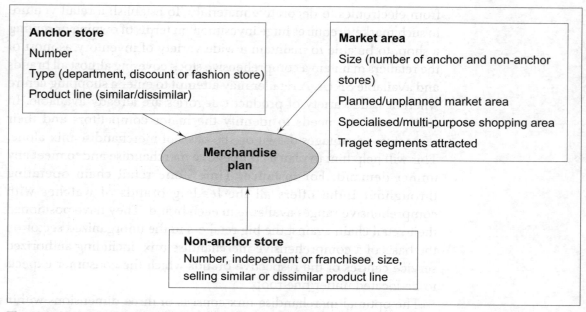

Fig. 7.9   Influence of competitive factors on merchandise plan

Criteria of Merchandise Classification

Merchandise can be clasified according to the following characteristes:

1. Unit value
2. Significance of each individual purchase to the consumer
3. Time and effort spent in purchasing by consumers
4. Rate of technological change (including fashion changes)
5. Technical complexity
6. Consumer need for service (before, during, or after the sale)
7. Frequency of purchase
8. Rapidity of consumption

The variety of the merchandise mix refers to the number of different merchandise lines that the retailer stocks in the store or department. Such lines are menswear, women's wear, children' clothing, toys, appliances, and household goods.

For any retail business its store image will guide the number of lines to carry, the price and quality range of merchandise within these lines, the lines that will be considered major lines, the complementary line or minor lines that should be carried, and so on. Space limitation and lack of funds for the investment in the inventories may be the major limitations to an expanded product offering. For example, in India most of the traditional eating joints faced with unexpected competition from the multinational chains, particularly McDonald's and Pizza Hut. In order to meet the competition they have added new product lines other than Indian cuisine, such as Chinese, Italian, Thai preparations, etc. In the same manner, most of the grocery stores in India started keeping the over the counter (OTC) medicines demanded by their customers and also provided them good margin in comparison to existing product mix. This has also enlarged the retail network for the pharmaceutical companies to distribute their products to immediate customers.

In India, most of the independent small retailers do not use a formalized merchandising system and inspite of that they are successful in managing optimal merchandise mix. To determine the inclusion and viability of any new product in the existing merchandise line, usually, retailers examine such offers on (see Fig. 7.10) three aspects:

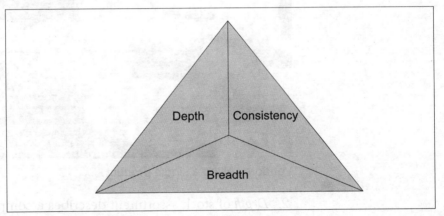

Fig. 7.10   Dimensions of merchandise line

1. *Breadth*, also called assortment, refers to the number of merchandise brands found in the merchandise line. Breadth is especially a problem for retailers selling private label brands.

   Therefore, a battle of the brands occurs when retailers, in determining the breadth of the product assortment, have their own products competing with the manufacturer's products for shelf space and control over display location. Merchandise decisions are constrained by the amount of money available to spend on inventory and the amount of space available in the store. For example, retailers dealing in consumer durables maintain an extensive range of brands in all the products (TV, Audio System and Refrigerators), particularly located in metros, whereas retailers in semi-urban settings have to run their business with a limited number of brands. On similar lines, most of the fashion department stores carry good stock of the private labels along with national brands in all the possible categories to not only tap the market segments but also to ensure financial viability of that particular product category.

Vendors selling a single product

2. *Depth* of stock assortment describes a comprehensive selection of brands, sizes, styles, colours, and prices within a particular category of product. In other words, it is the average number of stock keeping units within each brand of merchandise line. Specialist stores prefer to provide deep assortment within narrow merchandise variety. Most of the supermarkets or bid retailers carry deep assortments in each merchandise lines.

3. *Consistency*, the third dimension of the retail merchandise mix, refers to how closely or compatible the product lines are related in terms of consumer purchasing habits and end use. A low degree of consistency is found where scrambled merchandising occurs. For example, in India, most of the retailers operating in the periodic shopping centres in urban and rural areas go for minimal

consistency in their product mix, in comparison to retailers with established infrastructure. Low consistency in merchandise mix is also a very common phenomenon in the case of consumer fairs during festive periods and at discount stores.

Vendors selling multiple vegetables

Retail stores' pattern of breadth, depth, and consistency will change over the time as the needs of the target customer market and the environment changes. Such changes lead to changes in the marketing mix, which has its impact on the merchandise mix.

Points to Consider for Devising a Strategic Merchandise Assortment Plan

1. Which product lines does your store intend to carry?
2. Which items or products within these lines does your store intend to carry?
3. How much width will your store carry?
4. How much depth will your store carry?
5. How much consistency will your store have?
6. How do you intend to use tools such as stock–turnover and stock–sales ratios to help your assortment planning?
7. How does the 80/20 principle apply?
8. How can you effectively use scrambled merchandising to help your store sales and profits?
9. How can your store create customer interest and differential advantage by the merchandise it offers?

After comprehensive decision on merchandise lines and their respective breadth and depth, a retailer is expected to work on a model stock plan. The assortment of items that will comprise the merchandise mix must then be planned. This final mix should be determined by a combination of creative and analytical thought.

Model Stock Plan

Model stock plan is a plan for maintaining adequate merchandise on hand. It characterizes the decisive items and their respective quantities that should be on hand for each merchandise line the retail business is dealing in, and is developed after the retailer decides what relative importance will be placed on each dimension of the merchandise mix. Model stock planning is a quantitative method, which provides guidelines on the size, colour, brand, and composition of stock that specify the exact nature of merchandise. Model stock planning comprises the following steps (Fig. 7.11).

Identify the Attributes Considered by the Customer in Purchasing the Product

For example, in case of a restaurant, the customer generally evaluates the offer on the basis of the nature of cuisine (Indian, Chinese, Mexican, South Indian, etc.) the nature of preparation (vegetarian or non-vegetarian food) and the respective offering in each case. In case of

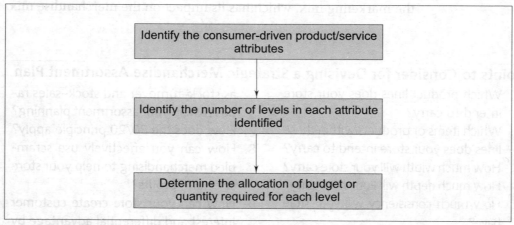

Fig. 7.11   Steps involved in model stock plan

garments, it depends on attributes like focus of the store on men's, women's, or kids' clothing, and the availability in terms of sizes, brands (national or private labels), and nature of garments—formal, casual, or ethnic. For example, Pantaloon store offers varied merchandise in terms of men's and women's garments and accessories, varied sizes and seasonal variations. However, it avoids giving due importance to the national brands in model stock plan as its research indicates that customers have a greater concern for the nature of products rather than the availability of brands.

Identify the Number of Levels Under Each Attribute

After identifying all possible attributes used by the customer to select the merchandise, retailers are required to list the levels available in the respective product category. At this stage the retailer prepares a list of the levels he intends to offer to his target segment keeping in view their preferences and offerings of the competitors. For example, Rajouri Garden central market in west Delhi has a number of leading restaurants like McDonald's, Bikaner, and Sagar Ratna offering a wide variety of quality food items to a largely Punjabi dominated area. The new retail chain, It's Only Paranthas (Punjabi stuffed chapati) proved to be a great success in a short time in such a competitive market as it only excelled in a specific product line by offering all possible levels in that category.

Similarly, retailers of white goods need to keep track of attributes preferred by customers and then plan an optimal merchandise mix. Retailers from unorganized sectors, selling high involvement product categories, depend on the experience of co-retailers and suppliers and the feedback of the customers to identify the relevant levels of attributes to plan the merchandise mix.

Allocate the Total Money or Units to the Respective Product Categories

This is the acid test for any retailer while planning for the optimal merchandise mix. It does not encompass the costs incurred for acquiring the merchandise but does include the ordering cost, transportation, and stocking cost. It is a well-known fact that after capital investment, major resources of the retailer are blocked in inventory. Therefore, optimal merchandise mix should meet the cost criterion at the retailer's end. In India, most of the retailers in the unorganized sector depend on wholesalers or big retailers trading in multiple product lines along with comprehensive brands. This saves their costs in terms of search and managing of various account heads. In the recent past, exclusive dealers for particular companies have gained recognition in the value chain. While allocating funds to each category and its respective variants, retailers take into consideration the turnover rate, demand trends, stocking costs, and economic costs due to a product being out of stock. At the same time, financial assistance in terms of trade discounts and cash discounts or an encouraging credit line motivates retailers to redesign the model stock plan.

Constraining Factors

Consumers need change, manufacturers develop new products, and progressive retailers are constantly adding new products and dropping old ones. The merchandise mix not only satisfies the customer's wants but also shapes those wants and influences the consumer's buying decision. Therefore, optimal mix depends on the trading area, the retail store is in operation and the retail format it has adopted, scale of operation, and segment of market it is serving. While introducing new offerings, manufacturers undertake greater risks, and retailers also develop merchandise mix under limitations on account of space, resources, etc. There are four constraining factors (see Fig 7.12) that influence the design of the optimal merchandise mix.

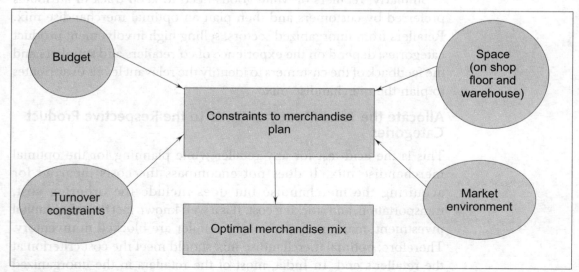

Fig. 7.12 Constraining factors influencing merchandise plan

Budgetary Constraint

A retailer has to work out the optimal merchandise mix for his customers on the basis of the resources available. There rarely will be enough financial resources to incorporate all three dimensions of variety, breadth, and depth. There is always a trade off to make from alternative merchandise lines to add, brands to select, and their respective SKUs. Retailers have a limited sum to invest in the stock or generating facilities to manage increased stock (warehouse, workforce, etc). These budgetary constraints are universal to all kinds of retail formats; only the intensity varies. The small retailer has either to arrange stocks against his own resources or credit extended by the suppliers; credit facility is not very popular among smaller retailers in India. Therefore, they plan their merchandise stocks according to their limited resources. However, retail outlets today in the organized sector avail of an effective bargaining position against suppliers and enjoy liberal support in making payments for the stock, and sometimes they collect payments after selling the products. For instance, most of the local brands in the FMCG sector initiate their distribution strategy by only placing their products with small retailers rather than bothering them for payments to be made for new merchandise. This provides suppliers with free shelf space as well as the goodwill of the retailers.

Retail formats also guide the adjustments to be made on account of budget franchised. Unorganized outlets are supposed to maintain limited stocks of the respective brands and their receptive stock keeping units as department stores are supposed to invest in various merchandised lines, along with extensive depth and breadth. For example, mega stores, in contrast to several smaller franchised outlets, have expanded product portfolios. From being a menswear—shirts and trousers—company, Pantaloon Retail has added to its credit several brands of ladies' and kids' wear. The women's brands are: Annabelle (western office/casual wear), Srishti (ethnic wear—salwar kameez, ready-made blouse), and Bare (casual wear for children/men/women). On the anvil are Agile (sports wear), AFL (a budget product), and Scottsville (winter wear). Apart from stocking its own brands, Pantaloon Retail outlets also stock other ready-made garment brands and fashion accessories.

Time Zone

Time Zone by Titan is the first retail chain offering multiple brands of watches from the franchised outlets. They have arrangements with retailers to display 60% of their stock along with an approved list of brands by the Titan management. Titan provides the additional margin, furniture, and fixture support to Time Zone franchisee in return of a premium and major shelf place allotted to its range. This kind of arrangement eases the decision-making at the end of retailer, as the allotment of shelf space is very clear.

Selling Space Constraint

Space available to a retailer is relatively fixed and must return a profit. If a retailer goes for depth or breadth, space requirement will increase. If variety is to be stressed, enough empty space is needed to separate the distinct merchandise lines. For instance, mobile vendors such as fruits and vegetable retailers normally deal in only one or two merchandise lines but with sufficient depth and breadth. On the same lines, department stores maintain a good variety of merchandise lines, along with comprehensive depth and breadth. A retailer has to consider about the warehouse space, along with shelf space, while deciding about the merchandise order. For instance, most of the small grocery and durable retailers do not have warehouse support; they have to stock in the store only. At the same time, the Indian retailers do not acknowledge shelf management in the unorganized sector as it has received recognition in Western countries. For instance, in case of some organized retailing of fashion products such as garments and watches, space is valued by the retailers and acknowledged in the optimal merchandise decision making.

Turnover Constraint

Turnover is an extremely important factor in buying and selling merchandise profitably. Pantaloon pushes for a stock turn of 40–50 times a year for its food items and once a month for ready-to-wear. A good turnover rate is an indication of good management since turnover is the result of intelligent buying based on sound assortment planning and realistic estimation. With the increase in the depth of the merchandise, more and more variants of the product are needed to be stocked to serve a large number segments. Increasing competition for the customers' spend and the rising costs squeeze profits. Improving turnover is one of the key ways to improve profit. Although mark-up is an important element of profit, it does not contribute to profit until merchandise is sold. Therefore, a retailer's merchandise mix should have the potential to generate high sales turnover. For instance, Pantaloon Retail (India) Ltd is making sustainable inroads by their Big Bazaar chain of discount stores. They are offering a variety of products all under one roof, which is bound to attract a lot of consumers, resulting in low turnover. Offering products and services such as a chemist, a photography shop, a bakery, automobile accessories, bicycles, and electrical hardware among other items, the range is vast and fulfils practically every need of the consumers under one roof. Such an extensive range helps to attract customers interested in multiple product shopping, which in turn provides good sales across all product categories.

Retailers are required to understand the sensitivity of their sales turnover to merchandise mix they are developing. For instance, its private labels such as Stop, Kashish, Life, and Carrot contribute 20% to the turnover of Shoppers' Stop.

Market Environment Constraints

It refers to the limitation on account of the target market residing in the area within walking or short-time distance to the store. Target market preferences and taste directs the development of optimal merchandise mix, as they are the final customers of the retail offer. If the final

---

LifeStyle Stores: Some Factors Responsible for Success

Instead of setting up different stores catering to different segments—the model used in the UAE—the company decided to put it all together under one roof and call it LifeStyle. The reason: the high cost of retail space did not justify separate stores in India.

From the beginning, the company concentrated on building up operating efficiencies so that it could cut costs from day one. To ensure this, the company monitored every item sold in the stores and take them off the shelves if they were not moving. For instance, LifeStyle closely monitors all fashion items for 30–45 days and then takes a call whether to order more or get rid of stocks by having a sale. Besides, it also concentrated on effective inventory and stock management. On an average, it keeps stocks of around 90 days and the stock turnaround is around 60–75 days.

Source: Surajeet Das Gupta 2003, Shopping in style, *Business Standard,* July 26.

Banglore Restaurants

Banglore restaurants used to prominently offer south Indian stuff in their outlets. In the recent past, Banglore has emerged as the hub of higher education centres and IT industry. Therefore, every year a good number of students and professionals from north India visit this region. This has brought the now spectacular change in the offerings of the restaurants. They have included a wide range of north Indian cuisine.

customers reject products, retailers may have to take substantial price reductions in order to get rid of compromised merchandise mix. Retailers have to consider the competitive environment and competitive dimensions prevailing in the trading area. This will help the store if required to position on the merchandise mix features such as variety, depth, and breadth. For example, Fab India, the ethnic cotton garment store, maintains extensive merchandise lines along with depth and breadth for both males and females. However, the W stores deal in working women fashion based on cotton with extensive depth and breadth. This has provided distinguished position to the two stores selling the same base material.

Constraining factors make it difficult to maximize all dimensions of the merchandise mix. However, if a retailer is going to lose customers, he should lose the less profitable ones by properly mixing its merchandise in terms of variety, breadth, and depth within the budget, space, turnover, and market environment constraints.

Decision Criteria to Select New Offers

1. Is the item useful to the target segment?
2. What will be the product profitability (gross margin or net profit)?
3. How much promotion and advertising support can be expected from the manufacturer?
4. Does the new offer duplicate an existing offering?
5. Is the new item compatible with the present product portfolio and store image?
6. Will the product help to build store traffic?
7. What has been the past experience with this manufacturer/wholesaler?
8. Are the appearance and the quality of the packaging satisfactory?
9. Does the expected retail price represent value to the consumer?
10. Has the item been test-marketed?

Types of Suppliers

A retailer can depend on one supplier or a combination of suppliers, as shown in Fig 7.13. There are a number of alternatives that retailers might consider as a suitable source of supply. Retailers are supposed to select an effective source of merchandise from various existing alternatives. Some of the options availed of by Indian retailers are discussed in the following sections.

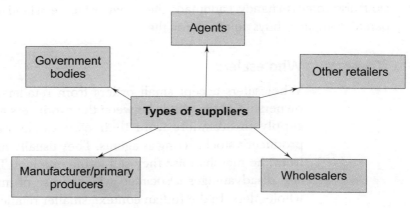

Fig. 7.13 Types of suppliers

Manufacturers and Primary Producers

This category sells cars, two-wheelers, gasoline and other related products, and consumer durables from company-owned stores (recent phenomenon in India). Large retailers regularly deal directly with a product manufacturer. Manufacturers will normally have a sales office or a showroom, either attached to a production unit or in a location that is convenient for retail customers. For instance, hosiery and woollen manufacturers from Ludhiana manage sales offices in Ludhiana and New Delhi to cater to the needs of the big retailers and wholesalers directly. At the same time in semi-urban towns most of the small-scale (shoes, cosmetics product, confectionery items) manufacturers approach the retailers to provide the required merchandise at their shop directly, such as bread, local made soaps, and handicraft items. In rural India, the local economy is sustained by direct selling of the produce by the manufacturers or retailers in the local or periodic markets.

LifeStyle: Effective Buying Management

LifeStyle has also focused on building direct relationships with manufacturers rather than buying products from middlemen. This reduces margins and enables the store to quickly pick up the products that it wants. Again, this enables it to have lower inventories. Its international clout also comes in handy. Landmark, the parent company, buys furniture for the entire group from Denmark and the Far East. Since it buys in bulk, it can sell much more cheaply. That apart, it can offer exclusive products as these are tailor-made to its designs.

Source: Surajeet Das Gupta 2003, 'Shopping in style', *Business Standard,* www.businessstandard.com, July 26.

Wholesalers

Wholesalers accept small orders from retailers. They actually take ownership of the goods between the producers and the retailer. They supply the retailers from their own stocks rather than from the producer's stock, acting as agents. They usually make attractive profits from the merchandise they sell to the retailers. There are advantages and disadvantages associated with the use of intermediaries such as wholesalers. In the Indian context, smaller retailers prefer to deal with the wholesalers dealing in a variety of products as they can purchase most of their merchandise from one shop. Small retailers are also not comfortable in dealing with company people of each product category or brands directly which they consider as a hindrance in their selling activity.

Agents

Agents provide purchasing and delivering facility to the retailers against negotiated commissions on the percentage of the total value of goods purchased. In some cases, product manufacturers also have agents who collect orders from the market. This is a very common source to retailers in the semi-urban areas or in and around major trading centres. Retailers depend on agents for weekly or fortnightly purchases from the major trading centres. For instance, the entire western Uttar Pradesh retailers buy local-made durables, ready-to-wear garments, decoration material, appliances, utensils, and stationery material from the Delhi markets such as Karol Bagh, Nai Sarak, Gufaar Market, and Chandni Chowk. At the same time, retailers selling ethnic women's wear such as sarees and salwar suits depend on Surat and south Indian markets.

This is advantageous to retailers on multiple accounts as they do not have to leave their shops to merchandise from different places and arrange for their transport. Agents are responsible for the safe transport of goods. In rural areas and smaller towns, retailers even bank on the informal set-up to acquire merchandise. Here they ask co-retailers to buy for them the required list of items and pay only transportation costs. No commission is paid for buying the goods. It is based on the mutual understanding among retailers working in proximity. In some cases, product manufacturers also have agents who collect orders from the market. Orders thus collected by multiple number of agents from various markets help manufacturers to effect economies of scale. They usually work on commission basis and may represent more than one producers. For instance, western UP rice manufacturers largely depend on the network of these agents to secure orders from adjoining cities and states. It saves the permanent cost of the sales force as they work on commission basis during the season.

Other Retailers

This category comprises retailers who operate on a larger scale. They cater to the needs of the immediate consumers along with the small retailers from contiguous areas, running their stores in interior localities of urban areas or in the rural areas. These retailers locate their shops in the main or central markets of the urban centres.

Government and Semi-government Source

Public distribution system acquires its entire stock of goods from the central government of India through various official state bodies such as the Food Corporation of India, Mother Dairy, and Safal. Several other state-specific co-operative societies sell their milk-based products, vegetables, fruits, and packaged processed food items through their own retail outlets and other grocery or supermarket stores.

Criteria for the Selection of Suppliers

Retailers regularly confront with the issue of locating a new supplier for the existing merchandise or identifying a new supplier for fresh merchandise introduced. A supplier's initial assessment will be made according to his ability to satisfy retailers in four main

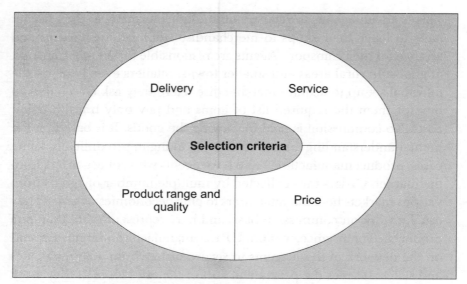

Fig. 7.14 Selection criteria for suppliers

areas (see Fig. 7.14) together with the kind of indicators that would determine the likelihood of supplier meeting criteria. The existing suppliers may be retained because they have given particularly good service in the past, or because there is no identifiable competition.

The main areas of supplier assessment criteria are:

Product Range and Quality

Retailers will assess the product range available with the supplier and the quality standard maintained while manufacturing or delivering. Retailers will consider the following parameters to judge the standing of a particular supplier: technical capability, design expertise, quality benchmarks, samples, and nil-defect delivery.

Price

Retailers will always have relative assessment of the different suppliers while deciding the purchase. At the same time, retailers as per the norms prevailing in their industry look forward to credit terms, payments options, penalties, discounts (cash and trade), and price levels and price points. Retailers will also evaluate the offer from the perspective of a consumer in terms of value for money and consistent price policy.

Delivery

In order to avoid sales loss, a retailer is generally interested in the assessment of a supplier's capacity to deliver ordered goods in time and as per specification. Retailers also evaluate the performance of the suppliers or gather information on these parameters to ascertain delivery capacity, such as minimum order quantities, lead times, workforce stability and response, and ability to collaborate on consumer-led response initiative.

Service

This encompasses all those facilities and support extended by the supplier to add value to the goods or services, or assistance in the sale of the goods. It includes pre- and post-sales services by the supplier. Retailers will be interested to assess the working of the supplier on parameters such as innovation, speed of new product or variant introduction, sampling service, marketing support (advertising and promotion), and handling queries and complaints.

A list of suppliers should be available and kept fully up to date, showing lines supplied by each. This will aid the process of review of suppliers and lines, so that suppliers performing well may be rewarded with larger orders.

Category Management

A category is the basic unit of analysis for making merchandising decisions. Products are naturally grouped into similar consumer taste preferences and product characteristics such as salty snacks, traditional sweets, cakes, pastry and cookies, etc. A category is an assortment of items that the customer sees as reasonable substitutes for each other. For example, retailers in ready-to-wear segment consider female and male clothing as one category. As they enjoy similar characteristics, retail marketing mix is designed on similar lines to a great extent. In the same way, grocery retailers have brought loose and packaged branded grocery items under one category.

Category management is the process of managing a retail business with the objective of maximizing the sales and profits of a category rather than the performance of individual brands or models.

It systematizes grouping of products into strategic units or category so as to better meet consumer needs and achieve sales and profit goals.

It directs retailers to devise merchandising strategy and to maximise the total return on the resources assigned. Most of the retail set-ups emerging in the organized sector are managing merchandise on these lines. However, the unorganized sector in India has worked considering most of their merchandise items as a set of categories in order to save on cost and time required in acquiring and to have best possible merchandise mix. For example, grocery retailers club most of their items on the basis of time of acquiring or the source (wholesaler or mobile vendor). Similarly, in India the entire set-up of Pan shops is catered by the mobile vendors (independent and company owned) who supply a set of items to retailers such as cigarettes, bidis, match boxes, chewing tobacco, and mints, which are grouped in one product category for convenience.

In the same manner, most of the retailers trading in cloth length and cut pieces approach merchandise management at their outlets as category management. They not only deal in women's and men's clothing but also in a range of variants in each category, which can be handled efficiently only by the following category management system.

Today, the relevance of category management is driven by the emergence of multiple number of brands in each product category, followed by an equal number of SKUs. For example, in a grocery store there might be five buyers for bathing soap (shelf space): Lux, Hamam, Boro Soft, Fair & Lovely, and Nirma. There are space, target customer preference, and investment constraints at the retailer's end. Therefore, retailers or concerned managers are responsible for working with a set of prospective vendors, selecting merchandise from multiple alternatives, pricing merchandise suitably, and co-ordinating the promotional campaigns.

The retailers in the unorganized retail set-up accomplish most of these tasks themselves with assistance from co-retailers, customers, suppliers, and past experience, as also feedback from sales people. In the organized retail sector, professionals take such decisions with the assistance of sales people, daily sales data, research and survey reports, etc.

For the success of any category management, retail business requires changes in the merchandising system and organizational commitment.

The homegrown quick-service restaurant (QSR) chain Nirula's has announced its entry into the consumer food category retail segment with the launch of a range of jams, sauces, condiments, chutneys, syrups, marmalades, tomato ketchup, chocolate fudge, and more under the brand Nirula's.

Advantages of Category Management

The following denote the advantages of category management.

Increased Sales

- Full category representation increases consumer demand and attracts new ones.
- The use of top-selling products increases sales per transaction.
- Increased sales result in substantial increase in profitability.

Reduced Inventory Investment

- Menu-based purchasing reduces the inventory and handling costs of additional, unnecessary SKUs.
- Purchasing efficiency increases dramatically.
- Order levels are more closely matched to sales, allowing reduced total inventory investment.

Improved Route and Warehouse Efficiency

- Route merchandising and product selection is simpler and comparatively more efficient.
- Warehouse order placement and product handling functions become relatively easier.
- Fewer SKUs and lower inventory levels lead to substantial reduction in warehouse labour strength.

The Essential Elements of Effective Category Management

- Category should be arranged as if consumers could stock the shelf themselves.
- Category composition should be on the basis of time, space, and product benefit.
- Category management should drive multiple item purchases.
- Category management is a dynamic, proprietary set of decisions, not a standard, universal, institutionalized practice.
- It is directed to create value for the consumer rather than facilitating relations between supplier and retailer.
- Category management plan should be based on the overall competitive environment in a specific trading area.

- Consumer data are helpful in evolving base for category management.

- Category management is a strategy of differentiation.

Drivers of Category Management

Pantaloon, a leading garment department store, has employed the concept of product (which it calls category management) management in its day-to-day merchandising function. The core assumption Pantaloon makes is that customers are more product-driven than brand-driven when they go shopping. A retail study confirms this — out of every 100 customers that enter a retail store to buy a specific product, 98 are not very particular about the brand. This is primarily because there are various factors like price, quality of the garment, texture, colour, and so on that influence a customer's choice of merchandise. So the customer's preference for a particular brand gets overshadowed by these other aspects, which lead to his ultimate decision. Thus, management of a category of merchandise is a more effective tool than managing individual brands.

Implementation of Product Category

Pantaloon's merchandising team is divided into the category management team and the merchandise management team. There is also a special design team. The

Pantaloon model differs from the others on category management, especially for the apparel segment. Most other models start with category management and finally end up with an individual selection of products across various classes, subclasses, and brands. Thus, brands do play an important role in the merchandising function of the store in other models. This is also due to the fact that most other stores deal with multiple brands and not with own store labels.

For example, John Miller is a brand of formal and semi-formal shirts, Bare is denim and casual wear brand, the Pantaloon brand represents only trousers, Knighthood is evening wear, Annabelle is western wear for women over 25, while Y? is western wear for women aged between 18 and 25. Thus, the significance of the brands is limited and even at the stage of brand management, the company deals mainly with a product category.

Source: www.eretailbiz.com

Merchandise Management Planning in Various Retail Segments

Speciality Retailers

Speciality goods are those for which customers have a preconceived need and for which they make an effort to come to the speciality store to purchase. Consumers usually will not accept a substitute for a speciality good. Here most of the items are fashion driven so replenishment goods constitute a very small fraction of the merchandise mix. Hence, the requirement is for an 'intelligent' merchandise planning where various factors will have to be accounted for, such as:

- Seasonality of demand
- Changing fashion
- Actual trends from the shop floor sales
- Market research for spotting early trends and competitor information

In the case of speciality retailers, the merchandise planning system requires a high degree of synergy with the ordering system in place. Merchandise at speciality stores is subject to markdowns and reductions as it has a very short life cycle. Retailers or planners in the speciality retail segment have to be guided by the element of intense competition owing to the following reasons:

- Overpopulated retail space
- Fast changing trends in fashion
- Constant threats and challenges from non-store marketers (catalogues, interactive TV, and now the Internet)
- Increasing significance of promotions and markdowns
- Emergence of discounters and other retail formats

These have led retailers to re-think their merchandise strategy and to re-design their merchandise mix. Some have resorted to super-specialization in categories which they think would be easier to sustain. For example, W is offering cotton-based comprehensive merchandise mix for the working women in metro only. They are today considered to be the best in this product category in their particular target market. On similar lines, FAB India's cotton-based clothing retail chain in NCR region offers a wide variety of items, basically hand-made. Their range comprises ready-to-wear for ladies, gents, and kids, and home décor material (from bedsheets to curtains). Therefore, the well-defined category has helped these stores not only to face competition from the unorganized sector but also to devise efficient merchandise management strategies.

Grocery and Food Retailing

These are basically known as convenience goods. It has been observed that consumers put a minimum amount of thought into the purchase of a known brand or whatever is available at the store. Some examples are toothpastes, bread, and eggs. The difference here as compared to speciality retailing is that most of the items are replenishment items and, hence, the driving force behind merchandise management here is the inventory management policies. The various replenishment policies being followed are discussed below.

Fixed Cycle of Replenishment

In this policy, replenishment takes place at predetermined time intervals, which are decided jointly by the retailers and suppliers. The fixed cycle of replenishment policy can be utilized for goods with the following characteristics:

- Predictable demand and sales pattern
- High transportation costs
- Batch production with large batch size
- Low inventory carrying costs

Continuous Replenishment

In this policy, replenishment levels are decided by the supplier and the retailer. Whenever inventory dips below the required level a purchase order is automatically generated leading to fulfilment. The continuous replenishment cycle policy is useful for goods with the following characteristics:

- Unpredictable sales pattern
- Goods for which historical data is not available to predict their sales pattern (Time series)
- The 'bread winners' for the retailer those goods which have a high retail margin—consumer necessity profile

Financial Objectives of Merchandising

Merchandise planning consists of establishing objectives and devising plans for obtaining these objectives. The objectives range from the corporate strategic objectives to the micro-level objectives regarding the merchandise assortment, stocking, and re-order.

Merchandise control involves designing the policies and procedures for collecting and analyzing merchandise data in order to determine whether the stated objectives have been achieved. Planning is the process of establishing performance guidelines, whereas control is the process of checking how well the management is following those guidelines.

Merchandise budget is a financial tool for planning and controlling the retailers' merchandise inventory investment. While the planning and control of the merchandise mix is directed at meeting the customer-oriented objectives, equally important in the merchandising process is the firm's financial objective of profitability. To ensure profitable operations, the retailer must use a merchandise budget in which sales volumes, stock levels, retail reductions, purchase orders, and profit margins are planned and controlled.

Merchandise management involves decisions related to inventory, which in turn is the largest investment for any retailer. In this context, the best merchandise performance measure is gross margin return on inventory (GMROI).

Gross margin return on inventory comprises a single measure for both inventory productivity and profit. The formula is as follows:
(Gross margin/Net sales) * (Net sales/Average inventory at cost) = (Gross margin)/Average inventory at cost)

Like return on assets, GMROI combines the effects of profits and turnover. It is important to use a combined measure so that departments or product category with variation in margin/turnover can be compared and evaluated. For example, within a department store, some departments (such as jewellery) are high margin/low turnover, whereas other departments (such as ready-to-wear garments) are low margin/high turnover. If the jewellery department's performance is compared to that of ready-to-wear section using turnover alone, jewellery would not fare well. On the other hand, if only gross margin was used, jewellery would be at an advantage.

GMROI is used to evaluate and control the performance of departments, merchandise, category, vendor lines, etc. It is also useful for management in evaluating the buyer's performance on the basis of gross margin ratio and inventory turnover ratio.

Evaluating Merchandise Performance

Retailers usually confront situations where they have to revise (drop or add) various SKUs, vendors, or departments during merchandise management. These decisions may be because of changes in consumer preferences, relationship with vendor, new arrivals, and poor performance of a particular merchandise. Causes responsible for the drop of a particular merchandise are inferior quality, excessive complaints or returns, too many repairs, and decreased sales and profits.

Three evaluative procedures to review the performance of merchandise are discussed below.

ABC Analysis

This method classifies the inventory into categories, proportional to the inventory's total cost, designated A, B, and C, or high, medium, and low rotation. At the same time, ABC analysis assists the management to merchandise by some performance measure to determine which set of items should never be out of stock, which items should be allowed to be out of stock occasionally, and which set of items should be dropped from the stock acquiring list. This not only provides information about relevance of merchandise to the retail store but also helps in the placement of merchandise (shelf space), budgeting, and revising the merchandise mix. It depends on the retailer or planner to select the unit of measurement such as department or SKU.

ABC analysis uses Pareto Principle of 80–20, where approximately 80% of the store's sales or profits are derived from 20% of the products.

A retailer has to first decide on the measurement criteria before ranking each SKU, category, or department. The measurement criteria can vary from contribution margin, sales in terms of money, sales in units, gross margin, and gross margin return on investment.

The usage of measurement criteria is subject to various factors such as unit of measurement. For example, sales figures of a jewellery department cannot be compared with sales figures of a kid's ready-to-wear department. Therefore, the best measurement criterion to measure performance of merchandise (SKU) is contribution margin.

Contribution margin = Net sales – Cost of goods sold – Other variable expenses

After ranking the entire merchandise mix on the basis of contribution margin or sales volume, retailers should devise a plan to deal with the respective category (A, B, or C) of merchandise. For example, the sales value of various brands of bathing soap and their respective SKUs is depicted in the general shape of the curve following Pareto principle in Fig 7.15.

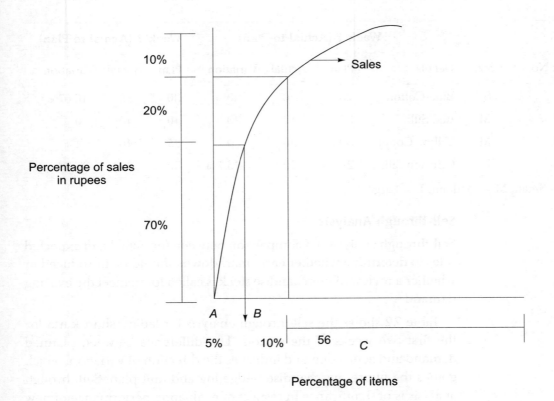

Fig. 7.15 ABC curve

Category A comprises those 5% of bathing soap SKUs which contribute 70% of sales. These SKUs should never be out of stock. This category represents the most significant amount of investment in inventory.

Category B represents 10% of bathing soap SKUs and an additional 20% of sales. This category comprises the items of secondary importance. Occasionally, these items will run out of stock because of limited investment made towards managing backup stock.

Items in category C represent 65% of SKUs but contribute only 10% of sales. The SKUs comprised in this category hold meaningless value in relation to the total inventory amount.

Table 7.2   Sell-through analysis for kurtas

Stock No.	Size	Details	Week 1 (Actual-to-Plan)			Week 2 (Actual-to-Plan)		
			Plan	Actual	Variation %	Plan	Actual	Variation %
K101	S	Blue-Cotton	25	20	−20%	30	35	16.67%
K102	M	Red-Silk	35	42	20%	40	40	0
K103	M	Yellow-Cotton	30	30	0	35	40	14%
K104	L	Crimson-Silk	24	20	−16.7%	30	22	− 26.7%

Size: S = Small; M = Medium; L = Large

Sell-through Analysis

Sell-through analysis is a comparison between the actual and expected sales to determine whether early markdowns should be introduced or whether a review of merchandise stock is called for to meet the existing demand.

Table 7.2 shows the sell-through analysis for ladies' short kurta for the first two weeks of the season. The difference between planned demand and actual demand indicates the direction of variation, which guides the future merchandise budgeting and unit plan. Sell-through analysis is of significance in respect of evaluating performance of new offerings or fashion-oriented products. After reviewing the performance of the various items in kurta category at the store, a retailer can plan for further ordering of the merchandise in case the items experienced generate favourable response and can go for markdowns for the items that experienced low demand. There is no well-established principle to determine future responses to new fashion offerings. In India, most of the retailers in the unorganized retail set-up depend on the feedback of co-retailers or demand of consumers and above all an assurance of return of merchandise if not sold.

On the other hand, in the organized retail set-up, vendors and retailers work hard an evolving a mechanism to ward off such risks which lead to loss of revenues in terms of stock out and markdowns. Today, most of the consumer goods companies are working on a fully integrated merchandise management system (MMS), which provides the tools to manage the entire retail cycle—from planning, buying, and receiving to transferring, distributing, and selling of goods to performance analysis and revised pricing then back to planning for the next season.

An effective merchandise management system provides a vital link between the actual customer demand, the store, and the distribution centre. Thus, the role of an MMS encompasses the following:

- Provides increased control of inventory management with tracking and reporting capabilities at all levels of the merchandising and organizational hierarchy.
- Provides sophisticated analysis tools to provide effective inventory control, sales tracking, merchandise analysis, financial management, and business planning.
- Helps in offering the right product, at the right store location, at the right time, at the right price, and in right quantity.

The integrated merchandise management system helps in achieving better margin percentages by:

- Reducing inventory and carrying costs in stores, and increasing the accuracy of orders by automating the reordering process based on projected sales algorithms.
- Providing access to better buying information, inventory availability and promotional pricing, thus improving operational margins through lower cost of sales.
- Enabling permanent linkages with markdowns/clearance or temporary markdowns with financial impact analysis and managerial authorization prior to implementing price changes.
- Enabling better return on investment by giving access to merchandising history so that markdowns can be planned based on prior performance.

Hence, product and merchandise management involves a detailed analysis of the strategic and financial aspects of the retail business. It also involves a deep understanding of the environmental and consumer-related factors that influence product selection and shopping behaviour.

Summary

Product and merchandise management is a critical aspect of retail business. Product management deals with all issues related to identification of the product type to be sold by the retailer. A related issue is brand management. It involves a decision as to the nature of retail brand and whether to opt for or avoid private labels. The key elements of a retail brand are: format, visual merchandising, location, experience, price, product assortment, and service.

Merchandise management is the analysis, planning, acquisition, handling, and control of the merchandise investments of a retail operation. Merchandise mix management covers decisions on a host of key parameters like merchandise variety, assortment, and support.

Merchandise budget is a financial plan that indicates how much to invest in product inventories, usually stated in rupees for a specific time frame. Model stock planning is a quantitative method, which provides guidelines on the size, colour, brand, and composition of stock that specify the exact nature of merchandise.

There are four constraining factors that influence the design of the optimal merchandise mix — budget, space, turnover, and market environment. Retailers or management are regularly confronted with the issue of locating a new supplier for the existing merchandise or identifying a new supplier for a new set of merchandise.

The main areas for supplier assessment criteria are product range, quality, price, delivery, and service. Category management is the process of managing a retail business with the objective of maximizing the sales and profits of a category rather than the performance of individual brands or models. A category is an assortment of items that the customer sees as reasonable substitutes.

The best merchandise performance measure is gross margin return on inventory (GMROI). Gross margin return on inventory comprises into a single measure both inventory productivity and profit. Retailers are usually confronted with a situation where they may have to revise (drop or add) a number of SKUs, vendors, or departments while managing their merchandise. In order to review the performance of merchandise two evaluative procedures are ABC analysis and Sell-through analysis.

Key Terms

1. **Assortment:** Selection of merchandise carried by a retailer. It covers both the breadth of the product categories and the variety within each category.

2. **Basic stock method:** Inventory level planning tool wherein a retailer caries more item than it expects to sell over a specified period.

3. **Category management:** Using merchandise management technique to improve their productivity. It focuses on product category results rather than performance of individual brands or models.

4. **Cross-merchandising:** The phenomenon where a retailer carries complementary goods and services so that shoppers are encouraged to buy more.

5. **Depth of assortment:** The variety in any product line stocked by a retailer.

6. **Fad merchandise:** Items that generate a high level of sales for a short period.

7. **Fashion merchandise:** Items that may have cyclical sales due to changing tastes and lifestyles.

8. **Forecast:** Projections of expected retail sales for a given time period.

9. **Generic brands:** No-frills goods stocked by retailers.

10. **Gross margin return on inventory (GMROI):** Shows relationship between total operating profits and the average inventory investment cost by combining profitability and sale-to-stock measures:

$$\text{GMROI} = \frac{\text{Gross margin in rupees}}{\text{Average inventory cost}}$$

11. **Gross profit:** Difference between net sales and the total cost of goods sold.

12. **Mass merchandising:** Positioning approach whereby retailers offer a discount or value-oriented image, a wide and /or deep merchandise assortment, and large store facilities.

13. **Model stock plan:** Planned composition of fashion goods, which reflects the mix of merchandise available based on expected sales. It indicates product lines, colours, and size distributions.

14. **Percentage variation method:** Inventory level planning method where beginning-of-month planned inventory during any month differs from planned average monthly stock by only one-half of that month's variations from estimated average monthly sales.

15. **Private brands:** Names designates by wholesales or retailers, which are more profitable to and are better controlled by retailers, and are not sold by competing retailers.

16. **Product life cycle:** The expected behaviour of a good or service over its life. The traditional cycle has four stages: introduction, growth, maturity, and decline.

17. **Scrambled merchandising:** Occurs when a retailer adds goods and services that may be unrelated to each other and to the firm's original business.

18. **Seasonable merchandise:** Items that sell well over non-consecutive time periods.

19. **Staple merchandise:** The regular products carried by retail outlets.

20. **Sock-to-sales method:** An inventory level planning technique wherein a retailer wants to maintain a specified ratio of goods on hand to sales.

21. **Stock turnover:** Number of times during a specified period, usually one year, that the average inventory on hand is sold.

22. **Week's supply method:** An Inventory level planning method wherein the beginning inventory equals several weeks' expected sales. It assumes inventory is in direct proportion to sales.

23. **Wholesaling:** Intermediate stage in the distribution process during which goods and services are not sold to final consumers but to the retailers.

24. **Width of assortment:** Number of distinct goods/service lines a retailer carries.

Concept Review Questions

1. What is the relevance of product management in retail business?
2. Discuss the key issues involved in retail product management.
3. Discuss the pros and cons of carrying the retailer's own brands.
4. Define merchandise management.
5. What are the methods used for determining merchandise budget?
6. Discuss the nature of suppliers and their selection criteria.
7. What are the merchandise performance measurement techniques?

Project Work Assignments

1. Analyse the retail branding strategies in a specific product category in the context of a retailer dealing in
   (a) Exclusively private label products
   (b) Multiple brands
   (c) Combination of private label and branded products
2. Identify the stages of merchandise planning and management giving the example of:
   (a) Grocery shops near your home/apartment
   (b) A department store
3. Compare the merchandise mix of
   (a) An independent retail firm with a franchised retail outlet operating in the same product category
   (b) Two leading fashion stores.
4. Identify the drivers guiding retailers' merchandise mix in a specific catchment area. Also provide the details of the catchment area concerned.

Case Study

Marks and Spencer

Marks and Spencer is one of UK's leading retailers of clothing, foods, homeware, and financial services serving 10 million customers a week in over 300 stores in UK. The company also trades in 30 countries worldwide through a network of around 544 stores. It has a group turnover in excess of £8 billion. It operates through Marks and Spencer stores in UK, Ireland, and Hong Kong, and through Marks and Spencer franchises worldwide. In USA it operates the *Kings Super Markets*.

The History

The Period 1884–1907 The company started in 1884 when Michael Marks, a Russia–born Polish refugee opened a stall at Leeds Kirkgate Market. Since he could not speak English, Marks laid out all of his merchandise into two groups and placed all those items costing a penny in one section and those costing more in the other. Signage board above the penny section, read 'Don't ask the price, it's a penny'. Marks targeted north England. The driving factor for this being that north England represented the transformation of Britain from an agrarian economy to a manufacturing-driven economy.

Initially, Marks avoided keeping any accounts. A single fixed price helped Marks in keeping all his calculations simple. The fixed price policy, however, put pressure on Marks to search a variety of high quality goods that could be sold for a penny.

In 1893, Michael moved to 20 Cheetham Hill Road, Manchester. In the following year, he opened a shop in the lower part of the same building.

With the rapid growth in the business, Marks realized the limitation of managing it alone; he began to search for a partner to share responsibilities and, hence, established a partnership with Tom Spencer. Thus was formed Marks and Spencer on September 28, 1894. Tom Spencer was a former cashier from the wholesale company IJ Dewhirst. In 1897, M&S shifted its headquarters from Wigan to Manchester.

In the first decade of its operation, Marks and Spencer outlets showed spectacular growth.

In terms of its management, three supervisors were in charge of visiting the bazaars, taking stock, supervising staff, expenditure and layout, and correcting deficiencies where they existed.

The Period 1907–1928 Marks died in 1907. In 1916, his son Simon became the chairman. By then Marks and Spencer (M&S) was a comprehensive variety retail chain.

London Penny Bazaar Co. was a major competitor for M&S. In 1914, it was bought for a sum of 15,000 pounds in cash. This move helped consolidate the position of M&S in London. After World War I, influenced by the competitors charging one dollar, M&S introduced the five-shilling price limit. In the chairman's words, 'The primary objective of the new merchandising policy was to discover, and where necessary create, a range and variety of goods, which had not been previously available at this price'. In 1920s, the company adopted the revolutionary policy of buying directly from manufacturers. In 1926, the company started selling textiles and in the same year it went public. Two years later, M&S launched its famous St Michael brand.

Year	City	Total Number of Outlets
1900	North England, South England, London	36
1903	North England, South England, London	40
1907	North England, South England, London	64

The Period 1928–1940 With the adoption of the new pricing and the resultant merchandising policy, there was a reduction in the range and variety of the merchandise offered from M&S stores. M&S shifted focus to high quality offerings and reduction in costs. From 1928 to 1932 over 70% of the items listed in the 1926 prospectus disappeared from the stores. The limited range of merchandise enabled M&S to increase the degree of specialization and make quicker responses to customer demand. This policy gave M&S stores a very special position in the retail sector and by the mid-1930s the company had become the largest retailer of textile products in Britain and Europe. In 1931, a food department was introduced selling produce and canned goods. However, throughout the 1930s, the sales of textiles continued to grow and the turnover multiplied more than three times between 1933 and 1939.

In 1930s, the company also introduced Café Bars in many stores. These provided cheap, hygienic, and nutritious mass catering. This was a valuable resource during the war making efficient use of scarce food.

In 1934, a scientific research lab was established headed by Dr Eric Kann. This was the first research lab of any British retailer, allowing the company to pioneer new fabrics.

The Period 1950–1980 By 1956, all goods were sold under the St Michael label. In 1956 the first St Michael branded chocolate was sold. In 1959, M&S became the first retailer to introduce the, 'No Smoking' rule in their stores.

In 1964, Simon's brother-in-law, Israel Sieff, became the chairman. It was during this period, from 1963 to 1972, that the company recorded a spectacular growth. The profit before taxes was almost 12% on sales, which was considered to be highly satisfactory in the retailing business. In 1965, M&S launched a major initiative to improve quality. Major stores were advised to send to the head office any defective goods either identified by M&S staff or returned by customers. After classifying the defects, manufacturers were invited to take a look at the merchandise. The exercise sent clear signals to manufacturers regarding the retailer's commitment to quality. Clothing sales accounted for almost 75% of M&S total sales in 1972.

In 1974 Indian and Chinese food items were introduced with dishes like *Chicken Korma* and *Lamb Rogan Josh.*

In 1985, the Marks & Spencer Chargecard was launched nationally. In 1986, the first edge of town store opened at the Metro Centre in Gateshead. During this time, furniture was added to the merchandise. This was supported by the launch of the Home Furnishing catalogue.

1990s and the Present By 1990 Marks and Spencer had 266 stores around the world. Marks and Spencer had adopted the policy of laying out all the merchandise for the customers to choose from (self-service). It has been acknowledged by Marks and Spencer that most retailers compete with one another in terms of quality of offerings, shopping convenience, displays, range of product lines, and brand portfolios. M&S depended on its team of designers working closely with the suppliers to create its own range of products. There had been the advent of new textile raw material during 1930s and 1940s. The company had reacted to this development by changing its product designs to suit these changes. Through its textile technologists and its merchandising departments, M&S ensured that at every stage of production the needs of the consumer were represented.

Marks and Spencer offered only one brand, St. Michael while other retailers offered a range of brands to their customers. Even though this limited the choice made available to the customers, Marks and Spencer felt that benefits outweighed costs. As a writer mentioned: 'To Marks and Spencer, the issue is not so much a question of choice as such, but rather whether or not the product in question can really satisfy the customer's needs.' The company assured customers that the products sold under this name were produced in accordance with the company's specifications on both materials and manufacturing methods. In spite of the high quality of St Michael merchandise, the company adopted a 'no questions asked' refund policy.

In case of pricing, M&S arrived at a price within the reach of the customer, independent of the current costs and selling prices. M&S then tried to find ways to develop products at a cost such that profits could be made. M&S had been a pioneer in advertising, with its slogan 'Don't ask the price, it's a penny' being one of the best of all advertising slogans. The St Michael brand name ranked among the most reputed brands of the world.

Product and Merchandise Management

The buying team at the head office takes decisions regarding introduction of new products. The buying team consisting of a selector, a merchandiser, a technologist, and a quality controller develops the product idea based on the interpretation of market needs. They are required to study materials, manufacturing processes required, and projected sales volume likely to be attained in the initial and final stages of the product's life cycle. The product then goes through a test marketing stage before the actual launch. Once the product is introduced, the company makes sure that it is available in sufficient volume to gain full market acceptance. M&S constantly reviews its product lines and regularly upgrades its merchandise.

M&S never hesitates in removing slow moving product lines. The fortnightly checking list, which provides sales information on all products, has been put to effective use in determining the performance of respective merchandise.

M&S always had direct contact with the manufacturers. M&S felt that manufacturers were not producing quality products in sufficient quantities at realistic prices that would appeal to customers. In order to solve this problem, M&S attempted to link together mass marketing and mass retailing to serve the customers effectively and efficiently. M&S is known as 'manufacturer without factories' working with suppliers who could be called retailers without stores'.

M&S established a Production Engineering Department in 1947. It helps manufacturers modernize their processes by giving advice on factory administration, layout, and any production problems. M&S found that lower prices could increase sales by 8–10 times. Higher volumes also enable M&S to place orders on a large scale. This also helps manufacturers to plan ahead for long runs. M&S attempts to ensure this crucial link between large-scale manufacturing and large-scale retailing.

Scientists and technologists at M&S are fully integrated into the commercial organization of the business and are active members of the buying department. M&S has gradually built up a team of qualified scientists and has extended and modernized laboratories in which new materials, processes, and finished goods are being developed.

Most of M&S merchandise is produced in Britain. However, it procures clothing from abroad when it cannot obtain the required quality in UK.

M&S has sometimes been criticized for using its strong bargaining power to squeeze the profit margins of manufacturers. The retailer has however maintained that it had a cooperative relationship with suppliers and helped them reduce their costs. A senior M&S executive is quoted to have said: 'Our suppliers have a responsibility towards us to produce high-quality merchandise, which will sell freely because of its good value. But we have an equal responsibility to our suppliers. Our responsibility is to ensure that, if a manufacturer or a producer is efficient, then he also makes a profit. It is essential that our manufacturers make profits which they can plough back into their businesses to buy the latest machinery, pay proper wages, implement decent staff amenities, introduce the newest technical aids and expand their plants to meet our increasing requirements and pay their shareholders.' Although M&S did not invest in manufacturing facilities, it invested substantially in technical support, management advice, and edu-cational processes, to bring the manufacturers' outlook and operating philosophy in line with that of M&S. One supplier remarked : 'When you tell someone that you supply to M&S, they look at you with a new respect because they know you have to be good.'

M&S' special way of buying came to be known as 'specification buying'. The company insists that the manufacturers work according to a list of detailed specifications drawn up by M&S regarding the materials and the processes employed. In order to carry out this task, the technologist at the buying team worked in close association with the manufacturer's technical personnel. M&S works out a detailed written specification with the manufacturer for each of its products. When the production process begins, two perfect specimens are sealed—one is sent to the maker and the other remains with M&S. The company rates even the slightest deviation from these specifications as a reject. At the same time, M&S also encourages ideas and improvements offered by suppliers.

In recent years, M&S has invested significantly in a sophisticated IT infrastructure capable of supporting the needs of both its staff and its customers.

In 2003, M&S enjoyed a turnover of around £ 7066 million from its UK operations and £ 681.3 million from its international division. The operating profit from UK operations was the £ 631.9 million while the international retail division contributed £ 43.5 million pounds.

1. Analyse the key aspects of the product and merchandising strategies followed by M&S.
2. Analyse the brand positioning of M&S as a result of its product and merchandising strategies.

3. What are the pros and cons of following an exclusively private label policy by M&S?

4. Given the nature of its merchandising policies and activities, discuss the tools that can be used by M&S for measuring its merchandise performance.

References

1. Mallik, P. 2001, 'Amul enters Pizza market', Indo-Asian News Service, www.rediff.com, July 23.
2. www.tata.com
3. www.the-week.com 2003, 'Emerging Stars of India', August 17.
4. www.imagefashion.com 2002, 'Footprints images' decade in the business of fashion', August.
5. www.delhimarket.com
6. www.travelmumbai.com
7. Gupta, P. 2002, 'Multinational fast-food majors outpace local peers', www.rediff.com, October 4.
8. Isabel Rodriguez-Gaite, 'The future of Private Label looks bright the world over', www.acnielsen.com.
9. www.eretailbiz.com
10. www.lucknowonline.com
11. *The Herald* 2003, www.canadaherald.com, September 30.
12. Das Gupta, S. 2003, 'Shopping in style', *Business Standard*, www.business-standard.com, July 26.
13. www.reachouthyderabad.com
14. www.retailyatra.com
15. Varley, R. 2001, *Retail Product Management*, Routledge, New York, pp. 76–85.
16. Brannen, W. 1981, *Practical Marketing for your Small Retail Business*, Prentice-Hall INC., Englewood Cliffs, New Jersey, pp. 34–50.

8 ATMOSPHERICS AND RETAIL SPACE MANAGEMENT

Learning Objectives

- To understand the role of atmospherics in retail business

- To evaluate the various components of store atmospherics

- To understand the techniques of retail space planning and the associated performance measures

- To explain the concept and techniques of visual merchandising

- To understand the use of colour, wall, and physical materials in the context of retail environment planning

- To identify the issues related with atmospherics in Internet retailing

Introduction

Atmospherics and retail space management are critical to any form of retail business. Their relevance emerges from the link between shopping behaviour and physical environmental factors. Physical environmental factors, for instance, influence the perception of shopping hours spent and the evaluation of merchandise. It, therefore, becomes important for the retailer to effectively plan and organize all the aspects related to atmospherics and retail space to be able to optimize scarce resources and improve profitability. Atmospherics refers to the physical characteristics associated with the store.

These characteristics include both interior and exterior elements, as well as layout planning and display. Display is popularly referred to as visual merchandising. Atmospherics plays a significant role in attracting customers to the store, improving the quality of service experience, creating a brand positioning for the outlet, and improving customer retention rates. Another equally significant but related concept is retail space management. Effective space management attempts to ensure optimum utilization of retail space along with convenience to customers and employees.

There are various aspects related to presentation, styling, and design that are used commonly across all the aspects of atmospherics and space management. Some of these are tools like lighting, colour planning, use of walls and physical materials. There are also emerging critical issues related to atmospherics in the context of Internet retailing. The effective use of technology and design is the key to higher clicks, browsing time, and sales.

Atmospherics

Atmospherics is referred to as a store's physical characteristics that are used to develop the retail unit image and draw customers. It describes the physical elements in a store's design that appeals to consumers and encourages them to buy.

Atmospherics can be classified in terms of exterior and interior atmospherics. Exterior atmospherics refers to aspects like store front, display windows, surrounding businesses, look of the shopping centre, etc. It is considered important to attract new customers. Interior atmospherics refers to aspects like lighting, colour, dressing room facilities, etc. It helps to enhance the display and provides customers with relevant information.

Importance of Atmospherics Planning

Atmospherics planning is increasingly gaining relevance in all kinds of retail set-ups. However, this is especially true for planned shopping centres and lifestyle stores. In a recent study on the cause of a breakdown in service at a travel agency, customers blamed the management when there was an untidy work environment. However, customers indicated a high level of store patronage when the work environment was tidy. Atmospherics plays an important role in creating a brand positioning for the outlet, attracting new customers, facilitating better organization of the store and its merchandise, and enriching the shopping experience.

Role of Atmospherics in Retail Strategy

Atmospherics plays the following roles in the retail strategy:

- Enhances the image of the retail outlet
- Attracts new customers
- Creates a definite USP
- Generates excitement
- Facilitates easy movement inside the store
- Facilitates access to merchandise inside the store
- Ensures optimum utilization of retail space
- Ensures effective and desired presentation of the merchandise
- Reduces product search time for the customer
- Reinforces the marketing communication of the outlet
- Influences the service quality experience

Atmospherics is an integral part of the service quality experience for the customer and visitor to the retail site. Physical surroundings, in service settings such as retail outlets, are vital cues to service quality expectations. The choice of fixtures, décor, and signage can greatly alter consumer perceptions of a store. Effectively placed signs can help to reinforce customers in their role in service encounters. Signs indicate services offered and often hang above or behind the service counters.

This enables even novice customers to quickly assess a business' service, helping to reduce the stress associated with having to ask questions. The choice of the sign's colour, size, and quality provides tangible cues to customers. From this information, they can set expectation levels regarding the kind of service that will be provided.

Another often overlooked, but vital, factor in atmospherics is employee attire. Uniforms, or similar attires for employees, help alleviate customer anxiety as they feel embarrassed to ask if somebody works there. It also reassures customers that the service employee is a professional. Quality of fixtures is a symbolic cue to the consumers.

Inexpensive and cheap fixtures may indicate that the retailer cuts corners, while overly expensive fixtures may indicate that the retailer is making large profits and over-pricing products. It is important that retailers carefully select the types and quality of the fixtures and décor used.

Signage, layout and furnishings all add to the ambience of the store and affect the store-browsing comfort of the customer. In-store elements such as colour, lighting, and music may have a bigger effect on purchase decisions than other marketing inputs such as advertising or point-of-purchase displays. Customers use scents and odours as cues to make inferences about retail locations. Aroma does not refer to immediately identifiable scents such as those emanating from a bakery or coffee shop, but rather ambient scents—those that do not emanate from a particular object but are present in the environment. These may affect perceptions of the store and its products. Studies have found that evaluations of overall retail store ratings were more favourable for scented stores than for unscented stores. Care must be taken to use appropriate aromas; otherwise a confusing situation may occur. Floral scents produce a positive result for outdoor products, but not for kitchen items. Background music enhances customer perception of the store's atmosphere and influences the amount of time a customer spends in a store. Fast paced music hurries customer browsing, while more relaxed music encourages relaxed browsing. An added benefit is that employees perform better when there is background music, which increases job satisfaction.

Immediate Effects of Retail Unit Environment

The three immediate effects of retail unit environment stimuli are pleasure, arousal, and dominance in the minds of the shoppers.

- *Pleasure/displeasure* is termed as affectual reaction of shoppers in service environment. This entails whether shoppers have perceived the environment as enjoyable or unenjoyable. For example, playing classical music in Hindi should enhance shoppers' enjoyment in specific kind of service settings in north India, whereas similar music could adversely affect shopping experience in retail units of Punjab.
- *Arousal* assesses the extent to which the environment stimulates the shoppers in a particular environment. Playing slow instrumental music may result in subdued activity level from customers in service settings such as restaurants, compared to no music or fast music.

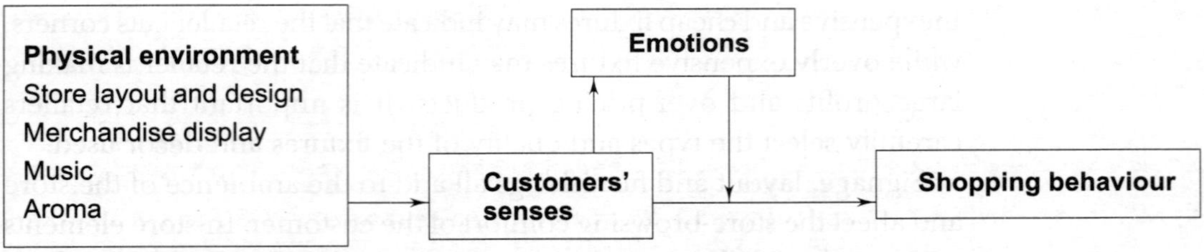

```
┌─────────────────────────────┐              ┌──────────────┐
│  Physical environment       │              │   Emotions   │
│  Store layout and design    │              └──────────────┘
│  Merchandise display        │                 ↑      ↓
│  Music                      │   ┌───────────┐              ┌─────────────────────┐
│  Aroma                      │──▶│ Customers'│─────────────▶│  Shopping behaviour │
│                             │   │  senses   │              └─────────────────────┘
└─────────────────────────────┘   └───────────┘
```

Fig. 8.1 Impact of physical environmental factors on shopping behaviour

Therefore, the nature of music in a specific retail environment can decrease or increase arousal.

- The third dimension is *dominance* that concerns whether customers feel dominant (in control) or submissive (under control) in the service environment. This is a feeling that could be related to environmental aspects like the height of the ceiling that makes one feel small (in control). The dominant colour in the store also creates a response. Individuals associate the colour red with active, assertive, and rebellious moods, whereas they associate blue with sedate tranquillity and a suppression of feelings. The nature of mood that needs to be potrayed, therefore, lies in the right choice of colour. This kind of decision is important in apparel retailing as well as furniture retailing since the choice of apparel as well as furniture greatly depends on the lifestyle of the targeted set of customers.

Environments could be constructed to encourage or discourage approach behaviours. For example, bright colours might encourage individuals to enter a fast-food restaurant, whereas uncomfortable seating might discourage long stays. The physical environment of a retail store has a considerable impact on the shopping behaviour of the consumers, as shown in Fig 8.1.

Key Components of Retail Atmospherics

Four key components of atmospherics in the retail context are:

1. Exterior atmospherics
2. Interior atmospherics
3. Store layout
4. Visual merchandising

All the above components are highly interrelated and appear to be organized in a complementary way. Many key aspects of atmospheric design like use of lighting, colour, and signage play an effective role in both interior and external atmospherics and also in visual merchandising. The dimensions of internal and external atmospherics are given in Fig. 8.3.

Similarly, the nature of physical materials used and wall planning play an important role in all the four components of atmospherics. For this reason some of the aspects like colour, wall planning, and nature of physical material used have been discussed separately in the chapter. Some of the key elements in each of the four components of retail atmospherics are shown in Fig. 8.2.

Exterior Atmospherics

Exterior atmospherics refers to all aspects of physical environment found outside the store. It significantly affects store traffic and sales. It is generated by all aspects of the store exterior. Store exterior includes store entrances, main board, marquee, windows, lighting, etc. Storefront of every retail store exhibits a specific image such as traditional, upmarket, or discount store to the shopper. In competitive markets, retailers can use the storefront as a strong differentiating factor and attract and target new customers.

Storefront is an important decision criterion for the new shoppers in unknown retail markets. Even many small town retailers try to balance and harmonize the various aspects of their store design including the storefront with consistent colours and nature of woodwork.

Elements of Exterior Atmospherics

- Storefront
- Marquee
- Entrances
- Display windows
- Height of building
- Size of building
- Visibility
- Uniqueness
- Surrounding stores
- Surrounding area
- Parking facilities

Four key aspects of exterior atmospherics—retail store entrance, display windows, marquee or signboard, and parking facilities—are discussed below.

Retail Store Entrance Store entrance provides prospective customers access to the retail outlet. Store entrance has to fulfil two important criteria—functional and aesthetic. In India, most of the traditional retail stores enjoy open entrance with no provision for entrance doors and security guards. In some leading markets, retailers or owners of the stores even stand outside and invite the passing shoppers to visit their stores and tell them about the availability of specific merchandise.

This clearly indicates that retail outlets are considered to be a part of the whole market set-up as there is no partition. In other words, doors are considered somewhat a restriction to entry. This phenomenon is still very common in the semi-urban townships of India, whereas in metros, retailers are trying to create a unique environment within their stores, which needs to be separated by doors.

New-age planned shopping centres and retail stores ensure accessibility to all customers, including those using wheel chairs, and also provide for the security of the store when it is closed. It is well researched that a wide opening for the store entrance is perceived as inviting by shoppers.

However, it is also considered a security risk because it does not offer protection from dust and rainy weather, and limits the scope for installing display windows. Fashion and food retailers prefer a semi-open entrance, which not only hinders accessibility but also ensures installation of window display. Retail units in enclosed shopping centres tend to prefer wide-open entrances as they are already secured from environmental threats. In India, most independent retailers prefer open entrances even in central district markets, which are open-market areas.

The funnel or lobby entrance increases the space for window display and welcomes prospective shoppers into the retail space without the commitment of stepping over the threshold. A standard doorway gives a more distinctive look to a retail store along with sufficient provision for window display to communicate with the shoppers. A limitation with standard entrance is restricted access, which may be handled effectively with a provision for an automatic door or positioning of security personnel.

In India, independent retailers prefer to have some pavement in front of their stores in order to place a part of their merchandise outside the store. This helps to draw attention and motivate shoppers to effect purchases. Here open entrances are obviously preferred by retailers.

The most common store entrance alternatives used by retailers are as follows:

- *Shutter-covered:* It is the most common storefront among Indian retail stores. The shutter is raised or removed during the working hours of the day. This is used because of security concerns and also because it ensures usage of the entire storefront.

- *Modular fabrication:* It is a one-piece rectangular or square entrance that may attach several stores.
- *Prefabricated structure:* It is a store frame prepared in a workshop and assembled at the store site.
- *Prototype storefront:* It is commonly used by franchisers and chains to maintain a uniform image of their stores.

Storefront of the prototype market Bombay Store in Bangalore

Number of entrances is one of the important dimensions of retail store entrance decision. A small independent retail store usually prefers one entrance, but in some cases they have provisions of backdoor entrance used prominently for receiving fresh stocks. On the other hand, large department stores or shopping centres operate with four or more entrances as they are supposed to attract a large number of visitors in comparison to independent stores. These retail units have to make sufficient arrangement of entrances for vehicular traffic to their stores also.

Retailers have also to give due weightage to the kind of walkways with the store entrance. Indian stores have no or very limited provisions for customers to enter the stores. Traditional shopping district centres have no provisions of walkways for grocery or pharmaceutical stores. Customers are attended across the counters.

Storefront of an independent retail store in Mumbai

However, traditional independent stores such as garment or jewellery are characterised with wide-open entrance with no walkways, enabling customers to step in directly. Walkways are important features of planned shopping centres or franchised/chain outlets, which cater to high-income sections of the market. Wide, well-decorated, and consistent with the interiors of the store, these have positive effects on the customer's shopping behaviour.

Display Windows Display windows are very common features among retailers dealing in garments and gift items. This feature is even prevalent among retailers in small towns. With the advent of new variants of display windows at local levels and also sponsored by the manufacturers for their authorized retail outlets, display windows are considered an important factor contributing to image-building of the store. For example, Titan Watches provides valuable inputs to Time Zone (first organized chain of retail stores in India) franchisers to install impressive moveable windows to display their merchandise, which not only communicate with prospective shoppers but also attract new customers to the store. During festive seasons, retailers display their selective merchandise along with their respective prices or discounts offered to attract pedestrian traffic, particularly the price-conscious shoppers.

Impressive window display by an apparel store

Retailers can avail of the maximum benefits of window display only through a consistent policy not only while installing them but also in their day-to-day management. The relevant factors that retailers or managers look into while deciding on various aspects of window display are number, size, shape, colour, material, theme of display, and the frequency of changes.

Marquee or Sign Board A marquee is usually a painted or neon light displaying the store name alone or mixed with trademark and other important information of a retail store at the storefront or entrance. In India, most independent retailers use painted tin boards placed outside the storefront. The quality of marquee influences the image of the store perceived by the customers. Pizza Hut, McDonald's, Barista, and Bombay Selection own widely acknowledged marque. Most of the manufacturers or suppliers sponsor marque for the independent retailers with the name of the proprietor along with their own brand names and trademarks. Storefront and marquee play an

Attractive marquee placed outside the Satyam Cineplex in Delhi

important role in enhancing the visibility of the retail unit by providing a clear view of the store to the pedestrian and moving vechicles.

Parking Facilities   Parking facilities play an important role in the success of a retail firm. The importance of parking facility is of great significance in urban shopping centres where the number of car owners is increasing day by day and people want to drive to shopping centres. Whereas most of the traditional shopping districts have no or limited arrangements of parking facility, most of the markets provide road pavements for this purpose. Limited or no parking facility in traditional centres is attributed to less than one per cent ownership of automobiles in India.

At the same time, Indian consumers prefer to purchase from the nearby shopping centres, which are conveniently approachable by walking or public transportation. Therefore, this aspect has remained neglected for long.

With the emergence of an automobile-owning shopping class, retailers, irrespective of their location in planned shopping centres or

---

Aspects of a Parking Facility

- *Spacious:* This facilitates movement of vehicles within the parking space and availability of parking space even during peak time.
- *Duration for parking :* The management can state the duration for which shoppers can park their vehicles.
- *Cost of parking:* It is the amount charged from the shoppers.
- *Security:* This is required to ensure

smooth passage of vehicles, to keep record of the cars exceeding allotted time duration, and ensure safety of the shoppers from criminals.
- *Underground or upstairs parking:* This provides a convenient location for parking where shoppers have to travel less from the parking place to the desired stores.

---

district centres or neighbourhood centres, are now providing adequate parking facility to their customers.

Interior Atmospherics

Interior atmospherics refers to all aspects of the physical environment found inside the store. Interior atmospherics affects sales, time spent in the store, and approach/avoidance behaviour of the target segment. Point-of-purchase interaction and retail unit decoration influences the customer and in turn sales of the retail unit. Some key ingredients of interior atmospherics are flooring, music, interior store design, level of cleanliness, etc. The layout and design of a retail centre and store (e.g., traffic flow, allocation of floor space, layout of merchandise, passages, aisle, traffic patterns, etc.) have been found to affect unplanned purchases and perceptions of price value.

A store's physical environments have an influence on shopping behaviour of customers through mediating emotional states. The retail unit environment contains various stimuli that might be perceived by the customer's senses and each stimulus offers many options with regard to shopping behaviour. For example, store music varies by volume, tempo, pitch and texture, and by the specific songs played. In addition, various individual stimuli can be combined to create a unique atmosphere. To project an upscale image, a retail owner/manager chooses folk music, modest colours, elegant perfumes, cool temperatures, inadequately displayed merchandise, and soft lighting.

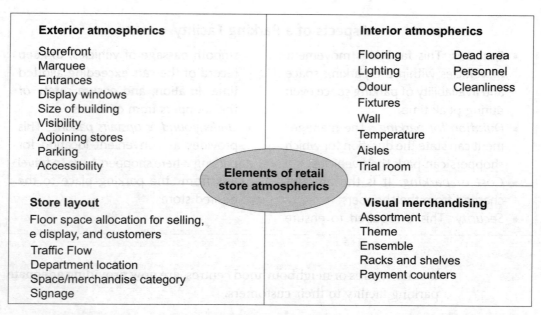

Fig. 8.2   Elements of retail store atmospherics

Interior Store Design   Conventional retailers design their stores in ways that produce specific emotional effects on shoppers, which in turn influence their shopping behaviour in favour of the retail store. Ghosh (1994, p.521) defines retail atmosphere as 'the psychological effect of feeling created by a store's design and its physical surroundings.' Furthermore, retail store image is one of the most powerful components of retail positioning strategy and one of the most powerful tools in attracting, influencing, and satisfying consumers. A retailer or manager is expected to design or redesign a store, with an objective of influencing customer's preferences, buying decisions, and shopping behaviours.

Retail store design covers store layout and space planning details issues. It is a well-known fact that store layout decisions certainly determine the issue of the amount of time that customers spend for shopping.

Interior design of stores is evolved by an intelligent combination of the following factors:

- Flooring
- Lighting
- Fixtures
- Temperature
- Colours
- Scents, sounds
- Wall textures
- Width of aisles

- Dressing facilities
- Dead areas
- Self-service
- Prices (levels and displays)
- Technology/modernization
- Vertical transportation
- Personnel
- Merchandise
- Cash register placement
- Cleanliness

Two critical aspects of store design—lighting and signage—are discussed below.

Lighting Lighting arrangement adds significant meaning to the entire retail store atmosphere. The basic purpose of the lighting arrangement is that the shoppers can see the merchandise with ease while the retail setting looks brighter and more attractive to customers.

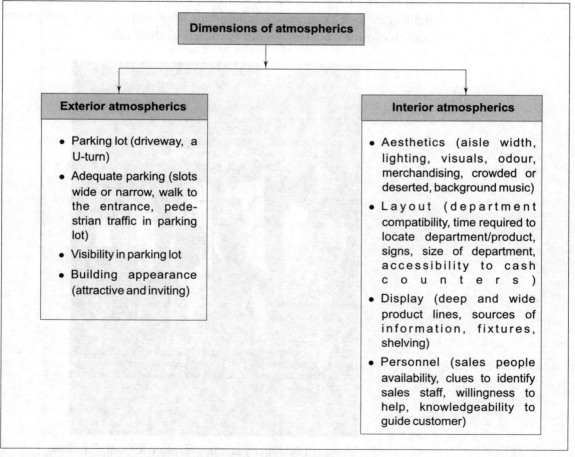

Fig. 8.3 Dimensions of interior and exterior atmospherics

Lighting affects the colour of the offerings on display in the retail store. For example, garments and jewellery retailers use lighting to display their products better. As customers prefer to evaluate the colour, texture, and design of such offerings with ease, there is need for adequate lighting. Poor lighting will make them uncomfortable in determining the parametres of the offerings, which in turn can lead to loss of sale. Research findings indicate that blue colour light is preferred in case of stores selling toiletries and white in the case of medical stores.

Retail units use various variants of lighting in accordance with their store image and positioning. For example, McDonald's uses bright lights in their stores as it keeps customers in high spirits and ensures a high activity level. On the other hand, Ruby Tuesday maintains a dull lighting, which ensures a subdued customer activity level and makes sure that most of them remain confined to their table.

Usage of lighting by an apparel store for merchandise display

Role of Effective In-store Lighting

- Improves visibility and attractiveness of the store and merchandise for the customers.
- Makes it easier to assess the colour of the merchandise.

- Eases the evaluation of the product attributes.
- Establishes the right mood.

Signage Visual cues meet most of the communication needs of customers in the shopping centres and retail stores. The location of a specific offering or department in large shopping centres is such information without which a shopper could get confused and disappointed, and finally perceive the particular store as being high on inconveniences.

Instruction board at a traditional eating joint in
the central business district of a city

Signages provide information regarding a store's policy in respect of returned goods, timing to return, prevailing discounts, etc. The type of signage used in terms of size, lettering, and colours, and the placement of signage are indispensable parts of the entire retail unit designing.

Most of the independent retailers in India place such signage boards near the cash counters, as most shoppers are found to place orders and make payments from this point of the store. For example, independent eating joints usually place the list of items available with their respective prices at the cash counters instead of offering individual menu cards.

In respect of the large department stores and shopping centres, marketers have to work out a balance between providing all the information a customer is looking for and cluttering the place with too many signage boards. Retailers or managers need to ensure that signages used in retail unit are complementary with the entire store design.

Music   Music is one of the key environmental variables that can influence shoppers. In a research done in the US, shoppers reported themselves (perception) as shopping longer when exposed to familiar music but actually shopped longer when exposed to unfamiliar music. Shorter times in the familiar music condition were related to time misperceptions. Environmental factors like music thus affect time spent in the store, propensity to shopping, and satisfaction with the shopping experience.

Store Layout

Store layout refers to the interior retail store arrangement of departments or groupings of merchandise. It is important for retailers to evolve a customer-friendly layout. This involves paying adequate attention to factors such as expected movement of the customers visiting the store and space allotted to customers to shop, and making adequate provision for merchandise display. These concerns are important as they contribute to the capital cost of the retail firm and also the overall image of the store.

Customer-friendly store layout is likely to motivate the shoppers to move around the store and shop more than what they had planned for. In India, many of the independent retailers have no or limited provision for customer movement within a store. Merchandise is displayed on the shelves and some beyond the vision of the customers. These are provided to them across the counter on request. For some of the smaller stores, at times, counters are placed at the store entrance. This is a very common practice with kirana (grocery) stores, garment stores, and medical stores. An example of such a store is Subhiksha. It reduces operational cost, wastage of space, and theft. This is in consonance with their strategy of providing merchandise at low prices to their customers.

On the contrary, many organized retail firms provide sufficient space within the store for customers and create a layout to facilitate a specific pattern of traffic movement. In most of the 'Do-It-Yourself' stores, customers expect comfortable space for movement and selection of goods they wish to buy or evaluate. Store layout depends on the kind of merchandise display planned by the retail management within the store. The placement of racks and shelves within the store determines the nature of space left for the customers to enjoy and organize their shopping. Too many racks and shelves in the store placed in a disorganized manner confuses the customer, makes it difficult for him to locate a particular merchandise, and hinders the movement of sales people and customers.

Most independent retailers prefer racks and shelves along the walls. This provides reasonable space within the store to place a larger quantum of stocks in the selling space. It may also be used to create the perception that the store carries a wide variety of merchandise. In many cases, low turnover merchandise is organized on the wall shelves and high turnover merchandise is displayed in mobile bins. The latter is also true for items with special promotional schemes and discounts. This is true for Big Bazar where large bins containing merchandise with special promotional schemes are dispensed throughout the store.

In planning the layout, it is important to consider issues related to logical sequencing and category adjacency. The merchandise layout plan should be created according to the shopping habits of customers at the store. In this context, *basics* are items that the customers will seek. *Seasonal* items are products that have a limited shelf life. These can be placed up front, on power walls or high-traffic areas. *Impulse* buys are best located in high-traffic areas and around the case.

Store layout planning involves decisions about allocation of floor space, product groupings, and nature of traffic flow, which can take the form of straight or grid traffic flow, free-form flow (curving) or racetrack flow. Some retailers also operate a storeyed layout to meet their specific requirements.

1. *Grid:* It is a commonly used system followed by conventional grocery stores as it facilitates planned shopping behaviour so that customers can easily locate products on their shopping list. Kirana and drugs store owners or managers commonly employ the grid layout. It comprises long gondolas with offerings positioned along aisles in a repetitive pattern. Grid arrangement is not very aesthetic but it ensures smooth shopping trips of shoppers within the stores. This layout is comfortable for the shoppers who are frequent visitors (weekly or bi-weekly) at the same store as this reduces their search cost of locating merchandise in stores. Grid design is considered cost-efficient by retailers in terms of space utilization; besides, aisles of same width and design permit easy movement of shoppers and carts. This design is considered to be the most space productive in terms of merchandise display. As most of the gondolas have large capacity (in terms of number of shelves), the amount of merchandise displayed on the floor is optimized in this layout. Grid layout saves expenditure on the fixtures, as it requires standard fixtures. The grid layout is shown in Fig. 8.4.

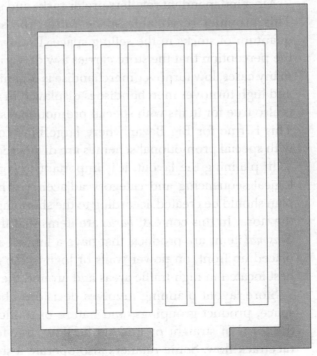

Fig. 8.4 Grid layout

2. *Free-form:* It offers convenience during shopping. It is also shown that it increases the time that consumers are willing to spend in the store. It is mainly used by large department stores (e.g., duty-free shops).

It is commonly used in small speciality stores and departments of large retail stores. In free-form layout, fixtures and aisles can placed asymmetrically. This provides informal setting to shoppers, which facilitates shopping and browsing. It is also referred to as 'boutique layout'.

The role of sales people on retail floor becomes crucial in this layout in comparison to grid or racetrack layout since customers are not drawn easily to stores in free-form layout.

Free-form proves costlier in terms of high probability of thefts, as sales people can't manage simultaneously two adjacent sections or departments. With such a layout, there is always a possibility of little or no arrangement of storage facility on retail floor, as one requires enough space area for merchandise display, as shown in Fig. 8.5.

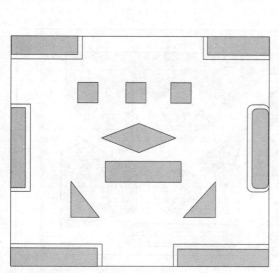

Fig. 8.5 Free-form layout

Fig. 8.6 Boutique layout

3. *Race track:* It offers an unusual, interesting, and entertaining shopping experience while also increasing impulse and promotional purchases. Customers visiting shops with this particular layout are required to navigate through specific paths and therefore, to visit as many store sections or departments as possible. They are, therefore, exposed to a large number of products and promotional materials. The race track layout is shown in Fig. 8.7.

Retail units with multiple departments opt for racetrack layout in order to attract shoppers to each department. It is also known as loop layout design. Racetrack provides an aisle to facilitate smooth flow of customer traffic with an access to the retail units multiple entrances. An aisle is supposed to give access to various specialized departments. Loop design encourages impulse purchasing, as shoppers are exposed to various departments during a particular merchandise purchase. For example, Big Bazaar and Pantaloon store in Gurgaon have adopted the racetrack layout for drawing customers to multiple sections, which are joined with a major aisle. Departments place fresh or new merchandise on the aisle to draw customers into departments and around the loop. Surface or colour of the aisle directs the shoppers within the retail store. The differentiation among various departments is based on the material or colour used in accordance with the store's internal décor.

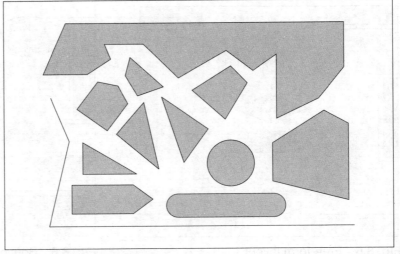

Fig. 8.7 Race track layout

4. *Storeyed layout:*   This is a very common variant of store layout design among Indian independent and leading retail chains in the organized sector. This type of layout not only provides the best utilization of floor area but also permits the retailer to set separate sections for different product categories. This arrangement provides comfort to the shoppers and also helps the retailers to manage the stock display effectively. Storeyed layout is popular among the leading fashion department stores and supermarkets in India, such as LifeStyle, Shoppers' Stop, and Saravana. This kind of layout saves a substantial amount of initial investment of the retailer or developer in a rising real-estate cost scenario in the emerging retail market in India.

Visual Merchandising

Visual merchandising, also referred to as display, is defined as the presentation of products in order to sell them. The initial point of interaction with a potential customer is in the window displays of the storefront. Good displays shout to the world that the retailer cares about his image and merchandise and, most importantly, about entertaining, informing, and educating his customers. The customers count upon seeing new things in the windows. Likewise, the interior of the store deserves the same attention as the windows. Frequent changes encourage the customer visiting his normal section to also wander about and discover additional novelties.

Visual merchandising includes various aspects such as: store floor plan, store windows, signs, merchandise display, space design, fixtures and hardwares, and the elements that come with it—which may be all too many to mention. Visual merchandising has been around since the dawn of civilization, when humans started selling merchandise to each others. When a retailer or a supplier arranged his goods to be more attractive to a customer, or when a farmer put the best of his harvest on the top of the basket for the consumers to see and touch, that was visual merchandising.

Visual merchandising, today, has become more sophisticated and all encompassing than was arranging of merchandise for easy access to customers. Visual merchandising techniques are put into practice right from designing the floor plan of the store to the beautiful mannequins that grace the store floor. With the speciality marketing

---

Benefits of Effective Display

- Entertains, informs, and educates the customer about the product/service in an effective and creative way
- Encourages a customer to wander about to discover novelties
- Re-affirms the store's image
- Arranges merchandise for easy access
- Draws the attention of the customer to enable him to take purchase decision within the shortest possible time and thus augment the shopping process.

- Establishes a creative medium to present merchandise in 3D environment, thereby creating a lasting impact and recall value
- Highlights merchandise to promote its sale
- Introduces and explains new products
- Gives ideas on how to use it
- Encourages the customer to enter the store and shop

---

of the 1990s, visual merchandising has become a necessity for the retail industry. It now envelops all aspects that go into creating and managing the overall visual presentation of the retail store environment. Specifically, it combines and integrates an understanding of merchandise presentation, display, and retail design. It is the art of presentation which brings the merchandise into focus. It is expected to educate the customers, create desire, and finally augment the shopping process. This is an area where the Indian retailers, particularly from the unorganized sector, lack adequate knowledge and expertise.

Organizing the Display An effective product placement strategy maximizes selling opportunities by creating a desire and invites the customer to pick up complementary or related items to the one already chosen. A planogram has been found very useful in organizing a co-ordinated display as it provides a schematic drawing of fixtures that illustrate product placement. Planogramming is an inventory control and merchandise display method that allows a retailer to maintain shelf inventory in an orderly way to improve efficiency and customer service. Organizing a display involves planning for three key aspects— deciding on the display theme or concept, identifying locations for it, and selecting and determining the nature of various display components.

Display concepts can be based on one or a combination of the following themes:

- Seasons
- Special occasions or holidays
- Colours
- Trends and activities (e.g., fishing, scrapbooking, rangoli, and collage, etc.)
- Themes (e.g., Victorian, children, ethnic, Western, construction, etc.)
- Events of the community

There are many locations within a store where displays can be set up. Some of them are:

- Front windows
- Small platform at the entrance
- End caps
- Display or product cases (for particular types of merchandise such as jewellery)
- Behind the check-out counter
- On counters or ledges
- Designated display areas (assigned levels of prominence due to traffic flow)

Factors Guiding Use of Merchandise Display Fixtures   When buying store fixtures and display merchandise for a retail store, a number of factors must be considered to be able to make the best possible choice. Some of the key factors are discussed below.

Product Placement Strategy

- Begin your product placement strategy by creating focal displays that introduce the section.
- Follow this by secondary focal display points that represent the merchandising unit. This influences the customer's eye movement and hence, where they walk.

Organizing Apparel Display: Sizing

- Do not size products on garment rods in walls with sizing rings.
- Sizing products, mixing colours and patterns together makes merchandise look as if it has been marked down for clearance.
- Since products stocked on store walls are viewed from a distance, items should be merchandised for maximum visual impact—first arranged by style, colourized within each style, and then sized without sizing rings.

- *Product line:* Characteristics of merchandise need to be considered while deciding the fixtures to be used for display. Wooden racks or shelves can be effectively used for apparel or packaged FMCG products. However, mirrored showcases are preferred for jewellery or gift items since they ensure better safety and presentation.

- *Customer profile:* Retailers have to take into consideration the profile and expectations of their target segment. Stores which primarily cater to functional rather than hedonistic needs do not require very fancy fixtures. Hence, they can reduce intensive investments in fixtures and pass on the benefits to the customers. Examples of such stores are kirana shops, chemist stores, and other neighbourhood stores. Many small eating joints and *dhabas* use inferior quality or low-cost furniture and fixtures. This is done keeping in mind the socio-economic profile of its customers and also the fact that customers do not yet expect *dhabas* to provide fancy and expensive décor. Stores targeting the high-end customers invest a lot in fancy and unique fixture designs and arrangements to generate an exciting and inviting store environment, thereby attracting customers and building their own store image.

- *Level of competition:* Level of competition is a significant factor in determining the kind of fixtures to be used by a retailer since it

Eating joint with minimal fixtures to attract the customers

provides him with a unique selling proposition (USP). For instance, most of the eating joints and garment stores in urban centres of

India were using very limited display options. However, with the advent of international players such as McDonald's, KFC, Marks and Spencer, Benetton, Levis, etc., the more upmarket retailers are pushed to refurbish their displays and interiors to keep pace with competition and continue to attract customers.

Components of Display   With a theme of the display determined and the location for it planned, the retailer needs to examine the components of the display. The various components of the display are as follows.

- *Wall displays* refer to slatwall panels and fixtures, gridwall panels and displays, slotted wall standards, face-outs, hangrails, and shelving.
- *Floor fixtures* are gridwall panels and accessories, garment racks, display cases and counters, metal shelving gondolas, floor and cube merchandisers. A dump display is merchandise displayed by being dumped or heaped in a pile, usually in a bin or on a table. Dump display can be used as bulk dump display and dump table display.
- *Display products* refer to mannequins and body forms, clear acrylic displays, and countertop and jewellery displays.
- *Supplies and equipment* include hangers and steamers, tagging supplies and labelers, packaging and shopping bags, etc.
- *Promotional items* include window signs and banners, sign holders and sign cards, and sales tags and tickets. These items should be used to enhance the product for sale or help in furthering the story or theme.
- *Lighting fixtures* include track lighting and accessories such as rope lights. It is important to use proper lighting to make the product 'pop' in the display. Incandescent spots are very effective here. Lighting needs to come from more than one direction for a balanced presentation.
- *Signage* should be professional, never handwritten, regardless of the size. A shelf tag is also a type of signage. It is a tag or sticker with merchandising information of what belongs in that place on the shelf or hook in the planogram or display. Bin tags, bin labels, peg tags, shelf labels, and planogram tags are some others types of signages. Shelf tags aid in the proper placement of product and frequently include price information for customers in lieu of price marking the individual items.

Wall displays   The popular wall displays are discussed below.

- *Slatwall* is the most popular wall system to display merchandise and maximize total use of wall areas. Slatwall panels and accessories allow complete versatility to display merchandise anywhere on the panel. Visually, the look of slatwall is very eye appealing, giving a clean, streamlined look. Slatwall accessories fit in grooves anywhere on the panel, allowing a retailer to set up displays exactly in accordance with their specific needs.

- *Slotted wall standards* are a long-established, effective means of displaying heavier merchandise, allowing you to display more merchandise on wall areas. Display hardware accessories such as

Slatwall wall fixture used for display of merchandise

shelving brackets, hangrail brackets, and face-outs provide organized, effective merchandise presentation. Slotted wall standards are available in regular-duty (with ½" slots) for medium weight loads, and heavy-duty (with 1" slots) for heavier items. For installation, simply screw the standards into the wall studs.

Organizing Apparel Display: Hangers

- Hangers should be hooked over bars and rods in the direction that makes them easiest for shoppers to remove.
- Since most people are right-handed, hangers should be hung so that they can be removed from the right or lifted toward the shopper's right.

Floor fixtures The important types of floor fixtures are as follows.

- *Gridwall panels and accessories* have become the most popular and versatile way to utilize both wall-mounted applications and free-standing floor displays. Gridwall panels are a durable, medium-weight system in a variety of panel sizes, which accept various display accessories for hanging, shelving, and merchandising products. To use as a wall system, the retailers may attach wall-mount brackets to the wall studs, and hang gridwall panels on the brackets, using four wall-mount brackets for each gridwall panel. To use as a floor system, the retailers may join gridwall panels together using joining clips or plastic cable ties, creating free-standing displays such as triangular three-way towers, four-way displays, and gondola style merchandising units. Gridwall panels are commonly used for display windows, trade shows, and markets, and can be set up side-by-side using attachable grid base legs, providing a large display space for merchandise presentation.
- *Garment racks and displayers* are beneficial to show and sell items using floor displays. Round racks, straight bar clothing racks, and high-capacity merchandisers are useful for holding a lot of merchandise in a limited amount of space. Two-arm and four-arm racks are popular, eye-catching displayers designed to create a visually powerful display of garments.
- *Display cases and counters* feature sturdy construction and durable low-pressure laminated finishes in solid colours and wood grain styles. It is one of the economical options with retailers as budget-priced display cases and counters are of an exceptional value, with the possibility of coordinated heights and widths to allow many possible layouts by using showcases, wrap counters, cash stands, and corner fillers. Line of display cases and counters depends on the requirements of the store and the available space for display cases and counters. Retailers have to decide on the display cases

and counters on the basis of material used, length or depth of the cases and counters required, and colour compatible with other fixtures.

Retailers use cases and counters with the provisions of show-cases having adjustable glass shelves, with options such as fluorescent lights, and locks to secure the products. Showcases are a very common feature at watch, gift, and jewellery stores.

- *Metal shelving gondolas* can display any number of products easily with total merchandising flexibility. Made of heavy gauge steel and built to last, they are one of the most effective and durable display merchandisers available. Gondolas have a beige baked enamel finish and pegboard backs.

They can be joined side-by-side to make a continuous run of shelving units and are available in both single-sided wall unit and double-sided floor units. Optional end display units can be added at each end of the floor units if desired.

Use of display case for merchandise display

Display products   The key product display fixtures are discussed below:

- *Mannequins and body forms* are essential for enhancing the appeal of the merchandise, making it easier for customers to visualize how clothing will look on them. Traditional life-size mannequins offer a flattering look to clothing and are the most effective way to sell merchandise. Body forms and mannequin alternatives such as torso forms, dress forms, and shirt forms are lower in cost, and are not full-body displays like mannequins. Cost-effective display stands with display hanger tops let you feature merchandise on counters, shelves, and as garment rack toppers.
- *Clear acrylic displays* offer many innovative fixtures, giving a clean look with the greatest eye appeal for the products. Made to display items on slatwall, gridwall, and countertop use, acrylic displays help you sell more merchandise and are excellent for many accessory items including jewellery. With clear acrylic displays such as shelves, trays, bins, sign holders, mirrors, easels, and display risers and cubes, there is a display available for almost every purpose.

    Black plush velvet countertop in jewellery displays are a low-cost, affordable way to display jewellery and accessories at their best. These are attractive with an upscale look, designed to display necklaces, bracelets, earrings, rings, and watches, great for use in showcases and store windows.

Promotional items   Window signs and banners are traffic-stoppers, and create an opportunity to draw a shopper's attention. Many retailers underestimate the powerful pull of an effective window sign. Before a retail store can sell merchandise to its shoppers, it has to entice them at first. This is where effective signs, banners, and promotional displays come in. Once a shopper is inside the store, a well thought out and effectively signed promotional interior can be a call to action for shoppers. Using promotional signs and sign holders, and colourful sales tags can plant a seed of interest in the customer's mind and help increase sales.

Lighting fixtures   One of the most important yet underused elements of visual merchandising is the proper use of lighting to highlight merchandise and displays. Track lighting enhances colour, and vivid colour sells merchandise. Track lighting can actually help enhance sales. Ambient lighting is the general lighting of a retail store, in many cases fluorescent lighting. Track lighting can be used for perimetre lighting to illuminate wall displays. Track lighting can also be used as accent lighting for highlighting specific merchandise, adding excitement, and drawing attention to the merchandise.

Interior lighting of the Ebony department store

Design Tools Employed to Attract Attention

There are five design tools employed to stop busy people in their tracks and cause them to really look at an eye-catching display.

- *Colour* is the first element that attracts attention in a display. It is important to choose the combinations carefully considering the colour of the product and the lighting environment.

- *Angles* direct the customer's eyes where the retailers want them to go. Varying heights of props and merchandise, angles of mannequin arms, free hanging graphics, light, or plants all create angles.

- *Motion* always creates interest and can be achieved by a fan, an electric train, the small motors of motorized displays, or blinking lights.

- *Simplicity* of the display sends a message of higher cost. Similarly, a large window, filled to the brim, suggests low prices.

- *Repetition* of an item says that the store really believes in that product and usually has a strong influence on the customer. If one of them is slightly askew or if an unusual prop is incorporated, even more interest is created.

Exterior lighting of the Ebony department store

Factors to Consider in Organizing an Effective Display   Factors like balance, rhythm, proportion, texture, harmony, and emphasis are important in organizing an effective display. The role of these factors and the techniques related to them are discussed below.

- *Balance*   It refers to an equality of optical weight and importance that creates a unified presentation. Balance could be of two kinds—formal and informal. Formal balance refers to symmetry. It is rigid and static but is simple and easy to use consistently. It helps keep wall displays organized and maintains uniformity. Informal balance is asymmetrical. It uses optical weight to balance the display. There is greater freedom to express movement and activity.

- *Rhythm*   Lines can lend a rhythmic feeling to any display or area. Various line shapes can be used to create rhythmic effects. Vertical lines send a message of dignity, strength, and height. Diagonal lines speak of action, effective mood-makers in sporting goods, and toy departments. Horizontal lines are more restful and remind us of landscapes. They also help to downplay the height of a room. Curved lines are graceful, relaxed, and indicate carefree movement and a sense of femininity. Hence, it is effectively used for bridal shops, maternity wear, and cosmetics. Repetition also creates a sense of visual rhythm. An instance of this is when merchandising message is repeated again and again.

- *Proportion*   It refers to the relationship between the apparent size, mass, scale, or optical weight of two or more objects. It can be

---

Organizing Apparel Display: Co-ordinated Merchandise

- Feature coordinated tops and bottoms on every wall section.
- A wall section featuring only T-shirts does not encourage multiple sales.
- Adding related accessories like hats, scarves, handbags, and shoes will further enhance wall presentations and support even greater sales opportunities.

- Hanging garments with similar sleeve lengths together on garment rods results in a cleaner and more appealing presentation.
- Varying sleeve lengths can be presented together on less visible floor fixtures if necessary.

---

used through the use of both contrasting sizes and consistency of sizes of objects.

- *Texture* Creating exciting and pleasing textures is important since people want to touch the merchandise. It sets the mood of the merchandise and the store. Texture can be both seen and felt.
- *Harmony* It is important to build the display such that it is in harmony with the whole store. The retailer should keep the whole store image and merchandising goals in mind when building displays. It is better to avoid little islands of brilliance that pay homage to the designer's cleverness when storewide design and harmony are likely to suffer.
- *Emphasis* Emphasis should always be on the merchandise. Hence, it should be in accordance with what will the display feature and how will it be communicated to the customer. Emphasis could be through the use of colour, dramatic lighting, signage and graphics, and strategic placements.

Visual Merchandising in India Unlike in the West, where visual merchandise receives the highest priority in commercial planning of a product, the Indian retail industry's understanding and practice of the concept of visual merchandise is inadequate. With the advent of foreign players and chain stores, independent retailers will have to compete purely on the basis of the competitive edge of the merchandise on display and visual merchandise will be a helpful tool in projecting the uniqueness of the products and will, thereby, increase the market access and sales. It is high time the Indian retailers opted for some new-age visual merchandise management in place of the traditional practice of display of merchandise. Still, majority of the retailers in the unorganized sector give limited importance to visual merchandise in the retail marketing mix.

Two interesting examples can be discussed in this context—Raymond's, the garment retail chain, and Parade, a retail store in Mumbai.

Raymond's, the first men's garment retail chain in India, has always taken visual merchandising seriously. Their management has hired a professional agency for consistent and picture-perfect window displays. They prefer a theme-based merchandise display that does not involve the use of expensive raw materials. They feel that a theme-based display provides the management with required flexibility and an opportunity to incorporate new ideas. Some time back they did a window display with a construction theme. However, it had to be scrapped because 'it failed to target the right clientele.'

The Raymond's have now appointed a professional agency to train the sales staff at their branches all over India by conducting workshops and slide shows. The management penalizes branch personnel who skip such training programmes. Most Raymond's stores ensure one huge deep window, which provides sufficient and attractive scope to display merchandise.

Parade, a boutique in an Andheri bylane in Mumbai, displays new stocks on hangers and places them in the windows for public view. The retailer does not bother himself with mannequins. This is a very common attitude among many of the independent retailers across product categories. They prefer spending on advertising rather than on window displays as they feel that most of the customers have specific requirements for which they inquire from the retailer as soon as they enter.

Store Space Management

Space and inventory are the two most important resources of the retail firm. The best possible allocation of the store space to departments, product categories, storage space, and customer space is a major challenge for the owners and managers of the store. Retailers acknowledge the importance of space management for the success of business. It has a two-way bearing on retail business—it not only attracts business by ensuring convenience to customers but also places the merchandise in accordance with the salespersons' work allocation.

Department store exhibiting space management

The key objectives of retail space management are:

- To obtain a high return on investment by increasing the productivity of retail space, which requires effective utilization of space for merchandise display and customer movement
- To ensure a compatible, exciting, and rational interface between the customer, merchandise, and sales people

Space, as a retail input, is fixed in supply with the retailer and is not easy to expand as it involves huge investments. Therefore, the allocation of the internal space among various heads is a challenging task for the retailer. He has to clearly allot the available space to provide the selling space, merchandise space, personnel space, and customer space.

Effective management of store space requires a sound understanding of the following factors:

- The nature of offerings, suppliers, and departments within the store
- The quantity of merchandise the store wants to carry and display
- The location and proportion of space allotted to different types of merchandise

Issues related to the nature of offerings, suppliers, and departments within the store are covered in the chapter on Retail Product and Merchandise Management. In this section we intend to discuss the other two aspects. The quantity of merchandise and space allotted to respective merchandise depends on the sales productivity of the particular merchandise and brand positioning of the retailer. Retailers' decision regarding the proportion of space to be allocated to specific merchandise is further guided by the following factors:

- Profitability of merchandise
- Merchandise display
- Placement of merchandise within the store
- Seasonal considerations

The space management decision also has an important influence on sub-decisions like:

- Location of various departments
- Arrangements between departments within the shopfloor
- Selection of layout with customer behaviour in mind
- Planned traffic flow of customers

For instance, independent retailers who follow the counter set-up restrict entry of customers in the store and provide a reasonable amount of space for merchandise storage and placement. They also keep free space within the store for smooth movement for the personnel to get material from the shelves and other storage places. However, in the more upmarket retail stores, a grid-iron layout provides the customers greater browsing space and enables them to collect the merchandise they want. Here the retailer can utilize the floor space for placing racks and shelves. This kind of space management is common in grocery stores or big supermarkets. If customers are more likely to stop, integrate merchandise, and wander back and forth, the free-flowing plan tends to be preferred. This is a very common feature in gift shops and apparel showrooms.

Grocery retailers locate more frequently purchased items such as bread, milk, eggs, etc. at the more easily accessible shelves, which lie in the front portion of the store. Less frequently purchased items such as shoe polish, detergents, etc. are placed deeper inside the store. Inconvenience caused to customers in locating desired merchandise leads to customer dissatisfaction, which in turn harms the image and sales of the store.

A study on the factors that influence a person's choice on where to shop identified that the ease with which a customer could find items in the store was particularly significant. The factor 'easy to find items' obtained the highest correlation with customer satisfaction. From customers' perspective the ideal design for space management is one that facilitates a comprehensive overview of all other parts of the store from any angle on the shopfloor. This would ease the process of trying to locate required groceries and, thus, simplify the shopping process.

In keeping with the requirement of ease of locating items, it would seem logical to suggest that the retail floor space should be located on one level only. Reasonably, one could expect the inconvenience of having to change floors with a basket of groceries without the aid of an escalator to have a severe impact on patronage turnover. The satisfaction factor 'ease of finding items and movement within the store, is subject to a good store layout, which enhances the appearance of the store and supports the positioning strategy of the firm.

For better store layout, retail space can be expanded, keeping in mind other factors, by including the first floor or a basement as part of the retail area to be accessed from the ground floor by an internal staircase.

Retail Performance Measures

Sales and profitability are considered established measures of success of a retail unit. Similarly, they can be used to measure the performance of retail space management. The measures of retail space performance indicate the productivity of retail space. The three commonly used retail space performance measures are sales per square metre or profit per square metre, sales per linear metre or profit per linear metre, and sales per cubic metre or profit per cubic metre.

Sales Per Square Metre or Profit Per Square Metre

It measures retail space performance on the basis of sales/profits according to the area of floor space covered (Fig. 8.8). This measure is convenient to use when only a single layer of merchandise is displayed and various types of fixtures are placed. This is a common measure for fashion retailing.

Sales Per Linear Metre or Profit Per Linear Metre

It measures retail space productivity on the basis of income generated by footage of shelf space allocated (Fig. 8.9). This measure is more suitable for the stores using multi-shelved fixtures such as a gondola or racks. It takes into consideration the linear metre value of a shelf rather than the area of space exposed in terms of the height value of a shelf.

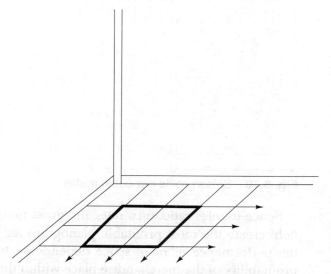

Fig. 8.8 Sales/profits per square metre

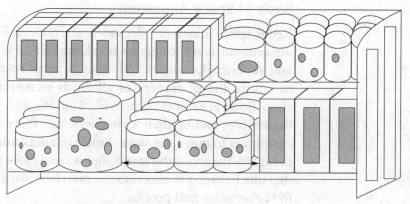

Fig. 8.9 Sales/profits per linear metre

Sales Per Cubic Metre or Profit Per Cubic Metre

It measures retail space performance on the basis of length, width, and depth of the fixtures placed in the store (Fig. 8.10). This measure is necessarily used by retailers in the frozen food business or those who place dump bins on the retail floor.

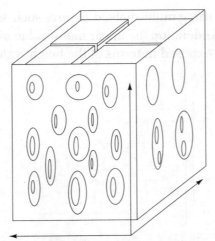

Fig. 8.10   Sales/profits per cubic metre

Space-to-sales ratio, turn rate, and gross margin ROI analyses can help create the most profitable planogram for the retailer. In effect, the performance of retail space depends on the levels of sales, the profitability of the merchandise place within the space, and the value of the retail space.

Basis of Space Allocation

Retail space allocation decisions are conceived and implemented at department level, category level, and SKU level in big department and supermarket stores. Whereas, a small retailer's major concern is to ensure the placement of all kinds of merchandise in the limited shop floor area and to provide smooth access to merchandise for themselves rather than customers, as there are no provisions for customers to enter the store. Small retailers normally place the goods in high demand on the lower shelves and close to the cash counters, so that one has speedy access to the merchandise in high demand, leading to higher sales and profits.

Similar concerns (sales and profits) guide department stores in the allocation of space to merchandise along with ensuring compatible movement for shoppers in accordance with their routine movement within the store.

Space allocation is the process of distributing the right amount of space to the right merchandise at the right time according to a detailed analysis of customer demand. It is fraught with tremendous complexity, spanning systems for data warehouses, distribution centres, transportation networks, and product planning.

Retailers normally depend on historical data or their experience for allocating space, which is common with retailers in the unorganized set-up. Sales and profitability are the two basic guiding principles used by retailers to arrive at space allocation decisions.

Sales as the Basis of Space Allocation

Retailers assign more space for merchandise that registers a higher volume of sale. Under this principle of retail space allocation, it is always favourable for retailers to have large stocks of goods which experience high demand to avoid stock-out situation and inconvenience to the customers. The fast-moving merchandise, such as bread and eggs at a grocery retailer, is not highly profitable in comparison to slow-moving merchandise but is required to maintain a desirable level of stock of merchandise to meet the demand for fast-moving merchandise. Retailers are supposed to evolve a balance between fast-moving merchandise and profitable merchandise while allocating retail space for various products.

Retailers have to decide about the sales data to be used for the allocation of space among merchandise. Three options available with retailers are historical sales data, market share, and projected sales.

Retailers tend to use historical sales data as it is easy to access and provides market inputs in terms of the preferences of the target segment. Sales data do not help to understand the emerging opportunities in terms of new product categories and do not incorporate the current and projected changes in the market. Data related to the share of the product sale as a proportion of its total turnover is important for space allocation. This share data is preferred by retailers due to its ease of access and the high value placed on fast-moving products by most retailers. However, it does not provide information on new or promising product categories, undermines local preferences, and may be an inappropriate input for selecting a product. Projected sales are advantageous to retailers as they take into consideration historical sales data, which exhibits preferences of its target segment and also incorporates sales estimates for new and promising product categories. The disadvantage of using projected sales data occurs when there is a major difference between estimated and actual sales.

Allocation of retail space among departments and product categories assumes that there is a relationship between the amount of space allocated and sales achieved. In other words, this relationship between the amount of space and sales recorded by merchandise is termed as space elasticity, which means that the sales of merchandise change in response to a change in the amount of space allocated to that particular merchandise. Research findings indicate that space elasticity is not consistent among product categories or across retail stores or departments. For example, for impulse products such as candies, snacks, and gifts, sale is positively related with increased space allocation in comparison to staple items such as rice or pulses. At the same time, some retailers need to allocate space in accordance with the number of SKUs for product categories, as consumers' purchase decisions depend on the availability of a particular SKU, such as lifestyle and fashion products.

Profitability as the Basis of Space Allocation

Retail space allocated on the basis of the sales-based methods is likely to influence sales positively rather than increasing profits. Profits are the prime objective of any business firm, as also of a retail unit, to meet the cost of goods, overheads, and take care of future expansion plans.

Therefore, profits are taken into consideration for determining the optimum allocation of retail space among various product categories. Product profitability is measured by gross margins and gross margin returns on investment, etc. Profitability returns help retailers allocate the quality and quantity of retail space to the profitable product categories and departments at a priority. It also keeps check on the retailer's unnecessary allocation of large space for the merchandise that would sell just as well in a limited place.

All profitable product lines are not fast moving, and allocating extra facings or shelves may not help in generating extra sales. In such cases, the quality of space plays an important role. The retailers can place high profit items in locations around the store that attract more customers.

The points discussed above for retail space allocation among product lines and departments depend on the specific needs of particular retailers. Retailers have to consider the objectives of their business, interest of their customers, and the nature of competition while deciding an allocation of retail space to various product lines and SKUs.

Walls as Retail Selling Tools

Walls are the most important and largest selling fixtures in the retailer's overall selling strategy. A wall meets several visual merchandising objectives:

- Captures shoppers' attention as they enter the retail space
- Wall displays draw shoppers farther into the store, exposing them to as many products as possible
- Communicates fashion information
- Encourages multiple purchases
- Acts as a way-finding (navigation) tool, guiding shoppers to products they have come to see and perhaps buy
- Forms the retail background, supporting store image by strategic use of a variety of interesting wall surfaces, paints, colours, and wallpapers that reinforce the retailer's atmospheric intent

Architecturally, walls are classified as perimetre walls and interior walls. Perimetre walls (outer walls) define the store's overall shape and support its basic construction. Perimetre walls are commonly divided and then merchandised by sections ranging in size from 4 to 60 feet (depending on the type of store). Strategically placed interior walls guide traffic, separate merchandising departments, and increase merchandisers' ability to present and display merchandise. These interior structures (sometimes called T-walls or divider walls) are also useful in defining and separating specific selling spaces and enclosing fitting rooms, restrooms, offices, and storage areas. Because of their large size, walls generally provide visual merchandisers with opportunities to create some of the most dramatic presentations in the store.

Walls can be used as destinations in the respective stores by dispersing traffic into selling departments and drawing shoppers toward merchandised walls. This offers advantages that have a positive impact on sales. Well-merchandised walls within the store help in the following ways:

- Shoppers will be exposed to more merchandise
- Once out of main traffic patterns, shoppers are more likely to spend time browsing through the store's entire merchandise assortment
- Once they've made their way to see the merchandise on the walls, customers will return to the main aisles
- On their return trip, they will see merchandise housed on the back side of floor fixtures

Merchandise Display and Wall Planning

Retailers can start merchandise display plan with bare walls. To ensure an impressive merchandise display, the retailer should know about the hooks and shelving needs.

While planning the wall display, it is important to know where customers' eyes usually focus. This height is slightly higher than the average eye level, somewhere around 5 feet 7 inches. This is why grocery stores put the items for which you will search, such as bleach, at a lower level. Items that they want to introduce to you are put at the eye level. All of the children's cereal is put on the lower shelves, at the child's eye level, so that they can drive their parents crazy asking for all of those sugary treats.

L'Oreal store with optimum usage of wall for merchandise display

Aspects of Effective Merchandise Wall Plan

- There should not be much bare space. Therefore, the retailer maximizes the opportunity to show his products and services.
- Similar products need to be put together. For example, packaging supplies as well as office supplies and gift supplies should be grouped together.
- Displays are intended to fill void spaces and are put at eye level whenever possible.
- Displays are used to fill the upper shelves where people cannot reach retail product, making sure not to cover any wall graphics.

- Avoid putting the products that do not move quickly or that get damaged easily due to the sun close to the front window.
- Keep in mind when you are displaying similar products that have a lot of colour and design; keep similar colours and designs together. For instance, if you carry a selection of gift bags, place different sizes of the same designs together, place the pastels together, put the bright colours together, and so forth.
- Since a clean store is such a priority, shelves should be cleaned weekly. You will want your customers to notice 'sparkle' as opposed to a cluttered and 'dull' look.

Colour Planning

Research has indicated many useful aspects related to colour and consumer perception of various colour themes. Red, yellow, and orange are considered warm colours. They indicate aggression, reminding one of fire and sun. Red is considered the colour of passion. Blues, greens, and some purple shades are considered cool colours. Blue speaks of cool restraint. These cooler colours are said to be relaxing and calm inducing, reminding us of clear skies and grassy meadows from at a distance. The emotions evoked by colours do not have to be communicated aloud; they are simply felt and absorbed in the subsconcionus because we share common experiences and reactions as humans. However, it must also be remembered that colour is also a cultural expression, meaning different things in different cultural contexts.

Colour Schemes

Various types of colour schemes can be organized to communicate the desired image. Some of these schemes are as follows.

Complementary Schemes

This involves two colours that are directly opposite to each other on the colour wheel, for example yellow and violet.

Split-complementary Schemes

This involves three colours—one central colour plus the two colours on either side of its complement; for example, yellow with red-violet and blue-violet.

Double-complementary Schemes

This uses four colours—two colours plus their complements; for example, yellow with violet and green with red.

Triadic Schemes

This colour scheme is implemented with three colours that are equidistant from one another on the colour wheel (they form a triangle when you look at the wheel). An example is orange, green, and violet.

Analogous Schemes (or Colour Families)

This scheme is implemented when two or more colours that are next to each other (adjacent) on the colour wheel are used; for example, yellow with yellow-green.

Monochromatic Schemes

This involves a single colour in different values and intensities (more white or grey blended into the basic colour). An example of this scheme is navy blue with medium blue and light blue.

While creating the colour scheme, it is important to keep in mind three important factors:

1. Combine the colours within each group to create colour schemes. Colours of the same intensity blend together harmoniously.
2. Do not combine colours from the various groups together, except for neutrals. Neutral colours can be combined with colours from any of the various colour groups.
3. The colours that do not blend harmoniously are not of the same intensity.

Organizing Apparel Display: Styles and Colour

Present just one style and one colour of an item per face-out. Featuring a single colour per face-out results in a clean, easy-to-shop presentation.

The Role of Colour in Retail Atmospherics

An effective colour plan performs the following functions:

- Communicates the desired aspects

Some Colours Used to Set the Mood for Events

- Christmas—red and green
- Halloween—black and orange
- Valentine's Day—red and pink
- Independence Day—red/white/blue

in US and UK; saffron in India; green in Pakistan
- Diwali—red, saffron, yellow, and green
- Eid—green

- Sets mood
- Emphasizes features
- Highlights a product
- Emphasizes seasonal aspects of the merchandise

Physical Materials in Store Designing

Interiors of any retail store are the result of materials used and their respective colours. In India, most of the retail set-ups, particularly in the unorganized sector, have neglected the decoration aspect of stores. It might be attributed to low customer expectation on that account and limited investment avenues with retailers.

With the emergence of organized retailing and well-aware customers, looking for compatible ambience, associate their shopping experience with the kind of retail format visited for purchasing. Therefore, retailers today, irrespective of whether they belong to the organized or unorganized set-up, are giving due importance to attract customers in a competitive environment.

The materials used in retail outlets are required to be strong in order to resist customer traffic, and colours must go well with not only the merchandise displayed but also with the entire store image. Some of the materials used in retail store designing are enumerated in Fig. 8.8. Retail store interiors should match with the kind of customer segment a retailer is targeting for his store. Most of the grocery stores in neighbourhood centres and colonies do not incur any major investment on material as most of the purchasing made by customers in these stores is across the counters, without the need to enter shops. At the same time, most of the *dhabas* do not carry out expensive interior decoration as they cater to the middle and lower income groups and customers looking for value for money rather than pleasant ambience. On the other hand, retail units intended to attract the customers from

SEC A are required to invest in interior decoration with exclusive material and inviting colours. For example, cineplexes in metros depict the usage of extraordinary quality of material in flooring, walls and partitioning, trims, furniture and fixtures, etc. Such materials have a positive influence on the buying decision of the segments that cineplexes or upmarket eating joints are attempting to target.

Type of material for flooring	Type of material for walls
Carpet (Designer, one-colour, multi-colour)	**Plaster** (Painter, raw paint effect)
	Glass (Opaque, tainted, coloured)
Wood work (Polished/unpolished)	
	Paneling (Wood, steel, dark, light, illuminated)
Tiles (Terra-cotta, Marble Golicha, White Mosaic, Grey Mosaic, Sunmica)	
	Ceramic tiles
Rubber/plastic	**Ruber/plastics**

Fig. 8.11 Materials used in retail store designing

Material used in the retail unit depends on multiple factors such as the kind of offerings the retail store deals in, cost of material and installing cost, traffic quality, and safety concerns.

Eating joints prefer to have ceramic and marble tiling as they are easy to clean. Whereas, a gift shop will have a good number of attractive display windows of glass along with impressive lighting to create an atmosphere of exclusivity for the shopper.

A retailer or a manager has to consider the investment aspect while acquiring and installing material for the store. Good quality material needs heavy investment not only initially but also on a recurring basis in respect of maintenance. At the same time, investment in material should go well with the store's image. Fashion stores, no doubt, have to have better décor in terms of impressive material for fixtures and fittings in comparison to discount stores. For example, Big Bazaar invests a limited amount in the quality of the material in comparison with the fashion department store *LifeStyle*.

Material used for flooring depends on the kind and strength of traffic that visits the store for shopping. For example, in restaurants and supermarkets, where customers visit in their shoes should have sturdy material on the floor. On account of safety measures, retailers must ensure that the flooring must not become slippery when wet. Retailers must also check that racks, shelves, and other display windows do not have edges, which can hinder shoppers' movement or hurt them.

Atmospherics in the Context of Internet Retailing

The evolution of the Web as a retailing medium makes it necessary for us to understand the implications of Web atmospherics. In the context of e-tailing, factors like website organization, server performance, product data, a search option, and shopping carts contribute to a positive Web shopping experience. The easy navigability of the website, for a shopper who wishes to buy through the net, is one of the first facilitating factors. Server performance directly affects the waiting time that is required for obtaining results of searches. The easy access to product data and a click- and browser-friendly search option add to the convenience of the surfer consumer. There is a negative correlation between waiting time and the evaluation of service satisfaction in brick-and-mortar retail stores. Though this can be mitigated through store atmospheric variables, the association is strong. Similarly, system response time is inversely related to computer user satisfaction (i.e., the longer the wait, the greater the dissatisfaction).

Demographic variables like age, stage of the life cycle, and gender may moderate perceptions of the convenience the Web provides and the choice of the channel to make a purchase. This means that the younger, unmarried segment of the population would have a better appreciation of the problems of Web purchasing and, therefore, may tolerate the disadvantages better than the older population.

The degree of perceived irritation induced by displeasing aspects of the Web-shopping environment would differ, based on the segment targeted. One of the better ways of segmenting the customers would be to track the frequency of shopping over the Web that would determine the tolerance/intolerance levels of Web atmospherics. In brick and mortar retailing, shopping is tending to move more towards shoppertainment, i.e., a large dose of social activity and entertainment, especially in a country like India. In the case of Web shopping, this is absent. The lack of a clear social dimension is not unexpected given that Web shopping is more of a solitary activity.

Inadequate instructions and complicated payment methods are areas that have a profound influence in the form of lost sales. Older age groups may get more irritated by a website that is not easy to read, thereby losing their way on the website and lacking confidence in product service.

This is because older consumers are more familiar with brick-and-mortar retailers where the product service may be assessed prior to purchase. Frequent shoppers on the Web are more irritated by the waiting time to check out. This makes sense since frequent shoppers are more experienced and may not tolerate delays. This is also true of the waiting time for a web page to load. Older consumers may be less irritated by the unpleasant visual surroundings in the location they shop on the Web, whereas the change of visuals and the attractiveness may be very crucial for young shoppers. Less frequent Web shoppers would be more irritated by unpleasant visual surroundings.

Atmospherics and space management are effective tools for managing retail business. However, to be able to employ them effectively, the specific objectives of retail business and understanding of consumer behaviour are a prerequisite.

Summary

Atmospherics and retail space management are important tools for success of retail business. They contribute to customer acquisition, retention through improved service experience, reduced costs, and higher overall profitability. Atmospherics is referred to as a store's physical characteristics that are used to evolve the retail store image, and attract and retain customers. It has four key components—interior and exterior atmospherics, store layout planning, and visual merchandising. Interior atmospherics refer to all aspects of physical environment found inside the store and include attributes such as interior flooring, interior store design, level of cleanliness, etc.

Exterior atmospherics refers to all aspects of physical environment found outside the store and includes attributes such as nature of store entrance, main board, marquee, window display, parking facilities, etc. Store layout refers to the interior retail store arrangement of departments or groupings of merchandise. Visual merchandising, also referred to as display, is defined as the presentation of products in order to sell them. Store space management deals with the best possible allocation and utilization of the store space to departments, product categories, storage space, and customer space. It is a major challenge for both owners and managers of the store.

Walls are the most important and popular fixtures in the retailer's tool kit. It communicates the image of the store besides helping arrange merchandise. Research has also indicated the multiple uses of colour and how it can be integrated into the entire store design and layout plan. It is important to organize the atmospherics according to the recommended colour schemes. Physical materials used in store construction and designing impact both the cost and presentation of the store interior and exterior. In the context of Internet e-tailing, factors like website organization, server performance, product data, a search option, and shopping carts all contribute to a positive Web-shopping experience.

Key Terms

1. **Accessibility:** The degree to which customers can easily get into, move around, and get out of a shopping centre.

2. **Atmospherics:** The design of an environment via visual communications, lighting, colour, music, and scent to stimulate customers' perceptual and emotional responses and ultimately to affect their purchase behaviour.

3. **Display merchandise:** Merchandise placed on various display fixtures for customers to evaluate.

4. **Dump bin:** Case display that houses piles of on-sale clothing, marked-down books, or other products.

5. **Feature area:** Section of the store that includes end caps, promotional aisles, free-standing fixtures, and mannequins to attract customers.

6. **Free-standing fixtures:** Display fixtures and mannequins located on aisles that are designed to attract shoppers.

7. **Gondola:** Island type self-service counter with tiers of shelves, bins, or pegs.

8. **Grid layout:** A type of store design in which merchandise is displayed on long gondolas in aisles with a repetitive pattern.

9. **Theme presentation:** A manner of presenting merchandise based on specific idea or image of the retail store.

10. **Marquee:** A sign used to display a store's name and/or logo.

11. **Planogram:** A diagrammatic presentation depicting the placement of merchandise in the store.

12. **Racetrack layout:** A type of store layout that provides major aisle to facilitate customer traffic that has access to the store's multiple entrances.

13. **Rack display:** Interior display that neatly hangs or presents products.

14. **Sales per cubic foot:** A measure of space productivity for stores that use multiple layers of merchandise.

15. **Sales per linear foot:** A measure of space productivity used when most merchandise is displayed on multiple shelves of long gondolas.

16. **Sales per square foot:** A measure of space productivity used by most retailers since rent

and land purchases are assessed on a per-square-foot basis.

17. **Selling space:** The section of a store set aside for displays of merchandise and interactions between sales people and customers.

18. **Storefront:** Total physical exterior of a retail store, including marquee or signboard, entrance, windows, lighting, and material used.

19. **Store image:** The way a store is defined in a shopper's mind.

20. **Store maintenance:** The activities involved with managing the exterior and interiors as also physical facilities associated with a store.

21. **Visual merchandising:** The presentation of products in order to sell them.

Concept Review Questions

1. Define atmospherics and its importance in retail marketing mix.

2. Give a brief account of a retail unit environment's influence on the shoppers' mental state.

3. Enumerate the key components of atmospherics and discuss each of them.

4. What is the relevance of store layout planning for a retail unit? Discuss any two types of store layout.

5. Define visual merchandising and discuss important components of visual merchandise to leverage its benefits.

6. What are the components of merchandise display fixtures? Give a brief account of any three.

7. Describe the major concerns of store space management and discuss retail space performance measures?

Project Work Assignments

1. Record the salient features of the atmospherics of three grocery stores (*kirana* stores) in your neighbourhood centre and identify their discriminating aspects.

2. Select two eating joints located in a central business district of your choice and record the responses of the customers visiting these joints to obtain their level of satisfaction or dissatisfaction from a retail unit's environment. Analyse the responses and suggest a suitable atmospherics and space planning outline for the concerned retailers.

3. Compare the various components of visual merchandising for the following:

    (a) two independent garment retailers located in a central business district,

    (b) two franchised garment stores located in a central business district, and

    (c) a fashion department store and a discount store.

4. Record the various types of display fixtures commonly used at the following stores:

   (a) Grocery store

   (b) Independent cloth retailer

   (c) Independent garment retailer

   (d) Franchised watch retailer

   (e) Independent watch retailer

   (f) Fashion department store

5. Visit the website of any Internet retailer of your choice. List and analyse the features that you appreciate and do not appreciate about the site?

References

1. Sivakumar, A. 2003, 'All that surrounding air', www.etretailbiz.com, March.

2. Nagasubramanian, M.M. 2003, 'Living it up', www.etretailbiz, Nov.

3. Uniyal, D.P. 2000, 'Atmospherics', *POP Today*, Oct.–Nov.

4. Sinha, P.K. 2003, 'The world within shop', www.thehindubusinessline.com, Jan. 3.

5. Ghosh, A. 1994, *Retail Management*, 2nd edn., The Dryden Press, New York.

6. Kotler, P. 1973-74, 'Atmospherics as a Marketing Tool', *Journal of Retailing*, 49, pp. 48–63.

7. www.retailyatra.com

8. www.fashionimages.com

9. www.brandequity.com

10. Berman and Evans 2002, *Retail Management: A Strategic Approach*, 8th edn., Pearson Education, New Delhi.

11. Levy and Weitz 2002, *Retailing Management*, Tata McGraw-Hill Publishing Co. Ltd., New Delhi.

12. Varley, R. 2001, *Retail Product Management*, Routledge, New York.

13. Kerfoot, S., Davies, B. and Ward, P. 2003, 'Visual merchandising and the creation of discernible retail brands', *International Journal of Retail & Distribution Management*, Volume 31, No. 3.

9   RETAIL PRICING

Learning Objectives

- To understand the impact of consumers, manufacturers, government, and competition in the retail pricing decision

- To discuss the various types of retail pricing objectives

- To analyse the retail pricing strategies and tools

- To develop an understanding of various concepts related to retail pricing

- To discuss various pricing techniques and methods

Introduction

Setting the right price can influence the quantities of various products or services that consumers will buy, which in turn determines the total revenue and the profit of the retail store. In the end, the right price for the product or service is the price that the consumer is willing to pay for it. Therefore, sound pricing decisions are important to successful retail business. Systematic and informed decisions regarding pricing strategies must be made while considering a wide range of issues.

Profitability of retail unit is subject to selling of merchandise for more than it has cost a retailer. The difference between the cost of the merchandise and the retail price is called the mark-up. Profitability is a prime objective of any retail firm. Profitability covers the cost of buying merchandise, costs of running business (rent, salary, maintenance cost), and finally the cost of investment for further expansion of the retail business.

Profitability of retail business is influenced by two factors: one, the profit margin on the offerings that are sold, and second, the cost involved in the selling of merchandise. These two factors directly influence the pricing of the merchandise store, which in turn influences the profitability of the store.

From consumers' perspective, price is always considered as an important feature of the entire offer in the purchase decision of a particular product. Retailers are required to understand the characteristics of the people who shop at their respective stores, reasons why they shop at their stores, and the degree of consistency between the price perception of consumers and the store's price philosophy.

Economy-conscious consumers look for low-price merchandise, whereas status-oriented consumers are lured by prestige brands and customer services more than the price. Convenience-seeking consumers are inclined to pay premium for such benefits as the location of the store, time taken to reach the shop, etc.

Therefore, understanding of the customer segment is important for the retailers in evolving the pricing strategy philosophy of the store. Pricing strategy philosophy contributes in the positioning of the store in the market and in turn gives the store an image, which provides it with an identity distinctive from the rest of the competitors in the market. A retailer patronizing high-end pricing philosophy believes prices must be set at above-average market levels due to attractive décor, grand atmospherics, distinctive products, super customer service, etc.

In low-end pricing philosophy, a retailer stresses on below-market average prices due to limited capital investment, low operating costs, special buys, tight controls, etc. A retailer following medium-pricing philosophy considers price factors neutral in their retail marketing mix in comparison to the relevance of other factors such as site of the store, operational hours, additional services, variety, etc.

Retailers depend on various alternatives to calculate prices of the products. Retailers from the organized sector in developed countries depend on data from National Retail Federation books, and Progressive Grocer. A large section of retailers in the unorganized sector in India adopt the average mark-up for products provided by the manufacturers.

Retailers are required to take into account the competition while determining the pricing strategy of its retail business.

External Influences on Retail Pricing Strategy

Apart from internal factors like costs, desired profit margin, etc., the price fixed by a retailer is also influenced by a number of external factors, shown in Fig 9.1. Using Porter's model to analyse these factors for strategic pricing, they can be broadly segregated into four 'forces'— customers, suppliers (manufacturers, wholesalers, and other suppliers), competitors, and government. These four factors or 'forces' have to be considered while determining the pricing strategy. In some cases, their influence may be inconsequential, while in others, the retailer may be totally constrained, as in the case of government regulations. The extent of influence may vary from industry to industry.

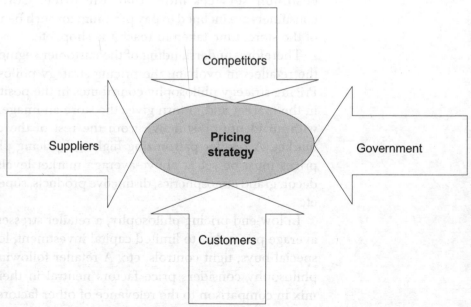

Fig. 9.1   External influences on pricing strategy

Customers

A retailer needs to understand the price sensitivity of customers that form his target segment. The price sensitivity of customers is based on various personal, social, or geographical factors and presents a major challenge for retailers while setting prices.

An interesting example in this case is of the Bangalore-based Rs 250-crore coffee chain, Cafe Coffee Day (CCD). It plans to expand its coffee bar chain and set up 200 stores across 60 cities before the end of 2004. CCD plans to reach cities like Kolhapur and Nagpur in the west, Hubli, Belguam, and Vizag in the south, Allahabad, Varanasi, Ambala, and Patiala in the north, Jodhpur and Mount Abu in Rajasthan, and Bhubuneshwar, Ranchi, Cuttack, Darjeeling, Guwahati, and Jamshedpur in the east.

CCD has chosen to increase its presence in the small cities, as it estimates that there is a huge demand waiting to be explored. The youth in small towns have adopted the lifestyles of their counterparts in metros. They are looking for self-expressive hangouts. With the existing supply chain and logistics across the country, it is a lot easier and economical to expand for CCD now; at the same time the low rentals increase profit margins. The only challenge the company feels is product pricing.

A cup of coffee at Rs 35 is accepted in metros but in small towns such price points may be difficult to sell. The company feels that it may not be possible to change prices in order to retain uniformity and also to build its image among the customers. Hence, it is banking on its decor, ambience, and experience to play a major role in pulling the crowds in small cities.

Pricing Strategy: Consumer-related Factors

- Is the price of the item very important to your target consumers? You need to know your customers' desires for different products and whether price is an important issue in their purchasing decision?
- Have you established a price range that people will pay for the product? What is the high and low price that the merchandise will have to fall within for someone to buy?
- Have you considered what would be compatible with your store's overall retail marketing mix, which includes merchandise, location, promotion, and services?
- Will trade-ins be accepted as part of the purchase price on items such as appliances and television sets?

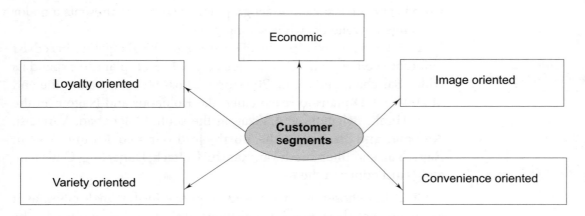

Fig. 9.2 Customer segments on the basis of price sensitivity

Customer Segments

Based on price sensitivity, customers can be divided into the following segments as discussed below.

Economic   They shop around for the lowest price available. They do not differentiate between various retailers on factors such as store image and service, other than price.

Convenience Oriented   They do not find the activity of shopping enjoyable. They shop when they have to. So, they prefer nearby locations, or minimum effort and time to be spent in shopping and, therefore, prefer Web shopping or shopping through catalogues. They are willing to pay higher prices for reduction in the shopping effort. So, they tend to prefer buying from websites such as www.phoolwala.com, or establishments such as Domino's Pizza where there are no delivery hassles and orders are quickly executed.

Image Oriented   These customers are not price conscious. They buy prestigious brands from value stores that offer high degree of customer service. So, they differentiate between various stores on the basis of image and the products they stock. They look for prestige value from their shopping. These customers prefer retailers such as Tiffany, Mehrasons, and Dewan Saheb, or restaurants like Ruby Tuesday.

Variety Oriented   These customers look for diversity in the product category they purchase. So, they tend to prefer retailers who have a wide range and assortment to choose from. They look for fair prices. Retailers that would attract such type of customers are Sears for tools and appliances, Nallis for sarees, etc.

Loyalty Oriented These customers purchase from familiar stores, where the owner or the retail personnel recognizes them. They want that they should be known, and they also look for strong relationships with the establishment or the personnel. They will pay slightly above average prices, or on the contrary they may look for discounts since they have been loyal to that retailer. Indian customers, generally, look for personalized transactions while buying jewellery.

One reason for choosing known retailers is the trust that comes with it. Such customers believe that if the retailer is known to them, he will not provide inferior or spurious products. Moreover, the price charged would also be fair. This aspect of consumer behaviour is somewhat peculiar to India because of the huge gray and duplicate goods market. It is not easy for the consumer to find out whether the product he is purchasing is authentic or not.

Also, retailers tend to charge different prices from different customers as most goods are unbranded and the customer cannot compare prices. Even when goods are unbranded, most of them are not widely available for the prices to be compared easily. Products such as toys, playing cards, plastic ware, etc. are mostly sold below MRP. Another reason why customers prefer known retailers is that such retailers are aware of a particular customer's tastes and preferences.

Also, the retailer knows the price band within which that customer would like to buy. Sometimes, the relationship is with the retail personnel and the customer may change the firm from which she purchases if that particular employee moves to a different shop. This is quite common in the case of barbers, where the customer is generally more concerned with the personnel than with the firm.

Another thing that a retailer needs to understand is the price elasticity of demand. Price elasticity is a measure of the responsiveness of demand to a change in price. If demand changes by more than the price has changed, the good is price-elastic. If demand changes by less than the price change, it is price-inelastic.

Difficult Comparison Effect

Customers are more sensitive to price when it is easy to compare competing offerings. A retailer cannot command higher prices on a well-known brand like Amul Butter, which is widely available and customers can easily compare prices. Retailers try to store unique offerings whose prices cannot be compared and, therefore, they can charge higher prices. Many retailers have developed their private-label merchandise.

This means that the brand name identifying the product is owned by the retailer rather than the manufacturer. For example, FoodWorld sells its own branded rice. It is very difficult for the customers to compare prices of private labels. However, retailers also need to store popular brands to meet customer demand.

Benefits/Price Effect

This defines the relationship between people's perception of the benefits they receive from a product and the price they pay for it. For some 'image' products, the customers are ready to pay higher prices even if the functional benefits are no different from other products. The benefit derived is in terms of ego-gratification and the recognition of the 'image' the product brings. For example, a customer would buy a Mont Blanc Pen at a much higher price even if a pen of similar quality is available at a lower price.

Sometimes, a product may fail even if it is priced lower because customers perceive it as lack of quality. They feel that since the product is available at a cheaper price, the manufacturer might have compromised with the quality.

Similarly, a high-price label may lead to better sales because customers believe that high price is often associated with high quality.

Situation Effect

Customers' sensitivity to price can differ depending on various other factors. For example, when people go on an outing to a hill station they do not hesitate to buy an item for double the price they would get it at in their local market. This is because this shopping is a part of the entire outing experience.

Many restaurants take advantage of the situation effect. Their lunches cost less than their dinners because customers expect to pay less for lunch. Retailers who wish to portray a 'high price high quality' image also take advantage of this effect by creating a plush atmosphere giving a rich look. On the other hand, 'low price' retailers maintain a utilitarian environment with sparse decorations. For example, many retailers in India do not install an air-conditioning system even when they can afford it because customers think that an air-conditioned shop must be charging higher prices. Thus, it is important for retailers to understand how various situations influence the price sensitivity of the customers.

Suppliers

It may happen that retailers and manufacturers have different objectives, which leads to conflict between the two. Generally, the cause of this conflict is the final prices set by the retailer. Both the retailer and the supplier (manufacturer) like to have control and want to price the product or services according to their own image, goals, and objectives. With the the advent of Internet, manufacturers are selling their goods directly to the final customer.

This also has resulted in a conflict between the retailer and the manu-facturer because the Internet prices are lower than what the retailer charges. So, the retailer feels that the manufacturer is infringing on the retailer's profits. Sometimes, introduction of a new product leads to conflict. If a new and better model is introduced, which renders the previous ones obsolete and is available at much lower prices, the re-tailer would not be able to clear his existing stock of the old models. This stock is virtually useless and the profits of the retailer can be seriously hit. If such a situation arises, the retailer has to increase the prices to cover any possible losses that may arise due to accumulation of obsolete stock.

Some manufacturers who want to have exclusive control over the prices at which goods are sold to the final customer go for an exclusive distribution network. Or, they sell directly to the customer through the manufacturer-owned outlets. In case of an exclusive distribution network, the retailer carries products of the particular manufacturer only. The manufacturer thus is able to exercise a fair degree of control. A mild strategy could be to avoid selling to price-cutting retailers. In any case, the manufacturer keeps a strict vigil on the retailer to make sure that goods are not being sold at prices that are detrimental to the interests of the manufacturer. Various control measures are devised to that end. For example, when the prices at which the goods are sold to the customer variy across different regions, the manufacturer generally incorporates some distinguishing features in the product. So, if products meant to be sold in one region are being sold in the other to take advantage of the price differential, the manufacturer gets to know of it.

Some manufacturers first estimate the price at which the goods would be sold to the customer and substract the required profit margin of the retailer/wholesaler to determine the selling price to the retailer. For example, if the estimated final price is Rs 100 and the accepted profit margin is 25% on sales, the manufacturer would sell to the retailer at Rs 75. So if the retailer buys at Rs 75, he can make a profit of 25% on the selling price of Rs 100, i.e., Rs 25.

The retailer also has his own methods of gaining control. Generally, retailers refuse to carry the supplier's product lines in case of a conflict. If the retailer is a volume buyer or crucial for some other reason, the retailer tends to have immense bargaining power. Sometimes, retailers also carry their private brands, which compete with the manufacturer's brands. The retailer would try to persuade the customer to buy the private brand as that is more beneficial. Retailers sometimes price the manufacturer's brands so high that their own brands are sold easily.

This is known as 'selling against the brand'. So, it may happen that while the manufacturer's well-known brands attract the customers to the shop, the customers walks out buying a private brand of the retailer. Then, the retailer also sells gray market goods. These gray market goods are branded products bought in foreign markets, purchased without proper payment of duty, or transshipped from other retailers. They may also be duplicate goods that have been made to look like branded products.

In some cases, they are pilfered or stolen goods procured without any invoice. For example, a mobile phone may be stolen and then re-sold in the gray market. Since such goods are purchased by retailers at prices that are much lower than that of the manufacturer's products, they are often sold to the customer at lower prices. Gray market goods sold by unauthorized dealers deprive the manufacturer of his share of profit.

If the retailer is influential enough, he can also ask for price guarantees, which protect retailers against possible price declines and hence help to maintain inventory values and profits. The retailer would like to opt for such guarantees when the suppliers are unknown or the products are new. For example, a supplier sells TVs to the retailer, and guarantees a retail price of Rs 8,000. If the retailer is unable to sell the TVs at this price, then the shortfall would be reimbursed by the supplier. So, if the retailer is able to sell the TV only at a price of Rs 7,500, Rs 500 would be paid by the supplier. Another kind of price guarantee is one in which the supplier guarantees that he will not supply a similar item to the retailer's competitor at a lower price. In some cases, the supplier may even guarantee that he would supply a particular item to that retailer only and nobody else.

Apart from the manufacturer or wholesalers, the other suppliers to the retailer are his employees, landlord, suppliers of fixed assets, etc. In some cases, it is possible that these parties affect the prices more than the wholesalers or manufacturers.

The following characteristics influence the bargaining power of a supplier:

- Number of suppliers, size of suppliers, and fragmented source of supply
- Number of substitutes for a particular merchandise
- The switching costs from one supplier to another
- The supplier's level of forward integration in order to obtain higher prices and margins

Competitors

In most cases, competitors are the most influential factor in determining the price. The competitive environment affects the freedom of a retailer to fix prices to a great extent. Competition can range from being perfect competition to a monopoly. A perfectly competitive market is the most competitive market imaginable.

Perfect competition is rare and may not even exist. In today's world there is so much competition that any individual buyer or seller has a negligible impact on the market price. Products are homogeneous. Information is perfect. Everybody is a price taker. Firms earn only normal profits, the bare minimum profit necessary to keep them in business. If firms earn more than that (excess profits), the absence of barriers to entry means that other firms will enter the market and drive the price level down until there are only normal profits to be made.

A monopoly is said to exist when the production of a good or service with no close substitutes is carried out by a single firm with the market power to decide the price of its output. In contrast with perfect competition, in which no single firm can affect the price of what it produces, typically, a monopoly will produce less, and sell at a higher price, than would be the case for the entire market under perfect competition.

It decides its price by calculating the quantity of output at which its marginal revenue would equal its marginal cost and then sets whatever price would enable it to sell exactly that quantity.

In practice, few monopolies are absolute, and their power to set prices or limit supply is constrained by some actual or potential near-competitors. An extreme case of this nature occurs when a single firm dominates a market but has no pricing power because it is in a contestable market, that is, if it does not operate efficiently, a more efficient rival firm will take its entire market away.

Anti-trust policy can curb monopoly power by encouraging competition. When there is a natural monopoly (when a monopoly occurs because it is more efficient for one firm to serve an entire market than for two or more firms to do so, because of the sort of economies of scale available in that market—a common example is water distribution) through regulation of prices, competition would be inefficient. Furthermore, the mere possibility of anti-trust action may encourage a monopoly to self-regulate its behaviour, simply to avoid the trouble an investigation would bring.

Monopoly is rare, and in most cases oligopoly exists. Oligopoly is when a few firms dominate a market. Often they can together behave as if they were a single monopoly, perhaps, by forming a cartel. Or they may collude informally by preferring gentle non-price competition to a bloody price war. Because what one firm can do depends on what the other firms do, the behaviour of oligopolists is hard to predict. When they do compete on price, they may produce as much and charge as little as if they were in a market with perfect competition. An example of oligopoly is the cola industry where there are only two major players, Coca Cola and Pepsi.

Somewhere between perfect competition and monopoly lies monopolistic competition, also known as imperfect competition. It describes many real-world markets. Perfectly competitive markets are extremely rare and few firms enjoy a pure monopoly; oligopoly is

---

Pricing Strategy: Competitor Considerations

- Do you know what your direct competitors are doing price wise?
- Do you regularly review the competitors' ads to obtain information on their prices?
- Do you do comparison shopping of competitors to obtain information on their pricing strategy?
- Have you considered how your competition will react when you enter the market place and how you will deal with their reactions?

---

more common. In monopolistic competition, there are fewer firms than in a perfectly competitive market and each can differentiate its products from the rest, perhaps by advertising or through small differences in design. Since customers also differentiate on factors like image, convenience, customer service, etc., each firm attempts to differentiate on such factors to avoid needless price-cuttings. These small differences form barriers to entry.

As a result, firms can earn some excess profits, although not as much as a pure monopoly, without a new entrant being able to reduce prices through competition.

Retailers generally avoid price-oriented strategies since competitors can copy them easily. If a particular retailer is successful with a price-based strategy, other players copy it in no time. Therefore, a retailer should consider price moves both from the short-term and long-term perspective. Sometimes, the competitive environment becomes so intense that a price war erupts. In such a case, the players in the market start reducing the prices one after another to attract customers. This happens recurrently and sometimes retailers start selling below cost. Once price wars start, they are difficult to end.

The airline industry in the US was virtually destroyed by price wars that resulted in loss of profits and even bankruptcies in the industry. The threat of new competitors will depend on the extent to which there are barriers to entry. These are:

- Economies of scale (minimum size requirements for profitable operations)
- High initial investments and fixed costs (real estate, franchise fee)
- Cost advantages of existing players due to experience curve effects of operation with fully depreciated assets

- Brand loyalty of customers
- Protected intellectual property like patents, licenses, etc.
- Inadequacy of important resources, e.g., qualified expert staff
- Access to supplier controlled by existing players
- Good customer relations of the existing players
- High switching costs for customers (jewellery stores, banks, etc.)

Government

Legal Issues

Legal issues affecting the retail environment can be broadly divided into two. One that affects the buying of merchandise, such as price discrimination and vertical price fixing, and the other that affects the customer (horizontal price fixing, predatory pricing, and bait and switch tactics).

Price Discrimination This means, when a vendor sells the same product to two or more customers at different prices. This discrimination can occur between the retailer and the customer or between the retailer and his vendor.

In the USA, price discrimination between vendors and their retailers is generally illegal, but there are three situations where it is acceptable. One, the manufacturer can charge different prices to different retailers if it is due to differences in cost of manufacture, sale, or delivery. These variances can result from the different methods or quantities in which such products are delivered. It is generally economical to sell or deliver in large quantities than in small ones as costs are distributed over a large number of units. So, vendors usually give quantity discounts to retailers who buy in huge quantities.

Another price difference that stems from varying methods of sale is the trade discount. Trade discount is the abatement given in suggested prices (list prices) to customers in different lines of trade (i.e., wholesalers and retailers). Wholesalers often receive lower prices for the same quantity purchased. This is legal because wholesalers perform more functions such as storing and transporting goods than retailers. Essentially, the manufacturers 'pay' wholesalers for servicing the retailers.

With the growth of large chain store retailers, the functions of the wholesalers are now performed by the retailers themselves. So they demand lower prices like wholesalers, which makes it very difficult for smaller retailers to compete.

The second exception is when the price difference is due to changing conditions affecting the market or for the marketability of the goods concerned. The third exception is when the differing price is made in good faith to meet a competitor's equally low price. For instance, if there is a particular market, which is very competitive and where local players are selling at very low prices, the vendor can sell its products in that market below the price charged in other markets.

Apart from the above three exceptions, a retailer should not ask a vendor for a price that will not be offered to his competitors on a proportional basis for similar merchandise to be purchased at about the same time. The legal issue of price discrimination between retailers and their customers is not very clear. Different customers would pay different prices after negotiations.

Vertical Price Fixing   It involves agreements to fix prices between parties at different levels of the same marketing channel (e.g., retailers and wholesalers). The agreements are usually to set prices at the manufacturer's suggested retail price. So pricing either above or below MRP is often a source of conflict.

Earlier, it was not allowed to sell below MRP to protect small retailers. It was believed that large chain retailers can sell below MRP because of their size advantage and this would force small retailers out of business. However, now it is allowed to sell below MRP.

However, retailers cannot sell above the MRP as it is not permissible under the existing law.

Horizontal Price Fixing   It involves agreements between retailers that are in direct competition with one another to have the same prices. Horizontal price fixing is always illegal since it suppresses competition and often raises the cost to the consumer. Suppose there are three stores in a locality. Two of them join hands and start selling groceries at very low prices as loss leaders. If the third store is selling only groceries, he would lose sales and would have to shut down the shop.

An exception to this rule is when geographically oriented merchants organize a special event.

Predatory Pricing   This means establishing merchandise prices to drive competition away from the marketplace and it is illegal. A retailer can, however, sell same merchandise at different prices at different geographic locations if the costs of sale or delivery are different.

In the Indian context, various government agencies exercise a strong influence on the price levels through legal and policy directives. As per the Weights and Measures Act, it is illegal to sell goods above MRP (maximum retail price). A customer can negotiate and purchase goods below MRP, but a retailer is not supposed to sell the product above the mentioned MRP. However, in practice, it is not uncommon to see goods being sold above the prescribed MRP. This, generally, happens where the firm is effectively in a monopoly condition. Like in the case of cinema halls where there is just one vendor selling soft drinks or roadside dhabas (food outlets) where another one is not located closeby.

Cigarette is one product that has been widely affected by the high taxation policy of governments all over the world. The governments have done this in order to reduce the consumption of cigarettes. In India, prices of cigarettes have been rising constantly, with the excise duties on cigarettes increasing each year from 1998 to 2001. Duties were left unchanged in 2002 giving some stability to prices. The current view in the industry is that cigarette sales are declining and that the smoking habit is no longer popular with the youth.

Developments in Retail Prices

Up to December 1990, producers of packaged goods in India had the option to print the price of the offerings on the package in two distinct ways:

- Retail price Rs..... (local taxes extra) and
- Maximum retail price Rs..... (inclusive of all taxes).

In the year 1990, the Ministry of Civil Supplies through its executive wing, the Department of Legal Metrology, directed change in Standards of Weights and Measures Act (Packaged Commodities Rules) to make all manufacturers print the maximum retail price inclusive of all taxes.

The concerned ministry revised the rules on the basis of complaints received from consumers as well as consumer organizations, alleging that retailers were over-charging consumers as they were adding on a cost to the printed price, under the guise of local taxes, even when the local tax was at a much lower rate.

Furthermore, in a market where different products have different rates of taxes, it made very difficult for consumers to check whether retailers were actually charging the correct amount of local taxes on the products they sold.

Consequently, all manufacturers, today, print a tax inclusive price on all packaged goods. This system has ensured that, by and large, there are no complaints by consumers on the issue of over-charging by retailers. However, certain other issues have come about, particularly in the area of under-charging by retailers.

Local taxes in the country mean the following taxes:

- *Central sales tax* by the union government
- *State sales tax* by the state, also called trade tax
- *Entry tax* by the state
- *Octroi* by the municipal or gram panchayat authority
- *Luxury tax* by the state

It is physically not possible for manufacturers to manufacture their product specifically for any one market, which has a unique tax rate. Consequently, they have to manufacture the product with one single rate, which is applicable all over the country and which must be a legal rate in every single state, municipality, and gram panchayat.

Pricing and Taxation

Maufacturers use two basic strategies to price their products while taking into account the various taxes.

Weighted Average Price

This system works if a manufacturer accepts that his profit margin will vary from state to state and municipality to municipality. This is normally unacceptable to any manufacturer. The manufacturer prints a price, exclusive of tax, and reimburses the actual taxes paid to his distributors, retailers, etc. Thus, the so-called nil tax price actually includes an element of tax built-in. Once again, the manufacturer has to accept varying rates of profitability from state to state.

Pricing for the Highest Tax Rate

The problem with pricing for the highest tax rate is that it means consumers in markets with lower tax rates have to pay a price which they are not interested in paying. The only people who gain in such a scenario are members of the trade. Very often, due to competitive pressures, members of the trade pass on this so-called additional margin to the consumers by charging the consumers a price lower than the print price.

In addition to state and local taxes, another factor which determines changes in price from state to state are accepted retail margins. Retailers in large cities, with very high overhead costs due to municipal taxes and land prices, require a higher percentage margin than retailers in smaller towns. Manufacturers, however, are not permitted to charge differential rates when making their sale.

They, therefore, build in a margin normally equivalent to the higher required margin, into their products. Retailers in smaller towns or those retailers who are willing to work with a lower margin then sell to consumers at prices lower than the printed price. The above are the main reasons why products in India often sell at prices lower than the printed price.

However, the important point to note is whether manufacturers should have the right, let alone the duty, to print the price for consumers on the goods they manufacture. The moment you let manufacturers print a price for consumers, it tantamounts to authorizing manufacturers to dictate their terms in respect of the profit the retailers and other members of the trade can get. This itself is violative of the very principles of free trade and, in fact, is also violative of the RTP section of the MRTP Act.

The next issue is ethical—whether retailers and manufacturers should be allowed to decide on their own profit margins or whether this margin should also be regulated by the government on a 'cost plus' basis. This controlled price system goes against the very principle of free market economies as it invariably results in inefficiencies, cost overruns, overstaffing, etc.

In the interest of consumers in India various consumer protection agencies have been petitioning the government to effect changes in the law in favour of prices being put on products only by the retailers and not by the manufacturers. Only then will the consumers know at what price goods can be purchased. This will create the right conditions for free market reforms to really work.

In order to protect the interest of consumers and retailers, in respect of price dissimilarities due to differences in the state and local taxes, the government is planning to introduce the value added tax (VAT) system throughout India. It has been in effect in some states such as Haryana.

Under the VAT regime, most items will attract a general VAT rate of 12.5%. This means that nearly all the items that currently fall in the sales tax brackets of 8–12% will be reassigned the 12.5% VAT rate. Also, all industrial inputs and essential goods will attract a 4% VAT, a rate that is roughly similar to current rates for most items.

Hence, the retailers who are dealing in commodities that are in the 8% bracket are greatly concerned as their items would be taxed at 12.5%. These include milk products, tea and coffee, electric bulbs, and toothpaste.

There is a strong possibility of prices being largely stable following the shift to VAT. The 8–12% sales tax is only the minimum stipulated (or floor) rate. Most states actually levy sales tax at far higher rates.

VAT is expected to subsume a variety of imposts—sales tax, work contract tax, lease tax, entry tax, purchase tax, turnover tax, and additional excise duty—the final incidence of tax on most commodities would not be substantially different when the effect of all these taxes is discounted. Southern and western states are the ones that tax goods at rates higher than the minimum sales tax rates in other parts.

For instance, Gujarat levies a 12% sales tax on milk products and 15% on tea, coffee and electric bulbs and Maharashtra levies a 13% tax on bulbs and tubelights. All these items are supposed to be taxed at 8% under the existing sales tax regime.

Similarly, Andhra Pradesh and Kerala levy a 20% tax on toothpaste and Tamil Nadu imposes a 16% tax on the item. Since toothpaste will now be taxed at 12.5% under VAT, prices are bound to drop. It is expected that for commodities for which the VAT rates are no different from the present sales tax rates, there could be a decline in retail prices because the cascading effect of taxes is plugged.

Also, VAT will do away with the price cushioning that is implicit in the current minimum retail price system. This is because the incidence of taxes paid in the entire retail chain would be clearly documented, giving manufacturers little scope to increase retail prices by manipulating the incidence of tax.

Retail Pricing Objectives

Retail pricing objectives or goals provide direction to the whole pricing process. Retailers are supposed to determine their objectives as the first step in pricing. When deciding on pricing objectives a retailer needs to consider: (1) the overall financial, marketing, and strategic objectives of the retail business; (2) the characteristics of product or brand; and (3) consumer price elasticity and price points; and (4) the resources available.

Broadly, there could be various pricing objectives such as market penetration, market skimming, return on investment, and early recovery of investments. Within these broad objectives a retailer may also try to fulfil the following specific objectives.

Profit Objective

The retail store may price its product with the objective of maximizing profits in the short run or long run or both. The objective of profit maximization must be studied carefully because it may lead to unethical practices such as overcharging or deceiving the customers. This in turn may lead to some form of intervention by either the government or consumer groups (NGOs).

At other times, the marketer may price his products with the objective of obtaining only a target rate of return on his investment. This is particularly so with products in the mature stage of the product life cycle.

Market Share Objective

The retailer or marketer may also price his product with the intention of increasing his market share or stabilizing his market share. He can set the price of his product lower than that of his competitors.

Competitor-oriented Objective

The retailer or marketer may price his product to counter any existing or prospective move by his competitors. A retailer may deliberately price its merchandise low to:
- discourage potential retailers from entering the market,
- expedite the exit of the potential competitors from the market,
- hasten the exit of the marginal firms, and
- spoil the market of retail competitors with an eye on getting future benefits.

With a low price, the marketer can prevent price-cutting by range.

At other times, the retailers may cooperate with his competitors by fixing a common price. A good example of this type of pricing is very common among traditional business centres in India where all retailers dealing in similar merchandise set similar common prices. This practice is common among retailers of beauty salons, garment retailers, and grocery, etc.

Buyer-oriented Objective

Another pricing objective adopted by a retailer may be buyer-oriented. The aim of such pricing is to maintain socially acceptable prices and be fair to customers. The prices of goods at super bazaars such as Margin Free (Kerela) and Rythu (Andhra Pradesh) can be considered buyer-oriented as these retail chains practice the professed pricing objectives of bypassing intermediaries and sharing savings with the ultimate consumers.

A buyer-oriented pricing objective can take the form of emphasizing the other elements of the marketing mix and reducing the importance of price. This is common in product categories which enjoy stable prices and whose retailers emphasize attributes of the merchandise rather than price. Most of the five-star hotels stress on the kind of ambience and services extended by their hotels as these are of prime concern to their customers.

Tanishq, the jewellery retail chain, emphasizes on the other elements of the marketing mix, such as heavier promotion and advertising, and highlighting the quality and the characteristics of their offerings primarily to justify the relatively high prices charged by them.

Government-oriented Objectives

The pricing of some products may be constrained by the existing laws or may be influenced by government action. The prices of petrol, grocery items, and vegetables in India are, to a large extent, controlled and influenced by government action. Consumer Protection Act, 1986, Indirect Tax, and MRTP Act provisions have a bearing on the pricing of the merchandise.

Product-oriented Objectives

The retailers or marketers, at times, make their offerings more 'visible' by means of pricing. Customers are usually attracted by the advertisements in newspapers highlighting special offers and discounts. This is especially true in an inflationary economy, which has made many people very price-conscious. With a lower price, the retail store can therefore catch the attention of buyers, and this will help him to introduce new offerings, increase the sale of weak products, or reduce his stock at the end of a season.

Key Retail Price Objectives

- To maximize long-and short-term profit
- To increase sales volume (quantity)
- To increase sales value
- To increase market share
- To obtain a target rate of return on investment (RoI)
- To maintain a proper image
- To discourage customers from becoming overly price-conscious
- To be perceived as fair by all parties
- To be consistent with setting prices
- To increase customer traffic during dull periods
- To clear out seasonal merchandise
- To match competitors' prices without starting a price war
- To promote a 'we-will-not-be-under-sold' philosophy
- To be regarded as the price leader in the market area by consumers
- To provide ample customer service
- To minimize the chance of government actions relating to price advertising and anti-trust matters
- To discourage potential competitors from entering the marketplace
- To create and maintain customer interest
- To encourage repeat business

Many of the retail stores in India such as Big Bazaar are using these pricing techniques. Products can also be made visible by means of a high price. This was practised in the cosmetics and jewellery trade, where people tend to associate high prices with better quality products and a higher status or image.

Based on the desire to achieve all or a set of such objectives, the retailer evolves various pricing policies, strategies, and short-term tactical initiatives.

Café Coffee Day: Drivers of Pricing Strategy

Café Coffee Day is part of India's largest coffee conglomerate, Amalgamated Bean Coffee Trading Company Ltd (ABCTCL), a Rs 250-crore ISO 9002 certified company and the first to roll out the 'coffee bar' concept in India with its first café in Bangalore. Café Coffee Day is India's only vertically integrated coffee company. Café Coffee Day's menu ranges from hot and cold coffees to several exotic international coffees, food items, desserts, and pastries. The coffee is attractively priced between Rs 16/- and Rs 65/- while food items and desserts are priced between Rs 15/- and Rs 60/-. This is attributed to two factors :

(a) to make in roads in this emerging market and

(b) to more effectively target their

market segment of college students and young professionals who have limited spending capacity. This is distinct from Barista whose market segment is more mature with higher pay-

ing capacity. This explains the more premium price of Barista products.

Source: www.retailyatra.com 2003, September 22

Retail Pricing—Approaches and Strategies

Pricing strategies affect both the margins and the positioning of a retailer. Various pricing strategies can be followed by the retailer depending on his business objectives, the influence of other external factors, and the impact of the pricing strategy on other aspects of the marketing mix.

Broadly, retailers adopt one of the three approaches in terms of pricing—discount orientation, at-the-market orientation, and upscale orientation. These approaches may be implemented using various pricing strategies. Discount orientation may take the form of every-day-low-pricing strategy or high–low strategy.

Upscale orientation is reflected in premium pricing strategies. At times it takes the form of skimming prices for certain product categories to be followed by penetration prices later on. At-the-market orientation is reflected in strategies that offer average prices for most products. While a store is likely to adopt a long-term approach in terms of pricing, most retailers also adopt short-term tactical pricing tools like coupons, rebates, etc.

Hence, while stores like *LifeStyle* and Arcus reflect an upscale pricing orientation they do offer rebates and discounts at various intervals. Similarly, many retailers tend to effect price reductions to pre-empt competition or achieve greater penetration. Some stores may adopt loss-leader pricing as a tactical move to stimulate additional store traffic while retaining their basic orientation towards at-the-market pricing.

Pricing Approaches

There are three retail pricing approaches based on the long-term objectives of the pricing decision. They are discount orientation, upscale orientation, and at-the-market orientation.

Discount Orientation

Here low prices are used as the major tool for competitive advantage. The store portrays a low status image and offers fewer shopping frills.

Profit margins are kept low to target price-based customers. The model works on high inventory turnover and lower operating costs. This is arguably the most common model in India because of the low per capita income and price consciousness. It is not uncommon to see affluent people buying from these low-price shops as Indians largely look for value for money. Frills can be sacrificed for some satisfactory price cuts. Roadside discount shops thrive in India where everything from clothes to perfumes is sold and the clientele is not necessarily the lower middle class. One such market is the Janpath market in New Delhi. However, with the advent of globalization, Indians are opening up and this seems to be changing.

At-the-market Orientation

A store with at-the-market orientation normally sets average prices. It offers solid service and a nice atmosphere to middle-class shoppers. Margins are average to good and it stocks moderate to above quality products. Since this model caters to the middle class, it has a huge target market. Moreover, as income increases, the price-based customers shift to these stores. Therefore, some discount retailers also own such a store to capture customers who would shift to a higher priced store as their income rises.

An example of such a store is Westside in India, which focussed on providing value for money merchandise for the entire family along with an international shopping experience. To reinforce this strategy Westside follows a 'store brand only' policy. This stems from the fact that a private label gives the company the flexibility to develop a range of merchandise that suits its customers, and to price it as per their philosophy of affordable pricing. Besides, a store brand also has the advantage of generating better margins for the company.

Westside: Price An Invitation to Wear Designer Wear

Westside, a leading fashion department store, has built good brand equity among consumers because of two reasons: style and reasonable prices, supported, of course, by the quality of its offerings. The range of products is modern and stylish at an affordable price. The store made a special effort to understand its customers in terms of demographics, and preferences in size, design, and, last but not the least, price, which has been acknowleged as the key decision variable in consumer shopping behaviour.

In particular Westside attempted to popularize designer wear, a new segment in clothes—dressy wear for parties and events. It really is a very small segment. Because of the limited numbers that sell at that price level, Westside felt it would be better to have established designers rather than do it itself. Today women aspire to own designer wear, but it is usually very high priced. In keeping with their USP, Westside wanted to make that segment affordable. Given its large number of stores, it is able to offer exclusive designs at competitive prices. And it is exclusive because the designer outfits at Westside are not available at any other store, including the designers' own.

Upscale Orientation

In upscale orientation competitive advantage is derived from the prestigious image of the store. The profit margins per unit are high, coupled with higher operating costs and lower inventory turnover. These stores usually stock distinctive product offerings and provide high quality service, building up customer loyalty. The products stored generally go with the image of the store. Such stores would stock Hugo Boss perfumes and Rado watches. It may be appropriate in situations of inelastic demand in which an organization decides to keep its prices high. The reasons for such a strategy might also include a growing super-premium segment of the market, overcrowding at the bottom-end of the market, or the desire to create a prestige image for the product.

Tanishq: From Premium to Popular Appeal

Tanishq has a successfully established retail chain in the very fragmented, very unorganized jewellery category. Tanishq is today rated as one of India's most aspirational brands of jewellery. Tanishq's marketing objectives were: first, drawing new customers into its sixty stores located across the country; and, second, building long-term relationships with its existing and increasing customer base. In order to achieve its marketing objectives, Tanishq appeals to all discerning consumers of jewellery in India, not merely to the elite. It believes that there are an increasing number of Indian women who seek the values and the benefits that a brand such as Tanishq offers—on account of trust and reliability, exquisite designs, and an International shopping experience.

All these are key differentiators in a jewellery market which is largely commodity-driven, which is led more by mass-market volumes than by differentiated design, which is hostage to a number of unethical practices ranging from underkaratage of gold to wrong certification of diamond quality. These differentiators provided by the Tanishq stores availed them to gain price premiums along with long-term relationship with their customers.

To them, Tanishq is a reflection of their own emerging lifestyle, a judicious blend of traditional values and a modern outlook, for which they can pay premium prices. Tanishq has positioned itself as a premium brand, but certainly not as a narrowly focused elitist brand. It caters to a wide segment of discerning consumers, and we believe that Tanishq offers a range of jewellery, which caters to various consumer segments.

For example, the entry points for the collection was just Rs 595, with more than 90 unique designs, including earring-pendant sets, neckwear, bangles, bracelets, chains, and rings. This concept took the market by storm.

Pricing Approaches and other Elements of the Retail Marketing Mix

The pricing approaches adopted by a retailer should be in accordance with the other elements of the retail marketing mix. Only then can the prices be sustained in terms of keeping costs under check. Besides, prices combine with all the other elements of the retail marketing mix to communicate the image of the retail outlet. Table 9.1 offers a representative list of the pricing approaches along with their complimentary retail mix strategies. This is only an indicative list and many retailers follow a different set of combinations to meet their specific requirements.

Table 9.1 Retail pricing approaches and other elements of the retail marketing

Retail marketing mix variable	Price below market price	Price at market price	Price above market price
Location	No parking, poor layout, inaccessible	Central business district, proximity to competition	Monopoly, compatible location to target segment
Service Attributes	Self-service, limited offerings, no sales	Support from sales people	Personalized attention to customers, home delivery, exchange facility, customized offerings
Assortment	Limited variety	Medium	Extensive assortment
Store Environment	Poor quality fixtures, imited space to move around, wall shelves, untidy	Compatible store environment	Inviting, impressive store décor, visual merchandise attractive

contd

contd

Nature of Brands	Unbranded, small manufacturers, loose quantities	Best-sellers	Exclusive name brands

Pricing Strategies

Following are the various pricing strategies followed by the retailer to meet his short- and long-term objectives. The adoption of these strategies is guided by the basic pricing approach of the retailer.

Every Day Low Pricing (EDLP)

EDLP has been popularized by large retailers like Wal-Mart, Home Depot, and Staples among others. This strategy entails continuity of retail prices below the MRP mentioned on the goods—in other words, at a level somewhere between the regular price at which the goods are sold and the deep discount price offered when a sale is held. So, low does not necessarily mean lowest. The price at a competing store where goods are on sale may be selling at lower prices.

However, in case of EDLP, these low prices are stable and not subject to a one-time sale. In India, many co-operative stores have adopted this strategy. One store that uses EDLP is Big Bazaar.

Here, goods are either sold below their normal prices, or some sales promotion scheme is available. For EDLP to work, volumes are necessary so that the store can negotiate with the manufacturers for bargain prices. The benefits of adopting an EDLP pricing strategy are given in Fig 9.3.

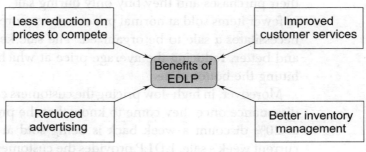

Fig. 9.3 Benefits of EDLP

Subhiksha: Essentials for a Discount Store

Subhiksha went for low real-estate costs, quick inventory turns, and informed customer buying, which have helped its meteoric growth. Subhiksha targets to become a Rs 1500-crore discount store chain by 2003.

Subhiksha has three separate godowns for stocking pharmacy products, unbranded groceries, and branded FMCGs. Subhiksha has a centralized purchasing system. This eliminates multiplicity of billings, which would occur if the stores were to make independent purchases. It buys directly from distributors who sell at only a small margin above the mill prices and from 150 odd manufacturing companies. It has a fleet of 10 tempos, which supplies its stores once a day. As the discount format requires holding costs to be at a minimum, all the stores are connected through an intranet to facilitate inventory planning.

Subhiksha makes spot payments against delivery, which enables it to get cash discounts. The supplier helps in inventory control and in return gets an improved cash flow.

Source: www.subhiksha.com

Some retailers have adopted a low-price guarantee policy where they guarantee that they will have the lowest possible price for a product. The guarantee usually promises to match or better any lower price found in the local market. If somebody is selling at a lower price, the retailer would refund the difference.

Benefits of EDLP   The following are the benefits of the EDLP strategy.

Less Reliance on Price Reduction to Compete   In high–low pricing, the goods that were selling for a particular retail price are sold at reduced prices during sale. This makes the customers conditioned to postpone their purchases and they buy only during sale. This is a vicious cycle as fewer items sold at normal prices means more piled up stock, which necessitates a sale to be organized. The sale keeps on getting bigger and better, reducing the average price at which goods are sold, thus hitting the bottom line.

Moreover, in high–low pricing the customers can have post-purchase dissonance once they come to know that the product they purchased at 20% discount a week back is being sold at 50% discount in the current week's sale. EDLP provides the customers with the satisfaction that they are paying a fair price for the product, and they tend to buy more frequently instead of waiting for the most beneficial sale to take place.

Reduced Advertising   Since prices are stable in EDLP, the retailer need not advertise frequently. In case of sale, which is held for a limited period, the retailer has to necessarily advertise so that more and more people visit the store to take advantage of the temporary low prices. Also, catalogues do not become obsolete since prices do not change so often.

Improved Customer Service   Stable prices also mean stable flow of customers in the store. In high–low pricing, the sales people generally fall short during sale time unless additional workforce is hired. In EDLP, the sales people are sufficient and, hence, are able to attend to customers properly.

Better Inventory Management   EDLP reduces the large fluctuations in demand that one experiences in high–low pricing. So, retailers can manage their inventory with more certainty.

It must be noted here that even though EDLP may provide stability in demand and easy forecasting of inventory, it does not make a large difference in many cases of stock-outs. Goods on sale are meant to be cleared as far as possible or reduced to zero. So, essentially, a storeowner 'wants' to achieve the situation of a stock-out. Moreover, as these goods are sold at low profit margins, stock-outs are not of much concern as not much profit is lost. Fluctuations are also experienced in EDLP due to other factors such as festivals. In fact, demand for a majority of products is seasonal in India due to the festive season.

High–Low Pricing

In high–low pricing, retailers offer prices that are sometimes above their competitor's ELDP, but they use advertisements to promote frequent sales. In the past, retailers would mark down merchandise at the end of a season to clear the stock. Grocery stores would only have sales when they were overstocked. Sale is very common in garment retailing.

A sale is organized at the end of a season to serve basically two purposes. One, goods that have not managed to get sold are disposed off. Otherwise, extra handling and storage expenses have to be incurred in respect of these goods. Moreover, there is no surety that they will

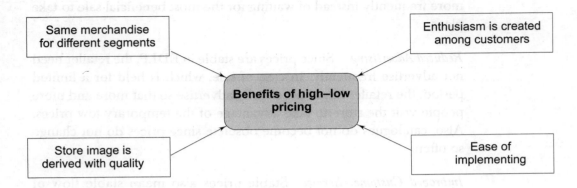

Fig. 9.4 Benefis of high–low pricing

get sold in the next season. Second, the sale provides an opportunity for a different target segment to visit the store. This segment is not very product conscious and would compromise on design, colour, etc., to buy cheaper. They also look for bargains where they are able to get a good quality product at sale prices. Nowadays, retailers also use sales to respond to increased competition and a more value-conscious customer.

High–low pricing is used by stores like *Lifestyle*. Each of these strategies has its own benefits, as shown in Fig 9.4. The benefits of EDLP are:

Benefits of High–low Pricing   The following are the benefits of high–low pricing.

Same Merchandise can be Used to Target Different Segments   The retailers use price skimming to target customers of various segments. When the merchandise is first put on display, it is sold at the maximum price. Fashion leaders and hard-to-fit customers buy at this price because they are less price-conscious or they fear that they would be unable to buy the same staff later on. Slowly, as sales in this segment are saturated, prices are lowered. More people enter the market, who are slightly more price conscious. Finally, at the end of the season, extremely price-conscious customers visit the store during deep discount sales. They are not much concerned about the design or sizes and look for value buys from whatever is left over. So, the store owner is able to use the same set of goods to target various segments of the market.

Enthusiasm is Created Among Customers A sale draws people to the store. This crowd helps in creating an atmosphere of excitement. The environment is such that people tend to purchase impulsively. During a sale, many retailers also use other supporting activities to create excitement. For example, product demonstrations or very short-term special prices. Many shoe retailers give free socks or shoe polish along with every pair of shoes purchased. This segment of customers also helps in improving the visibility of the store.

Image of Quality is Created In an EDLP policy, the customer may assume that since prices are low throughout the year, the store must be compromising on quality or service somewhere. However, in high–low pricing, even during a sale, the customer uses the original highest price as the reference. So, he or she tends to think that the merchandise stored is of high quality.

Difficult to Implement EDLP EDLP can be used primarily for known branded products so that the customer can compare the prices in the market, or, frequently purchased commodities whose prices the customers are aware of. So, EDLP cannot be implemented in every store. Moreover, implementation of EDLP requires large volumes so that the store can bargain with the suppliers for prices.

The pricing strategy of a retailer would lie along a continuum from EDLP to high–low pricing. However, retailers use other pricing practices also along with their basic strategy. In fact, very few retailers have a clear cut, simple to understand pricing strategy. It differs from time to time, product to product, and location to location. Nothing wrong about it as there are some products that are suited to EDLP and some are not. Some of the pricing practices used by retailers are:

Pricing Issues and Store Policies

- Setting the price must be compatible with the retailers' established store policies and their desired image.
- Will a one-price system, under which the same price is charged to every purchaser of a particular item, be used on all items or is the price negotiable with the customer?
- Will odd-ending prices such as $1.97

and $44.95 be more appealing to customers than even-ending prices?
- Will consumers buy more if multiple pricing, such as 2 for $8.50, be used?
- Should any loss leader product pricing be used?
- Will price lining—the practice of setting up distinct price points and then marking all related merchandise at these points—be used?

- Would price lining by means of zones be more appropriate than price points?
- Will prices include applicable taxes for customer convenience?
- Will cent-off coupons be used in newspaper ads or mailed to selected consumers on some occasion?
- Would periodic special sales, combin-

ing reduced prices and heavier advertising, be consistent with the store image the retailers are seeking?
- Has the impact of various sale items on profit been considered?
- Will 'rain-checks' be issued to consumers who come in for special sale merchandise that is temporarily out of stock?

Loss Leader Pricing

Retailers sometimes price particular fast moving products at a lower price to attract customers to the store. Once the customers are in the store, they can be persuaded to buy more profitable products. For example, a retailer can sell eggs cheaper than other competing stores so that customers consider him while purchasing groceries.

Since the customer is also likely to buy milk, bread, flour, etc. along with eggs, these products are priced slightly higher. So, the profit foregone on eggs is less than that recovered on other items of groceries.

Sometimes, the fast moving products are sold at cost price or even at a loss. So, these are also called loss leaders. If the sales of other profitable products is insufficient to cover the losses incurred on sales of loss leaders, then this strategy can backfire.

Generally, those items are priced higher whose prices cannot be easily compared by the customers. Therefore, easily available branded products are not considered. The retailer, normally, chooses his own store brands for higher pricing. Items such as pulses, rice, flour, etc. are priced higher because it is also not easy to compare the price against the quality offered by other stores.

It is also important to understand that consumers respond differently to such promotions and price cuts. A study by Sanjay K. Dhar and Peter E. Rossi has investigated the role of retail competition, retail strategies, and demographics in determining consumer response to such promotions. The results revealed that consumers who shopped at stores with an EDLP pricing strategy were less sensitive to short-term price cuts than consumers at high–low pricing stores.

In markets with greater retail competition, there was greater price sensitivity, making consumers more responsive to price cuts. More competition made it easier to compare prices across national brands.

Higher income consumers seemed less likely to respond to price cuts, but more likely to use feature ads and in-store displays to save time and effort in searching for better prices. The study shows that older consumers were more sensitive to displays and features than to price, and private label buyers were more price sensitive than other buyers.

Skimming Pricing

Price skimming is a pricing strategy in which a retailer sets a relatively high price for a product or service at first, then lowers the price over time. It allows the firm to recover its sunk costs quickly before competition steps in and lowers the market price. There are several potential problems with this strategy:

- First, it is effective only when the firm is facing an inelastic demand curve.
- Price changes by any one firm can be matched by other firms resulting in a rapid growth in industry volume. Dominant market share will typically be obtained by a low cost retailer that pursues a penetration strategy.
- The inventory turn rate can be very low for skimmed products.
- Skimming encourages the entry of competitors. When other retailers see the high margins available in the industry, they may decide to quickly enter.
- The retailer could gain negative publicity if he lowers the price too fast and without significant changes in product profile. Some early purchasers may feel cheated. They may feel it would have been better to wait and purchase the product at a much lower price. This negative sentiment may be transferred to the retailer as a whole.
- Besides, high margins may make the retail organization inefficient. There may be no incentive to keep costs under control. Inefficient practices will become established, making it difficult for the retailer to compete on value or price.

Penetration Pricing

Penetration pricing is the pricing technique of setting a relatively low initial entry price, a price that is often lower than the eventual market price. The expectation is that the initial low price will secure market acceptance by breaking down existing brand loyalties. Penetration pricing is most commonly associated with the marketing objective of increasing market share or sales volume, rather than short term profit maximization.

The advantages of penetration pricing to the retailer are:

- It can result in fast diffusion and adoption. This can achieve high market penetration rates quickly. This can take the competition by surprise, not giving them time to react.
- It can create goodwill among the all-important early adopter segment. This can create valuable word-of-mouth publicity.
- It creates cost control and cost reduction pressures from the start, leading to greater efficiency.
- It discourages the entry of competitors. Low prices act as a barrier to entry.
- It can create high stock turnover.

The main disadvantage with penetration pricing is that it establishes long-term price expectations for the product and image preconceptions about the retailer. This makes it difficult to eventually raise prices. It is also claimed that penetration pricing attracts only the switchers (bargain hunters) and that they will switch away from the retailer as soon as prices are increased.

There is much controversy over whether it is better to raise prices gradually over a period (so that consumers do not notice) or employ a single large price increase (which is more efficient). A common solution to this problem is to set the initial price at the long-term market price but include an initial discount coupon. In this way, the perceived price points remain high even though the actual selling price is low. Another potential disadvantage is that the low profit margins may not be sustainable long enough for the strategy to be effective.

Price penetration is most appropriate when:

- Product demand is highly price-elastic.
- Substantial economies of scale are available.
- The product is suitable for a mass market.
- The product is likely to face stiff competition.
- There is inadequate demand in the low elasticity market segment for price skimming.

Price Lining

Price lining refers to the offering of merchandise at a number of specific but predetermined prices. Once set, the prices may be held constant over a period of time and changes in market conditions are adapted to by changing the quality of the merchandise. A limited number of predetermined price points are set at which merchandise may be offered for sale, e.g., Rs 79.50, Rs 109.50, Rs 149.50.

Psychological Pricing

Psychological pricing is a method of setting prices intended to have special appeal to consumers. Prestige pricing, reference pricing, odd–even pricing, and traditional pricing are all different types of psychological pricing.

Prestige Pricing   Prestige pricing uses high prices to convey a distinct and exclusive image for the product. It refers to charging a high price for a product or service where it is judged that this in itself will give it prestige and make it much sought after.

It refers to the practice of setting a high price for a product throughout its entire life cycle—as opposed to the short-term 'opportunistic' high price of price skimming. This is done in order to evoke perceptions of quality and prestige in the product or service.

For products for which prestige pricing may apply, the high price is itself an important motivation for consumers. As incomes rise and consumers become less price sensitive, the concepts of 'quality' and 'prestige' can often assume greater importance as purchasing motivators. Thus, advertisements and promotional strategies focus attention on these aspects of a product, and, not only is a 'prestige' price sustainable, it also becomes self-sustaining. Retailers of various services like beauty parlours and hair saloons at times price their offerings in this manner, an example being Habeebs in Delhi. Even various clubs like Gymkhana Clubs and DLF Golf Club price their products to indicate exclusivity.

Similar strategy is followed by five-star hotels like Taj and Radisson in terms of their menu offerings. For instance, a glass of coke at Radisson could cost close to Rs 75–100 and Kababs at its famous Kabab Factory at Rs 800–1000.

Reference Pricing   It uses consumers' frame-of-reference that is established through previous experience of purchasing the sports product or through high levels of information search.

Traditional Pricing   It uses historical or long-standing prices for a sports product to determine the pricing.

Odd–Even Pricing   It is setting prices at odd numbers (e.g., $9.95) to denote a lower price or a 'good deal' or setting prices at even numbers (e.g., $10.00) to imply higher quality. Because odd prices are associated with lower prices, they are typically used by retailers who either sell at below the market or at the market prices. Retailers selling above the market price usually end their prices in even numbers that have come to denote quality. Many discounters like Big Bazar in India and Wal-Mart in the USA use odd prices to denote lower prices. Many retailers in Japan use even pricing to denote quality—a critical issue with Japanese consumers.

Retailers believe that greater than expected demand occurs at such prices. Some theories about the cause of such an effect are as follows.

- For simplicity the consumer ignores one or more of the least significant digits; amounts like $ 6 and $ 7 are more easily handled than $ 6.95, and ignoring part of a number is easier than proper rounding; this effect is enhanced when the cents are printed smaller. Even though the cents are seen and not totally ignored, they may subconsciously be partially ignored. Odd pricing is also believed to suggest to consumers that goods are being sold at the lowest possible price (Harper 1966). Many retailers believe that the more specific a statement is, the more inclined people are to believe it (Schwartz 1973).

- By using odd prices, a retailer may thus convey an image of honesty which would not be achieved by charging a slightly higher round figure. Other explanations for the effect of odd pricing includes a belief that 'circles attract the eye', thereby drawing consumers to the digit 9, and that customers like to receive change. However, despite the apparent plausibility of some of these explanations, they are largely based on speculation rather than objective evidence (Kreul 1982; Dodds and Monroe 1985).

- Now that consumers are used to odd psychological prices, other prices look odd. Another advantage is that in most cases the consumer does not hand over the exact amount and therefore has to be given change. This reduces the risk of personnel stealing from the shop owner by not recording a sale on the cash register and pocketing the money, in the case that the customer does not require a receipt.

Multiple Unit Pricing

Retailers use multiple unit pricing to encourage additional sales and to increase profits. The gross margin that is sacrificed in a multiple unit sale is more than off-set by the savings that occur from reduced selling and handling expenses.

Bundled Pricing

Bundled pricing occurs in the case of the retail sale of otherwise distinct and identifiable products for one non-itemized price that does not vary and is non-negotiable based on the selection of the products made by the purchaser. It is the practice of offering two or more different products or services at one price. Price bundling is used to increase both unit and rupee sales by bringing traffic into the store. It can also be used to sell less desirable merchandise by including it in a package with a product of great demand. For example, a hotel can offer a two-days stayfor Rs 5000 inclusive of lunch, even though separately these two items (stay and lunch) would cost more than Rs 5000. In many cases, a retailer may bundle a set of extra-large T-shirts with large size T-shirts to promote the sale of the slow moving item. A similar strategy is sometimes used for low selling shoe sizes.

Pre-emptive Pricing

Pre-emptive pricing is a strategy which involves setting low prices in order to discourage or deter potential new entrants to the retailer's market, and is especially suited to markets in which the retailer does not enjoy any market privilege and entry to the market is relatively straight-forward.

By deterring other entrants to the market, a retailer has time to:
- Refine/develop the merchandise
- Gain market share
- Reduce costs of operations (through sales/experience effects)
- Acquire name/brand recognition, as the 'original' supplier/retailer

Extinction Pricing

Extinction pricing has the overall objective of eliminating competition, and involves setting very low prices in the short term in order to 'undercut' competition, or alternatively repel potential new entrants. The extinction price may, in the short term, be set at a level lower than even the suppliers own cost of production, but once competition has been extinguished, prices are raised to profitable levels. Only retailers dominant in the market and in a strong financial position are able to survive the short-term losses associated with extinction pricing strategies, and benefit in the longer term.

The strategy of extinction pricing can be used selectively by firms who can apply to certain product 'lines'. The low price of a product at one end of the product range might attract new purchasers to the product line, and sales of different, more profitable items might increase. When implemented for particular products it becomes quite similar to loss-leader pricing.

Perceived-value Pricing

It is a method of pricing in which the seller attempts to set the price at the level that the intended buyers value the product. It is also called value-in-use pricing or value-oriented pricing. If the perceived value is high, the retailer can charge a premium price for the product.

The example of well-established traditional independent retailers in small townships can be cited in this respect. They charge a premium price on their offerings because of the quality and variety offered to their customers. Kala Mandir, the ethnic women apparel store in Ludhiana, provides exclusive collection of sarees and ladies suits to their customers at prices above the market average. A small fashion retailer, Style Looks in Ludhiana deals in fashion garments inspired by movies or film personalities. Therefore, it charges a price premium from its customers who are willing to pay extra for the desired merchandise. The premium in the above cases is not perceived as such due to the perceived incremental value offered by the retailer.

Demand-oriented Pricing

A method of pricing in which the seller attempts to set price at a level that the intended buyers are willing to pay. It is also called value-in-use pricing or value-oriented pricing.

Fixed and Variable Pricing

Most firms use a fixed price policy, i.e., they examine the situation, determine an appropriate price, and leave the price fixed at that amount until the situation changes, at which point they go through the process again. The alternative has been variable pricing, a form of first degree price discrimination, characterized by individual bargaining and negotiation and typically used for highly differentiated items, such as real estate, unbranded garments, fresh vegetables, and fruits. In India, there are certain markets which are well known for bargaining, e.g.,

Gaffar market in Delhi, Fashion Street in Mumbai, Ranganathan Street in Chennai.

There are some shops in markets like Sarojini Nagar and Lajpat Nagar in Delhi which specifically advertise that they do not bargain and have a 'Fixed Price'. In South Africa, the 'flea markets' specifically advertise in big block letters 'We Bargain'.

Tactics for Fine-tuning the Base Price

Following are some of the tactics used by retailers to fine-tune the base price.

Coupons

These are documents that provide a right to the holder to purchase at a reduced price or entitle him or her to a discount on the product. This is, therefore, a kind of selective discounting. The coupons are disbursed by retailers through various means, depending on the type of customers that they want to target, economy of distribution, etc. Sometimes coupons are issued in newspapers, and people can cut them out and show them at the retailer's outlet to avail of a discount.

Coupons can also be given along with the purchase of a particular product or purchases above a certain amount. For example, anybody who buys a television would get a coupon entitling him to avail of a discount on microwave oven. Or, anybody who buys goods worth Rs 5,000 would get a coupon to purchase Rs 500 worth of goods free of cost.

Coupons are used to attract customers to buy for the first time, convert those first-time customers to regular ones, and induce large purchases and increase usage. However, some believe that coupons make the customers purchase in advance at cheaper rates, thus, adversely affecting sales of future periods.

Rebates

Rebate is basically money returned to the buyer on the basis of some portion of the purchase price. The buyer would return the empty packaging or anything that would serve as a proof of purchase and the retailer/manufacturer returns the mentioned amount to the buyer.
For example, one scheme could be that if the empty pack of a washing powder is returned, the buyer would get 10% discount on his future purchase. Or, if the pack is worth Rs 50, on returning the pack, the buyer would be returned Rs 5. Rebates are used when the price is

---

Rain Check

These are given to customers in the event of a stock-out. They are written promises that the store will sell the merchandise that is out of stock at sale prices as and when the merchandise arrives. This practice is not common in India. So if a rain check is not given, the customer benefits from coming to the store early and purchasing. If the customer is unable to get merchandise of his choice, he has to settle with whatever is available.

---

large, because for small amounts the handling costs do not justify rebates.

Rebates are preferred by retailers over coupons because for rebates they do not need to incur distribution and operational costs. Since it is up to the customer to bring the proof of purchase and redeem the discount, the retailer has to incur no effort. Moreover, some customers fail to redeem these proofs and it results in dummy discounts. That is, the customers are being given rebates and they can avail of these if they so wished, thus giving an impression that a discount was being given. However, when they fail to furnish the proof required for getting the discount, at the end of the day, no discount is given. So, effectively the retailer can generate the 'feel-good' factor related to a discount without giving anything away.

Whatever strategy the store follows, it is important to provide value to the customer for his money. A low-price shop would not work if the goods fail to satisfy the customer's expectations. Naturally, a customer would expect that a product purchased from a low-price shop would perform sub-optimally compared to the one purchased from an upscale shop. The customers would not expect a Rs 100 watch to last forever. But still they would not expect it to break down the very next day. So, it is extremely vital for a store to find out this price to value equation. This aspect would be understood in greater detail when we discuss the methods that stores use to fix prices.

Price Increase

If price is increased after the merchandise has been put on the shelf, it may lead to customer dissatisfaction. But when the purchase price of a particular product increases rapidly, the retailer has to consider an upward revision of prices. Since the cost of the inventory increases, the selling price also needs to be increased to maintain profitability.

Backup Stock

This is the inventory used to prevent a stock-out if demand exceeds forecast or goods are delayed. The quantity to be kept as backup stock is decided by the store keeping in mind its own particular conditions. Other factors remaining the same, a store whose supplies are reliable and timely would need less backup stock compared to the one whose supplies are erratic and undependable.

In order to minimize customer dissatisfaction, the original label should be removed completely.

Pricing Strategy and Private Label Brands

Store brands offered by organized grocery retailers are giving the big FMCG brands a run for their money. In India, as elsewhere, private labels are driving growth and market penetration across various categories like grocery, packaged food, and even homecare items. A study by Economic Times (2004) reports that these brands are cheaper by 20–25% than the organized FMCG majors in the marketplace.

Attractive pricing had helped these brands catch the customer's eye. The margins on own-store brands are nearly two-and-half times higher than those on regular FMCG brands. Food, grocery, and tobacco account for 72.2% of the total Indian retail market. Store brands owned by Food Bazar, the food retail division of Pantaloon Retail (India), are steadily gaining market share. This is to a large extent driven by the performance of inhouse Food Bazar brands. Hence, they have started thinking of launching new products under different brand names. The company sells salt, tea, masala, and pulses under the Food Bazar label and, dal and spices under the Premium Harvest label.

The company's in-house brands have garnered a market share in the range of 25–40% at its existing stores. Food Bazar's in-house tea brand, which is 20–30% cheaper than major FMCG brands, has cornered a 40% market share. In the salt category, the Food Bazar brand has cornered a market share of 40–45%. The company has launched a premium health salt in the price range of ordinary iodised salt from Tata Chemicals and HLL.

It is believed that retail chains are offering products at cheaper prices through direct tie-ups with tea gardens and salt refineries.

Similar strategies are being followed by major retail chains like FoodWorld, Shubhiksha, and Nilgiris. Ability to offer customers better value for money is attributed to better management of supply chain and logistics. Wide options in everything including snacks, grocery items such as *atta*, salt and grains, and other household food products, coupled with attractive discounts and free gifts, seem to have appealed to the customer.

Setting Retail Prices

To set retail prices, it is important to understand some of the concepts and calculations related to it, basic methods employed for setting prices, and factors such as price elasticity and price sensitivity, which impact the effectiveness of the pricing strategy.

Concepts and Calculations for Setting Retail Prices

The price that a customer pays for an offering comprises two main components: the cost of the offering or the price that retailers pay to a supplier/manufacturer, and the gross profit margin, which is, the selling price minus the cost of the product. Fig. 9.5 gives an example of setting retail price for a product.

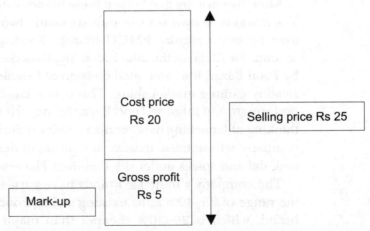

Fig. 9.5　The retail selling price

In the retail business, the cost of goods (costs of acquiring products) includes the price paid for the merchandise, handling, freight charges, and import duties. Operating expenses include rent, wages, advertising, utilities, and supplies.

Mark-up is the difference between the price you pay for the product and the selling price. The mark-up can be established as a percentage of the cost or as a percentage of the retail price. A price based on mark-up percentage on cost is determined by adding a percentage of cost to the cost of goods as follows:

Cost of shirt Rs 20.00 × Mark-up 25%

= Mark-up amount Rs 05.00

Cost of shirt Rs 20.00 + Mark-up amount 5.00

= Selling price Rs 25.00

Mark-up percentage is expressed as a percentage of cost, that is,

(Mark-up amount ‚ Cost of goods) × 100

A more common mark-up strategy in retail is to base the mark-up on the retail price. Divide the cost of the product by the mark-up percentage as follows.

A retailer can decide to use a standard mark-up percentage for all the merchandise or have different mark-ups for different products. The key is to make sure the average mark-up or gross margin is enough to cover the operating expenses and meet its target profit margins. When establishing the mark-up on a particular merchandise, two points should be noted:

- The cost of the merchandise used in calculating markup consists of the base invoice price for the merchandise plus any transportation charges minus any quantity and cash discounts given by the seller.
- Retail price, rather than cost, is ordinarily used in calculating percentage mark-up. The reason for this is that when other operating figures such as wages, advertising, and profits are expressed as a percentage, all are based on retail price rather than on the cost of the merchandise being sold.

Traditionally, price has been determined by adding a bit of profit to the cost of goods. However, more often than not, pricing is not as simplistic as that.

Some common terms that are used when fixing price, based on accounting figures, are disscussed below.

Cost of Goods Sold Cost of goods sold (COGS) includes all costs incurred to bring the goods to a saleable condition. Only costs that relate to goods actually resold are considered. In other words, COGS does not consider costs relating to goods remaining unsold. Since COGS takes into consideration every expense incurred to bring the goods to the point of sale, it includes other expenses besides the invoice cost of goods moved out of stock. COGS is the largest expense incurred by a retailer and the price is generally determined by adding a margin for other expenses plus profit to service and replace the capital. COGS would typically include:

(a) The purchase cost of all the goods that have moved out of stock (This movement may be the result of sales, or theft, breakage and other losses. This purchase cost is the price charged in the purchase invoice. Trade discounts given in the invoice are considered and therefore subtracted from the purchase price. However, cash discounts are not considered.)

(b) Taxes charged in the invoice

(c) Expenses incurred to bring the goods to the point of sale such as carriage inwards (freight), travelling expenses incurred by the buyer to purchase the goods, etc.

(d) Depreciation on the remaining stock at the end of the period

(e) Transfers from other departments or branches

Therefore, (COGS) can be calculated by the formula:

Opening stock (at cost or market price, whichever is lower)

+ Purchases and additions during the year (after including the costs as detailed above)

– Closing stock (valued on the same basis as opening stock)

The stock is valued at cost or market price, whichever is lower, because prudence is observed in accounting for profits. Even if the market price is above the cost, the stock is valued at cost, the unearned profit to be realized on sales not being considered. If the market price of the stock has fallen below cost, it is assumed that the stock would have to be sold at the lower market price, and the potential loss is accounted for immediately.

The method of valuation for opening and closing stock has to be the same to ensure consistency.

Net Sales This is the total sales figures adjusted for goods returned by customers and allowances. Net sales is, therefore, gross sales less returns and allowances.

Gross Margin (or Gross Profit) It is the difference between net sales and the cost of goods sold. Net sales means sales adjusted for any goods returned.

Percentage Gross Margin (or Gross Profit Percentage) This is the gross margin expressed as a percentage of net sales:

(Gross margin, Net sales) × 100

Mark-up and Margin   *Mark-up* is a percentage of the cost. *Margin* is the same rupee amount as mark-up, but expressed as a percentage of the selling price.

Example

Item costs Rs 20.00; it sells for Rs 25.00.

Mark-up is Rs 5.00 or 25% of the cost.

Margin is Rs 5.00 or 20% of the selling price.

Another pricing practice among retailers is to price merchandise according to the suggested retail price recommended by the manufacturer. This is the easiest way to determine prices, but can get cause into trouble if the margin between the cost of goods and the suggested retail price is not enough to cover operating costs. The income of the retail business is determined on the basis of the gross profit margins and number of goods sold.

This provides resources to incur expenditure towards the stock purchases, meeting operating costs, and investing funds for expansion of business. In order to achieve desired success in retail business, setting of prices by retailers is important. Retailers are expected to take into account these factors while setting prices of their offerings:

- Owner's returns
- The portion of rent going for storage space
- Maintenance and repairs
- The costs of business services (such as accounting and legal services)
- Advertising and promotion costs, insurance premiums, interest payments, etc.

Points to Consider Calculating Planned Initial Mark-up

- Have you estimated sales, operating expenses, and reductions for the next selling season?
- Have you established a profit objective for the next selling season?
- Given your estimated sales, expenses, and reductions, have you planned initial mark-up? The initial mark-up percentage is calculated by adding the operating expenses, planned reductions (markdowns, stock shortages, and employee/customer discounts), and profits together, and then dividing this total by net sales and planned reductions.
- Different initial mark-up figures may have to be used for various lines of merchandise or services, particularly when different lines have different characteristics from others.

Characteristics of Merchandise to Consider while Calculating Planned Initial Mark-up

- Did you get a 'good deal' on the wholesale price of the merchandise?
- Is this item at the peak of its popularity?
- Are handling and selling costs relatively great due to the product being bulky, having a low turnover rate, and requiring much personal selling, installation, or alterations?
- Are relatively large levels of r e d u c - tions expected due to markdowns, spoilage, breakage, or theft?
- Will customer services such as delivery, alterations, gift wrapping, and installation be free of charge to customers?

Other Factors to be Considered while Deciding on Initial Mark-up

- Are additional mark-ups called for because wholesale prices have increased or because the item's low price causes consumers to question its quality?
- Should purchase discounts to special groups be given?
- When markdowns appear necessary, have other alternatives been considered first (i.e., merchandising out of the problem)?
- Has an attempt been made to identify the cause of markdowns?
- Has the relationship between timing and size of markdowns been taken into account?
- Would a schedule of automatic markdowns after merchandise has been in the stock for specified intervals be appropriate?
- Is the size of the markdown 'just enough' to stimulate purchases?
- How is the seasonality of products allowed for?

Mark-down This is a reduction on the normal selling price. Sometimes, a particular line of goods is not moving; therefore, the retailer reduces the price on such goods to make them attractive to the customers.

Mark-down = Normal selling price − reduced selling price

Margins vary from product to product. On goods like furniture, margins tend to be high. These goods have low turnover and high margins are required to cover the stocking costs. On the other hand, lower margins are charged on high turnover products, such as convenience goods.

Mark-downs should be discussed in greater detail because of their importance to the retailer. There is a tendency to use mark-downs indiscriminately to clear non-moving stocks. One needs to understand the various uses of mark-downs and factors that ultimately result in a mark-down.

Use of Mark-downs

- Correctional mark-downs are used to encourage customers to respond more satisfactorily to a line. For example, if a new product has been launched, it may be sold at a reduced price to induce customers to purchase it.
- Operational mark-downs are used to sell off obsolete, end-of-season goods, or goods that are damaged, shopworn, and broken. For example, if a lot of crockery has been chipped, then it can be sold at a reduced price.
- Promotional mark-down is used to increase sales by offering the customers the incentive of lower prices.
- Correctional mark-down is used to correct errors resulting from wrong pricing, buying, or selling.

Causes of Mark-downs

Mark-downs resulting from buying errors:

- Overbuying caused due to incorrect demand forecasting, or buying more than the current stock requirement.
- Wrong buying. The colour, style, sizes, etc. of the goods purchased may not be suitable keeping in mind the preferences of the customers. Or the retailer might have bought novelty goods that failed to click.
- Buying at the wrong moment. Goods are bought too early or too late, or they are received too late for sale.
- Individualistic or 'pet buying'. A person in charge of purchases may buy some products just because he has a liking for them, even though such products are not popular.
- Failure to examine incoming stock for defects.

Mark-downs resulting from pricing errors:

- The initial price has been set too high.
- Competitors' prices have not been considered while setting the initial prices.
- The initial markdown has been too small.

Mark-downs resulting from selling errors:

- Failure to display merchandise properly, i.e., in the right location, with proper decoration
- Careless handling of the goods resulting in their deterioration. For example, a salesman has to show the displayed pair of shoes to each and every customer that walks in. If those are not handled properly, these may have to be sold as shop-worn stock.

Mark-downs are not only due to errors, but also because of uncontrollable causes such as:

- Weather conditions. A warm winter may drastically reduce the sales of sweaters resulting in a huge unsold stock.
- Economic conditions. Sales of expensive goods and consumer durables may decline during an economic recession.
- Display items that have been kept on display for a long time tend to become discoloured and unattractive.

Methods for Setting Retail Prices

Wal-Mart is also under constant pressure from political groups on account of its imports, which is, as per estimates, one tenth of direct US imports. Generally, one of the following three methods could be used for setting retail prices—cost-oriented, competition-oriented, and demand-oriented method.

Cost-based Method This is the most fundamental method of setting prices. The retailer adds a standard markup to the cost of goods to arrive at the selling price. This is a fairly simple approach and easy to implement. However, it ignores the prices set by competitors and the demand for the product.

Competition-based Method This method means closely matching the prices of competing retailers. This method is very easy to implement, as it does not need demand forecast as in the case of demand-oriented pricing. Also unlike cost-oriented pricing, it does not require cost figures or their analysis.

However, competition-oriented pricing is reactive rather than proactive. A retailer merely follows his competitors and cannot differentiate himself from his peers. So, the retailer depends on his competitors for his pricing decisions. It does not allow a retailer to maximize profits because demand and costs are not considered while pricing.

Retailers can price either above, below, or at parity with the competition. A low-cost provider would try to price below competition while a retailer with high quality image, unique merchandise, etc., would price above competition. Stores like Shoppers' Stop, which has a significant brand image, sell above the competitor's prices.

Competition-related Issues to be Resolved before Setting Prices

- Should your overall strategy be to sell at the prevailing market prices or do you want to work at an above-the-market or below-the-market strategy?

- Should competitors' temporary price reductions ever be matched?
- Could private-brand merchandise be obtained in order to avoid direct price competition?

Competitive Markup Method for Pricing—an Example

The competitive markup method is used to price the goods similar to those of the competitors. In effect, the markup is controlled by competitors and it fluctuates as a consequence of what the competitors are charging for their products and services. In this example, let us use the same operating cost and net sales numbers that we used in the previous example.

If the retailer knows that his competitors are using a 50% average markup on everything they sell, the profit expectations from his store would be:

Profit = (Competitive markup × Net sales) − (Total operating costs)
= (.50 × $250,000) − ($75,000)
= $50,000

Price Rationalization to Fight Competition and Increase Profits

Starting from Restaurant International's Pizza Hut, the Bhartiya group-promoted Domino's Pizza India Ltd, and Subway, to the home-grown Pizza Corner, Nirula's, and Saravana Bhavan are dropping prices and playing the value-for-money card. Almost all fast-food chains are adopting popular pricing strategies. McDonald's India recently dropped prices of several of its popular menu items by as much as 20–25%. A communication exercise initiated by the chain highlights 'price points of convenience' – Rs 10, Rs 15, and Rs 20. While the company is projecting it as a 'promotional exercise for a few products

in some cities', most believe that it is a strategy that is here to stay.

The Bistro Hospitality-promoted Thank God It's Friday (TGIF) chain dropped prices by about 20% a couple of months ago. Interestingly, this is the first significant large-scale price reduction exercise undertaken by the chain since it began operations in India in 1996. They claim that it is the indigenisation of ingredients, to a large extent, which has made this possible.

Similarly, Barista Coffee Company dropped its prices by about 25% in 2003. Its strategy was driven by the need to drive volumes and increase footfalls. The company claimed that after the price reduction exercise, visits had increased by over 40%. The company also indicates that there could be further price reduction in the future.

Domino's, too, is pegging high hopes on its thin crust pizza—currently being offered free with any large pizza, or for Rs 39 along with mid-sized pizzas. It expects double digit growth from the above strategy.

The above strategies are essentially the result of branded food chains looking for incremental sales and higher footfalls in the backdrop of stiff competition and changing consumer tastes.

Source: R. Bhushan 2003, 'Popular Pricing Catches up with Food Chains Too', *Business Line*, www.thehindubusinessline.com, December 18.

Demand-oriented Pricing Method

Demand-oriented pricing should ideally be used along with cost-oriented pricing. When these two are used in conjunction, the retailers can not only consider their profit structure but also the impact of price changes on sales. For example, if the customers are insensitive to price (the demand is price inelastic), an increase in prices would result in higher profits, as sales would decrease insignificantly. Similarly, if customers are price sensitive, a decrease in prices would actually result in greater profits, as sales increase much more to offset the decrease in prices. Demand-oriented pricing, therefore, seeks to maximize profits.

Consumer Response to Prices

While setting retail prices, it is important to understand the impact of various price points on demand. In this context, the various price elasticities need to be factored in for the calculation of price. While price elasticity is a characteristic of the product price, sensitivity is a characteristic of the consumer. Price sensitivity in turn affects price elastisity.

Price Elasticity

Price elasticity of an offering plays a key role in price fixing. Price elasticity determines the extent to which the demand for an offering responds to a change in price. Retailers are required to find out whether customers would continue to buy their offerings even when the price is high, i.e., whether a significantly more numbers of customers will buy the product if the price is low.

If an offering is price elastic, a change in price will cause an even larger change in the quantity demanded. This usually means that if a retailer lowers price of its merchandise, the quantity demanded of a product or service will increase. However, some products may see an increase in demand as prices are raised due to a perception of higher quality and luxury.

The retailers should take due care in setting the price of price elastic products. If the item is more expensive than the competitors', be sure there are added features and benefits to make up for the difference. If the retailer is selling a price-inelastic product or service, a change in price will cause less of a change in quantity demanded. So, whatever price you charge, your demand will be relatively stable. Items that are price inelastic usually have no similar items available, and no substitutions for the products exist. Because of this, proprietors with price inelastic products have the ability to charge a higher price.

Price Elasticity of Food Offered by Indian Dhabas

Most of the *dhabas* set prices of their offerings at reasonable and attractive levels. They realise that their offerings are price elastic with the presence of the multiple outlets of same kind in the vicinity. In case customers intend to pay more, they prefer to visit upmarket restaurants, where they can enjoy the ambience along with the seemingly hygienic surroundings.

Price Sensitivity

To determine retail prices, the price sensitivity of the customers needs to be determined. Price sensitivity is influenced by a number of factors such as substitute awareness effect and income effect.

Substitute Awareness Effect

When there are a lot of substitutes available to the customers, and comparing prices among them is easy, the price sensitivity is high. The customers can switch easily if they perceive that the price they are paying is high.

Total Expenditure Effect

The customers are price sensitive when the expenditure incurred on a particular product is high. The expenditure is large both in terms of absolute rupees as well as a percentage of the customers' income.

Pricing is a critical decision for the retailer. Pricing strategy must be determined after considering the business objectives and the various external factors that impact the validity of the decision. The increasing role of technology (like point-of-sale and back-end automation) in retail business is also offering a set of varied alternatives to the retailer to fine-tune prices in accordance with market segment and merchandise features.

Summary

Pricing is a critical decision for the retailer and influences the effective realization of all other retail marketing goals. Various consumer, supplier, government, and competition-related factors affect the pricing decision of the retailer, who can use various pricing approaches. The most popular ones are discount orientation, market orientation, and upscale orientation. Based on the basic pricing approach, a retailer can design his pricing strategy. Pricing strategy can be a combination of some or all of the following strategies: every day low price, high–low price, skimming pricing, penetration pricing, loss-leader pricing, price lining, psychological pricing, bundled pricing, fixed and variable pricing, perceived value pricing, demand-oriented pricing, multiple unit pricing, preemptive pricing, and extinction pricing. Tactics like coupons and rebates can be used to fine-tune the base price.

The role of pricing strategy in the context of private label brands is also discussed. In India, as elsewhere, private labels are driving growth and market penetration across various categories, like grocery, packaged food, and even home-care items.

To set retail prices, it is important to understand the various concepts and methods to calculate and set the prices. Prices can be fixed on cost-based, competition-based or demand-based methods. Price elasticities and consumers' sensitivity to various price levels should also be considered while setting retail prices.

Key Terms

1. **Additional mark-up:** Increase in a retail selling price above the original mark-up when demand is high or there is increase in costs.
2. **Additional mark-up percentage:** Re-ferred to total rupees additional markups as a percentage of net sales.

Additional mark-up percentage

$$= \frac{\text{Total rupees additional mark-ups}}{\text{Net Sales (in Rupees)}}$$

3. **Bundled pricing:** When a retailer combines several units in one basic price.
4. **Competition-oriented pricing:** It is a strategy in which a firm sets prices in accordance with competitors'.
5. **Cost-oriented pricing:** It is referred to as a pricing approach in which retailers sets a minimum price acceptable to the firm so it can attain a targeted profit goal.
6. **Demand-oriented pricing:** It is referred to as a pricing approach by which a retailer sets prices based on consumer desires. It determines the range of prices acceptable to its target segment.
7. **Flexible pricing:** Strategy enables consumer to bargain over-selling prices, those consumers who are good at bargaining obtain lower prices than those who are not or avoid bargaining.
8. **Gross margin:** It is the difference between net sales and the total cost of good sold. It is also called gross profit.
Gross margin = Net sales – Total cost of good sold
9. **Gross profit:** It is the difference between net sales and the total cost of good sold. It is also known as gross margin.
Gross profit = Net sales – Total cost of good sold
10. **Horizontal price fixing:** It is an agreement among manufacturers, wholesalers, or retailers to set certain prices. This is considered illegal.
11. **Leader pricing:** It is observed when a retailer advertises and sells selected items in its good/service assortment at less than the usual profit margin. The goal is to increase customer traffic and in turn sales.
12. **Loss leader:** When a retailer prices its offerings below cost to lure more customer traffic. Loss leaders are restricted to some state minimum price laws.
13. **Mark-up:** It is the difference between merchandise costs and retail selling price.
14. **Mark-up pricing:** It drives cost-oriented pricing wherein a retailer sets prices by adding per unit merchandise costs, retail-operating expenses, and the desired profit.
15. **Markdown:** It is referred to as a reduction from the original retail price of an offering to meet the lower price of another retailer, tackle inventory overstocking, clear out old stock of merchandise from shop floor, and increase customer traffic.
16. **Market penetration:** It is a pricing strategy in which the retailer seeks to achieve large revenues by setting low prices and selling high unit volume.
17. **Market skimming:** It is a pricing strategy wherein firms charge premium prices and attract customers less sensitive to price than to service, assortment, and status.
18. **Multiple-unit pricing:** When a retailer offers discounts to customers who buy in quantity or who buy products in a bundle.
19. **One-price policy:** It is a pricing strategy wherein a retailer charges the same price to all customers buying an item under similar conditions.
20. **Predatory pricing:** It is a pricing strategy where large retailers sells goods and services at very low prices with an objective to reduce competition, thus causing small retailers to go out of business.
21. **Prestige pricing:** A strategy where a retailer assumes consumers will not buy goods and services at a price deemed too low. It is based on the price–quality association.

22. **Price elasticity of demand:** Sensitivity of customers to price changes in terms of the quantities bought.

$$\text{Elasticity} = \frac{\dfrac{\text{Quantity a} - \text{Quantity b}}{\text{Quantity a} + \text{Quantity b}}}{\dfrac{\text{Price a} - \text{Price b}}{\text{Price a} + \text{Price b}}}$$

23. **Price lining:** It is a practice whereby retailers sell offerings at a limited range of price points, with each point representing a distinct level of quality. It is prevalent in commodity market.

24. **Variable pricing:** It is a pricing strategy wherein a retailer alters prices to coincide with fluctuation in costs or consumer demand.

25. **Vertical price fixing:** It occurs when manufacturers or wholesalers seek to control the retail prices of their goods and services.

Concept Review Questions

1. What is the relevance of pricing strategy in the overall retail marketing mix?
2. Analyse the various types of retail-pricing objectives.
3. Discuss the influence of various external factors on the determination of retail price.
4. What is the difference between margins and mark-up. Explain using an example.
5. Discuss the various pricing approaches available to the retailer.
6. What are the various retail pricing strategies? Discuss any three pricing strategies in retailing.

Project Work Assignments

1. Identify and compare the retail pricing objectives of
   (a) two independent retailers operating in the same product category, and
   (b) two retail chain stores (franchised) operating in the same product category.
2. Identify the external factors influencing the pricing strategy of the following retail firms:
   (a) A *kirana* store in a neighbourhood centre
   (b) An independent retailer in a central business district
   (c) A retail chain (select as per the availability)
3. Identify the strategic pricing approach adopted by the three independent retailers in a central business district in a particular product category. Also list the differences in their respective strategies and drivers for the same.
4. Identify and analyse the pricing strategies followed by department stores and leading independent stores in a specific product category and a similar catchment area.
5. Select two leading department stores in your city and compare their pricing strategy for their respective private label products.

Case Study 1

Margin Free Market Private Ltd

Subhiksha in Chennai, Margin Free in Kerala, Bombay Bazaar in Mumbai, RPG's Giant in Hyderabad, and Big Bazaar in Kolkata, Hyderabad, and Bangalore have one thing in common—they all price their products below MRP. Discount stores are slowly arriving in India and industry insiders feel they will spearhead a revolution in organized retailing. On the list of top retailers in the world, quite a few are discounters. Around 60% of the business abroad comes from this format. Incidentally, the largest retailer in the world, Wal–Mart, is a discount store.

Margin Free was registered as co-operative society in 1993 in Kerala and entered the supermarket business in 1994. It is run by the Consumer Protection and Guidance Society, a charitable organization based in Thiruvananthapuram. Today, it has emerged as India's number one supermarket chain with 150 stores and a turnover of Rs 450 crores. Margin Free purchases directly from manufacturers at ex-factory price and sells at lower prices than the MRP, as it eliminates the margin accrued in the traditional manufacturer–stockist–wholesaler–retailer network.

Margin Free takes extreme care while pricing the products through its entire stores. It has employed software which evaluates the price by minimizing profits. Every store is computerized and utilies the software to determine the pricing. This helps in ensuring that the products are rationally priced.

Margin Free has found exceptional success in its scalable franchised model. It is now looking to upgrade to a central warehouse concept, which will help it manage growth further. The success of Subhiksha and Margin Free indicate that the discount war will hot up in the coming months but it will be the customer who will emerge as the final winner.

Margin Free also gets an average credit of 20–22 days from suppliers, which it sells, on an average in 10 days, thereby even earning a notional interest on its sales also. Its strategy has made it flush with funds, which can finance further expansion. Margin Free uses its customer base as a bargaining power to strike discount deals. Any dealer who wants to set up a Margin Free store has to buy at least rupees one lakh worth of share of the main Margin Free holding company. Margin Free has a consumer base of 6 lakhs and it sells them consumer cards at Rs 40 per year. Customers who buy using this card get discounts on bulk purchases and also on government subsidized products like Rs 2 per kg rice.

The stores are now opting for a major expansion drive. A key part of this is the introduction of private labelling, which is the season's flavour in the retailing industry. For the purpose they have shortlisted 15 items—all generic labels like rice, sugar, etc.—and will add to the list in future.

Hence, they will be in a better position to provide quality stuff at considerably low prices within easy reach of an average middle-class family. For example, a packet of tea which sells for an MRP of Rs 120 at one of the corporate retailers, will be available for Rs 90 at the Margin Free stores.

The chain is now planning to open huge Margin Free hyper markets. The first such hyper market, featuring an array of wares and spread over 50,000 square feet of well-laid out space, is planned to open at Ernakulam. The two other hyper markets would be opened in Thiruvananthapuram and Kozhikode.

If the success of retail activity is measured in the number of outlets, the existing 240-odd chain of franchisees must have already made Margin Free the largest 'pure retail chain' (as distinct from retailers who are manufacturers) in the private sector. Even going by the number of footfalls, the Kerala-based retailer must have already beaten competition by a handsome margin.

The hyper markets will feature almost all conceivable retailing products under one roof—textiles, leather, cosmetics, provisions, electronic goods, consumer durables, grains, and grocery. As for ambience and class, they are most likely to resemble the Giant retailing chain operating out of Hyderabad and other cities.

The hyper market would not dabble in imported items—Chinese or otherwise — that are flooding the retail market right now. The co-operative society is in the process of mobilizing resources for the hyper market initiative.

It plans to rope in outside investments over and above what the Consumer Protection and Guidance Society hopes to raise on its own.

The Society chose Ernakulam first because it happens to be the most commercialized city in the state. Also, the comparable purchasing capacities are higher there. The nomenclature for the hyper market has a Margin Free prefix to it, seeking to build on the enormous trust that the discount chain has been able to build over a span of eight years of existence.

The management feels that the Margin Free retail chain has been able to earn the whole-sale trust of consumers in a very short span. However, in its journey to success, the Margin Free stores have made life slightly uncomfortable for entrenched interests who have, on one hand, been fleecing consumers and, on the other, resorting to indiscriminate under-invoicing to avoid tax. The latter leads to loss of crores of rupees in realisable revenue for the state government.

Every month, Margin Free is opening up to 12 stores and the number has grown to 241 at last count. The chain has spread to literally all parts of Kerala. It has seven franchisees in neighbouring Tamil Nadu already and two in Karnataka. The overall turnover has grown to Rs 600 crore.

1. What has been the role of pricing strategy in the success of Margin Free Markets?

2. What are the salient features of Margin Free Market pricing strategy?

3. Analyse the external and internal factors that have made it possible to sustain the present pricing strategy of Margin Free Market?

4. Discuss the limitations of the existing pricing strategy of Margin Free Market? Suggest appropriate changes?

Case Study 2

Wal-Mart Discount Store

Wal-Mart stores are the flagship retail division of Wal-Mart Stores, Inc. Wal-Mart is a national discount retailer offering a wide variety of general merchandise. The stores offer pleasant and convenient shopping in 36 departments including family apparel, health and beauty aids, household needs, electronics, toys, fabrics and crafts, lawn and garden, jewellery, and shoes. In addition, some Wal-Mart stores offer a pharmacy department, garden centre, snack bar or restaurant, vision centre, and one-hour photo processing for customer convenience.

The company was founded with the opening of the first Wal-Mart in Rogers, Ark. The stores operate on an 'Every Day Low Price' philosophy and are able to maintain their low price structure through, among other things, conscientious expense control. While other major competitors typically run 50 to 100 advertised circulars per year, Wal-Mart produces only 12–13 major annual circulars. The cost savings associated with fewer circulars are passed on to the customer through lower shelf prices every day.

By 1990, it had become America's top retailer. It entered the international market for the first time with the opening of a unit in Mexico City. In 1996, it entered China and in 1998 it entered Korea through a joint-venture agreement. In 2003, Wal-Mart was named by Fortune magazine as the most admired company in America.

The growth of Wal-Mart discount stores represents a major shift in the shopping habits of 'Middle America.' Shoppers are patronizing the major discount department stores as their primary retail format. A recent study of shoppers stated that most consumers planned or prefered to spend more of their dollars at discount stores than in any other retail format.

Wal-Mart Culture

The Wal-Mart culture created by its founder, Sam Walton, is based on three basic beliefs:
1. Respect for the individual
2. Service to our customers
3. Strive for excellence

Wal-Mart has strived for exceeding customer expectations. They believe they can exceed customer's expectations better than any other retailer in the world. They feel that this can be accomplished only if they work together as a team. They do this with a highly diverse working staff.

Wal-Mart believes in helping people make a difference. They commit to all sorts of socially responsible activities among the communities. After all, all of their associates come from the surrounding communities. They do all of this and commit to offer the lowest prices around.

Sam Walton credits a manufacturer's agent from New York, Harry Weiner, with his first real lesson about pricing:

'Harry was selling items of ladies wear for $2 a dozen. We'd been buying similar pieces of clothing from Ben Franklin for $2.50 a dozen and selling them at three pairs for $1. Well, at Harry's price of $2, we could put them out at four for $1 and make a great promotion for our store.'

'Here's the simple lesson we learned ... say I bought an item for 80 cents. I found that by pricing it at $1.00, I could sell three times more of it than by pricing it at $1.20. I might make only half the profit per item, but because I was selling three times as many, the overall profit was much greater. Simple enough. But this is really the essence of discounting: by cutting your price, you can boost your sales to a point where you earn far more at the cheaper retail than you would have by selling the item at the higher price. In retailer language, you can lower your markup but earn more because of the increased volume.'

Sam's adherence to this pricing philosophy was unshakeable, as one of Wal-Mart's first store managers recalls:

'Sam wouldn't let us hedge on a price at all. Say the list price was $1.98, but we had paid only 50 cents. Initially, I would say, "Well, it's originally $1.98, so why don't we sell it for $1.25?" And, he'd say, "No. We paid 50 cents for it. Mark it up 30%, and that's it. No matter what you pay for it, if we get a great deal, pass it on to the customer." And of course that's what we did.'

And that's what Wal-Mart claims, it continues to do - work to find great deals to pass on to its customers.

The key aspects of the pricing philosophy followed by Wal-Mart are as follows:

Wal-Mart's Pricing Philosophy

The lower the price, the larger the quantity you will sell. Just because your profit margin is smaller per item, you will sell more in the long run at a lower price; thus looking at the end profit to be more rewarding.

Every Day Low Price

Because Wal-Mart's customers work hard for every dollar; they can expect to pay the very least for every item every day. It is not a sale; it is a great price you can count on every day to make your dollar go further at Wal-Mart.

Rollback

This is Wal-Mart's commitment to cut prices on its everyday low prices at every chance it gets. It strives to pass the savings to its customers. 'When our costs get rolled back, it allows us to lower our prices for you. It began in 1992 as a way of reminding customers that they were not resting on simply Every Day Low Prices.'

Special Buy

These are exceptional values where a consumer might get a larger quantity for the same everyday low price. This happens usually while supplies last. Wal-Mart has combined the retail and service end to create an incomparable retail superstore. They have all sorts of services within their establishments. They provide eye- glass care, photo, banking, portrait studios, auto care, cellular phone service, hair care services, and many others. All of this is added to better fit the needs of their consumers. This is why their new tag line is 'the one stop shop.' With America growing in size everyday, it becomes more crowded to get around and a place like Wal-Mart is a huge convenience to many shoppers.

Retail Format Preferred by Holiday Shoppers

The company had been quite successful with its 80,000 to 120,000 sq. ft marts. In 1988, the company opened its first supercentre in Washington. These stores were expected to offer a full-service grocery store.

The supercentre approach meant that Wal-Mart would provide truly one-stop shopping for not just for local, but for regional shoppers too. The long-standing retail theory that shoppers will not shop for both grocery and clothing in the same trip has been proven false in this new environment, and shoppers come to the large stores more as an 'event' than as a needed chore. Shopping frequency is now often two or three times a week and the projected market radius (catchment area) to supercentre is up to 40 miles. The leading competitor, Kroger company officials accept that it is a pity, the third- and fourth-ranking food retailers in a town where a Wal-Mart supercentre opens up will not survive. What impresses the large food chain managers is Wal-Mart's ability to provide products at a lower cost. Their distribution system technology is state-of-the-art, and the resulting advantage, for the consumer, of a full selection and lower cost is thus far an unbeatable combination.

Wal-Mart's influence on Downtown Stores

Wal-Mart's impact on downtown retail has been alarming. With the advent of Wal-Mart franchises, business of *High Streets market* suffered heavily. But for the value Wal-Mart produced, in the form of more jobs, consumer savings, and expanded trade, the loss of *Main Street life* seemed an incidental price to pay.

The long-term impact of Wal-Mart is less clear. Some downtown businesses in cities where Wal-Marts have located have benefited from the increased draw of customers. Others have suffered because of the new competition for their customers' dollars.

A study of Illinois towns indicated that the infusion of a large discounter store in a community dramatically increased the retail market area and draw for that particular town. It may be assumed that Wal-Mart's market analysts consciously looked for sites where there was already economic growth, but it is more likely that locating a new Wal-Mart store in a community generated the resulting economic growth.

One speciality shop merchant states, Wal-Mart has actually helped their business by drawing shoppers in from a larger area. A new business owner did not feel the threat, for he saw Wal-Mart and *Kmart* catering to elderly customers, while downtowns are still appealing to younger customers. Wal-Mart management added value by creating hundreds of thousands of jobs. Because of this millions of people are better off today. Wal-Mart considers small-town merchants were not doing a very good job of taking care of their customers. Wal-Mart store in a town attracts customers from the variety stores. Wal-Mart with their low prices has ended an era of 45% mark-ups and limited selection.

In US alone, Wal-Mart has a total of 1568 discount stores, 1258 supercentres, and 29 neighbourhood markets. Outside US, it has 942 discount stores, 238 supercentres, and 37 neighbourhood markets.

What's Next?

Wal-Mart management is planning a shift in its strategy of aggressively keeping prices low. It has felt that in the recent period lower prices at Wal-Mart do not appear to be bringing in increased volumes as in the past—for December, 2003 sales were at the lower end of its forecasted range. Other retailers, in contrast, appeared to be meeting or exceeding their holiday sales expectations.

Wal-Mart is also under constant pressure from political groups on account of its imports. As per estimates, one tenth of direct US imports from China go to Wal-Mart. Hence, highly skilled manufacturing jobs get shipped overseas and U.S. workers are forced into low-paid jobs as retail clerks or into hawking foreign-made wares. Wal-Mart is also reviewing its pricing strategy because of import prices, which have begun to edge higher. To counter political criticism and the potential shoppers' boycott, Wal-Mart is planning to purchase more US-made goods, or increase benefits and salaries. To make up for those rising costs it may have to raise prices.

1. Discuss the retail marketing mix of Wal-Mart and the role of its pricing strategy in this context.

2. What is the role of merchandise mix and its management on the pricing strategy of Wal-Mart?

3. What is the impact of Wal-Mart on downtown retailers? On which retail dimensions they can compete with Wal-Mart?

4. Analyse the pricing strategy of Wal-Mart.

5. Suggest the future approaches to pricing strategy for Wal-Mart in the context of the recent socio-economic and political challenges.

References

1. Kreul, L.M. 1982, 'Magic numbers: Psychological aspects of menu pricing', *Cornell Hotel and Restaurant Administration Quarterly*, Volume 23, No.1, pp. 70–75.

2. Dodds, W.B. and Monroe, K.B. 1985, 'The effect of brand and price information on subjective product evaluations', *Advances in Consumer Research*, Volume 12, pp. 85–90.

3. Harper, D.V. 1966, *Price Policy and Procedure*, Harcourt Brace & World, USA.

4. Schwartz, D.J. 1973, Marketing Today—A Basic Approach, Harcourt Brace Jovanovich, USA.

5. www.euromonitor.com/Cigarettes_in_India

6. Vijayraghavan, K. and Sabarinath M. 2004, 'Private labels peel big brands out of stores', *The Economic Times*, Wednesday, January 21.

7. Dhar, S.K. and Rossi, P.E., 'Why Responsiveness to Retail Promotions Varies Across Retailers', gsbwww.uchicago.edu/news/capideas/summer02/retailpromotions.html

10 RETAIL PROMOTION STRATEGY

Learning Objectives

- To understand the role and impact of retail promotion strategies
- To understand the steps involved in developing a retail promotion programme
- To analyse the various methods of advertising and sales promotion employed by the retailer
- To understand the tools and techniques of personal selling
- To understand the role and impact of publicity for the retail organization

Introduction

Retail promotion is broadly defined as all communication that informs, persuades, and/or reminds the target market or the prospective segment about marketing mix of the retail firm. The retailers seek to communicate with customers to achieve a number of objectives. These objectives include increasing store traffic by encouraging new shoppers to visit the store, increasing share-of-wallet for all shoppers or specific groups among them, increasing sale of a given product or category, and developing the store image or the retail brand. The retailers communicate with customers through many vehicles: advertising, sales promotion, publicity, and personal selling. This chapter focuses on all four of these vehicles, i.e., the promotion mix.

The promotion mix is managed by the retail firm's marketing and advertising department. Such kind of structure is common in the case of multi-chain department stores or company-owned retail chains. In case of small independent retailers, small retail chains, and franchisees, the promotion mix is largely organized with the support of the manufacturer/supplier in terms of material, ideas, and funds. In some cases, retailers and manufacturers pool in resources for effective promotional strategy.

Advertising, sales promotions, and personal selling are examples of paid impersonal communications. The various types of communication methods are shown in Fig. 10.1. The responsibility of personal selling predominantly lies with the sales personnel and, in case of small retail outlets, with the owner himself. Personal selling is the cornerstone of the promotion strategy for the Indian retail industry, especially in the unorganized sector. The key advantage with the retail sector is the opportunity of face-to-face interaction with customers. Hence, it has the advantage of utilizing various facets of personal selling to personalize the promotion efforts.

Advertising is a form of paid communication and it uses impersonal mass media like newspapers, magazines, TV, radio, direct mail, etc. In recent years, retailers of all sizes and from various geographical locations have started utilizing a wider set of media vehicles for their promotion efforts. Use of print media by independent retailers in small townships was limited to some local newspapers and magazines published by local societies. However, the key advertising media was word-of-mouth communication generated through personal selling efforts and the purchase experience itself. With changing times, small retailers have begun to use local cable TV networks and have increased the use of regional newspapers. On the other hand, retailers from the organized sector and those operating in metros make greater use of all the available communication media.

Sales promotions is another form of paid impersonal communication, which offers additional value and incentive to the customer. It not only encourages the customers to visit the store but also promotes trial and repeat purchases. Some of the popular sales promotion activities are special events, in-store demonstration, coupons, and contests. Publicity is an un-paid form of communications that provides information about the retailer through the media.

McDonald's promotion strategy indicates the relevance of using knowledge of target customers, clarity of business objectives, and effective selection of communication media to evolve a powerful business strategy. The present focus on kids in promotional strategies of retailers or marketers is attributed to a major shift to nuclear families in the 1990s. When there were more joint families, it used to be the head of the family who used to take most decisions. In smaller families, the opinion of all family members became relevant in most purchase-related decisions. The role of children as influencers, persuaders, and information providers has been strongly witnessed in purchase decisions regarding entertainment and leisure-related products like resorts, movies, theme parks, tourist destinations, and eating joints.

	Impersonal	Personal
Paid	Advertising Store atmosphere Visual merchandising Sales promotion	Personal selling
Unpaid	Publicity	Word-of-mouth

Fig. 10.1   Communication methods

Selection of Promotion Mix

Retailers usually employ a combination of advertising, sales promotion, personal selling, and publicity to achieve promotional and business objectives. The degree and nature of usage of each of the promotion methods depends on the objectives of the retail firm, product, market profile, and availability of resources. For example, McDonald's extensively relies on advertising in the national and local newspapers, and national television channels. Haldiram, the Delhi-centric food chain, primarily relies on point-of purchase (POP) material, neon signs on the restaurant exterior, and lately FM radio channels for its promotions. Table 10.1 gives a comparative analysis of all the promotion methods.

Retail banking industry makes extensive use of all promotion methods inluding television, print media, and personal selling. It also manages to generate publicity by sponsoring and organizing business meets and seminars. Small retailers generally depend on point-of-purchase material provided by the companies which provide the merchandise. Promotion mix employed by the retailers should be compatible with the desired store image, provide scope for modification if need arises, and fit within the budget allocations. Therefore, various retail promotion methods can be compared on the basis of the degree of control, flexibility, credibility, and cost associated with them.

Control

Retailers can exercise greater control when using paid versus unpaid methods of promotions. Communication methods like advertising, sales promotion, and store atmosphere provide control on message content and time of delivery.

Flexibility

Personal selling depends largely on individuals like the sales personnel for its content and delivery. Hence, this method of promotion is most flexible since every sales person has his own personality, way of talking, dealing with the customers, making presentations, etc.

Credibility

Publicity and word-of-mouth are delivered through independent sources, which makes them more credible compared to paid information sources. There is a greater likelihood of the receiver believing such information.

Cost

Publicity and word of mouth are classified as unpaid communication methods, but they incur cost for stimulation. Creating an event that merits significant news coverage can be costly for the retailer.

Table 10. 1 Comparison of promotion methods

	Control	Flexibility	Credibility	Cost
Paid impersonal				
Advertising	■	☐	☐	▨

contd

contd

	Control		Flexibility	Credibility	Cost
Sales Promotion	■	☐			☐
Sales Atmosphere	■	☐		▨	
Paid personal					
Personal Selling	▨		■	☐	▨
Unpaid Impersonal				▨	
Publicity	☐		☐		☐
Unpaid personal					
Word-of-mouth	☐		☐	▨	☐

■ High		▨	High to moderate
▦ Moderate		☐	Moderate to low
Low			

Promotion Mix of LifeStyle International at Phoenix, Mumbai

LifeStyle International is a part of $600 million Landmark Group, the Dubai-based retail conglomerate. LifeStyle offers a wide range of merchandise in apparel, footwear, children's wear, lifestyle products, furniture, and households. LifeStyle store at Mumbai employed an integrated mix of promotion strategy comprising publicity, advertising, events, and sales promotions. Mahima Choudhary, leading Indian movie star, unveiled the second, two storeyed, 50,000 sq.ft department store in Mumbai. LifeStyle highlights the concepts of 'fashion' and 'style' in their entire advertisement compaign regarding their product mix, which is compatible with their target consumers. LifeStyle also projects, through various communication mediums, their outstanding ambience and display, which attracts footfalls to have a distinctive shopping experience under one roof. To announce its new store opening at Phoenix, LifeStyle has announced an exciting range of promotions throughout the month, such as scratch and win and 'Stay True-Don't Blend in Nights' at leading clubs like Fire-n-Ice, Velocity and Cirkus—where well-known DJ's like DJ Nasha, DJ Freeze and Akbar Sami will be playing through the night and guests stand to win gift vouchers and prizes from LifeStyle.

Source : www.retailyatra.com

Promotions by Westside

Westside does brand building through advertisements in the media, but they emphasize more on their in-house promotions, which peak during the three main festive seasons: summer, Diwali, and Christmas. A sum of Rs 20 crore had been allocated for advertising and promotions. The promotions are mostly theme based, with matching decorations, live bands, and other attractions. So last year's Westside show had a Hawaiian theme and this year the chain has gone the 'Wild West' way. This is followed by a 'heavy' media burst across print, out-doors, cinema theatres, and Fashion TV. Trent has signed cricketer Yuvraj Singh as the brand ambassador for the Westside chain for three years.

Advertising

Advertising is recognized as an indispensable tool of promotion. It has acquired a lot of significance in the national and international markets. With the advent of globalization and liberalization its imperativeness in the Indian retail sector has increased as a result of competition, latest technologies, and the rapidly changing consumer lifestyles.

Earlier, advertising mainly portrayed the role of an information tool providing requisite information about jobs, birth–death, and engage-ments, etc. However, today advertising not only provides limited prod-uct details, it also provides information about its attributes, place of availability, and the price range. Advertising is a very important link between the sellers and buyers. In this age of intense competition, it is important to stimulate sales, which can be done by attracting prospec-tive customers and retaining old customers to buy the product through the mechanism of advertising.

Advertising has generally been defined as the dissemination of information concerning an idea, product, or service to induce action in accordance with the intent of an advertiser. The American Marketing Association defines it as 'any paid form of non-personal presentation of ideas, goods and services by an identified sponsor'. Based on the these conceptualizations, advertising can be understood as follows:

- *Paid form of communication*—They appear in television, newspapers, magazines, Internet, hoardings, etc. for communicating information to prospective customers.
- *Non-personal presentation of message*—Advertising lacks face-to-face direct contact with customers. It involves non-personal salesman-ship and can be used as complementary to personal selling.
- *Issued by an identified sponsor*—It involves disclosure of the name of the sponsor and, hence, prevents the possibility of any distortion and manipulation in the intended message. It should disclose the sources of opinions and ideas which it presents.

Objectives of Advertising

The fundamental objective of advertising is to sell something—a product, service, or an idea—but in addition to this objective it is utilized to achieve certain other objectives. For Example, Benetton, the retail fashion chain, effectively uses advertising to reposition its stores as a part of a well-conceived promotion mix strategy.

The major objectives of advertising are listed as follows:

- To promote a new product
- To support the personal selling programme
- To reach out to people not accessible to salesmen
- To enter a new market for attracting customers
- To manage competition in the market by stimulating sales
- To enhance the goodwill of the retail organization
- To improve dealer relations
- To warn the public against imitation of the retailer's products

The Benetton Makeover: Promotion Strategy

DCM Benetton recently launched its pilot 'Baby-on-Board' store, which targets mothers-to-be and kids, as well as the 'Accessories' and 'Adults-Only' store in Gurgaon. The Baby-on-Board store, which is targeted at young urban upwardly mobile parents, has a product line which includes infant and maternity wear, educational toys, strollers, car seats, fashion for moms-to-be, newborns, babies, and kids up to 12 years of age. The Accessories store, on the other hand, sells luggage, bags, sunglasses, and vanity cases, while the Adults-Only store showcases Benetton's apparel collection for men and women. DCM Benetton has redesigned stores as per its international format and also repositioned the brand from a casual wear brand to a wardrobe option, the company is now looking at targeting a niche audience through its concept stores. It now has 85 exclusive outlets across the country. The company decided against using below-the-line promotions or sales promos to promote their concept stores. The marketing mix was conservative. They started with a mood-oriented campaign in print and then looked at promoting the stores. These stores in mega malls and high streets are advertisements in themselves, largely due to the overall ambience and the depth of the product offering. Benetton carries two types of campaigns — product-specific and corporate. The focus of each campaign is different. A product-specific campaign highlights Benetton's collections and hence, seasonal, corporate campaigns are generally undertaken once in 12–18 months to showcase larger issues affecting the world. In India, however, the company focuses only on the product campaign. The company planned to invest 5% of its projected sales in advertising.

Benetton's promotion strategy is contrary to the findings of KSA Technopak. It states the importance to have below-the-line promotions and sales promotions to promote the stores. 'The brand has to communicate with its target audience. It cannot depend on walk-ins and ambience.'

Benetton's repositioning of its stores from a casual wear brand to an international wardrobe option has worked well for the company with the existing promotion strategy.

Source: A. Shashidhar 2003, 'The Benetton Makeover', *Business Line*, August 27.

Benetton store

Significance of Advertising in the Retail Sector

Advertising is not only the provider of information about products, services, and availability at different retail locations, but also an important link in the retail sector between the advertiser and the receiver of the message. Its imperativeness has increased in this era of 'globalization and liberalization' around the world. It has certain benefits not only for the manufacturers and traders but for the retailers as well. Raymonds, the apparel retail chain, primarily used television and print advertising to promote the experiential aspects associated with shopping at its stores.

Raymonds: 'The Complete Man'

Promotional strategy has a salient role in the building up of a store's image. In all cases, the product and its utility is important, but the way the product is cultivated in the minds of the consumers is also equally important.

In retail, it is not only the product but also the entire retail environment along with its peripherals—such as store ambience, packaging, promotions, how sales people communicate about the shopping experience—which together go to build a brand image for the retail store. For example, Raymonds, through its 168 Raymonds showrooms across India, is portraying the brand, which comes across in its the communication strategy. The catch-line of 'The Complete Man' advertised extensively on electronic and print media got reflected not only in the products on offer but also in the retail environment in which it is offered.

Benefits of Retail Advertisements for Customers

- It helps in creating awareness among the customers about the existence, prices, and availability of products at different locations for the satisfaction of their wants.
- It educates customers about new products and their diverse uses.
- It increases the utility of existing products.
- It encourages the manufacturers to improve the quality of products through research and development. It ensures the supply of products of better quality to customers.

Types of Advertising

There could be various types of advertisements based on the target customers, advertising objective, as the message, also shown in Fig. 10.2.

Consumer-oriented or Persuasive Advertising

It surrounds our daily lives and provides stimulus to purchase various products or services. It helps in maintaining a regular demand and attracts a lot of attention and preference of the customers. The major objectives of consumer-oriented advertising are as follows:

- Information to consumers about new products
- Holding consumer patronage against intensified campaign by rivals
- Teaching customers about the usage of the product
- Promoting a contest or a premium offer
- Establishing a new trade character

The retailers selling lifestyle products that are high on experience attributes such as fashion and personal care products, health clubs, etc. build a distinctive appeal in their ads to approach the well-defined

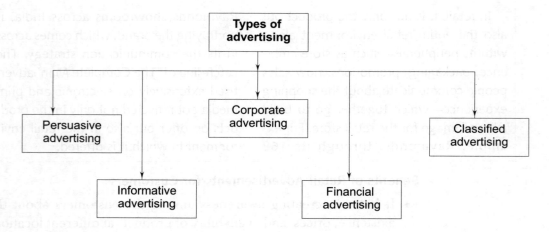

Fig. 10.2　Types of advertising

niche segment. Examples of such ads come from Wills Lifestyle, the ITC owned apparel retail chain, and five-star and seven-star hotels and resorts.

Informative Advertising

Purchases of durable products are generally erratic and often too expensive to buy, so the buyer requires elaborate information about them. Hence, the retailer and the manufacturer spend a huge amount on informative advertising.

Institutional or Corporate Advertising

Its main motive is to build a corporate image. In corporate advertising an attempt is made to highlight the achievements and objectives of the retail organization. The institutional advertising campaigns have the following objectives:
- Creating the corporate image
- Building up retailer prestige
- Emphasizing the services and facilities provided by the outlet
- Increasing consumer friendliness and goodwill towards the retail organization

---

Corporate Advertising: the HDFC Way

HDFC Bank has tied up with Business To-day, the leading business magazine, to sponsor 10,000 copies of the magazine in each metro. The cover of the sponsored

copies would be the 'December 2003' issue of Business Today, which rated HDFC
Bank as the best bank in the country. On
the opposite side, there is an advertorial,
which talks about HDFC as a 'one-stop
financial supermarket'. These copies are
to be circulated among top corporates and
high-networth customers of the Bank.

Financial Advertising

It refers to advertisements by various financial institutions like Standard
Chartered Bank, ICICI, etc. They provide information about the
investment opportunities and the risks and benefits associated with
them. Recently, HDFC bank evolved a mix of sales promotion and
advertising to attract new customers and retain its existing customer
base that has been fast getting eroded by competition from banks like
the ICICI and the State Bank of India.

Classified Advertising

It refers to messages, which are placed under specific headings and
columns in various magazines and newspapers, e.g., *Furniture for sale*,
Situations vacant, etc.

Advertising Campaign

An advertising campaign comprises a series of advertisements, with
the same theme over a period of time and across ads. There are different
ad copies of campaigns. They are self-contained and independent but
thematically related. The campaign can be at the local, regional, or
the international level. The pioneering campaigns introduce new
products and the competitive campaigns emphasize superiority for
retaining the present market or expanding it by increasing the
consumption by sizing up the customers of a competitive brand. The
two major types of advertising campaigns are as discussed below.

Vertical Co-operative Advertising

This type is planned when the retailers and other channel members
(usually manufacturers) share the advertising budget, e.g., if a manufacturer pays up to 40% of the retailer's cost for advertising or a fixed
amount as decided on a prior basis. In other words, we can say that
the manufacturer subsidizes some of the retailer's advertising that features a manufacturer's brand. Manufacturers extensively support most
of the mom-and-pop stores and independent retailers since the latter
lack the professional expertise and financial resources to undertake a

campaign on their own. Therefore, the quantum and nature of manufacturers' or suppliers' support for advertising becomes an important variable for retailers in his brand-stocking decision.

There is good temptation among the retailers to undertake vertical co-operative advertising since the monetary expenses are off-loaded on the manufacturer or supplier. Some retailers tend to forget that good advertising constitutes an investment and should primarily be used to increase revenues from customers and not just from vendors. Besides, in case of a retailer-driven advertising the retailer can exercise considerable control over the focus and content of the ad. Hence, the retailers must realize that it is better to get return on money with vertical advertising or by paying the advertising costs themselves, which help to achieve the objectives.

Vertical Advertising

In order to increase chocolate penetration, confectionery major Cadbury India Ltd has rolled out a portfolio of customized marketing and communication initiatives at the retail end. The key thrust area is to speed up brand mobility at the retail level. Promotion strategy incorporated to explore and foray into non-traditional channels, frequent consumer visits, innovative point-of-sale and point-of-purchase initiatives, unique merchandising plans, and newer formats of product delivery. As part of the point-of-sale initiative for brands like Chocki, a huge retail exercise is being undertaken especially near schools, as children are the core target group for the product. Point-of-sale plays a key role in promoting impulse product sales. This is true for chocolates, as they are bought largely on impulse and are meant for out-of-home consumption. The company ensures that retailers' visual merchandising strategy attempts to:

• Communicate values of chocolate at the highest experiential level, with the help of posters, flyers, and other POP material
• Reinforce Cadbury's ownership of that experience
• Establish and drive category relevance, and concurrently Cadbury's dominant position
• Motivate and engage consumers with the desire and anticipation to participate in the category

In addition to such a promotion strategy, the company is also supporting small retailers by providing PET jars, display-cum-dispensing outers, hangers, and sheet metal dispensers for grouping and displaying the cluster of products. The retailers value the company support on account of point-of-sale material, in-shop visibility, shop-front signages, and outdoor. Point of purchase material focuses on 'appetite-appeal' visuals as a stimulus, followed by a call to action. The company believes that through participative promotional strategies with retailers they can garner a bigger bite of the market share in this competitive chocolate segment.

Source: Tarun Narayan, 'Cadbury Rolls Out Slew Of Retail , *The Financial Express.*

Horizontal Co-operative Advertising

This type is launched when two or more retailers come together to share the cost of advertising leading to a joint promotion of events or sales that benefit both parties. For example, in Connaught Place and Rajouri areas in New Delhi a mega sale is organized every year in which all the retailers advertise their brands together. They are good business traffic generators that boast the image of the entire shopping centre. This also helps to counter competition from the other emerging and established shopping centres.

Steps Involved in Retail Advertisement Campaigns

'Unless your campaign contains a big idea, it will pass like a ship in the night'.   —*David Ogilvy*

An advertising campaign is of great significance to an organization's future, and a careful consideration of various factors like the psychology of buyers, market requirements, competition, product features, funds allocation for promotion and effectiveness of advertising media is required. The steps involved in the implementation of an advertising campaign are given in Fig. 10.3.

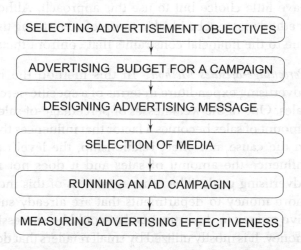

Fig. 10.3   Steps in an advertising campaign

Selecting Advertisement Objectives

It should be in compliance with the retailer's objectives and should be a part of the promotion mix. The ads could focus on one or more of the following aspects:

- Age of the store
- Location of the store
- Types of goods sold
- Level of competition
- Market size
- Supplier support

Although the ultimate goal of advertising is to generate additional sales, the identification of group goals calls for careful investigation of market, product, consumer, and competitors.

Advertising Budget   A well-designed retail advertising campaign requires proper budgetary allocation for advertising. The appropriation of advertising budget must be determined with direct reference to advertising objectives.

Four widely used methods for determining the expenditure on a retail campaign are discussed below.

Affordable Method   Many small retailers use this method in which they set the budget at a 'reasonable' level—that which they can afford. At times this leads to inadequate appropriation of budget. Some retailers have little choice but to use this approach. Although, the affordable method may not be ideal in terms of advertising theory, it is defensible due to the financial constraints that confront the smaller retailers.

Percentage-of-sales Method   In this method the retailer budgets the advertising expenditure in terms of a specific percentage of forecasted sales. One of the weaknesses of percentage-of-sales method is that the amount of sales becomes a factor that influences the advertising outlay. In the cause and effect relationship, the level of advertising should influence the amount of sales and it does not reflect the retailer's advertising goals. The other weakness of this method is that it gives more money to departments that are already successful and fails to give money to departments that could be successful with a little extra money. It is mostly utilized by small retailers that do not use ad agencies and lack the sophistication required to adequately implement the task and objective approach.

Festival-driven Timing of Advertisement

Retailers from the organized and unorganized sector, especially those with formats like Shoppers' Stop, Pyramid, LifeStyle, Bombay Selection, Time Zone, and Haldiram's, increase overall spending on the advertisement in terms of creating new ads and increasing its frequency of display. These increased investments are made with an eye on the festival seasons such as Diwali, Christmas, and New Year. This phenomenon is common throughout the world.

Objective and Task Method In this method a retailer establishes the advertising objectives and then defines the tasks required to achieve them after estimating the cost of performing those tasks. When all the costs are totalled the retailer has his advertising budget ready. In short, this method begins with the retailer's advertising objectives and then it determines the cost to achieve these objectives.

Competitive-parity Method In this method the retailer allocates the advertising budget at a level at which the competitors spend for the same kind of time periods and campaigns.

The affordable, percentage-of-sales, and competitive-parity methods have the advantage of simplicity, but they fail to recognize the important contribution that effective advertising can make to improve sales. When they are applied they look backward rather than forward. Whereas, the objective and task method forces a firm to look ahead and assesses the benefits and costs of advertising.

Designing Advertising Message The advertising message must appeal to the target audience, and is conveyed through the advertisement copy. The creative decisions are important for retailers as advertising messages seek immediate action from the consumer and have a short life span.

The advertising messages, prepared through the advertisement copy, can be used to gain attention, create interest, arouse desire, and secure buying action. Certain factors should be considered while designing the ad copy :
1. Attention value
2. Memorizing recall value
3. Suggestion value
4. Conviction value

McDonald's AD Design

Initially McDonald's tried to position its stores as a special place to visit, with the baseline 'McDonald's mein hain kuch baat' in their advertisements. The objective of the advertisement was to attract the customers to try the McDonald's experience. However, over the years, with increased acceptance of McDonald's by customers, the company realized there was a need to evolve a comprehensive communication strategy and move on from trying to encourage people to visit them for the first time to making McDonald's a regular experience. As they are already established and many people have already visited them and know what McDonald's is all about, they have changed their baseline to 'Toh aaj McDonald's ho jaye'. In this ad campaign they stressed about an everyday experience, not the first time visit. The focus was to encourage their customers to visit McDonald's more often with their family members and have an enjoyable eating.

---

5. Educational value
6. Instinctive appeal value

Selection of Advertising Media   Today's retailer has many media alternatives from which he can select. In the past, retailers primarily focused on print (newspaper, magazines, and direct mail), radio, and outdoor media. Now retailers have started focusing on other media like television and Internet as well. The most frequently repeated television ads are of Fun Republic, Essel World, and PP Jewellers, which aim at attracting the urban population, especially the tourist crowd. While newspapers and television can be effectively used for communication aimed at the total market, radio, direct mail, magazines, and Internet can be easily targeted towards specific audiences. The recent popularity of FM radio is significant in this regard with some of the popular ads being for Mehrasons Jewellers, Shyam Garments, PVR movies, and many other food and entertainment centres.

In the Indian context, the most popular retail advertising media have been in the form of outdoor media like billboards, posters, and neon signs. Most Indian markets, traffic intersections, bus stops, and railway platforms are littered with such advertisements. Their biggest advantage for retailers is in terms of the lower costs and localized coverage. Another very popular advertisement channel for the Indian retailers has been the local TV networks in terms of the marquee that floats continuously on the screen and is used by many local level shops.

Many retailers in the unorganized sector also employ the use of a vehicle with a loud speaker to spread the advertising message. Some beauty parlours, health clubs, food joints, and pharmacies popularly employ the use of flyers to provide information on their launch, sales promotions, or any special benefits.

Running an Advertisement Campaign   It involves the execution of advertising programme which should be in accordance with the advertisement goals and the budget. The task can be entrusted to a department that is created within the retail organization or an outside advertising agency. It is advisable to run pre-test of an advertisement before releasing it commercially so that, if needed, any modifications can be done in the advertisement copy itself.

Measuring Advertisement Effectiveness   The retailers are interested to know the result of advertising due to the considerable amount of money, time, and resources spent on them in order to know

Table 10.2.   Ad spend of the US retail industry

Advertising Media	Ad Spend in 1998 (million US dollars)
Total	11,572.5
Outdoor	178.4
Radio	
Network radio	105.8
Spot radio	462.3
Magazines and Newspapers	
Consumer magazines	526
Sunday magazines	124
Local papers	5556.9
Sunday papers	267.4
Television	
Network TV	1131.5
Spot TV	2729.7
Syndicated TV	113.9
Cable TV networks	275.8

Source: www.retailindustry.about.com

whether the advertisement campaign has been successful in meeting the objectives. Measuring the effectiveness of advertising is a complex and challenging task. It includes two main components, namely communication effectiveness measurement and sales effectiveness measurement. According to research findings, probably no more than 0.2% of total advertising expenditure is used to achieve an enduring understanding of how to spend the other 99.8%. It is frequently observed that good planning and targeting of advertising can ensure its effectiveness.

The effectiveness of an advertisement is measured for a variety of reasons:

1. To determine the success of the campaign objectives with respect to advertisement objectives
2. To determine the effectiveness of an advertisement to ascertain which layout or illustration is the best
3. To determine the strengths and weaknesses of various media and media plans

Pre-tests need to be conducted to find out whether the information presented in the message meets the purpose of the ad. If the ads are not potentially effective they have to be modified. Two important methods used for this purpose are as follows:

- *Readability studies:* These are conducted for different socio-economic and geographical backgrounds to find the comfort level of reading the advertisement.
- *Eye-movement analysis:* Eye movement of respondents are recorded when advertisements are shown to them on screen and the results are analysed to assess the level of viewing pleasure of the viewers.

Post-advertisement tests to measure advertising effectiveness   are administered after the advertisement has been released. They help to know whether the advertisement meets the objective or not and if any changes are required to be made. The various measures taken into account are as follows:

- *Recall tests:* These are aimed at assessing how many people remember the advertisements. The respondents are shown some of the previously run advertisement compaigns and are asked to recall which part of it they remember. From this, they conclude that the better the people recall the advertisements the more the people will purchase the products. Recall tests are also called recognition, readership, and viewership tests and are used at the pre-testing stage.

- *Concurrent tests:*   They are conducted at the time when the consumer is exposed to the advertisement.
- *Response tests:*   The advertisement can include response coupons urging the reader to place the order to seek information.
- *Attitude change test:*   These tests are designed to modify the attitude or opinion of potential customers in a manner that customers are inclined to buy the retailer's products.

The sale effectiveness of advertising can also be used for this purpose. There are two approaches frequently used by retailers. One is the historical approach, in which the relationship between past sales data and advertising expenditure during the corresponding period is analysed. The other is the experimental approach, in which the advertising message and expenditure in different regions/locations is established and the relationship between sales and various advertising variables is analysed. Independent retailers in the unorganized sector depend heavily on their own experience rather than formal measuring tools to evaluate effectiveness. Increased number of product and store-related inquiries and footfalls are common indicators of ad effectiveness.

Media Selection

Media selection involves finding the most cost-effective media to deliver the desired number of exposures to the target audience. In the desired number of exposures the advertiser seeks a certain response from target audience, e.g., a certain level of product trial and the level of brand awareness among the audience. The effect of exposures on audience depends on reach, frequency, and impact.

- Reach (R): It includes the different persons or households that are exposed to a particular media schedule at least once during a specified time period.
- Frequency (F): The number of times within the specified time period that an average person or household is exposed to the message.
- Impact (I): The qualitative value of an exposure through a given medium.

The relationships between reach, frequency, and impact is captured through the following concepts:

- Total number of exposures (E): It is the reach times the average frequency, i.e., $E = R * F$. This measure is referred to as gross rating points (GRP).

- Weighted number of exposures (WE): It is the reach times frequency times average impact, i.e., $WE = R * F * I$

The media planner has to figure out, with a given budget, the most cost-effective combination of reach, frequency, and impact. Reach is most important for launch-purchased products, flanker brands, extensions of well-known brands or infrequently purchased brands, or going after undefined target market. Frequency is most important where there are strong competitors, a complex story to tell, high consumer resistance, or frequency–purchase cycle.

Table 10.3 Major media types

Media	Advantages	Limitations	Examples
Newspapers	Flexibility; timeliness; good local market coverage; broad acceptance; high believability	Short life; poor reproduction quality; small 'pass-along' audience	The Hindustan Times, The Times Of India, The Indian Express
Television	Combines sight, sound, and notion; appealing to the senses; high attention; high reach	High cost and clutter; fleeting exposure; less audience selectivity	Zee TV, Sony, Star TV, DD Metro
Direct mail	Audience selectivity; flexibility; no ad competition within the same medium; personalization	Relatively high cost; 'junk mail' image	E-mail/ Letter/fax
Radio	Mass use; high demographic and geographic selectivity; low cost	Audio presentation, lower attention than television; non-standardized rate structures; high exposures	Radio 98.3 FM, Vividh Bharti
Magazines	High geographic and demographic selectivity; credibility and prestige; high-quality reproduction; long life; good 'pass-along' readership.	Long ad purchases lead time; waste circulation; no guarantee of position	Business World, Femina, India Today, Cosmopoltian

contd

contd

Media	Advantages	Limitations	Examples
Outdoor	Flexibile; high repeat exposure; low cost; low competition	Limited audience selectivity; creative limitations	Hoardings, posters, banners, neon signs, baloons
Yellow pages	Excellent local coverage; high believability; wide reach; low cost	High competition; long ad purchase lead time; creative limitations	Tata Press Yellow pages
Newsletters	high selectivity; full control; interactive oppournities	High cost	Mall Times by Ansal Plaza, New Delhi
Brochures	Flexibility; full control; can dramatize messages	Overproduction leads to run away costs	Be:, John Player
Telephone	Many users; to opportunity give a personal touch	High cost unless volunteers are used	Just Dial Services, MTNL
Word-of-mouth	No cost; from consumers, for consumers, by consumers; enhances reputation	No control; decides its own course (positive or negative); Needs hard to counteract the negative	Local retailers, professional services (medical, financial analysis)
Flyers	Inexpensive; easy to administer, no frills required; use pictures; easy to change; wide coverage	Mistaken for junk; limited life; limited information can be communicated	Small retailers, restaurants
Vehicle signs	One-time cost; visible 24*7; find place on business and personal vehicles; use words or pictures	Limited space to display; owner may object; durability is limited;	Car showrooms, accessories stores, auto services
Internet	High selectivity; interactive possibilities; relative low cost	New media with a low number of users in some countries	Yahoo, Rediff, India times

Selecting Specific Media Vehicles

The retailers or their media planners usually make a choice from alternative media categories by taking into account factors like target audience, media habits, product profile, message compatibility, and costs. Retailers or marketers need to review periodically the impact and cost of various media types available. In the recent past, Indian retailers started using different media channels. Earlier, a good number of media channels like TV and radio used to serve a limited purpose for the retailers making their use generally unattractive. The major media vehicles are given in Table 10.3.

These days, leading chains along with independent retailers are using modern electronic media extensively along with other conventional media vehicles such as newspapers, magazines, posters, banners, flyers, etc. The retailers operating certain speciality stores are also exploring viable use of latest techniques like advertorials and infomercials.

The advertorials are print ads that offer editorial content and are difficult to distinguish from routine news stories in newspapers or magazines while infomercials are TV commercials of 30 minutes duration packed with advertisements for various products.

The most popular and readily available media is the store itself which effectively employs store atmospherics to powerfully convey the desired image and message. Alongwith the usage of promotional vehicles such as price tags, displays, packaging material, supermarkets also sell the space on their floors for company logos, occasionally experimenting with shelves and introduction of 'video carts'. Even in the best selling paper books, theatres, and movie videotapes, the written material which consists of annual reports, data sheets, and catalogues increasingly carry ads, and many companies even mail audio/ videotapes of their products to prospective customers.

Many large and small retailers use sponsorships to communicate their message and also obtain the desired publicity. VLCC, the health and beauty chain, co-sponsored the Miss India Contest for the year 2004. Many banks in the retail sector sponsor business meets and management seminars. Food chains like McDonald's, Domino's, and various other independent food retailers in major towns and cities extensively sponsor school and college events, local music shows, and 'melas'. Many small retailers also sponsor local level religious events like 'jagratas' in North India, Durga Pooja in West Bengal, Ganesh Chaturthi in the west, and religious discourses by well-known religious leaders throughout the country.

Women in India Trust Print Media

Magazine and newspaper advertisements carry the most amount of influence for female consumers in India, according to the results from the latest research 'What Women Want' by Images. Of the 891 working women covered in the study,

62.6% said they were influenced by ads in the print media, which they often viewed as more trustworthy when compared to other media. 13.1% said print ads influenced them, and only 22.2% thought they were never influenced. Results from the extensive survey could have a far reaching impact on a market currently opening up to foreign direct investment from publishers. Point of purchase (PoP) ads were said to be the next biggest influence, with 26.3% of India's female workforce citing them as influential and 8.1% saying they were often influenced. Electronic media was considered to be the next most influential followed by outdoor advertising. Surprisingly, TV was said to have the least influence, with more than 60% of respondents saying they never took any notice of broadcast commercials.

Source: www.exchange4media.com

The retailer or concerned media planner must look for the most cost-effective media vehicles within the chosen media type. The planner has to rely on media measurement services, which estimate the composition, audience size, and media cost. The key factor to be considered here is the size of circulation, effective audience, and the exposed audience.

Media planners calculate the cost per thousand persons reached by the vehicle. The media planner ranks each magazine by cost per thousand and favours magazines with lowest cost per thousand for reaching target consumers. The various criteria applied to cost per thousand measures are audience quality, audience attention probability, and the magazine's editorial quality. Media planners are increasingly using more sophisticated measures for increasing effectiveness and employing them in mathematical models to arrive at the best media mix. Many advertising agencies use computer programs to select initial media and then make further improvements based on subjective factors.

Popular Media Vehicles Used in the Indian Retail Sector

There is a whole range of vehicles for promotions available to the retailers to choose from. While selecting a particular set of materials for the publicity, retailers have to consider factors such as cost of the selected material, compatibility with their objective, and the rest of the communication strategy. Most Indian retailers rely on vehicles like leaflets, posters, banners, wall paintings, magazines, flyers, direct mails, etc. Television is primarily used by retail chains in the organized sector. They largely have a standardized offering across outlets and, hence, find it cost effective to approach a wide audience through television advertising. Examples of such chains are McDonald's, Domino's, and Pizza Hut. The popular media vehicles are discussed below.

Leaflets or Flyers

Retailers to promote specific activities and events use leaflets or flyers. They have a short shelf life, so they are most useful for marketing specific activities such as opening of a new outlet or off-season sale rather than conveying information the retailer wants customers to retain for a long time. Leaflets inserted into other publications such as newspapers and magazines may never get any further than the person who first receives them. With increased usage of leaflets by marketers, lots of cluttering takes place in terms of number of messages of a similar kind. Therefore the effectiveness of leaflets for a desired objective has to be ensured before using them. Retailers have to give due weightage to the designing of the message.

Posters/Calendars

Retailers use posters to promote specific activities and events, or as free gift to other channel members, especially their loyal customers. This is a very common practice among small retailers in India associated with the festive season of Diwali or New Year. Recently, even the most established retail chains such as banks and other professional houses opted for it. Many posters do not even make it to a wall. One has to incorporate the taste and preferences of their customers while designing the calendar if it has to make any positive impact on the customer's psyche. Retailers need to include contact details on posters and calendars.

Booklets

Retailers from the organized sector can afford this costly mode of communication. It is effective in case of products or services which are intense on information, such as banking, real estate practitioners, fashion designers, and insurance services. Most of the retailers selling consumer durables depend for such support on respective manufacturers rather than investing themselves. The retailers should avoid the temptation to cram too much information into a booklet to lower the production values—this often results in the booklet being difficult to read and can portray a negative image.

Direct mail

Retailers can opt to send out regular, targeted letters as part of their communication strategy. Direct mail advertising includes postcards, catalogues, brochures, e-mail, and single letters. This technique is considered to be effective at the time of introducing new products and informing about prospective sales and or special discounts. Direct mail advertising is recommended for retail firms with a wide selection of merchandise like furniture, music, insurance, clothes, etc. It is a great way to keep your current customers aware of new products, services, or sales. It can also be used as a promotional tool for new customers.

This is a relatively cost-effective way of reaching audiences and one can achieve a much more direct tone of voice. Direct mail letters should be personalized and should be short and to the point, with strong opening and concluding paragraphs. Leading retailers such as Shoppers' Stop and other retail chains in the organized sector use this medium to communicate about new arrivals, seasonal discounts, and previews sales.

Magazines

Magazines are considered to be an effective medium to advertise to the target segment. For example, a retailer selling baby products could put an ad in *Parenting* or *Health and Nutrition*. If retailers are in home fashion products, they can advertise in magazines such as *Society Interiors* and *Inside Outside*. Due to the large reach of magazines, this type of advertising is effective for a large retailing chain with a wide customer base. Local and regional magazines also play a crucial role in respect of the small retailers in townships. These are published by market associations or religious bodies.

Local Cable Channels

With the advent of the local cable TV channels, most of the small retailers, basically located in central business districts, use this medium to communicate about their offerings and promotions to their target segment more effectively. Most of the retailers realize cable network is comparatively less costly in comparison to newspapers and pamphlets, and proves to be more effective as most of the family members can be covered through this media. It serves well to launch a new retail outlet, new product range, and above all any promotion or discount information in the catchment area. The retailers can avail of great degree of flexibility of the medium by making changes in the message as need arises or according to the feedback received.

Billboards

It is one of the most famous and convenient media used by retailers in urban areas to communicate their offerings to the people in their catchment area. Most of the leading retailers of the city place their billboards at railway stations or bus stands and at the entrance of the city by road.

They are available in various sizes, which to a certain extent gives an idea about the stature of the store in the city. Billboard advertising is also a great way to direct people to a store or shopping centre. Retailers to place their billboards have to pay some local taxes to the local government bodies or private owners, whose place is used to place

Billboard for a computer centre

the billboards. Billboards are an effective medium of advertising for restaurants, hotels, car rental companies, shopping centres, adventure parks, and any type of business that deals with travelling customers.

Exclusive billboard by a leading city jeweller

Wall Paintings

This is the most traditional media used by the small retailers in the villages and townships in India. As it includes cost of paint and the low fee charged by painters, retailers usually get the walls of deserted buildings painted at the outskirts of the city with the name of the store and address. This mode is commonly used these days even by the leading marketers. Wall painting is a durable form of media with limited degree of flexibility to change the content of the communication.

Banners

Retailers use banners regularly for immediate benefits, such as to make the customers aware about the new arrivals, promotional schemes, or launch of the new store. Banners are messages displayed on cloth, plastic, or hard board. Banners can be wall mounted or ceiling mounted both indoors and outdoors. The cost involved is limited but it provides ample mobility to the retailers to display their banners.

Banners displayed in a central business district mart

Deciding on Media Timing

In choosing media, advertisers face a macro-scheduling problem and a micro-scheduling problem. The micro-scheduling problem involves scheduling the advertising in relation to seasons and business cycle whereas the micro-scheduling problem deals with allocation of advertising expenditures within a short period to obtain maximum impact. The timing pattern considers three factors which are buyer turnover, purchase frequency, and forgetting rate. Buyer turnover expresses the rate at which new buyers enter into the market; higher the rate, more continuous should be the advertising. Purchase frequency is the number of times during a period that the average buyer buys a product. Higher the purchase frequency, more continuous the advertising should be. Forgetting rate is the rate at which buyers target the brand; higher the forgetting rate, the more continuous advertising should be. In launching of new product, the advertiser has to chose between ad continuity, concentration, fighting, and pulsing.

Deciding on Geographical Allocation

A company has to allocate its advertising budget over a time and space. The company makes 'national buys' when the ad is placed in nationally circulated magazines, TV networks, and it also makes 'spot buys' when the time is purchased in regional editions of magazines. These markets are called areas of dominant influence (ADIs) or designated marketing areas (DMAs). The term 'local buys' refers to radio, newspapers, or outdoor sites.

Sales Promotion

Sales promotion is one of the most important promotion strategies followed by retailers. Sales promotion refers to communication strategies designed to act as a direct inducement, an added value, or incentive for the product to customers. It is traditionally designed for immediate (short-term) increase in product sales. Sales promotion efforts are designed to assist the other promotional activities undertaken by a store. Advertising and publicity may create the desire but its conversion into sales can be achieved only by sales promotion through its short-term incentives. Sales promotion involves activities that may shape buying patterns, attract new customers, or increase sales. It tends to encompass everything that falls outside advertising, publicity, and direct marketing, although these might be used to deliver sales promotions.

Sales promotion provides extensive tactical measures to marketers to manage internal or external impediments to sales or profits. Internal impediments could arise from unsold stock, which may be going out of fashion, or stock of damaged material. External impediments to profits and sales could arise from impending entry of competition into the market, bad reviews in the press, etc. Retailers during the summer of 2004 were concerned about the decline in footfalls due to school exams, general elections and, above all, the cricket series between India and Pakistan. Retailers from the food and beverages sector came up with very effective promotional campaigns to overcome this challenge.

Gini & Jony: Promotions through Word-of-mouth

Kids apparel brand Gini & Jony, launched in 1980, is a unisex brand catering to both boys and girls in the age group between 2 and 16 years. The product portfolio comprises t-shirts, shirts, jackets, cargos and jeans for boys, and Jamaicans, dungarees, skirts, co-ordinates t-shirts, and capris for girls. Its recent addition is Toddlers, a complete range of garments for infants. It is also foraying into new categories to make it a one-stop shop for kids. The latest addition to Gini & Jony's portfolio is the accessories launch, which comprises the footwear and eyewear collection. To achieve overall sales growth for kids apparel, the management has decided to enter into tie-ups with celebrities in the area of drama and dance. For instance, the company is planning to enter into an arrangement with the dancing schools of Shiamak Davar and acting schools of Raell Padamsee, whereby discounts could be offered to consumers. Such promotional exercises will have a positive word-of-mouth along with awareness among the target segment Gini and Jony is looking for.

Source: P. Chatterjee 2003, 'Kids apparel brand Gini and Jony shifts creative account', *Business line*, Thursday, Nov 06.

Print advertisement by Gini and Jony

Sales Promotion to Answer Exams, Election, and Cricket fever

Cricket, exams, and elections affect the retail business to a great extent in India. In particular, when they hit the scene together. No doubt elections or exams bring big business for many sectors but for the food and beverages (F&B) retail industry, they spell low footfalls and sharp decline in sales. First, for most food majors, a high percentage of its customer base is teenagers, who are busy with board exams during this time of the year. Secondly, cricket confines a large customer base of these outlets to home/office. Leading food retailers foresee the loss of 5–10% in profits because of cricket, exam, and poll. Major retail outlets such as Pizza Hut, Subway, Barista, and Pizza Corner have conceived their promotional schemes with cricket theme in common to bring customers in, increase footfalls, and convert those footfalls into profitable footfalls by offerings deals and goodies.

Yum! Restaurants International, the parent company of Pizza Hut, for instance, managed to beat the negative impact of exam and cricket by launching unique promotions. For example in 2003, in addition to exam season slack there was the World Cup in the March-April period. At this point, they launched the Tandoori range of pizzas and intelligent marketing initiatives such as the Pooch World Cup blast, and clocked a 20% increase in sales. Similarly, Barista focused on student-based promotions to increase the offtake and negate any disadvantage from loosing out on sales during this lean period. In particular, they highlighted in their communication a delivery facility, which appealed to the target segment 'confining to home/office'; this increased delivery sale, as during the cricket season and the elections a large number of consumers like to enjoy great food within the confines of their homes and offices. Accepting cricket as the national passion, Barista Coffee participated in the same by running promotions across India and creating parallel buzz on the cricket fever.

One can observe that most of the retailers use promotions around the events to meet the external challenges effectively and reap sound benefits.

Source: P. Kaul, www.financialexpress.com

It is commonly perceived that sales promotion only deals with offering discounts. However, sales promotion is a much broader concept than this. It can include the provisions for sampling or learning opportunities, joint promotions or collaborations with third party networks, special events, giveaways and competitions, discounts, incentives, value adding, and rewards. Good sales promotions can be an inexpensive way of increasing awareness, of reaching to new buyers, or extending the buying choices of existing customers. Because sales promotions often involve working with other organizations, they can open doors into the wider community. By building mutually beneficial relationships, it can be used for paving the way for sponsorships.

Drivers of Promotions

Big retail chains across the country such as Shoppers' Stop, Westside, Pantaloon Retail (India), LifeStyle, Ebony Retail Holdings, Globus, and The Home Stores leave no stone unturned to woo the consumers during the festive season. It is normal for retail chains to offer attractive freebies and discounts during the festive season. Drivers for festive bonanza are two-fold. One is to cash in on increased festive season spending. Second is more bottomline-driven, with loss-making stores looking to wipe out losses. In other words, retail chains obviously want to push out stocks and inventories to avoid loss on account of excess inventory and low turnover.

Source: R. Bhusan 2003, 'Retailers Shower Freebies this Festive Season', *Business line*, Saturday, Oct. 18.

Objectives of Sales Promotion

Sales promotion efforts are generally designed to assist the other communication activities undertaken by a store. For example, awareness may be generated through advertising but sales promotion may be used tactically to overcome any resistance to purchase. The desire may be created by advertising, but its conversion into sales would be done by sales promotion by offering a short-term incentive. Thus, a quicker sales response results from sales promotion.

The various objectives of sales promotion can be summed up as follows.

Stop and Shop

Customers who are just passing by, with no intention of purchasing, would be encouraged to enter the store. The promotional activity may be such that it does not directly hint at a purchase, but just a free trial. For example, free hairstyling done using a hair gel sold by the store.

Shop and Buy

Once the customers have been persuaded to enter the store, they have to be convinced to purchase by presenting the merchandise in such a manner that the customer feels a desire to buy. For example, the store could offer a money-off voucher with the hair gel bottle or the customer would be entitled to get a shampoo if they purchase the hair gel.

Buy Bigger

The promotional activity aims to persuade the customers to buy in a greater quantity or buy other products in addition. For example, customers who buy a bigger pack may be entitled to enter into a contest or they can get a free gift or customers who purchase merchandise more than a specified amount would get similar benefits.

Repeat purchase

The final objective is to encourage customers to return again and again to the store. This is achieved by instilling loyalty among the customers through previous purchases. The goodwill can be created by schemes like continuity programmes or store cards. Regular customers are offered cards whereby after a certain amount of purchases they are entitled to a gift, for example, a trip to Mauritius.

Sales can basically be increased by two methods. Either the number of transactions is increased or the size of the average sale is increased. This can be achieved by a number of activities; some of them are listed below.

- Increasing the number of transactions:
  (i) Sales promotion methods can be used to persuade more people into the store and convince them to buy.
  (ii) Point-of-sale incentives can be improved to generate quicker sales response.
- Increasing the size of the average sale:
  (i) Promotions can be introduced on high-margin goods, so the overall profitability improves.
  (ii) Customers may be encouraged to buy more quantities by offering them various incentives.

Supplier-originated Sales Promotions

Sales promotions can originate from two sources—suppliers or the retail store itself. The suppliers can initiate various sales promotion activities at their end. The retailer is not actively involved in them. The retailer plays no part in such promotional activities; he sells the merchandise as usual, with no significant efforts and expenses from his end. He does not play any role in designing such activities.

In-store Activities

The following are the main in-store promotional activities.

Price-off Pack The product is sold at a reduced price from its normal selling price. This is in the form of a discount, where a customer has to pay less to purchase a product. Usually, it is mentioned on the pack that a certain amount is 'off'. For example, a one litre bottle of cola may say 'Rs 10 off!' So, if the bottle normally sells at Rs 50, the customer now has to pay only Rs 40 for the same.

Premiums   These are in the form of small gifts that a customer gets on purchasing a product. The gifts are usually attached to the pack, or inside the pack. For example, the customer could get a jigsaw puzzle inside a pack of cornflakes, or a free mug with the purchase of a health drink.

Self-liquidating Premiums   In these schemes, the customer has to write to the supplier for the gift, enclosing empty packets, bottle crowns, etc. of the product plus some money. Basically, the customer provides some proof of purchase along with some money. For example, the scheme could be:

5 bottle crowns + Rs 25 – One cap
10 bottle crowns + Rs 35 – One purse
15 bottle crowns + Rs 50 – One watch

The gifts are likely to be bought in bulk by the supplier, giving him the benefit of large discounts. Thus, the per unit purchase price is low enough to be covered by the profit on all extra sales made. And since the customer also sends in some amount of money, the purchase price is easily covered. Another advantage is that these gifts serve as promotional materials, as the name of the supplier is usually mentioned on them.

Personality Promotions   Many companies use show-business personalities to endorse their products. The suppliers tend to associate the charisma associated with these personalities with their products. The idea being that the customer would be attracted towards purchasing the product. However, the appeal of these personalities may be declining because so many companies use the same celebrity models. Therefore, the customer is not able to associate that person with a single product. So, many companies now use personalities selectively to avoid overexposure. For example, T. N. Sheshan, the former Election Commissioner, was used by Safal vegetables since he did not appear for any other product and he had an honest and upright image. Therefore, people would tend to believe his statements.

Competitions   The information about these competitions is usually printed on the packs. The customer needs to follow the instructions and apply. Generally, proof of purchase (maybe in the form of empty packs) is required to participate in the competition, but not necessarily so. 'Britannia khao, World cup jao' was one such promotional scheme. The advantage to the supplier is that the budget is known well in advance, the requisite number of prizes being pre-arranged. Also, the supplier can get a decent amount of publicity when he announces the winners and the prizes.

Co-operative Promotions Sometimes, two or more products share and fund a joint in-store promotion. For example, shaving foam and after shave lotion.

Sampling The customers are given product samples for free. This is usually an in-store activity. Sometimes, a demonstrator may also be present to explain the product. These samples aim at inducing trial of the product. These products are such that customers, if left on their own, would be reluctant to spend money and give them a try. The product may be entirely new and customers may have little knowledge about them. For example, soya bean milk, exotic mushrooms, etc.

Coupons Price-off coupons are printed on the pack or in store handouts, and the customers can use them to save substantial amounts on their next purchase of the brand. The effectiveness of this type of promotion can be significantly reduced if the store allows the coupon to be redeemed for different products. This is called 'malredemption'.

Buy One, Get One Free The customer can get two units of the product at the price of one. Or another variant could be that he buys three packets and gets the fourth one free. Sometimes, the customers have to send the empty packets to the supplier for getting their free products. This may not be very effective and enticing due to the hassles involved in it for the customers. However, it reduces the cost of promotion because of the low 'redemption rate'. Of the many customers who buy the product, very few would send the empty packet back to the supplier and redeem their gift.

Multi-packs Here two or more packs are attached and sold for a better and attractive price than the price of the items singly. It would be 'economical' for the customers to buy a pack of three as it is available at the price of two packets. Thus, the price per unit of the product is reduced for the customer. For example, one Maggi noodles packet free with the purchase of four, or one gets three soaps at the price of two. Frequently, a 'stretched' version of the pack obviates the extra shelf space required. Such schemes are popular in toiletries and drinks.

In-store Salespersons   The supplier provides his own personnel to explain the benefits of the displayed products to the customers. These personnel persuade the customers to purchase by clearing their doubts and mentioning the advantages that their product has over other products. An example would be 'demonstrators' used in the electrical white goods market. For such schemes to work effectively, further inducement may need to be offered such as reduced prices. Once the customer shows his interest in the product, the salespersons can take off from there and complete the sale. Any doubts and questions that arise in the minds of the customers can be cleared then and there, thus overcoming the resistance. This promotion is used selectively, normally in supermarkets, department stores, etc. The number of customers visiting must be large enough to cover the costs involved.

Even though the retailer is not actively involved, he has to be well informed for achieving the planned objectives of promotional schemes. That is, the retailer needs to see over the collection and redemption of coupons, reorganization of the store layout, shelf displays, etc.

Point-of-purchase (PoP) Display Material

Most suppliers produce sales-aid materials which are placed near the products to attract customers and induce them to purchase. Examples of this type of material are:

- Leaflets—These provide details of the product, the advantages of a particular retailer's products over the competitor, unique features and benefits, price, etc. For example, leaflets providing information about a particular model of a car are kept in a car showroom.

- Special fittings—The products are kept in the special racks or stands provided by the suppliers. For example, racks provided by toothbrush suppliers, dry-battery stands, glass case for watches, etc. These fittings make the product prominent compared to other products kept in normal racks. As these fittings are large and attractive, and kept at conspicuous places, they attract the attention of the customers.

- Demonstrators—Sometimes demonstrators are used in this context. For example, a children's product may use a person dressed as their logo (for example a teddy bear) in the store. Such a person can give away samples of the product or stand near the rack storing the product to induce purchases.

Many retailers use the display material provided by suppliers very selectively due to the danger of producing a cluttered and uncoordinated retailing environment. If every supplier wants his individual rack to be placed in the store, it would lead to a much disorganized environment. And since every supplier has his distinct looking stand, the store would lose its consistency in appeal. In some cases, the suppliers and retailers collaborate to produce a mutually acceptable point-of-sale display material.

Advantages of Sales Promotion

The key advantages of retail sales promotions relate to its eye-catching appeal and distinctive value offer associated with it. Its key advantages are listed below:

- It often has eye-catching appeal.
- Themes and tools can be distinctive.
- The consumer may receive something of value such as coupons of free merchandising.
- Impulse purchases are increased.
- It helps to draw customer traffic and maintain loyalty to the retailer.

The major disadvantages of sales promotion are:

- It may be difficult to terminate certain promotions without adverse customer reactions.
- The retailer's image may be hurt if corny promotions are used.
- Sometimes frivolous selling points are stressed rather than retailers' product assortment, prices, customer services, and other factors.
- Many sales promotions have only short-term effects.

Steps in Designing Retail Sales Promotions

It is important to evolve a well-designed promotion plan to be able to obtain its key benefits. For this purpose, the following steps can be employed by the retailer:

Promotions Lead to Footfalls

Barista experienced 20% increased footfalls in the financial year 2002-2003. Such impressive growth in footfalls is attributed primarily to running a lot of in-store promotions throughout the year and price cuts on offerings. The net sales at the end of the year was a whoping Rs 60 crores, a 25% increase over the last year's sales, and average footfalls of 1.2 million a month.

1. Set goals
2. Analyse benefits
3. Design the offer
4. Identify the sources for promotion
5. Design the response and follow-up

Set Goals

This should be determined on the basis of the long-term goals of the retail organization—which might be to attract audiences from a particular socio-economic group, increase first-time customers, and so on. It should also be determined by the particular needs of a specific promotion scheme and contextual factors like time of the year—Diwali, Christmas, wedding season, Valentine's Day, etc. The specific promotion policies of the retail organization and the concerned manufacturer should also be kept in mind.

Analyse Benefits

In identifying possible sales promotions, it is important to ensure that everyone involved, including the customer, benefits.

The benefits might be in the form of:
- Access to customer information due to the creation of database of the users of the promotion activity
- The 'feel good' factor the promotion may create both for the customer and the manufacturer
- Reinforcement of the retailer's image
- Provision of rewards to customers
- Stimulation to trial
- Increased sales
- Value addition, special offers, cheaper prices, learning opportunities, etc. offered to customers, especially loyal shoppers.

Design the Offer

The promotion offer can be designed around one or a combination of the following.

Experience Providing a unique experience can involve offers like dinner with a celebrity, free tickets to some sports event or movies, etc. These days most of the retailers, particularly in the lifestyle segment,

Wills Lifestyle Store Expereince

Wills Lifestyle used the mix of publicity by providing opportunity to their customers to walk down the ramp with leading celebrities at the launch of their summer collection. Fashion icon Sushma Reddy and Nethra Raghuraman, a leading dancer, participated in the fashion show. The unique show, christened 'Fashion Factor', was organized for the patrons (loyal customers). Every customer who walked into the showroom, irrespective of age, was invited to the ramp to do his or her fashion statement in her own style. The event began with the 'strike a fashion pose', where the customers had to perform a catwalk and pose for the camera, and then a written round with five questions called the 'fashion quotient' was conducted to judge the customer's fashion IQ. The selected finalists were asked to do the 'cool catwalk' in their choicest apparels that they could pick up from the store followed by an interactive session with the super models. In the end, the winners walked out smiling with attractive gift hampers.

Such events help the retail chain to retain and increase the spending of the existing customer base and also in attracting new customers through positive word-of-mouth of their own patrons and publicity in media.

Promotion with a Difference

Globus has phased out the 'Redeemable Points' concept and brought in the 'Privilege Club' concept, where members are entitled to a slew of benefits and offers at various exclusive outlets like nightclubs and restaurants in cities where Globus is present. This has not only added newness to their promotional scheme but also added value to their promotional programmes by extending the usage of schemes across its set of retail outlets. It has provided them added advantage to attract new customers and retain the existing customer base.

are devising their promotion mix to extend experiential benefits rather than some economic benefits. This helps retailers to communicate with their privileged segment more effectively.

Premium or Value Adding   This can be achieved through a mixture of packaging or add-on offers and might include best seats at a movie theatre or play, dinner and hotel accommodation at one of the well-known resorts or hotels, free massage and makeover at one of the parlours, signed copies of books or catalogues, etc.

Ebony: Mega Discount Offers on Branded Products

Ebony, India's premier department store, launches 'Ebony Sale' at regular intervals, announcing attractive discounts. The sale usually lasts for a month and gives the customers an opportunity to buy branded products and private labels at affordable prices. Besides flat rate discounts, Ebony offers attractive discounts on branded products like Blackberry, Koutons, Vibe, Louis Philippe, Basics, Ebony, etc. Special gifts on the purchase of household items and discounts on the kid section make this a unique sale and has positioned it ahead of other department stores. The objective of Ebony is to give their customers quality products at affordable prices and this sale gives them the opportunity to purchase good brands at great prices.

Discount Involves Price Reduction All of the above give the customer incentives to feel a part of the retail organization. It is important to avoid the 'Wait there's more' approach. It is also important to be creative in both the offer and the delivery. Make sure the offer is easily understood and that it appears to be and is genuine. There is some evidence to suggest that incentives in the form of competitions, even discounts to a range of other events, show mixed results in converting switchers to loyalists. However,, incentives such as magazine subscriptions or preferential treatment have been found to be very effective in generating loyalty. Well-designed discount offers, targeted at new or infrequent shoppers, can sometimes produce spectacular results provided the offer seems personalized. Independent retailers and retail chains offer festive and off-season discounts every year. For example, Pitambari Saris offered a flat discount of 20% on the entire collection at their outlets in Adhchini and East Patel Nagar, New Delhi. Bombay Selection offered 50% discount on their entire collection at all stores in Delhi. This phenomenon is very common even in the semi-urban areas of India.

Some of the retail sales promotion offers are shown in table 10.4.

Table 10.4. Types of retail sales promotion offers

Offer	Examples
Premium packages	Reserved parking, valet parking, welcome drink, invitation to preview sales, etc.

contd

contd

Offer	Examples
Membership schemes	Frequent flyer, frequent guest, and frequent shopper programmes with special prices and privileges
Discount packages	Price offs, buy-one-get-one-free, volume sales/group bookings, etc.
Lifestyle packages	Babysitting and creche services, home delivery services available 24 hours.
Incentives	Gifts like key rings, calendars, and diaries given on purchase or to frequent shoppers.

Promotional Incentives During Festival Season

- Ebony's 'Ebony Aao, Gift Uthao' promotion, for example, has a Diwali bonanza which includes assured gifts, besides points on purchases ranging from slabs of Rs 500 to Rs 60,000.
- The Tata group's Westside chain of stores is running a 'festival of delights', which comprises a bumper prize of Rs 15 lakh and Tanishq jewellery worth Rs 1 lakh, apart from offering the usual 'assured' gifts on purchases at different price slabs.
- The Globus chain's 'simply kharido aur sona paao' (buy and win gold) promotion has 1-g, 2-g , and 5-g gold coins on offer, a luxury cruise on Star Cruises, and even a Maruti Versa.
- Shoppers' Stop offered an incentive-based promotional scheme named 'The Glitter, Glamour and Gifts festival' for womenonly during the Diwali festival week. The festive offer provides shoppers an opportunity to earn while they shop. If they buy goods worth Rs 5,000 of Christian Dior brand they get free lipstick, 50 ml of cleanser and mascara worth Rs 2,500, and purchase of Rs 1000 worth goods from L'Oreal would help them get a coffee set free.

Wills Lifestyle: Gift Vouchers

ITC's Wills Lifestyle, a nationwide retail chain of exclusive speciality stores, presented 'Occasions', a range of exclusive gift vouchers. These gift vouchers are redeemable against a tempting range of Wills Classic formal wear, Wills Sport relaxed wear, Wills Clublife evening wear, and fashion accessories.

Salient features of the 'Occasion' exclusive gift vouchers'

- Presents the perfect gift for any occasion
- Comes with a 'message card' that can be personalized
- A flexible gifting option in a wide range of denominations: Rs 250; Rs 500; Rs 2000; Rs 5000; Rs 10000
- Gives the recipients the freedom to choose a gift of their choice
- Available and redeemable at all 49 ITC's Wills Lifestyle stores
- A tempting choice of formal, relaxed, and evening wear for men and women

Impressive Gift Voucher by Wills Lifestyle

Identify Sources of Sales Promotion

Identifying sources of sales promotion involves evaluating the various media to distribute and display the message. The analysis related to the media and vehicle for advertising equally applies here. However, we discuss below some of the more popular sales promotion tools used by a retailer.

Inserts   Brochures or fliers could be inserted into almost anything: newspapers, magazines, telephone, paper deliveries, any kind of bill (though the recipient is not necessarily in a receptive frame of mind), shopping bags with purchases of books or CDs.

Flyer Distribution   This can be done through volunteers or students with a small monetary incentive. To implement this systematically, the retailer should list locations including good parking spots on easily understood routes and distribute the flyers to the passers by. Even sponsors can distribute the flyers among their staff and clients. Some more ideas for the same are as follows:

- Postcards or business cards neatly folded into the bill
- Beer mats or up-market coasters for wine bars
- Bookmarks—bookstore chains and libraries might slip them into books being sold or borrowed.
- Hotels might also consider attaching a flier to the front of newspapers that are delivered to the room.
- Fliers inserted into ticket envelopes when they are mailed or when renewals go out for memberships.

Archive   Build pride in the retail orgabization's achievements with a wall or hall of honour, featuring past posters or photographs. They become part of a collective memory and are powerful.

Displays Window display is the most critical sales promotion tool for retailers. Many discount or special offers and the products to which they relate find a place on the window display. They play a useful role in reinforcing the campaign.

Blackboards and White Boards Some food and coffee joints frequently use black boards and white boards to provide information on their special offers as well as some messages like 'thought for the day'. An example here is of Barista outlets across the country.

Joint Promotions There could be one-off themed networks that match with the specific promotion activity. An example could be price-off coupons for McDonald's along with the movie ticket of Harry Porter given by a multiplex in Delhi. Similar deals could be worked out with fast-food restaurants, credit card companies, travel agencies, local fitness clubs, and educational institutions. The advantages are two fold. First, they reduce the fear of the unknown in case of a lesser known partner, and second, it is cash cheap.

Events An event can be a form of sales promotion in case it is used to attract new customers or increase sales. The shop window performance might be a ploy to attract media coverage, and the open day might be a mechanism to increase attendance from students. Outdoor events—a regular feature for some retailers—are often justified on the basis that they help in building a new customer base. Lifestyle retailers organize fashion shows to promote their merchandise and,

---

Barista: Promotion Tie-ups

Barista Coffee Company Ltd, as part of its marketing strategy, is planning to rope in entertainment, consumer goods, and music companies, which include the US-based Bose Corporation, Swatch, and International Travel House for promotional campaign. The objective behind the move is to leverage co-marketing opportunities and alliances to offer greater value to its consumers. Barista launched a consumer promotion whereby on the purchase of a Barista coffee worth Rs 150, consumers can avail of a Lacoste gift voucher worth Rs 500 and a Lacoste calendar. Barista also does promotions with Elle 18. Elle 18 launched a collection of coffee-coloured lipsticks and have named it after Barista beverages. Such association helps both the firms involved in the promotional programme. For Elle 18, the objective was to build a platform for their range of coffee coloured lipsticks, and for Barista, the objective was to associate with the brand and attract their consumers.

HDFC Promotions: Objectives

HDFC Bank has renewed its focus on promotional activities such as organizing school-level painting competitions, sponsoring business meets and freebies, etc. as an important ingredient of their communication strategy along with electronic and print ads. The objective of the promos is not just acquisition of new customers, but also creating product awareness, enhancing usage, and providing value-adds to its customers to reward them for their faith and loyalty. The promo is titled "Wheels of Fortune". This promo is targeted at all those customers who avail a personal loan, or car or two-wheeler loan. There will be a lucky draw at the end of the promo and the winners would get exotic prizes. A school-level painting competition on wildlife across cities was also planned to promote the Kids Advantage account.

therefore, sales. Globus, Wills Lifestyle, and Provogue exclusive retail chains organize regular shows before the formal launch of their summer and winter collections.

Fashion show in progress at an exclusive Provogue showroom

Designing the Response and Follow-up

Sometimes promotional tools do not realize their full potential because the response mechanism is too complicated or unclear. It should be easy to respond by ticking a box, picking up the phone, handing over the coupon, and so on. There is a risk in giving people too many

Organizing Effective Sales Promotion

The following are some tips for organizing effective sales promotion:

- Protect and enhance your image through the kinds of sales promotions you choose and by controlling the messages as far as possible.
- Seal all promotions with third parties with letters of agreement.
- Success is in the details—you may generate ill will through sales promotions that create expectations you can't deliver or are poorly executed at the point of sale.

- Take a strategic approach to your sales promotions programme; sales promotions designed only to sell slow-moving stock may damage your image. Always include sales promotion in your early marketing plans.
- Sales promotions can be time-costly, so reap the rewards of your efforts by ensuring you do not lose that valuable customer after the event.
- Maintain the novelty value of sales promotions. It is tempting to repeat successful formulae but repetition can deliver a diminishing return.

choices, as it can take too long to work out what to do. On the other hand, customers like offers to be as flexible as possible.

When the retailer designs a response plan for sales promotion, the prime consideration is: Is it easy for the customer?

Other key things to remember are:

- How will the target customer for the offer be identified?
- Would it be possible to keep the customer's name and address for the future?
- Is the sales promotion method foolproof and will it reflect well on the retail organization?
- Can the logistics of the programme be easily managed?

Personal Selling

Personal selling involves oral communication with one or more perspective customers for the purpose of marketing and sales. Like advertising, the objectives of personal selling is also informing, persuading, and reminding the consumer about the market offering. However, in the retail context, personal selling also plays the important role of building relationship and trust with the customers.

Objectives of Personal Selling

The objectives of personal selling can be demand-oriented and/or image-oriented. The former focuses on pushing sales for the product

Table 10.5 Objectives of personal selling

Personal selling objectives		Operative in situations
A	Demand-oriented objectives	
1	Information	To explain goods and services attributes
		To provide answers to the questions and queries
		To investigate for any further probing/questioning
2	Persuasion	To convert a suspect into prospect
		To placate dissatisfied customers
		To outsmart competition by clearly distinguishing attributes of goods and services from those of competitors
3	Reminding	To follow-up after purchase
		To follow up when repeat buying is near
		To sell complementary items, e.g., a site seeing tour with the hotel room
B	Image-oriented objectives	To maintain good appearance by all front line executives
		To be respected by the employees, customers, and the public firms
		To follow up the selling practices accepted by the marketing environment

while the latter attempts to build the store image. Demand-oriented objectives can relate to providing information, persuading the customer, and reminding him about the products, services, and the related experience. Image-oriented objectives relate to building the retail brand and generating trust among customers and the larger community. The various objectives of personal selling are shown in Table 10.5.

The major objectives of personal selling are to:
- Persuade customers to purchase
- Stimulate sales of impulse items or products related to a consumer's basic purchases
- Complete transaction with customers
- Provide feedback and information to the decision-makers
- Provide adequate level of customer services and maintain customer satisfaction

Types of Personal Selling

Retail personal selling can be classified as either taking the order or getting the order. In both the types, sales personnel are involved. An order-taking salesperson engages in routine clerical and sales functions, such as setting displays, placing inventory at the shelves, answering simple inquiries from customer, filling up the order form, and ringing up the sales. This is a type of in-store sale and it is normally a mix of self-service and some service personnel on the floor.

An order-getting salesperson is involved in informing, persuading, taking order, and closing a sale activity. Repeat buy of the customers is normally the result of the efforts of the order-getting sales personnel. These are the true sales employees that close the sales activity starting from the grass root level, or, in the other words, they complete a cold call. They usually sell high-priced products like real estate, autos, apparel, appliances, etc.

The need for effective personal selling has been observed in case of complex and information-intensive products and services and where trust, involvement, customization, and convenience are critical to the purchase decision. Hence, personal selling is quite common in case of financial and insurance products due to the complexity and information-intensity of the product along with the need to reassure the client. Most banks and insurance companies generally approach the clients at their residence for the purpose. Now some Indian banks like SBI and ICICI are also approaching their walk-in customers to sell their insurance products. Therefore, the next time you visit the neighbourhood State Bank of India (SBI) branch, do not be surprised to see the staff there in suits and ties, flashing their visiting cards to attract business from walk-in customers.

Similarly, retailers of high-involvement product categories like personal care products, durables, and customized product/service providers rely largely on personal selling to aid the customers in their selection process. It is also employed to heighten the comfort factor and make the customers feel important. Most salespersons in the unorganized retail sector in India make it a point to approach the customer as soon as he enters the shop with statements like 'What are you looking for?', 'Please be seated', 'New stuff has arrived', etc. Some markets have the tradition of almost all retailers inviting customers to enter their shop as soon as they spot one passing by.

Network Selling at Work in Rural India

FMCG major Hindustan Lever established an alternative retail format in late 2000 to sell its products through women self-help groups who operate like a direct-to-home team of saleswomen in areas where HLL's conventional sales system does not reach.

HLL evolved Project Shakti to reach areas of low access and low market potential. The project currently covers all districts of Andhra Pradesh and Karnataka, reaching almost 5,000 villages through 800 self-help groups (SHGs). The company intends to extend the model across Madhya Pradesh, Gujarat, and Uttar Pradesh in 2003. It is looking at the Tamil Nadu market too. It is estimated that 30% of the FMCG business comes from villages with a population less than 2,000. The Shakti model trains women from SHGs to distribute HLL products of daily consumption such as detergents, toilet soaps, and shampoos—the latter's penetration being only 30% in rural areas. The women avail of micro-credit through banks. Each Shakti dealer covers 6–10 villages, which have a population of less than 2,000. The company is creating demand for its products by having its Shakti dealers educating consumers on aspects such as health and hygiene. HLL registered incremental sales of Rs 1 crore a month each in Andhra Pradesh and Karnataka where it has covered the whole state. *Source:* Vinay Kamath 2003, *Business Line*, New Delhi, April 25.

In the organized sector, some retail outlets with self-service facilities minimize the use of personal selling to push their products. They, instead, rely on the product display or brochures (menu display in case of restaurants) to do the same. The organized sector retailers in the area of consumer durables, high-end products, and lifestyle stores extensively use personal selling, both to satisfy the informational needs and to heighten the experience factor.

Identifying and Overcoming Objections during the Selling Process

In any selling process, identifying and overcoming objections from the prospect is a key factor for its success. Objections can be defined as any hindrance voiced by the prospect which prevents the salesman from moving to the next step in the sales process or from closing the sale. Objections which sales people mostly face tend to be in the form of skepticism, misunderstanding, and stalling. The best way to handle objections is to appear as a knowledgeable, interested salesperson whose mission is to help the prospect achieve his objectives and goals. It is important to respond to objections positively and respect the prospect's actions as legitimate concerns.

Personal selling at work in rural India

Skepticism may arise from all or any of the following:

- *Promising too much too soon*
- *Failing to gain rapport:* It is required that the salesman listens and responds effectively.
- *Not asking the right questions:* The salesman should try to know enough about the prospect's needs to be able to ask relevant questions.
- *Not fully answering questions:* The prospect's questions should not be thought of as 'dumb'. Salespersons should not avoid questions just because they think of them as trivial.
- *Coming off as defensive:* If the salesperson appears to be defensive to an objection, the prospect may be turned off completely. He should always respond enthusiastically, not defensively.
- *Not client-centred:* If the salesperson speaks in general terms and does not address the specifics of the prospect's objection, the salesperson has not been able to give an answer the prospect was looking for.
- *A perceived lack of time :* If the salesperson rushes through his sales pitch or does not give enough consideration to the prospect's concerns, it could make the prospect feel uneasy. It is important not to linger endlessly on any one point and also not to give any quick answers either.

Objections related to *misunderstanding* may result from any of the following three factors:

- *Inadequate definition of the need:* A good salesman has the ability to define and solve problems. By understanding the prospect's situation, he is better able to offer the help or answers needed by the prospect. It is important to take time to get the facts and offer the solutions necessary to close the sale.
- *Inadequate goal definition:* A salesperson should know the prospect's goal before he tries to suggest a path. If his main concern is to obtain regular supplies of a particular type of rice, speak in terms of providing the same rather than trying to improve his recipe. Help him to hit his goal.
- *Inadequate definition of benefits and features:* A salesperson should provide specific examples of how the prospect will benefit from the product or service. He should not give vague answers to specific problems.

If the prospect seems to be *stalling,* the reason might be one of these:

- The prospect is not the decision-maker—if this is the situation, find out who the decision-maker is and ask to meet with that individual or give the opportunity to the prospect to speak with the decision-maker. Many retailers permit their customers to use their telephone for the purpose. Many apparel and jewellery retailers encourage their regular customers to take the selected products home to obtain the approval.
- He is not sure on your product—ask probing questions to determine what the problem is. 'Are you not sure about our pricing?' 'Are you concerned about our ability to deliver?' 'What is holding you back in making your decision?'
- He wants to explore other alternatives—find out what his criteria are for the selection. A salesman should also try to determine what kind of information the prospect is looking for.
- He is too busy to talk right now—ask him what his schedule is and when you can return or call him back. Also, it might be good to find out if the prospect is serious about the purchase or just biding his time.
- The product is beyond the stated budget of the prospect—this provides an excellent chance for the salesman to show him the cost-benefit. Besides, the retailer should be willing to adjust his policies, especially regarding credit and payment terms, to take

care of such concerns. In the organized sector retailing in India, 'purchase on credit' facilities are largely driven by the manufacturer/supplier, while in the unorganized retail sector they are largely driven by the retailer himself. Hence, there are many examples of retailers in small towns providing garments and durables to their trusted customers on credit.

Effective Personal Selling Tips

Some do's related to personal selling are as follows:

- Always maintain a positive attitude and be enthusiastic.
- Always remember that objections are a natural part of the sales process and should not be considered as a personal affront.
- Always maintain good eye contact, even when under fire.
- Always listen closely to an objection.
- Always acknowledge the objection and then give your point of view.
- Always be prepared to prove your position with testimonials, references, and documentation.

Publicity

Publicity (at times referred to as public relation) entails any communication that fosters a favourable image for the retailer among its public. It can be non-personal or personal, paid or non-paid, and sponsor controlled or non-sponsor controlled. Publicity is a non-personal form of promotion where messages are transmitted through mass media, the time or space provided by media is not paid for, and there is no identified commercial sponsor. Public relation is beneficial for both small and large retailers as large retail houses can spend a lot on publicity by organizing events, shows, etc., whereas small retailers can also draw attention easily with less budget. Some methods of developing public relations or getting publicity for small retailers are:

- Eliminate junk mail to editors: Press release should be limited to some extent only, which can increase the chances of getting coverage.
- Follow time limitation: Only should know how much time an editor will spend to determent the utility of your item. So the title and headline of the release should be interesting.
- Through TV: Small retailers can give their ads through local cable TV channels.

Effective PR Plan

The following aspects must be considered to formulate an effective PR plan:

- Evaluating the current PR situation
- Developing the public relations strategy
- Knowing the target
- Identifying PR topics
- Developing messages
- Developing a media list
- Developing an event list
- Identifying editorial opportunities
- Announcing news
- Writing the press release
- Pitching the story
- Choosing a unique angle

There are many other ways to promote the store through public relation at lower costs.

Objectives of a public relations strategy can be summarized as follows:

- To increase the awareness of the retailer and his strategy mix
- To maintain or improve company's image
- To demonstrate innovativeness
- To minimize total promotion costs
- To present a favourable message in a believable manner

Mahima Chaudhary at the launch of a fashion store in mumbai

Types of Publicity

Public relation or publicity can be broadly classified as positive and negative publicity. Further classifications can be as follows.

Planned Public Relation

A retailer outlines its activities in advance, strives to have media report on them, and anticipates that certain events will result in media coverage. Community services like donations and social sales, and introduction of new goods and services are some of the activities which lead to media coverage.

Unexpected Publicity

It takes place when the media reports on a firm without any advance notice about the media coverage. TV and newspaper reporters may anonymously visit stores and rate their performance for the coverage.

Complementary Publicity

Sometimes media reports about a firm in a complimentary manner with regard to the excellence of its retailing practices.

Retail promotion needs to be organized with due understanding of the retail business and its positioning. The financial resources required and the impact of the promotion strategy on the brand image of the store and the products retailed by it must also be considered. Hence, a promotion strategy must go hand in hand with the brand stocking decision. Many retailers are effectively utilizing the Internet to reach wider markets. Witness the case of small *paan* vendors in Mumbai, sweet vendors across the country, and providers of varied gift items and services like cards, florists, and childcare consultants. The diversity of media and the promotional strategies used by Indian retailers is a reflection of the vibrant retail canvass of India.

Summary

Retail promotion is broadly defined as all communication that informs, persuades, and/or reminds the target market or the prospective segment about the marketing mix of the retail firm. The various promotion methods include advertising, sales pro-motion, personal selling, and publicity. All of these have their unique focus and must be used intelligently. Advertising is a form of paid, non-personal communication. Personal selling is a form of personal, paid communication. Publicity is a form of unpaid, non-personal communication. Sales promotion can employ any or all of the above to achieve its short-term tactical objectives. The types of promotional strategies can be distinguished on the basis of control, flexibility, credibility, and cost associated with them.

Advertising is generally defined as the dissemination of information concerning an idea, product, or service to induce action in accordance with the intent of an advertiser. The various types of advertising can be classified as consumer-oriented or persuasive, informative, institutional or corporate, financial, and classified advertising. Some advertisement campaigns can take the form of vertical co-operative advertising or horizontal co-operative advertising depending on sharing of the campaign expenses with the manufacturer/supplier or other retailers. The popular media vehicles for advertising are television, radio, print, flyers, brochures, telephone, walls, banners, posters, internet, etc.

Sales promotion refers to communication strategies designed to act as a direct inducement, an added value, or incentive for the product to customers. It is traditionally designed for immediate (short-term) increase in product sales. Sales promotion efforts are designed to assist the other promotion activities undertaken by a store. Sales promotions are designed to attract new customers, induce repeat purchase or increase share of wallet of customers. Many sales promotion activities are driven and sponsored by manufacturers and suppliers. Some examples are price-off schemes, premiums, coupons, competitions, etc. Many retailers also organize and sponsor events to advertise their sales promotion activities.

Personal selling involves oral communication with one or more perspective customers for the purpose of marketing and sales. Its objectives can be demand-oriented and/or image-oriented. Personal selling activities can be classified as order taking or order getting. This is the most powerful promotion tool available with the retail sector due to its unique opportunity for direct interaction with the customers.

Publicity or public relations is a non-personal form of promotion where messages are transmitted through mass media, the time or space provided by media is not paid for, and there is no identified commercial sponsor. While this media does not afford the possibility of controlling the communication and the message, many retailers use it effectively by organizing and sponsoring news-generating events and activities.

Key Terms

1. **Advertising:** Paid, non-personal communication, transmitted through out-of-store mass media by an identified sponsor.

2. **Store image:** Represents how a given retail store is perceived by consumers and others.

3. **Personnel selling:** Oral communication with one or more prospective customers to make sales.

4. **Point-of-purchase display:** Interior display that provides shoppers with information,

adds to store atmosphere, and serves a substantial promotional role.

5. **Publicity:** Any non-personal from of public relations, whereby messages are transmitted by mass media, the time or space provided by the media in not paid for, and there is no identified commercial sponsor.

6. **Retail promotion:** Any communication by retail store that informs, persuades, or re-members the target market about the marketing mix of the retail store.

7. **Sales promotion:** Includes all other paid communication activities other than advertising, public relations, and personal selling that stimulate consumer purchases and retailer performance.

8. **Word of mouth:** Happens when one customer talks to others.

9. **Contest:** Promotional activity in which customers or prospective customers compete for rewards through games of chance.

10. **Coupons:** Entitles the holder to a reduction in the price of a product or service.

11. **Infomercial:** A TV programme that mixes entertainment with product demonstration and solicits orders placed by telephone from customers.

12. **Promotion mix:** A communication programme made up of advertising, sales promotion, website, store atmosphere, publicity, personnel selling, and word of mouth.

Concept Review Questions

1. What is the significance of retail promotion strategy in the entire retail marketing mix?
2. Define retail promotion strategy and also state all the components of promotion strategy.
3. What are the types of advertising? State each with relevant examples from the retailing industry?
4. What are the stages of an advertising campaign?
5. Discuss the selection criteria used by marketers to choose a particular medium or a mix of media types.
6. Describe the various advertising vehicles used by Indian retailers.
7. What is the role of sales promotion and personal selling in the Indian retailing sector?
8. Discuss the relevance of publicity for retailers and shopping centres in detail.

Project Work Assignments

1. Evaluate the promotion strategy of the three fashion department stores in your city.
2. Compare the sales promotions carried by an independent retail store, a retail chain, and a franchised outlet in food and fashion category.
3. Devise an advertising campaign for a lifestyle store and professional service providers (such as medical practitioners, interior designers, etc.).
4. Analyse the implications of manufacturer-driven promotions for retail business. Discuss in respect of two retail formats of your own choice.

5. A leading restaurant of your city has been besieged with negative publicity regarding its hygiene standards. Propose an effective promotion strategy to overcome this problem. His promotion budget cannot exceed Rs 50,000.

Case Study

McDonald's Promotion Strategy in India

McDonald's, the global fast food giant, entered India in October 1996. Today it has retail outlets in Mumbai, Delhi, Pune, Ahmedabad, Vadodara, Ludhiana, Jaipur, Noida, Faridabad, Doraha, Manesar, and Gurgaon. Its first restaurant opened on 15 April 1955 in Des Plaines, Illinois, USA. Forty eight years down the line, they are the world's largest food-service chain with more than 30,000 restaurants in 100 countries, serving more than 46 million customers every day.

McDonald's in India have specially developed a range of 100% pure vegetarian food along with a non-vegetarian range. In fact, even the mayonnaise used in the items is eggless. Taking into account the Indian palate, they have prepared the choicest of products using spices favoured by local customers. When they entered India, they encountered competition everywhere in every possible form. McDonald's efforts were aimed purely at driving traffic in. Towards this end, promotions and consumer offers were the order of the day. On an average, McDonald's puts back 5% of the total sales revenue into marketing.

Objectives of Promotion Strategy

The key objectives of McDonald's promotion strategy were to, as they say, 'Get them in. Trade them up. Get them back'.

Hence, the first and foremost objective was to make consumers step into McDonald's outlets. The second objective was to shift the consumers to McDonald's core products (the Veg Burger with cheese, the McChicken Burger with cheese, and Fillet-o-Fish) by increasing sampling and showcasing the value aspect of McDonald's. The third objective was to increase the frequency of visits by making the McDonald's brand experience unique and memorable.

Target Segment and Positioning

McDonald's was positioned as a family restaurant. Extra care had been taken to make the restaurants children-friendly, by providing play areas wherever possible so that the parents could relax and have a good time when they were visiting McDonald's.

McDonald's has been targeting both Sec A and B, because 'that's where the volumes lie'. No wonder the company has been targeting kids quite persistently. It is the children who drive the going out and eating out patterns in families. McDonald's strategy is obviously to make the eating-out function the focus of these outings.

Looking at it, McDonald's is focusing on all the three objectives discussed above. Promotions and offers are still regular features, something that is dictated by increased penetration. At the same time, the value aspects are constantly being addressed as more SEC B families come into the fold. Indianization is an important factor in reaching this segment. Its management claims, 'SEC B is a critical mass for us. That's why even our communication is very Indian. And all through this, the focus has to be on educating the consumer about the finer points of McDonald's and on building the brand.'

By 1998 McDonald's had achieved a sufficient level of success in inducing trial of its offerings. It then realized that it was time to educate consumers about its core strengths such as quality, service, hygiene, and, of course, products. There was a strong perception of McDonald's being an expensive place that needed to be corrected. However, McDonald's was interested in highlighting not only the economic value but also the experiential aspect at their stores. In this context, they attempted to ensure that every employee strove to provide 100% customer satisfaction for every customer on every visit. This included friendly and attentive service, accuracy in order taking, and anticipation of customer's needs. They also provided hostesses who would keep circulating in the lobby helping children and adults alike with straws, napkins, soufflé cups, sauce sachets, etc., and any other assistance that they required.

Role and Use of Advertising

McDonald's realized that advertising does help in building brand recall, but advertising alone could not sustain a brand. The McDonald's management claimed that 'the products that we serve are of international standards and we believe that our brand has grown because we deliver our promise, we sustain the quality, and experience promised to the consumers in our advertisements in the restaurants.'

Based on the evolution of its business objectives, McDonald's continuously revised its advertising strategy. As a result, they felt that they had developed a strong base of repeat customers. Their customer base has increased substantially since they started operations. In the period 1996–2000, McDonald's experienced very high trials from first-time customers—averaging 77–80%. Since then, they have tried to move away from inviting trials and have focused on building customer loyalty.

Ad Campaign Launched   When they started operations in India, McDonald's tried to position itself as a place to visit, with the tag line 'McDonald's mein hain kuch baat' in their advertisements. This had an aura of mysticism whereby people were encouraged to try the McDonald's experience. However, over the years, having obtained consumer acceptance, McDonald's felt the need to evolve its communication strategy. Hence from trying to encourage people to visit them, they tried to move on to making McDonald's a regular experience. New ads were run with the tag line 'Toh aaj McDonald's ho jaye'. Here they were talking about an everyday experience, not the first time visit. It was an encouragement to their customers to visit them more often with their family and enjoy their time out.

The experience aspect was reinforced through its ad campaign where you have a small boy in an uncomfortable situation, unable to remember a poem. Once he enters a comfortable atmosphere (in McDonald's) everything fell into place for the kid.

In 2003 the company felt the need to focus on building its brand. It launched an advertisement campaign with the tag line 'I'm lovin' it' in the Indian subcontinent. The campaign was launched in India from 5 October 2003, and was used concurrently in 100 nations across the world. As a result of this campaign, it expected to improve its revenues in India by 15%.

Media Strategy   McDonald's focused more on the electronic media since most of their outlets are placed in big cities, which are visited by good number of people from the neighbouring towns. Hence, their target segment can be effectively reached through the electronic media. McDonald's ads talk about emotions, family ties, and fun, and all these have a high visual appeal. Its management believes that advertisements create more impact if they are seen and heard at the same time. The fun-filled atmosphere which customers can identify with when in McDonald's can be created only on the electronic media. McDonald's does not generally use the print media.

Promotional Activities Aimed at Kids
World over McDonald's has positioned itself as a family restaurant and children have been an integral part of its promotion focus. It tries to ensure that its restaurants are child friendly where children feel comfortable and the entire family can come and have a good time. In the 1990s India saw a major shift to nuclear families. When there were more joint families, it used to be the head of the family who used to take most decisions. In smaller families, everybody's opinion started mattering, whether it was for buying a fridge or a TV or whether it was for going out. The child became an integral part in purchase decision-making. Today, the child does influence the decisions of parents as has been proved by research. Hence, focusing on kids gelled well with the sociological profile of its target customers.

Keeping kids in mind, McDonald's did away with sombre colours in favour of rich, vibrant ones. Even the paintings that once tended to be abstract were replaced with things children could relate to. McDonald's runs promotional schemes that involve children. For instance,

some time back, they had organized a Happy Meal Carnival in all their restaurants, where a child could pick a toy of his choice from among 45 toys and win amazing prizes every time. The focus of this promotion was to enhance the family experience.

Recently, McDonald's redesigned its 'Happy Meal' programme with new marketing activities within McDonald's restaurants across the country. The objective behind the move was to engage customers with innovative experiences while providing them with McDonald's products within its restaurants.

For this purpose, McDonald's India entered into a tie-up with Hewlett-Packard (HP) whereby on the purchase of a 'Happy Meal', a mother was able to get a picture clicked with her child free of cost and take home happy memories. It was designed to be a fun-filled activity, where the mom dresses up her child in a costume in one minute. If it is a boy, the costume is 'Galidor' and if it is a girl, she has to don the 'Hello Kitty' costume.

As part of the new Happy Meal programme, McDonald's India also provided an option of substituting aerated beverage (Coke) with a small McShake for Rs 8 or more. Apart from this, it has created a platform for offering an affordable menu called 'Happy Price Menu' whereby McDonald's products such as McAloo Tikki, Chicken McGrill, Pizza McPuff, and Soft Serve Small (hot fudge and strawberry) would all be priced at Rs 20 each, all inclusive of taxes. In order to create awareness about the new marketing activities, McDonald's has launched the 'I'm loving it' campaign on television to show that any small excuse is a good enough reason to come to McDonald's. There are six such 'excuses' or 'bahanas' that are planned to be aired.

Juhi Chawla: A date with McDonald's

What does Juhi Chawla do when she's in a hurry and needs a quick bite? Why, go to Mickey Dee's, of course. And that's slang lingo for McDonald's. She's already checked out the outlet at Linking Road and CST in Mumbai. And she wanted to check out the new one at Charni Road. So, in she rushed to her new BMW with hubby Jay and drove down to the joint for a veg burger and a Coke. Of course, the star sat in her car while gentleman Jay went out to get her meal. And then Juhi had her own theory on why you should eat a veg burger while it is still hot. 'Because it tastes like rubber when it's cold,' the Chirpy Chawla informed us. As if we didn't know already. But we'll keep it in mind. Maybe, the food trivia experts will be interested.

Source: News clipping from Times of India, April 23, 2004.

Beef Scoop!

Political activists staged a demonstration before the head office of the McDonald's in South Delhi protesting the alleged use of beef flavouring by the international fast food giant in its French fries. The party later submitted a memorandum addressed to the Indian government, demanding closure of all the outlets across the country stating that in a country where 80% of the population worships the cow, one cannot go on with this kind of a controversy. The Store Manager, Thane, stated that the company had suffered losses to the tune of Rs 20 lakhs due to the ransacking of the outlet in Thane. 'The agitators', the Store Manager stated, 'should have discussed the reports that first came in stating that McDonald's vegetarian products contained beef extracts. It was too early to decide whether to file any cases against the protesters'.

McDonald's Clarifies

The McDonald's in India soon after issued a clarification asserting that none of its products, including French fries, contained any beef or pork extract. McDonald's India had taken adequate precautions to avoid untoward incidents in all its outlets in the country, it said.

'All our restaurants are open. We have taken all precautions,' the Managing Director of the McDonald's said. Dismissing any negative effect on its sales, the Managing Director added, 'In India we don't serve any beef or pork in our menu as we are extremely sensitive to the Indian culture and religious sentiments.'

McDonald's in India, it was stated, was a locally-owned company and respected the local culture and religious sentiments and will continue to do so in future. There is complete segregation, the company added, of their vegetarian and non-vegetarian products right from the suppliers' end, till it reaches customers in the restaurants. Finally, the company remarked that the Central Food Technology Research Institute tested the products and McDonald's in India was committed to build a relationship of trust with its customers.

Source: www.expressindia.com 2001, May 5.

1. Discuss McDonald's promotion strategy in terms of the promotion and media mix and the nature of campaign. How does it serve the business purpose?
2. Identify and evaluate the different stages of its promotion programme.
3. Analyse McDonald's media strategy in terms of managing negative publicity and suggest alternative promotion strategies to manage such eventualities in future.

References

1. Berman and Evans 1989, *Retail Management: A Strategic Approach*, Macmillan Publishing Company, New York, NY.
2. Lusch and Dunne 1990, *Retail Management*, South-Western Publishing Co., Cincinnati, HO.
3. Levy and Weitz 2002, *Retailing Management*, Tata McGraw-Hill Publishing Company Ltd, New Delhi.
4. Chatterjee, P. 2003, 'Kids apparel brand Gini & Jony shifts creative account', *Business Line*, Thursday, Nov 06.
5. Shashidhar 2003, 'The Benetton Makeover', *Business Line*, August 27.
6. Narayan, T., 'Cadbury Rolls Out Slew Of Retail', *The Financial Express*.
7. www.retailyatra.com
8. www.financialexpress.com
9. www.excahnge4media.com
10. www.mona-advertising.com
11. Kamath, V. 2003, 'HLL Shakti', *Business Line*, New Delhi, April 25.
12. Parsons, A.G. 2003, 'Assessing the effectiveness of shopping mall promotions: customer analysis', *International Journal of Retail & Distribution Management*, Volume 31, No. 2.
13. Peattie, S. 1998, 'Promotional competitions as a marketing tool in food retailing', *British Food Journal*, Volume 100, No. 6.

11

RELATIONSHIP MARKETING IN RETAILING

Learning Objectives

- To understand the concept of relationship marketing and how does it apply to the retail sector

- To understand the various types of relationship marketing efforts

- To analyse the nature of customer service as part of relationship marketing efforts

- To understand the nature and role of loyalty programmes in building and maintaining relationship with customers

- To analyse and compare loyalty programmes across sectors

- To appreciate the role of employees in building and maintaining customer relationships

Introduction

Relationship marketing refers to all marketing activities directed towards establishing, developing, and maintaining successful relational exchanges. The theories and concepts of relationship marketing draw upon a number of distinct areas including service quality, services marketing, customer retention economics, and issues related to interpersonal and social interaction. However, the practice of relationship marketing is as old as marketing and selling.

The relationship marketing philosophy suggests that, at a macro level, retail organizations should consider their impact across a broad range of market relationships in the value chain.

These markets are customers, local bodies (govt and non-govt), suppliers, and internal customers (employees). All these markets require adequate attention and importance from the retail units to build a profitable and fruitful relationship. A specific marketing strategy is also needed to address groups within these markets. The objective of relationship marketing is to attract, maintain, and enhance customer relationships with the existing and potential customer. Many retailers and marketers have now acknowledged the relevance of relationship marketing in retail strategy.

Relationship marketing is implemented through various components such as rewards, customer services, and involvement of customers in planning and execution of retail strategy. Retail stores that enact a system of rewards but neglect to have a focus on customer service fail. Only those retailers that deliver genuine benefits, based on intimate knowledge about their customers, and create a 'customer-first' mentality at all levels of their service reap the ultimate benefit: customer loyalty.

Relationship marketing, at a theoretical level, emerged in the 1990s and has ever since become an important marketing tool due to the compulsions of competition, globalization, and the emergence of more knowledgeable and demanding customers. In consumer products marketing, it is the function of retailing that has attracted the most obvious interest in the development of relational strategies. In the organized retail sector, the popularity of store loyalty cards is provided as an evidence of the wide take-up of relationship marketing in this field. It comes as no surprise that retailers, today, are interested in relational strategies.

The intimate nature of the relationship the industry shares with the ultimate consumer (compared to businesses further back in the distribution chain) suggests that the closer the retailers get to the customers, the better they can provide the services the customers seek.

The 'moment of truth' in consumer goods and services marketing is seen as that point when the consuming public comes face-to-face with the point of supply. As it is the retailer who most often manages this interaction and who, historically, has gone beyond the mere 'service

Indicators of Effective Relationship Marketing in Retailing

- A high level of trust between consumer and retailer
- A high level of commitment between consumer and retailer
- A long time horizon (and length of relationship)
- Open communication channels between both parties with free exchange of information
- Retailer having the consumer's interest at heart
- A commitment to quality for both parties
- An attempt by the retailer to favourably lock-in or retain the customer

encounter', their potential interest in relational strategies becomes even more apparent.

The retailers or marketers need to have a better understanding of customers at an individual level. They should provide to the consumers specific product-related information and deliver goods targeted to their specific needs. Through this, marketers develop long-term annuity streams that translate into worthwhile profits.

Customer service is a vital part of relationship marketing. High level of customer service and satisfaction forces the suppliers and customers to have high 'switching costs'. Customer commitment is crucial for market share retention of any product, brand, or store, which is the result of effective relationship marketing. A customer who has committed loyalty to a single seller for a return of some 'valued reward' is not going to satisfy a competitor's grab for additional sales.

The Evolution of Relationship Marketing

Customer relationship management (CRM) had its origins in two unrelated places. One was in the US where it was driven by technology. Under the direction of marketers, information technology and statistical algorithms were developed to increase the efficiency and effectiveness of selling what a company makes. This popularly came to be referred to as database marketing. CRM systems such as call centres, websites, customer service and support teams, and loyalty programmes were used to manage the relationship with customers.

The second place where the CRM concept developed was in business to business(B2B) marketing in Scandinavia and northern

Europe. The IMP (Industrial Marketing and Purchasing) Group has been instrumental in developing our understanding about the nature and effects of building long-term, trust-based relationships with customers. These are managed by the marketing and sales departments.

They may be based as much on the structural ties between companies as they are on personal relationships among managers. Here, the emphasis is on understanding customer needs and then solving problems or delivering benefits that create demonstrable customer value. While information technology is important in this style of CRM, it is designed to support rather than drive the customer relationship. The types of relationship that develop here are often deep and meaningful—for both the retailers and the customers involved.

In the latter half of the 1990s, the focus of database marketing began to shift to relationship marketing. Marketers and retailers started using improved information technology to regularly communicate with a firm's customers and to base product offerings as per the consumer's buying behaviour.

Computer linkages aid communication among channel members and also have the added effect of creating a relationship between a buyer and a seller. There is an economic and non-economic incentive for both entities to remain committed to the relationship.

Relationship marketing in retailing has emerged out of two major considerations:

1. at a macro level, the recognition that marketing influences a wide range of areas including customer, employee, supply, internal, referral, and 'influencer' markets such as the governmental and financial markets; and
2. at the micro level, the recognition that the nature of interrelations with customers is changing. The emphasis is on moving from a transaction focus to a relationship focus.

Relationship marketing is different from transactional marketing. The differences between transactional marketing and relationship marketing are given below.

Transactional marketing	Relationship marketing
Focus on single sale	Focus on customer orientation
Orientation on product features	Orientation on product benefits

contd

contd

Transactional marketing	Relationship marketing
Short-time scale	Long-time scale
Little emphasis on customer service	High customer service emphasis
Limited customer commitment	High customer commitment
Moderate customer contact	High customer contact
Quality is a concern of production	Quality is the concern of all

Thus, relationship marketing is different from the old concept of marketing, which used to be based more on increasing the customer base. Relationship marketing focuses on using relational strategies to acquire customers, retain them, and enhance relationship with them. In fact, as per Pareto's Law, 80% of the total sales comes from 20% of the customers, and, thus, relationship marketing attempts to optimize the resources for the retailer by retaining the most profitable of the customers.

The retailing industry plays an important role in the success of relationship marketing as it serves as the major link between the supplier and customers. Therefore, it engages, maintains, and enhances the relationship with the ultimate entity of the value chain, which in turn determines the success of all the members of the value chain. The retailers have always acknowledged the importance of long-term relationship with customers in their business.

Relationship Marketing Strategies in Retailing

Relationship marketing (RM) strategies refer to any effort that is actively made by a seller towards a buyer, and is intended to contribute to the buyer's customer value above and beyond the core product and/or service efforts received, and can only be perceived by the buyer after continued exchange with the seller. Hence, RM strategies attempt to provide benefits to the buyer above and beyond the core service performance.

For instance, many traditional Indian retailers treat their regular customers in a warm and personal way and also provide them with special benefits in terms of home delivery, discounts, etc. These benefits are an attempt to provide benefits above and beyond the core service performance.

Relationship marketing strategies could be a combination of one or all of the following benefits:

- Personalization benefits
- Special treatment benefits
- Rewards
- Communication benefits

Fig 11.1 shows the components of relationship marketing strategies.

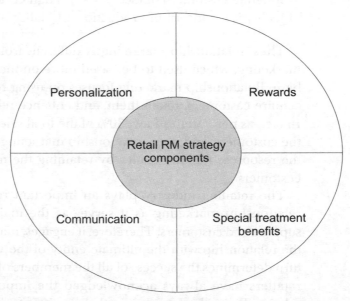

Fig. 11.1. Components of retail relationship strategy

Personalization

Personal exchanges between buyers and sellers are important in influencing the quality of relationship. This is by no means surprising given the fact that relationships are inherently social processes. In certain situations, buyers may develop buyer–seller relationships resembling personal friendships. There are certain 'personalized shoppers' who highly appreciate personal contact in the store. In fact, the social interaction afforded by shopping sometimes works as a prime motivator for some consumers to visit retail establishments. These persons consider retail encounters as valuable sources of social contact.

The term personalization describes the social content of the interaction between service employees and their customers. Personalization refers to the way in which employees relate to customers as people—cold and impersonal at one end, and warm and personal at the other. Consequently, personalization can be regarded as a means of showing recognition and respect for the other party. Examples of social relationship benefits include feelings of familiarity, personal recognition, friendship, and social support. One of the suggested ways of valuing a buyer's uniqueness as an individual is to address him by his name as people feel good when someone remembers their names at a later point in time. Sales practitioners often stress the importance of remembering and using customers' names. Other indicators of personalization efforts are employees' attempts to get to know a customer as a person, their efforts to engage in friendly conversations, and their exhibition of personal warmth. This corresponds to the feeling of 'being included in the communication process' and of 'being liked and treated with respect'.

Personalization leads to a positive impact in terms of increasing trust in the seller/store, customer satisfaction with the relationship, and repeat purchase.

Special Treatment Benefit

Consumer focus and selectivity, i.e., all consumers do not need to be served in the same way, is a key aspect of relationship marketing. If a consumer receives personalized, customized service from retailer A but not from retailer B—and if this service is valued—then the consumer will be less likely to leave retailer A for B. Customers, generally, perceive such customization efforts as preferential treatment not normally provided to the other customers.

The retailers can distinguish between at least two identifiable customer segments: loyal customers and non-loyal customers. Differentiating between loyal and non-loyal buyers enables a seller to address a person's basic human need to feel important. Most retailers use core service upgradation and service augmentation as ways to provide special treatment benefits to customers in return for their loyalty.

Differentiation refers to the fact that loyal customers are provided with extra recognition in terms of better service and additional efforts that are not being made to other, non-loyal customers. By not differentiating between loyal and non-loyal customers, retailers waste resources in over-satisfying less profitable customers, while under-satisfying more valuable, loyal customers.

Communication Benefits

Communication is often considered as a necessary condition for the existence of a relationship. A seller's communication with a buyer conveys his interest in the buyer and serves to strengthen the seller's relationship with him.

Efforts to 'stay in touch' with the customers have been identified as the key determinants of relationship enhancement in retailer–customer relationship. It is generally recognized that buyer–seller relationships become stronger when the ease and volume of exchange between buyers and sellers increase.

The intense levels of buyer–seller communication (1) increases the probability of discovering behaviours that generate rewards, (2) enhances the prediction of behaviour of the other party and clarifies each other's roles, (3) leads to easier discovering of similarities between parties, and (4) encourages feelings of trust, special status, and closeness.

Generally, communication strategies as part of relationship marketing efforts refer to directed communication to the customers as against mass-media communication, which does not afford selectivity. However, it does not include face-to-face interaction, which forms part of the personalization efforts by the retailer. Many retailers adopt direct mail, e-mail, telephone, and SMS as means to interact with their loyal customers or members of loyalty programmes.

Rewards

Providing customers with tangible rewards is often referred to as 'level one relationship marketing'. This level of relationship marketing relies primarily on pricing incentives and money savings to secure customers' loyalty. It implies that clients earn extra based on purchasing performance. As opposed to the previously discussed relationship efforts, rewarding efforts are of a more functional, economic nature.

Psychologists have long been interested in the role of rewards in behavioural learning and modification. According to Skinnerian exchange theory, any behaviour that is rewarded will tend to be repeated, whereas behaviour that is punished is likely to be curbed. Since various types of consumer rewarding programmes imply reinforcements that are promised and provided, consumers can be persistently conditioned for long periods of time as a result of receiving rewarding relationship efforts.

Frequent flyer programmes, customer loyalty bonuses, free gifts, personalized discount coupons, and other point-for-benefit 'clubs' are examples of these efforts. Trying to earn points on such things as hotel stays, movie tickets, and car maintenance would help customers to remain loyal, regardless of service enhancement or price promotions of competitors.

However, it is important to remember that rewarding efforts generally do not lead to sustained competitive advantages given the reality that price is the most easily imitated element of the marketing mix, that some customers may react opportunistically, and that already-loyal customers may be 'unnecessarily' rewarded. Nevertheless, rewarding strategies can lead to sustainable competitive advantages if such strategies are not short-term promotional give-aways, but planned and implemented parts of a larger loyalty management strategy.

Rewards should be designed to promote long-term behaviour and discourage short-term deal-seeking behaviour. Rewarding efforts refer to structured and planned marketing efforts that should encourage loyal behaviour, distinguishing it from short-term oriented sales promotions.

Relationship Marketing in the Organized vs. Unorganized Retail Sector

Broadly the organized retail sector can be divided into two segments: in-store retailers, who operate in fixed point-of-sale locations, located and designed to attract a high volume of walk-in customers, and non-store retailers, who reach out to the customers at their homes or offices.

The organized retailers provide various standardized services to their customers. Large retail formats with high quality ambience and courteous and well-trained sales staff are the distinguishing features of these retailers. In most of the cases, they have a wide range of merchandise stocked with them so that the customers can have their pick.

Also, in most cases, customers are required to choose from the available items themselves and forward all the merchandise to a cashier. These retailers have a wide reach and cater to customers of a very large geographical area. People visit these stores not only for shopping but also for having a nice time outside their homes.

The unorganized retailers, especially in India, comprise the *kirana* or small independent stores located in neighbourhood centres and central business districts of a city. These stores have a limited reach in the sense that people living in a particular locality visit stores in their own colony. The USP of these stores is the locational convenience they provide to their customers. They provide customized services to their customers and also go to the extent of procuring merchandise and delivering them to their customers on order.

In the context of Indian traditional retail formats, one can comfortably establish the significance of relationship marketing in the success of a retail store, particularly the relationship between retailers and customers. The existence of a sound relationship between these two entities (retailers and customers) comprehensively suggests the importance of the present unorganized retail network in India in the entire value chain.

The role of retailers is not surely defined in terms of delivering the core goods and services their customers are looking for; they also have to build their image and role in accordance with the needs and purchasing, and usage behaviour of their customer segments. For example, most of the general stores (*kirana*) located in the neighbourhood centres or locality lanes not only extend locational convenience to the customers but also establish a comfortable relationship between shoppers and service providers.

Customers, on a regular basis, inform about their ever-changing needs to the retailers and also provide them with feedback about the products used. On the other hand, retailers conceive their entire product mix according to the needs of their target segment. They may include such services as home delivery, taking order over phone (extending such services for minimal bill), returns and adjustments (even if suppliers do not provide), offering product on order, credit services, etc. to add value to their core products and also to satisfy consumer needs.

It is a common feature of transactions between customers and retailers not to discuss issues such as brand, SKU, price, and quantity to be delivered, as a retailer is used to delivering merchandise according to the given parameters for ages. The retailers in small towns and localities are considered part of the customer's family—these two entities with their respective families regularly interact at social-political gatherings.

Retailers depend for extra resources, to meet the payments of suppliers and company, on their trusted customers, who in turn do not even charge interest on such friendly loans. Such quality relationships help the two parties in economic and non-economic terms to a great extent. One cannot measure the nature and quantum of benefits extended by such relationships in the unorganized sector.

These relationships are not only confined to grocery retailers dealing in convenience goods but also include those selling shopping or speciality goods such as garments, jewellery, and other durables. In such a retail set-up, the retailers have a significant say in the selection of goods—as most of the customers are not well aware of such high-value products. They, therefore, depend on retailers rather than on brands.

Such dependence is the result of the relationship one enjoys with a particular retailer. For example, most of the rural customers prefer to buy such durables from the urban centres, and as they are new to the place, they rely on the advice of their friends, relatives, or the retailer of the product category himself to help them make the right purchase.

The strength of the relationship enjoyed by retailers with customers has provided them with the bargaining power in the value chain, particularly in developing economies where organized retailing is at a nascent stage. Sound relationship between the two is mutually beneficial both economically and non-economically.

Relationship marketing (RM) efforts in terms of personalization, communication, special treatment, and rewards find expression in the form of specific retailer focus on customer service and/or loyalty programmes. Hence, retailers' efforts for personalization, communication, and special treatment benefits are implemented through customer service strategies of retailers (Fig 11.2).

Similarly, communication, special treatment benefits, and rewards are implemented through loyalty programmes—quite popular in the

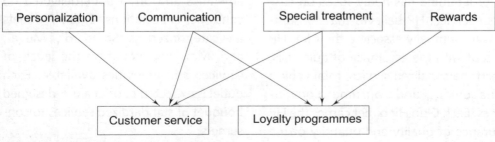

Fig. 11.2   RM efforts and strategies

organized retail sector. In the sections that follow, we discuss implementation of RM strategies through customer service focus and loyalty programmes.

Customer Service in Retailing

Marketing is concerned with the exchange relationships that exist between a retailer and its customers. Quality and customer service are the key elements in this relationship. Today's competitive environment requires a retailer to understand and properly apply the concept of relationship from the perspective of the customer and other channel members. This will ensure that:

- customers strongly believe that the retailer offers good value for money; and
- all the channel members (including the customers) would like to do business with that retailer.

The challenge for a retail unit is to bring three critical areas, namely marketing, customer service, and quality, into closer alignment. Relationship marketing attempts at bringing these three areas together.

Customer Service as part of Club HP Programme

HPCL is India's second largest integrated oil refining and marketing Company. It has launched a loyalty programme by the name of Club HP. The Club HP concept has been developed after an exhaustive research of over a year, which encompassed collating feedback from more than 13,000 respondents from 9 key markets across the country. Besides reward points, the programme has a key focus on customer service. HP believes that consumers will eventually associate the Club HP concept with the assurance of quick fills, expert, personalized service, total vehicle management, and consumer conveniences. Each Club HP outlet carries the HP assurance of quality and quantity of the products on offer. The Club HP concept also recognizes the fact that the consumer today gives high priority to vehicle care at petrol stations and simultaneously expects other value added services. Club HP, which offers the twin benefits of vehicle care coupled with customer care, departs from the recently witnessed trend which gave higher importance to consumer amenities and often underdelivered on consumer expectations. Club HP outlets are categorized as 'Standard', 'Mega', and 'Max' depending on the levels of services and amenities available. Each outlet is expected to offer a pre-designed bouquet of standardized services to consumers.

Peters and Waterman drew a lot of attention to the efforts that top performing companies were placing on 'getting closer to the customer' in their book *In Search of Excellence.* In the financial services sector of the UK, virtually every major player in retail financial services has adopted some form of 'customer care' programme.

Different retailers have different views on the nature and package of customer services offered to the customers. It is essential to have a distinct store ambience and an attractive atmosphere to attract high-income customers to a speciality store, whereas store ambience will not be a major issue for retail stores in neighbourhood centres catering to the middle-income class consumers.

Quality of the product or services is a must as customers will not accept an inferior quality product. Even though a retail store may be very good in developing relationship with customers, with poor quality core products or associated services it cannot exercise relationship marketing. On the contrary, a strong customer service will enhance relationship marketing between a retailer and a customer.

In the same manner, the composition and relevance of the services extended to customers varies across product categories, target segments, and competitive market structures. For example, with the advent of private financial institutes after the liberalization of the Indian economy, the customers have started experiencing a totally new set of services offered to them by banks. New offers comprise right from wide product portfolio to multiple associated services to enhance their comfort and convenience with financial management, which was not the case earlier.

Customer service refers to a rightful blend of activities involving all areas of retail business, which combine to deliver and invoice the store's products or services in a fashion that is perceived as satisfactory by the customer and which advances the store's objectives. It also implies timeliness and reliability of getting products or services to customers in accordance with customers' expectations. Customer service, therefore, can be seen as a process which provides time and place utilities for the customer and which involves pre-transaction, transaction, and post-transaction considerations in relation to the exchange process with the customer.

The provision of quality customer service involves an understanding of what a customer wants and eventually buys, and determining how additional value can be added to the products or services being offered.

However, the implementation of customer service varies considerably from one retail unit to another.

In this context, it is important to discuss the focus on customer service by the small independent retailers in India. The customers favour the small retailer for the low prices and services he offers. A small retailer provides all those services which supermarkets normally do not. This has increased competitiveness in the trade.

The increased competitiveness has improved customer service levels, which are reflected in the wide-ranging facilities being offered by him. Such facilities include telephone order system, credit facilities, home delivery, and branded products procured on order (in case of stock-outs). More importantly, he is available next door; most often the owner himself is present to offer personalized service. In this way, he is able to develop a strong relationship with his customers who, over a period of time, become extremely loyal.

The small retailer has ensured convenience, which is the basic platform on which a supermarket positions itself. Large, organized retailers agree that small retailers are a powerful lobby to stand up against and have been difficult to dislodge. In fact, the small retailers have forced supermarkets to offer the same range of services, such as telephone order and other personalized services, which defeats the very purpose of the supermarkets. Supermarkets generate greater revenues when they get the customer or the traffic into the store as it facilitates impulse purchases.

Customer Service: Managing Gaps Between Expectation and Performance

When customers' expectations are greater than their perceptions of the delivered product or service, customers are dissatisfied and feel that the quality of the retailer's service is poor. Thus, retailers need to reduce the service gap (the difference between customers' expectations and perceptions of customer service) to improve customers' satisfaction with their service. Table 11.1 gives an overview of certain situations that stimulate customers to evaluate the service quality in a retail setting. There are four important dimensions that customers employ to judge the effectiveness of customer services provided by retailers, which are:

1. Knowledge: The difference between consumer expectations and the retailer's perception of customer expectations

2. Standards: The difference between the retailer's perceptions of customers' expectations and the customer service standards it sets

3. Delivery (Actual performance): The difference between the retailer's service standards and the actual service provided to customers

4. Communication: The difference between the actual service provided to customers and the service communicated in the retailer's promotion programme

These four dimensions determine the quality of customer service extended by the retailers or marketers. The retailer's objective is to enhance the performance on account of the aforesaid dimensions by reducing differences in each of the four components of customer service satisfaction.

Thus, the key to improving service quality is to (1) understand the level of service customers expect, (2) set standards for providing customer service, (3) implement programmes for delivering service that meets the standards, and (4) undertake communication programmes to inform customers about the services offered by the retailer.

Table 11.1: Situations stimulating customers to evaluate service quality in retail setting

Situation	More satisfying experience	Less satisfying experience
Unavailable service—customer asks for a particular merchandise but discovers that the retailer does not have it.	Manager apologizes for not having the merchandise and offers to get it for him the next day.	No explanation, no apology and no assistance.
Employee response to slow service—customer waits for two weeks for the ATM card to be delivered when a three-day delivery was promised.	Employee apologizes and promises to allow the use of company's credit card for one year for free.	Employee says after every three days that the card will be delivered in the next three days.
Employee response to service failure —customer	Employee replaces all of them and expresses apologies for the	Employee suggests that they were in a good shape when customer

contd

contd

Situation	More satisfying experience	Less satisfying experience
finds a few broken CD covers in the packet and returns them asking for a replacement.	inconvenience caused.	left store and that the customer damaged them and is trying to fool the retailer.
Response to a special need—customer comes into the store with a lot of luggage and says he cannot keep them out.	Employee offers him a cart to keep the luggage and asks a helper to accompany the customer while he is shopping.	Employee suggests customer keeps the luggage outside or come some other time when he does not have any luggage.
Response to admitted error—customer leaves a bag in store after making purchases.	Employee notifies the customer and then delivers the bag to customer's place.	Employee waits until customer discovers the bag is missing and returns to store to get it.
Attention paid to customer—customer has problems locating a particular size of shirt and asks for assistance.	Employee accompanies him to the place where he can get the desired shirt and patiently answers all his queries.	Employee acts as if customer is a bother and just points out the place for him.

Knowledge Gap   The most critical factor in providing effective and efficient customer service to the consumers is that the retailers or marketers need to have comprehensive knowledge of customers' expectations. Lack of accurate information about customers' need and expectation leads to faulty preparation of retail strategy. This lack of information can result in poor decisions, which might leave a bad impression on the customers who visit the retail store.

For example, a grocery store may put everything on display so that a customer chooses what he wants, but it may fail to realize that customers in the locality prefer being served personally. Therefore, what the store should have done is to keep staff to take orders from the customers and serve them over the counter. To develop a better understanding of customer expectations, retailers and marketers need to:

- undertake customer research,
- increase interaction between retail managers and customers, and
- improve communication between managers and employees who provide customer service.

Bharat Petroleum: Focus on Courteous Service

Bharat Petroleum (BP) believes that customers choose vendors on their value perceptions, which include quality, reliability, and expertise. In this context, it has implemented a Quality and Quantity (Q&Q) Programme, which focuses on courteous service to each customer. Bharat Petroleum feels that each time the customer drives into the forecourt of the petro-station he needs to be recognised and acknowledged, greeted with a smile, made to feel special, and cared for. It may perhaps take three or four fills for the customer to notice an improvement in Q&Q. But his first exposure to exemplary courtesy and personalized service will make an instant impact, resulting in reinforced consumer confidence and positive referrals.

Service Standards   Having gathered information about customers' expectations and perceptions of the products and services provided by the retailers or marketers, the next step is to use this information to set standards (benchmarks) and develop systems for delivering high-quality service.

Service standards should be based on customers' perceptions rather than internal operations. For example, a mail order house may require its employees to answer a phone call after not more than two rings. However, the customer may not be concerned with the time he has to spend over phone. Instead, he may be concerned with the time it takes to deliver the merchandise ordered. The retailers, in order to establish service standards, need to incorporate the following aspects:
- committing their store to providing high-quality service,
- developing innovative solutions to service problems,
- defining the role of service providers (sales people, cashier, designers, etc.)
- setting service goals, and
- measuring service performance.

Performance (The Delivery Gap)   Merely setting standards and communicating the same would not help unless a retailer takes steps to meet the set standards. The retailer must try to deliver in excess of what is expected by the customers to earn their loyalty and, thus, profits. In order to deliver goods and services as promised and expected by customers, retailers need to take the following steps:
- Give service providers the necessary knowledge and skills.
- Provide instrumental and emotional support.
- Improve internal communication and reduce conflicts.
- Empower employees to act in the customers' and firm's best interests.

Communication The fourth key factor that influences the quality of customer service provided by a retailer is the difference between the actual service provided to customers and the service communicated in the retailer's promotional compaign. Overstating the services offered raises customers' expectations. Then, if the retailer does not follow through, expectations exceed perceived service and customers end up dissatisfied.

For example, a supermarket gives calendars to its customers every year on the occasion of New Year. Customers will feel dissatisfied if they do not get the calendar in a certain year. Raising expectations too high might bring in more customers initially, but it can also create dissatisfaction and reduce repeat business if the expected level of service is not maintained.

For example, ICICI Bank has attracted customers through an extensive advertising campaign regarding its innovative product profile, luxurious ambience, helpful sales staff, and above all convenient and effective services. But with the unexpected increase in the number of customers the established infrastructure could not provide the services as communicated to the customers.

Loyalty Programmes

Corporate expenditure on loyalty initiatives are booming: the top 16 retailers in Europe, for example, collectively spent more than $1 billion in 2000.

Bases of Loyalty Programmes

Retailers focus on loyalty programmes since it is believed that:
- Loyal customers are cheaper to serve, therefore more profitable.
- They are willing to pay more for a given bundle of goods.
- They act as effective marketers for the store's offerings.

Loyal Customers are Cheaper to Serve Customers who almost invariably do business in high volumes know their value to the company and often exploit it to get premium service and price discounts. On the other hand, retailers may not be required to invest to attract, maintain, and communicate with loyal customers as they are already predisposed to search for information on new arrivals, services, and developments of the store in comparison to customers who are not loyal.

Loyal Customers are Willing to Pay More for a Given Bundle of Offerings   Many proponents of loyalty programme argue that customers who stick to one business entity do so because the cost of switching to another supplier is too high, which not only comprises economic but also psychological stress. They will, therefore, be willing to pay higher prices up to a point to avoid making the switch or try some other store. Contrary to this, customers expect, and get, some tangible benefits for their loyalty.

A number of theories could explain this phenomenon. First, loyal customers generally are more knowledgeable about product offerings and can better assess their quality. That means they can develop solid reference prices and make better judgements about value than sporadic customers can. Perhaps more fundamental, though, is the fact that customers seem to strongly resent companies that try to profit from loyalty. Finally, it is impossible these days to get away with price differentiation for any length of time. Remember how close Amazon came to destroying its brand when it attempted to charge different prices to different customers for the same DVDs.

They Act as Effective Marketers for the Store's Offerings   The frequent customers are also the strongest advocates for patronization of a particular retail store. The word-of-mouth marketing is very effective, and many stores justify their investments in loyalty programmes by seeking profits not so much from the loyal customers as from the new customers the loyal ones bring in.

Apparently, the link between customer longevity and the propensity to market by word-of-mouth was not that strong. But when we looked at attitudinal and actual loyalty separately, the results were intriguing. Customers who scored high on both loyalty measures were 54% more likely to be active word-of-mouth marketers and 33% more likely to be passive word-of-mouth marketers than those who scored high on behavioural loyalty alone.

The results of a survey of the corporate service provider's customers produced similar if less striking results: customers who exhibited high level of both behavioural and attitudinal loyalty were 44% more likely to be active marketers and 26% more likely to be passive word-of-mouth marketers.

Identifying the Loyal Customers

In order to formulate an effective marketing programme to cater loyal customers profitably and effectively, retailers need to have a proper understanding of their customers' demographic and psychographic characteristics, and shopping behaviour.

But the biggest challenge faced by marketers is to identify or classify the loyal set of customers from the entire set of customers the business is catering to. The most common way to sort customers is to score them according to how often they make purchases and how much they spend. Many tools can be used for that; one of the most familiar is called RFM (which stands for recency, frequency, and monetary value). Mail-order companies, in particular, rely on this tool to assess whether a customer relationship merits further investment.

To understand how methods like RFM work, let us imagine for the sake of simplicity that a retailer focuses on just two dimensions, recency and frequency of purchase. Retailers or marketers measure recency by finding out from their database if the customer bought anything in the last six months, a year ago, or more than a year ago, assigning a higher score to the more recent purchases.

It then measures how frequently the customer made purchases in each of these three time frames—twice or more, once, or never—assigning a score in a similar way. Then it adds the two scores together. In general, the more items a customer purchases and the more recent the transactions, the higher the overall score and the more resources the company lavishes on the person. In actual practice, many companies weight the scores in favour of recency.

Scoring approaches of this kind result in significant over-investment in lapsed customers. Customers who purchase very intensively but only for a brief period have high RFM scores even though they have stopped buying from the store. This results in poor investment on the part of the business due to the assessment tool that they use.

Customer loyalty is the cornerstone of the independent stores that are so prevalent in Indian retail industry. It is an in-built composition of the relationship enjoyed by two entities, namely customers and retailers. The retailers running such stores have accepted long back the importance of maintaining sound relationships with customers.

Bombay Selection

Bombay Selection, an apparel store chain operating in Delhi and Gurgaon, has been in business for a few decades. They have built a loyal clientale over the years. They have a tradition of remembering the names of their regular customers as well as their family details and purchase pref-erences. They do not operate a formal loyalty programme. Rather loyal customers are given upto 10–20% discount on an informal basis. This they feel is far more than what they obtain by way of reward programmes. Besides it saves the effort to record and update points.

They look after their best customers really well because they are the ones who generate the most business and profits. These stores do not have technological support to identify or classify the profitable, loyal, or non-profitable customers, but they depend on manual records or experiences.

At the same time, they know all the customers personally and what they buy regularly and, therefore, anticipate their needs and reward those who generate the most profits. These stores do not insist on loyalty cards or bill receipt to extend benefits in future. They usually prefer to reward their regular and profitable customers on every purchase made without or with limited formalities or paper work.

The other drawback of scoring methods like RFM is that the monetary value component is almost always based on revenue rather than on profitability. Whereas, retailers are more interested in profitability than in revenues. Specifically, we need an estimate of the average profit earned on each customer in any typical purchase period (per period profitability). To estimate a customer's future profitability, simply multiply his average periodic profit figure by the probability that the customer will still be active at the end of that period.

Table 11.2: Choosing a loyalty strategy

Status	Short-term customers	Long-term customers
High profitability	**Butterflies** • Good fit between company's offerings and customers' needs • High profit potential	**True friends** • Good fit between company's offerings and customers' need • Highest profit potential

contd

contd

Status	Short-term customers	Long-term customers
	Actions: • Aim to achieve transactional satisfaction, not attitudinal loyalty • Milk the accounts only as long as they are active • Key challenge is to cease investing soon enough	*Actions*: • Communicate consistently but not too often • Build both attitudinal and behavioural loyalty • Delight these customers to nurture, defend, and retain them
	Strangers • Little fit between company's offerings and customers' needs • Lowest profit potential	**Barnacles** • Limited fit between company's offerings and customers' needs • Low profit potential
Low profitability	*Actions*: • Make no investment in these relationships • Make profit on every transaction	*Actions*: • Measure both the size and share of wallet • If share of wallet is low, focus on up- and cross-selling • If size of wallet is small, impose strict costs controls

Loyalty programmes are the means of encouraging customers to stay and not to switch to a competitor or elsewhere. Loyalty is all about the creation of a continuing perception of comparatively superior value while meeting the changing customer needs and the continued adherence of individual customers.

On this basis, customer loyalty can only exist if there is a competitive market. Unless the customer remains connected, the service provider can do nothing more and cannot profit from adding further value. The basic priority is that the customer stays. The key loyalty drivers identified and patronized by Department's are: quality, service, value, and cleanliness.

For non-retailers, the 'C' would more aptly stand for convenience (e.g., how easy is it to place a catalogue order or a stock trade). Until those four elements are in good shape, it is probably best to defer the introduction of a loyalty programme. Table 11.2 shows the various loyalty strategies.

To qualify, a loyalty programme must:

- Require customers to enroll
- Provide rewards, discounts, or services based on a customer's spending patterns
- Communicate benefits customers can receive from specific purchasing behaviours

Requirements to be Met by Loyalty Programmes

A set of criteria that should be observed when drafting a loyalty programme:

- Enrolments must be voluntary.
- Rights and obligations must be stated clearly and in writing on conclusion of an agreement.
- Information registered must be administered in an ethically proper manner.
- There should be proportional and undifferentiated earning of bonus.
- No rules should be established concerning expiry limits.

Programmes are typically delivered in one of the three following ways:

- *Frequent shopper card without credit linkage:* Shoppers scan card at the time of purchase to get real-time discounts. Cards are often used for making payments, particularly at grocery stores, as against cheques.
- *Store credit card with tiered membership benefits:* Rewards and incentives encourage or reward higher spending levels. Benefits often include 'cardholder only' sales and promotions based on customer's spending levels.
- *Co-branded credit cards (e.g., Visa, MasterCard) with accrued rewards and other benefits based on spending:* Often provide differentiated rebates to consumers based on purchases in store versus elsewhere (e.g., 5% cash back for gas purchases, 1% back for all other purchases).

Classification of Loyalty Programmes

On the basis of ownership and management, loyalty programmes may be classified as multi-sector loyalty programmes, single-operator, multi-partner programmes, and true coalition programmes (Fig 11.3).

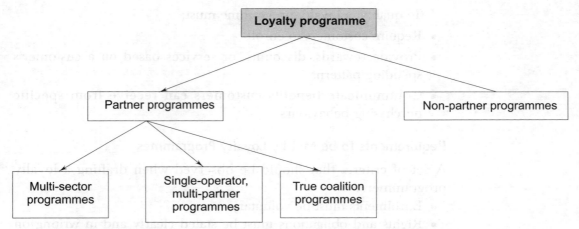

Fig. 11.3   Types of loyalty programmes based on ownership and operation

Multi-sector Loyalty Programmes   There are un-partnered loyalty programmes and partnered programmes (called 'coalitions'). Within the partnered category of programme, there are two main types of multi-partner programmes that have proved their value time and again: true coalition programmes and single operator programmes that include other partners.

Single-operator, Multi-partner Programmes   Tesco's Clubcard is an example of a single-operator programme that involves other partners. The programme is owned and run by Tesco. However, Clubcard holders can collect points when buying from various partners in the programme, such as Alders, Beefeater, Marriott, and National Tyres. Vidal Sassoon is an example of redemption partner.

True Coalition Programmes   For example, Air Miles and Nectar are true coalition programmes. The programme management is independent of any of the partners. The partners have contracts with the operators of the programme to issue and/or redeem the currency of the programme, and only have access to data harvested by the programme through its operator.

Affinity Loyalty Programmes

The important objectives of affinity loyalty programme are:
- Rapid and wide market penetration
- Delivery of attractive and an optimal combination of incentives
- Building multiple communication channels

The success of partnered loyalty programme depends not only on the design and execution of loyalty programme but also the role and terms of the entities involved. The critical factors for the success of partnered loyalty programme are:

- Interest in the programme
- Limited number of cards to carry
- Provision for members to earn points quickly
- Greater variety of incentives (rewards)
- Concentrated, coherent communication and promotions
- Economical on account of time and cost involved in development
- Database run and managed by professionals
- Collaborative marketing campaigns
- Wide penetration

Use of Loyalty Card Data

The retailer loyalty card is of great help to gather data about customers. This provides extensive understanding about customer (e.g., cost insights, customer retention rates at different spending levels, response to offers, and new customer conversion rates), followed by optimal marketing action and follow-up analysis. In other words, a loyalty card is primarily an information card from which follows better decision-making in both marketing and cost-reduction.

Some business firms realized that the major beneficiary of their loyalty card programmes was not their marketing department but their real estate department that was looking for locations for new stores. For example, not just how far customers travelled to their stores but also how many customers' spending changed as the distance varied. This was of significant importance to the real estate department as they evaluated new store sites.

The information related aspects of loyalty cards are potentially more important than their apparent reason for existence. With the current trend towards micro-marketing, the requirement for highly accurate information at an individual level has increased significantly.

Although loyalty cards have been in existence for a reasonable period of time, there is a sense that the industry is still very much on the edge of the information and targeting opportunities provided by these cards. Loyalty card data is used on a very selective basis in category management and ECR programmes, although most manufacturers would probably like greater access to the information sets.

Coupled with this, the retailers may have difficulties in manipulating data sets due to their size and complexity. In the FMCG markets, even frequently purchased goods have reasonable inter-purchase intervals resulting in the requirement for substantial back data to fully evaluate the purchase patterns. Analysis of the data poses its own problems. If we view loyalty card data as essentially very large, partial, continuous panels, they must have a requirement for similar treatment in order to ensure that the final data sets are accurate.

Examples of issues that should be faced are new and lapsed card holders, multiple card holders in the same store, the accuracy of demographic information, and the treatment and understanding of classic panel concepts such as trial, repeat purchase, and switching.

Loyalty card data gives excellent information about the customer base, that is, the card holders' behaviour in a store. They do, however, omit the non-holders and information on the purchasing outside of the store. In order to address this, it would be appropriate to use existing continuous panel data to match and provide a context for consumers' purchasing behaviour elsewhere.

It is ironic that while loyalty card data is undoubtedly a very effective tool for one-to-one marketing, the data cannot measure loyalty because they lack the competitive context.

Relationship Rewards as Part of Loyalty Programmes

Reward drives behaviour. We teach our pets how to behave by rewarding them when they behave correctly, and by not rewarding them when they do not. Reward the behaviour that you want and do not reward the behaviour that you would like to discourage, and behaviour will follow reward—within reason.

Use of Customer Data

The uses that customer data collected through loyalty cards can be put to are:

- Customer shopping behaviour profiling
- Customer lifestyle and demographic profiling
- Customer product preferences and repertoire
- Customer targeting and differentiation
- Best customer marketing and win-back
- Product category relationships and cross-selling
- Planning and merchandising
- Pricing policies

Source: The Loyalty Guide, 2004

But, paradoxically, while a big reward reinforces desired behaviour better than a small reward, when rewards are discontinued, those who have received big rewards are more likely to return to the old buying pattern than those who received small rewards. So the warning is clear: never let your best customers feel that you are withdrawing privileges from them.

It follows from this that reward is a crucial part of any loyalty programme. It has to be desirable enough to change the behaviour of customers. In fact, if the reward is really well chosen, it will be attractive to the target group of customers, and not attractive to customers who are not really valuable to the business.

It also has to be affordable, and balancing the two sides of the desirability/affordability equation is tricky. Our report examines the key functions of a loyalty reward, offering sound advice on what consumers might value, and what might disappoint them. It also walks you through the properties or attributes that are always found in successful loyalty rewards. There are various types of rewards such as a simple discount, a more targeted discount, points which lead to a gift from a catalogue or later money-off offer, or even extra services. There has to be some means of recognizing each customer at the point of sale.

Department stores such as Saks Fifth Avenue and Neiman Marcus reward their important customers with attractive gifts and other benefits to encourage them to continue being loyal. A retail consultant once remarked that upscale stores are 'shooting for a class of people who spend $6000 for a dress. You have to coddle these people constantly because you cannot afford to lose even a few of them as customers.'

Following are some details of the rewards offered by various retail organizations:

- Neiman Marcus inaugurated retailing's first customer loyalty programme in 1984, InCircle. The members of the programme earn one point for every dollar spent at the store. A minimum of 5,000 points is required to become a member of InCircle Rewards, which includes special privileges alongwith the eligibility to redeem gifts.
- Saks Fifth Avenue recently invited its 40 platinum members (who spend at least $ 10,000 per year) to dinner at a top New York restaurant with their spouses and friends. Among the invited guests were designer Donna Karan, who personally offered to help the guests select their spring wardrobe at Saks.

- Several airlines, including Northwest and Delta, are offering bonus points if you check in for your flight before you get to the airport. The process is simple; you log on, plug in your flight information and reward programme PIN, and print out a boarding pass. The bonus is usually 1,000 points.

Loyalty programmes are known for some of their more obvious effects—such as increase in spending (and therefore customer lifetime value) and better retention—but they can also achieve a number of other things that impact the company's business strategy, operational efficiency, human resources policy, and more. For example, customer acquisition, up-selling and cross-selling, intelligent deselection (getting rid of unprofitable customers), winning back defected customers, selection of new outlet locations, reducing advertising costs, stock planning and merchandising, getting competitive responses right first time, setting pricing policies, building lasting relationships, and enabling true 'best customer marketing'.

The reasoning is simple—as a general rule, retailers have found that the best customers have:

- The lowest defection rates
- The lowest processing costs
- The highest gross profit yields

Customers are loyal or otherwise for many different reasons: some are loyal from choice, some are loyal because both parties have invested time and effort in building a relationship, while some are loyal because their needs are met or exceeded, and others because the relationship is profitable to both sides.

A number of factors play a part in influencing the loyalty and commitment of customers, such as the quality and value of the retailer's core offering, levels of customer satisfaction, 'elasticity' inherent in the sector or product category, other competitors in the market, and even social, demographic, and geographical influences.

Factors for Success of Loyalty Programmes

Some critical factors that govern the success or failure of any loyalty or relationship-based marketing initiative are listed below:

- Do not aim for a quick fix.
- Empower your loyalty team.

- Make it a long-term project.
- Know your customers.
- Acquire new customers.
- Provide attainable, affordable rewards.

- Measure your costs and returns.
- Recover your costs.
- Communicate properly.
- Create barriers for competitors.
- Keep it simple.

A successful programme needs to have participation of all the channels in the customer relationship to attain measurable objectives. A programme needs to have the following characteristics to attract and meet the objectives of a loyalty programme:

- *Visibility:* A loyalty programme must be highly visible regardless of the channel. A website can show special offers for programme members, a catalogue can feature the programme prominently and shoppers in the store should be asked if they would like to join. Cross-promotional materials should be present and easily obtainable.
- *Simplicity:* To succeed, a loyalty programme must be easy to use in all channels. Minimize the fine print; the more the customers have to figure out, the less they like the programme.
- *Value:* The balance of reward and recognition must establish value in the customer's mind and motivate incremental purchases. Programme rewards should be credited regardless of where the customer prefers to shop. And while the price of merchandise should be consistent across all channels, do not be afraid to offer incentives to encourage customers to try a new shopping experience.
- *Trust:* Keep the promises made by the loyalty programme. If the promise is for a personalized, highly valued service, do not bombard programme participants with meaningless offers that obviously are available to everyone.
- *Communication:* Communication with the loyal customers plays an important role at every stage from engagement to maintenance. There are many more communication channels available today than there were before the rise of interactive and electronic media such as the Internet and mobile telecommunications.

Communication with consumers and other businesses can take place by mail, telephone, fax, text message (SMS), multimedia message (MMS), e-mail, instant messaging (IM), voice over IP (VoIP), Internet chat rooms, websites and bulletin boards, and other Internet-based systems including video conferencing and meeting sharing systems such as the Microsoft (www.microsoft.com) Netmeeting service. Each has different cost implications to the business, and different perceived benefits to the consumer.

Building any degree of customer loyalty online, whether through websites or through e-mail, is a challenge. Although many loyalty programmes have a Web presence in the form of an online account management interface, a reward redemption catalogue, or a sign-up form, those do not represent truly Internet-based loyalty.

For example, the UK's Nectar coalition loyalty programme has a very useful and consumer-friendly website but the programme itself is essentially a bricks-and-mortar retail programme. In contrast, the online auction site eBay is an online business that has set up a number of loyalty and incentive initiatives, which aim to drive desired patterns of behaviour through its website. Both are successful within their respective fields.

Sector-specific Loyalty Programmes

Different sectors are viewing and approaching loyalty differently, and are at different stages of development, both in business terms and in the minds of consumers. Moreover, there are regional, national, and international variations and forces at work, which drive and determine the direction of loyalty programme in specific geographical areas of operation.

Supermarkets and General Retail Supermarkets face intense competition, not only from other supermarkets but also from warehouse clubs, supercentres (like Wal-Mart), and convenience stores. Today, leading supermarkets are among the most sophisticated retailers in the world. They lead most other sectors in customer data collection and analysis, in stock management, in level of customer service and in retail innovation. Which sector will be the first to widely adopt RFID technology? Or 'smart' shopping carts? Or self-scanning of purchases? Or in-store kiosk-based information and sales points? Most likely the supermarkets.

In general retail in the organized sector, the pressing need now is to focus on what drives loyalty programmes, what customers actually prefer, and what the future is likely to bring. Most retailers accept that they need to know more about their customers, and that the knowledge should be centrally recorded so that it is available to employees when they need it.

In the unorganized sector, largely populated by small independent retailers, the focus is on providing loyal customers with personalized service and preferential treatment. There is no formal rewards system. However, regular customers are provided with discounts on an informal basis. In fact, in certain high-risk and high-relevance product categories like jewellery and high-end consumer durables, consumers form strong relationships with their preferred retailer. At times, the relationship spans generations and is shared by a huge set of relatives. There is a deep sense of trust both ways—in terms of receiving good quality at reasonable prices for the customer and receiving full payment and long-term loyalty for the retailer.

Telecom   The overall telecom market around the world has been volatile over the past two years, with non-telecom firms joining the battle for consumer communications spend—including internet service provision—and governments deregulating the market, and of course the innovation of number portability. In the meantime, firms in the mobile telecoms sector have been developing their offerings beyond communications into the financial services sector, through 'm-payments' and 'm-cash' (mobile payment systems). Airtel's Recharge Rewards Programme and MTNL's loyalty programmes are described below.

Airtel's Prepaid Recharge Rewards Programme   The Recharge Rewards Programme provides extra talk time to the pre-paid subscribers depending upon the recharge option opted for as described below. The scheme was available and open for all existing and new pre-paid subscriber(s) during the period from Aug 6, 2003 March 31, 2004 and only operated in the Kolkata circle.

Under the offer, the subscriber recharging his/her subscription was entitled to an additional percentage of free calling value based on the value of recharge coupon as mentioned below:

- On 4th recharge coupon 4% of the calling value of the 4th recharge coupon
- On 8th recharge coupon 8% of the calling value of the 8th recharge coupon
- On 12th recharge coupon 12% of the calling value of the 12th recharge coupon
- On 16th recharge coupon 16% of the calling value of the 16th recharge coupon

- On 20th recharge coupon 20% of the calling value of the 20th recharge coupon and 20% of the calling value of every subsequent 4th recharge coupon thereafter.

The offer was available on recharge coupons from Rs 300 onwards only. The additional calling value was to be credited to the subscribers' account on recharging with an Airtel prepaid coupon. An automatic SMS confirming the credit of the bonus talk time was to be sent to the subscriber. If a subscriber recharged during the grace period, then his recharge history was to be considered from the programme beginning date for the rewards programme. The bonus talk time earned for recharge on a particular number was to lapse if that number ceased to exist for that particular subscriber.

MTNL'S Schemes to Reward Loyal Customers MTNL has launched schemes rewarding its loyal customers with bonus points that could be redeemed for attractive gifts. The company plans to give points for loyalty, usage, early payment of bills, and for using unified services. MTNL's biggest challenge was to retain customers in view of the increasing competition, hence the launch of the loyalty programme.

Through its new schemes, MTNL will offer incentives such as Internet account for 250 hours, attractive cordless phones and virtual credit cards (VCC) of Rs 1,000. A customer who accumulates 550 bonus points is entitled for a VCC of Rs 108; for 1,100 points he will get a VCC of Rs 216; for 2,700 points the entitlement is either for a VCC of Rs 540 or an Internet account of 100 hours. For 5,400 points, subscribers are entitled for an Internet account of 250 hours or a VCC card of Rs 1,080. For 10,000 points, a customer can get a cordless and customer line identification phone. For 25,000 points, MTNL will give a CDMA connection to the subscriber. All existing customers with no outstanding dues would get 100 bonus points from the day of launch. There will be a special bonus for customers using MTNL services for over a year.

Those who are with MTNL for over five years will get a bonus of 125 points. The subscribers who come back to the MTNL network will get 100 points. Recommending MTNL to any new subscriber would entitle a customer 50 bonus points.

The bonus point system is also expected to encourage the use of MTNL phones. For instance, if a customer makes 1,300 calls in a month, he is entitled to 100 bonus points. A subscriber can earn up to

1,750 points in a month through usage. MTNL hopes that its customers would find these schemes very attractive and, hence, it would be able to maintain a good growth rate in terms of subscribers and revenues.

Travel and Entertainment   A great deal has happened in the travel and entertainment sector in the past few years, with particular emphasis on increasing both the visit frequency and providing compelling offers and gifts to encourage loyalty. Airlines, hotels, restaurants, and even car rental firms have focused on improving customer service and offering more relevant options to encourage consumers to buy more of what they want.

In the following section we discuss the details of the loyalty programme run by PVR in Delhi and its surrounding areas.

PVR CLUB   Priya Village Roadshow (PVR), the company that runs a chain of multiplex theatres in the national capital region (NCR), also operates a loyalty programme for its patrons. It is called the PVR Club. Only members are allowed to buy tickets online. They can even have the tickets delivered to their doorstep, and enter exciting contests and win fabulous prizes. Members also have the option of subscribing to the weekly PVR newsletter with lots of exciting events, movie charts, and news about PVR.

The PVR Club membership is free. To become a member, the concerned person has to just click on the registration link on the PVR home page and fill out a simple form. The user name and password entered by him while registering is required to access the site.

The next level of membership is called the PVR Club Class Membership level. Besides buying tickets online and entering exciting contests to win fabulous prizes, the Club Class Member can also maintain an online account, earn points for every ticket transaction in the loyalty programme, and redeem them against exciting gifts. They also have the option of subscribing to the weekly newsletter. To become a PVR Club Class Member, the concerned person must open his online account with a minimum balance of Rs 500 (using credit card) at the time of registration.

There is also a PVR Kids Club. It is a unique club created specially for kids. It has listings and schedules of all the children's movies and members can book the tickets online. There are special contests for children with great prizes to be won. To be eligible for membership, the kid must be 14 years or below.

Financial Services   Looking at the financial services sector, the industry is at a very peculiar stage of its customer relationship development graph across the world, with much of the most recent progress being made in the United States, Canada, and Europe (including the UK). But even these countries do not have all of the answers yet. In this context, it is important to discuss the role of credit and debit cards as loyalty building tools for the financial services as well as the other retail sectors of the economy.

Credit and Debit Cards as Relationship Building Tools   Co-branded and affinity programmes are usually based on a credit card. They burgeoned in the 1990s. But, while they are still popular with consumers and card issuers alike, the market in some regions has become somewhat mature. A co-branded card is the result of a partnership between an issuing bank and a co-branding partner which could be any commercial organization (such as an airline, automobile association, retailer, insurance company, or motor manufacturer). One example of a co-branded card is the UK's GM Platinum Card issued by HDFC Bank.

An affinity card is similar except that the partner is not a commercial organization, but is generally a non-profit making organization like a club, association, charity, or professional body. One example is the Amnesty International Visa Card issued by the Cooperative Bank. The affinity cards allow the issuer to mine the potential of the database of members of an already formed non-commercial group.

The affinity group itself benefits from extra funds, as a fee is usually paid by each member who enrols for a card, and then a percentage of each transaction's value is also garnered. Most importantly, affinity cardholders feel good because they are positively helping a cause close to their hearts, so they are likely to use the card in preference to other cards they might have.

However, chip-based credit cards (smart cards) open up the field for loyalty programmes. The chip used to handle the financial side of the card has enough space to run other programmes on it as well. This means that not only can the card issuer provide its own loyalty programme, but the card can be used to carry other programmes as well. Visa International has already launched a standard card, entitled VS3, for loyalty schemes and other applications operating on Visa credit and debit cards.

Meanwhile, MasterCard International has also taken steps towards the development of standards for smart card applications and offers development assistance to its card issuers. Although, smart cards in the field of loyalty have been discussed openly for quite some time, the market is still young and there's plenty of room for innovators to succeed.

Use of Co-branded Cards in the Financial Services Industry   Virtually all credit card companies are attempting to offer additional value to their customers by providing co-branded cards. Co-branding with an essential service provider, say a telecom operator, a fuel company, or an insurance company, seems to be an ideal way to create product differentiation and at the same time build customer loyalty.

Co-branded cards offer tremendous value to customers as they are empowered with special value-added offers, such as rebates and discounts to attract new customers, encourage usage, and build stronger ties with customers. Successful co-brands have doubled the spends, resulting from the rewards attraction offered to card holders, which is much more than non-co-branded cards. Co-branded cards also generate higher retention of customers because of the rewards linked to these cards.

The Air Sahara-Visa co-branded card, for example, has been a huge success with Air Sahara customers as it is linked to miles and other special benefits like frequent upgrades to business class. The HDFC believes that co-branded cards definitely go a long way in offering additional value and customer retention. However, credit companies have to react to customer needs while deciding on their co-brand strategy.

However, in spite of the market's inclination towards entering into co-branding strategies and coming up with value propositions for customers, it is important to work out the impact on revenues. With the cluttering of many such schemes, the revenues have not gone up appreciably.

Fuel Retailing   The forecourt sector (fuel retailers, that is, 'petrol' to the Briton or 'gasoline' to the American) was one of the first sectors to become involved in loyalty programmes. In fact, in the early 1990s, some people equated loyalty programmes with forecourt programmes. But the market soon tarnished as consumers began to expect tokens or coupons on the forecourt, and very little 'interest factor' was added over time.

Now, to be successful, a forecourt loyalty programme has to do far more than simply provide a small rebate that can be saved up and redeemed for a reward once or twice a year. To attract and hold the customer's attention has become increasingly difficult—it has to offer genuine benefits that remain interesting over time.

BPCL has launched some new products, such as a new fuel blend, multiple facilities at its outlets, and a new partnership to reach out to its best and loyal customers in a targeted, customized manner.

This was relationship marketing paying off in the best way possible as the economics of going direct started to become attractive in addition to the immense marketing benefits. For instance, when BPCL launched its high performance fuel 'Speed' in mid 2002, it could immediately make an offer to specific segments of PetroBonus members who fit the Speed target audience profile, offering them bonus PetroMiles for fueling up with Speed. The luxury of having a database of members, an open channel to communicate with them, and an accepted and widely used programme currency mechanism to reward them proved an enormous advantage to BPCL in marketing many products and services.

Hospitality Industry   A hospitality chain should have a mix of both kinds of properties (business and leisure), small as well as large, priced in different ranges, to allow a guest to redeem their points as per his disposition. Business travellers earn their points at business destinations at the cost of the company, while they redeem points during their leisure travel, which is often at their own expense; thus, the chain strength with wider options should be the prime focus before a business traveller signs on the dotted lines.

Most of the loyalty programmes have business travellers around 90%. The percentage again depends on different programmes and their structures. Business travellers must review the areas or cities of their travel, whether national or international.

They are not likely to get many benefits from stand-alone chains, as compared to chains with properties scattered all over the world. Another important factor that should be checked for is the user friendliness and communication of the programme, which is necessary. A programme should be accessible and well administered. Hotels do have leisure hotels, but business hotels are revenue generators. Most loyalty programmes are geared for the business traveller.

Business travellers are frequent travellers, who have their company booking them into hotels all across the world. In case they make a decision to be loyal to a particular chain, the hotel's loyalty programme subsequently rewards them with items for personal effects and various rewards listed under a respective programme, which are directly proportionate to the number of points earned.

It makes better sense to be part of a loyalty programme and enjoy its perks with no added effort. Besides, for all business travellers such programmes are extremely beneficial when business travellers wish to redeem their points on a leisure stay. This way they can enjoy the best of both worlds.

The Marriott programme, especially the 'gold passport', is internationally acclaimed as the best such programme worldwide. The Taj started its loyalty programme only last year, but now that the teething problems are over, given a year their programme will be at par, if not the best.

A chain that has tentatively decided on the number of people it wants on the programme, out of the entire database, helps it to have an idea about the target in terms of number of guests/customers to enroll and to fix a reward percentage that the traveller would like to part with. The management focuses on enrollment of as many business travellers as possible so that the base is firm.

Simultaneously, this provides estimates regarding the cost of running the programme and, most importantly, to have the right software in place so as to track the points at each and every hotel in the chain. For this, administrative machinery and call centres have to be flawless. Then it would get into the execution stages, where a company needs to communicate the intricate details and reward factors of the programme.

The programme may extend rewards of various kinds; for example, hotel stays, merchandise, upgrades, bottle of wine, and the like are packaged together and a loyalty programme is prepared. Waving off the membership fee can also allure guests. As a guest builds his percentage points, chances of him switching to other hotels get remote. Loyalty programmes also target at point accumulation, which builds a wall around the customer and increases the cost of switching.

There are various add-ons, but primarily they all focus on making the guests feel more at home and more important than they would feel at any other facility. The common add-ons are upgrades, discounted tariffs on weekends, and special promotions. From time to time, depending on the strategy and game plan, one keeps adding on and taking off from the programme.

In the section that follows we discuss the loyalty programme of Taj Group of Hotels.

Taj Hotels InnerCircle Programme   Taj InnerCircle is a privileged guest programme run by the Taj Group of Hotels. It is a rewards programme with two options—the Epicure Plan and the Taj InnerCircle Junior League.

The Taj InnerCircle programme has three membership levels, with a member beginning as a Blue member and moving up the membership ladder to Silver and then on to the premium Gold membership level. The more one stays and dines at The Taj, the easier it gets to move up from Blue through Silver to Gold. The level of service benefits increases with each membership level. A guest enrolls as a Blue member. The Blue membership is valid as long as there are eligible transactions worth 100 points in a two-year period.

To move up to Silver, 250 points need to be earned in a continuous period of 60 days. To retain the Silver status, 1,000 points need to be accrued in every subsequent period of 24 months. To move upwards to the Gold tier, the highest level, 2,000 points need to be earned in a

Membership levels	Minimum requirement/ upgrade	Renew	Incentive value
Blue	N/a	100 points in 24 months.	Earn points at the rate of 1 Taj InnerCircle point for every Rs 100 spent (net after taxes)
Silver	250 points in a continuous period of 60 days	1,000 points in 24 months	Points accrual at the rate of 1point for every Rs 80 spent (net after taxes)
Gold	2,000 points in 12 months	1,000 points in 12 months	Gold card members earn points at the rate of 1 point for every Rs 80 spent (net after taxes)

12-month period. To renew the Gold membership, 1,000 points need to be accrued in every subsequent 12-month period.

Benefits for Blue Members: Points are earned against charges accrued on room stay, restaurant charges, mini bar, and room service as well as usage of telephone, fax, laundry, and business centre facilities. Rewards are for points accrued ranging from 1,000 points to 25,000 points.

Benefits for Silver Members:
- Priority wait list, easier check-in and check-out facilities
- Double occupancy at no extra cost
- 10% discount on published tariff at all Taj Leisure Hotels
- 10% discount on telecommunication facilities
- 15% discount on laundry services
- 10% discount on use of the business centre facilities
- Fruits and flowers in the room
- Free entry to select Taj Night Clubs on Wednesday nights—these Taj Night Clubs include Incognito (Taj Bengal, Kolkata), Insomnia (Taj Mahal, Mumbai), My Kind Of Place (Taj Palace, New Delhi), and Club Polaris (Blue Diamond, Pune)
- Priority reservation at Taj restaurants
- Complimentary use of health club and steam or sauna facilities during your stay at Taj hotels

Benefits for Gold Members:
- All Silver service benefits
- Non-alcoholic welcome drink
- Preferred daily newspapers at metro hotels

The Epicure Plan—an optional add onto the Taj InnerCircle—is an exclusive dining plan that offers Taj InnerCircle members special privileges and rewards, based on food and beverage spends. The members of the plan receive a 'Smart' membership card, which is embedded with a microprocessor that allows for instant recording, updating, and redemption of points. The members earn Epicure points for expenditures incurred on food and beverages by visiting Taj restaurants in India.

A part of the Taj InnerCircle, Taj InnerCircle Junior League is the frequent guest programme of Taj Hotels Resorts and Palaces. Specially designed for kids between 5 and 12 years old, the Taj InnerCircle

Junior League is a fun way to enjoy the Taj experience. The child has the opportunity to participate and learn in interesting ways at the many Taj workshops conducted at the hotels that include theatre acting, dancing, painting, voice modulation, computers, swimming, karate, yoga, and cricket, besides others.

As a Taj InnerCircle Junior League member, a child will earn points every time he or she, with or without family, stays or dines at any of the participating hotels, coffee shops, or cake shops. These points can be exchanged for holidays at exciting Taj destinations or gifts like delicious chocolates, special stationery, walkmans, and music synthesisers. The various fun choices find mention in the Rewards Booklet.

Loyalty Programmes in the Franchise Retail Format   The franchise retail format faces a distinct set of challenges in the successful launch and operation of a loyalty programme. While the coordinated planning and execution of marketing campaign is required from the entities, parties to the loyalty programme, funding issues relating specifically to loyalty programmes in the franchise retail format become a challenge and a constraint for their successful implementation.

In most franchise agreements, franchisees pay a fee to the franchisor. This fee traditionally supports mass-marketing activities such as television, radio, print advertising, and promotional activities throughout the year. The consolidation of these marketing efforts through the franchisor is generally recognised as being a far more efficient and effective method than any single franchisee could have achieved independently. In the same manner, the effective and efficient management of the loyalty programme depends on the franchisor in the franchising format. The major points of difference between the two entities are regarding resources for the programme and management of the loyalty 'breakage' or point value.

Barista Launches 'Brewards'

Barista, the speciality coffee bar chain, has launched a loyalty programme, 'Brewards', for its regular customers. The coffee bar issues smart cards to its loyal customers, which they can use for discounts.

The Coffee Card will offer flat discounts of 12.5% for students and 10% for others. Customers can also accumulate 'value points' and redeem them for free beverages. Apart from this, those with the cards will also get invited to various events. Bangalore is the first city to get the Coffee Cards and these can be used at all outlets there. They claim to have a target of issuing 10,000–15,000 cards and that eventually the loyalty programme will be offered in other cities too.

Managing Loyalty Programmes

Loyalty programmes involve a good amount of resources such as money, human resources, technology, etc. The return value on loyalty programme is well documented and easy to understand, but the real return value of retention in loyalty programmes takes time; most return on investment (RoI) models for loyalty programmes take at least a year to show any results.

The promise of a strong RoI in loyalty is an output of the investment made in the initial period of the loyalty programme. The franchisor, in order to raise the participation of franchisee in the programme and its returns, would expect them to share the cost of the programme. It will not be in favour of the franchisor to conceive and operate the programme by employing its own resources.

The franchisor needs to understand the business model of the independent retailer, in particular the one followed by them before joining franchising agreement. As independent owners of their retail unit, they most likely practice their own loyalty and customer service initiatives established for generations. For example, leading independent jewellers provide major discounts at the spot to their regular customers on every purchase made, as they know they will visit their store for big purchases during marriages and festivals. In the same manner many of the Indian independent retailers, across product categories, prefer their own informal customer services and reward schemes. Therefore, it sounds illogical to retailers to contribute towards the common loyalty programme. There are also issues regarding the basis on which the contributions will be made by the franchisee outlets under the franchisor.

In such circumstances, the franchisors need to be aware of the importance of consistency of rewards and customer services from outlets under one brand name. They can also highlight that such provisions will give them an opportunity to increase the number of customers shopping at their store and thereby increase their profits.

Managing the Loyalty 'Breakage' or Point Value

Most loyalty programmes have a significant amount of 'breakage' that is earned but never redeemed. Breakage or currency in loyalty programmes does not occur for a year or more after a transaction materializes. It is always difficult to have the exact breakage percentage at the outset of a programme. Many programmes use breakage to fund planning and execution of marketing.

The usage of these funds should be laid clearly and transparent so that franchisees do not perceive breakage as a tool being used by the franchisor to simply increase profits.

Role of Employees in Store Loyalty

Lately, the market forces have challenged the theory of store loyalty. The dynamic business environment provides ample alternatives to customers to shop at every stage from the shopping centre retail format to the retail store format (independent, speciality, etc.), so much so that they may buy from one store today and shift to another tomorrow. Not that they think that the earlier store was bad, but it is the luxury of variety which the customers enjoy.

The customer service, impetus on the quality of offerings, and pricing play an important role along with other components of retail mix. But to keep the customers engaged, it is necessary for the employees to be engaged. By engagement one means dedication and commitment from the employees, which will ensure that the customers come back.

The concept of an engaged employee becomes important especially for the retail businesses. In this industry, the level of services by the employee determines store patronage by the customers.

The retailers in the organized sector are meeting challenges on multiple fronts on account of employee, including recruitment, training, experience, and retention.

Employee retention has become important for the retail players in the organized sector. With the competition heating up in this sector, the retailers now face a peculiar problem of limited supply of experienced and trained manpower. Most of the retailers facing major constraints in their expansion plan are in need of trained manpower.

Even as employees are trained by the company, there is no guarantee whether the company will be able to retain them given the competition not only from the retail sector but also from other sectors like BPOs (business process outsourcing). Therefore, the time spent in training means that others take the share of responsibility and may not be able to service the customers adequately given the pressure.

Pantaloon Retail India: Employees for Customer Loyalty

Pantaloon Retail India Ltd is clear when it hires personnel for the job—they should have the right attitude; the skill sets can come later or rather can be built up. The attitude herein is the value systems which the employee brings , which should fit with that of the company. But the selection of the candidates also depends on various retail formats of the company. The key differentiation of the formats like Pantaloon, Big Bazaar, Food Bazaar, and Gold Bazaar are also kept in mind. Thus, a hypermarket format like Food Bazaar and Big Bazaar is high on price and less on services, but Pantaloon is the reverse because customers frequenting the store expect a certain level of service at the store. Therefore, at Pantaloon, it is imperative for the associates to put themselves in the customers' shoes and attend to them. This they feel is a question of attitude. The criteria for selection focus more on communication skills and understanding the local environment rather than academic qualifications. For this reason most retailing companies hire from the immediate neighbourhood as such a person understands the environment and is therefore able to serve the customers better.

Retailers have to have engaged and committed manpower to have engaged customers. And to create an engaged employee requires time and effort. The effort is to provide the employee with the right skills to perform the responsibility, and takes time to build a long-term employee–store relationship, which ensures loyalty.

To build commitment within the employees, the companies need to assess whether adequate tools are being provided to enable them to do their job well. And loyalty comes by improving the work life and looking at the career progression. The tools that the company needs to provide are product knowledge and behavioural skills.

Remuneration Monetary remuneration plays a significant role in attracting and retaining the trained and competent workforce. Especially, given the relative young age group profile which take up jobs at the front end of the retail formats. For the 21–23 year age group, the lure of more money makes them shift jobs not only within the retailing but also jump into other high paying sectors. Also many of them leave to pursue higher studies because they see it as a job and not as a career.

The retailers and marketers have to initiate the two-way policy theme to meet this problem. There is a need to take care of the short-term and long-term interest of employees to build employee's trust and loyalty. The short-term measure is more pay and the long-term measure is constant training to equip the workforce with new techniques enabling them to upgrade. The short-term technique is a double-edged sword as more pay means that the company incurs higher employee costs. But higher pay is the carrot, which definitely does help. The monetary compensation is important but along with that a company needs to tell the employees the career progression. The increase in salary comes with growth, and as the employees grow with the company, they earn more.

The retailers along with monetary benefits also provide a comfort factor. The comfort level includes the benefits and services which the retailer provides to ensure that the employees are on a consistent learning curve.

Summary

Relationship marketing strategies in the organized retail sector have become extremely important lately with a spate of loyalty programmes and focus on customer service. However, small independent retailers have long practised the building up of relationship in marketing in a formal and personalized way.

Relationship marketing efforts aim to provide four types of benefits to customers —personalization, communication, special treatment benefits, and rewards. The term personalization has been used to describe the social content of interaction between service employees and their customers. Personalization can be regarded as a means of showing recognition for the other party.

Personalized treatment refers to the fact that loyal customers are provided with extra recognition in terms of better service and additional efforts that are not being made to other, non-loyal customers.

Communication strategies as part of relationship marketing efforts refer to direct communication with the customers as against mass-media communication, which does not afford selectivity. Rewards rely primarily on pricing incentives and money savings to secure customers' loyalty.

Customer service refers to the complex of activities involving all areas of retail business which combine to deliver and invoice the store's products or services in a fashion that is perceived as satisfactory by the customer and which advances the store's objectives. It also implies timeliness and reliability of getting products or services to customers in accordance with customers' expectations.

Many retailers operate loyalty programmes. They can take the form of frequent shopper programmes without credit linkage, store credit cards with tiered membership, co-branded cards, and affinity programmes.

Key Terms

1. **Relationship marketing:** Marketing with the conscious aim to develop and manage long-term and/or trusting relationships with customers, distributors, suppliers, or other parties in the marketing environment.

2. **Customer defection:** A consideration in calculating customer lifetime value. Specifically, it measures how long a certain customer is expected to remain within a portfolio and in what time horizon that customer is expected to generate value.

3. **Customer service:** The complex of activities involving all areas of retail business which combine to deliver and invoice the store's products or services in a fashion that is perceived as satisfactory by the customer and which advances the store's objectives. It also implies timeliness and reliability of getting products or services to customers in accordance with customers' expectations.

4. **Operant conditioning:** A theory associated with Skinner. It refers to the process of altering the probability of a behaviour being emitted by changing the consequences of the behaviour.

Concept Review Questions

1. Discuss the concept of relationship marketing how it relates to transactions marketing.
2. Discuss the various types of relationship marketing efforts and how they translate into a relationship marketing strategy.
3. Analyse the various customer service strategies operative in retailing.
4. Identify the key objectives and aspects of retail loyalty programmes. How can the design of retail loyalty programmes be improved?

Project Work Assignments

1. Devise a loyalty programme for (a) a small independent apparel retailer (b) an apparel chain store.
2. Evaluate the loyalty programme of any pharma retail store of your choice in the organized sector. How does its strategy compare with that of a small chemist in the same locality.
3. Select a department store each in two different product categories in your city. Compare and contrast their relationship marketing strategies. Specifically evaluate the impact of market conditions, product category issues, and customer preferences.
4. Select a neighbourhood store and evaluate its customer service strategy and its role in enhancing customer relationships.

Case Study

Loyalty Programme—BPCL

Petroleum Sector in India

Three companies, Indian Oil Corp. Ltd (IOCL), Bharat Petroleum Corp. Ltd (BPCL), and Hindustan Petroleum Corp. Ltd (HPCL), dominate the petroleum retail sector in India with about 93% market share among them.

These players cater to a market of about 40 million vehicles (approx. 77% two wheelers, 13% cars in 2002) on Indian roads with a retail network of over 15,000 outlets across the country. The petroleum retail sector in India recently experienced fundamental changes in the way business is being done.

The sector has moved away from government control and towards market forces, a move that has brought competition from private players and renewed customer focus.

The Changing Shopping Experience

The changing shopping experience and the rise of loyalty programmes have seen parallel development in the Indian retail context. The retail experience at petroleum stations were only functional in nature, with the station being nothing more than a place to get petrol, and cash the preferred payment mode.

In recent times, the outlets have been transformed to complete facelift, with new multi-fuel dispensers, better-trained attendants, impressive and attractive atmospherics, and comprehensive service elements. The product offering has widened to include blended fuels, branded fuels, high-octane fuels, lubes, groceries, and more.

The outlet itself is expanding to include grocery stores, cafes, bank ATMs, internet kiosks, etc., giving the customers more reasons to spend time and money at a location that offers more than just fuel. Credit cards, debit cards, and loyalty cards are also widely accepted.

These changes have given sufficient reasons to consumers to build preference among the three companies (IOCL, BPCL, and HPCL) and their brands. As consumers have begun to express their preferences, the companies have entered an inevitable battle for business through relationship-building initiatives, including loyalty programmes.

BPCL Leader in Loyalty Programme

A customer who joins BPCL's loyalty programme by making a one-time payment of Rs 250 is issued a Petro Card. It is a pre-paid debit card and can be used to fill in fuel from any BPCL outlet in the country.

The customer pays the money to the dealer and this amount is 'loaded' or transferred to his Petro Card account. Fuel worth a minimum of Rs 500 can be 'loaded' each time. This card can then be used to fill in fuel till the amount is exhausted. Each time the card is swiped for filling fuel, the amount in the bill is debited from the card.

On the other hand, payment made through a credit card attracts a surcharge on the amount indicated in the bill. Moreover, each time the card is used to fill in fuel, the consumer gets bonus points or 'petro miles', which he can exchange for attractive gifts.

The Petro Card was introduced to reward our loyal customers and also to ensure that they stay with us. The feedback has been excellent and we already have 20,000 Petro Card holders in the city. We also run promotional schemes, under which Petro Card users are given higher bonus points,' says a BPCL official. BPCL officials point out that the Petro Card scheme, launched on an experimental basis at Chennai in 1999, now has almost one million members countrywide.

Today, it is one of the most successful 'loyalty' programmes in the market. One of the key factors in its success has been the provision of 'card reader machines' at almost 70% of its outlets across the country to enable the use of the Petro Card.

During Onam last year, the company had organized a promotional scheme for 15 days, and this had attracted many new customers. Consumers can also avail themselves of a 5% discount by using the Petro Card to shop at 'In and Out' convenience stores of BPCL.

While the Petro Card is meant for owner-drivers, there is also the Fleet Card for those who run car rental services. While BPCL has taken an early lead in the market, other oil companies are also offering loyalty programmes to consumers. The Indian Oil Corporation (IOC) has a special programme to reward those customers who buy fuel with money and Hindustan Petroleum (HP) has its own card, 'HP Smart 1', on which 'reward' points can be converted to free fuel.

Benefits of the Loyalty Programme

PetroBonus is the largest loyalty programme in India. It rewards customers for all purchases at the Bharat Petroleum PetroBonus Outlets.

PetroBonus offers you the convenience and security of paying through electronic purse, with the added opportunity to earn valuable rewards and enjoy exclusive benefits, when you consolidate all your fuel and convenience store purchases at Bharat Petroleum's PetroBonus Outlets.

Customers can load money at the Bharat Petroleum PetroBonus Outlets and use the Petro Card to purchase fuel, lubricants, and all items sold in the In&Out Stores. Each time customer use the Petro Card to make payments, you would earn Loyalty Points called Petromiles, which you can redeem for Gifts and Rewards. The Loyalty Points are stored on the card, which also has advanced security features. The PetroBonus programme has been a continuously evolving programme and looks forward to providing you with added benefits and services.

Transaction Fee

There is no transaction fee levied on any of transactions with Petro Card. The Petro Card is not associated with a bank and functions independently. Thus, there is no fee attached for doing any transaction from a Petro Card.

Petromiles

Petromiles are the points earned when the customer makes a transaction through a Petro Card. Customers earn Petromiles when they load money on their Petro Card as well as when they buy using the Petro Card. The table given below indicates the Petromiles earned when customers spend their pre-loaded money on various items available in Bharat Petroleum PetroBonus Outlets:

Amount spent/item	Petromiles earned
Rs 100 spent on Petrol	15 Petromiles
Rs 100 spent on Speed	25 Petromiles
Rs 100 spent on Speed 93	30 Petromiles
Rs 100 spent on Diesel	15 Petromiles
Rs 100 spent on 2T Mix Petrol	18 Petromiles
Rs. 100 spent on Lubricants	250 Petromiles
Rs. 100 spent at the In&Out or Bazaar Stores	100 Petromiles

Even when a customer buys a loaf of bread with his Petro Card at a Bharat Petroleum PetroBonus Outlet, he earns valuable Petromiles. The application forms are available at Bharat Petroleum PetroBonus Outlets. The enrolment fee is Rs 250/-, which can be paid by cash at any of the participating Petrol Pumps.

BPCL also focused on using new interactive media to improve the PetroBonus experience while improving efficiencies. BPCL created a dedicated website for PetroBonus and used the web and e-mail for surveys, online campaigns, points statements, rewards catalogues, etc. in a two-pronged strategy of e-mail database building and widening of the online and e-mail offering. With the mobile boom, SMS-based services are on the rise.

The situation today is that PetroBonus has reached a critical mass that gives it immense power, with the road ahead seeing technology and analytics playing an ever-greater role in increasing operational efficiencies and deepening the relationship with the customers through interactivity and flexibility.

There are problems to be sorted out for sure and the competition nipping BPCLs feet could well have an advantage in being leaner. This competition, as it turns out, is not just from similar loyalty programmes by other petroleum companies, but equally from the emergence of co-branded programmes with banks, which are shaping this quickly maturing market.

Emerging Competition

For the other two players, IOCL and HPCL, customer loyalty programmes did not happen until mid-2002. Both of these companies focused their initial marketing efforts on building their retail outlet brand and services before launching a range of card-based programmes.

Also, both companies took the co-branded route, tying up with banks that were also looking to launch their petrol loyalty programmes. The entry of the banks into this space brought about the next wave of loyalty programmes, with a fresh set of offers for the customers.

The credit- and debit-card-based programmes offered the customers all the facilities of a regular credit/debit card in addition to a host of specific services including transaction fee waivers, surcharge waivers, insurance overage, discounts, increased point earnings opportunities, fuel for points, etc.

These programmes leveraged the wide acceptance of the credit/debit card as a payment device and an established reader network. The 'smartcard' format found relatively few takers, with most new launches preferring to ride on the existing card reader network of the magnetic strip-based credit/debit cards.

Two other developments in basic programme formats were the introduction of Fleet card and network loyalty programmes. On the Fleet card front, BPCL was again the pioneer, launching SmartFleet in February 2001, followed by IOCL's PowerPlus in January 2002.

These programmes gave fleet owners the option of giving drivers pre-loaded cards which allowed better MIS, transaction tracking, and points earnings. Network loyalty also came into the picture when IOC launched a co-branded card with MyShoppe, a network loyalty programme with a number of retail chain affiliates. The second wave gave the arena vitality as companies launched programmes with fundamentally different formats, giving the consumers an array of options to choose from.

At a time where evolutionary patterns seen in Western markets are getting replicated in India but with a shortened timeframe, this is a good indicator that one will see companies quickly launching every possible structural variant and then heading towards a period of maturity that gives them a chance to improve efficiencies and then reinvent themselves.

Challenges

With all three major players in the petroleum retail sector coming out with a good number of card-based loyalty programmes, this indicates that it will be difficult for the players to differentiate their respective loyalty programmes. New entrants are still pondering over launch decision, and planning a variety of new offerings that will strive to capture new prospects and focus on becoming the 'second card' in the pocket that slowly edges out the old card through aggressive and innovative marketing.

The drivers that govern loyalty programme success are also changing. For most of the players in the industry, coverage is the key driver. The more cities and outlets they launch their programme in, the larger their member base naturally grows. After coverage begins to hit a plateau, data and analytics will take centre stage as companies plunge into the deep end of data mining for elusive insights to drive their campaigns.

Technology upgrades will feed the efficiency and interactivity demand. New partnerships will move towards more niche segments that target lifestyle or special interest groups. Finally, creativity and innovation will bring the sizzle that gives the market vitality.

In the large and complex market that India is, direct and loyalty marketing can thrive in the many opportunities present. The fast growing urban population is getting increasingly Westernized, but the diversity within the people remains an opportunity for micro segmentation and targeted campaigns to follow. Petrol retail has tasted blood with loyalty programmes, and the many miles to go are sure to be marked by initiatives that would make marketing history.

1. Analyse details of the BPCL loyalty programme. Relate the programme to the market context.
2. What are its key benefits for the customer and how does it fit in with BPCL's marketing mix?
3. Suggest relationship programme strategies for the competitors of BPCL. How can they evolve differentiation in their loyalty strategies?
4. How can BPCL's programme be enhanced/modified to face future challenges?

References

1. Clark, R. 2004, 'Running and setting up a loyalty scheme—what to find out, and how', Published by The Wise Marketer in April.

2. www.thewisemarketer.com

3. www.businesstravellerindia.com, 'Strength of A Chain Should Be the Prime Selection Criterion' Excerpts: Zaid Farooqui, Director, Sales and Marketing and Loyalty Programmes, Taj Group of Hotels.

4. *The Financial Express* 2004, 'BEST PRACTICE: Getting Employees To Build Customer Loyalty', Saturday, Feb 28.

5. Gairola, M. 2004, 'MTNL offers freebies to its users' *The Economic Times*, February 8.

ANNEXURES

Annexure I   The Shops and Establishment Act

The Act, in essence, is a state legislation. It seeks to regulate the working conditions of workers in the unorganized sector, including shops and establishments which do not come under the Factories Act Regulations. The rules and regulations regarding working hours, rest intervals, overtime, holidays, termination of service, maintenance of shops and establishments, and other rights and obligations of the employer and employees are laid down in the Act.

Objectives

To provide statutory obligation and rights to employees and employers in the unorganized sector, i.e., shops and establishments.

Scope And Coverage

- A state legislation; each state has framed its own rules for the Act.
- It is applicable to all persons employed in an establishment with or without wages, except the members of the employer's family.
- A state government can exempt, either permanently or for a specified period, any establishment from all or any of the provisions of this Act.

Main Provisions

- Compulsory registration of shop/establishment within 30 days of commencement of work
- Communication of closure of the establishment within 15 days from the closing of the establishment
- Lays down the hours of work per day and week
- Lays down guidelines for spread-over, rest interval, opening and closing hours, closed days, national and religious holidays, and overtime work
- Rules for employment of children, young persons, and women
- Rules for annual leave, maternity leave, sickness, and casual leave, etc.
- Rules for employment and termination of service
- Maintenance of registers and records and display of notices
- Obligations of employers
- Obligations of employees

When to Consult And Refer

- At the time of the start of an enterprise
- When framing personnel policies and rules

   The Bombay Shops and Establishment Act, 1948, is appended as a specimen.

The Bombay Shops and Establishment Act, 1948

Registration: Form A—Within 31 days of its commencement
Renewal of registration: Form B—Last date 15th December
Notice of Change: Form E

I. Fees for Registration and Renewal of Registration Certificate

Category of Establishments	Fees
Commercial establishment	Rs 50/-
Shops having employee	Rs 50/-
Shop having no employee	Rs 50/-
Residential hotel	Rs 50/-
Restaurants and eating houses	Rs 50/-
Theaters and other public places	Rs 50/-
Amusements or entertainment	Rs 50/-
NB: Cheque to be drawn in favour of 'Municipal Corporation of Greater Mumbai'.	

II. Fees for Notice of Change, to be Submitted along with Form E

Shops and establishment having	Registration fees per year	Fees for renewal of regis -tration certificate per year	Trade refuse charges per year
Nil Employees	Rs 50/-	Rs 50/-	Rs 150/-
1 to 5 Employees	Rs 150/-	Rs 150/-	Rs 450/-
6 to 10 Employees	Rs 300/-	Rs 300/-	Rs 900/-
11 to 20 Employees	Rs 600/-	Rs 600/-	Rs 1800/-
21 to 50 Employees	Rs 1500/-	Rs 1500/-	Rs 4500/-
51 to 100 Employees	Rs 3000/-	Rs 3000/-	Rs 9000/-
101 and above Employees	Rs 4000/-	Rs 4000/-	Rs 12000/-

Starting a Business: India

Nature of Procedure (2004)

	Proc. #	Duration (days)	US$ Cost
• Obtain pre-approval of name, have documents vetted	1	7	10.41
• Stamp the Memorandum and Articles of Association	2	2	25.40

- File for registration   3   9   193.60
- Make a seal   4   7   10.41
- Obtain PAN   5   60   1.35
- Obtain TAN   6   45* 0
- File for sales tax   7   15* 2.60
- Register for Profession Tax   8   2*   0
- Register with the Mumbai Shops and   9   2*   20.82
  Establishment Act
- File for EPF   10   2*   0
- File for ESIC   11   1*   0
  Total: 11   89   264.59

This procedure runs simultaneously with previous procedures.

The Bombay Sales Tax Act, 1959

Registration Under the Bombay Sales Tax Act, 1959

A dealer engaged in the activity of manufacturing, importing, buying, and selling of goods needs to register under the Bombay Sales Tax Act, 1959.

Why registration? Obtaining a certificate of registration is a legal obligation. It also enhances the prestige of a trader in the market.

Who is liable for registration? A dealer engaged in the activity of manufacturing, importing, buying and/or selling of goods is liable for registration.

When to apply for registration? Application to be submitted within 30 days of exceeding the prescribed turnover of the sales or purchases in any financial year.

What are the prescribed turnover limits? Prescribed limits of the turnover are as follows:

Type of applicant	Limits effective after 1-05-98	
Manufacturer	(i)	Total T.O. of sales or purchases exceeds Rs 1,00,000/-
	(ii)	T.O. of taxable sales or purchases exceeds Rs 10,000/-
	(iii)	Value of any good whether taxable or not manufactured by him exceeds Rs 10,000/-
Importer	(i)	Total T.O. of sales or purchases exceeds Rs 1,00,000/-
	(ii)	T.O. of taxable sales or purchases exceeds Rs 10,000/-
	(iii)	Value of any good whether taxable or not brought by him into the state exceeds Rs 10,000/-
All other dealers	(i)	Total T.O. of sales or purchases shall exceed Rs 2,50,000/-
	(ii)	T.O. of taxable sales or purchases exceeds Rs 10,000/-

contd

contd

Type of applicant	Limits effective after 1-05-98
Voluntary	(i) Turnover limits are not applicable
Registration	(ii) Advance of Rs 30,000/- is required to be paid, which is adjustable towards dealer's liability of tax, interest, penalties

Consequences of Non-registration   If you do not register yourself and discharge the obligations under the law, you are liable for prosecution resulting in a maximum imprisonment for 12 months or fine or both.

Where to apply?   The sales tax officer having jurisdiction over your area. In Mumbai, the registration branch is situated at Vikrikar Bhavan, 1st floor, Mazgaon, Mumbai -10.

How to register?   Contact the nearest sales tax authority for guidance. Fill in Form No. 1, which is the application for registration and pay a sum of Rs 100/- towards registration fee. Also affix the application with two copies of your recent photograph. The authorities will verify the veracity of the entries made by you in the application form and issue you the registration certificate.

What are the requirements for registration?   Required documents are:
- Books of accounts and statement of sales/purchases
- Statement of applicant in duplicate
- Partnership deed/memorandum of articles of association
- Confirmation of residential address/place of business
- Rent receipts of place of business and residence (consent letter if sub-tenant), bank account, etc.
- Ration card/election identity card/driving licence of the proprietor/partners/directors
- Latest passport size photograph of the applicant, which is required to be signed before the registration officer
- Certificate/licence under The Municipal Act, The Factories Act, the Shops and Establishment Act, etc., as applicable
- Copy of the assessment order under income tax if any
- Required court fee stamp on CST registration application, and court fee stamp or chalan for BST application
- Any other details on demand to prove the genuineness of the applicant

What is voluntary registration?   A certificate of registration can be obtained without exceeding the turnover limit under the Voluntary Registration Scheme. An amount of Rs 30,000/- is required to be deposited for voluntary registration, which is adjustable towards a dealer's subsequent liability of tax, penalty, and interest.

Is new registration required if place of business is shifted?   Yes. New registration certificate is required on shifting of place of business even from one pin code to another pin code.

Is new registration required on change in constitution?   Yes. New registration certificate is required if there is a change in constitution, such as partnership to proprietorship or proprietorship to pvt ltd company.

What are the advantages of registration?

- You will be entitled to collect the sales tax payable by you. An unregistered dealer cannot collect tax , even though tax is payable by him.
- Tax exemptions on purchases is available only to a registered dealer.
- Incentive in the form of sales tax exemption/deferral etc. are available only to the registered dealers.
- A preferential treatment is always given to a registered dealer in case of selection for govt/ semi-govt contracts.
- If registered under the Central Sales Tax Act also, you are entitled to purchase from outside the state of Maharashtra at a concessional rate of tax at 4% on C form declaration.
- Registration enhances the prestige of a trader in the market.

What are the Disadvantages of Non-registration?

- Taxes cannot be collected even though payable
- No exemptions admissible on taxes paid for purchases
- No benefits such as exemption or deferral under the incentive schemes
- Possibility of non-consideration of tenders for government, semi-government contracts
- Purchases at concessional rates not available against declarations such as C Form
- Invites action for levy of penalty and prosecution, which may lead to fine and conviction upto 1 year imprisonment.

Specimen Copy

FORM PRESCRIBED UNDER THE TAMIL NADU GENERAL SALES TAX RULES, 1959

FORM XI

(See Rule 40)

ISSUED UNDER THE TAMIL NADU GENERAL SALES TAX ACT, 1959 (Tamil Nadu Act of 1959)

Declaration under rule 45 of Tamil Nadu General Sales Tax Rules, 1959

To

The Registering / Assessing Authority / Joint / Deputy Commercial Tax Officer.

I/We .... (Name) of .... (address) carrying on the business(es) known as .... at .... And other places in the State of Tamil Nadu and holding Registration Certificate No. ....dated...........Issued under the Tamil Nadu General Tax Act 1959, by............................... (designation and jurisdiction of the Registering Authority) do hereby declare that I/Thiru.. son of .... residing at .... whose signature is appended below and who am/is .... mention here the status or designation of the said concern shall be deemed to be the Manager of the said business(es) at all places within the State of Tamil Nadu for the purpose of the said Act and shall at all times comply with the provisions of the said Act and the rules made there under.

1.This supersedes the declaration filed already in favour of Thiru ....

Signature of the Manager :

Place :

Signature :

Date :

Name :

Status :

Here enter one of the following as may be applicable:

(a) The guardian/trustee or on behalf of ....

(b) A Hindu undivided family known as ....

(c) An association / club / society known as ....

(d) A firm known as ....

(e) A private limited company known as ....

(f) A public limited company/co-operative society known as .... The declaration shall be signed in the case of :

1. A Hindu undivided family—by its Manager.

2. An association/club or society—by its president or Chairman and the Secretary

3. A firm—by the partners having a total share of not less than 50%.

4. A private limited company—by all its Directors or where there are no Directors, by the authorized representative of the company nominated by the Chairman, viz. public, limited company or co-operative society by the Managing Agents, or, where there are no Managing Agents, by the Managing Director or the Chairman of the Board of Directors and the Secretary.

Annexure II   Sales Tax: A Note

Sales tax is a tax levied on sale of goods. The liability to pay sales tax arises on making sale of goods. In India, the law for levying sales tax is provided in the Central Sales Tax Act, 1966. This act was passed by the Parliament and applies to the entire country. The main objectives of this act are:

1. To formulate the principles to determine as to when sale or purchase of goods takes place (i) in the course of inter-state trade or commerce, (ii) outside a state, or (iii) in the course of import into or export from India
2. To provide for the levy, collection, and distribution of taxes on sales of goods in the course of inter-state trade or commerce
3. To declare certain goods to be of special importance in inter-state trade or commerce
4. To specify the restrictions and conditions in respect of state laws, which impose taxes on the sale or purchase of such goods of special importance

The CST Act, being a central act passed by the Parliament, regulates and provides for levy of sales tax on the sale and purchase of goods made in the course of inter-state trade or commerce. Sales and purchases made within a state are regulated by the sales tax law of each individual state. For example, in the state of Maharashtra, the Bombay Sales Tax Act, 1959 provides for the levy of sales tax on sales made within the state of Maharashtra.

Similarly, other states also have their own sales tax laws for levying sales tax on intra-state sales or purchases of goods. Generally, the CST Act does not deal with sales made intra-state. However, in respect of certain declared goods such as oil seeds, sugar, pulses, crude oil, etc., the CST Act imposes restrictions on the powers of the state governments to levy sales tax even in respect of intra-state sales.

Accordingly, sales can broadly be classified into three categories:

- Intra-state sales, i.e., sales within the state
- Sales during import and export
- Inter-state sales

The provisions of the CST Act apply only in respect of inter-state sales and not intra-state sales or import or export sales.

Definitions

It is essential to understand the meaning of certain terms used in the CST Act. For the purpose of the Act, certain terms have been defined in the Act itself and the meaning of these terms will be as per the definition only and not as per the ordinary meaning of the term. However, where a particular term has not been defined, it will have the same meaning as ordinarily understood.

Business includes

- Any trade, commerce, manufacture, or any adventure or concern in the nature of trade, commerce or manufacture, whether or not such trade, commerce, manufacture, adventure or concern is carried out with the motive to make gain or profit and whether or not, any gain or profit accrues from such trade, commerce, manufacture, adventure, or concern

- Any transaction in connection with or incidental or ancillary to such trade, commerce, manufacture, adventure, or concern

Dealer means any person who carries on, whether regularly or otherwise, the business of buying, selling, supplying, or distributing goods, directly or indirectly, for cash or for deferred payment or for commission, remuneration, or for other valuable consideration, and includes:

- A local authority, body corporate, company, co-operative society or other society, club, firm, Hindu Undivided Family (HUF), or other Association of Persons (AOP), which carries on such business.
- A broker, commission agent, or any other mercantile agent, by whatever name called and whether of the same description as herein before mentioned or not, who carries on the business of buying, selling, supplying, or distributing goods belonging to any principal, whether disclosed or not. An auctioneer who carries on the business of selling or auctioning goods belonging to any principal, whether disclosed or not and whether offer of the intending purchaser is accepted by him or by the principal or by the nominee of the principal.
- A government, whether or not in the course of business, which buys, sells or supplies, or distributes goods, directly or otherwise, for cash or for deferred payment or for commission, remuneration, or other valuable consideration shall except in relation to any sale, supply, or distribution of surplus, unserviceable or old stores, or materials or waste products, or absolute or discarded machinery, or parts or accessories thereof be deemed to be a dealer for the purpose of this Act.

Sale means transfer of any property or goods from one person to another for cash or for deferred payment or for any other valuable consideration and includes the transfer of goods on hire-purchase or other system of payment by instalments but does not include a mortgage or hypothecation, or charge or pledge on goods.

Accordingly, consignments to agents or transfer of goods to branches or other offices does not amount to sale for the purpose of the CST Act. Sale price means an amount payable to a dealer as consideration for the sale of any good less any sum allowed as cash discount according to the practices normally prevailing in the trade but inclusive of any sum charged for anything done by the dealer in respect of goods at the time of or before the delivery thereof. However, it does not include freight or delivery cost or cost of installation where such cost is separately charged.

Declared goods means goods declared under Section 14, which are of special importance in inter-state trade or commerce. The important ones among them are:

- Cereals
- Coal in all forms excluding charcoal
- Cotton in unmanufactured form
- Cotton fabrics and cotton yarn
- Crude oil
- Hides and skin
- Iron and steel
- Jute
- Oil seeds
- Pulses

- Man-made fabrics
- Sugar
- Unmanufactured tobacco
- Woven fabrics of wool

Inter/Intra-state Sales

The CST Act has imposed certain restrictions on the powers of the state governments to impose taxes on declared goods inside the states.

Sale or Purchase in the Course of Inter-state Trade or Commerce

A sale or purchase of goods shall be deemed to take place in the course of an inter-state trade or commerce if the sale or purchase occasions movement of goods from one state to another or is effected by the transfer of documents of title to the goods during their movement from one state to another.

Explanation 1

Where the goods are delivered to a carrier or other bailee for transmission, the movement of goods shall, for the purpose of clause 2 above, be deemed to commence at the time of such delivery and terminate at the time when delivery is taken from such carrier or bailee.

Explanation 2

Where that movement of goods commences and terminates in the same state, it shall not be deemed to be a movement of goods from one state to another merely because of the fact that in the course of such movement, the goods do not pass through the territory of any other state.

Ashok of Ambala sells goods to Bhaskar of Bangalore in Ambala. Such sale is not an inter-state sale since the goods do not move from one state to another. Ashok of Mumbai sells and despatches goods to Bhaskar of Calcutta. This is inter-state sale of goods since goods move from one state to another under the contract of sales. Ashok of Delhi sends goods by railways to Bhaskar of Mumbai. Bhaskar sells the goods to Chetan of Mumbai and transfers the document of title (railway receipt) during their movement from Delhi to the state of Maharashtra. This is inter-state sale since the documents of title are transferred while the goods are being moved from one state to another.

Sale or Purchase Inside the State

A sale or purchase of goods shall be deemed to take place inside the state if the goods are within the state.

- In case of specific or ascertained goods, at the time the contract of sale is made (specific or ascertained goods means goods which are identified and agreed upon at the time when the contract of sale is made).
- In case of unascertained or future goods, at the time of appropriation of contract of sale by the seller or by the buyer, whether the ascent of the other party is prior or subsequent to such appropriation(e.g., agreement to buy mangoes, which are still growing on the trees, at a future date).

Explanation

Where there is a single contract of sale or purchase of goods situated at one or more places, the provisions of this sub-section shall apply as if there were separate contracts in respect of the goods at each of such places.

A sale or purchase of goods, which is not within the state as per the above provisions will be treated as taking place outside the state. The purpose of determining whether the sales have taken place within the state or outside the state is very important for levying central sales tax as under the CST Act tax is leviable only on sales in the course of inter-state trade or commerce.

Inter-state sales involve two or more states. It is necessary to determine the state in which the sale or purchase of goods takes place as that becomes the appropriate state for the purpose of levying and collecting central sales tax.

Charge of Sales Tax under the Central Sales Tax

Section 6 of the Central Sales Tax Act focuses on the imposition and collection of the central sales tax. The section states that a dealer is liable to pay sales tax on all sales of goods, other than sale of electrical energy, effected by him in the course of inter-state trade or commerce during any financial year. However, no sales tax can be levied under the CST Act in respect of the following:

- Inter-state sale of electrical energy
- Sales in the course of import and export
- Intra-state sale of goods
- Sales made in respect of goods on which sales tax is exempted by a notification in the official gazette, provided all conditions prescribed under the notification are fulfilled
- Subsequent sale of goods which are exempted from sales tax under the laws of the relevant state or chargeable to tax at a lower rate, if sold within the state
- Subsequent sale of goods by transfer of documents

Subsequent Sales

Subsequent sale refers to the sale of goods after the first time they have been sold. For example, A, a manufacturer, sells a radio to B, a dealer. B sells it to a consumer, C. In this case, sale of A to B is the first sale and all other sales made after this sale are subsequent sales. Under the CST Act, sales tax is levied at a single point only (first sale) and no sales tax is payable on subsequent sales. Subsequent sale during the movement of goods from one state to another shall be exempted from the levy of central sales tax if the following conditions are satisfied:

- Sale should be either to the government or a registered dealer.
- Sale should be of the same goods during their movement from one state to another, i.e., the goods should not undergo a change in the course of transport.
- Sale should be effected by the transfer of documents of title to the goods such as railway receipt, lorry receipt, etc., which are freely transferable from one dealer to another by endorsement.
- Subsequent dealers are required to obtain necessary certificates in the prescribed form from their vendors, e.g., Form C from purchaser and Form D from government.

- Where subsequent sale is to a registered dealer other than the government, the sale should be only of those goods which are mentioned in the certificate of registration of the dealer intended for the purpose of resale and manufacturing or processing of goods for resale or mining or generation of electricity.

For example, Bhaskar of Bangalore ordered from Ramesh of Rajkot to sell and despatch 100 radios. Ramesh despatched the goods to Bhaskar of Bangalore by road. Instead of taking delivery, Bhaskar transferred the lorry receipt to Chetan of Bangalore. Sale by Bhaskar to Chetan is an inter-state sale because it was effected by a transfer of documents to title, i.e., lorry receipt.

In the above case, if Chetan instead of taking delivery transferred the lorry receipt to Dable of Bangalore, the sale between Chetan and Dable is still a subsequent sale and may enjoy the benefit of Section 6 subject to the fulfillment of the other conditions mentioned above.

Ashok of Ahmedabad ordered from Babu of Bombay 100 radios. Babu despatched the goods to Ashok by road. Instead of taking delivery of goods, Ashok transferred the lorry receipt to Ingle of Indore. This is inter-state sale by documents of transfer. Ashok should obtain Form E1 from Babu of Bombay, and Form C from Ingle of Indore. Babu charges CST against Form C from Ashok. A will not charge any CST to Ingle. In such cases, it should be noted that the transfer of documents of title must take place before taking delivery of goods for it to be treated as subsequent sales in the course of inter-state trade or commerce. Once the buyer has taken delivery of goods, there is no document left for transfer and it will not be treated as subsequent sale in the course of inter-state trade or commerce.

Tax Rates and Filing of Returns

Every dealer who sells goods in the course of inter-state trade or commerce to the government will be liable to concessional CST of 4 %, provided the government gives a certificate in Form D appropriately filled and signed by a duly authorized officer of the government. The concessional rate of 4% is also applicable in the case of sales to a dealer who is registered under the CST Act on the date of sale, provided :

- The goods sold must be of the class or classes specified in the certificate of registration of the registered dealer purchasing the goods.
- Such goods are meant for resale or are to be used in a manufacturing process or as packing material.
- Purchasing dealer must give a prescribed declaration, i.e., Form C to the selling dealer.
- Office stationery, office furniture, or books and periodicals purchased for office use cannot be purchased at a concessional rate of 4% against Form C since it is not for the purpose of resale nor is it used in the manufacturing process or as packing material.
- Raw material, plant and machinery, tools, moulds, and packing materials can be purchased at a concessional rate of 4% against Form C.

A dealer of declared goods who is not registered under the CST Act (unregistered dealer) shall be liable to pay central sales tax at the rate twice the rate of sales tax applicable to the sale or purchase of such goods inside the appropriate state in the course of inter-state trade or commerce. In case of sale of goods other than declared goods, CST will be 10% or the rate applicable to the sale or purchase of such goods inside the appropriate state, whichever is higher.

Goods may be taxed at the lower rate of 4% or be exempted from CST under the following circumstances.

- Where under the sales tax law of the appropriate state no tax is payable on the sale or purchase of such goods, no CST is payable even in the case of inter-state trade or commerce in relation to that state.
- Where under the sales tax law of the appropriate state tax is payable on the sale or purchase of such goods at a rate lower than 4%, CST is payable at that lower rate even in the case of inter-state trade or commerce in relation to that state.

The appropriate state government may grant exemption from CST or may reduce the rate of tax with reference to any goods or a class of goods for any person or classes of persons through notification in the official gazette. The exemption may be granted to any one dealer or a class of dealers. It may be absolute or conditional, total or partial.

Filing of Returns

Category	Form No	Periodicity
Dealers having a tax liability of less than Rs 20,000 in the previous and current year	III-B III-BB	Annual, Annual
Dealers having a tax liability of more than Rs 20,00 in the previous year but less the Rs 20,000 in the current year	III-B III-BB	Monthly, Annual
Dealers having a total tax liabilty of more than Rs 2,000 in the previous year	III-BB	Annual
Newly registered with no previous year	III-B	Monthly

Month	Due Date
March	25 April
April	25 May
May	25 June
June	25 July
July	25 August
August	25 September
September	25 October
October	25 November
November	25 December
December	25 January
January	20 February
February	20 March

Annexure III   The Consumer Protection Act, 1986: A Note

Introduction and Definitions

A consumer is a user of goods and services. Any person paying for goods and services which he uses is entitled to expect that the goods and services are of a nature and quality promised to him by the seller.

The earlier principle of 'Caveat Emptor' or 'let the buyer beware' which was prevalent has given way to the principle of 'Consumer is King'. The origin of this principle lies in the fact that in today's mass- production economy where there is little contact between the producer and the consumer, often the sellers make exaggerated claims and advertisements, which they do not intend to fulfill. This leaves the consumer in a difficult position with very few avenues for redressal. The onset of intense competition also made the producers aware of the benefits of customer satisfaction and, hence, by and large, the principle of 'consumer is king' is now accepted.

The need to recognize and enforce the rights of consumers is being understood and several laws have been made for this purpose. In India, we have the Indian Contract Act, the Sale of Goods Act, the Dangerous Drugs Act, the Agricultural Produce (Grading and Marketing) Act, the Indian Standards Institution (Certification Marks) Act, the Prevention of Food Adulteration Act, the Standards of Weights and Measures Act, the Trade and Merchandise Marks Act, etc., which to some extent protect consumer interests. However, these laws required the consumers to initiate action by way of a civil suit, which involved lengthy legal processes proving to be too expensive and time consuming for lay consumers. Therefore, the need for a more simpler and quicker access to redressal of consumer grievances was felt and, accordingly, it led to the legislation of the Consumer Protection Act, 1986.

Objects of the Consumer Protection Act, 1986

The preamble to the Act states that the Act was legislated to provide for better protection of the interests of the consumers and for that purpose to make provisions for the establishment of consumer councils and other authorities for the settlement of consumer disputes and for matters connected therewith.

The basic rights of consumers as per the Consumer Protection Act (CPA) are:
- The right to be protected against marketing of goods and services, which are hazardous to life and property
- The right to be informed about the quality, quantity, potency, purity, standard, and price of goods or services so as to protect the consumers against unfair trade practices
- The right to be assured, wherever possible, and have an access to variety of goods and services at competitive prices
- The right to be heard and be assured that consumers' interests will receive due consideration at appropriate forums
- The right to seek redressal against unfair trade practices or restrictive trade practices or unscrupulsous exploitation of consumers
- The right to consumer education

The CPA extends to the whole of India except the state of Jammu and Kashmir and applies to all goods and services unless otherwise notified by the central government.

Definitions of Important Terms

Before studying the provisions of the CPA, it is necessary to understand the terms used in the Act. Let us understand some of the more important definitions.

Complainant means:

- a consumer; or
- any voluntary consumer association registered under the Companies Act,1956 or under any other law for the time being in force; or
- the central government or any state government, who or which makes a complaint; or
- one or more consumers where there are numerous consumers having the same interest.

Complaint means any allegation in writing made by a complainant that:

- An unfair trade practice or a restricted trade practice has been adopted by any trader.
- The goods bought by him or agreed to be bought by him suffer from one or more defects.
- The services hired or availed of or agreed to be hired or availed of by him suffer from deficiency in any respect.
- The trader has charged for the goods mentioned in the complaint a price in excess of the price fixed by or under any law for the time being in force or displayed on the goods or any package containing such goods.
- Goods which will be hazardous to life and safety when used are being offered for sale to the public in contravention of the provisions of any law for the time being in force, requiring traders to display information regarding the contents, manner, and affect of use of such goods.

Consumer means any person who:

- buys any good for a consideration which has been paid or promised or partly paid and partly promised, or under any system of deferred payment (e.g., hire purchase or installment sales) and includes any other user of such goods when such use is made with the approval of the buyer but does not include a person who obtains such goods for resale or for any commercial purpose; or
- hires or avails of any services for a consideration which has been paid or promised, or partly paid and partly promised, or under any system of deferred payment and includes any beneficiary of such services when such services are availed of with the approval of the first mentioned person.

For the purposes of this definition, 'commercial purpose' does not include goods bought and used by a consumer exclusively for the purpose of earning his livelihood by means of self-employment.

Goods means goods as defined in the Sale of Goods Act, 1930. Under that Act, goods means every kind of movable property other than actionable claims and money, and includes stocks and shares, growing crops, grass, and things attached to or forming part of the land, which are agreed to be severed from land before sale or under the contract of sale.

Service is defined to mean service of any description which is made available to potential users and includes the provision of facilities in connection with banking, financing, insurance, transport, processing, supply of electrical or other energy, board or lodging or both, housing construction, entertainment, amusement or the purverying of news or other information but does not include the rendering of any service free of charge or under a contract of personal service.

Consumer dispute means dispute where the person against whom a complaint has been made denies or disputes the allegation contained in the complaint.

Restrictive trade practice means any trade practice which requires a consumer to buy, hire, or avail of any good, or as the case may be, services as a condition precedent for buying, hiring, or availing of any other goods or services.

Unfair trade practice means unfair trade practice as defined under the Monopolies and Restrictive Trade Practices Act. The MRTP Act has defined certain practices to be unfair trade practices.

Defect means any fault, imperfection or shortcoming in the quality, quantity, potency, purity, or standard which is required to be maintained by or under any law for the time being in force or under any contract, express or implied, or as is claimed by the trade in any manner whatsoever in relation to any good.

Deficiency means any fault, imperfection or shortcoming or inadequacy in the quality, nature, and manner of performance, which is required to be maintained by or under any law for the time being in force or has been undertaken to be performed by a person in pursuance of a contract or otherwise in relation to any service.

Redressal Machinery under the Act

Consumer Protection Councils

The interests of consumers are enforced through various authorities set up under the CPA. The CPA provides for the setting up of the Central Consumer Protection Council, the State Consumer Protection Council, and the District Forum

The Central Consumer Protection Council

The central government has set up the Central Consumer Protection Council, which consists of the following members :

(a) the minister in charge of consumer affairs in the central government who is its chairman, and

(b) other official and non-official members representing varied interests.

The Central Council consists of 150 members and its term is 3 years. The council meets as and when necessary but at least one meeting is held in a year.

The State Consumer Protection Council

The State Council consists of :

(a) the minister in charge of consumer affairs in the state government who is its chairman, and

(b) other official and non-official members representing varied interests.

The state council meets as and when necessary but not less than two meetings are held every year.

The CPA provides for a three-tier approach in resolving consumer disputes. The District Forum has jurisdiction to entertain complaints where the value of goods/services complained against and the compensation claimed is less than Rs 5 lakhs, the State Commission for claims exceeding Rs 5 lakhs but not exceeding Rs 20 lakhs, and the National Commission for claims exceeding Rs 20 lakhs.

The District Forum

Under the CPA, the state government has to set up a District Forum in each district of the state. The government may establish more than one district forum in a district if it deems fit. Each District Forum shall consist of :

(a) a person, who is or who has been qualified to be a district judge, who shall be its president;

(b) two other members who shall be persons of ability, integrity, and standing, and have an adequate knowledge or experience of or have shown capacity in dealing with problems relating to economics, law, commerce, accountancy, industry, public affairs, or administration, one of whom must be a woman

Appointments to the State Commission shall be made by the state government on the recommendation of a selection committee consisting of the president of the State Commission, the secretary of the law department of the state, and the secretary in charge of consumer affairs.

Every member of the District Forum holds office for 5 years or up to the age of 65 years, whichever is earlier, and is not eligible for re-appointment. A member may resign by giving notice in writing to the state government whereupon the vacancy will be filled up by the state government.

The District Forum can entertain complaints where the value of goods or services and the compensation, if any, claimed is less than Rs 5 lakhs. However, in addition to jurisdiction over consumer goods and services valued up to Rs 5 lakhs, the District Forum also may pass orders against traders indulging in unfair trade practices, selling defective goods, or rendering deficient services provided the turnover of goods or value of services does not exceed Rs 5 lakhs.

A complaint shall be instituted in the District Forum within the local limits of whose jurisdiction

(a) the opposite party or the defendant actually and voluntarily resides or carries on business or has a branch office or personally works for gain at the time of institution of the complaint; or

(b) any one of the opposite parties (where there are more than one) actually and voluntarily resides or carries on business or has a branch office, or personally works for gain, at the time of institution of the complaint, provided that the other opposite party/parties acquiescence in such institution or the permission of the Forum is obtained in respect of such opposite parties; or

(c) the cause of action arises, wholly or in part.

The State Commission

The Act provides for the establishment of the State Consumer Disputes Redressal Commission by the state government in the state by notification. Each State Commission shall consist of:

(a) a person, who is or has been a judge of a High Court, appointed by the state government (in consultation with the chief justice of the high court) who shall be its president;

(b) two other members who shall be persons of ability, integrity, and standing, and have an adequate knowledge or experience of or have shown capacity in dealing with problems relating to economics, law, commerce, accountancy, industry, public affairs, or administration, one of whom must be a woman.

Every appointment made under this shall be made by the state government on the recommendation of a selection committee consisting of the president of the state commission, secretary of the law department of the state, and secretary in charge of consumer affairs in the state.

Every member of the District Forum holds office for 5 years or up to the age of 65 years, whichever is earlier, and is not eligible for re-appointment. A member may resign by giving notice in writing to the state government whereupon the vacancy will be filled up by the state government.

The State Commission can entertain complaints where the value of goods or services and the compensation, if any, claimed exceed Rs 5 lakhs but do not exceed Rs 20 lakhs.

The State Commission also has the jurisdiction to entertain appeal against the orders of any District Forum within the state.

The state commission also has the power to call for the records and appropriate orders in any consumer dispute which is pending before or has been decided by any District Forum within the state if it appears that such District Forum has exercised any power not vested in it by law, or has failed to exercise a power rightfully vested in it by law, or has acted illegally or with material irregularity.

The National Commission

The central government provides for the establishment of the National Consumer Disputes Redressal Commission. The National Commission shall consist of:

(a) a person, who is or has been a judge of the Supreme Court, appointed by the central government (in consultation with the chief justice of India), who shall be its president;

(b) four other members who shall be persons of ability, integrity, and standing, and have an adequate knowledge or experience of or have shown capacity in dealing with problems relating to economics, law, commerce, accountancy, industry, public affairs, or administration, one of whom must be a woman.

Appointments shall be made by the central government on the recommendation of a selection committee consisting of a judge of the Supreme Court to be nominated by the Chief Justice of India, the Secretary in the Department of Legal Affairs, and the secretary in charge of consumer affairs in the Government of India.

Every member of the National Commission shall hold office for a term of five years or up to seventy years of age, whichever is earlier, and shall not be eligible for reappointment.

The national commission shall have the jurisdiction

(a) to entertain complaints where the value of the goods or services and the compensation, if any, claimed exceeds Rs 20 lakhs;

(b) to entertain appeals against the orders of any state commission; and

(c) to call for the records and pass appropriate orders in any consumer dispute which is pending before or has been decided by any State Commission where it appears to the National Commission that such commission has exercised a jurisdiction not vested in it by law, or has failed to exercise a jurisdiction so vested, or has acted in the exercise of its jurisdiction illegally or with material irregularity.

Complaints may be filed with the district forum by:

- The consumer to whom such goods are sold or delivered or agreed to be sold or delivered, or such service provided, or agreed to be provided

- Any recognized consumer association, whether the consumer to whom goods sold or delivered or agreed to be sold or delivered, or service provided or agreed to be provided, is a member of such association or not

- One or more consumers, where there are numerous consumers having the same interest, with the permission of the District Forum, on behalf of or for the benefit of all consumers so interested
- The central or the state government

On receipt of a complaint, a copy of the complaint is to be referred to the opposite party, directing him to give his version of the case within 30 days. This period may be extended by another 15 days. If the opposite party admits the allegations contained in the complaint, the complaint will be decided on the basis of materials on the record. Where the opposite party denies or disputes the allegations or omits or fails to take any action to represent his case within the time provided, the dispute will be settled in the following manner:

I. *In case of dispute relating to any goods:* Where the complaint alleges a defect in the goods which cannot be determined without proper analysis or test of the goods, a sample of the goods shall be obtained from the complainant, sealed and authenticated in the manner prescribed for referring to the appropriate laboratory for the purpose of any analysis or test whichever may be necessary, so as to find out whether such goods suffer from any other defect. The appropriate laboratory would be required to report its finding to the referring authority, i.e., the District Forum or the State Commission within a period of 40–45 days from the receipt of the reference or within such extended period as may be granted by these agencies.

Appropriate laboratory means a laboratory or organization:

(i) recognized by the central government;
(ii) recognized by a state government subject to such guidelines as may be prescribed by the central government;
(iii) any such laboratory or organization established by or under any law for the time being in force, which is maintained, financed, or aided by the central government or a state government for carrying out analysis or test of goods with a view to determining whether such goods suffer from any defect.

The District Forum/State Commission may require the complainant to deposit with it such amount as may be specified towards payment of fees to the appropriate laboratory for carrying out the tests. On receipt of the report, a copy thereof is to be sent by the District Forum/State Commission to the opposite party along with its own remarks.

In case any of the parties dispute the correctness of the methods of analysis/test adopted by the appropriate laboratory, the concerned party will be required to submit its objections in writing in regard to the report. After giving both the parties a reasonable opportunity of being heard and to present their objections, if any, the District Forum/State Commission shall pass appropriate orders.

II. *In case of disputes relating to goods not requiring testing or analysis or relating to services:* Where the opposite party denies or disputes the allegations contained in the complaint within the time given by the District Forum/State Commission, it shall dispose of the complaint on the basis of evidence tendered by the parties. In case of failure by the opposite party to represent his case within the prescribed time, the complaint shall be disposed of on the basis of evidence tendered by the complainant.

Limitation Period for Filing of Complaint

The District Forum, the State Commission, or the National Commission shall not admit a complaint unless it is filed within two years from the date on which the cause of action has arisen. However, where the complainant satisfies the Distict Forum/State Commission that he had sufficient cause for not filing the complaint within two years, such complaint may be entertained by it after recording the reasons for condoning the delay.

Powers of the Redressal Agencies

The District Forum, State Commission, and the National Commission are vested with the powers of a civil court under the Code of Civil Procedure while trying a suit in respect of the following matters:

- the summoning and enforcing attendance of any defendant or examining the witness on oath;
- the discovery and production of any document or other material producible as evidence;
- the reception of evidence on affidavits;
- the requisitioning of the report of the concerned analysis or test from the appropriate laboratory or from any other relevant source;
- issuing of any commission for the examination of any witness; and
- any other matter which may be prescribed.

Under the Consumer Protection Rules, 1987, the District Forum, the State Commission, and the National Commission have the power to require any person:

(i) to produce before and allow to be examined by an officer of any authorities such books of accounts, documents, or commodities as may be required and to keep such book, documents, etc., under its custody for the purposes of the Act;

(ii) to furnish such information which may be required for the purpose by any officer so specified.

They have the power:

(i) to pass written orders authorizing any officer to exercise the power of entry and search of any premises where these books, papers, commodities, or documents are kept if there is any ground to believe that these may be destroyed, multiliated, altered, falsified, or secreted. Such authorized officer may also seize books, papers, documents, or commodities if they are required for the purposes of the Act, provided the seizure is communicated to the District Forum/State commission/National commission within 72 hours. On examination of such documents or commodities, the agency concerned may order the retention thereof or may return it to the party concerned.

(ii) to issue remedial orders to the opposite party.

(iii) to dismiss frivolous and vexatious complaints and to order the complainant to make payment of costs not exceeding Rs 10,000 to the opposite party.

Remedies Granted under the Act

The District Forum/State Commission/National Commission may pass one or more of the following orders to grant relief to the aggrieved consumer:

- To remove the defects pointed out by the appropriate laboratory from goods in question

- To replace the goods with new goods of similar description, which shall be free from any defect
- To return to the complainant the price or, as the case may be, the charges paid by the complainant
- To pay such amount as may be awarded by it as compensation to the consumer for any loss or injury suffered by the consumer due to negligence of the opposite party
- To remove the defects or deficiencies in the services in question
- To discontinue the unfair trade practice or the restrictive trade practice or not to repeat them
- Not to offer the hazardous goods for sale
- To withdraw the hazardous goods from being offered for sale
- To provide for adequate costs to parties

Appeals

Any person aggrieved by an order made by the District Forum may tender an appeal to the State Commission in the prescribed form and manner. Similarly, any person aggrieved by any original order of the State Commission may appeal to the National Commission in the prescribed form and manner. Any person aggrieved by any original order of the National Commission may appeal to the Supreme Court.

All such appeals are to be made within 30 days from the date of the order. The concerned appellate authority may entertain an appeal after the said period of 30 days if it is satisfied that there was sufficient cause for not filing it within the prescribed period. The period of 30 days is to be computed from the date of receipt of the order by the appellant.

Where no appeal has been received against any of the orders of the authorities, such orders would be final. The District Forum, the State Commission, or the National Commission may enforce respective orders as if it were a decree or order made by a court of law and in the event of their inability to execute the same, they may send the order to the court for execution as if it were a court decree or order.

Penalties

Failure or omission by a trader or other person against whom a complaint is made or the failure of the complainant to comply with any order of the State Commission or the National Commission shall be punishable with imprisonment for a term which shall not be less than one month but which may extend to 3 years, or with a fine of not less than Rs 2,000 but which may extend to Rs 10,000, or with both.

However, if it is satisfied that the circumstances of any case so require, then the District Forum or the State Commission or the National Commission may impose a lower fine or a shorter term of imprisonment.

Annexure IV   The Prevention of Food Adulteration Act, 1954

The Prevention of Food Adulteration Act, 1954 aims at making provisions for the prevention of adulteration of food. The Act extends to the whole of India and came into force on 1st June 1955.

What is Adulterated Food?

An article of food shall be deemed to be adulterated

(a) if the article sold by a vendor is not of the nature, substance, or quality demanded by the purchaser or which it purports to be;

(b) if the article contains any substance affecting its quality or if it is so processed as to injuriously affect its nature, substance, or quality;

(c) if any inferior or cheaper substance has been substituted wholly or partly for the article, or any constituent of the article has been wholly or partly subtracted from it, so as to affect its quality or if it is so processed as to injuriously affect its nature, substance, or quality;

(d) if the article had been prepared, packed or kept under insanitary conditions whereby it has become contaminated or injurious to health;

(e) if the article consists wholly or in part of any filthy, putrid, disgusting, rotten, decomposed or diseased animal or vegetable substance or being insect-infested, or is otherwise unfit for human consumption;

(f) if the article is obtained from a diseased animal;

(g) if the article contains any poisonous or other ingredient which is injurious to health;

(h) if the container of the article is composed of any poisonous or deleterious substance which renders its contents injurious to health;

(i) if the article contains any prohibited colouring matter or preservative, or any permitted colouring matter or preservative in excess of the prescribed limits;

(j) if the quality or purity of the article falls below the prescribed standard, or its constituents are not present in standard proportions, or its constituents are present in proportions other than those prescribed, whether or not rendering it injurious to health.

Thus, addition of water to milk amounts to adulteration, within the meaning of sub-clauses (b) or (c).

When are Foods Misbranded

An article of food shall be deemed to be misbranded

- if it is an imitation of, or is a substitute for, or resembles in a manner likely to deceive, another article of food, and is not conspicuously labelled so as to indicate its true character,

- if it is falsely stated to be the product of any place or country,

- if it is sold by a name which belongs to another article of food,

- if it is so coloured, flavoured, coated, powdered, or polished as to conceal any damage to the article or to appear of greater value than it really is,

- if false claims are made for it upon the label or otherwise,

- if, when sold in sealed or prepared packages by its manufacturer, the contents of each package are not conspicuously and correctly stated on the outside thereof,

- if the package containing it is deceptive with respect to its contents, in any manner, such as label, statement, design, or device, which is misleading,

- if the package containing it, or the label thereon, bears the name of a fictitious individual or company as the manufacturer or producer of the article,

- if it purports to be, or is represented as being for special dietary uses, unless its label bears the prescribed information concerning its dietary properties,
- if it contains any artificial flavouring, colouring, or chemical preservatives without declaring the same on the label, or in violation of the requirements of this Act and the rules made thereunder, and
- if it is not labelled in accordance with the requirements of this Act and the Rules made thereunder.

Preservative means a substance which when added to food is capable of inhibiting, retarding, or arresting the process of fermentation, acidification, or other decomposition of food.

Prohibitions and Restrictions

Prohibition on the Manufacture, Sale, etc. of Certain Food Articles

No person shall manufacture, store, sell, or distribute
 (i) any adulterated food,
 (ii) any misbranded food,
 (iii) food articles to be sold under licence without fulfilling the conditions of the licence,
 (iv) any food article the sale of which is prohibited by the food (health) authority in the interest of public health,
 (v) any food article in contravention of any other provision of the Act or the Rules, (see 'Conditions for Sale'), or
 (vi) any adulterant.

The act of storing an adulterated article of food would be an offence only if storing is for sale. The sale of a part of the stored article constitutes an offence distinct and independent from the offence of storing for sale.

Prohibition on use of Certain Expressions While Labelling of Edible Oils and Fats

The package, label, or the advertisement of edible oils and fats shall not use the expressions super-refined, extra-refined, micro-refined, double-refined, ultra-refined, anti-cholesterol, cholesterol fighter, soothing to heart, cholesterol friendly, saturated fat free, or such other expressions which are exaggerations of the quality of the product. (Rule 37 D).

Prohibition on the Sale of Certain Admixtures

For example, cream which has not been prepared exclusively from milk, milk which contains any added water, ghee which contains any added matter not exclusively derived from milk fat, a mixture of two or more edible oils as an edible oil and turmeric containing any foreign substance, etc. (Rule 44).

Prohibition on the use of acetylene gas (carbide gas) in artificially ripening of fruits (Rule 44 AA).

Prohibition on the sale of food articles coated with mineral oil, except in accordance with the permitted standards (Rule 44 AAA and Appendix B).

Restriction on the sale of ghee having less than specified Reichert value except under the 'AGMARK' seal (Rule 46).

Prohibition on the sale of admixtures of ghee or butter, or on its use as an ingredient in the preparation of an article of food (Rule 46).

Any food item resembling honey, but not pure honey, shall not be marked 'honey' (Rule 45).

Restriction on the sale of kangra tea, except only after it is graded and marked in accordance with the provisions of the Agricultural Produce (Grading and Marketing) Act, 1937 and the rules made thereunder. (Rule 44E).

Conditions for the sale of flavoured tea—only by those manufacturers who are registered with Tea Board and the package bearing the label, 'FLAVOURED TEA' (Common name of permitted flavour, percentage and registration no.) (Rule 44G).

Restriction on the sale of common salt: No person shall sell or offer or expose for sale, or have in his premises for the purpose of sale, common salt for direct human consumption unless the same is iodized. (Rule 44H).

Restriction on the use and sale of artificial sweeteners, except that saccharin sodium can be added to carbonated water, supari, pan masala, and pan flavouring material within the specified maximum limit and aspertaine may be sold for diabetic use under medical advice. (Rule 47).

Prohibition on the sale of permitted food colours, i.e., synthetic colours, or their mixtures or any preparation of such colours, except under a licence. (Rule 48A).

Prohibition on the sale of permitted food additives, except only under the ISI certification marks. (Rule 48C).

Prohibition on the use of Coumarin and Dihydro Cocumarin, Tankabean (Dipteryl Adorat) and B-asarane and Cinamyl Authracilate as flavouring agents. Any extraneous addition of flavouring agent should be mentioned on the label attached to any package of food so flavoured in capital letters in the following manner:
'CONTAINS ADDED FLAVOUR'

Restriction on the Use of Preservatives

Addition of Class I preservatives, i.e., common salt, sugar, dextrose, glucose (syrup), spices, vinegar, or acetic acid, honey, and edible vegetable oil in any food is not restricted provided that the food article to which the preservative has been added conforms to the specifications laid down in Appendix B.

Class II preservatives such as benzoic acid and its salts, sodium diacetate and sodium, potassium and calcium salts of lactic acid, etc. can be used only restrictively. Use of more than one Class II preservative is prohibited.

Conditions for the Sale of a Food Article

Every utensil or container used for manufacturing, preparing, or containing any food or ingredients, and second-hand tin containers for packaging of edible oils and fats, meant for sale, shall be maintained in a clean and sanitary condition, away from impure air or dust, properly covered at all times, and such utensils or containers shall not be used for any other purpose. Use of rusty containers, improperly tinned copper or brass containers, containers of aluminium or plastic not conforming to ISI specifications, etc. in preparation of food is also prohibited. Besides, certain special conditions for sale of certain articles such as asafoetida, salseed fat, lactic acid, edible oils, katha, margarine, milk powder, etc. have also been laid down.

With effect from 22 Feb. 1995, persons shall sell powdered spices only in a packed form. No person shall sell or serve food in any commercial establishment in plastic articles used in catering and cutlery, unless the plastic material used in catering and cutlery articles conform to the food grade plastic.

Purchaser may have the Food Analyzed

A purchaser of any article of food, or a recognized consumer association, may also get an article of food analyzed by the public analyst on payment of the prescribed fees, provided that the vendor is informed of this intended action at the time of purchase. Thereafter, the purchaser or the consumer associations have to follow the procedures mentioned by the food inspectors. If the article of food is found to be adulterated, the fees paid by the purchaser or the association shall be refunded.

Offences and Penalties

- Import, manufacture, storage, sale, or distribution of any food article which is adulterated by allowing its quality or purity to fall below the prescribed standard, or is misbranded, or is in contravention of any provision of the Act. Penalty is minimum imprisonment of six months that may extend up to 3 years and a minimum fine of Rs 1,000.
- Import, manufacture, storage, sale, or distribution of any adulterant not injurious to health. Penalty is minimum imprisonment of six months that may extend up to 3 years and minimum fine of Rs 1,000.
- Preventing a food inspector from taking a sample or exercising his powers. Penalty is minimum imprisonment of six months that may extend up to 3 years and minimum fine of Rs 1,000.
- Giving a false warranty in writing in respect of any food article. Penalty is minimum imprisonment of six months that may extend up to 3 years and minimum fine of Rs 1,000.
- Import, manufacture, storage, sale, or distribution of any food article, which is adulterated within the meaning of any of the Sub-clauses(e) to (l) of Section 2(ia); or any adulterant which is injurious to health. Penalty is minimum imprisonment of one year that may extend up to 6 years and minimum fine of Rs 2,000.

- Sale or distribution of any food article containing any poisonous or other ingredient injurious to health, which is likely to cause death or grievous bodily harm. Penalty is minimum imprisonment of three years that may extend up to life and minimum fine of Rs 5,000.

Annexure V   The Standard of Weights and Measures Act, 1976

The Standard of Weights and Measures Act, 1976 was enacted to establish standards of weights and measures, to regulate inter-state trade or commerce in weights, measures, and other goods, which are sold or distributed by weight, measure, or number, and to provide for matters connected therewith or incidental thereto. The Act extends to the whole of India.

Sale and Distribution of Goods in Packaged Form

When commodities are sold or distributed in packaged form in the course of inter-state trade or commerce, it is essential that every package must have a:
- a plain and conspicuous declaration thereon showing the identity of the commodity in the package,
- the net quantity in terms of the standard units of weights and measures and if in Nos, the accurate number therein,
- the unit sale price of the commodity and the sale price of that particular package,
- the names of the manufacturer and also of the packer or distributor should be mentioned on the package.

In this regard, the Packaged Commodities Rules (PCR) were framed in 1977. These Rules extend to the whole of India and apply to commodities in the packaged form which are, or are intended or likely to be sold, distributed, delivered, offered, displayed for sale, distribution or delivery, or which are stored for sale or distribution or delivery in the course of inter-state trade and commerce.

Exemptions

The following are the items on which the PCR, 1977 are not application:-

1. Any raw material for the use of industrial purpose only.

2. Any part or material used in any workshop or service station repairing bicycle, tricycle and motor cycle.

3. Fast food items packed by restaurant/hotel etc.

4. Drugs/medicines covered under Drug Control Order, 1955.

5. Agriculture farm products in packet of above 50 kg.

Packages for Retail Sale

1. Packaged commodities meant for retail sale, distribution, or delivery shall contain items only

in standard quantities as specified in the third schedule of the Act.

2. Every package shall bear thereon or on a label securely affixed thereto, a definite, plain, and conspicuous declaration giving the name and address of the manufacturer or where the manufacturer is not the packer, the name and address of the manufacturer and packer, the name and net quantity of the commodity in weight, measure or number, as the case may be, the month and year in which the commodity is manufactured or pre-packed, and the retail sale price of the package. Where size of the commodity is relevant, the dimensions thereof shall also be given in the package.

3. Besides, every package shall bear conspicuously the name and address of the manufacturer; where the manufacturer is not the packer, the package shall bear the name and address of the manufacturer and the packer; and where the commodity is manufactured outside India but is packed in India, the package shall also contain the name and complete address of the packer in India.

4. Certain commodities have been exempted from the printing of the declaration of sale price. These are uncanned packages of vegetables, fruits, fish, or meat.

5. With effect from 1 Jan. 1996, in case of soft drinks, ready to serve fruit beverages, or the like, the retail sale price shall be printed either on the crown cap or on the bottle or on both.

6. The rules specify the size of the font, etc. on the principal display panel on packages so that the details provided thereon can be easily examined by the customer.

7. Any manufacturer or packer of vanaspati, ghee, and butter oil shall declare the net quantity by weight with its equivalent in volume or vice versa w.e.f. 1 Jul. 1995.

Wholesale Packages

Every wholesale package shall bear thereon a legible, definite, plain, and conspicuous declaration giving the name of the manufacturer or of the packer, the identity of the commodity contained in the package and the total number of retail packages contained in that wholesale package or the net quantity in terms of the standard units of weight, measure, or number of the commodity.

Packages for Export

Every package for export shall have conspicuous declaration that it is intended for export and the name and address of the manufacturer or packer provided the importer has no objection to such indications.

In addition, the identity of the commodity contained and its net weight, measure, or number shall also be declared on the package.

Where an export package contains two or more individually packaged or labeled pieces of the same or different commodities, the number and description of such individual packages and the net weight, measure, or number of commodities in each shall also be clearly displayed.

Export packages from all the countries shall not be sold in India unless the manufacturer or packer has repacked or re-labeled the commodity for domestic sale.

Packed Commodities Imported into India

All pre-packed commodities imported into India shall carry:
- name and address of the importer,
- generic or common name of the commodity packed,
- net quantity in terms of standard unit of weight and measure without applying standard sizes prescribed under the third schedule,
- month and year of packing in which the commodity is manufactured or packed or imported, and its retail sale price,

The importer shall be responsible for making these mandatory declarations in either of the following manners:

(i) printed on a label securely affixed to the package; or

(ii) made on an additional wrapper and imported package may be kept inside the additional wrapper; or

(iii) printed on the package itself; or

(iv) made on a card or tape affixed firmly to the package or container and bearing the required information.

Price Tags and Stickers

- No manufacturer, packer, wholesaler, or retail detailer shall sell any packaged commodity at a price exceeding its retail sale price.
- Where any tax payable in relation to a packaged commodity is revised, it shall not be sold at a price exceeding the revised retail sale price communicated by the manufacturer or packer.
- The manufacturer or packer shall communicate by at least two advertisements in the newspaper such price revision, whether there is an increase or decrease in the retail price of any pre-packed commodity.
- The revised retail price shall be charged in relation to packages which were pre-packed in the month in which such tax had revised or fresh tax had been imposed or in a month following thereto.
- Where the revised prices are lower than the price marked on the package, the commodity shall be sold at the revised price irrespective of the month of packing.
- The retail sale price of any packed commodity indicated on the package or a label affixed thereto, shall not be obliterated, smuggled, or altered by any person.
- No additional label should be stuck on a package even with manufacturer's logo or trademark. However, affixing of a price sticker to indicate a retail sale price less than the MRP declared by the manufacturer is not a violation of the rules, provided that the declaration made by the manufacturer is not obliterated.

The manufacturer or packer shall not alter the price on a wrapper once printed and used for packaging.

Offences and Penalties

Offence	Penalty
1 Use of non-standard weights or measures or numeration	1 Imprisonment up to 6 months or fine up to Rs 1,000/- or both. For second or subsequent offence, imprisonment up to 2 years and also fine.
2 Quotation, etc. in non-standard weights and measures	2 Fine up to Rs 2,000/-. For the second or subsequent offence, imprisonment for a term up to 3 years and also fine.
3 Sale, etc. of unverified weights and measures	3 Fine up to Rs 10,000/-. For the second or subsequent offence imprisonment up to 7 years and also fine.
4 Sale, etc. of packaged goods not conforming to provisions of Sec. 39	4 Fine up to Rs 5,000/-. For second or subsequent offence imprisonment up to 5 years and also fine.
5 Contravention of any other provision of the Act	5 Fine up to Rs 2,000/-

Annexure VI   The Sales of Goods Act, 1930

The Sale of Goods Act, 1930 governs the contracts relating to sale of goods. It applies to the whole of India except the state of Jammu and Kashmir.

The contacts for sale of goods are subject to the general principles of the law relating to contracts, i.e., the Indian Contract Act. A contract for sale of goods has, however, certain peculiar features, such as transfer of ownership of the goods, delivery of goods, rights and duties of the buyers and sellers, remedies for breach of contract, and conditions and warranties implied under a contract for sale of goods. These peculiarities are the subject matter of the provisions of the Sale of Goods Act, 1930.

Elements of Sale, Sale Contract, and Goods?

A contract of sale of goods is a contract whereby the seller transfers or agrees to transfer the property in goods to the buyer for a price. It thus includes both an actual 'sale' and an 'agreement to sell', which have been distinguished later.

'Goods' means every kind of movable property other than actionable claims and money, and includes stocks and shares, growing crops, grass and things attached to or forming part of the land, which are agreed to be severed from land before sale or under the contract of sale.

A 'sale' must be distinguished from an 'agreement to sell' since the legal implications of the two terms are vastly different. A contract, wherein the property in the goods is transferred from the seller to the buyer, the contract is called a sale, but where the transfer of property in the goods is to take place at a future time, or subject to some conditions, thereafter to be fulfilled, it is called an agreement to sell. An agreement to sell becomes a sale when the time elapses or the conditions are fulfilled subject to which the property in the goods is to be transferred.

Effects of Destruction of Goods Already Contracted

There are various kinds of goods and the parties have various options to agree about the delivery of the goods. What shall be the fate of a contract if the goods are perished or destroyed?

Destruction before Making of Contract Where in a contract for sale of specific goods, at the time of making the contract, the goods, without the knowledge of the seller, have perished or become so damaged as to no longer fit their description in the contract, the contract shall become null and void. This is based on the rule of impossibility of performance. Since the subject matter of the contract, which is one of its essential ingredients, itself is destroyed, the contract cannot be carried out.

'Perishing of goods' includes not only complete destruction of the goods when the seller has been irretrievably deprived by the goods or when the goods have been stolen or have in some other way been lost and are untraceable, but also when the goods become un merchantable, i.e., when the goods have lost their commercial value.

Destruction after the Agreement to Sell but before Sale Where in an agreement to sell specific goods, if subsequently the goods, without any fault on the part of the seller or buyer, perish or become so damaged as to no longer fit their description in the agreement, the agreement shall become void, provided the goods perish before the ownership and risk passes to the buyer. This rule is based on the ground of impossibility of performance.

If the title to goods has already passed to the buyer, he must pay for the goods though the same cannot be delivered.

Documents of Title to Goods

A document of title to goods is one which entitles and enables its rightful holder to deal with the goods represented by it as if he were the owner. It is used in the ordinary course of business as a proof of the ownership, possession, or control of goods. It authorizes the possessor to receive the goods. It also confers a right on the possessor to transfer the goods to another person, by mere delivery or by proper endorsement of the delivery.

Cash memo, bill of lading, dock warrant, warehouse keeper's or wharfinger's certificate, lorry receipt (L/R), railway receipt (R/R), and delivery order are some examples of documents of title to goods.

Express and Implied Conditions/Warranties : A Sale

Conditions and warranties may be express or implied.

Express conditions and warranties are those which are expressly provided in the contract.

Implied conditions and warranties are those which are implied by law or custom. These are mentioned in the contract of sale, unless the parties agree to the contrary.

Condition as to Title   In every contract of sale, unless the circumstances of the contract are such as to show a different intention, there is an implied condition on the part of the seller that :

- in case of a sale, he has a right to sell the goods, and
- in case of an agreement to sell, he will have a right to sell the goods at the time when the property is to pass.

The term 'right to sell' contemplates not only that the seller has the title to what he purports to sell, but also that the seller has the right to pass the property. If the seller's title turns out to be defective, the buyer may reject the goods.

Condition as to Description   In a contract of sale by description, there is an implied condition that the goods shall correspond with the description. The term 'sale by description' includes the following situations:

- The buyer has not seen the goods and buys them relying on the description given by the seller.
- The buyer has seen the goods but he relies not on what he has seen but what was stated to him and the deviation of the goods from the description is not apparent.

Packing of goods may sometimes be a part of the description. Where the goods do not conform to the method of packing described (by the buyer or the seller) in the contract, the buyer can reject the goods.

Condition as to Quality or Fitness   Where the buyer, expressly or by implication, makes known to the seller the particular purpose for which goods are required, so as to show that the buyer relies on the seller's skill or judgement, and the goods are of a description which it is in the course of the seller's business to supply (whether or not as the manufacturer of producer), there is an implied condition that the goods shall be reasonably fit for such purpose. In other words, this condition of fitness shall apply if:

- the buyer makes known to the seller the particular purpose for which the goods are required,
- the buyer relies on the seller's skill or judgement,
- the goods are of a description which the seller ordinarily supplies in the course of his business, and
- the goods supplied are not reasonably fit for the buyer's purpose.

Condition as to Merchantability   Where the goods are bought by description from a seller, who deals in goods of that description (whether or not as the manufacturer or producer), there is an implied condition that the goods shall be of merchantable quality.

Merchantable quality ordinarily means that the goods should be such as would be commercially saleable under the description by which they are known in the market at their full value.

Condition as to Wholesomeness   In case of sale of eatable provisions and foodstuff, there is another implied condition that the goods shall be wholesome. Thus, the provisions or foodstuff must not only correspond to their description, but must also be merchantable and wholesome. By 'wholesomeness' it means that goods must be for human consumption.

Condition implied by Custom or Trade Usage   An implied warranty or condition as to quality or fitness for a particular purpose may be annexed by the usage of trade. In certain sale contracts, the purpose for which the goods are purchased may be implied from the conduct of the parties or from the nature or description of the goods. In such cases, the parties enter into the contract with reference to those known usage. For instance, if a person buys a perambulator or a medicine, the purpose for which it is purchased is implied from the thing itself; the buyer need not disclose the purpose to the seller.

Conditions in a Sale by Sample   A contract of sale is a contract for sale by sample where there is a term in the contract, express or implied, to that effect. Usually, a sale by sample is implied when a sample is shown and the parties intend that the goods should be of the kind and quality as the sample is.

Conditions in a Sale by Sample as well as by Description   A vast majority of cases in which samples are shown are sales by sample as well as by description. In a contract for sale by sample as well as by description, the goods supplied must correspond both with the sample and with the description.

Implied Warranties

A condition becomes a warranty when
(a) the buyer waives the conditions or opts to treat the breach of the condition as a breach of warranty; or
(b) the buyer accepts the goods or a part thereof, or is not in a position to reject the goods.

Implied Warranty of Quiet Possession   In every contract of sale, unless there is a contrary intention, there is an implied warranty that the buyers shall have and enjoy quiet possession of the goods. If the buyer's right to possess and enjoy the goods is in any way disturbed due to the seller's defective title, the buyer may sue the seller for damages for breach of this warranty.

Implied Warranty of Freedom from Encumbrances   The buyer is entitled to a further warranty that the goods shall be free from any charge or encumbrance in favour of any third party not declared or known to the buyer before or at the time when the contract is made. If the buyer is required to discharge the amount of the encumbrance, it shall be a breach of this warranty and the buyer shall be entitled to damages for the same.

Transfer of Property in Goods

The property in the goods is said to be transferred from the seller to the buyer when the latter acquires the proprietary rights over the goods and the obligations linked thereto. 'Property in Goods' which means the ownership of goods, is different from 'possession of goods', which means the physical custody or control of the goods.

The transfer of property in the goods from the seller to the buyer is the essence of a contract of sale. Therefore, the moment when the property in goods passes from the seller to the buyer is significant for following reasons.

Ownership   The moment the property in goods passes, the seller ceases to be their owner and the buyer acquires the ownership. The buyer can exercise the proprietary rights over the goods.

For example, the buyer may sue the seller for non-delivery of the goods or when the seller has resold the goods, etc.

Risk Follows Ownership   The general rule is that the risk follows the ownership, irrespective of whether the delivery has been made or not. If the goods are damaged or destroyed, the loss shall be borne by the person who was the owner of the goods at the time of damage or destruction. Thus, the risk of loss prima facie is with the person with whom the property is.

Action Against Third Parties   When the goods are in any way damaged or destroyed by the action of third parties, it is only the owner of the goods who can take action against them.

Suit for Price The seller can sue the buyer for the price, unless otherwise agreed, only after the goods have become the property of the buyer.

Insolvency In the event of insolvency of either the seller or the buyer, the question whether the goods can be taken over by the official receiver or assignee will depend on whether the property in goods is with the party who has become insolvent.

Essentials for Transfer of Property   The two essential requirements for transfer of property in the goods are as follows.

Goods must be Ascertained   Unless the goods are ascertained they (or the property therein) cannot pass from the seller to the buyer. Thus, where there is a contract for the sale of unascertained goods, no property in the goods is transferred to the buyer unless and until the goods are ascertained.

Intention to Pass Property in Goods must be There   In a sale of specific or ascertained goods the property in which is transferred to the buyer at such time as the parties to the contract intend it to be, regard shall be had to the terms of the contract, the conduct of the parties, and the circumstances of the case.

Types of Contracts (With Regard to Delivery of Goods)

There are various types of contracts from the point of view of the delivery of goods.

F.A.S. or F.A.R. Contract   F.A.S. stands for 'Free alongside Ship' and F.A.R. stands for 'Free Along with Rail'. Under F.A.S. or F.A.R. contracts, the seller is required to deliver the goods alongside the ship or rail named in the contract and to notify the buyer that the goods have been so delivered. The property in the goods passes to the buyer when the seller delivers the goods alongside the ship or rail. Thereafter, it is the buyer's duty to arrange for the contract of affreightment and insurance of the goods while in transit.

F.O.B. or F.O.R. Contracts   F.O.B. stands for 'Free on Board' and F.O.R. stands for 'Free on Rail'. In a F.O.B. (or F.O.R.) contract, the seller is required to deliver the goods on board (or on rail), as named in the contract. Thus, the seller has to bear all expenses up to and including shipment of goods on behalf of the buyer, who is responsible for their freight, insurance, and subsequent expenses.

Thus, as soon as the goods are put on board, the property in them passes to the buyer. This will be so even if the goods are not specific or ascertained. The buyer is liable to pay the price even if the goods are lost in transit. The property in goods shall, however, not pass if the seller reserves the right of disposal.

C.I.F. Contract   The words 'C.I.F.' stand for cost, insurance, and freight. A C.I.F. contract is a type of contract wherein the price includes cost, insurance, and freight charges. Under a C.I.F. contract the seller is required to insure the goods, deliver them to the shipping company, arrange for their affreightment, and send the bill of lading and insurance policy together with the invoice and a certificate of origin to a bank. The documents are usually delivered by the bank against the payment of seller since he continues to be the owner of the goods until the buyer pays for them and obtains the documents. The property in the goods passes to the buyer on the delivery of documents. The buyer is equally protected as he is called upon to pay only against the documents and the moment he pays, he obtains the documents which enable him to get delivery of the goods. If in the meantime the goods are lost neither the buyer nor the seller is put to loss, whoever is the owner at the time of the loss can recover it from the insurer.

Ex-ship Contracts   Under an 'ex-ship contract the seller has to deliver the goods to the buyer at the port of destination. In such contracts the property in the goods does not pass until actual delivery. The goods are at the seller's risk during the voyage. It is therefore for the seller to insure the goods in order to protect his interest. The seller is to pay the freight, or otherwise release the ship owner's lien and to furnish the buyer with a delivery order or an effectual direction to the ship owner to deliver.

Rights Against the Goods

Where the property in the goods has passed to the buyer:

Right of Lien   'Lien is the right to retain possession of goods until certain charges in respect thereof are paid. An unpaid seller who is in possession of the goods is entitled to retain them until the payment of the price, in the following cases:
(a) when the goods have been sold without any stipulations to credit.
(b) when the goods have been sold on credit, but the term of credit has expired.
(c) when the buyer becomes insolvent.

Where the goods have been sold on credit, the right of lien shall remain suspended over the period of credit and shall revive on the expiry of that period.

The right of lien is linked with possession of the goods and not with the title. It is not effected even if the seller has transferred the documents of title till he remains in possession of the goods. However, if the buyer has further transferred the documents of title to a bona fide purchaser the seller's lien is defeated.

Right of Stoppage in Transit   The right of stoppage of goods in transit is enjoyed by an unpaid seller after he has parted with the possession of the goods. The seller has the right to resume possession of the goods while they are in the course of transit and to retain them until payment or tender of the price.

The right of stoppage in transit is available to an unpaid seller when the buyer becomes insolvent and the goods are in transit.

The buyer is said to be 'insolvent' when he has ceased to pay his debts in the ordinary course of business or cannot pay his debts as they become due whether he has committed an act of insolvency or not.

Right of Resale The rights of lien and stoppage in transit would not have been of much value if the seller had no right to resell the goods, because the seller cannot continue to hold the good indefinitely. Section 54 provides an unpaid seller with a limited right to resell the goods.

An unpaid seller may resell the goods

- when the goods are of perishable nature, without giving any notice to the buyer, of the resale,
- in case of other goods, when after giving a notice to the buyer of his intention to resell the goods, the buyer does not pay the price within a reasonable time; and
- where the seller has expressly reserved the right of resale in the contract. No notice to the buyer is required in that case.

where the property in the goods has not passed to the buyer:

Right of Withholding Delivery Where the property in the goods has not passed to the buyer, the unpaid seller has the right to withhold delivery of the goods, which is similar to and co-extensive with his rights of lien and stoppage in transit which he would have had if the property had passed.

Rights Against the Buyer Personally (Seller's Remedies Against buyer for Breach of Contract) Besides the above rights against the goods, an unpaid seller has certain rights against the buyer personally. The seller enjoys the following rights in personam (also known as remedies for breach of contract).

Suit for Price When the property in the goods has passed to the buyer, and the buyer wrongfully neglects or refuses to pay the price, the seller is entitled to sue him for the price.

Where under a contract of sale the price is payable on a certain day irrespective of delivery or passing of property, and the buyer refuses or neglects to pay on that day, the seller may sue him for the price.

Suit for Damages for Non-acceptance Where the buyer wrongfully neglects or refuses to pay for the goods, the seller may sue him for damages for non-acceptance.

Suit for Damages for Repudiation of Contract before the Date of Delivery Where the buyer repudiates the contract before the date of delivery, the seller may adopt any of the following two courses of action, viz.

(a) The seller may treat the contact as rescinded and sue the buyer for damages. This is also known as 'damages for anticipatory breach'. The damages will be assessed according to the prices prevailing on the date of breach.

(b) The seller may treat the contract as subsisting and wait till the date of delivery. The contract remains open at the risk and for the benefit of both the parties. If the buyer subsequently chooses to perform, there shall be no damages; otherwise he shall be liable to damages assessed according to the prices on the day stipulated for delivery.

Suit for Interest The seller may recover interest or special damages whereby law interest or special damages may be recoverable.

Buyer's Remedies Against Seller for Breach of Contract A buyer also has certain remedies against the seller who commits a breach. These are described below:

Suit for damages for non-delivery   When the seller wrongfully neglects or refuses to deliver the goods to the buyer, the buyer may sue the seller for damages for non-delivery. This is in addition to the buyer's right to recover the price, if already paid, in case of non-delivery.

Suit for price Where the buyer has paid the price and the goods are not delivered to him, he can recover the amount paid.

Suit for Specific Performance   When the goods are specific or ascertained, a buyer may sue the seller for specific performance of the contract and compel him to deliver the same goods. The court orders for specific performance only when the goods are specific or ascertained and an order for damages would not be an adequate remedy. Specific performance is generally allowed where the goods are of special significance or value, e.g., a rare painting, a unique piece of jewellery, etc.

Suit for Breach of Warranty   When there is a breach of warranty by the seller, or when the buyer elects or is compelled to treat the breach of condition as breach of warranty, the buyer cannot reject the goods. The buyer may (a) set up the breach of warranty in extinction or diminution of the price payable by him, or (b) sue the seller for damages for breach of warranty.

Suit for Damages for Repudiation of Contract before the Due Date   When the seller repudiates the contract before the date of delivery, the buyer may adopt any of the following two courses of action.

He may treat the contract as rescinded and sue the seller for damages. This is also known as 'damages for anticipatory breach'. The damages will be assessed according to the prices prevailing on the date of breach.

He may treat the contract as subsisting and wait till the date of delivery. The contract remains open at the risk and for the benefit of both the parties. If the seller subsequently chooses to perform, there shall be no damages; otherwise he shall be liable to damages assessed according to the prices on the day stipulated for delivery.

Suit for interest   The buyer may recover such interest or special damages as may be recoverable by law. He may also recover the money paid where the consideration for the payment of it has failed.

In the absence of a contract to the contrary, the court may award interest to the buyer, in a suit by him for the refund of the price in case of a breach on the part of the seller, at such rate as it thinks fit on the amount of the price from the date on which the payment was made.

Rights and Duties of the Buyer

The rights and duties of a buyer under the Act may be summarized as follows.

	Rights		Duties
1.	To have delivery of the goods as per the contract (Secs 31 and 32)	1.	To accept the delivery of goods, when the seller is willing to make the delivery as per the contract (Sec. 31)
2.	To reject the goods when they are not of the description, quality, or quantity as specified in the contract (Sec 37).	2.	To pay the price in exchange for possession of the goods

contd

contd

	Rights		Duties
3.	To repudiate the contract when goods are delivered in instalments without any agreement to that effect [Sec. 38 (1)]	3.	To apply for delivery of the goods (Sec. 35)
4.	To be informed by the seller when the goods are to be sent by sea route so that he may arrange for their insurance [Sec. 39 (30]	4.	To demand delivery of the goods at a reasonable hour [(Sec. 36 (4)]
5.	To have a reasonable opportunity to examine the goods for ascertaining whether they are in conformity with the contract (Sec. 41)	5.	To accept delivery of the goods in instalments and pay for them in accordance with the contract [Sec. 38 (2)]
6.	To sue the seller for recovery of the price, if already paid, when the seller fails to deliver the goods	6.	To bear the risk of deterioration in the course of transit, when the goods are to be delivered at a place other than where they are sold (Sec. 40)
7.	To sue the seller for damages if the seller wrongfully neglects or refuses to deliver the goods to the buyer (Sec. 57)	7.	To inform the seller in case the buyer refuses to accept or reject the goods (Sec. 43)
8.	To sue the seller for specific performance	8.	To take the delivery of the goods within a reasonable time after the seller tenders the delivery (Sec. 44)
9.	To sue the seller for damages for breach of a warranty or for breach of a condition treated as breach of a warranty (Sec.59)	9.	To pay the price, where the property in the goods are passed to the buyer, in accordance with the terms of the contract (Sec. 55)
10.	To sue the seller the damages for anti-cipatory breach of contract (Sec. 60)	10.	To pay damages for non-acceptance of goods (Sec. 56)
11.	To sue the seller for interest where there is a breach of contract on the part of the seller and price has to be refunded to the buyer (Sec. 61)		

Rights and Duties of the Seller

The rights and duties of a seller, under the Act, may be summarized as follows.

	Rights		Duties
1.	To reserve the right of disposal of the goods until certain conditions are fulfilled [Sec. 25 (1)]	1.	To make the arrangement for transfer of property in the goods to the buyer

contd

contd

2.	To assume that the buyer has accepted the goods where the buyer (i) conveys his acceptance; (ii) does an act adopting the sale; or (iii) retains the goods without giving a notice of rejection, beyond the specified date (or reasonable time) in a sale on approval. (Sec. 24)	2.	To ascertain and appropriate the goods to the contract of sale
3.	To deliver the goods only when applied for by the buyer (Sec. 35)	3.	To pass absolute and effective title of the goods to the buyer
4.	To make delivery of the goods in instalments, when so agreed [Sec. 39 (1)]	4.	To deliver the goods in accordance with the terms of the contract (Sec 31)
5.	To exercise lien and retain possession of the goods until payment of the price [Sec. 47 (1)]	5.	To ensure that the goods supplied conform to the implied /expressed conditions and warranties
6.	To stop the goods in transit and resume possession of the goods until payment of the price [Sec. 49 (2) and 50]	6.	To put the goods in a deliverable state and to deliver the goods as and when applied for by the buyer (Sec 35)
7.	To resell the goods under certain circumstances (Sec. 54)	7.	To deliver the goods within the time specified in the contract or within a reasonable time and a reasonable hour [Sec. 36 (2) and (4)]
8.	To withhold delivery of the goods when the property in the goods has not passed to the buyer [Sec. 46 (2)]	8.	To bear all expenses of and incidental to making a delivery, i.e., up to the stage of putting the goods into a deliverable state [Sec. 36 (5)]
9.	To sue the buyer for price when the property in the goods has passed to the buyer or when the price payable on a certain day, in terms of the contract, and the buyer fails to make the payment (sec 55)	9.	To deliver the goods in the agreed quantity [Sec. 37 (1)]
		10.	To deliver the goods in instalments only when so desired by the buyer. [Sec 38 (1)]
		11.	To arrange for insurance of the goods while they are in transmission or custody of the carrier. [Sec. 39 (2)]
		12.	To inform the buyer in time when the goods are sent by a sea route so that he may get the goods insured [Sec. 39 (3)]

Annexure VII   The Essential Commodities Act, 1955

This is an Act to provide, in the interests of the general public, for the control of production, supply, and distribution of, and trade and commerce in, certain commodities.

It was enacted by the Parliament, in the sixth year of the Republic of India in the following manner:

1. Short title and extent

(1) This Act may be called the Essential Commodities Act, 1955.

(2) It extends to the whole of India.

2. Definition

In this Act, unless the context otherwise requires,

(i-a) 'Code' means the Code of Criminal Procedure, 1973 (2 of 1974)

(ii-a) 'Collector' includes an additional collector and such other officer, not below the rank of sub-divisional officer, as may be authorized by the collector to perform the functions and exercise the powers of the collector under this Act.

(a) 'Essential commodity' means any of the following classes of commodities:

  (i) cattle fodder, including oil-cakes and other concentrates;
  (ii) coal including coke and other derivatives;
  (iii) component parts and accessories of automobiles;
  (iv) cotton and woollen textiles;
  (iv-a) drugs [In this sub-clause, 'drug' has the meaning assigned to it in clause (b) of Section 3 of the Drugs and Cosmetics Act, 1940 (23 of 1940)].
  (v) foodstuffs including edible oilseeds and oils;
  (vi) iron and steel, including manufactured products of iron and steel;
  (vii) paper including newsprint, paper board, and straw board;
  (viii) petroleum and petroleum products;
  (ix) raw cotton, whether ginned or unginned, and cotton seed;
  (x) raw jute;
  (xi) any other class of commodity which the central government may, by a notified order, declare to be an essential commodity for the purpose of this Act, being a commodity with respect to which the Parliament has the power to make laws by virtue of entry 33 in list III of the seventh schedule to the constitution.

(b) 'food-crops' include crops of sugarcane;

(c) 'notified order' means an order notified in the official gazette;`

  (cc) 'order' includes a direction issued thereunder;

(d) 'State Government', in relation to a union territory, means the administration thereof;

(e) 'Sugar' means

  (i) any form of sugar containing more than 90% of sucrose, including sugar candy;
  (ii) Khandsari sugar or bura sugar or crushed sugar, or any sugar in crystalline or powdered form; or

(iii) sugar-in-process in vacuum-pan factory or raw sugar produced therein.

(f) Words and expressions used but not defined in this Act and defined in the code shall have the meanings respectively assigned to them in that Code.

Specimen State Amendments

Retailers are required to keep a regular track of amendments to the Act that are made from time to time.

Himachal Pradesh

After sub-clause (vi) of Clause (a) of Section 2, the following new sub-clause inserted, namely:
(vi-a) Packing cases made wholly or partly of wood, card board, or straw.

[H.P. Act 1 of 1992]

Maharasthra

(i) After the words 'the context otherwise requires', the following clause shall be inserted, namely:
(a-i) 'Controller' in Greater Bombay means the Controller of Rationing and includes any Deputy or Assistant Controller of Rationing, and elsewhere means the Collector of the District and includes any Assistant or Deputy Collector or District Supply Officer within his respective jurisdiction.

(ii) After clause (b), the following clauses shall be inserted, namely:
(ba) 'Holder' in relation to any agricultural land, means the person in actual possession of such land and includes a company or other body corporate, firm, association, joint family, or body of individuals in joint possession of such land;
(bb) 'Holding' means the aggregate of all lands in possession of a holder.

[Mah. Act 1 of 1976]

Comments Cement is essential commodity. Amrit Singh v. State. 1995 Cri.L.J. 3771 (Delhi)

3. Power to control production, supply, distribution, etc. of essential commodities

(1) If the Central Government is of the opinion that it is necessary or expedient to do so for maintaining or increasing supplies of any essential commodity or for securing their equitable distribution and availability at fair prices, or for securing any essential commodity for the defence of India, or for the efficient conduct of military operations, it may, by order, provide for regulating or prohibiting the production, supply, and distribution thereof and trade commerce therein.

(2) Without prejudice to the generality of the powers conferred by sub-section (1), an order made thereunder may provide
(a) for regulating by licences, permits, or otherwise the production or manufacture of any essential commodity;
(b) for bringing under cultivation any waste or arable land, whether appurtenant to a building or not, for the growing thereon of food crops generally or of specified food-crops, and for otherwise maintaining or increasing the cultivation of food crops generally, or of specified food-crops;

(c) for controlling the price at which essential commodity may be bought or sold;

(d) for regulating by licences, permits, or otherwise the storage, transport, distribution, disposal acquisition, use or consumption of any essential commodity;

(e) for prohibiting the withholding from sale of any essential commodity ordinarily kept for sale;

(f) for requiring any person holding in stock, or engaged in the roduction, or in the business of buying or selling, of any essential commodity

    (a) to sell the whole or a specified part of quantity held in stock or produced or received by him; or

    (b) in the case of any such commodity which is likely to be produced or received by him, to sell the whole or a specified part of such commodity when produced or received by him, to the Central Government or a State Government, or to an officer or agent of such Government, or to a Corporation owned or controlled by such Government, or to such other person or class of persons and in such circumstances as may be specified in the order;

Explanation 1. An order made under this clause in relation to foodgrains, edible oilseeds, or edible oils, may, having regard to the estimated production in the concerned area of such foodgrains as edible oil-seeds, and edible oils, fix the quantity to be sold by the producers in such area and may also fix, or provide for the fixation of, such quantity on a graded basis, having regard to the aggregate of the area held by, or under the cultivation, of the producers.

Explanation 2. For the purpose of this clause, 'production' with its grammatical variations and cognate expressions includes manufacture of edible oils and sugar.

(g) for regulating or prohibiting any class of commercial or financial transactions relating to foodstuffs or cotton textiles, which, in the opinion of the authority making the order, are, or, if unregulated, are likely to be, detrimental to the public interest;

(h) for collecting any information or statistics with a view to regulating or prohibiting any of the aforesaid matters;

    (i) for requiring persons engaged in the production, supply, or distribution of, or trade and commerce in, any essential commodity to maintain and produce for inspection such books, accounts, and records relating to their business and to furnish such information relating thereto as may be specified in the order;

    (ii) for the grant or issue of licences, permits, or other documents, the charging of fees thereof, the deposit of such sum, if any, as may be specified in the order as security for the due performance of the conditions of any such licence, permit, or other document, the forfeiture of the sum so deposited or any part thereof for contravention of any such conditions, and the adjudication of such forfeiture by such authority as may be specified in the order;

(j) for incidental and supplementary matters, including, in particular, the entry, search, or examination of premises, aircraft, vessels, vehicles, or other conveyances and animals, and the seizure by a person authorized to make such entry, search, or examination -

(i) of any articles in respect of which such person has reason to believe that a contravention of the order has been, is being, or is about to be committed and any packages, coverings, or receptacles in which such articles are found;

(ii) of any aircraft, vessel, vehicle, or other conveyance or animal used in carrying such articles, if such person has reason to believe that such aircraft, vessel, vehicle, or other conveyance or animal is liable to be forfeited under the provisions of this Act;

(iii) of any books of accounts and documents which, in the opinion of such person, may be useful for, or relevant to, any proceeding under this Act and the person from whose custody such books of accounts or documents are seized shall be entitled to make copies thereof or to take extracts therefrom in the presence of an officer having the custody of such books of accounts or documents;

(3) Where any person sells any essential commodity in compliance with an order made with reference to Clause (f) of sub-section (2), there shall be paid to him the price thereof as hereinafter provided

(a) where the price can, consistently with the controlled price, if any, fixed under this section, be agreed upon, the agreed price;

(b) where no such agreement can be reached, the price, calculated with reference to the controlled price, if any;

(c) where neither Clause (a) nor Clause (b) applies, the price calculated at the market rate prevailing in the locality at the date of sale.

(3-A)(i) If the Central Government is of the opinion that it is necessary to do so for controlling the rise in prices or preventing the hoarding of any foodstuff in any locality, it may, by notification in the Official Gazette, direct that notwithstanding anything contained in sub-section (3), the price at which the foodstuff shall be sold in the locality in compliance with an order made with reference to Clause (f) of sub-section (2) shall be regulated in accordance with the provisions of this sub-section.

(ii) Any notification issued under this sub-section shall remain in force for such period not exceeding three months as may be specified in the notification.

(iii) Where, after the issue of a notification under this sub-section, any person sells foodstuff of the kind specified therein, and in the locality so specified, in compliance with an order made with reference to Clause (f) of sub-section (2), there shall be paid to the seller as the price thereof-

(a) where the price can, consistently with the controlled price of the foodstuff, if any, fixed under this section, be agreed upon, the agreed price;

(b) where no such agreement can be reached, the price calculated with reference to the controlled price, if any;

(c) where neither Clause (a) nor Clause (b) applies, the price calculated with reference to the average market rate prevailing in the locality during the period of three months immediately preceding the date of the notification.

(iv) For the purposes of sub-section (c) of Clause (iii) the average market rate prevailing in the locality shall be determined by an officer authorized by the Central Government in this behalf, with reference to the prevailing market rates for which published figures are available in respect of that locality or of a neighbouring locality; and the the average market rate so determined shall be final and shall not be called in question in any court.

(3-B) Where any person is required, by an order made with reference to Clause (f) of sub-section (2), to sell to the Central Government or a State Government or to an officer or agent of such Government, or to a Corporation owned or controlled by such Government, any grade or variety of foodgrains, edible oil seeds, or edible oils in relation to which no notification has been issued under sub-section (3-A), or such notification having been issued, has ceased to be in force, there shall be paid to the person concerned notwithstanding anything to the contrary contained in sub-section (3), an amount equal to the procurement price of such foodgrains, edible oilseeds, or edible oils, as the case may be specified by the State Government, with the previous approval of the Central Government having regard to

(a) the controlled price, if any, fixed under this section or by or under any other law for the time being in force for such grade or variety of foodgrains, edible oilseeds, or edible oils;

(b) the general crop prospects;

(c) the need for making such grade or variety of foodgrains, edible oilseeds, or edible oils available at reasonable prices to the consumers, particularly, the vulnerable sections of the consumers; and

(d) the recommendations, if any, of the Agricultural Prices Commission with regard to the price of the concerned grade or variety of foodgrains, edible oilseeds, or edible oils.

(3-C) Where any producer is required by an order made with reference to Clause (f) of subsection (2) to sell any kind of sugar (whether to the Central Government or a State Government, or to an officer or agent of such Government, or to any other person or class of persons) and either no notification in respect of such sugar has been issued, under sub-section (3-A) or any such notification, having been issued, has ceased to remain in force by efflux of time, then, notwithstanding anything contained in sub-section (3) there shall be paid to that producer an amount thereof , which shall be calculated with reference to such price of sugar as the Central Government may, by order, determine, having regard to

(a) the minimum price, if any, fixed for sugarcane by the Central Government under this section;

(b) the manufacturing cost of sugar;

(c) the duty or tax, if any, paid or payable thereon; and

(d) the securing of a reasonable return on the capital employed in the business of manufacturing sugar;

and different prices may be determined from time to time for different areas or for different factories or for different kinds of sugar.

Explanation For the purposes of this sub-section 'producer' means a person carrying on the business of manufacturing sugar.

(4) If the Central Government is of opinion that it is necessary so to do for maintaining or

increasing the production and supply of an essential commodity, it may, by order, authorize any person (hereinafter referred to as an authorized controller) to exercise, with respect to the whole or any part of such undertaking engaged in the production and supply of the commodity as may be specified in the order, such functions of control as may be provided therein and so long as such order is in force with respect to any undertaking or part thereof -

(a) The authorized controller shall exercise his functions in accordance with any instructions given to him by the Central Government, so, however, that he shall not have any power to give any direction inconsistent with the provisions of any enactment or any instrument determining the functions of the persons in charge of the management of the undertaking except in so far as may be specifically provided by the order; and

(b) The undertaking or part shall be carried on in accordance with any directions given by the authorized controller under the provisions of the order, and any person having any functions of management in relation to the undertaking or part shall comply with any such directions.

[Sub-sections (4-A), (4-B) and (4-C) to Section 3 inserted by Act 14 of 1967 Section 2 ceased to have effect from 31-3-1968.] Repealed by Act 56 of 1974, Section 2 and Schedule I.

(5) An order made under this section shall

(a) In the case of an order of general nature or affecting a class of persons, be notified in the Official Gazette; and

(b) In the case of an order directed to a specified individual be served on such individual

(i) by delivering or tendering it to that individual; or

(ii) if it cannot be so delivered or tendered, by affixing it on the outer door or some other conspicuous part of the premises in which that individual lives, and a written report thereof shall be prepared and witnessed by two persons living in the neighbourhood.

(6) Every order made under this section by the Central Government or by any officer or authority of the Central Government shall be laid before both the Houses of Parliament, as soon as possible, after it is made.

Bihar

In Section 3 of the Act:

(a) in sub-section (2), for clause (f), the following clause shall be, and shall always be deemed to have been, substituted, namely: '(f) For requiring any person holding in stock, or engaged in the manufacture or production of, or in the business of buying or selling of, any essential commodity to sell the whole or a specified part of the quantity held in stock or manufactured or produced, or caused to be produced by him, or received or likely to be received by him in the course of the said business, to the Central Government or a State Government or to such other person or class of persons and in such circumstances as may be specified in the order.

Explanation An order relating to foodgrains made with reference to this clause

(i) may specify the prices, fixed by the Central/State Government in this behalf, after taking into account the recommendation, if any, of the Agricultural Prices Commission and with the prior concurrence of the Central Government as the amount which shall be paid for the foodgrains required to be sold under the order;

(ii) may fix or provide for the fixation of the quantity to be sold by a producer with reference to the area under cultivation and the availability of irrigation for production of the particular foodgrain to which the order relates and also fix or provide for the fixation of such quantities or a graded basis having regard to the aggregate area held by or under the cultivation of different producers;

(b) In sub-section (3), for clause (c), the following clauses shall be and shall be deemed always to have been substituted, namely:

(c) In case of foodgrains, where neither clause (a) nor clause (b) allies, the price, if any, specified in the said order;

(d) Where neither clause (a), nor clause (b), nor clause applies, the price calculated at the market rate prevailing in the locality at the date of sale;

(e) In sub-section (3-B), after clause (a), the following clause shall be, and shall be deemed always to have been, inserted, namely:

(aa) in the case of foodgrains, where no controlled price is fixed by an order made with reference to clause (c) of sub-section (2), the amount specified in the said order made with reference to clause (f) of sub-section (2) for such grade or variety of foodgrains; or [Bihar Act IX of 1978].

Maharashtra

In Section 3 of the principal Act:

(i) In sub-section (2), for clause (f), the following clause shall be, substituted and shall be deemed always to have been, substituted, namely:

(f) for requiring any person holding in stock or likely to hold in stock or engaged in the manufacture or production or processing of, in the business of or buying or selling, any essential commodity to sell, the whole or a specified part of the quantity or the essential commodity held in stock or likely to be held in stock by him or manufactured or produced or processed or likely to be manufactured or produced or processed by him or received or likely to be received by him in his business of buying or selling to the Central Government or the State Government or to an officer or agent of any Government or to such other person or class of persons and in such circumstances as may be specified in the order.

Explanation An order made under this clause in respect of foodgrains may fix or provide for fixation of the quantity to be sold by a producer with reference to the nature and extent of his holding or the land revenue payable by him with certain weightages, which may be prescribed for certain crops or lands enjoying irrigation or other facilities and also fix or provide for fixation of the quantity to be sold on a graded basis having regard to the size of the holdings of different producers.

(ii) In sub-section (3), for clause (c), the following clause shall be substituted, and shall be deemed always to have been substituted, namely: '(c) Where neither clause (a) nor clause (b) applies, in the case of foodgrains, the amount, if any, specified in or calculated in accordance with the order made under clause (f) of sub-section (2) read with sub-section (3-B), and in the case of any other essential commodity, the price calculated at the market rate prevailing in the locality at the date of sale.'

(iii) For sub-section (3-B), the following sub-section shall be substituted, and shall be deemed always to have been substituted, namely: '(3-B) Where, by an order made with reference to clause (f) of sub-section (2), any person is required to sell any grade or variety of foodgrains, edible oilseeds, or edible oils to the Central Government or a State Government or an officer or agent of such Government or a Corporation owned or controlled by such Government or to a person or class of persons specified in the order, and either no notification in respect of such foodgrains, edible oilseeds, or edible oils has been issued under sub-section (3-A), or any such notification having been issued, has ceased to remain in force by efflux of time then, notwithstanding anything contained in sub-section (3), there shall be paid to the person concerned an amount determined by the Central Government or the State Government, as the case may be,

(a) having regard to the controlled price, if any, fixed under this section or by or under any law for the time being in force for such grade or variety of foodgrains, edible oilseeds, or edible oils, or

(b) having regard to the prices recommended by the Agricultural Prices Commission for the concerned essential commodity, where no controlled price in relation to such commodity has been fixed by or under any law for the time being in force. [Mah. Act 1 of 1976].

Orissa

In Section 3 of the Act:

(i) In sub-section (2), for clause (f), the following clause shall be and shall be, deemed always to have been, substituted, namely:

(f) For requiring any person holding in stock or engaged in the manufacture or production of, or in the business of buying or selling any essential commodity to sell the whole or a specified part of the quantity held in stock or manufactured or produced, or caused to be produced, manufactured or produced, by him, or received or likely to be received by him in the course of the said business, to the Central Government or a State Government, or to an officer or agent to such Government, or to such other person or class of persons and in such circumstances as may be specified in the order.

Explanation An order relating to foodgrains made with reference to this clause -

(i) may specify the prices, fixed by the State Government in this behalf, after taking into account the recommendations, if any, of the Agricultural Prices Commission and with the prior concurrence of the Central Government, as the amount, which shall be paid for the foodgrain required to be sold under the order;

(ii) may fix or provide for the fixation of the quantity to be sold by a producer with reference to the area under cultivation and the availability of irrigation for production of a particular foodgrain to which the order relates, and also fix or provide for the fixation of such quantities on a graded basis having regarded to the aggregate area held by or under the cultivation of the different producers.

(ii) In sub-section (3), for clause (c) the following clauses shall be and shall be deemed always to have been substituted, namely:

(c) in the case of foodgrains, where neither clause (a) nor clause (b) applies, the price, if any, specified in the said order

(d) where neither clause (a) nor clause (b) nor clause (c) applies, the price calculated at the market rate prevailing in the locality at the date of sale.

(iii) In sub-section (3-B) after clause (i), the following clause shall be inserted and shall be deemed always to have been inserted, namely: (i-a) In the case of foodgrains where no controlled price is fixed by an order made with reference to clause (c) of sub-section (2), the amount specified in the said order made with reference to clause (f) of sub-section (2) for such grade or variety of foodgrains; or [Orissa Act 8 of 1976].

Uttar Pradesh

In sub-section (2) in clause (f), after Explanation 1, the following Explanation shall be inserted, namely:

'*Explanation 1-A* An order made under this clause in relation to rice may, having regard to the milling capacity of a rice mill, fix the quantity to be sold by the licensed miller and may also fix or provide for the fixation of such quantity on a graded basis.' [U.P. Act 16 of 1978]

In sub-section (2), after clause (f), the following clause shall be inserted, namely:

(ff) for preventing the hoarding of any essential commodities'   [U.P. Act No. 9 of 1974].

In sub-section (3), for clause (c), the following clause shall be substituted and shall be deemed always to have been substituted, namely:

(c) In the case of foodgrains, where neither clause (a) nor clause (b) applies, the amount, if any, specified in the said order made with reference to clause (f) of sub-section (2);

(d) Where neither clause (a), nor clause (b), nor clause (c) applies the price calculated, at the market rate prevailing in the locality at the date of sale.' [U.P. Act 18 of 1975].

Comments Prosecution duty bound to establish knowledge on the part of the accused, and by his merely being a driver, by establishing that the fuel tank did contain kerosene, such knowledge could not be established. Abdul Jabbar v. State of Maharashtra. 1995 Cri.L.J. 3446, (Bom.)

Sale of Adulterated Cement Damaged stoned cement not cement–Proceedings quashed. Sri Mahadev Ch. Mazumder v. State of West Bengal and others. 1994 Cri.L.J. 3808 (Calcutta)

Black Marketing Breach of distribution and control order regarding sugar received under licence–Accused liable for punishment. State of Madhya Pradesh v. Chahaganlal s/o. Ramlal Dholi. 1993 Cri.L.J. 1495 (M.P)

Formulation Includes even one bulk drug where that one bulk drug by itself is treated as a medicine. Balakrishna Pillai and another v. M/s. Matha Medicals and others. 1991 Cri.L.J. 448 = 1991(1) JT 123 = 1991(1) Rec Cri R 263 = 1991 SCC (Cri) 461 = AIR SCW 1991 SC 349 (S.C)

Food Grains Sold in Anticipation of Licence Absence of any intentional contravention of Section 7 - Conviction set aside. Shiker Chand v. State of Rajasthan, 1994 Cri.L.J. 760 = 1994(2) Rec Cri R 337 = 1994 (2) CCJ 207 (Raj.)

4. Imposition of duties on State Government, etc.

An order made under Section 3 may confer powers and impose duties upon the Central Government or the State Government or officers and authorities of Central Government or the

State Government, and may contain directions to any State Government or to officers and authorities thereof as to the exercise of any such powers or the discharge of any such duties.

5. Delegation of powers

The Central Government may, by a notified order, direct that the power to make orders or issue notifications under Section 3 shall, in relation to such matters and subject to such conditions, if any, as may be specified in the direction, be exercisable also by
- (a) such officer or authority subordinate to the Central Government; or
- (b) such Government or such officer or authority subordinate to a State Government as may be specified in the direction.

6. Effect of orders consistent with other enactments

Any order made under Section 3 shall have effect notwithstanding anything inconsistent therewith contained in any enactment other than this Act or any instrument having effect by virtue of any enactment other than this Act.

6-A. Confiscation of essential commodity

(1) Where any essential commodity is seized in pursuance of an order made under Section 3 in relation thereto, a report of such seizure shall, without unreasonable delay be made to the Collector of the district or the Presidency town in which such essential commodity is seized and whether or not a prosecution is instituted for the contravention of such order, the Collector may, if he thinks it expedient to do so, direct the essential commodity so seized to be produced for inspection before him, and if he is satisfied that there has been a contravention of the order he may order the confiscation of
- (a) the essential commodity so seized;
- (b) any package, covering or receptacle in which such essential commodity is found; and
- (c) any animal, vehicle, vessel, or other conveyance used in carrying such essential commodity:
    provided that without prejudice to any action which may be taken under any other provision of this Act, no foodgrains or edible oilseeds seized in pursuance of an order made under Section 3 in relation thereto from a producer shall, if the seized foodgrains or edible oilseeds have been produced by him, be confiscated under this Section;
    provided further that in the case of any animal, vehicle, vessel, or other conveyance used for the carriage of goods or passengers for hire, the owner of such animal, vehicle, vessel, or other conveyance shall be given an option to pay, in lieu of its confiscation, a fine not exceeding the market price at the date of seizure of the essential commodity sought to be carried by such animal, vehicle, vessel, or other conveyance.
(2) Where the Collector, on receiving a report of seizure or on inspection of any essential commodity under sub-section (1), is of the opinion that the essential commodity is subject to speedy and natural decay or it is otherwise expedient in the public interest so to do, he may
- (i) order the same to be sold at the controlled price, if any, fixed for such essential commodity under this Act or under any other law for the time being in force; or

(ii) where no such price is fixed, order the same to be sold by public auction:
Provided that in the case of any such essential commodity the retail sale price whereof has been fixed by the Central Government or a State Government under this Act or under any other law for the time being in force, the Collector may, for its equitable distribution and availability at fair prices, order the same to be sold through fair price shops at the price so fixed.

(3) where any essential commodity is sold, as aforesaid, the sale proceeds thereof, after deduction of the expenses of any such sale or auction or other incidental expenses relating thereto, shall

(a) where no order of confiscation is ultimately passed by the Collector,

(b) where an order passed on appeal under sub-section (1) of Section 6-C so requires, or

(c) where in a prosecution instituted for the contravention of the order in respect of which an order of confiscation has been made under this section, the person concerned is acquitted,

be paid to the owner thereof or the person from whom it is seized.

Annexure VIII   Service Tax Provisions: Retailers

Service tax is a relatively recent phenomenon. As the name suggests, it is a tax on services rendered. Economics does not bifurcate between production of goods and rendering of services. Both are productive activities which enhance a nation's income. Excise duty is levied on goods manufactured in India. Therefore, several economists are of the view that if excise duty is payable on goods manufactured, a similar duty must be levied on services rendered. This has given rise to the concept of service tax, i.e., a tax on services. It is similar to excise duty in the sense that it is an indirect tax. The person rendering the service is the person who is liable to pay service tax. He may recover the service tax from the person who has availed of the services.

Service Tax in India is governed by the provisions of the Finance Act, 1994 as amended from time to time. The said service tax provisions have come into effect from 1st July, 1994. However, the Central Government, by notification in the Official Gazette shall specify the dates from when service tax is leviable on various services. The service tax provisions apply to the whole of India except the state of Jammu and Kashmir.

Definitions

Certain terms have been defined in the Finance Act, 1994 for the purpose of levy of service tax. Some of the most important ones are given below:

'Actuary' has the meaning assigned to it u/s 2(1) of the Insurance Act, 1938. For a person to be an actuary, he must possess the prescribed qualifications.

'Advertisement' includes any notice, circular, label, wrapper, document, hoarding, or any other audio or visual representation made by means of light, sound, smoke, or gas.

'Advertising agency' means any commercial concern engaged in providing any service connected with making preparation, display, or exhibition of advertisement and includes an advertising consultant.

'Air travel agent' means any person engaged in providing any service connected with the booking of passage for travel by air.

'**Appellate tribunal**' means the Customs, Excise, and Gold (Control) Appellate Tribunal constituted under Section 129 of the Customs Act, 1962.

'**Architect**' means any person whose name is, for the time being, entered in the register or architects maintained under section 23 of the Architects Act, 1972, and also includes any commercial concern engaged in any manner, whether directly or indirectly, in rendering services in the field of architecture.

'**Assessee**' means a person liable for collecting the service tax and includes his agent.

'**Authorized service station**' means any service station or centre, authorized by any motor vehicle manufacturer, to carry out any service or repair of any motor car or two wheeled motor vehicle manufactured by such manufacturer.

'**Banking**' shall have the meaning assigned to it in clause (b) of section 5 of the Banking Regulation Act, 1949.

'Banking company' shall have the meaning assigned to it in section 45A(a) of the Reserve Bank of India Act, 1934.

'**Banking and other financial services**' constitutes, the following services provided by a banking company or a financial institution including a non-banking financial company or any other body corporate, namely:

- financial leasing services including equipment leasing and hire purchase by a body corporate,
- credit card services,
- merchant banking services,
- securities and foreign exchange (forex) broking,
- asset management including portfolio management, all forms of fund management, pension fund management, custodial depository, and trust services, but does not include cash management,
- advisory and other auxiliary services including investment and portfolio research and advice, advice on mergers and acquisitions, and advice on corporate restructuring and strategy and
- provision and transfer of information and data processing.

'**Board**' means the Central Board of Excise and Customs constituted under the Central Boards of Revenue Act, 1963.

'**Broadcasting**' has the meaning assigned to it in clause (c) of section 2 of the Prasar Bharati (Broadcasting Corporation of India) Act, 1990 and includes programme selection, scheduling or presentation of sound or visual matter on a radio or television channel that is intended for public listening or viewing, as the case may be, and in the case of a broadcasting agency or organization, having its head office situated in any place outside India, includes, the activity of selling of time slots or obtaining sponsorships for broadcasting of any programme or collecting the broadcasting charges on behalf of the said agency or organization, by its branch office or subsidiary or representative in India, or any agent appointed in India, or by any person who acts on its behalf in any manner.

'**Broadcasting agency or organization**' means any agency or organization engaged in providing service in relation to broadcasting in any manner and, in the case of a broadcasting agency or organization, having its head office situated in any place outside India, includes its branch office or subsidiary or representative in India or any agent appointed in India or any person who acts on its behalf in any manner, engaged in the activity of selling of time slots for broadcasting of any programme or obtaining sponsorships for programme or collecting broadcasting charges on behalf of the said agency or organization.

'Beauty treatment' means face and beauty treatment, cosmetic treatment, manicure, pedicure or counselling services on beauty, face care or make-up.

'Beauty parlour' means any establishment providing beauty treatment services.

'Cab' means a motor cab or maxi cab.

'Cable operator' shall have the meaning assigned to it u/s 2(a) of the Cable Television Networks (Regulation) Act, 1995.

'Cable service' shall have the meaning assigned to it u/s 2(b) of the Cable Television Networks (Regulation) Act, 1995.

'Cargo handling service' means the loading, unloading, packing, or unpacking of cargo and includes cargo handling services provided for freight in special containers or for non-containerized freight, services provided by a container freight terminal or any other freight terminal, for all modes of transport and cargo handling services incidental to freight but does not include handling of export cargo or passenger baggage or mere transportation of goods.

'Caterer' means any person who supplies, either directly or indirectly, any food, edible preparations, alcoholic or non-alcoholic beverages or crockery and similar articles or accoutrements for any purpose or occasion.

'Clearing and forwarding agent' means any person who is engaged in providing any service, either directly or indirectly, connected with the clearing and forwarding operations in any manner to any other person and includes a consignment agent.

'Computer network' has the meaning assigned to it u/s 2(1)(j) of the Information Technology Act, 2000.

'Consulting engineer' means any professionally qualified engineer or an engineering firm who, either directly or indirectly, renders any advice, consultancy, or technical assistance in any manner to a client in one or more disciplines of engineering.

'Convention' means a formal meeting or assembly which is not open to the general public and does not include a meeting or assembly the principal purpose of which is to provide any type of amusement, entertainment, or recreation.

'Courier agency' means a commercial concern engaged in the door-to-door transportation of time sensitive documents, goods, or articles utilizing the services of a person, either directly or indirectly, to carry or accompany such documents, goods or articles.

'Credit rating agency' means any commercial concern engaged in the business of credit rating of any debt obligation or of any project or programme requiring finance, whether in the form of debt or otherwise, and includes credit rating of any financial obligation, instrument, or security, which has the purpose of providing a potential investor or any other person any information pertaining the relative safety of timely payment of interest or principal.

'Custom house agent' means a person licensed, temporarily or otherwise, under the regulations made under subsection (2) of Section 146 of the Customs Act, 1962.

'Data' has the meaning assigned to it u/s 2(1)(o) of the Information Technology Act, 2000.

'Dry cleaning' includes dry cleaning of apparels, garments or other textile, fur or leather articles.

'Dry cleaner' means any commercial concern providing service in relation to dry cleaning.

'Electronic form' has the meaning assigned to it in clause (r) of sub-section (1) of Section 2 of the Information Technology Act, 2000.

'Event management' means any service provided in relation to planning, promotion or organizing or presentation of arts, entertainment, business, sports, or any other event and includes any consultation provided in this regard.

'Event manager' means any person who is engaged in providing any service in relation to event management in any manner.

'Facsimile (FAX)' means a form of telecommunication by which fixed graphic images, such as printed texts and pictures, are scanned and the information converted into electrical signals for transmission over the telecommunication system.

'Fashion designing' means any activity relating to conceptualizing, outlining, creating the designs, and preparing patterns for costumes, apparels, garments, clothing accessories, jewellery, or any other article intended to be worn by human beings and any other service incidental thereto.

'Fashion designer' means any person engaged in providing service in relation to fashion designing.

'Financial Institution' has the meaning assigned to it in Section 45-Ic of the Reserve Bank of India Act, 1934.

'General insurance business' has the meaning assigned to it in Section 3 (g) of the General Insurance Business (Nationalization) Act, 1972.

'Goods' has the meaning assigned to it under Section 2(7) of the Sale of Goods Act, 1930.

'Health and fitness service' means any service for physical well-being such as sauna and steam bath, turkish bath, solarium, spas, reducing or slimming salons, gymnasium, yoga, meditation, massage (excluding therapeutic massage), or any other like service.

'Health club and fitness centre' means any establishment, including a hotel or resort, providing health and fitness service.

'Information' has the meaning assigned to it in Section 2 (1)(v) of the Information Technology Act, 2000.

'Insurance agent' has the meaning assigned to it in clause (10) of Section 2 of the Insurance Act, 1938.

'Insurance auxiliary service' means any service provided by an actuary, an intermediary or insurance intermediary or an insurance agent in relation to general insurance business, or life insurance business and includes risk assessment, claim settlement, survey, and loss assessment.

'Intermediary or insurance intermediary' has the meaning assigned to it in sub-clause (f) of clause (1) of Section 2 of the Insurance Regulatory and Development Authority Act, 1999.

'Insurer' means any person carrying on the general insurance business or life insurance business in India.

'Interior decorator' means any person engaged, whether directly or indirectly, in the business of providing by way of advice, consultancy, technical assistance, or in any other manner, services related to planning, design or beautification of spaces, whether man-made or otherwise and includes a landscape designer.

'Leased circuit' means a dedicated link provided between two fixed locations for exclusive use of the subscriber and includes a speech circuit, data circuit, or a telegraph circuit.

'**Life insurance business**' has the meaning assigned to it in Section 2 (11) of the Insurance Act, 1938.

'**Magnetic storage device**' includes wax blanks, discs or blanks, strips or films the purpose of original sound recording.

'**Management consultant**' means any person who is engaged in providing any service, either directly or indirectly, in connection with the management of any organization in any manner and includes any person who renders any advice, consultancy or technical assistance, relating to conceptualizing, devising, development, modification, rectification, or upgradation of any working system of any organization.

'**Mandap**' means any immovable property as defined in Section 3 of the Transfer of Property Act, 1882 and includes any furniture, fixtures, light fittings, and floor coverings therein let out for consideration for organizing any official, social, or business function. Section 3 of TOPA defines immovable property as not including standing timber, growing crops, or grass.

'**Mandap keeper**' means a person who allows temporary occupation of a mandap for consideration for organizing any official, social, or business function.

'**Manpower recruitment agency**' means any commercial concern engaged in providing any service, directly or indirectly, in any manner for recruitment of manpower, to a client.

'**Market research agency**' means any commercial concern engaged in conducting market research in any manner, in relation to any product, service or utility including all types of customized and syndicated research services.

'**Maxi cab**' has the meaning assigned to it in clause (22) of Section 2 of the Motor Vehicles Act, 1988. Under the said clause, 'maxi cab' means any motor vehicle constructed or adapted to carry more than 6 passengers but not more than 12 passengers, excluding the driver, for hire or reward.

'**Motor cab**' has the meaning assigned to it in clause (25) of Section 2 of the Motor Vehicles Act, 1988. Under the said clause, 'motor cab' means any motor vehicle constructed or adapted to carry not more than 6 passengers, excluding the driver, for hire or reward.

'**Non banking finance company**' has the meaning assigned to it in clause (f) of Section 45-I of the Reserve Bank of India Act, 1934.

'**On-line information and database access or retrieval**' means providing data for information, retrievable or otherwise, to a customer, in electronic form through a computer network.

'**Pager**' means an instrument, apparatus or appliance which is a non-speech, one, way personal calling system with alert and has the capability of receiving, storing and displaying numeric or alpha-numeric messages.

'**Photography**' includes still photography, motion picture photography, laser photography, aerial photography and fluorescent photography.

'**Photography studio or agency**' means any professional photographer or a commercial concern engaged in the business of rendering service relating to photography.

'**Policy holder**' has the meaning assigned to it in clause (2) of Section 2 of the Insurance Act, 1938. Under the said clause, policy holder includes a person to whom the whole of the interest of the policy holder in the policy is assigned once and for all, but does not include an assignee thereof whose interest in the policy is defeasible or is for the time being subject to any condition.

'**Port**' has the meaning assigned to it in clause (q) of Section 2 of the Major Port Trust Act, 1963.

'Port services' means any service rendered by a port or any person authorized by the port, in any manner, in relation to a vessel or goods.

'Practising chartered accountant' means a person who is a member of the Institute of Chartered Accountants of India and is holding a certificate of practice granted under the provisions of the Chartered Accountants Act, 1949 and includes any concern engaged in rendering services in the field of chartered accountancy.

'Practising cost accountant' means a person who is a member of the Institute of Cost and Works Accountants of India and is holding a certificate of practice granted under the provisions of the Cost and Works Accountants Act, 1959 and includes any concern engaged in rendering services in the field of cost accountancy.

'Practising company secretary' means a person who is member of the Institute of Company Secretaries of India and is holding a certificate of practice granted under the provisions of the Company Secretaries Act, 1980 and includes any concern engaged in rendering services in the field of company secretaryship.

'Rail travel agent' means any person engaged in providing any service connected with booking of passage for travel by rail.

'Real estate agent' means a person who is engaged in rendering any service in relation to sale, purchase, leasing or renting, of real estate and includes a real estate consultant.

'Real estate consultant' means a person who renders in any manner, either directly or Indirectly, advice, consultancy or technical assistance in relation to evaluation, conception, design, development, construction, implementation, supervision, maintenance, marketing, acquisition, or management, of real estate.

'Recognized stock exchange' has the meaning assigned to it in clause (f) of Section 2 of the Securities Contracts (Regulation) Act, 1956.

'Scientific or technical consultancy' means any advice, consultancy, or scientific or technical assistance, rendered in any manner, either directly or indirectly, by a scientist or a technocrat, or any science or technology institution or organization, to a client, in one or more disciplines of science or technology.

'Securities' has the meaning assigned to it in clause (h) of Section 2 of the Securities Contract (Regulation) Act, 1956.

'Security agency' means any commercial concern engaged in the business of rendering services relating to the security of any property, whether movable or immovable or of any person in any manner and includes the services of investigation, detection, or verification, of any fact or activity, whether of a personal nature or otherwise, including the services of providing security personnel.

'Ship' means a sea going vessel and includes a sailing vessel.

'Shipping line' means any person who owns or charters a ship and includes an enterprise which operates or manages the business of shipping.

'Sound recording' means recording of sound on a magnetic storage device and editing thereof in any manner.

'Sound recording studio or agency' means any commercial concern engaged in the business of rendering any service relating to sound recording.

'Steamer agent' means any person who undertakes, either directly or indirectly :

- To perform any service in connection with the ship's husbandry or dispatch including the rendering of administrative work related thereto
- To book, advertise, or canvass for cargo or on behalf of a shipping line
- To provide container feeder services for or on behalf of a shipping line

'Stock broker' means a stock broker who has either made an application for registration or is registered as a stock broker in accordance with the rules and regulations made under the Securities and Exchange Board of India Act, 1992.

'Storage and warehousing' includes storage and warehousing services for goods including liquids and gases but does not include any service provided for storage of agricultural produce or any service provided by a cold storage.

'Sub broker' means a sub-broker who has either made an application for registration or is registered as a sub-broker in accordance with the rules and regulations made under the Securities and Exchange Board of India Act, 1992.

'Subscriber' means a person to whom a telephone connection or a pager has been provided by the telegraph authority.

'Taxable service' means any service provided:

- To an investor by a stock broker in connection with the sale or purchase of securities listed on a recognized stock exchange
- To a subscriber by the telegraph authority in relation to a telephone connection
- To a subscriber by the telegraph authority in relation to a pager
- To a policy holder by an insurer carrying on general insurance business in relation to general insurance business
- To a client by an advertising agency in relation to advertisements in any manner
- To a customer by a courier agency in relation to door-to-door transportation of time-sensitive documents, goods, or articles
- To a client by a consulting engineer in relation to advice, consultancy, or technical assistance in any manner in one or more disciplines of engineering
- To a client by a custom house agent in relation to the entry or departure of conveyances or the import or export of goods
- To a shipping line by a steamer agent in relation to a ship's husbandry or dispatch or any administrative work related thereto as well as the booking, advertising, or canvassing of cargo, including container feeder services
- To a client by a clearing and forwarding agent in relation to clearing and forwarding operations in any manner
- To a client by a manpower recruitment agency in relation to the recruitment of manpower in any manner
- To a customer by an air travel agent in relation to the booking of passage for travel by air
- To a client by a mandap keeper in relation to the use of a mandap in any manner including the facilities provided to the client in relation to such use and also in services, if any, rendered as a caterer
- To any person by a tour operator in relation to a tour
- To any person by a rent-a-cab scheme operator in relation to the renting of a cab

- To a client by an architect in his professional capacity in any manner
- To a client by an interior decorator in relation to planning, design, or beautification of paces, whether man-made or otherwise in any manner
- To a client by a management consultant in connection with the management of any organization in any manner
- To a client by a practising chartered accountant in his professional capacity in any manner
- To a client by a practising cost accountant in his professional capacity in any manner
- To a client by a practising company secretary in his professional capacity in any manner
- To a client by a real estate agent in relation to real estate
- To a client by a security agency in relation to the security of any property or person, by providing security personnel or otherwise, and includes the provision of services of investigation, detection, or verification of any fact or activity
- To a client by a credit rating agency in relation to credit rating of any financial obligation, instrument, or security
- To a client by a market research agency in relation to market research of any product, service, or utility in any manner
- To a client by an underwriter in relation to underwriting in any manner
- To a client by a scientist or a technocrat or any science or technology institution or organization, in relation to scientific or technical consultancy
- To a customer by a photography studio or agency in relation to photography in any manner
- To a client by any commercial concern in relation to holding of convention, in any manner
- To a subscriber by the telegraph authority in relation to a leased circuit
- To a subscriber by the telegraph authority in relation to communication through telegraph
- To a subscriber by the telegraph authority in relation to communication through telex
- To a subscriber by the telegraph authority in relation to a facsimile communication
- To a customer by a commercial concern in relation to online information and database access or retrival or both in electronic form through computer network in any manner
- To a client by a video production agency in relation to video tape production in any manner
- To a customer by an authorized service station in relation to any service or repair of motor cars or two wheeled motor vehicles in any manner
- To a customer by a body corporate other than the body corporate refered in the point marked above in relation to banking and other financial services
- To a customer by a beauty parlour in relation to beauty treatment
- To any person by a cargo handling agency in relation to cargo handling services.
- To a subscriber by a cable operator in relation to cable services
- To a customer by a dry cleaner in relation to dry cleaning
- To a client by an event manager in relation to event management
- To any person by a fashion designer in relation to fashion designing
- To any person by a health club and fitness centre in relation to health and fitness services
- To a policy holder by an insurer carrying on life insurance business in relation to life insurance business
- To a policy holder or insurer by an actuary or intermediary or insurance intermediary or insurance agent in relation to insurance auxilliary services concerning life insurance business

- To a customer by a rail travel agent in relation to booking of passage for travel by rail
- To any person by a storage or warehouse keeper in relation to storage and warehousing of goods

'Tour' means a journey from one place to another irrespective of the distance between such places.

'Tourist vehicle' has the meaning assigned to it under Section 2(43) of the Motor Vehicles Act, 1988.

'Tour operator' means any person engaged in the business of operating tours in a tourist vehicle covered by a tourist permit.

'Underwriter' has the meaning assigned to it in Section 2(f) of the SEBI (Underwriters) Rules, 1993.

'Underwriting' has the meaning assigned to it in Section 2(g) of the SEBI (Underwriters) Rules, 1993.

'Vessel' has the meaning assigned to it in Section 2(z) of the Major Port Trusts Act, 1963.

'Video production agency' means any professional videographer or any commercial concern engaged in the business of rendering services relating to video-tape production.

'Video-tape production' means the process of recording of any programme, event, or function on a magnetic tape and editing thereof in any manner.

Levy of Service Tax

Charge of Service Tax

Service tax will be levied on taxable services on and from the date on which the service tax is to be levied as notified by a notification in the official gazette in respect of different taxable services. The list of taxable services is given in the definition of taxable services. Service tax cannot be levied on any service which is not included in the list of taxable services. The intention of the government is to gradually increase the list of taxable services until most services fall within the scope of service tax. The rate of service tax is 5% of the value of the taxable services.

Valuation of Taxable Services for Charging Service Tax

For the purposes of levying service tax, the value of any taxable service shall be the gross amount charged by the service provider for such service rendered by him and includes:

- The commission received by the air travel agent from the airline
- The commission, fee, or any other sum received by an actuary or intermediary or insurance intermediary, or insurance agent from the insurer
- The reimbursement received by the authorized service station from manufacturer for carrying out any service of any motor car or two wheeled motor vehicle manufactured by such manufacturer
- The commission or any amount received by the rail travel agent from the railways or the customers but does not include
- Initial deposit made by the subscriber at the time of application for telephone connection or pager or facsimile, or telegraph, or telex, or for leased circuit
- The cost of unexposed photography film, unrecorded magnetic tape or such other storage devices, if any, sold to the client during the course of providing the service

- The cost of parts or accessories, if any, sold to the customer during the course of service or repair of motor car or two-wheeled vehicle
- The airfare collected by air travel agent in respect of service provided by him
- The rail fare collected by rail travel agent in respect of service provided by him

Taxable service accordingly
- in relation to the services provided by an advertising agency to a client, shall be the gross amount charged by such agency from the client for services in relation to advertisements.
- in relation to the service provided by a courier agency to a customer, shall be the gross amount charged by such agency from the customer for services in relation to door-to-door transportation of time-sensitive documents, goods, and articles.
- in relation to the services provided by a manpower recruitment agency to a client, shall be the gross amount charged by such agency from the client in relation to the recruitment of manpower in any manner.
- in relation to the services provided by an air travel agent to a customer, shall be the gross amount charged by such agent from the customer for services in relation to the booking of passage for travel by air excluding the airfare but including the commission, if any, received from the airline in relation to such booking. The central government has exempted air travel agents from paying so much of the service tax leviable on them as is in excess of the commission received by the air travel agent from the airline for booking of passage for air travel.
- in relation to the services provided by a mandap keeper to a client, shall be the gross amount charged by such keeper from the client for the use of mandap including the facilities provided to the client in relation to such use and also the charges for catering, if any. The central government has exempted mandap keepers from paying so much of the service tax leviable on them as is in excess of the amount of service tax calculated on 60% of the gross amount charged from the client by the mandap keeper for the use of mandap including the facilities provided to the client in relation to such use and also for catering charges. This exemption is available only where the mandap keeper also provides catering services and the bill indicates that it is inclusive of charges for the catering service.
- in relation to the services provided by a tour operator to a client, shall be the gross amount charged by such operator from the client for services in relation to a tour and includes the charges for any accommodation, food or any other facilities provided in relation to such tour. The central government has exempted tour operators from paying so much of the service tax leviable on them as is in excess of the amount of service tax calculated on 40% of the gross amount charged from the client by the tour operator for services provided in relation to a tour, where the tour operator provides a package tour to any person and the bill indicates that it is inclusive of charges for such a tour.
- in relation to the services provided by a real estate agent to a client, shall be the gross amount charged by such agent from the client for services rendered in connection with the sale, purchase, leasing, or renting of real estate including any advice, consultancy, or technical

assistance relating to evaluation, conception, design, development, construction, implementation, supervision, maintenance, marketing, acquisition, or management of real estate.

- in relation to the services provided by a security agency to a client, shall be the gross amount charged by such agency from the client for services rendered in connection with the security of any property or person, and includes services of investigation, detection or verification of any fact or activity including services of providing security personnel. The central government has exempted security agencies from the whole of service tax leviable on the gross amount of charges on a client in relation to services of providing safe deposit lockers or security or safe vaults for security of movable property.

Payment of Service Tax

Every person providing taxable service to any person must pay service tax at the prescribed rate (8% of value of taxable services) within the prescribed time period.

However, in respect of some taxable services notified by the central government in the official Gazette, the service tax is to be paid by some other person (who will be mentioned in the notification) in such manner as may be so prescribed. The provisions of service tax in such cases will apply as if the person who is so responsible for collection and payment of service tax is the tax payer and not the service provider.

Procedures and Assessment

Registration   Every person liable to pay the service tax must, within the prescribed time and in the prescribed manner and form, make an application for obtaining service tax registration number to the superintendent of central excise having jurisdiction over him.

Furnishing of Returns   Every person liable to pay service tax shall himself assess the tax due on the services provided by him and shall furnish to the superintendent of central excise , a return in the prescribed form and prescribed manner at the prescribed frequency.

Assessment   The superintendent of central excise may, on the basis of the information contained in the return, verify the correctness of the tax assessed by the assessee on the services provided.

The superintendent of central excise may require the assessee to produce any accounts, documents, or other evidence as he may deem necessary for verification as and when required.

The superintendent of central excise, after considering such accounts, documents, or other evidence, and after taking into account any relevant material which he has gathered, if he is of the opinion that service tax has escaped assessment or has been under-assessed he may refer the matter to the assistant commissioner of central excise (ACCE) or, as the case may be, deputy commissioner of central excise (DCCE), who may pass such order of assessment as he thinks fit.

Best Judgement Assessment   In case :

- any person fails to file a return of service tax within the prescribed time limit; or

- any person who having filed a return fails to comply with the terms of a notice; or
- the ACCE / DCCE is not satisfied with the correctness or the completeness of the accounts of assessee, the ACCE / DCCE may, after taking into account all the relevant material which he has gathered, by an order in writing, make the assessment of the value of taxable service to the best of his judgment and determine the sum payable by the assessee or refundable to the assessee.

Forms

Form	Used for
ST-I	Application for Registration
ST-2	Form of Certificate of Registration
ST-3	Quarterly Return of Service Tax
ST-3A	Memorandum of Provisional Deposit
ST-4	Appeal to Commissioner (Appeals)
ST-5	Appeal to Appellate Tribunal by tax payer
ST-6	Memorandum of Cross Objection to be Submitted to the AppellateTribunal
ST-7	Application to Appellate Tribunal by the CEO
TR-6	Treasury Challan for paying Service Tax

Form ST-1

Application for Registration Under Section 69 of the Finance Act, 1994

(32 of 1994)

1. Name of the Assessee :
2. Address of the Assessee :
2A. PAN Number :
3. Address of the premises to be registered :
4. Category of the service :
5. Fax / telex and phone number :
6. Form of organisation (individual/company/ :
   parternsip etc.) :
7. Additional information required int he case of stoock-
   broker
   (a) Name of the member, with code No. :
   (b) Name of stock exchange registered with :
   (c) Date of admission of membership :
   (d) Whether member of more than one stock
       exchange? If so, please give name of the stock
       exchange with code number :
   (e) Registration number allotted by Securities and
       Exchange Board of India (copy of certificate of
       registration may be enclosed or a copy of applciation
       for registration with SEBI may be enclosed) :
8. I/We _____ agree to abide by all the provisions of Service
   Tax Rules, 1994, and any order issued.
9. I/We _____ declare to the best of my/our knowledge and belief
   that the information furnished herein in true and complete.

Place :
Date :

Signature of assessee or his
authorized representative

Hints for filling in Form ST-1

- This form has to be furnished by the assessee to Central Excise Office where his jurisdiction falls.
- Form can be signed by assessee or his representative.
- This form is to be filed for each premises separately or regional office or head office as the case may be where central billing is not adopted and business is carried from more than one place.

- Fresh application should be made by any person (transferee) who has purchased the existing business of a registered service provider.
- No time limit was prescribed for making an application for registration but w.e.f. 16-10-98, according, to Service Tax (Amendment) Rules, 1998, application should be made within a period of thirty days from the date on which Service Tax is levied.
- If taxable service is provided from more than one premise and billing is centralized, the assessee may opt for registering only the premises from where centralized billing is done.
- Where the assessee is providing more than one taxable service, he may name a single application mentioning therein all the taxable services.
- Proof of address / residence / premises from where business is carried may be demanded and should be attached to the form.
- For partnership firms, department can ask for a copy of partnership deed as an evidence of partnership, which may be supplied.
- In case of a limited company, power of attorney and copy of the Memorandum and Articles of Association should be submitted.

Form ST-4

Form of Appeal to collector of Central Excise (Appeals) Under Section 85 of the Finance Act, 1994 (32 of 1994)

1. No. _____ of _____ 20_____
2. Name and Address of the appellant
3. Designation and Address of the Officer passing the _____ decision or order appealed against and the date of decision or order
4. Date of Communication of the decision or order_____ appealed against to the appellant
5. Address to which notice may be sent to appellant
5(a) (i) Period of Dispute
   (ii) Amount of service tax, if any, demanded for _____ the period mentioned in col. (I)
   (iii) Amount of refund, if any, claimed for the _____ period mentioned in Col. (I)
   (iv) Amount of interest
   (v) Amount of penalty
   (vi) Value of the taxable service for the _____ period mentioned in col. (I)
6) Whether service tax or penalty or interest or all the _____ three have been deposited
6(a) Whether the appellant wishes to be heard in person
7. Refund claimed in appeal

Statement of Facts

Grounds of Appeal

Signature of the authorized   Signature of the Appellant
representative, if any

Verification

I, _____ the appellant, do hereby declare that what is stated above is true to the best of my information and belief.

Verified today, the _____ day of _____

Place :

Date :

Signature of the authorized   Signature of the Appellant
representative, if any   or his authorised representative

Notes : The form of appeal including the statement of facts and the grounds of appeal shall be filed in duplicate and shall be accompanied by a copy of the decision or order appealed against.

Hints for Filling in Form No. ST-4

- ST-4 is to be used for appeals against assessment order passed under sections 71, 72, or 73 or denying his liability to be assessed or by an order levying interest or penalty.
- Appeal shall be presented within 3 months from the date of receipt of the order.
- Form should be verified in the prescribed manner.

Form ST-5
Form of appeal to the Appellate Tribunal under Section 86 of the Finance Act, 1994(32 of 1994)

In the Customs, Excise and Gold (Control) appellate Tribunal

Appeal No . _____ of _____ 19 _____

_____ Appellant

vs

_____ Respondent

(1) The designation and address of the authority passing the order appealed against.

(2) The number and date of the order appealed against.

(3) Date of communication of a copy of the order appealed against.

(4) State/Union Territory and the Commissionerate in which the order/decision of assessment/ penalty /interest was made.

(5) Designation and address of the adjudicating authority in cases where the order appealed against is an order of the Collector (Appeals).

(6) Address to which the notices may be sent to the appellant.

(7) Address to which the notices may be sent to the respondent.

(8) Whether the decision or order appealed against involves any question having a relation to the value of the taxable service for purposes of assessment; if not, difference in tax or tax involved, or amount of interest or penalty involved, as the case may be.

    8(A) (i) Period of dispute.

       (ii) Amount of tax, if any, demanded for the period mentioned in item (i).

      (iii) Amount of refund, if any, claimed for the period mentioned in item (i).

      (iv) Amount of interest involved.

      (v) Amount of penalty imposed.

(9) Whether tax or penalty /interest is deposited; if not, whether any application for dispensing with such deposit has been made (a copy of the challan under which the deposit is made shall be furnished).

    9(A) Whether the appellant wishes to be heard in person.

(10) Reliefs claimed in appeal.

Statement of Facts

Grounds of Appeal

(i) _____

(ii) _____

(iii) _____

(iv) _____

_____   _____

Signature of authorized   Signature of the Appellant

representative, if any

Verification

I, _____ the Appellant, do hereby declare that what is stated above is true to the best of my information and belief.

Verified today, the _____ day of _____ 19 _____

_____   _____
Signature of authorized   Signature of the Appellant
representative, if any   or his authorised representative

Notes :

(1) The appeal including the statement of facts and the grounds of appeal shall be filed in quadruplicate and shall be accompanied by an equal number of copies of the order appealed against (one of which at least shall be certified copy).

(2) The Form of appeal shall be in English (or Hindi) and should set forth, concisely and under distinct heads, the grounds of appeal without any argument or narrative and such grounds be numbered consecutively.

(3) The fee of Rs. 200 required to be paid under the provision of the Act shall be paid through a crossed bank draft drawn in favour of the Assistant Registrar of the Bench of the Tribunal on a branch of any nationalized bank located at the place where the bench is situated and the demand draft shall be attached to the Form of appeal.

Hints for filling in Form No. ST-5

- To be filed by an assessee aggrieved by an order passed by Commissioner of Central Excise u/s 84 or an order passed by a Commissioner of Central Excise (Appeal) u/s 85.
- Appeal should be made in quadruplicate.
- Four copies of order appealed against must be attached of which one or more should be certified copy.
- Filing fee is Rs 200.
- 4 copies of memorandum of cross objections should also be filed.
- Appeal should be filed within 3 months of the date on which the order sought to be appealed against is received.
- The form should be verified in the prescribed manner.

Summary Tables
Summary of Obligations under Service Tax

Sr. No.	Obligation	Frequency	Time Limit	Form to be used
1.	Payment of service tax	Monthly	For corporates and other (not individuals or firms) assessees, by 25th day of the following month	TR-6 Challan
2.	Payment of service tax	Quarterly	For individuals and firms, by 25th of the following month of the quarter ended	TR-6 Challan
3.	Registration under service tax rules	Only once at the time of registration	Within 30 days from the date on which tax is levied or business is commenced.	Form ST-1
4.	Grant of certificate of registration by CEO	Only once at the time of receiving application for registration	Within 7 days of application otherwise, it will deemed to have been granted	Form ST-2
5.	Return of service tax (in triplicate)	Half yearly	Within 25 days of end of each half year	Form ST-3/ST-3A
6.	Provisional deposit of service tax	Monthly or quarterly and as per Rule 6 (4) and 6(5)	Not prescribed	Form ST-3A
7.	Appeals to Commissioner of Central Excise (Appeals)	If required by assessee	3 months of the receipt of order sought to be appealed	Form ST-4
8.	Appeals by the assessee against the order of Commissioner of Central Excise (Appeals) to the Appellate Tribunal	If required	3 months of the receipt of order sought to be appealed	Form St-5 Form ST-6
9.	Appeals by the Board against the order of Commissioner of Central Excise (appeals) to the Appellate Tribunal	If required	3 months of the receipt of order sought to be appealed	Form ST-7

Summary of Effective Dates, Rates, and Scope of Service Tax at a Glance

Applicability of Service Tax Since	Service/Service provider	Taxable Amount	Rate of Service Tax
1/7/94	Insurance Service	Total amount of the premium received by the insurer from policy holders.	5%
1/11/96	Courier Service	Gross amount charged by courier agency from the customer in relation to taxable services	5%
1/11/96	Advertising Services	Gross amount charged by such agency from the customer in relation to taxable services	5%
1/11/96	Radio Pager Services	Gross total amount (including adjustments from any deposits) received by the telegraph authority.	5%
16/7/97	Clearing and Forwarding Agent's Services	Gross amount charged by such agent from the client for taxable services	5%
7/7/97	Manpower Recruitment Agency Services	Gross amount charged by such agency from from the the client for such services	5%
1/7/97	Air Travel Agent's Services	Gross amount charged by such agent excluding the airfare but including the commission received from the airline in relation to to booking.	5%
1/7/97	Mandap Keeper's Services	Gross amount charged by mandap keeper from the client for the use of mandap including the facilities provided to the client in relation to such use and also the charges for catering if any.	5%
16/10/98	Real Estate Agents of Consultants	Gross amount charged by such agency or consultant from the client for such services.	5%
1/7/2001	Authorized Service Stations	Gross amount charged by service provider including reimbursements received from manufacturer and excluding cost of parts/accessories sold	5%

Summary of Services on which service tax was levied and summary of services on which Service Tax was levied and subsequently withdrawn/exempted

Effective Service

Period

16-11-1997 to Goods Transport Operators
1-6-1998

1-8-1997 to Outdoor Caterers
1-6-1998
1-8-1997 to Pandal or Shamiana Contractors
1-6-1998
1-9-1997 to Tour Operators
17-7-1998
16-7-1997 to Rent-a-Cab Scheme Operators
27-2-1999
16-10-1998 to Mechanized Slaughter Houses
29-2-2000

Summary of Punishments/Penalties relating to Service Tax

Sr. No.	Offence/Default	Penal Provisions
1.	Delayed payment of service tax	Simple interest at the rate of one and a half per cent for every month or part of a month by which such crediting of tax or any part thereof is delayed.
2.	Failure to pay service tax	In addition to paying service tax and interest, not less than Rs 100 but which may extend to Rs 200 for every day du-ring which the failure conti-nues. However, the penalty shall not exceed the service tax assessee has failed to pay.
3.	Failure to furnish prescribed return	Penalty which may extend to an amount not exceeding Rs 2000 for each failure.
4.	Suppressing value of taxable service	In addition to service tax and interest, a sum which shall not be less than, but which shall not exceed twice the amount of service tax sought to be evaded.
5.	Failure to register service	In addition to paying service tax and interest, a sum of Rs 500/- for failure to make application for registration where service tax is applicable will be payable.
6.	Failure to comply with notice	A sum which shall not be less than 10% but which shall not exceed 50% of the amount of the service tax that would have been avoided.

Summary of persons liable to pay Service Tax

Sr. No.	Taxable Service	Person(s) Liable
1.	Stockbroker	Every stockbroker who is a member of a recognized stock exchange.
2.	Telephone Services	Director General of Posts and Telegraphs, Mahanagar Telephone Nigam Ltd and any other person who has been granted a licence by the Central Government.

contd

contd

Sr. No.	Taxable Service	Person(s) Liable
3.	General Insurance Services	Chairman/Managing Directors of General Insurance Corporation of India, National Insurance Com-pany Ltd, New India Assurance Company Ltd, Oriental Insurance Company Ltd, United India Insurance Company Ltd or any other person carrying on general insurance business who has obtained a certificate of regist-ration under Insurance Act, 1938.
4.	Courier service	Every courier agency raising the bill for services rendered to a client by such agency.
5.	Advertising Services	Every advertising agency which raises the bill for services rendered to a client by it.
6.	Radio Pager Services	Same as in (2) above.
7.	Customs House Agents	Every custom house agent which raises the bill for services rendered to a customer.
8.	Steamer Agents	Every steamer agent which raises a bill for services rendered to a shipping line.
9.	Consulting Engineers	Every consulting engineer who raises a bill for services rendered to a client by him.
10.	Clearing and Forwarding Agents	Every person who engages a clearing and forwarding agent and by whom remmuneration or com-mission (by whatever name called) is paid for such services to that agent.The burden has been shifted to clearing and forwarding agent in light of the Supreme Court judgement in Laghu Udyog Bharti case
11.	Manpower Recruit-ment Agents	Every manpower recruitment agency which raises a bill for services rendered to a client by such agency.
12.	Air Travel Agents	Every Air Travel Agent who books the passage for travel by air for a passenger.
13.	Goods Transport Opera-tors Services (Exempted by Notification No. 49/48, 2nd June, 1998)	Every person who pays or is liable to pay the freight or transpor-tation charges either himself or through his agent for the transp-ortation of goods by road in a goods carriage.
14.	Outdoor Caterers (with drawn by Notification No.49/98, 2nd June, 1998)	Every outdoor caterer who raises the bill for services rendered to a client by such caterer.

contd

contd

Sr. No.	Taxable Service	Person(s) Liable
15.	Pandal or Shamiana Contractor Services (withdrawn by Notification No.49/48, 2nd June, 1998)	Every pandal or shamiana contractor who raises a bill for services rendered to client by such contractor.
16.	Mandap Keeper's services	Every mandap keeper who raises the bill for services rendered to a client by such mandap keeper.
17.	Tour Operators (Exempted by Notification No.52 dated 8th July, 1998 till 31-3-2000)	Every tour operator who raises the bill for services rendered to any person by such operator.
18.	Rent-a-cab Scheme Operators (Exempted vide Notification No.3/99 dated 28-2-1999 till 31-3-2000)	Every rent-a-cab scheme operator who raises a bill for services rendered
19.	Architects	Every architect who raises a bill for services rendered to a client by him/her.
20.	Interior Decorators	Every interior decorator who raises a bill for services rendered to a client by him or her.
21.	Management Consultants	Every management consultant who raises a bill for services rendered to a client by him/her.
22.	Chartered Accountants	Every practising chartered accountant who raises a bill for services rendered to a client by him/her in respect of specified services.
23.	Company Secretaries	Every practising company secretary who raises a bill for services rendered to a client by him/her in respect of specified services.
24.	Cost Accountants	Every practising cost accountant who raises a bill for services rendered to a client by him/her in respect of specified services.
25.	Private Security agencies	Every private security agency which raises a bill for services rendered to a client by such agency.
26.	Real Estate Agents and Consultants	Every real estate agent or consultant which raises a bill for services rendered to a client or customer.
27.	Market Research Agencies	Every market research agency which raises a bill for the services rendered to a client by such agency.
28.	Credit Rating Agencies	Every approved credit rating agency which raises a bill for services rendered to a client.
29.	Underwriters	Every recognized underwriter who charges underwriting commission or fee from the client for the underwriting done.

contd

contd

Sr. No.	Taxable Service	Person(s) Liable
30.	Mechanised Slaughter Houses (Exempted by Notification No.2/2000 Service Tax dated 1-3-2000)	Mechanized slaughter houses undertaking slaughtering of bovine animals at Rs.100/- per animal.
31.	Scientific and Technical Consulting Services	Professional scientist / technocrat or any intsitute or organization engaged in science / technology rendering services to a client
32.	Photography Services	Professional photographer or studio or agency rendering service to a customer
33.	Convention Services	Commercial concern rendering such service to a client
34.	Telex Services	Telegraph authority rendering such services to clients
35.	Telegraph Services	Telegraph authority rendering such services to clients
36.	Online Information and Data Base Access/Retrival Services	Commercial concern rendering such service to a customer
37.	Video Tape Production Services	Video producing agency providing such service to a client
38.	Sound Recording Services	Sound recording studio or agency providing such service to a client
39.	Broadcasting Services	Broadcasting agency or organization providing such service to a client
40.	Insurance Auxilliary Services	Actuary or intermediary or insurance intermediary or insurance agent providing service to a policy holder or insurer
41.	Specified Banking and Financial Services	Banks, financial institutions, NBFCs rendering such specified services to clients
42.	Port Services	Port or any person authorized by a port providing such services to a client
43.	Services to Lease Circuit Line Holders	Telegraph authority rendering such services to clients
44.	Authorized Service Stations	Authorized service stations for service of motor vehicles including 2-wheelers
45.	Facsimile Services	Telegraph authority rendering such services to clients

Due Dates

Due Dates for Service Tax Assessees
Registration:
Within 30 days from the date on which service tax is levied or within 30 days of commencement of business, whichever is later.

Payment
- Payable by individuals, proprietary concerns, partnership firms:

Payable on amounts Payable by:
Received during the quarter

1st April to 30th June: 25th July
1st July to 30th September: 25th October
1st October to 31st December: 25th January
1st January to 31st March: 25th April
- Payable by persons other than individuals, proprietary concerns, partnership firms:

Payable on amounts Payable by:

Received during the month:

April 25th	May
May 25th	June
June 25th	July
July 25th	August
August 25th	September
September 25th	October
October 25th	November
November 25th	December
December 25th	January
January 25th	February
February 25th	March
March 25th	April

- Returns

For the half year: to be filed by

1st April to 30th September 25th October
1st October to 31st March 25th April

Service Tax Latest Update

The service provided by hotels as *mandap keepers* has been exempted from service tax up to 31.3.2002, where services include catering service, i.e., supply of food along with any service in relation to use of mandap and the bill issued for this purpose indicates that it is inclusive of charges for catering services. Food for this purpose means a substantial and satisfying meal, and hotel means a place that provides boarding and lodging facilities to public on commercial basis. Non-commercial photography studio or agency has been exempted from service tax vide notification 13/2001-Service Tax dated 27.12.2001 amending the earlier notification 6/2001- Service Tax dated 9.7.2001. The earlier notification had exempted a photography studio or agency which is not registered under the law relating to shops and establishments or any other law for the time being in force. The recent notification substitutes the words 'other than a commercial concern' in place of 'which is not registered under the law relating to shops and establishments or any other law for the time being in force'. The effect of this amendment is that only non-commercial photography studio or agency will now be exempt from service tax.

INDEX